THE ILLUSTRATED ENCYCLOPEDIA OF

STAMPS
& COINS

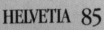

THE ILLUSTRATED ENCYCLOPEDIA OF
STAMPS & COINS

The ultimate visual reference to over 6000 of the world's best stamps and coins
and a professional guide to starting and perfecting a spectacular collection

Full advice on getting the most out of these popular pastimes, from making your
first acquisitions to organizing and caring for your collection. With 6000 colour images

DR JAMES MACKAY

HERMES
HOUSE

This edition is published by Hermes House, an imprint of Anness Publishing Ltd
Hermes House, 88–89 Blackfriars Road, London SE1 8HA; tel. 020 7401 2077; fax 020 7633 9499
www.hermeshouse.com; www.annesspublishing.com

Anness Publishing has a new picture agency outlet for images for publishing, promotions or advertising.
Please visit our website www.practicalpictures.com for more information.

Publisher: Joanna Lorenz
Editorial Director: Helen Sudell
Project Editor: Catherine Stuart
Senior Production Controller: Claire Rae
Design: Nigel Partridge
Text Editor: Beverley Jollands
Photography: Martyn Milner and Mark Wood

ETHICAL TRADING POLICY
At Anness Publishing we believe that business should be conducted in an ethical and ecologically
sustainable way, with respect for the environment and a proper regard to the replacement
of the natural resources we employ.
As a publisher, we use a lot of wood pulp in high-quality paper for printing, and that wood
commonly comes from spruce trees. We are therefore currently growing more than 750,000 trees
in three Scottish forest plantations. The forests we manage contain more than 3.5 times the number
of trees employed each year in making paper for the books we manufacture.
Because of this ongoing ecological investment programme, you, as our customer,
can have the pleasure and reassurance of knowing that a tree is being cultivated on your behalf to naturally
replace the materials used to make the book you are holding. For further information about this scheme,
go to www.annesspublishing.com/trees

Previously published as two separate volumes, *The Complete Guide to Stamps and Stamp Collecting* and *The
Complete Guide to Coins and Coin Collecting.*

*Page 2, central image: Swiss miniature sheet celebrating 150 years of the "Seated Helvetia" on stamps, and
commemorating her appearance on the country's original coinage (pre-Euro), as represented by a silver 5 francs.*

Note:
The stamps and coins reproduced in this book do not appear at their actual size, and readers should
treat the images as representative of actual dimensions. A small defacing bar has been added to
mint issues of stamps, where applicable, to indicate that they are a reproduction.

PUBLISHER'S NOTE
Although the advice and information in this book are believed to be accurate and true at the time of going
to press, neither the authors nor the publisher can accept any legal responsibility or liability for any errors
or omissions that may have been made.

CONTENTS

COINS 256

A GUIDE TO COLLECTING COINS 260

THE WORLD DIRECTORY OF COINS 346

INTRODUCTION

Philately and numismatics, the art of collecting stamps and coins respectively, are universally the most popular of the acquisitive hobbies. Most people tend to concentrate on one or the other, but a surprising number take a keen interest in both. Despite their considerable differences in longevity, stamps and coins do share some historical ground. It could be argued that both achieved mass distribution thanks to reforms in favour of smaller change and affordable postage, placing these acquisitions into the hands of the lower classes as well as the wealthy.

THE POPULARITY OF COINS

Coin collecting has a much longer history than its sister hobby, with origins in the days of ancient Rome. It regained popularity during the Renaissance, when the coin cabinets of wealthy aristocrats were likely to contain classical coins as well as the handsome silver issues of their own time. Among subsequent generations, numismatics became the pursuit of educated men raised in the classical

Below: A miniature sheet from Gibraltar celebrating the introduction of the new Euro coinage, 2001.

tradition; not surprisingly, they too had a particular attachment to the coins of Greece and Rome.

With the possible exception of the United States, where coin collecting gained widespread popularity from the early 19th century onward, numismatic tradition generally remained the pastime of the elite until the 20th century. In the United Kingdom, the hobby gathered momentum in the late 1960s, largely due to the imminent decimalization of the national currency.

The growing number of enthusiasts has brought about some important commercial changes. Four decades ago, for example, there were very few new issues aimed at the collector's market. Today, the vast majority of mints and numismatic bodies produce periodical sets, proofs and special issues on a regular basis, catering to a growing market and also stimulating it.

THE APPEAL OF STAMPS

Philately, by contrast, is a relatively young hobby, although, within a decade of the British Penny Black being launched as the very first adhesive postage stamp, people began to form collections of these alluring pieces of paper. At first, stamp collecting was

Above: The Israeli definitive stamps of 1948 and 1951 reproduced ancient Jewish coins.

generally perceived as a pastime for young women or schoolboys, but from 1866 onward it acquired the kind of serious consideration given to numismatics and, for those who took an interest in the intricacy of "advanced philately", was seen as more of a science than a recreation. Such was the appeal and accessibility of the hobby, it soon eclipsed its once more eminent sibling in terms of popularity.

In response to this increased demand for new and fascinating stamps, many national governments and postal administrations seized the opportunity to establish philatelic bureaus and sales departments to manage the design and promotion of their postal products. In more recent years, coin production has been organized along similar lines, a factor that has possibly encouraged some philatelists to take up the practice of coin collecting as well.

DUAL INTEREST

It is perhaps inevitable that an eager interest in one hobby would lead naturally to an affection for the other. Formerly, philatelists collected any new stamps they could get their hands on, but today many choose, for practical reasons, to restrict their interests to a small group of countries or perhaps even a single country. Within this degree of specialization, it is logical to extend an interest from stamps to other

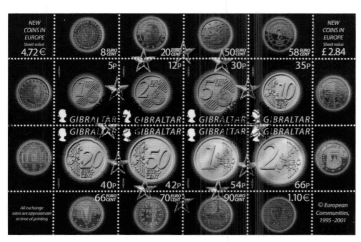

Above: 5 kreuzer stamp (left) on an Austrian coin of 2000 celebrating the 150th anniversary of Austrian stamps. The world's first adhesive stamp (right), the Penny Black, reproduced on a crown from the Isle of Man. A special technique was used to simulate the black appearance of the stamp.

Above: Australian maximum card, uniting themed stamp, stationery and postmark, celebrating 100 years of the Perth Mint. The commemorative stamp reproduces the obverse and reverse of the first gold sovereign struck there in 1899.

attractive, accessible items of similar historical importance, such as stamped letters, rail tickets or bank notes.

The change in trading patterns have also made an impact. At one time there were many stamp shops; today there are few, but, in spite of this, the actual number of dealers has multiplied. Instead of fixed premises with high overheads, most dealers now opt to do business with customers on-line, or meet at fairs and exhibitions. These events are likely to accommodate those buying and selling coins as well as stamps, plus related collectables such as coin tokens and postcards.

Below: A commemorative German cover known as a Numisblatt, *which incorporates both stamps and coins.*

CROSSING BOUNDARIES

While there are currently very few coins reproducing actual postage stamps, there is, by contrast, a large number of stamps depicting coins. This is not a new phenomenon by any means. Back in 1860, the Australian colony of Victoria introduced a 5-shilling stamp reproducing the obverse (or "head") of the British "Gothic crown" of 1847. In fact, the stamp outlived the coin, continuing in circulation until 1897. In 1863 Tasmania began issuing stamps that reproduced the figure of St George and the Dragon from the famous reverse ("tail") of the British sovereign. The same design appeared on the 5-drachma stamps of Crete in 1900, and later on a Greek issue of 1964. Although the choice may seem surprising, it actually shows how philatelic and numismatic themes can unite different countries. Although renowned as an English patron saint, George was, in fact, a Christian martyr born in Asia Minor – hence the Cretian and Greek celebrations. Moreover, the motif of George slaying the dragon is a striking metaphor of good triumphing over evil, and, as such, has also appeared on stamps issued by Sweden and Romania.

COLLECTING TODAY

Today, philinumismatic memorabilia has generated a hobby with a solid core of enthusiasts. This has not, of course, been lost on the various philatelic and numismatic administrations powering the industries. In recent years, stamps and coins have often been combined in souvenir or commemorative covers, spurred on by the success of the *Numisblatt* (below-left).

Whether your passion is for stamps or coins, or both, this compendium will offer inspiration and guidance to all new collectors, and some colourful commentary to those who simply want to learn more about how these artefacts came into being. Remember that both stamps and coins were designed to be used and handled – so they are as much a history of the people who purchased or exchanged them as the countries and heads of state whose identities they carry. The story of how stamps and coins both contributed to, and reflected, the social and economic changes of their time is often "written" into their outward appearance, and the art of "reading" the characteristics of your collectables is therefore perhaps the greatest gift a collector can attain. Exactly how to do this is just one of the many practical aspects of the hobbies explained in the pages that follow.

SVERIGE **KR 10**

C.G. PILO PINX.   1991   CZ SLANIA SC.

Czeslaw
Slania
70 ÅR

E. JERN DEL   1991   CZ SLANIA SC.

SVERIGE **KR 10**

C.G. PILO PINX.   1991   CZ SLANIA SC.

GUSTAF III:s KRONING 1772

KR 10 SVERIGE

C.G. PILO PINX.   1991   CZ SLANIA SC.

LATVIJA 12

HARK THE HERALD ANGELS SING
CHRISTMAS ISLAND
INDIAN OCEAN

POSTAGE
2½
PAKISTAN

1ᵈ   1ᵈ
1962
INDEPENDENCE
JAMAICA

EGYPT
8P

STAMPS

The following pages present a colourful history of the adhesive stamp, and examine its continuing appeal and global importance. This part of the book is divided into two chapters. The former looks at the development of the stamp, from its radical birth in Victorian England to its subsequent impact on global communications. See how revolutionary developments in design, production and purpose generated a wealth of collectable material, from postmarks on ships' letters to "Cinderella" issues. The second chapter traces, through superb colour images, the global history of stamps, from the very first definitive issues to the latest modern incarnations. Organized country-by-country, every stamp-issuing nation in the modern world is represented, and the chronological treatment makes it easy for the enthusiast to compare, at a glance, the stamps of past and present.

Left, clockwise from top: Swedish miniature sheet of 1991, Egyptian stamp of 1985, Jamaican stamp of 1962, Pakistani stamp of 1948, Christmas Island stamp of 1969, Chinese stamp of 1949, Latvian stamp of 1997. Above, left to right: Canadian stamp of 1865, Kenyan stamp of 1964, Polish stamp of 2000, Indian stamp of 1948, Rio Muni stamp of 1962.

INTRODUCING STAMPS AND PHILATELY

Philately, to give stamp collecting its proper name, has been called "the king of hobbies and the hobby of kings" – alluding to the fact that George V and Edward VIII of Britain, Carol of Romania, Alfonso XIII of Spain and Farouk of Egypt were all enthusiasts. The most famous non-royal head of state who was a lifelong philatelist was Franklin Delano Roosevelt. In *The Second World War* Winston Churchill has left a description of President Roosevelt engrossed in his hobby. In May 1943 the two statesmen were staying at Shangri-la, Roosevelt's mountain retreat in Maryland:

> The President had been looking forward to a few hours with his stamp collection. General "Pa" Watson, his personal aide, brought him several large albums and a number of envelopes full of specimens he had long desired. I watched him with much interest and in silence for perhaps half an hour as he stuck them, each in its proper place, and so forgot the cares of State.

All too soon, however, Bedell Smith arrived with an urgent message from Eisenhower. "Sadly F.D.R. left his stamp collection and addressed himself to his task…"

When American GIs entered Hitler's mountain lair at Berchtesgaden in May 1945 one of them retrieved the Fuhrer's stamp album, but it was actually a volume prepared for him for geopolitical reasons, with the stamps of the British Empire arranged to show the Nazi leader the rich prizes that would one day fall into his grasp. There is no evidence that Hitler took a personal interest in stamps, although the Third Reich was quick to harness this medium for propaganda.

WHY COLLECT?

Different people take an interest in collecting stamps for different reasons. Schoolteachers used to encourage the hobby because it stimulated an interest in history and geography, but most collectors are initially attracted by those fascinating little pieces of paper, inscribed in exotic languages, with unfamiliar currencies and views of far-away places. Although stamp collecting is an acquisitive hobby, you do not have to spend any money on it at the outset; the stamps from the letters of friends, relatives and work colleagues will get you off to a flying start.

However, by investing a little more time and money in the hobby, you may soon find yourself on a unique and absorbing journey. In this book we take a look at the various methods of starting a collection and the ways in which it can be developed to suit your own interests and requirements. We discuss the mechanics of collecting, including various tools, equipment, albums and accessories that can greatly enhance the

Above: Definitive sets of mounted stamps are widely available to purchase, and are often favoured by collectors who organize their stamps by country.

systematic development of a collection. You should always remember that stamps are fragile things, originally designed to do no more than perform postal duty once and then be discarded. We look at the best ways to house these delicate treasures so that they are protected from the adverse effects of heat, humidity, sunlight and atmospheric pollution, and how to make sense of their arrangement – chronological or thematic – on the pages of an album.

FINDING YOUR NICHE

There are many ways of personalizing a stamp collection. Many collectors begin with a modest idea and then find they lean naturally towards a particular aspect of a country, period or theme. You may enjoy playing the detective, delving into the background of each issue to find out the reasons for the

Left: A 1947 stamp from Monaco showing Roosevelt at his stamp collection. It was designed by Pierre Gandon and does not set a good example for stamp collectors, for its subject is about to scuff the stamps with the cuff of his shirt. It must be presumed that Gandon exercised some artistic licence.

Right: A multi-tiered collectable bearing an Egyptian stamp, a contemporary Army Post stamp and a cancellation made by British field post handstamp E 602 in 1940.

introduction of a change of colour or watermark, why one design was introduced or another hastily scrapped, or why one printer lost the contract and another gained it.

The diligent collector need not limit the search to adhesive stamps. Until the early 20th century collectors indiscriminately took everything associated with the postal service, including stickers and labels, postal stationery and anything that remotely resembled a stamp. These sidelines fell out of favour as stamps became more prolific, but in recent years they have once again become legitimate subjects for study and competitive exhibition. Many of the world's finest collections now encompass much of the ancillary material associated with the production and issue of stamps, from postal notices, leaflets, brochures and other ephemera, to artists' drawings, printers' proofs, colour trials and actual stamps overprinted "SPECIMEN" or endorsed in some other manner to prevent postal use. Add to these items the souvenir folders produced by stamp printers, presentation packs sold by postal administrations, first day covers and souvenir postcards, not to mention the analysis of the stamps themselves, and you will find yourself embarked on a vast and interesting project.

FINANCIAL RETURNS

Every collector dreams of one day stumbling across a cache of ancient letters franked with stamps of immense rarity. Many of the fabulous gems of philately were discovered by ordinary people, even children, and the story of these rare finds and their subsequent history as they advanced in value every time they changed hands is the very stuff of romance and adventure.

Today, stamp dealing is a global business; thousands of people make a decent living from trading in stamps and no modern postal administration can afford to ignore the revenue accruing from philatelic sales. Philately is one of the few hobbies to offer its followers the opportunity to make a profit at the

end of the day. Advice on buying is essential, as are tips on the best methods of disposal and on gauging the value of your stamps, whether solo or part of a larger collection.

The rise of online dealing has taken stamp buying and selling to a new level. All kinds of collectors – from the amateur just starting out to the professional seeking a rarity to complete a prize-winning exhibit – correspond across the globe and undertake bidding wars on international auction sites. Such is the scale of the new e-shopping culture that many philatelic societies now enable members to participate in club trading circuits via email.

GETTING INVOLVED IN THE HOBBY

Philately is highly organized, with clubs and societies at local, regional, national and worldwide levels. Many offer online membership to draw collectors from far and wide, and are an excellent source of information and contacts.

Exhibiting remains a popular objective for the many collectors who like to show off their treasures. The beginner of today, making his or her first display to the local stamp club, may one day aspire to win an international gold medal. This book gives advice on arranging and annotating your collection, and on the different approaches to displaying material, depending on whether the collection is arranged on traditional lines (by country or period) or topical, or perhaps devoted to telling a story, postal history or sidelines such as air, war or charity issues.

A WORLD OF STAMPS TO CHOOSE FROM

Every country in the modern world has produced stamps at some time. At present there are some 240 countries that issue distinctive stamps, and there are at least three times that number of

Above: This attractive first flight cover of the Italian Airmail Service, issued on 16 May 1917, bears what is generally recognized as the world's first official airmail stamp. Augmented further by its historic cancellation, this cover has all the elements of a highly collectable piece.

"dead" countries, which no longer exist as political entities or have changed their name, but which have left their mark in the stamp album.

The World Directory of Stamps, which follows the Guide to Collecting chapter, provides a survey of all the existing countries that currently issue stamps, as well as many obsolete entities – former German, Italian and Indian states, for example – that issued them. Some countries are grouped according to common links in their political and philatelic histories, while others stand alone in the extent of their contribution to philately. In addition to tracing the cultural and economic shifts of the modern world, these intricately designed pieces of paper are a testament to the sheer volume of material available to today's collector.

Below: A historic Madras War Fund charity label produced during World War I to raise funds for a hospital ship.

A GUIDE TO COLLECTING STAMPS

People have been collecting adhesive stamps ever since they first appeared in 1840. While the methods of prepaying postage have diversified considerably since the very first mailing of a letter bearing a Penny Black, most countries continue to appreciate the revenue to be gained from the sale of adhesive stamps and first day covers to collectors. The result is that the number of new issues generated each year now exceeds 10,000. This chapter is divided broadly into three key sections. The first takes a look at how stamps have originated and evolved, and how differences in the use of paper, ink, perforations and watermarks may considerably affect the value of two stamps that look the same. The second section discusses the various methods of collecting – from tools and display techniques to choosing a theme to unite your stamps and stationery – and looks at the choice of what there is to collect, from airmail, sea mail and military posts to the study of the postmarks relating to a country, region or even a single town. Finally, we trace the evolution of philately from its inception in the 1850s, and explain how to reap the rewards of a diverse and exciting hobby in an age of technological innovation – whether making contact with fellow collectors around the globe, bidding online for rarities, or researching the history of an unusual stamp.

Above, from left: Olympic philately is one of the largest branches of thematic collecting. It is little surprise that Greece, which issued these three stamps in 1968, 1972 and 1906, is so prolific on this subject.

WHAT ARE STAMPS?

We usually think of postage stamps as small pieces of printed, gummed paper, but in fact stamps, labels and seals have evolved in response to various postal functions, and a wealth of distinctive formats – and affiliated stationery – now exist.

Left: A United States commemorative celebrates the centenary of its country's stamps in 1947.

THE ORIGINS OF POSTAL SERVICES

Almost as soon as writing evolved, communications of a sort came into being. Postal services were certainly in existence in China as long ago as 4000 BC and in Egypt and Assyria a millennium later. The Chinese and Egyptian services were confined to imperial court circles, but in Assyria the service was open to the mercantile class as well. Not only are these ancient services well documented in contemporary chronicles, but actual examples of letters have survived, in the form of clay tablets bearing messages written in cuneiform (wedge-shaped) script. An immense hoard of such correspondence was discovered at Kultepe in Turkey in 1925 and included clay tablets dating from at least 2000 BC.

Below and right: Cuneiform writing on a Mesopotamian clay tablet, dating from the 21st or 20th century BC; this was celebrated on an Austrian stamp of 1965 issued for the Vienna International Philatelic Exhibition.

EARLY POSTAL SERVICES

A regular postal network was established by Cyrus the Great in Persia in about 529 BC, and detailed descriptions of it were written by the Greek historians Herodotus and Xenophon, both of whom commented on the speed and efficiency of the horse relays that carried letters to the furthest reaches of the Persian Empire.

By this time, the Chinese had a highly sophisticated network of post relays. In the 13th century Marco Polo described the imperial service as having over 25,000 relay stations, but as late as 1879 it was still confined to the court, and the general public were barred from using it on pain of death.

The Chinese were also the first to use paper as a writing material, by the 2nd century BC. The Romans wrote their letters on wax tablets and later on thin sheets of wood,

Right: A medieval Latin manuscript on another Austrian stamp of the WIPA series of 1965.

while the Egyptians favoured papyrus. Parchment was the preferred medium in Europe until the 15th century, when paper was introduced from China via Asia Minor and the Byzantine Empire.

By the Middle Ages there were many postal services in Europe, but none was in general use. They operated almost exclusively for trade guilds (such as the Metzger Post of Germany, which served the guild of butchers), the merchants of the Hanseatic League, Venice and

Above: Postmen from the Middle Ages to more modern times are depicted on stamps of Austria, USA, Belgium and France.

the Italian city states, the universities and the great religious houses. When state services were instituted, these gradually died out or were merged with them.

THURN AND TAXIS MONOPOLY

By the 15th century the Holy Roman Empire had an efficient postal service operated by the Counts of Thurn and Taxis, whose range extended from the Baltic to the Adriatic and from Poland to the Straits of Gibraltar. The service survived into the era of adhesive stamps, and issued these in various states of Germany until 1867, when the Thurn and Taxis family (which had backed Austria, the losing side, in the

Seven Weeks' War of the previous year) was forced to give up its postal monopoly to Prussia, receiving 3 million thalers in compensation. The family business had lasted over 420 years, and the last hereditary Grand Master of the Posts died in 1871. (The 500th anniversary of this first great international post was celebrated by a joint issue of stamps in five countries in 1990.)

National postal services evolved from communications established to keep rulers in touch with regional governors. Sometimes a temporary service would be organized to serve the monarch while campaigning against enemy countries. In Britain, Henry VII had such a service in the late 15th century while fighting in Wales and Ireland. Out of the temporary arrangement set up when Henry VIII went to war against the Scots came the rudiments of the service along the Great North Road. Charles I opened the Royal Mail to the general public in 1635 as a way of raising money without recourse to Parliament (which he had dissolved), and the service was completely overhauled after the Restoration of the monarchy in 1660.

Below: A Roman cursus publicus *mail coach on an Austrian stamp of 1959, a "ball-wagon" designed to thwart robbers who would fall off after leaping aboard (Denmark, 1951) and the Bath–London mail coach on a British stamp of 1984.*

EARLY AMERICAN POSTS
The first postal service in America was established in November 1639, when Richard Fairbanks of Boston became Postmaster to the Massachusetts Bay Colony. Services were organized in Virginia (1657), New York (1672), Connecticut (1674), Philadelphia (1683) and New Hampshire (1683), and were united in 1691 under Thomas Neale as Deputy Postmaster General (under the Postmaster General in London). He was responsible for the handling of all mail arriving from abroad and destined for the various British settlements in North America.

Internal postal services originally radiated from the capital city, but by 1680 cross posts provided a more direct route. The first domestic service was organized by Duncan Campbell of Boston in 1693, operating between there and New York. Other routes, linking Philadelphia to Newport, Virginia (1737) or New York (1742), Boston to Albany, Baltimore to Annapolis and Philadelphia to Pittsburgh, were amalgamated in 1792. The year also saw the first regular exchange of mail between the USA and neighbouring Canada.

CONVEYING MAIL
Mail in the Roman Empire was conveyed by the *cursus publicus* ("public course") using light carts that rattled over paved roads, but the breakdown

A Postal Dynasty
In 1952 Brussels hosted the 13th Postal Union Congress. Belgium marked the occasion with a set of 12 stamps portraying members of the princely family known as the Counts of Thurn and Taxis, who operated an international postal service from 1490 to 1867.

of the infrastructure in the Dark Ages meant that for many centuries most mail was carried by foot or horse posts. This continued well into the 19th century – the term "postmaster" originally meant a horse-hirer. When the age of steam dawned in the 1830s, however, mail by rail began to supersede horses and coaches, just as sailing packets gave way to the first steamships. Although the modes of transport were becoming speedier, the cost of sending or receiving letters remained prohibitively high until 1840, when national postal services underwent revolutionary change.

Left: A US 2c stamp of 1869 showing a Pony Express rider.

Below: A block of four showing historic mail transport, issued for the 20th Congress of the Universal Postal Union in 1989.

BIRTH OF THE ADHESIVE POSTAGE STAMP

On 22 August 1839 the British Treasury was authorized to implement a plan for an affordable postal service, put forward by the reformer Rowland Hill (1795–1874). Seeking inspiration, the Treasury announced a competition for designs and suggestions as to how prepayment of the new Penny Postage might be shown. Prizes of £200 and £100 were offered for the best design and the runner-up. This was widely publicized and eventually drew some 2,700 entries. Although prizes were awarded, none of the winning entries was actually used. One design showing the head of Queen Victoria was submitted by Sir George Mackenzie of Coul, Ross-shire. Recently discovered in the Royal Collection at Buckingham Palace, it is now regarded as the prototype for the first stamp, the Penny Black of May 1840.

Sir Rowland Hill
Born at Kidderminster in 1795, Hill trained as a schoolmaster but also involved himself in social improvements and colonization projects before turning to postal reform in the 1830s. His plan for uniform penny postage was adopted in January 1840, precipitating the use of adhesive stamps.

THE FORERUNNERS OF THE POSTAGE STAMP

All the elements that made up the first stamps were in fact already in existence. Revenue stamps embossed on blue paper had been around since 1694. They were attached to parchment documents by means of lead staples, secured at the back by small rectangular pieces of white paper – the size of the future Penny Black – bearing the crowned royal cipher, and they even had plate numbers and corner letters, just like the early postage stamps.

Newspapers were subject to a tax as a means of raising revenue, often for defence, although they were allowed free transmission by post. It was the extension of this levy to the American colonies in 1765, via the Stamp Act, that helped to trigger the opposition which culminated in the War of Independence a few years later. From 1802 onwards many taxes were denoted by adhesive labels. Indeed the tax stamps applied to patent medicines were not unlike some of the essays submitted in the Treasury competition.

The adhesive labels denoting prepayment of freight charges are thought to have been used by shipping and freight companies

Above: A tax stamp embossed on blue paper and fixed with a lead staple.

Below: An adhesive label used to secure the back of the lead staple (left) and an impressed newspaper tax stamp of the American colonies, 1765 (right).

152

Above: The first issues of the Penny Black (top left) and Twopence Blue (bottom), as they appeared in May 1840, with an illustration of the crown watermark (top right).

from about 1811, though none is now extant. So the concept of using adhesive stamps to denote prepaid mail was a natural development.

POSTAL REVOLUTION
The Penny Black and Twopence Blue, introduced in May 1840, were a team effort, conceived by Hill, drawn by Henry Corbould from the effigy sculpted by William Wyon for the Guildhall Medal of 1838, engraved by Charles and Frederick Heath and recess-printed by Perkins, Bacon of London. The rose engine used to engrave the background was patented by the American engineer Jacob Perkins, who had devised a method of engraving steel plates to print banknotes that were proof against forgery.

The new-fangled stamps were slow to catch on. At first they were on sale only at stamp offices operated by the Board of Stamps and Taxes, and postmasters had to obtain a licence to sell them. Until 1852 the public had the option to prepay postage in cash, and such letters bore a red postmark to indicate this. Letters could still be sent unpaid, but attracted a double charge of 2d per half ounce.

WORLD FIRSTS

Brazil is generally credited with being the first country to follow Britain's lead, with its celebrated Bull's Eyes of 1843. In fact the New York City Dispatch Post was using 1c stamps portraying George Washington a year earlier. Henry Thomas Windsor, the proprietor of this private local service, was an Englishman who imported the idea from his native country.

The Swiss cantons of Basle, Geneva and Zurich adopted stamps in 1843–5. In 1845 the US Post Office (USPO) authorized postmasters to issue their own stamps, and two years later the first federal issue consisted of 5c and 10c stamps portraying Benjamin Franklin (first Postmaster General of the USA) and George Washington respectively. Every American definitive series from then until 1981 included a representation of Washington, though Franklin was dropped after 1965.

In 1847 Mauritius was the first British colony to adopt adhesive stamps, although Trinidad had a local stamp that year, for mail carried by the *Lady McLeod*, a steamship

Right: Obverse of the 1838 Guildhall Medal, sculpted by William Wyon.

Below: A miniature Isle of Man sheet of 1990, showing the evolution of the Penny Black.

Above: The Brazilian 90 reis stamp of 1843, nicknamed the Bull's Eye.

Below: The first stamps issued for use throughout the USA: the 5c Franklin and 10c Washington of 1847.

run by a private company. Although this showed the ship it was not the first pictorial design to be produced. As early as 1843 the Broadway Penny Post of New York had a stamp showing a steam locomotive.

Bermuda adopted adhesive stamps in 1848, the postmasters of Hamilton (W.B. Perot) and St George's (J.H. Thies) producing them by striking their hand-stamps on gummed paper.

Above: The 1d Post Office stamp of Mauritius, 1847, and the Bavarian 1 kreuzer, 1849.

Right: The Belgian Epaulettes issue of 1849.

Below: Switzerland's Double Geneva cantonal stamp of 1843, the world's first discount stamp – 5c each or the double for 8c.

In 1849 Bavaria, Belgium and France produced their first stamps and the first decade ended with stamps extending to Austria, Austrian Italy, British Guiana. Hanover, New South Wales, Prussia, Saxony, Schleswig-Holstein, Spain, Switzerland and the Australian state of Victoria. New South Wales had anticipated Britain's adoption of prepaid postage by introducing embossed letter sheets as early as 1838, but adhesive stamps lagged behind by 12 years.

Thereafter, the use of adhesive postage stamps spread rapidly. In 1851 Baden, Canada, Denmark, Hawaii, New Brunswick, Nova Scotia, Sardinia, Trinidad and Württemberg joined the stamp-issuing entities. In 1852 another 11 countries adopted the system, including the Indian district of Scinde (now part of Pakistan), the first country in Asia. With the arrival of the celebrated triangular stamps of the Cape of Good Hope in South Africa in 1853, stamps had spread to every inhabited continent.

ISLE OF MAN   058321

1840·THE PENNY BLACK·1990

THE PARTS OF A STAMP

A postage stamp is the sum of many different parts and processes, and two issues that look the same on the surface may in fact conceal subtle variations. An American 32c issue of 1995–7, known to collectors as the Flag Over Porch issue, illustrates this point. To the untrained eye, these stamps look very similar, but their additional features make them really quite different. Although the same printing process (multicolour photogravure) was used throughout, the stamps were produced by four different printers: Avery-Dennison, J.W. Fergusson & Sons, Stamp Venturers, and the Bureau of Engraving and Printing. There are also differences in the gum: some have gum arabic on the back, which has to be moistened, while others have a self-adhesive backing. Some of the stamps were issued with phosphor tagging to assist electronic sorting and cancellation, while others were not. Fortunately the paper was the same throughout and there were no watermarks to contend with, but different qualities of paper and watermarks in many older issues can dramatically affect the value of seemingly similar stamps.

Above: Superficially these 32c Flag Over Porch stamps of the USA are the same, but they were produced by different printers; they are either conventionally gummed or self-adhesive, and are taken from sheets or coils.

PHOSPHOR TAGGING

The 32c Flag Over Porch stamps are all of much the same value, whether in mint (unused) or used condition, but sometimes a very slight variation can make a vast difference to a stamp's worth. Phosphor is used in Britain to distinguish second and first class mail, the stamps having one or two bands, or an all-over coating detected only with an ultraviolet lamp. The British halfpenny stamp of 1971 may be found with two phosphor bands (in sheets) or a single central band (in coils and booklets) and both types are very common. However, in 1972, a prestige booklet in honour of the Wedgwood pottery legacy included a halfpenny stamp in a mixed pane (the term for a page of stamps) with a single phosphor band at the left side only. Today it is catalogued at 100 times the price of the normal versions.

PERFORATION

Rows of holes are punched out of the sheet between the stamps to make them easy to separate, and variations in perforation are the feature that usually distinguishes stamps. Their size and spacing varies, and a gauge is used to measure the number of holes in a length of 2cm/3/4in. Stamps may be comb-perforated, when three sides are punched at a time, or line-perforated, producing a characteristic ragged effect at the corners.

Before true perforation was perfected in the 1850s, stamps were sometimes rouletted: the paper was pierced by blades on a wheel, but not punched out. This method has survived intermittently to the present day but is more usually confined to postal stationery and stickers. Although perforation is redundant in self-adhesive stamps, it is often retained, in the form of die cuts, for aesthetic reasons.

WATERMARKS

The commonest form of security device, watermarks can usually be detected by holding stamps up to the light. Very few countries now use them, but until the 1970s they were widespread. British stamps of the period 1953–67 may be found with three different watermarks or none at all.

When it is necessary to compare different watermarks a detector is required. The traditional method was

During the first decade of their existence, adhesive stamps were cut, or even torn, from a sheet by the local postmaster. Then, during the 1850s, Henry Archer invented a machine to perforate stamps by punching rows of holes along the white spaces between the stamps to ease separation. This perforating machine (left) is one of the few working Victorian examples left in the world. The Penny Red (above right) issued in 1854, shows a triple perforation – an example of the early teething problems experienced with the new-fangled perforators.

Left: This block of Polish stamps of 1919 was perforated by a comb machine: the regular holes intersect perfectly.

to place the stamp face down on a polished black surface and apply a drop or two of benzine, which momentarily renders the stamp transparent. Nowadays there are various electric devices that are more effective.

PRINTING METHODS

Stamps are printed by a number of different processes, so it's important to recognize their salient characteristics.

The earliest stamps, and most US stamps until the 1970s, were recess-printed from steel or copper plates with the design cut into them (a process sometimes described as intaglio). These can be recognized by the slight ridges (as on a banknote) that result from the paper being forced under great pressure into the recesses of the plate. The opposite process is relief-printing or letterpress, often called typography by philatelists, in which the lines of the design on the plate are raised. Ink is

Above: A miniature sheet issued by New Caledonia in 1999 shows reproductions of its first stamp, produced using five different printing processes.

rolled across them and pressed into the paper, producing a smooth surface but often with the design showing through on the back of the stamp.

British low-value stamps were printed by letterpress until 1934, when photogravure was adopted. For this the plate is engraved photographically, allowing fine gradations of tone. When magnified the image can be seen to consist of fine lines due to the screening process. It was first used by Bavaria in 1914 and became popular in the 1930s. In recent years it has given way to multicolour offset lithography, perceived as a cheaper and more reliable process, whereby the image is chemically applied to the printing plate and the ink is "offset" on to a secondary medium, such as a rubber mat, before being transferred to the paper. The image is made up of fine dots.

A few stamps from 1847 onwards were embossed, with the portrait or emblem in relief. Recent attempts to create three-dimensional effects have given rise to laminated-prismatic stamps, stamps in metal foil, images raised by thermography, and holograms.

The Many Lives of a Famous Stamp

1   2   3   4

The Austrian 1s stamp holds the world record for being printed using four different processes at different times. Designed by H. Strohofer to mark the 800th anniversary of Mariazell Basilica, it began life on 22 June 1957 [1], engraved by G. Wimmer and recess-printed (intaglio). On 25 October 1957 it was re-issued as the first denomination in a new definitive series devoted to buildings. This issue [2] was typographed (letterpress), retaining Wimmer's name in the margin. It is similar to the first: the chief differences are the solid value tablet (the intaglio version has criss-cross lines) and the clouds, which are stippled rather than cross-hatched. The rest of the series, as it gradually appeared, was lithographed, and a version of the 1s in this process appeared in January 1959, easily distinguished by the omission of the engraver's name and the lighter colour [3]. Finally a smaller format was adopted for the version of February 1960 printed in photogravure by the British printer Harrison and Sons of High Wycombe [4]. Apart from the Allied occupation set of 1945 (printed in Washington), this was the only Austrian stamp printed outside the country.

STAMPS FOR EVERYDAY USE

In 1840, when the first stamps were issued, there was only one kind, intended to prepay the postage on ordinary letters. When registered mail was introduced a year later, the British Treasury ruled that the 6d fee had to be prepaid in cash, as registration was not classed as a postal service. It was only in the early 20th century, as postage stamps designed to prepay a range of different services became increasingly available, that the permanent issues came to be known as "definitives".

Britain has retained the small upright format of the Penny Black for the vast majority of definitives, and today every denomination, from 1p to £5, is the same size. However, at various times since 1867, larger sizes have been used for the higher values, while the first ¹/₂d stamp, issued in 1870, adopted a small horizontal format, half the size of the 1d stamp. Because most early definitives portrayed a head of state, the upright shape came to be known as the portrait format.

DEFINITIVE SERIES
In establishing a definitive series, most countries followed Britain's lead, although Canada pioneered a horizontal (landscape) format in 1851 for its

Above: One year after the birth of the British penny postage, the Penny Red and "improved" Twopence Blue replaced the original 1840 designs, as part of the Post Office's bid to stamp out postal fraud. While effigies of rulers continue to be adapted or created anew by their designers, the basic format of many "portrait" definitives worldwide remains exactly the same.

Above: Canada issued its first stamp, the Threepenny Beaver, in 1851.

Below: Africa's first stamp: The Cape of Good Hope Triangular of 1853.

Threepenny Beaver, and this shape was later adopted by New Brunswick (1860) and the USA (1869).

The British colonies in North America were innovative in the matter of shape: New Brunswick started with a diamond format in 1851, while Newfoundland's first series (1857) adopted square or triangular shapes as well as a larger portrait size, with a corresponding landscape format from 1865. The Cape Triangular (1853) is said to have been adopted to help semi-literate postal workers sort the mail, though this is unlikely as all Cape stamps up to 1864 were of that shape.

SALE OF DEFINITIVES
British stamps were printed in sheets of 240, so that a row of twelve 1d stamps could be sold for 1s and the full sheet for £1. This pattern was followed in those dominions and colonies that used sterling currency, but elsewhere sheets of 100 or 200 were the norm. In recent years, the tendency has been to produce much smaller sheets, notably in

Above: A portion of a self-adhesive US booklet by Stamp Venturers, 1995–6.

Germany, where sheets of ten are now issued with decorative margins, a marketing ploy to encourage philatelists to collect complete sheets rather than single stamps. In the USA sheets of 20 or 18 are now common.

AMERICAN PORTRAITS
The subject matter of definitive stamps has also broadened considerably in the past half century. From 1847, US policy was to portray dead presidents and politicians and occasionally other historic figures. The series of 1918 revived the landscape format, briefly used in 1869 for $2 and $5 stamps portraying Benjamin Franklin; this was expanded in 1922–5, when all denominations from 20c to $5 used the horizontal shape to show landmarks, scenery and a buffalo to best effect.

The series of 1938 again portrayed dead presidents. The denominations up to 22c portrayed the president of the

Above: Definitive designs: a UK Machin (left) flanked by a Scottish "country" definitive (right).

corresponding number (for example, the 17th president, Andrew Johnson, was shown on the 17c stamp). Most American definitives since 1954 have broadened the scope to include men and women prominent in many different fields.

NATIONAL THEMES

Monarchical countries such as Britain and Spain prefer a uniform series with a single portrait of the ruler. Indeed, the effigy of Elizabeth II, designed by Arnold Machin, has adorned British stamps since 1967 and several hundred different varieties have now been issued. For their low value stamps, the Scandinavian countries and the

Above: Small format definitives issued by St Lucia, 1912 (left) and Sudan, 1921 (right).

Below: Dominica's 1923 series coupled a royal portrait with a colonial emblem.

Postwar German Definitives

The division of Germany after World War II into the Federal Republic, the Democratic Republic and West Berlin resulted in separate issues of stamps in each area. West Germany's definitive stamp designs ranged from the symbolic (posthorns) to presidential portraiture before settling on the themes of technology and famous buildings. West Berlin featured famous Berliners and architecture, while the Democratic Republic favoured socialist celebrities and communist symbolism.

Netherlands have a penchant for designs based on the numerals of value. Norway's Posthorns have been in longest continuous use, since 1871, but Denmark's Wavy Lines are not far behind. Higher values, however, stick to royal portraits. Republics such as France, Switzerland and Portugal prefer allegorical figures.

Above and right: Pictorial definitives from Italy (castles), Austria (religious foundations) and Australia (cartoons).

Below: Historic ships appeared on the Barbados series of 1994–8.

PICTORIAL DESIGNS AND MULTICOLOUR STAMPS

Definitives depicting scenery and the occasional fauna and flora became popular in the late 1890s, beginning with New Zealand, Tonga and Tasmania and spreading to the Latin American countries. By the 1930s the colonies of the British and French empires were indulging in bicoloured pictorials.

The advent of multicolour photogravure, and later offset lithography, broadened the scope in the postwar era, and fully pictorial definitives became the fashion. At first these sets had a mixture of subjects but as the tendency to change sets more frequently has developed, such sets have usually adopted a specific theme, such as birds, flowers, insects or wild animals. Other subjects that have proved very popular include women's costume (Austria), antique furniture (Hungary), coins (Portuguese India) and civic arms (Lithuania).

Definitives are produced in vast quantities – even the Penny Black of 1840–1 ran to some 72 million – but technical alterations during the production, or changes in postal rates, can produce elusive items that soar above their peers in philatelic value.

SHEETS, COILS, BOOKLETS AND STATIONERY

Definitives were always issued in sheets until the 1890s, but other methods of providing stamps have since come into use. In that decade several companies on both sides of the Atlantic devised machines that would dispense stamps. Some were coin-operated but others were intended for use in large company mailrooms, saving staff the time it took to tear up sheets.

COILS AND SHEETS
At first coils of stamps were made up from strips cut from sheets, with parts of the margins used to join one strip to the next; specialists like to collect the coil-join pairs. Later, special printings of stamps from rotary presses produced continuous reels, giving rise to joint line pairs, with a narrow vertical line of colour where the ends of the printing plate met as they were curved round the cylinder. In many countries coils are numbered sequentially on the back of every fifth or tenth stamp in the row.

Apart from the lack of perforations on opposite sides, either vertically or horizontally, coil stamps can be distinguished by their sideways watermark (in Britain) or two or more different stamps side by side to make up the value paid. Similar multivalue coil strips were produced in Britain and later in South Africa in connection with offers made by the *Reader's Digest*.

Left: A US coil of 1912, with private perforations.

Below: A US coil pair of 1983, showing the vertical joint line.

Above: The cover of a British booklet of 1920, advertising Harrods department store.

Right: A Canadian booklet of Flag stamps, 2004.

Sometimes a different theme is used for definitives in coils and sheets. Thus the USA features prominent Americans on sheets and modes of transportation on coils; Germany has portrayed famous women on sheets and landmarks on coils.

Automatic stamps, pioneered by the Frama company of Switzerland in the 1970s, are dispensed by inserting a coin in the slot and using a keypad to tap out the value of the stamp required. The earliest Frama labels were very prosaic, in shades of red ink, but they have become multicoloured and pictorial. Similar systems are operated by Klussendorf (Germany), Creusot (France), Epelsa (Spain) and others.

BOOKLETS AND MINIATURE SHEETS
Booklets of stamps were pioneered by Luxembourg (1895), spread to the USA (1902) and Britain (1908) and are now universal. The stamps are often imperforate on two or more adjoining sides and may be found with inverted watermarks (in Britain) or with different stamps or advertising labels side by side. Originally, booklets were stitched, often with advertising on the covers and interleaves, but in most the panes are now stuck to the cover in a style

developed by Sweden. Britain pioneered the prestige booklet in the 1970s, with mixed panes of definitives as well as combinations of regional stamps or special issues.

Luxembourg also pioneered miniature sheets (1921–3), which have spread around the world. One or more stamps, sometimes forming a large composite design, are set in a decorative margin, with the image on the stamp often projecting out to the edges of the sheet.

POSTAL STATIONERY
These collectables include all kinds of envelopes, letter sheets, postcards and wrappers with some kind of stamp printed on them.

Stamped letter sheets denoting prepayment of postage were in use in Sardinia by 1818. Although the "stamp" actually represented a tax, they were allowed to pass through the post without further charge, so they are often regarded, in Italy at least, as the world's first stamps. Other countries, such as New South Wales (1838),

Below: A composite sheetlet of 12 stamps issued by the United Nations in 1998 for International Year of the Ocean.

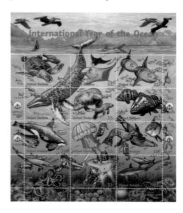

The Mulready Envelope

William Mulready was the designer of Britain's first postal envelope, issued in 1840 but withdrawn in 1841. Its rather pompous decoration, portraying Britannia sending forth her winged messengers to all parts of the far-flung British Empire, inspired a satirical poem in *Punch* magazine and numerous lampoons, resulting in its withdrawal but also triggering off a craze for pictorial stationery.

Above: On this Australian booklet pane of 1967, 4c stamps were uprated to 5c.

Russia and Finland (1845) and some German states (1845–8), had similar stamped sheets long before resorting to adhesive stamps. Even Rowland Hill pinned his faith on wrappers and letter sheets designed by his friend William Mulready, issuing adhesive stamps only as an afterthought. The "Mulreadys" gave way to envelopes bearing an

Left and below: Impressed stamps from a 2002 Italian commemorative postcard and a US airmail postcard issued in 1981.

embossed stamp (the Penny Pink, which continued in use until 1902). Special envelopes with crossed blue lines for registered mail were adopted in 1878 and "Official paid" stationery, pioneered by the USA, spread to most countries by the early 1900s. Stamped postcards were invented in Austria in 1869, offering cut-price postage, and spread abroad a year later despite reservations about the messages being read by postal workers and servants.

OTHER STATIONERY

Newspaper wrappers with printed stamps developed in the 1870s. Lettercards – cards folded and sealed along the outer edges by perforated strips that were torn off by the addressee – were first used in Belgium (1882), while Newfoundland (1912) alone produced reply lettercards, with a smaller card inside. Britain briefly flirted with postnotes, folded sheets with an impressed stamp, in 1982. Telegram forms with impressed or embossed stamps were once common.

Special stationery used by government departments has included jury citations and vaccination certificates.

Distinctive stationery for use by armed services or prisoners of war is of particular interest to collectors of military postal history. Austria and prewar Czechoslovakia made enthusiastic use of prestamped postcards for tourist publicity. In Australia, prestamped envelopes and postcards are often employed to commemorate events not deemed to merit adhesive stamp issues.

Since the 1970s there has been a trend towards stationery with a device indicating that postage has been paid, without specifying the amount. Instead the class of postage is expressed, overcoming the need to reprint stationery every time postal rates are increased.

Below: The world's first stamped postcard, issued by Austria in 1869.

COMMEMORATIVE AND SPECIAL ISSUES

The notion that stamps could be used for purposes other than merely to indicate that postage had been paid was slow to catch on. In 1876 the USA produced envelopes with embossed stamps to celebrate the centenary of the Declaration of Independence, but the idea was not adopted for adhesive stamps until the Columbian Exposition in 1893. In the interim, a German local post, the Privat Brief Verkehr of Frankfurt-am-Main, issued a stamp in July 1887 in honour of the Ninth German Federal and Jubilee Shooting Contest. The following year several local posts issued mourning stamps following the deaths of German emperors, William I and his son Frederick III. Many other German local posts had commemorative stamps (including one from Breslau to celebrate the Jewish New Year), but Germany itself did not issue any such stamps until 1919.

FIRST GOVERNMENT ISSUES
In May 1888 New South Wales celebrated the centenary of the colony with a long series captioned "One hundred years". The stamps remained in use for 12 years, undergoing numerous changes in colour, watermark and perforation. Most commemorative issues since that time, however, have been on sale for a short time only, and in some cases from restricted sales outlets. Britain's first adhesive commemorative stamps, for example, publicizing the

Left: The first adhesive commemorative stamp was issued by Frankfurt-am-Main in July 1887, on the occasion of a shooting contest.

Right: New South Wales celebrated its centenary with a commemorative set, issued in May 1888.

Above: The first Mother's Day stamp, released by the USA in 1934, aptly used Whistler's portrait of his mother.

Below: Marshall Islands stamp, 2004.

British Empire Exhibition at Wembley in 1924–5, were sold only at the exhibition's post offices.

Commemoratives spread throughout the world. Hong Kong overprinted a stamp in 1891 for the colony's 50th anniversary; El Salvador and Nicaragua issued sets in January 1892 to mark the 400th anniversary of Columbus's arrival in America; Montenegro produced Europe's first commemoratives, overprinting the definitive series in 1893 to mark the quatercentenary of printing; and the Transvaal issued Africa's first commemorative in 1895, to mark the adoption of penny postage.

Not only are commemoratives issued with increasing frequency to honour historic events and personalities, as well

as to publicize current events of national or international importance, but often the subject of the commemoration is used as an opportunity to issue a set of stamps. Thus the maiden voyage of the *Queen Mary 2* in 2004 was the pretext for a set of six stamps depicting famous British ocean liners.

SPECIAL ISSUES
Many postal administrations now augment their definitives with "special issues", a term that covers anything with a restricted lifespan. These issues are generally thematic in nature, often all of the same denomination and increasingly printed side by side in the same sheet. They include stamps for Christmas, Easter, Mother's Day and

many other such occasions, as well as sheetlets or booklets containing greetings stamps, covering everything from the birth of a baby to "Get well soon" or "I love you, Mom".

STAMPS AND PHILANTHROPY

Philately is the only collecting hobby able to support good causes of all kinds, through the medium of stamps that include a sum payable either to charity in general or to a specific organization. Such stamps are known generally as charity stamps (although in the USA they have been described more accurately as semi-postals, as only part of the charge goes to the postal service).

The concept originated in Britain in 1890, when pictorial envelopes were issued to celebrate the golden jubilee of penny postage. They were sold for 1s but were valid for only 1d postage, the other 11d going to the Rowland Hill Benevolent Fund for Post Office Widows and Orphans.

In 1897–1900 some of the Australian colonies – New South Wales, Queensland and Victoria – issued stamps for Queen Victoria's diamond jubilee or Boer War funds, selling them for 1s, 2s or 2s 6d but providing postal validity for only 1d, 2d or

2½d. The example was followed by Russia and Romania in 1905, but without the outrageously high premiums. These stamps, like the Australians, were issued for specific charities, notably the Russo-Japanese War of 1905, but when the idea spread to other parts of Europe, proceeds were devoted to ongoing good causes, especially child welfare. The stamps issued by Switzerland from 1913 for child welfare, inscribed in Latin "Pro juventute", consisted of short sets, usually with a specific subject. Later this concept was extended to other good causes, bearing the inscription "Pro patria" ("For the fatherland").

WELFARE STAMPS

Germany began issuing welfare stamps (*Wohlfahrtsmarken*) in the 1920s and later added stamps with the inscription "*Weihnachtsmarke*" ("Christmas stamp") or "*Jugendmarke*" ("Youth stamp"). The concept continues to this day. The Netherlands produce stamps inscribed "*Voor het kind*" ("For the child") or "*Sommerzegel*" ("Summer stamp"). Since 1929 New Zealand has issued stamps for children's health camps. Some countries, such as Yugoslavia and Portugal, had charity tax stamps whose use was compulsory

Above: Stamps in aid of the Ludwigshafen explosion disaster in 1948 and New Zealand health camps (1949).

Right: A Netherlands Antilles definitive overprinted for the relief of Dutch flood victims in 1953.

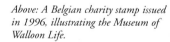

Above: A Belgian charity stamp issued in 1996, illustrating the Museum of Walloon Life.

at certain times, and even issued special postage due labels with which to surcharge mail not bearing the stamps.

Excessive premiums brought charity stamps into disrepute and the actual charity portion is now seldom more than 50 per cent of the postal value. Britain, which started the ball rolling in 1890, did not issue a charity stamp until 1975 (for health and handicap funds), while the USA's first charity stamp (raising money for breast cancer research) appeared in 1988.

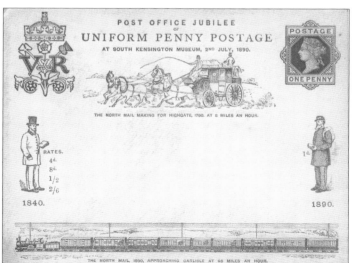

Left: The envelope for the golden jubilee of penny postage contrasted mail communications in 1840 and 1890.

AIRMAILS AND SPECIAL SERVICE STAMPS

Sending messages by air goes back to the 5th century BC, when inscribed arrows were used during the siege of the Corinthian colony of Potidaea. Messages carried by kite date from AD 549 in China, and pigeons have been used since the Siege of Leyden in 1575. The first balloon message was carried by Vincenzo Lunardi in September 1784, and the first official airmail was carried between La Fayette and Crawfordsville, Indiana, by the balloon *Jupiter*, on 17 August 1859.

Above: A French stamp of 1955 showing a balloon flight during the Siege of Paris in 1870.

Right: Private 5c stamp for mail carried by the balloon Buffalo, *1877.*

FIRST AIR MAIL STAMPS
The first regular air service was set up during the sieges of Metz and Paris in the Franco-Prussian War in 1870–1, for which special message forms were inscribed "Par Ballon Monté" ("By

Left: This 1959 US airmail stamp marked the centenary of the Jupiter *balloon flight.*

Below: Loading mail on to the biplane Horatius *at Croydon, south of London, in the early 1930s.*

manned balloon"). Within five years of the first faltering flight by the Wright Brothers in 1903, mail was being flown by plane from Paris to St Nazaire. In 1909 the Peruvian aviator Jorge Chavez carried the first airmail between two countries: Switzerland and Italy.

The first air stamp was a private 5c label produced in 1877 by Professor Samuel King for use on mail carried by his balloon *Buffalo* from Nashville, Tennessee, and showed the balloon in flight. In 1898 1s stamps were issued

in connection with the Original Great Barrier Pigeongram Service in New Zealand. Semi-official stamps for souvenirs flown by heavier-than-air machines at aviation meetings were first issued in 1909 at Bar-sur-Aube, France.

MAIL CARRIED BY AIRCRAFT
India organized the world's first mail service by aircraft (Allahabad to Naini, February 1911), closely followed by Britain, Denmark, Italy and the USA. These services had special postmarks but used ordinary stamps. The USA was the first country to issue a stamp depicting an aircraft, in 1912, but it was part of a parcel post series and had no relevance to airmail. Several other countries featured planes on non-airmail stamps in 1914–15.

Italy produced the first airmail stamp, overprinted for the Rome–Turin service in 1917. The first definitive air stamps were issued by the USA in 1918 and featured the Curtiss Jenny biplane. The 24c with inverted centre was the first airmail error. Thousands of airmail stamps have been issued since, though nowadays many that are specific to airmail rates are no longer thus inscribed.

The Inverted Jenny
The USA released a set of three stamps in 1918 depicting a Curtiss JN-4, popularly known as the Jenny. The 24c was printed with a red frame and a blue centre, but one sheet of 100 was discovered with the centre inverted – one of the greatest American rarities.

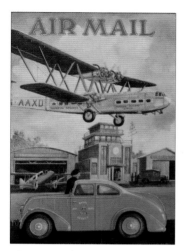

Above: Airmails have spawned colourful stationery over the years. As shown by this postcard, it was popular to include illustrations of the planes themselves.

Below: Collectable airmail cigarette cards featured the famous pilots of the day and historic airmail planes.

Colombia, Germany, Mexico and Thailand had lightweight airmail stationery from 1923 onwards, but air letter sheets, or "aerogrammes", were pioneered by Iraq in 1933, followed by Britain (1941) and other countries after World War II. The first British aerogrammes were used for mail sent to prisoners of war and were inscribed in English, French and German.

"BACK OF BOOK" STAMPS

Stamps that were neither definitive nor commemorative but intended for special services have traditionally been tacked on the end of the main listing in stamp catalogues. They are therefore known as "back of book" stamps (BOB for short), a phrase that originated with American collectors. The largest group are not strictly postage stamps at all, but labels indicating that money has to be recovered from the addressee, either because an item is unpaid or under-paid, or because some special fee (such as customs duty) has to be collected. These are known as postage due labels, although many of them are inscribed "To pay" in the relevant language.

Because they are used internally, few of these stamps bear a country name, and identifying them by their inscriptions or currency is often a headache for inexperienced collectors. Most are quite functional in design, with numerals of value, but more recent issues tend to be pictorial. They were pioneered by France in 1859 and gradually spread around the world.

Stamps for Parcels, Express Delivery and Other Services

Belgium produced the world's first parcel stamps in 1879, but many railway and freight companies had been using them since the 1840s, if not earlier. Britain's only stamps in this category were definitives overprinted from 1883 onwards for use on government parcels. The USPO introduced a parcel service in 1912 and briefly issued a series of red stamps, mainly depicting aspects of postal communications.

Special and express delivery stamps have appeared mainly in Latin American countries but also in Canada and the USA. The latter also issued stamps denoting special handling in 1925–9. Distinctive stamps for registration, sometimes incorporating a serial number, were issued by Canada, Liberia, Montenegro, the USA, Australian states and several Latin American countries.

Official stamps are those provided for the use of government departments. Stamps for separate departments were issued by the USA, Britain, South Australia and Argentina, but elsewhere all-purpose stamps were produced. Definitives were also overprinted or perforated with initials for this purpose. Stamps inscribed or overprinted to

Above: The 1968 US $1 stamp enabled servicemen overseas to send parcels home at a special rate.

Below: Postage due labels from the USA (1879) and Yugoslavia (1948), the latter applied to mail not bearing the compulsory Red Cross charity stamp.

denote a tax on mail during wartime were pioneered by Spain (1874–7) and widely used in World War I.

Stamps have also been produced for many other purposes, such as advice of delivery (Colombia), concessional letters (Italy), journal tax (Austria), late fee (Latin America), lottery or prize draw (Japan and Norway), marine insurance (Netherlands) and newspapers (Austria, New Zealand, USA).

Right: Advice of delivery stamp from Montenegro, 1895.

Below: Parcel postage due label, USA, 1912.

HOW TO COLLECT STAMPS

Armed with a few essential items and some knowledge of stamp care and mounting, the ways you can organize a collection are limitless. Sometimes the choice of what to include seems too great, but, as explained here, there are logical ways to narrow the focus.

Left: An Egyptian "stamp on a stamp", issued in 2004 for the 25th anniversary of the Philatelic Society.

STARTING A COLLECTION

There are many different reasons why people take up stamp collecting. A lucky few may inherit a collection from a parent or relative, so they can get off to a flying start and just carry on where the previous owner left off, but most people have to start from scratch. It may be as simple as seeing a particularly eye-catching stamp on an item in your own mail, perhaps from an interesting place you once visited, or depicting a subject that fascinates you, or that is related in some way to your profession or to a school project. The desire to keep it might just be enough to trigger off the notion of forming a stamp collection with a related theme.

We are by nature acquisitive animals, given to collecting items that may serve no utilitarian purpose but which are nontheless decorative or desirable. As collectable objects, stamps offer variety, rarity, scholarly interest and aesthetic appeal. Ever since the Penny Black first appeared, stamps have been admired and hoarded by collectors for their aesthetic qualities as miniature works of art and masterpieces of engraving, and as exponents of cultural and political ideals.

Below: The theme of the Europa stamps in 2004 was holidays, exemplified by this stamp from Guernsey.

Above: Pictorial stamps from China and Hungary in 2004 illustrate the popular themes of birds and animals.

PHILATELY TODAY

Not so many years ago most pieces of mail that came into the average household bore adhesive stamps, and it was a relatively easy matter to clip stamps off envelopes. Before long you had the nucleus of a collection, mostly stamps of your own country, but augmented with the occasional foreign stamp culled from holiday postcards or, in some cases, from correspondence sent to the workplace. The chances are that your local town had one or more stamp shops with attractive displays of the world's latest issues in the window to tempt passers-by.

Adhesive stamps are now virtually confined to social mail such as personal letters and postcards, as most business

Above: Shops dealing in goods for the stamp collector are fewer than they were, but those remaining are often well stocked and helpful. As they are almost always run by keen philatelists, they are great places to get advice if you are just starting out. Most stamp shops stock starter packs, interesting collections of stamps, and equipment for the specialist.

and "junk" mail bears meter marks or some other indication that postage has been prepaid by a bulk mailer. Meter marks and PPIs (postage paid impressions) do have their own devotees, but they lack the universal appeal of adhesive stamps. Because stamps are now not very plentiful on mail this particular incentive to start a collection, especially among children, may not be so great as it was. However, this does not mean that philately is becoming less popular. On the contrary, postal

Below: Presentation packs, often collected as mementoes by the non-philatelist as well as the keen collector, are an important source of revenue for philatelic bureaux.

administrations all over the world now spend a small fortune on advertising on television and in the press, as well as producing lavish brochures and sales literature promoting an ever-increasing number of special issues and first day covers. The response comes mainly from adults, many of whom may have collected stamps as children and given up the hobby, but returned to it later. Yet philatelic bureaux are also keen to issue stamps bearing themes of interest to children and young adults, and the prospect of swapping issues with a fellow collector – at a local stamp club or via internet contact – establishes philately as a great interactive pastime.

BE AN INDIVIDUAL

Despite the high-pressure sales tactics, not every newcomer to the hobby slavishly collects the offerings of the national philatelic bureaux. Many start out along that road but quickly tire of following the herd and decide to assert their individuality.

What impels them to continue with stamps may be determined by many other factors. They may be attracted to the stamps of another country because of holidays, military service or business connections there, the latter being particularly useful for continuing and developing the collection. In America, while most philatelists collect US stamps, many are drawn to the country from which their ancestors emigrated. The stamps of Israel and the Vatican are immensely popular with Jews or Roman Catholics for religious reasons. And it may simply be the lure of far-off places that explains the popularity of stamps from places such as Pitcairn and Tristan da Cunha.

These are the main reasons for embarking on a straightforward country collection. You begin with the latest issues, sign up to a dealer's new issue service or perhaps get your stamps and first day covers direct from the philatelic bureau of your chosen country, and gradually work back in time, filling in the gaps with purchases from dealers or bidding at auction: all these methods are discussed more fully later.

It is often the case that children begin with a general collection, embracing the stamps of the whole world and including anything that looks remotely like a postage stamp. As they grow older and the difficulty of attempting to form a meaningful collection on such a broad scale becomes apparent, collectors gradually narrow their interests and begin to specialize in a single country or even a particular reign or period.

In the past half century, however, other forms of collecting have developed. Paramount is the collecting of stamps according to the subject or purpose of issue, regardless of the country of origin. Others have developed an interest in postmarks and graduated to postal history, studying and collecting cards, covers and other pieces of mail, not primarily for their adhesive stamps but because of their cancellations and other postal markings.

Left: One of a set of 12 issued by the Vatican in 1946, celebrating the 400th anniversary of the Council of Trent.

Below: A stamp promoting tourism for the Pitcairn Islands, 2004.

Every Stamp Tells a Story

Every stamp tells us something about its country of origin, but occasionally the postmark reveals a bigger story. This Irish cover was salvaged from the fire that burned down the Rotunda, Dublin – itself being used as a temporary GPO after the main office was destroyed during the Easter rising of 1916.

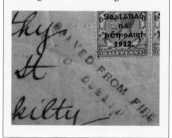

TOOLS AND TECHNIQUES

Like any other hobby, stamp collecting requires certain basic essentials, aids and tools. If you buy a starter kit you will find that most, if not all, of these items are included, although as you progress in philately you will probably want to add more advanced versions, as well as other gadgets.

The most obvious necessity is a magnifying glass – the higher the magnification the better. For handling stamps, a pair of tongs or tweezers with flattened "spade" ends is a must. To distinguish the subtle differences between stamps you will need a perforation gauge. These range enormously in sophistication (and price), from the basic transparent plastic model with dots or lines to electronic gauges. Similarly, watermark detectors range from a small black tray to machines with lights and filters. An ultraviolet lamp is used to detect different fluorescence and types of phosphor bands.

WHERE TO FIND STAMPS

Sooner or later you are going to be confronted with used stamps in their raw state, still attached to pieces of envelopes or postcards, either clipped off your own mail or purchased in bulk from a dealer who gets his supplies from the various charities that save stamps to raise funds. Banks and mail-order firms are other good sources. You

Above: It is possible to buy world stamps in bulk from a stamp dealer at a relatively low price. Many of these will still be attached to pieces of envelope, or postcards, and will require careful detaching with the aid of a few useful tools before they are mounted.

will find details of the latter in any monthly stamp magazine.

Postal administrations have also got in on the act. In many countries stamps were not affixed to parcels but were

KEY
1 *Stamp catalogue*
2 *Colour key*
3 & 4 *Perforation gauges*
5 *Large magnifying glass*
6 *Sliding stamp magnifier*
7 *Small plastic tongs*
8 *Larger metal tongs*
9 *Small scissors*
10 *Starter pack of stamps*
11 *Small magnifier*
12 *Stamps attached to pieces of envelope.*

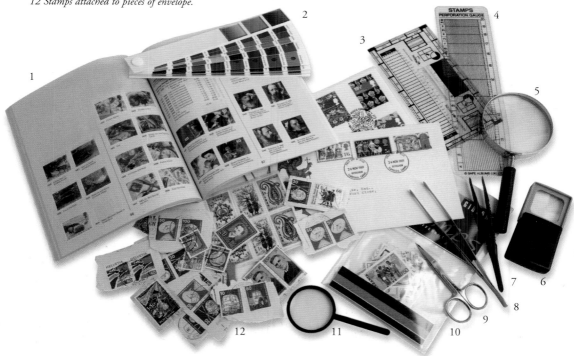

Perforation Gauge

Invented in the 1860s, a perforation gauge measures the number of holes in a space of 2cm (³/₄in). You simply lay the stamp alongside the rows of holes on the gauge until you find the one that fits. This will give you a "perf measurement".

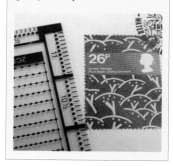

Step-by-Step Soaking Sequence

1. Float the stamps face upwards in a basin or large bowl of lukewarm water. Do not soak them.

2. The stamps will curl away from the paper almost immediately, but you can test this by gently lifting a corner.

3. Remove the stamps from the water and, with care, use the tweezers to detach from the paper completely.

4. Lay the stamps face down on the top half of a clean sheet of white porous paper to dry.

5. Fold the bottom half of the white paper so that it rests over the top of the stamps, then place the folded sheet between layers of newspaper.

6. Place heavy weights on top and leave for 24 hours before removing the dried stamps and sorting into packets. They are now ready to mount in an album.

attached to cards that accompanied the parcel to its destination. The cards were then retained by the post office for some time before being scrapped. The stamps, clipped off the cards, eventually found their way into bags sold to dealers and collectors by the kilo – hence the term "kiloware" which is often applied loosely to any mixture of used stamps on paper sold by weight.

DETACHING STAMPS

Once you have sifted through the mixture and selected the stamps you wish to retain, they have to be carefully parted from the envelopes. In the days

Below: When trimming the attached paper around self-adhesive stamps, take care not to damage the perforations, as this detracts from their value.

when most stamps were recess-printed in monochrome, collectors would quite happily drench them in hot water – but not any more, for modern stamps are printed by less stable multicolour processes on glossy paper with a high chalk content, with fugitive inks and phosphor bands that would be damaged by total immersion. The soaking procedure described above holds good for the vast majority of self-adhesive stamps, which now have a water-soluble backing. However, some issues from the 1980s, notably from France, the USA and Australia, are backed with a rubber-based adhesive, which defies soaking. All you can do with these is keep them on their paper, trimmed neatly.

HOUSING A COLLECTION

One of the real joys of philately is the satisfaction gained from organizing a motley collection of stamps, covers and postal titbits into a logical, attractive format that can be pored over with pride and interest. Those collectors new to the hobby tend to be familiar with the preprinted fixed-leaf album, where individual spaces for stamps are effectively "drawn" on the page, but there are in fact a wealth of alternative housing options, some of which may not even be designated specifically for stamps. Before purchasing a home for your stamps, you should always reflect upon the type of material you wish to mount: will your collection contain only singles and pairs, or larger items such as First Day Covers and

Below: There are many ways of mounting stamps and stationery for display. Black-backed glassine sheets (left), with clear plastic sleeves already in place, are proving increasingly popular thanks to their user-friendly qualities. To house individual stamps, "Hawid strips" (centre foreground) can be cut to any shape or size, while photo corners (in the red box) are useful for mounting larger pieces of postal stationery. Traditional stamp mounts and pages with a grid pattern offer yet another means of affixing stamps to the page.

miniature sheets? How would you like the material to appear on the page: evenly-spaced individuals affixed using a discreet mount, or slotted into a clear plastic pouch – and against what kind of background? Will you require the flexibility of removing pages later? How much text do you plan to add: a simple label, or a lengthy caption?

CHOOSING AN ALBUM

My very first stamp collector's outfit contained a *Whirlwind* album – small, stapled card covers embellished by a picture of a Spitfire fighter, enclosing pages bearing dotted lines ruled into squares with names of countries and a few illustrations in the headings. A packet of transparent, gummed hinges, a packet of 50 assorted world stamps and the *XLCR Stamp Finder* (a 28-page pocket encyclopedia covering stamps of the world, priced 4d if sold separately) completed the kit that got me started on the right lines.

To this day most albums in starter kits are of the fixed-leaf variety, with printed pages facing each other. They are the most basic and the cheapest, and their chief drawback is their inflex-

Above: Removing the pages from a spring-back album.

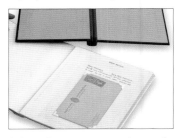

Below: Once the pages are removed they lie flat for easier mounting and writing.

ibility – there is never enough space for the stamps of the more popular countries, while many other pages remain depressingly empty. Also, stamps mounted on facing pages have a habit of catching on each other's perforations if the pages of the album are turned carelessly.

Loose-leaf albums provide the means for expansion and it is advisable to graduate to one of these at the earliest opportunity, once you have decided in which area you wish to specialize. The most basic form is the spring-back type, in which the pages are held firmly in place by powerful springs in the spine. To remove or insert pages, the boards of the binder are folded back to release the spring. This is simple and easy to do, but frequent usage over a period,

Above: Removing a page from an album with a multi-ring binder.

Below: Photo corners are used to mount postcards, covers and miniature sheets.

together with the temptation to cram too many pages into the binder, weakens the springs and then the pages are not held as firmly as they should be. The other snag with spring-backs is that it is impossible to lay the pages flat when the album is open.

Peg-fitting albums have the advantage that the pages lie flat, but every time you wish to insert a new page somewhere all the pages before it have to be taken off the pegs and then threaded back on again. This is the system adopted in the most expensive albums, which usually have glassine sheets attached to the front of each page to provide additional protection for the stamps mounted on them.

Less expensive are the albums with a multi-ring fitment. Release the catch and the rings break open so that fresh pages can be inserted wherever you wish without disturbing the others. These albums also lie flat when open. The leaves provided with them have a row of holes punched on the left side to fit the rings. A similar system is used in ring binders intended for holding

A4-size cards slipped into plastic sleeves, and increasingly this type of binder is being adopted by collectors, especially those who prefer to generate their album pages on a computer. For larger pieces of postal material, such as first day covers, clear "photo corners" can be mounted on punched sheets of card to hold them in place on the page.

If you do adopt this system, you must make sure that the cards, if white, do not contain artificial bleaching agents, and that the sleeves are chemically inert, otherwise either may do long-term damage to your stamps.

HINGELESS MOUNTING SYSTEMS

Previously, all stamps, mint or used, were affixed to the page by means of small pieces of transparent paper, gummed on one side. The mount was folded in half and moistened, so that one part adhered to the top of the back of the stamp and the other to the page. The best quality hinges were double gummed so that they peeled off the stamp without damaging it, although some trace of the hinge was inevitable.

In the 1950s, however, a desire for unmounted mint stamps developed in Europe and has now become universal. Dealers encourage this by the wide price differential between unmounted and mounted mint. One solution is to

Hawid Strips

If you are anxious to preserve the value of your mint stamps, you can try the clear- or black-backed mounts known generically as "Hawid strips" (after the German inventor, Hans Widemeyer). The stamps just slot into these, and they certainly enhance the appearance of mint stamps, but unless you are prepared to pay extra for the ready-cut packs they have to be trimmed to size and are fiddly to use.

select mint stamps from the corner of the sheet, with a strip of marginal paper attached, and to affix the hinge to the selvage. Thus the stamp remains unmounted mint, though the page may look untidy as a result.

Below: A stockbook, with transparent strips and clear interleaving, is useful for storing stamps awaiting mounting.

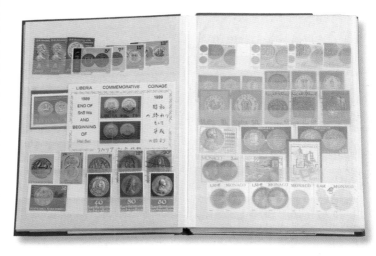

MOUNTING STAMPS FOR DISPLAY

When stamp albums became popular in the 1860s the best of them – fixed-leaf, of course – had printed outlines of the appropriate shape for every postage stamp of the world then known to exist, with the denomination and colour of the stamp in each space. By the 1870s some albums even attempted to illustrate the stamps as well, although the images were often rather crude. The ultimate de luxe albums of the late 19th and early 20th centuries were those with spaces and illustrations on the right-hand page and catalogue descriptions and technical data on the left-hand page. They were sumptuously bound in full morocco leather and fitted with a heavy brass lock.

Above: A fast-bound printed album, with stamps mounted on facing pages.

ONE-COUNTRY ALBUMS

As the number of stamps increased, such albums became less practicable. As late as the 1940s, Minkus of the USA was still offering the "Master Global" album with a space for every stamp since 1840, but this was a philatelic dinosaur and was eventually killed by its sheer bulk. By that time

some publishers, notably Schaubek of Germany, were producing one-country albums along similar lines and this fashion continues to the present day with several companies in America and Europe offering a comprehensive range of such loose-leaf albums, together with annual supplements. The ultimate is

the one-country hingeless album with clear mounting strips already in place over each illustration. The collector with plenty of money but perhaps limited time to devote to the hobby can subscribe to the new issues from a philatelic bureau and merely tip them into the appropriate page.

Although simple, this method is unlikely to appeal to collectors for whom the pleasure of the hobby comes not from acquiring new specimens, but from arranging them, mounting them in albums and annotating them to suit their individual taste. To them, a blank album page, adorned with nothing more than the feint squares that provide a guide to keeping the rows of stamps straight, is a challenge to be faced with enthusiasm. Avoiding the rigid constraints of the printed album, these collectors relish the opportunity to express their individuality, not only by the manner in which they lay out the stamps on the page, but also in the methods adopted to annotate them, demonstrating their technical expertise as well as their calligraphic skills.

Below: An album page showing a World War I cover mounted with photo corners and neatly annotated by hand.

Below: A page of Austrian stamps in hingeless mounts, accompanied by manuscript captions.

Mounting Pairs and Blocks

Multiples can be mounted with hinges if they are in used condition, otherwise Hawid strips can be cut to fit. Provided at least two corners of the block are imperforate, photo corners can be used without blunting the perforations.

Above: A page from a beginner's printed album of the 1950s.

Above: A balanced arrangement of Tuva stamps of different shapes.

LAYING OUT STAMPS

It's a good idea to spread out the stamps you intend to mount on the page and move them around until you achieve a balanced effect. Do not attempt to cram too many stamps on to the page – a common mistake of even experienced collectors. Of course, if you wish to display an entire definitive series you may be constrained by the number of stamps in the set, although the average definitive range

Below: A late 19th-century printed album with a space for each stamp.

consists of about 15–20 stamps. Longer sets, such as the Prominent Americans or Transportation coils, would require two or three pages at least, while the prolific Machin series of Great Britain could fill an entire album.

Try to avoid rows containing the same number of stamps, especially if they are all of the same size and format. Most sets are a mixture of horizontal and vertical formats and stamps for the highest denominations are often larger, but where they are all the same size you can impart some variety by laying out the rows to form a pyramid.

Commemoratives and special issues may present more of a problem, but also offer greater leeway to indulge your artistic skills. Less rather than more should be the keynote. In some cases you may need a row for each stamp, pair or short set, but sometimes you can get two single issues side by side.

ANNOTATING THE PAGES

The number of stamps you can display on a page is also dependent on the amount of annotation you plan to add. The basic data would be the date of issue and the title of the set or stamp. Then you could add the names of the designer and printer and the printing process used. Further information might include details of perforation and watermark, captions for each stamp and even some notes on the reason for the issue, such as additional denominations or changes of colour necessitated by increased postal rates. It is a good idea to map out the text on a scrap sheet to ensure you get the balance right.

If you are annotating the page by hand you should use a fountain pen or a drafting pen, and preferably black ink. Never use a ballpoint pen because the ink may smudge, and pencilled notes will simply fade.

ADVANCED DISPLAY TECHNIQUES

In a stamp album it is permissible to mount appropriate first day covers and souvenir cards. For a more specialized study ancillary material might include original artwork, essays and rejected designs, die and plate proofs and colour trials, as well as covers, cards and wrappers for registered mail and airmail, illustrating the actual usage of the stamps. As well as a straightforward set you would have separate pages for a range of shades, in chronological order of printing, strips and blocks of stamps to show such marginal markings as plate or cylinder numbers, printers'

imprints, alphanumeric controls indicating the year and sequence of printing, or multiples illustrating the exact position of plate flaws and other varieties occurring in the sheet. Information on these topics of interest to the advanced collector will be found towards the end of this section.

The more specialized a collection, the more writing-up is likely to be involved. In extreme cases a single stamp might be mounted on a page with several hundred words of annotation to explain the technical minutiae that make this specimen extraordinary.

INCLUDING POSTAL EPHEMERA

The collectable material associated with the lifespan of a postal service or a particular stamp is often described as "ephemera". For example, a cover or entire letter from the "pre-stamp" era might require all kinds of additional material to illustrate details of the route taken from sender to recipient, the computation of the postal charges and other fees (such as registration or express delivery) and any infringements of the regulations that necessitated a fine or some kind of endorsement in manuscript or by handstamp. Other related ephemera might include press cuttings, photographs or engravings.

The inclusion of collateral material, as it is known, is at the discretion of the individual. At one time, too much of this in relation to the actual piece of mail was frowned on, but it is now positively encouraged and is even regarded as a separate class, known as social philately, in competitions. In this area, considerable ingenuity is required to incorporate bulky and even three-dimensional items, as the notion of philately is stretched to the limit.

Above: A corner of a sheet showing two strips of the Spirit of 76 US stamps, with "Mail early" slogan and Mr Zip.

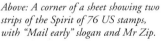

Below: Plate block of the $5 US definitive of 1975, featuring a railway conductor's lantern.

Above: Reconstruction of a quarter sheet of New Zealand stamps issued in 1893, displayed to show the advertisements printed on the reverse of the stamps.

Right: Picture postcard of the German battle cruiser Derfflinger, *scuttled at Scapa Flow in 1919, with a postcard bearing the ship's postmark.*

Above: A US $4.40 booklet of 1985 containing stamps showing seashells.

virtually impossible to think of a topic that has not been depicted on a stamp somewhere, at some time. Thematic collecting has liberated philately from the constraints of collecting stamps solely by country.

SUBJECT COLLECTING

The basic idea of thematic collecting is to group stamps according to the subject of the design. When the American Topical Association was formed in 1949 its primary aim was to provide members with checklists of stamps showing different subjects. Today, the ATA has over 50,000 members in almost 100 countries, and has published countless booklets detailing a wide range of different subjects. These have been basic lists enabling collectors to locate the stamps of their chosen subject with the aid of a standard stamp catalogue. However, in recent years major catalogue publishers have begun to produce thematic catalogues, fully illustrated and often in colour.

These catalogues follow a well-trodden path and cover such popular subjects as ships, aircraft, trains, cars,

Below: Chinese and Greek stamps for the railway enthusiast – but you have to look hard to spot the locomotives in the background of the designs.

Above: A Marshall Islands sheet of 50 showing US warships named after each state, from Alabama to Wyoming.

flowers, animals, birds, insects, sports, religion and fine art, as well as such international movements as the Red Cross or the Boy Scouts. There are even catalogues that list all the stamps depicting fungi, seashells and insects such as butterflies, and catalogues that deal exhaustively with ball games or the Olympics. However, many of these categories are broad and it is important to define limits within your chosen subject. It would be impossible to collect every stamp that showed a bird, for example; it makes more sense to focus on individual species that appeal to you, such as robins or puffins.

EUROPA STAMPS

Stamps inscribed "Europa" began to be issued in 1956, and have become one of the mainstays of pictorial subject collecting. Originally, the stamps were confined to the six countries of the European Coal and Steel Community (France, Germany, Italy, Belgium, the Netherlands and Luxembourg). During the 1960s their administration was taken over by the European Conference of Posts and Telecommunications (CEPT), now known as PostEurop, and the scheme has expanded to countries from Greenland to Turkey and the

Ukraine. At first the stamps had identical designs but in the 1970s this gave way to individual interpretations of a common theme.

You can either collect all the stamps with "Europa" in their inscription, or take those Europa stamps that fit the subject you are collecting. In 2004, for example, the theme of the Europa stamps was holidays. Some countries (such as Ireland) opted for tourist attractions such as scenery and landmarks, while others concentrated on sailing, swimming or just lounging on the beach. Many stamps have more than one element in their design. The primary subject will be very obvious, but often there is a secondary subject, perhaps tucked away in the border or the background, and it is the sharp-eyed philatelist who recognizes it who gains points for observation and originality in competitive exhibitions.

Right and below: Stamps from Slovenia, Latvia, the Czech Republic and Greece expound on the holiday theme of the 2004 Europa stamps.

PURPOSE-OF-ISSUE COLLECTING

This branch of thematics, which is also known as incidental philately, deals with the building of a collection around a particular event. A classic example might be a periodical celebration such as an anniversary, but occasionally a single event in history is chosen as a theme.

Anniversaries were among the first of the "global" themes to adorn stamps and labels. The first time stamps were issued in several countries to mark an event occurred in 1892–3, when the United States and several countries of Latin America celebrated the 400th anniversary of the first voyage of Columbus to the New World. In 1897–8 seven countries of the British Empire issued 56 stamps among them to mark Victoria's diamond jubilee; although Britain did not issue stamps, a number of commemorative labels were produced. Around the same period Portugal and its colonies celebrated the exploits of Vasco da Gama. Issues marking the 450th and 500th anniversaries of Columbus, and numerous others on this theme from Spain, Italy and the Western Hemisphere in between, make this one of the largest subjects in this category.

OMNIBUS EDITIONS
Identical commemorative sets issued simultaneously in many territories became fashionable in the French and British Empires in the 1930s. Sets from

Below: A Portuguese stamp of 1894 marked the 400th anniversary of the voyage of Vasco da Gama to India.

numerous colonies and protectorates celebrated the Colonial Exposition in Paris (1931) and the silver jubilee of George V (1935). With uniform designs differing only in the country name and denomination, these set the pattern for many other omnibus issues until the 1970s. Since then, different motifs within an overall uniform style have been preferred. Royalty remains a popular subject, as seen in birthday and jubilee editions and numerous memorial issues for Diana, Princess of Wales.

THE CONQUEST OF SPACE
Space is a vast, global topic with many different strands to be explored, from the Chinese invention of rockets to the Apollo moon landings and beyond, the probes of Mars and Venus and the development of the Hubble telescope. The space race between the USA and the USSR could be illustrated not only

Above: British royal portraiture in stamps has developed enormously, from the restrained, two-colour intaglio pictorials of George V's silver jubilee in 1935 to the multicolour photogravure and offset lithographic stamps of recent years, celebrating Elizabeth II's golden jubilee in 2002 and paying tribute to the Queen Mother following her death.

by stamps but also by souvenir covers and postcards. A straightforward subject collection might consist of the different types of spacecraft, while purpose-of-issue collecting could concentrate on the Apollo 11 mission of 1969 and the stamps that celebrated anniversaries of Neil Armstrong's first "step for mankind", or the issues around the world that mourned the victims of the Columbia and Challenger disasters. The exploration of space might be linked to the devel-

Above: A se-tenant pair *– with two designs printed side by side – from the German Democratic Republic, marking the flights of Vostok V and VI in 1963.*

opment of the telescope and the science of astronomy. All these aspects now form a distinct branch of the hobby, under the title of astrophilately.

OLYMPIC PHILATELY

In 1896 Greece hosted the first modern Olympic Games and issued a set of 12 stamps, from 1 lepton to 10 drachmae. Although designed, engraved and printed in France, they were wholly Greek in concept. Apart from the 1d and 10d, which depicted the Acropolis and the Parthenon respectively, the designs were derived from ancient Greek sculptures of athletes, or statues symbolizing the spirit of the Games.

Greece produced a second Olympic set in 1906 but this precedent was not followed by any other host

Right: A pre-publicity stamp for the Melbourne Olympic Games of 1956.

Below: A Greek miniature sheet publicizing the Athens Olympic Games, 2004.

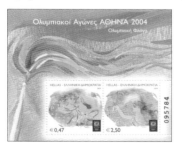

country until 1920, when Belgium issued a set of three, establishing an enduring trend whereby the host nation issues stamps to mark the event. In 1932 the USA became the first country to issue stamps for the Winter Olympics as well. In 1954–5 Australia broke new ground by issuing stamps as advance publicity for the Melbourne Games of 1956. This tradition has now reached the point at which countries begin issuing pre-Games stamps as soon as the winning bid is confirmed.

The Games now include around 30,000 participants, and if you take into account all the stamps marking the anniversaries of national Olympic committees, as well as the stamps and postal stationery provided for the use of the International Olympic Committee in Switzerland, plus souvenir cards and covers, it is not hard to appreciate what a huge subject this has become.

SOCCER STAMPS

If the Olympic Games dominates world sport, the World Cup Football Championship (first held in Uruguay in 1930) is not far behind. Like the Olympics, the World Cup takes place every four years and is now almost as prolific in stamp terms. In the interim, however, the European Cup is beginning to rival the global championships in terms of the outpourings of stamps from participants and non-participants eager for revenue from portraying the great soccer stars. In addition, FIFA, the International Federation of Association Football, celebrated its centenary in 2004 and virtually every affiliated country issued stamps to mark the occasion. There have been stamps for women's football (Nigeria and Sweden), children's soccer (Alderney) and even one-legged football (El Salvador).

Above: This sheetlet from Niger in 2000 was one of a series charting each decade of the 20th century.

Left: One of the stamps issued by Sweden to celebrate the FIFA centenary of 2004 portrayed famous women footballers.

OTHER THEMES

Other aspects of purpose-of-issue collecting are more focused, with worldwide issues for United Nations campaigns, the 75th anniversary and centenary of the Universal Postal Union (UPU) in 1949 and 1974, Rotary International (1955 and 1980), the Millennium (2000–1) and memorial issues for leaders of international renown, such as Franklin D. Roosevelt (1945) and Winston Churchill (1964–5). Many nations brought out iconic stamps to mourn the assassination of President John F. Kennedy in 1963, followed by another set to mark the first anniversary.

The First Olympics

Commemorative stamps were still a novelty in 1896, and a long set with a high face value, as issued by the Greek authorities to mark the Athens Olympics of that year, was roundly condemned at the time. Today, however, the series is highly valued and is the key set for any collection with an Olympic theme.

CHOOSING THEMES AND TELLING STORIES

The third distinct branch of topical collecting offers the greatest scope for the collector's individuality, because it involves selecting and arranging material in such a way that it tells a story. Certain topics in this field are extremely popular because of the range and availability of stamps associated with them.

Raw material for a collection illustrating "The American Dream", for example, is to be found in the definitive sets portraying presidents and other prominent figures, numerous commemoratives or special issues and, in recent years, *se-tenant* strips or entire sheets of different stamps featuring outstanding personalities, from country and western singers to choreographers. More manageable US themes might be "How the West was Won" or "The conflict between North and South." There are also many stamps rather more overt in their promotion and def-

Above: Commemorative and special US issues, usually priced at the domestic letter rate, publicize all aspects of American life. This group highlights youth: the Boy Scouts, Girl Scouts and the National Apprenticeship Program. Even the Automobile Association stamp (1952) stresses the youth angle.

Suffragette Mail
A suffragette nails the colours to her mast before a demonstration (left). Some members of the suffragette movement in Britain actively targeted public services, such as the postal network, in a bid to draw attention to their campaign. In some cases, public works buildings were set on fire, while other campaigners resorted to more prosaic, local vandalism to make a point. The envelope below was a victim of such an attack: it was heavily damaged when a suffragette poured ink into the letterbox of an unpopular household.

inition of the American way of life, bearing iconic images and inspiring messages to the people of the country.

DIDACTIC STAMPS

Almost from their inception, American stamps have had a didactic element, teaching migrants from many lands something of the customs, history and geography of their adopted land. Stamps "saluted" young Americans with carefully contrived issues highlighting the importance of useful, beneficial activity, such as the Boy and Girl Scouts stamps. The American work ethic was hammered home in numerous celebratory portraits of the blue-collar industrial worker, on issues such as those depicting rail and automobile engineers, postal workers, rangers, apprentices and the country's "future farmers".

In contrast to these, more recent issues address health concerns such as obesity and poor levels of fitness by actively promoting physical exercise. A rather idealized version of the American woman as "homemaker" features on several issues, while others champion peace, liberty and diplomacy.

THE TOURIST TRAIL

Another popular approach to creating a narrative collection is to describe a tour around a country, island or even an individual city, illustrating it with appropriate stamps.

Paris and Berlin are excellent subjects for such treatment, because France and Germany (and especially West Berlin when it issued its own stamps) have produced numerous stamps showing everything from panoramic views to individual landmarks. Washington and London might present more of a challenge but it is surprising how many stamps from other countries have portrayed their prominent features. New York City would be much harder. Of course, there are many stamps of the world showing the famous downtown skyline, but only a handful mourned 9/11 with views of the ill-fated Twin Towers. Stamps from many countries marked the New York World's Fairs in 1939 and 1964. The USA issued a stamp in 1953 for the tercentenary of the city, contrasting the Dutch town of New Amsterdam with the modern skyscrapers. New York's Coliseum (1956), University Library (1981), Stock Exchange (1992) and the Brooklyn (1983) and Verrazano Narrows (1964) bridges have all appeared on American stamps, but they are overshadowed by the numerous stamps from the USA and elsewhere featuring the Statue of

Below: Stamps from Nauru in the central Pacific showed solidarity with the USA in the wake of 9/11.

Liberty, an interesting theme in its own right, particularly for collectors concerned with iconography in stamps.

POLITICAL MATTERS

Many countries and regimes have used stamps extensively as political propaganda. Fascist Italy started this trend in the early 1920s but it was taken to new levels by Nazi Germany, and by the countries in the communist bloc when the Cold War was at its height. An interesting collection could be made of the propagandist stamps issued by the former German Democratic Republic, and the means by which it sought to denounce the ideals of the West. From 1940 onwards, the United States has issued many stamps that promote democratic ideals, contrasting the four freedoms enshrined in its constitution with the oppression of the nations then under Nazi occupation or – later – behind the Iron Curtain.

Some stamps, such as those issued by the Isle of Man, vividly illustrate the struggle to win votes for women, featuring portraits of the leaders of the suffrage movement, or the campaigns in many parts of the world to achieve racial equality and civil rights for all. In countries such as Britain, exponents of universal suffrage actually targeted the postal services as part of their national campaign, and remnants of the graphic vandalism exist to this day.

The range of topics with a quasi-political slant is enormous, ranging from the rise and fall of the Roman Empire to the collapse of communism in the 1990s. The French Revolution and its worldwide repercussions and

Above: Many stamps of the GDR commemorated the Nazi death camps, and also portrayed victims of the Holocaust (left).

Below: An American patriotic label from the Cold War era.

the power struggle that led to World War I are themes that lend themselves well to a philatelic treatment.

COLLATERAL MATERIAL

To illustrate a story in real depth, it's important to look beyond the stamps themselves. Increasingly, related material is being brought into play. First day covers (special envelopes bearing stamps cancelled on the first day of issue) and maximum cards (postcards with an appropriate stamp affixed to the picture side, cancelled by a matching postmark) augment mint stamps, but you can also include non-postal labels (sometimes called poster stamps), perhaps commemorating an event or anniversary, or even advertising diverse products in connnection with the event. Pictorial meter marks and postmarks are other items that can be effective in a thematic display.

COLLECTING POSTAL HISTORY

In its broadest sense, postal history encompasses the study of the development of the posts over the centuries. In practice, as a branch of philately, it embraces the collecting of everything pertaining to the transmission of mail, from the cuneiform tablets of ancient Assyria down to the junk mail that popped through your mailbox today. Although postal services of some kind have been around for thousands of years, no one thought of studying the ephemera and artefacts associated with them until the late 19th century – well after the adoption of adhesive stamps and postal stationery.

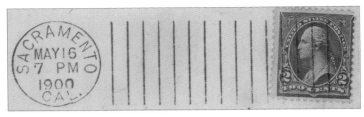

Above: An early example of an American machine cancellation, dated 1900, appears adjacent to a 2c George Washington stamp.

Below: "Dumb cancels" (those that do not contain a town or country name) appear in many forms, the impressions often made from shapes cut into cork.

CANCELLATIONS

The earliest philatelists preferred to collect mint stamps; the cancellation was considered merely to be something that detracted from their appearance. By the 1870s, however, a few collectors were beginning to take note of the cancellations as well as other markings on mail, such as datestamps, charge and explanatory marks, and route and transit marks, which appeared mainly on the backs of the envelopes.

In Britain, some dedicated individuals even travelled round the country trying to persuade postmasters and counter staff to give them impressions of their date stamps, a

Above: A Pearson Hill parallel motion cancelling machine dating from about 1865.

practice that was regarded in official circles with the gravest suspicion. Although such impressions, on otherwise blank pieces of paper, seem rather childish, had they not been preserved many of the marks would be otherwise unrecorded. The advent of the parcel post in 1883 gave an impetus to postmark collecting, although it was not until 1904 that every post office in the UK was equipped with a datestamp.

Postmark collecting as a hobby developed around the same time in the USA, where collectors were fascinated by the astonishing range of postmarks.

Above and right: A flag cancellation from Boston in 1898 shows the origin of the seven wavy lines found in machine postmarks everywhere. Such postmarks are immensely popular with American collectors as an adjunct to the many stamps featuring the Stars and Stripes.

It was left to the initiative of each postmaster to devise a mark that suited his fancy, and as well as circles and stars there were numerous pictorial cancellations, cut from pieces of rubber or cork. Around the turn of the 20th century, countless US post offices had

Above: Twin datestamps are typical of the French Daguin cancelling machine.

Below: A dated postmark of Versailles, France, from the pre-stamp era.

machines generating a cancellation whose obliterator took the form of the Stars and Stripes. It is from these "flag cancellations" that the wavy lines in most machine cancellations are derived.

PRESERVING POSTMARKS

The craze for picture postcards from the 1890s to World War I provided an abundance of raw material. Sadly, collectors of the period often cut out the postmark, even cutting into the stamps to achieve a neat little square. This vandalism has destroyed the value of many otherwise rare items. Nowadays collectors keep postcards intact. In the case of ordinary envelopes it is generally sufficient to cut out the stamp and postmark, leaving a generous margin all round. Machine cancellations and slogans are usually kept in strips. Registered, express or other covers subject to special handling, as well as underpaid items surcharged prior to delivery, should be kept whole.

Postmark collecting as a sideline to philately became immensely popular in the period after World War II, when increasing use was made of slogan cancellations that were changed at frequent intervals. Firms would sell the wastepaper from their mailrooms by the sackload for a nominal sum, and this was a fertile source of new material.

Many post offices were still cancelling stamps by hand at that period, but from the 1970s mail was increasingly concentrated and mechanized. Letters and cards are nowadays often transported over long distances to a central automatic processing centre or mechanized letter office, and the cancellations have relatively little relevance to the place where the mail originated. This is true not only of the more industrialized countries such as the USA, Britain, France and Germany, but also of many other countries, which, until quite recently, allowed most post offices to cancel their outgoing mail. It is still possible to get a rubber stamp applied to covers and cards at post office counters in Canada and the USA, but in Britain the only way you can now get a mark distinctive to each office is by tendering a letter or card for posting, and asking for a certificate to confirm this. At one time, a charge was applied for this, but the service is now free.

FROM METER MARKS TO ELECTRONIC POSTAGE

Postage meters were pioneered by Norway and New Zealand in the early 1900s and spread throughout the world from 1922 onwards. Meter marks, which were once despised by philatelists, have become popular in recent years, either as a branch of postal history or as an adjunct of topical collecting (mainly for the pictorial element in their design). Even permit mail markings and postage paid impressions (PPIs), which are extensively used on business mail and bulk mailings, have their devotees: one person's junk mail may be another's collectable material. It is now even possible to download postage through a computer and generate electronic stamps.

Above: A curious machine cancellation from the Netherlands uses a pattern of dots instead of the usual wavy lines.

Below: Postal history of the future – a postage stamp generated by computer.

Pictorial Meter Marks

From the outset, meter marks offered business users the opportunity to incorporate a slogan showing the company emblem or advertising its products. This also applied to the marks used by offices at local and national government level, and they have often been used to convey road safety or public health messages. Much sought after today are the early meter marks from the United Nations, showing the headquarters building in the "stamp" and the logo and slogans alongside it.

LOCAL PHILATELY

An increasingly popular approach is to concentrate on the philately and postal history of your own town, district, county, state or province. Obviously the various postmarks from your own area will form the core of such a collection, but it is often surprising how much other paraphernalia is available. Some of these categories, such as local stamps of express and parcel companies, private posts, telegraph and telephone stamps, poster stamps and labels, are discussed in more detail later in this section, but by focusing your search for material on a specific locality you will give greater significance to items of this kind.

Above: Stamps issued by three local posts operating in New Zealand, many serving specific regions. Private stamps such as these often yield local markings, which may also be of interest to collectors.

Left: A parcel stamp issued by the Ardrishaig Mail Service, Scotland, in 1956.

Below: Stamps of the Llechwedd Railway, Wales, with souvenir postmark and cachets, 1980.

Above and right: Stamps issued by two of the private posts that operated during the protracted British postal strikes of 1962 and 1971.

WHERE TO BEGIN

You may be lucky enough to live in an area that has made its own distinctive contribution to philately. For example, people living in Oxford or Cambridge, England, could specialize in the stamps and stationery used by the various colleges between 1871 and 1886, when the stamps were deemed to be infringing the monopoly of the Postmaster General and banned. Keble College, which had been the first to issue stamps, celebrated its centenary in 1970 with a souvenir stamp, known on intercollegiate covers. The British postal strikes of 1962 and especially 1971 (when over 200 services briefly flourished) gave rise to private stamp issues in many localities.

In Britain the old railway companies had distinctive newspaper and parcel labels. These were followed by railway letter stamps, sanctioned by the government, from 1891 to 1922, and many of these are of great local interest, especially used on covers with the undated cancellations of local railway stations. On a similar theme, many bus companies had their own parcel stamps, and some still do.

Above: Stamps issued by Keble College, part of Oxford University in England, for the college messenger service in 1871 and 1970.

the 1870s and its use eventually spread around the world. Until recently, stamp collectors tended to regard punctured

Below: Perfins from Argentina and Britain; the latter is a Board of Trade device on a stamp of 1887.

PERFINS

Stamps were sometimes perforated with the initials of organizations as a security measure, to prevent pilferage or misuse. This kind of device, known as a perfin, was adopted in England in

the rarest, and thus most desirable, marks are those applied to mail damaged as a result of a train crash.

IDENTIFYING INSCRIPTIONS

Special postmarks were devised in every country to denote railway mail. The commonest form was an inscription with two or more names, indicating the termini and perhaps an intermediate station en route. Various initials are another clue, and it is important to spot such designations as "ST" (sorting tender), "SC" (sorting carriage), "RPO" (railway post office) or "TPO" (travelling post office). Inscriptions in other languages may include the words *ambulant* (French), *ambulante* (Portuguese), *ambulancia* (Spanish), *Bahnpost* or *Eisenbahn* (German), *banen* (Danish and Norwegian), *jernbanwagen* (Swedish) or abbreviations such as AMB or EISENB. Some marks used by the old German States were inscribed *"Fahrendes postamt"* (literally "Travelling post office").

Subsidiary inscriptions include "Up" or "Down" in British postmarks, indicating the direction of the mail train, while "Day" or "Night" shows the service. German postmarks often include a numeral preceded by "Zug" or "Z", indicating the identification number assigned to the actual train.

Above: French TPO postmarks can be recognized by their scalloped edge and two place names.

Above: Spanish TPO marks are octagonal, bearing the abbreviation "Amb" for ambulancia *(moving).*

Right: German TPO marks are rectangular or oval, with two names and even a train ("Zug") number.

While the railway postmarks used in Britain, Canada and the USA conform to the patterns for datestamps in general, many European countries have favoured distinctive patterns. Austria, Germany and Czechoslovakia used large horizontal oval shapes, whereas French TPOs traditionally have a scalloped edge. In Spain and Portugal the postmarks are octagonal and the Low Countries use a horizontal rectangle.

WHEN RAILWAY MARKS DO NOT MEAN RAILWAY MAIL

Because of the immense popularity of railway mail, and the premiums paid for covers and cards whose postmarks show that they were carried by rail, it is important not to confuse the railway marks with others that appear to have a rail connection, but do not in fact indicate railway mail.

Many postmarks include words that mean "railway station", such as *Bahnhof* or *Hauptbahnhof* (German), *gare* (French), *stazione* or *ferrovia* (Italian) or *stasjon* (Norwegian). These merely indicate a post office that happens to be located at a railway station,

rather than mail transported by train.

In fact, collecting covers, cards and parcel labels from such station post offices has become quite a study in its own right, but even here some caution has to be exercised. Many country post offices in Scotland included the word "Station" in their name. Of course, the post office may actually have been in the station at one time but in most cases places such as Annbank Station and Drymen Station were villages in their own right. With the closure of many railway lines, the station names have become redundant and the villages have changed their names: these examples are now known respectively as Mossblown and Croftamie.

Below: Many of the preserved railway lines in the UK issue their own stamps, complete with special cancellations and souvenir cachets.

COLLECTING WARTIME MAIL

It is remarkable that even at the height of the worst conflicts, the mail still manages to get through. The Universal Postal Union was the only international organization that continued to operate reasonably smoothly throughout both World Wars, often relying on elaborate routing of mail through neutral countries. Of course, a vast quantity of mail was trapped as the tide of war ebbed and flowed and it was several years before some could be safely delivered.

FPO AND APO POSTMARKS

Special provisions for the handling of letters to and from soldiers and sailors in wartime date from the Napoleonic Wars, and many distinctive postmarks were employed by both sides. The British and French had efficient facilities for the smooth collection and delivery of forces' mail during the Crimean War (1854–6) and from then on special postmarks were employed in virtually every campaign.

A varied, almost chaotic, range of postmarks appeared during the Boer War (1899–1902) but by the outbreak of World War I a system of field post offices (FPO) was in place and this has continued to the present time, with regular numbers identifying the location of units at home and overseas.

Left and below: An Austrian field postmark of 1915 and a letter to Geneva from French troops in Holland during the Napoleonic War.

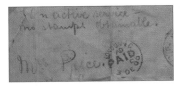

Above: Two APO cancellations dating from 1900 during the Boer War. The scrawl across the top envelope points out that "no stamps [were] obtainable", while the hand stamp below explains that the envelope was "recovered from mails looted by the Boers on June 8".

The transmission of mail to and from soldiers in the American Civil War (1861–5) was often haphazard, but enlivened by a wealth of patriotic covers. A regular service by army post offices (APO) emerged during the Spanish-American War (1898) and was greatly expanded in World War I. The APO system continues today, with numbers identifying offices in Iraq, Afghanistan and other trouble spots.

Below: A stamp postmarked in July 1939 at Camp de Septfonds, a French internment camp for Spanish refugees during the Civil War.

Above: In Britain, the Home Postal Centre in Nottingham was the hub of mail distribution for much of World War II. This clerk is checking a vast index that gave the location of units.

Air raid mail

These two pieces of postal ephemera – a badly damaged newspaper wrapper and a remarkably clean envelope with stamps intact – both survived the carpet-bombing raids targeting southern England in World War II. Note the missile-shaped postmark, applied to wartime mail delayed by enemy action, shown on the bottom envelope.

NAVAL MAIL

Since the mid-19th century a system of special postmarks for military and naval mail has been developed by almost every country around the world. The Franco-German War of 1870–1 and the Pacific War of 1878–83, involving Bolivia, Chile and Peru, yielded a rich crop of military markings, as well as provisional stamps intended for use by the victors in conquered territory.

Naval mail constitutes an enormous area of philately in its own right. While the French and German navies had distinctive datestamps for each warship, the US Navy often resorted to ships' names and other inscriptions set between the obliterating bars of rubber stamps. British vessels, in contrast, retained their anonymity for security reasons. Mail landed from these ships was marked with a handstamp or machine cancellation which read "Received from H.M. Ships". This was altered in World War II to "Post Office Maritime Mail" so as not to exclude deliveries from Allied ships. In World War I each ship was responsible for censoring outgoing mail and a wide variety of marks was employed; these have enabled students to identify many of the individual ships.

Left: Postmark from the German warship Deutschland, *which was interned at Scapa Flow in 1919.*

Below: A World War II cover from England to neutral Switzerland, examined and resealed twice by both British and German censors.

For security reasons, mail landed from warships during World War I was not cancelled by the ordinary postmarks of seaports; instead various dumb cancels were employed on handstamps, in the form of barred circles, concentric circles or crosses. Even cancelling machines had their normal inscriptions replaced by crosses or plus signs. Canada took this concept a step further in World War II, using daters in machine cancellations, devoid of any names or locations.

OCCUPATION, INVASION AND LIBERATION

Occupation stamps were first issued by the German Federal Commissioners in the duchy of Holstein in 1864, following the invasion by Austrian and Prussian forces. It was, incidentally, when the Allies fell out over the administration of the duchies of Schleswig and Holstein that the Seven Weeks' War of 1866 erupted, resulting in many different *Feldpost* markings on both sides. The distinctive stamps for use in occupied territory alone constitute a formidable branch of philately, but the range of covers, postcards and distinctive postmarks is almost infinite.

Special military stationery ranges from the Franco-Prussian and Russo-Turkish wars of the 1870s to the forces' air letter sheets used in Iraq in 2004. Special provision for stamps, stationery and postmarks in connection with the invasion of other countries dates from the 1930s and includes material relating to the Italian invasions of Abyssinia (1936) and Albania (1939), the German invasion of Czechoslovakia (1938–9), Memel, Danzig and Poland (1939), the Hungarian invasion of Slovakia (1938) and Ruthenia (1939). An interesting sideline is the partial erasure of postmarks by the conquerors, cutting out the indigenous version of placenames in bilingual datestamps.

In World War II the Allies made provision for liberation stamps and postal stationery in the aftermath of the landings in Sicily, Italy and Normandy. Stamps were also issued for the Allied

Above: A World War II patriotic cover sent by a soldier in Florida to Canada, transmitted free.

Below: A cover sent from the Cromarty naval base, with the name and date replaced by crosses for security reasons.

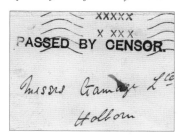

Military Government of Germany in 1945. The stamps of the countries of South-east Asia and the Pacific that were overrun by the Japanese were overprinted following invasion, pending the issuing of distinctive stamps by the occupying power.

SIEGE AND UNDERGROUND POSTS

Distinctive postmarks and cachets are known from various towns under siege, from Paris (1870) to Przemysl (1915); even Mafeking had its own stamps (1900). Underground posts were operated by guerrillas in the Philippines, partisans in Italy and Yugoslavia, and the Boy Scouts during the Warsaw Rising of 1944 (with crude postmarks showing the Scout emblem, carved from half a potato). Internees and prisoners of both World Wars, and even the inmates of the Lodz Ghetto, Theresienstadt and Dachau concentration camp had their own stamps and stationery. Censorship is an enormous subject, with a vast range of re-sealing labels and examiners' marks.

COLLECTING AIRMAIL

The distinctive stamps and stationery devised for mail transported by air has yielded a huge crop of collectable material, and occupies a branch of the hobby known as aerophilately. Yet it is the vast history of the service itself, spanning some two centuries, that often prompts collectors to take a closer interest in this field. Behind the post-marked envelopes and first flight covers are fascinating accounts of some of the most daring, innovative and bizarre methods of carrying mail ever devised.

BALLOON POSTS

It was not long after the first hot-air balloon flights by the Montgolfier brothers in France and Vincenzo Lunardi in Britain that attempts were made to carry mail by balloon. In 1807 during the Peninsular War, propaganda leaflets were dropped over the French lines, and thus began a branch of postal history known as "psywar" (psychological warfare) that is of immense interest to airmail buffs as well as military postal historians.

The first commercial balloon posts were organized during the sieges of Metz and Paris in 1870–1. Of the 65 balloons flown out of Paris, six were

Left and above: A Swiss stamp celebrating the first round-the-world balloon flight (1999), and the launch of balloons during the Siege of Paris (1870–1).

Right and below right: The Graf Zeppelin moored at Los Angeles on 26 August 1929, following a 79-hour Pacific crossing, and one of three US stamps issued to celebrate its Europe–Pan-American flight in 1930.

captured by the enemy, two were blown out to sea and never seen again and the others made safe landings and delivered their precious cargo of letters. These balloons came down all over the place, including one that landed at Lifjeld in Norway, having flown 3,142km/1,952 miles in 14 hours: its record airspeed of 241kph/150mph was not broken until 1915.

Unmanned free balloons were occasionally used to transmit mail during World War I but in the interwar period they were mainly associated with the souvenir mail carried by contestants in the Gordon Bennett balloon races (for which special stamps were also issued). The trouble with free balloons was that they went wherever the wind blew and it was only in 1999 that a balloon capable of reaching the steady airstream in the upper atmosphere could circumnavigate the world, a feat celebrated by a special cover from Switzerland.

Experiments with dirigible balloons by Santos Dumont in Brazil and Count Ferdinand von Zeppelin in Germany led to the airships of World War I and the giant zeppelins of the 1920s and 1930s, which achieved epic transatlantic, polar and global journeys. Zeppelin mail has a large number of devotees, and items include the charred covers from the ill-fated *Hindenburg*, which crashed in New Jersey, in 1937.

The Birth of the US Airmail Service

In 1918, the US Army was persuaded to lend pilots and planes to establish air routes for mail delivery. Within a few years, the service was a thriving commercial enterprise, with airlines dispatching mail at affordable rates.

Above: A souvenir cover from the first night mail flight between Sweden and Croydon, England, in 1928.

HEAVIER-THAN-AIR MACHINES

Within five years of the first flight by the Wright Brothers in 1903, mail was being carried by aircraft in France. Sir Walter Windham, a British pioneer of aviation, organized the first official airmail between Allahabad and Naini, India, in February 1911 and swiftly followed this with the Coronation Aerial Post between London and Windsor in September. Denmark, Italy and the USA all had official airmails launched in the same month.

Mail flown over sea between two countries began with Augustin Parla's flight of July 1913 between Florida and Cuba, and this was followed by the

Above: A cigarette card featuring an "Empire" class flying boat.

Below: US Postmaster James A. Farley helps to stack mail delivered from a flying boat on 22 November 1935.

Above: A first flight cover from the gold-mining town of Herb Lake to The Pas in Manitoba, Canada, 1937.

flight of January 1914 between Buenos Aires and Montevideo by Teodoro Fels. Five years later John Alcock and Arthur Whitten-Brown made the first successful non-stop crossing of the Atlantic, flying from St John's, Newfoundland to Clifden, County Galway, Ireland. Ironically, the postal covers that were salvaged from the wrecks of the earlier, unsuccessful competitors in this endeavour now rate much more highly than those from the successful flight.

The heyday of pioneer airmails was the 1920s, when many countries made their first attempts to organize air routes, and the postal subsidies were a major factor in their success. Large countries such as Canada, Australia, Brazil and the USA were in the forefront of this development. In addition to first flight covers with colourful cachets and postmarks, airport dedication souvenirs were produced, notably in the USA where local airports proliferated in this period.

In the 1930s the great transoceanic air routes became commercially feasible, and their development was duly charted by the special covers and postcards associated with the Clipper flying boats. There were also ingenious attempts by France and Germany to accelerate sea mail by using small aircraft catapulted from the decks of ocean liners as they drew near to land. In 1928 France even issued special stamps for this service operated by the liner *Ile de France,* while the catapult mail from the German ships *Bremen* and *Europa* (1929) was marked with distinctive cachets.

HELICOPTER MAIL

Conventional aircraft required a lengthy runway, but the problem of short take-off and landing was solved by the development of the autogiro in the 1930s. Souvenir covers associated with this short-lived aircraft are known from England, Spain, Australia, Canada and the USA between 1934 and 1939. The autogiro was eclipsed by the helicopter, which was developed during World War II and first used to carry mail at Los Angeles in July 1946. At first helicopter flights were confined to emergencies, but in the UK regular commercial mail services were inaugurated in East Anglia in June 1948.

FROM PIGEONGRAMS TO ROCKET MAIL

Carrier pigeons have been used to convey urgent messages since the days of ancient Greece, but the first regular commercial service was organized during the Siege of Paris in 1870–1. More than 300 birds flew messages into the beleaguered city. At first, handwritten flimsies were attached to them but later microfilm *pellicules* were used. The pigeons were taken out of Paris aboard manned balloons. Pigeongrams were widely used in New Zealand from 1896 and in India from 1931 to 1941.

Mail-carrying rockets were devised in Austria and Germany in 1928–31 and were used extensively in India between 1934 and 1944, while Cuba even issued a special stamp for a rocket mail service in 1939.

Below: A cover from the first official helicopter mail flight, from Lowestoft to Peterborough, in 1948.

CINDERELLA PHILATELY

Everyone is familiar with the story of Cinderella, neglected and mistreated by her ugly stepsisters, but transformed by her fairy godmother into the belle of the ball. The parallel between Cinderella and the byways of philately is close, and it is appropriate that the sidelines of the hobby, once despised and ignored, have now developed a strong following and, in fact, form a major branch of philately with its own societies. Many of these have websites where members discuss literature on the subject, specialized auctions and insuring expensive collectables. A list of useful addresses for the aspiring Cinderella philatelist is included at the end of this chapter.

ALBUM WEEDS
Back in the 19th century, when stamp collecting was still in its infancy, collectors did not have at their disposal a

wealth of handbooks and monographs, let alone the priced catalogues that are now easily available, or the infinite mass of data on the internet. They therefore operated on the principle of "if it looks like a stamp, stick it in the album". Among these were forgeries and utterly bogus issues, produced solely to defraud collectors. The Reverend R.B. Earee coined the term "album weeds" in the 1870s and such fabrications were the first to go, but many years later philatelists realized that it was important to study forgeries, if only to help collectors distinguish between the genuine and the false.

The brothers Norman and Maurice Williams wrote many books on philately from the 1930s to the 1970s. In one of them, aimed at youthful beginners, they illustrated a range of stamp-like objects – labels, fiscals, telegraph stamps, Christmas seals and the

Above: A Frama label (automatic machine stamp) issued by New Zealand.

Right: A self-adhesive service indicator label used at British post office counters in 2004.

like – declaring sternly, "These have no place in a stamp album." Ironically, the Williams brothers were assiduous collectors of all things Cinderella and for many years were the joint editors of *The Cinderella Philatelist*.

BEYOND THE CATALOGUE
What is the definition of a philatelic Cinderella? The short answer is anything that is not listed in the standard stamp catalogues. However, this simple answer has to be qualified, for general stamp catalogues often omit items that do find a place in the more specialized catalogues, and quite often what the editor decides to include is arbitrary. For example, some catalogues, especially in Europe, list and price automatic machine stamps, often known as ATM (from the German term *Automatenmarken*), but sometimes referred to loosely as Framas, after the Swiss company that pioneered them. In Britain they are referred to as vending machine labels, and that last word tends to be applied to anything that is not a stamp – despite the fact that the Penny Black and other early British stamps were described in their own sheet margins as labels.

Right: The £5 stamp used on British Army telegraphs, and a Victorian label for securing the lead seal on the tax stamps affixed to legal documents.

Below: A page from Collecting Postage Stamps *by L.N. & M. Williams (1950), giving examples of "what not to collect".*

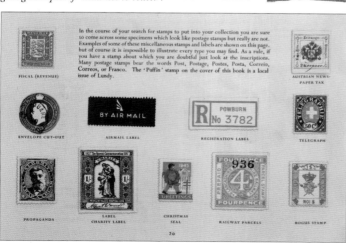

Civil War Cinderellas

These patriotic labels were created around 1861 by the Federal government during the American Civil War. They were produced in sheets (size unknown) of at least 9 images in *se-tenant* blocks. The right-hand image displays one of the labels in place, bound to the envelope by means of a town cancellation – a rare occurrence. The biblical reference shown at the top of this mounted label (Job 39:21) reads: "He paweth in the valley, and rejoiceth in his strength; he goeth on to meet the armed men." Any literate person in those days would have understood its relevance to the war.

Service Indicator Labels – The New Cinderellas?

Postage dues are not postage stamps, as they do not indicate that postage has been prepaid, and for that reason they are strictly termed labels – yet they are invariably included in stamp dealers' catalogues. The distinction between "stamps" (items included in the catalogues) and "labels" (ignored by the catalogues) is becoming more and more blurred. In recent years, for example, the UK has adopted service indicator labels, computer-printed at the point of sale, and these have now virtually ousted the higher denominations of conventional stamps. They prepay postage and perform all the functions of traditional stamps, yet they are completely ignored by the catalogues. Collectors, on the other hand, have had the good sense to realize that these things are just as worthy of study and collecting as the pretty pictures known as commemorative and special issues, most of which never perform any actual postal duty and merely serve to raise revenue for the postal services.

Many other countries operate a similar system. In the USA, in particular, such self-adhesive labels have been available at postal counters for many years. In fact, the difference between conventional stamps (more and more of which are produced to generate philatelic sales) and operational labels (which are gradually usurping the traditional role of stamps in prepaying postage) is becoming difficult to define. Catalogues continue to list, price and illustrate stamps whose status is questionable and which, in many instances, never see the country from which they purport to come, while ignoring the increasing number of "service labels" that now play a vital part in the smooth operation of the mails.

Both Scott (USA) and Gibbons (UK) list the labels involved in an experimental self-service mailing system that was tried in Washington and Kensington, Maryland, in 1989–90. Gibbons describes them simply as machine labels, whereas Scott more accurately refers to them as computer-vended postage. While Gibbons illustrates and describes them, Scott lists and prices them in some detail. These different approaches are also evident in the case of the more permanent issues in use since 1992.

Neither catalogue gives space to the parcel stamps of Belgium and the Netherlands, denominated by weight, or the range of special service labels produced by Germany, all of which cost money and indicate the service provided. The moral here is "ignore the catalogues". If you are specializing in a particular country, everything to do with the postal service deserves an equal place in your collection.

POSTAGE PAID IMPRESSIONS

Businesses, local authorities and mail order companies, which at one time used a postal frank, meter mark or bulk posting prepaid in cash denoted by a special red postmark, now make extensive use of systems such as permit mailing (in the USA) or postage-paid impressions (in most other countries). These impressions, handstruck or printed, are applied either directly to the cover, card or wrapper, or to a self-adhesive label. An increasing number of postal administrations now encourage local businesses to custom their own design, upon which they will be issued with an identification number. Thanks to their propensity for unique thematic appeal and pictorial motif, PPIs have already gained many devotees, and may indeed be Cinderellas of the future.

Above: These two triangular stamps are "phantom" issues – a popular branch of Cinderella philately. They were created by a Viennese stamp dealer, S. Friedl, to commemorate the discovery of a group of glacial islands during an Austro-Hungarian expedition attempting to reach the North Pole in 1872–4. The green item names "Cap Pest", the yellow refers to "Cap Wien". The pair is much sought after by collectors of polar issues.

SOCIAL PHILATELY

This is the newest branch of the hobby of stamp collecting, having originated in Australia in the late 1990s. In 1999 a competitive class for social philately was inaugurated at the Melbourne International Philatelic Exhibition. The concept spread to the Northern Hemisphere shortly afterwards, when it was included in the London Stamp Show of May 2000. It is basically a reaction against the strictures of the traditional and thematic philately classes in national and international competitions, which disqualified exhibitors if they strayed off the straight and narrow path laid down by the rules.

If an exhibitor included items that were not strictly stamps, either mint or affixed to covers or cards, the exhibit was severely marked down. More and more collectors were finding these restrictions increasingly irksome. They felt that – far from detracting from their displays – the judicial inclusion

Below: A page from a collection devoted to the floating mail of St Kilda.

of non-philatelic items, such as ephemera or photographs, that were relevant to the stamps made the exhibit far more interesting, especially to the general public, who would not necessarily appreciate a show devoted to stamps alone. There was a very real danger of philately becoming esoteric and elitist, and the gulf between the "pot hunter" dedicated to winning competitions and the ordinary collector was becoming wider every year. More importantly, however, as competitive philately became more rarefied and confined, the potential for attracting and recruiting newcomers to the hobby decreased sharply. Competitive displays were beginning to appear boring to many collectors, let alone the general public.

A NEW WAY TO COLLECT

Recognizing this problem, the organizers of philatelic shows tentatively suggested an Open Class where anything was permissible and entries were judged by popular vote. However, this merely represented an extension of the existing system and ran the risk of becoming subject to similar rules and regulations if aspiring winners hoped to progress beyond it.

It was the collector Pat Grimwood-Taylor, exhibiting for the very first time at Melbourne in 1999, who became the apostle of a new style. She scooped a gold medal at the exhibition and subsequently conducted a seminar on the subject in London, for which the British Philatelic Trust (BPT) produced an attractive pamphlet under the title *What is SOCIAL PHILATELY?* Marking further recognition for the new concept, the definition hinged on the aim of presenting a historical story or illustrating the relevance or impact of a postal system – official or otherwise – within a society.

Straight away, the two fundamental differences between social philately and other forms of collecting were made

clear. You do not necessarily have to be an expert philatelist (though a knowledge of the basic techniques of the hobby is a help) and, more importantly, you can include many types of non-philatelic material and ephemera (such as maps, prints, coins, medals, cigarette cards and banknotes) in your collection to make it tell the story.

USING POSTAL HISTORY

The BPT leaflet went on to expand its theme, explaining that you can tell the story of the development of a town or country by using stamps, actual letters and documents of all kinds. Local postal historians have probably been doing this for many years, expanding their interests far beyond the strict boundaries of postal markings and covers or postcards.

Leaflets and mini-posters announcing changes in postal rates or the opening or closure of post offices are strictly relevant, but what about press-cuttings containing human interest stories such as postal workers being bitten by dogs or retiring after 60 years in the service? This kind of material had always previously been something of a grey area, considered suitable for a talk to a local philatelic society, but not for inclusion in a competitive display.

In studying the postal history of a town or locality, the philatelist inevitably becomes immersed in the social and economic development of the place, amassing plenty of material that is fascinating but not actually relevant to the story of the posts. Social philately allows the collector to probe the background of a historic event, or chain of events, and include both conventional and non-conventional philatelic material to tell the tale.

A PERSONAL STUDY OF ST KILDA

Relating this to my own experience, and arising out of time I spent with the British Army on the remote island of St Kilda in 1959–61, I formed a collection of that island's postal history that eventually ran to nine volumes. From the outset, however, I was not content merely to acquire covers and postally used postcards bearing the single-circle datestamp, or even explore

Below: Another page on the floating mail of St Kilda, showing a letter sent in this manner in 1897 and a photograph of an original "mailboat" complete with sheep's bladder float.

by-ways such as the island's unique floating mail, airdrops, emergency helicopter flights or mail carried from St Kilda by French lobster-boats and Spanish trawlers that ended up in Camaret-sur-Mer or San Sebastian.

I added maps, ranging from that of Martin Martin, the first visitor to describe the island in detail in 1698, to a contemporary flight plan for one of the earliest airdrops in 1959. Ephemera in the collection ranged from leaflets produced by the National Trust for Scotland (who now own the island) to a spoof certificate purporting to be from King Neptune and retrieved from a bottle washed up on the shore. This was one of several thousands launched off the east coast of the USA in 1959 as a stunt celebrating the bicentenary of the Guinness brewery; most of the bottles came ashore in America but some drifted all the way across the Atlantic on the Gulf Stream. This find also gave me the opportunity to include a Guinness bicentenary beer-bottle label, arguably the first commemorative of its kind, which had been included with Neptune's parchment inside the bottle.

FLOATING MAILS

The earliest letter I possess from St Kilda dates from 1738. It has no wrapper or postmark and would probably have been disqualified in any conventional postal history display, despite its immense historical interest. It is a letter written by Lady Grange, who was kidnapped in Edinburgh by friends of her ex-husband and eventually imprisoned on St Kilda for fear that she would expose her husband's implication in a Jacobite plot. Her letter, written in ink "from the soot of my lamp and mine awin blood", was discovered three years later in a half-buried whisky bottle on the beach at Baleshare, an island of the Outer Hebrides. It eventually found its way to the addressee, her cousin in Edinburgh, but by the time he took action the poor woman had been moved to the Isle of Skye, where she

Above: Newspaper cuttings are a useful adjunct to a social philately collection.

Right: Parchment found in a Guinness bottle launched in the 1950s.

died. This letter, and the covering note from the tenant of Baleshare, form the basis of my own social philately display of the floating mails of St Kilda, developed by the islands in the 1870s and continuing until 1930 when the island was evacuated.

Reoccupied by the RAF and the Army in 1957, and regularly visited since by work parties from the National Trust for Scotland, St Kilda has been the scene of many "mailboat" or "tin can mail" launches over the past 45 years. Some have been picked up on the west coast of the Hebrides within 48 hours, while others were recovered more than three years later, as far away as eastern Iceland and north Norway, Orkney and Shetland.

Although the collection includes stamps, postmarks, cachets, charge marks, mixed franking of British and Norwegian stamps and even postage due labels (on covers recovered abroad and treated as unpaid because British stamps are not valid in Norway), the bulk of the display is devoted to photographs of launches and recoveries and a mass of press cuttings and articles about this remarkable phenomenon. It is entirely two-dimensional because I have not yet acquired one of the actual mailboats, consisting of a piece of driftwood hollowed out to form the hull, attached to an inflated sheep's bladder.

FORGERIES, FANTASIES AND POSTAL FRAUD

The subject of stamp forgery attracts collectors, not simply because of the tales of derring-do often attached, but also due to the challenge presented by comparing the likeness between real and fake. Forgery has dogged stamp-issuing authorities since the birth of the Penny Black. In fact, British authorities hired an American inventor, Jacob Perkins, who devised a rose engine capable of producing such an intricate background that the forger would be deterred. In fact, only one attempt to forge the Penny Black was detected, and that was such a poor travesty that it was easily spotted.

VICTIMS OF STAMP FORGERY

Countries where cheaper processes such as letterpress and lithography were in use, or where postal authorities paid

Above: In a bid to beat the forgers, the Twopence Blue was issued with check letters in all four corners in July 1858. The combination of numbers identified each stamp's position in a printed sheet.

Below: These British 6d stamps were produced in doubly fugitive ink with the value surcharged in red letters – another attempt to deter fraudulent use.

less attention to good intaglio engraving, often fell victim to forgery. The earliest attempts at forgery were usually intended to defraud the revenue.

Yet even the British postal service was not exempt from this humiliation. The 1s stamp was forged in 1872–3 and vast quantities were passed off as genuine at the Stock Exchange (where this denomination was commonly used on telegrams), but the crime did not come to light until 1898, by which time the trail had gone cold. It was thanks to the vigilance of philatelists that the forgery was detected at all, because the counterfeiters had used combinations of corner letters that did not exist in the genuine stamps. Although the Post Office placed its faith in the check letters as a deterrent to forgery, postal staff apparently never gave them a second glance. Today, the Stock Exchange forgeries fetch higher prices at auction than the genuine stamps, such is the demand for them.

Postal forgeries continue to this day. In recent years British and French definitives have been forged for sale to the public at discount prices, and it was for this reason that elliptical perforations were introduced, the theory being that forgers might produce a passable imitation of a stamp but they would never get the perforations right.

FAMOUS FORGERS

Once philately became an established hobby and definite market values emerged for the scarcer stamps, it was inevitable that the stamp trade should be infiltrated by unscrupulous people who turned to forgery as a means of robbing gullible collectors. The activities of such master forgers as François Fournier, Erasmus Oneglia, Jean de Sperati, S. Allan Taylor and Albert C. Roessler are well documented in literature such as Varro E. Tyler's *Philatelic Forgers: Their Lives and Works* (1976) and, indeed, some important collections of their wares have been formed.

Many forgers achieved notoriety in their day. S. Allan Taylor, an American born in Ayrshire, Scotland, in 1838, was known as "the Prince of Forgers" and produced hundreds of fakes and forgeries during the latter half of the 19th century, some of which were assumed to be authentic for many decades. He put his own portrait on bogus charity and local post stamps, and a self-likeness of the mature Taylor was incorporated into a label produced by a short-lived group of admiring Cinderella philatelists, the S. Allan Taylor Society.

An accomplished forger of more recent times, the Italian Jean de Sperati (1884–1957) was the most technically competent of his peers, producing some 566 forgeries purporting to originate from more than 100 countries.

Bogus Bill

Abkhazia, which seceded from Georgia, briefly had a genuine postal service with distinctive stamps, but long after the secession was suppressed stamps continued to appear in its name, including a notorious miniature sheet showing President Clinton and Monica Lewinsky. Georgia even apologized to the Clinton family and offered them a free holiday at the Black Sea resort of Soukhumi in recompense.

Above: Genuine and forged versions of the French 25c Hermes, the latter produced by British Intelligence.

He even wrote books on the art of philatelic forgery, in which he expressed his contempt for the "experts" who had tried to foil his efforts.

COLLECTING FORGERIES

Many of these colourful characters had a taste for risk and illegality, and no doubt relished the thrill of creating immaculate forgeries that fooled even the most diligent of postal watchdogs. But there are other instances of forgery,

Below: Bogus stamps attributed to South Moluccas, New Atlantis, Albania, Atlantis and Sedang.

A Dishonest Postmaster

Fraudulent usage of postal material does not always involve the forgery or manipulation of stamps. This rare envelope, shown here front and back, which eventually arrived at Everest Base Camp in 1936, informs the recipient that their letter "Suffered detention in Gangtok post office owing to the Postmaster's failure to affix postage stamps and to forward them in time. The Postmaster has been sent to jail for his offence."

where the primary motive – financial gain – appears to lack a well thought out plan. Where stamps are plentiful and cheap in the genuine state, it does not seem to have been worth the forger's expertise to perpetrate such imitations. Nevertheless this is not as unusual a phenomenon as might be thought. Many stamp clubs have a forgery collection, which members may consult in order to check doubtful specimens in their own collections.

Many of the forgeries produced in the 19th century would fool no one nowadays, either because the wrong printing process was used (such as lithography instead of intaglio) or because the draughtsmanship was relatively crude, but it must be remembered that 19th-century collectors did not have the well-illustrated reference works so readily available nowadays. The study of forgeries is germane to any specialized collection, which explains why forgeries often fetch high prices at auction, even when clearly exposed for what they are.

PROPAGANDA FORGERIES

Arguably the most desirable of all forgeries are those that were manufactured by various belligerents in wartime as part of a propaganda campaign. During World War I, Britain forged German and Bavarian stamps, which were affixed to letters or cards dropped in enemy or neutral countries to give the impression of coming from Germany while disseminating subtle propaganda or defeatist literature. This worked well enough to encourage the British to repeat the exercise in World War II, but this time they produced clever parodies of Nazi stamps as well. Stamps of the Vichy French regime portraying Marshal Petain were also forged by the British.

The Germans were adept at creating propaganda forgeries of British stamps, including a large number of George VI definitives overprinted "Liquidation of Empire" and the parody of the 1937 Coronation stamp, with Stalin replacing Queen Elizabeth.

BOGUS STAMPS

The term "bogus" describes stamps that are pure fantasies, often purporting to come from non-existent countries. This was a favourite ploy of conmen in the late 19th century, using such stamps to lure investors in fictional colonial projects. Sadly, these fabrications have their modern counterparts. The break-up of the Soviet Union in the 1990s proved to be a fertile ground for a host of bogus issues, aimed at unsuspecting philatelic buyers.

FIRST DAY COVERS AND SPECIAL POSTMARKS

In the 1930s, when postal administrations began announcing impending issues of stamps (instead of just putting them on sale without warning), collectors got into the habit of mailing covers to themselves with the latest stamps purchased on the day they became available. Before that decade was out many countries were cashing in on the growing popularity of this trend by providing special postmarks for use on the first day of issue.

FIRST DAY COVERS

Both stationers and stamp dealers published attractive envelopes to accompany the new issues, and by the 1940s many postal services were getting in on this act as well. By 1950 the collecting of first day covers – or FDCs as they are known for short – was well established, although it was not until 1963 that the British Post Office began to produce first day postmarks and souvenir envelopes.

This field has now developed to such an extent that most collectors acquire both a mint set and the appropriate FDC for each new issue. In addition to the special handstamp or machine cancellation authorized by the postal service for each issue, many dealers, cover producers and organizations (such as the charity or public body connected with a particular stamp issue) sponsor first day handstamps. In Britain, for example, as many as 40 sponsored postmarks may be associated with each new issue.

SPECIAL POSTMARKS

Though the use of operational datestamps on ordinary mail has declined, the fashion for special handstamps remains undiminished. These originated in the mid-19th century, when temporary post offices were set up at major agricultural fairs and exhibitions and gradu-

ally extended to all manner of events, from conferences to sports and race meetings. At these post offices a specially worded postmark was invariably applied, but since the 1960s it has become more usual merely to have a posting box at such events, the mail being cancelled at the nearest main post office. Many countries use pictorial postmarks as a form of local publicity and they exist both as handstamps and as machine cancellations. Postal administrations sometimes offer special

Right: First day covers from Gibraltar and the Czech Republic – on the latter both the pictorial panel and the postmark complement the stamp.

Below: The cartoon character Phil Stamp finds a humorous angle on British stamps issued in 2004.

Above: An Indian stamp from 2004 whose motif is matched on the first day postmark.

postmarks automatically to customers who set up standing orders, but in other countries the collector still has to write to the individual post office and send items for reposting.

THE PHILATELIC DOCUMENT

France pioneered the philatelic document in 1973, originally as a means of raising funds for its National Postal Museum. The document consists of a sheet describing a particular issue, with a stamp affixed and cancelled by a special postmark. The concept has spread to the USA and many other countries in recent years. Pre-stamped envelopes and postcards are also often produced in connection with stamp exhibitions and are avidly collected with the appropriate stamps and cancellations.

CHOOSING BETWEEN POSTMARK AND PICTURE

Around the beginning of the 20th century, when picture postcard mania was at its height, collectors attempted to match the picture on the card with a postmark relevant to it. However, there was something rather disappointing about mounting the souvenirs of your

Below: A French philatelic document bearing the Gaston Lagaffe cartoon stamp, with pictorial postmark and background text.

Above: The back and front of a Swiss postcard that has the stamp on the picture side.

foreign vacation in an album but being unable to see the stamp and postmark as well as the picture. This problem was solved by sticking the stamp in the top right-hand corner of the picture side and hoping that the post office would indulge your eccentric behaviour by applying the postmark.

In Britain this informal practice was officially banned until the 1970s, but other countries were more obliging and France and Germany even had special explanatory marks, struck on the address side, to explain that the adhesives were on the picture side, thus avoiding the surcharging of the card as if it had been sent unpaid.

MAXIMUM CARDS

In the 1930s, when stamps had become much more pictorial in concept, the notion arose of affixing a stamp to a postcard with a relevant picture and then getting the stamp cancelled at an appropriate place. Indeed, many postal administrations and philatelic bureaux encouraged this by producing special cards to accompany each new issue of stamps, and providing a service for cancelling them on the picture side. Such

cards are known as maximum cards because they offer the maximum of a picture, a stamp and a postmark that can all be seen at a glance when mounted in an album. While these items are important adjuncts to thematic collecting, they are now studied and collected in their own right under the name of maximaphily.

Although the British Post Office began to permit maximum cards only in 1970 (in connection with the Philympia stamp exhibition held that year), it took the idea a step further in 1973, when it introduced postcards that reproduced commemorative or special issue stamps. These are known as PHQ cards (from the initials of Postal Headquarters), and are collected either in unused condition or with the appropriate adhesive and matching first day cancellation on the picture side. Ironically, PHQ cards were very slow to catch on with collectors, and this limited circulation means that some examples now change hands for three-figure sums.

Left and below: Maximum cards from the Faroes and Australian Antarctic.

Below: British PHQ card for the English first class definitive.

POSTER STAMPS

The term "poster stamps" was devised in the interwar period, when multicolour lithography was frequently used to create posters in miniature for the promotion of tourism. The description of such items as "stamps" is in fact a misnomer, because although they resemble stamps in appearance these bright, colourful and attractive labels have no connection with the postal services. They were produced by tourist boards, chambers of commerce and even private individuals. They were also extensively

Right: A poster stamp produced for the Leipzig Fairs of 1906–7.

Above: Something of a philatelic first, the Shakespeare Penny Memorial label both commemorated the Bard's birth and sought to fund a new theatre.

Below: A label publicizing the Pan-American Exposition in 1901.

employed to advertise the products of many companies, especially after the concept of brand names and trademarks developed in importance in the late 19th century.

COMMEMORATIVE LABELS

Although commemorative postage stamps did not materialize until the late 1880s, labels that celebrated historic personalities or documented important events were in existence many years earlier. The first of these was an embossed medallic label produced for an exhibition in Vienna; although it bore the effigy of the Emperor Ferdinand it was a private production by Apollo Kerzen-Fabrik. In 1851 a label was issued in connection with the Great Exhibition in London; in fact, there is a theory that it was devised to frank the correspondence of Royal Commissioners, but it is of such great rarity that little is known about it.

All of the early labels were produced in connection with international fairs and exhibitions, but in 1860 a label portraying Garibaldi celebrated his expedition to Sicily as part of the campaign for the unification of Italy. Garibaldi was also the subject of a label in 1863 mourning his defeat at Aspromonte. The first label to mark a historic anniversary was produced in England in 1864. Inscribed with the legend "Shakespeare Penny Memorial", it portrayed the Bard himself and celebrated the 300th anniversary of his birth. As the inscription implies, it was also intended as a fundraiser for the projected Memorial Theatre at Shakespeare's birthplace, Stratford-upon-Avon, completed in 1879.

Up to 1873 very few labels were recorded each year, but when Vienna hosted the International Exhibition that year there were embossed scalloped

Below: A French patriotic label of 1915 recalling the Revolution (left) and a German patriotic label of the same year captioned "God punish England!"

labels for the various commissioners, as well as the label reproducing the gold medals awarded, with the effigy of the Emperor Franz Joseph on the obverse.

A NEW CENTURY

The generation of commemorative labels reached its zenith at the Exposition Universelle in Paris in 1900. This exhibition, to celebrate the achievements of the previous century and progress in the next, was the greatest of the world's fairs at that time, and resulted in the issuing of many hundreds of different labels.

By the end of the 19th century, production of commemorative labels had grown enormously, with publishers producing sets of colourful labels for every conceivable occasion. The labels for the Paris show could be divided into general publicity, the numerous series that featured the landmarks and scenery of Paris, the issues of the many French learned societies, the labels published by companies advertising goods displayed at the fair and the *timbres recompensés*, reproducing the various gold, silver and bronze medals. In addition, A. Baguet alone produced five sets of labels, 40 in all, honouring each of the national pavilions. Some students of poster stamps have devoted a lifetime solely to collecting the different labels from the Exposition Universelle.

The first phase of poster stamps ended with the onset of World War I but over the next four years the publicity labels of the earlier years gave way to long sets showing regimental flags, portraits of military and naval heroes and all the weird and wonderful weaponry conjured up by the conflict. Inevitably France and Germany vied with each other in the production of labels, which moved effortlessly from publicity to propaganda.

TOURIST PUBLICITY

The return to peace saw a dramatic change in the labels. By the 1920s the notion of commemorative postage stamps was well established, and consequently far fewer labels of a com-

memorative nature were produced. It was now that the publicity element came into its own with the rise of cheap foreign travel. Tourist organizations were quick to perceive the benefits of advertising through this medium. Many of the rather garish posters of the period were automatically reduced to the medium of poster stamps and adorned envelopes containing promotional leaflets and brochures. There was an attempt in continental Europe to produce booklets of different scenic labels, but this fashion was already waning when the outbreak of World War II killed it off.

PHILATELIC EXHIBITIONS

One sphere in which the poster stamp has held its own, despite the vagaries of fashion or the competition from postage stamps, is in philately itself. The first issue in this connection consisted of a series of 1pf stamps of the Circular Post of Frankfurt-am-Main in 1887, available in five different colours. Since this time,

Right: A Swiss tourist label publicizing autumn holidays.

Below: A sheetlet depicting views of the Smithsonian Institution in Washington, DC.

Above: Prewar poster stamps from Tournoel in France and Newquay in Cornwall, England.

every national and international philatelic exhibition has spawned a shoal of labels, and latterly miniature sheets, used either as advance publicity stickers or as mementos of the show. They provide a colourful adornment to the various covers and postcards produced for the occasion, and augment the commemorative stamps with their pictorial cancellations.

SOCIETIES

The collecting of poster stamps is closely affiliated to Cinderella philately, and you may get information on significant issues from the societies devoted to that field. There are, however, organizations and exhibitions devoted predominantly to the study and collection of poster stamps. The American Poster Stamp Society offers membership and a regular bulletin. An address for the society can be found at the end of this chapter.

CHARITY SEALS AND LABELS

From the Shakespeare Penny Memorial label of 1864, an increasing number of labels were devised to raise money for good causes. Although many are not official postage stamps, and may not be listed in catalogues, their often colourful and highly visual designs make them of natural interest to collectors.

Left: The Prince of Wales's Hospital Fund label, 1897.

Below: World War I charity fundraising labels from New Zealand and Russia.

Right: Einar Holboell, who devised charity seals, was portrayed on a Belgian anti-TB stamp in 1955.

THE QUEEN'S COMMEMORATION

Queen Victoria's diamond jubilee of 1897 yielded several sets of purely commemorative labels, but there was a particular issue that stood out on account of its intricate design.

Line-engraved by De La Rue (who produced the British postage stamps) the issue consisted of 1s and 2s 6d labels, each depicting the allegorical figure of Charity aiding poor children. At the top was the inscription "1837 The Queen's Commemoration 1897" but at the foot was the facsimile signature of the Prince of Wales (the future

Edward VII) and the words "Prince of Wales's Hospital Fund". Although these labels had no postal validity they had the tacit support of the Post Office and were intended to adorn letters and postcards – so long as they were kept well away from the proper postage stamps. Used examples are scarce, suggesting that most were purchased to keep as souvenirs of the jubilee.

The success of the venture induced the promoters to issue 5s and 10s labels as well, but this was going too far and not surprisingly the high values are of the greatest rarity today. The resultant fiasco put a damper on attempts to repeat the exercise and it is significant that no fundraising labels appeared in Britain at the time of the Boer War (1899–1902). There was a belated resurgence during World War I though the idea found greater favour in India and Australia than it did in Britain. Nevertheless, charity labels are among the most enduring of the Cinderellas on a worldwide basis, despite the fierce competition from charity stamps.

CHRISTMAS AND EASTER SEALS

It was in December 1904 that a Danish postal official, Einar Holboell, came up with the notion of producing labels to

be affixed to the envelopes of greetings cards, the money thus raised being given to the national anti-tuberculosis fund. His idea was enthusiastically endorsed by the Danish Post Office, which even arranged for the Christmas seals to be sold at post offices. The scheme was taken up by the other Scandinavian countries the following year. At first a single design was produced annually, but in more recent years different motifs have appeared on each label, often forming a composite design covering the sheet. Holboell has himself been portrayed on charity stamps of Denmark and Belgium.

The labels spread to the Faroes, Iceland, Greenland and the Danish West Indies (now the American Virgin Islands), and from there spread to

Above: A booklet containing French anti-TB Christmas seals.

Below: This Swedish envelope bears the 1903 Christmas seal alongside a stamp.

Korean Charity Labels

It is easy to detect the American influence on these labels for Boys Town and Girls Town charities in Korea, which by the 1960s were caring for almost 4,000 orphans in the cities of Pusan and Seoul.

Above: Even charity seals occasionally carried commercial advertising. This French booklet pane promotes various items, such as toothpaste, in its margins.

many other countries, notably Canada, Mexico, the USA, France and South Africa. In the last two countries the seals were produced in booklets, which

Below: A bilingual pair of Christmas seals from South Africa (1938).

Above: A Danish Christmas seal (1904) and a Thorvaldsen Foundation seal from Iceland (1953).

Below: An Easter seal produced by the St John Ambulance Brigade, 1970.

were sold at post offices. French stamp booklets carried commercial advertising on the top and bottom margins, and this practice was extended to the charity labels, often with incongruous results. A factor unifying most Christmas seals, no matter where they are issued, is the red Cross of Lorraine, the international emblem of the anti-tuberculosis campaign.

In the 1940s the concept was extended to Easter seals, which were sold in aid of funds for the handicapped. Recurring themes of these labels were the Easter lily or a crutch to symbolize the disabled. In New Zealand, however, Easter seals support the St John Ambulance movement and incorporate the Maltese Cross emblem. In recent years many other charities have begun producing their own versions of Christmas and Easter seals to raise funds for cancer research, epilepsy and the prevention of blindness, while organizations like the Red Cross issue charity labels in many lands that can be used all year round.

CHILDREN'S CHARITIES

A group of charity labels with a strong thematic appeal is that devoted to the care of orphans and homeless children. The vast majority of Easter seals come into this category, notably the American labels showing disabled children overcoming their handicap, accompanied by slogans such as "I'm a fighter" or "Back a fighter".

The best known of the children's charities producing annual labels is Boys Town in Nebraska, founded by Father Edward Flanagan. Many of its

Above: Christmas seals from Boys Town, Nebraska and Cal Farley's Boys Ranch, Texas.

Left: Dürer's "Praying Hands" on a Christmas seal of the Omaha Home for Boys.

labels feature the poignant figure of a boy with a youngster asleep round his neck, saying, "He ain't heavy, Father, He's m' brother." Based on a real incident that has since been immortalized in a statue, this motif is the logo of Boys Town. Separate labels exist for affiliated Boys' and Children's home charities.

Below: Charity labels issued by France and Spain. The French Red Cross label (left) raised funds for military hospitals during World War I; the Spanish "2 pesetas" was one of a number produced in the 1930s and '40s to help provide for the widows of postal workers.

FISCAL STAMPS AND SPECIAL SERVICE LABELS

Adhesive stamps and labels issued to denote dutiable goods, payment of a licence, or simply bearing special instructions to customs or to postal authorities, are among the most diverse of Cinderella collectibles.

FISCAL STAMPS

Adhesive stamps embossed on deep blue "sugar-bag" paper were used for revenue purposes at the Board of Stamps and Taxes in London from 1694 onwards. They were an innovation imported by William of Orange from his native Holland, where they had been in use since the early 17th century. Later fiscal stamps (known as revenue stamps in the United States) were embossed directly on to boxes and bottles containing patent medicines, or the wrappers of dice, while the elaborate device on the ace of spades in a deck of cards was, in fact, a tax stamp.

The excise duty on a wide range of articles, from hair powder to gloves, was indicated by such stamps. Adhesive stamps were produced in perforated sheets for matchboxes, tobacco and

Left: A British 3d postage stamp over-printed for use as an additional medicine duty stamp.

Above: A patent medicine tax stamp, used to seal pill boxes.

Below: Fiscal stamps of the Cape of Good Hope and Malta.

cigarettes, wines and spirits, entertainment duty and even phonograph records. The range of fiscal stamps in Britain in the 19th and early 20th centuries was enormous, from additional medicine duty during World War I to travel permits and unemployment insurance. As a result of the Local Stamp Act of 1869 there were even revenue stamps of purely local validity, from Alderney to Winchester, and separate issues for Scotland and Ireland. Savings stamps, introduced in many countries in World War I, continued until the 1970s and have since been replaced by individual issues by banks and public utilities.

A similar pattern operated in many other countries, with a wide range of national duties and numerous taxes

Below: A US cigarette tax stamp portraying De Witt Clinton, a documentary stamp featuring a battleship, and an Ohio vendor's receipt stamp.

Below: The US migratory bird hunting stamp for 1954: the design was changed annually to feature different species.

Bomb Warning
Perhaps the most sombre labels in current use are those of the Israel Postal Authority, inscribed in Hebrew, English, Arabic and Russian, warning the recipient of a parcel that if there is any suspicion that it contains a bomb it should be taken to the police.

imposed at cantonal or communal level. In the USA it was illegal to use a revenue stamp for any purpose other than the specific tax inscribed on it, and up to 1862 there was a proliferation of stamps for many duties. Thereafter a general issue of documentary stamps by the Bureau of Internal Revenue could be used indiscriminately with the exception of the distinctive stamps applied to proprietory articles, such as matches and medicines, introduced in 1871. In 1962 the centenary of the documentary stamps was marked by what is probably the world's first commemorative revenue stamp, and facilities were exceptionally made for it to be used on first day covers. The use of such stamps ceased in 1967.

In 1934 the USA introduced migratory bird hunting permits and stamps denoting payment of the fee. In addition, many individual states have their own annual migratory hunting stamps.

TELEGRAPH, TELEPHONE AND TELEVISION STAMPS

At one time there were separate issues of stamps for telegrams in many countries, as well as the issues of the private

Above: Telegraph stamps issued by Britain, Spain and Tangier.

Left: A British telephone stamp of 1884.

telegraph companies. In Britain, the National Telephone Company even had its own stamps (1884–91) portraying its chairman, Colonel Robert Raynsford-Jackson. They were used as an early method to pay for telephone calls at local offices, to avoid the need for an exchange of money. The stamps were finally withdrawn from use in 1891, due to the Post Office's belief that they could be confused with normal postage stamps. Despite this, special stamps were used until relatively recently in some countries to help people save towards the cost of a TV licence.

POSTAL SERVICE LABELS

Labels denoting specific postal services originated in the 1870s when Germany and Sweden introduced stickers bearing names of towns and serial numbers for use on registered packets. The system was later extended to the serial labels affixed to the cards that accompanied parcels. In Britain, distinctive parcel labels were issued to every post office from 1883 to 1916, but registration labels were not adopted until 1907, although the UPU had decreed this in 1881. Distinctive serial labels have also been used for certified mail (USA) or recorded delivery (UK), with

equivalents in most other countries. In recent years labels distinctive to each post office have been largely replaced by a national series of barcode labels. Resealing labels for damaged or broken packets and explanatory labels marked "Deceased", "Gone away" and "Return to sender" in different languages are also to be found.

AIRMAIL *ETIQUETTES*

France pioneered special stickers for airmail in 1918, and for that reason they are still generally known to collectors by the French term *etiquettes*. Their use is on the increase as it is now mandatory to affix them to all letters and cards going abroad by air. In many countries nowadays their place has been taken by A-Priority labels, although these retain the general pattern of white inscriptions on a blue background. In such countries there is usually the equivalent of a second-class service denoted by white on green B-Economy labels. The Postal

Above: Reasons for non-delivery are explained in English, Afrikaans and French on this South African label.

Below: A pre-stamped postcard from the Åland Islands, bearing an airmail "priority" sticker, issued in 2004.

Union Congress at Madrid in 1920 decreed the introduction of green labels for Customs declaration and these, in various modifications, are still in use, generally inscribed in French and a national language. For dutiable goods on which the tax has been paid there are labels inscribed in French "*Franc de droits*" (Free of dues).

LABELS FOR SPECIAL TREATMENT

At various times from the late 19th century there have been special labels for express and special delivery services, warning labels affixed to parcels of eggs or containing fragile or perishable substances, and even labels for packages containing live creatures, pathological specimens or radioactive materials. There are also stickers to mark parcels containing Braille reading material for the blind. These labels often conform to an international convention of easily recognizable symbols, such as a wine glass (fragile), a rabbit (live animals), the staff of Aesculapius (pathological specimens) or a blind person carrying a white stick.

Right: A label from the Czech Republic for use on parcels containing live animals.

Right: An early United States Customs label.

Below: An insured parcel card for a dispatch from Vienna to Berne in 1911, bearing an impressed 10 heller stamp.

LOCAL STAMPS AND PRIVATE POSTS

The stamp catalogues of the 19th century included postage stamps of all kinds, whether issued by government posts or local services operated by private enterprise. Later, the sheer number of government issues forced all but a few highly specialized one-country catalogues to drop nearly everything else. Thus the stamps of the many local and private posts were consigned to limbo.

CARRIERS STAMPS
US carrier stamps are among the only semi-official issues that continue to be listed. These local stamps originate from the period before 1863, the year the US Post Office finally established a general town delivery. For some 20 to 30 years prior to this, the gap was filled by numerous local dispatch posts known as "carriers", many employees of which later worked for the government as part of the national postal network. In 1842, a 3c carrier stamp became the first ever stamp to be issued under government

Above: Two stamps used for the Chesterfield Scouts Christmas post.

Left: Shotts Scouts in Lanarkshire, Scotland, produced this 75th anniversary stamp for their 1998 Christmas postal service.

authority, thanks to the merging of a private firm, City Despatch Post, and the state-run New York City Carrier Department. US carrier stamps are comprehensively listed in the Scott *Specialized Catalogue of U.S. Stamps*, but ignored everywhere else.

In Germany, from the 1860s to 1900, the Reichspost did not provide a service for commercial mail and printed matter such as circulars, and it was left to private operators to fill the gap. Over 200 services came into existence, many functioning within a single town and others maintaining a nationwide network. In March 1900 they were nationalized and absorbed into the Reichspost. Their heyday was the 1880s and 1890s and they pioneered various issues such as commemoratives, mourning stamps and Christmas or New Year greetings stamps. Similar local services, complete with distinctive adhesives and pre-stamped stationery, operated in Denmark, Norway and Sweden during the same period.

ZEMSTVO POSTS
By far the largest network of local posts was that operating in tsarist Russia. The imperial post served only the cities and

larger towns, and in 1864 local authorities were empowered to establish their own postal services in rural districts and to link them to the imperial service. The stamps issued by these local posts are popularly known as "zemstvos" (from the Russian word for a unit of local government). Vetlonga established its service in 1865 but the honour of issuing the first stamps went to Schluesselburg the following year. From 1870 onwards the zemstvo posts were given a completely free hand in matters of design and some of the most colourful stamps of the 19th century resulted.

By the time these services were closed down as a result of the 1917 uprising by the Bolsheviks, many

Right: A Russian zemstvo stamp from Lebedyansk, showing the civic emblem, a swan.

The World's Rarest Stamp
There are quite a few stamps of which only a solitary example has been recorded, but this zemstvo stamp, issued in June 1869 by Kotelnich, in the Viatka province north-east of Moscow, is truly unique, since only half the stamp is now known to exist. It consisted of a right-hand square that was affixed to the letter while the left-hand portion was intended to be retained by the sender as a receipt. Strangely, the complete stamp was illustrated in the catalogue published in the 1880s by the Belgian dealer, Jean-Baptiste Moens.

Left and below: Two undenominated stamps, depicting Benjamin Franklin and the American eagle, produced in 1861–3 to denote the 1c charged for delivering mail from US post offices to householders. Their use was confined to New York, Philadelphia and New Orleans.

Above: The British Customs and Revenue Act of 1881 provided for stamps that served both postal and fiscal purposes. The Penny Lilac, inscribed "Postage and Inland Revenue", was widely used on bills and receipts as well as mail until 1902, providing a wealth of material for advanced study, hence its nickname: the Poor Man's Penny Black.

FLAWS AND VARIETIES

Apart from the inks, papers and processes that distinguish the work of one printer from another, the advanced collector must pay attention to the stamps themselves. Each printing method creates its own little quirks, resulting in minor blemishes in the stamps that are known to collectors as "flaws". They may be constant, appearing in the same plate or cylinder position throughout the print-run, such as the "screwdriver" flaws – white gashes caused by damage to the plates. Constant flaws help specialists to reconstruct entire sheets, a process known as "plating". Flaws may also be ephemeral, such as "confetti" flaws – patches of white on some stamps caused by small pieces of paper (often the fragments punched out by the perforators) adhering momentarily to the plate.

Weaknesses in line engraving can be corrected, causing a slight doubling of lines known as a "re-entry". Varieties in photogravure stamps can be corrected manually but the result is still obvious and is known as a "re-touch".

Flaws and varieties are best collected in positional blocks to show their relation to the sheet margins. Controls and cylinder blocks are generally kept in corner blocks of six (three by two) and arrow markings in blocks of four.

MARGINAL MARKINGS

Specialists are also preoccupied with the paper that surrounds sheets of stamps because of the useful information it contains. Back in 1840 the sheets of Penny Blacks included the plate number and instructions regarding the correct attachment of the stamp to the letter as well as the price per row (1s) or sheet (£1). From 1881 until 1947 British stamps bore a control letter alongside numerals indicating the last two digits of the year.

American and Canadian stamps had control numbers referring to the plates released to the printers. De La Rue stamps often had a numeral in a chamfered rectangle, the "current number", which indicated the order in which a plate was printed. Other sheet markings include arrows (to guide the counter clerks in dividing up the sheets in their stock), the printer's imprint or logo, and the exact date of printing.

Thick bars were inserted in the margins in 1887 to prevent wear on the plate. Known as "jubilee lines" (because they first appeared in the jubilee definitives of that year) they are a feature of British stamps to this day. Sheets of stamps in the early 20th century often had strange cuts in the jubilee lines, believed to be made by the printers to

Below: Part of a sheet of Welsh Scenery 43p stamps (2004) showing cylinder numbers, colour dabs and the sale date.

Above: A stamp from Israel's Ottoman Clock Tower series (2004) showing an accountancy mark in the right margin and a tab below.

identify certain plates. This feature sometimes forms part of the product description on sheets up for auction.

Modern offset litho and photogravure stamps have cylinder numbers in one margin and "traffic lights" (the printer's colour dabs) in the other. The stamps of many countries have the cumulative values of each row printed at the top or bottom to assist accounting. These "reckoning numbers" are not only helpful in plating but are often slightly changed and thus help to identify a particular printing.

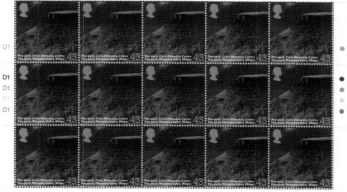

Sale Date 15-Jun-2004

A GLOBAL HOBBY

From its origins in the late 18th century, stamp collecting has emerged as the world's largest and most universal hobby. It is thought that more than 50 million people around the globe now collect, from crowned heads to schoolchildren.

Left: A famous philatelic commemorative produced for an American-hosted exhibition of 1926.

THE ORIGINS OF THE HOBBY

Philately is an extremely interactive pastime, supported by a strong network of societies, magazines, study circles, websites, web-based discussion groups, and exhibitions of interest to both the amateur and the specialist. Some clubs, such as the Invalid and Lone Collectors Society in Britain, exist to establish links between collectors living in remote areas or who, perhaps due to ill health, lack the opportunity to meet others sharing their interest. For the serious collector, there are stamp auctions and dealers' bourses where the outstanding rarities have been known to change hands for seven-figure sums.

EARLY COLLECTORS

Perhaps surprisingly, the earliest stamp collection was put together long before adhesive postage stamps (as we know

Below: Female postal workers examine love letters sent on St Valentine's Day. Despite frivolous portraits such as these, many 19th-century women took a serious interest in stamps, and some became avid pioneers of philately.

them today) came into existence. As long ago as 1774, John Bourke, then Receiver-General of the Stamp Duties in Ireland, started a collection of revenue stamps shortly after they were introduced in that country. However, the father of stamp-collecting in the accepted sense was Dr John Edward Gray, Keeper of the Zoological Department of the British Museum. He took a very close interest in postal reform and was one of several people who later challenged Rowland Hill's claim to have invented stamps.

On the day the Penny Black went on sale (1 May 1840) Dr Gray purchased some examples of the stamp, which he kept as mementoes of a historic occasion. He subsequently added the Twopence Blue when it appeared on 8 May, and collected other stamps as soon as they were issued.

In 1862 he was the compiler of one of the earliest stamp catalogues, and he also published sets of gummed titles, intended for collectors to cut up and use as headings for the pages of their stamp albums.

Apart from Dr Gray there must have been other men and women who were quick to perceive the innate interest in these tiny scraps of paper and began forming collections of them. By 1850, when stamps from about 20 countries had appeared, and the number of issues

Left and above: The first page of the inaugural issue of The Stamp Collector's Magazine, *February 1863, and a page advertising the sale of readers' stamps, labels and covers.*

in circulation had reached three figures, stamp collecting was well established as a hobby. As early as 1842 references to this strange new craze began to appear in newspaper and magazine articles. More significantly, advertisements of stamps wanted or for sale were being published by 1852. In that year a Belgian schoolmaster is said to have started encouraging his pupils to collect stamps, to improve their knowledge of geography.

Stanley Gibbons

Edward Stanley Gibbons was born in the same year as the Penny Black (1840) and began trading in stamps in 1856 from his father's shop in Plymouth, having purchased a collection of South African stamps from two sailors who had just returned to the port. Stamp trading apart, he led a colourful life, marrying five times.

THE FIRST DEALERS AND CATALOGUES

The hobby was certainly well established in Belgium by 1854, by which time Louis Hanciau and Jean-Baptiste Moens (who later became leading dealers) were avid enthusiasts. Edward Stanley Gibbons began dealing in stamps in 1856, a window of his father's pharmacy in Plymouth being devoted to mouth-watering bargains. Nine years later he published his first catalogue, the forerunner of the extensive range of general, specialized and thematic catalogues now on offer.

Oscar Berger-Levreult and Alfred Potiquet both began publishing catalogues in France in 1861 and not long afterwards there were regular magazines devoted to the hobby. One of the earliest was *The Stamp Collector's Magazine*, which first appeared in February 1863, and contained in its opening pages a very vivid account of the open-air selling and swapping of stamps conducted in Birchin Lane, Cheapside, in London, and the similar al fresco meetings of "timbromaniacs" held in the gardens of the Luxembourg and the Tuileries in Paris.

THE BIRTH OF PHILATELY

Timbromania, the original pseudo-scientific name for the hobby (from the French word *timbre*, a stamp), was soon replaced by something more dignified, if less easy to pronounce. Again it was a Frenchman, Georges Herpin, who coined the word "philately", but his logic was as faulty as his grasp of Greek. He tried to convey the idea of something on which no tax or charge was due because it was prepaid (*philos* = love, *a* = not, *telos* = tax), and thus ended up with a word that meant a lover of no taxes. Some have argued that "atelophily" would be more correct. Significantly, the Greeks themselves use the term *philotelia*, which omits the negative element, implying that stamp collectors are lovers of taxes rather than of the stamps that signify their payment.

FIRST STAMP CLUBS

Among the pioneer collectors was the Reverend F.J. Stainforth, who organized the first indoor meetings when the police began to discourage the obstruction caused in Birchin Lane. In the 1860s collectors met on Saturday afternoons in his rectory at All Hallows Staining in the City of London – its Dickensian ring is hardly surprising as it features in Dickens's novel *Dombey and Son*. The gatherings included Charles W. Viner, editor of *The Stamp Collector's Magazine*, Mount Brown, who published an early catalogue, Judge Philbrick and Sir Daniel Cooper, who became president of the Philatelic Society, London, when it was founded in 1869. A society had been formed in Paris in 1864 but it did not last long. The London society, now the Royal Philatelic Society, is still in existence and, if not the biggest, is certainly the most prestigious in the world.

Although stamp collecting is sometimes regarded as a male-dominated hobby, women have always played a prominent role in the field. Among the earliest female enthusiasts were Charlotte Tebay, who helped organize the earliest London exhibition, and Adelaide Lucy Fenton, who was a prolific contributor to the stamp magazines but, like some female novelists of an earlier generation, preferred to write under the masculine pen name of "Herbert Camoens".

The English school of philately was noted for its general approach, whereas the French school had a more scientific bent, paying greater attention to the minute variations in stamps. It was one of their number, Dr Jacques-Amable Legrand, who invented the perforation gauge in 1866 and wrote the earliest treatise on watermarks a year later.

Below: A society for young philatelists was, indeed, the brainchild of a young philatelist. Fred Melville was just 17 when he established the group in 1899, following his disappointment at being rejected as a member of the London Philatelic Society on account of his age. The first meeting is believed to have been held in a shop in Clapham, South London, and the Junior Philatelic Society went on to become the National Philatelic Society, which celebrated its centenary in 1999.

ORGANIZED PHILATELY

Stamp collecting endured a sticky patch in the 1870s (*The Stamp Collector's Magazine* ceased publication in 1874, and its rival *The Philatelist* in 1876, for lack of support), but somehow it managed to keep going and steadily gained ground in the 1880s. By then it was well established throughout Europe and North America, with numerous dealers and stamp auctions.

GROWTH OF STAMP CLUBS
The reason for the loss of interest in the 1870s was probably the paucity of stamp clubs; without the interaction of fellow enthusiasts, many of the original collectors lost heart and gave up. The resurgence of the hobby began in continental Europe, where a national philatelic society was revived in France at the end of 1875.

A stamp club had started in New York in 1867 but soon faded into oblivion and it was not until 1886 that the American Philatelic Society (APS) was formed. Chartered by Congress in 1912, it is now the world's largest stamp club, with its headquarters and

magnificent library in State College, Pennsylvania. About the same time the Manchester Philatelic Society was established in England. The Edinburgh & Leith Philatelic Society, founded in 1890, was almost entirely composed of expatriate German businessmen and for the first three years the minutes were recorded in German. By the beginning of the 20th century there were 34 philatelic societies in the UK, a score in the British colonies, a dozen in the USA, 19 in continental Europe and nine in Latin America.

EARLY STAMP EXHIBITIONS
In 1887 the first stamp exhibition took place at Antwerp. Two years later similar shows were organized in New York, Amsterdam and Munich. In 1890 – the golden jubilee of adhesive postage stamps – exhibitions were staged in Vienna, Birmingham, Edinburgh and Leeds as well as London (for which some of the earliest special postmarks were produced). Undoubtedly such exhibitions attracted the general public and drew many new recruits.

Below: The American Philatelic Society, established in 1886 as the American Philatelic Association, has hosted annual conventions for many years.

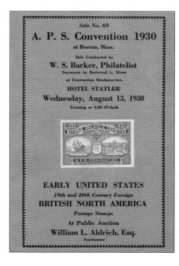

World Fair Stamps
New York's fair of technology and science, held from 1939 to 1940, brought hope to an era of international tension. A commemorative stamp was issued by the USPO in the Fair's first year. Some participating countries, such as Iceland, issued postage stamps to fund their attendance at the two-year global exhibition. The Centennial Stamp Exhibition was one of many around the world that marked the centenary of the Penny Black.

Philatelic literature, including handbooks and monographs as well as general catalogues, had grown to such an extent that, by 1889, the Munich exhibition included more than 500 volumes. The first exhibition devoted to stamps of particular countries took place in 1893 when the Philatelic Society of London staged a show of British India, Ceylon and the West Indies. The Society's exhibition the following year was dedicated to rare stamps in general.

The first London exhibition in 1890 had been a major landmark. Although the centenary exhibition in 1940 was muted as a result of the outbreak of World War II, it set the precedent for

If you decide to sell to a dealer you may be in for quite a shock. What he offers you may be only a fifth of what you paid – sometimes less – especially if you are trading in your entire collection rather than selected items. The reason for this large differential between buying and selling price is mainly economic. When appraising a collection, dealers ignore all the common stamps (of which they will already have a large stock that is slow to turn over) and will base their valuation on the scarcer or more expensive individual items. Selling stamps this way, however, means that you get cash on the spot – useful if you need money in a hurry.

FINDING THE RIGHT DEALER

For every dealer with a retail shop there are probably 100 whose business is postal or by appointment only. Some of the world's largest dealers operate in quite a modest manner, acting on behalf of a few very wealthy clients who will regularly spend large sums with them. They are truly international, traversing the world in search of major rarities, relying on their laptops, bidding at auctions online and emailing clients to set up new deals.

At the other end of the scale are the vast majority of dealers, who are content to make a modest living, meeting potential customers on the fair circuits, which have now largely superseded the retail shops. Others have found niches specializing in certain countries or types of material, sending out price lists to regular clients and laboriously making up approval booklets in which stamps and covers are mounted and priced.

Apart from the excellent directories of dealers published by such bodies as the American Stamp Dealers' Association (ASDA) and the Philatelic Traders' Society (PTS) in Britain, the easiest way to contact a dealer specializing in your field is to scour the classified advertisements in the philatelic magazines. If yours is a popular subject the choice of dealers will be bewildering, but whatever your interests – no matter how esoteric –

somewhere there will be at least one dealer specializing in them. As a rule, the dealers with a retail shop tend to hold general stocks as they have to cater to all tastes, whereas the postal dealers are more likely to concentrate on specific subjects. Many of them are leading authorities in their chosen speciality and you can usually rely on their judgment and integrity.

AUCTIONS

The stamp auction is where the best stamps and postal history material come up for sale, and this is where you are most likely to find entire collections and specialized studies that can form the basis for further expansion, as well as the more choice single items that fill that long-felt want.

If you attend a sale, make sure you know before it begins what your spending limit is, and stick to it. Too often, a couple of bidders get carried away in their reckless attempt to secure a coveted item and one ends up paying well over the odds. You also need to remember that most auctions nowadays charge a buyer's premium (usually 15 per cent) and that a general consumer tax may be payable on that, so the net sum you have to fork out on a purchase could turn out to be substantially more than your final bid.

It is also possible to place your bid by post. In this case you need to state the maximum you are prepared to pay on each lot and the auctioneer will let you have it at the next step above the highest room bid or the next highest postal bid to yours.

If you have good material to dispose of, selling at auction offers the best method of ensuring the maximum return, but bear in mind that the auctioneer takes a percentage of the sum realized, and many months may elapse between sending stamps to the auction and the sale itself, as material has to be appraised, lotted and described, catalogues printed and dispatched to prospective bidders, and then all the paperwork after the sale completed before you receive a remittance.

Above: An early auction catalogue. The first auction devoted entirely to stamps was held in Paris in 1865. Five years later, the American philatelist J. Walter Scott (founder of the Scott philatelic empire) organized his first sale in New York, and by the 1880s stamp auctions were a regular occurrence, with firms established solely to generate philatelic sales. Although London was dominant for many years, today there are many excellent stamp auctions in Geneva, Sydney, Singapore and Hong Kong.

PHILATELIC BUREAUX

Virtually every national postal administration now operates a philatelic bureau, selling stamps, postal stationery, FDCs and other products direct to collectors, and all transactions can be made by credit card. You pay only face value for your purchases, plus a small handing charge in many cases, but this ensures you get everything relevant to your chosen country, and sometimes a bonus such as a proof or special print unavailable across the post office counter. Bureaux produce annual catalogues of back stock as well as their own magazines, usually quarterly, announcing forthcoming issues, often with excellent background stories.

PHILATELY ONLINE

We are living in the heart of an IT revolution that impacts on every aspect of our lives, from split-second global communications to online shopping and banking, and information retrieval. Stamp collecting is also currently being transformed by the advent of the internet, with countless societies, clubs, magazines, dealers, auctioneers and centres of research offering online facilities to assist in the expansion and refinement of collections.

In addition to the ever-growing number of internet research outlets, there are also numerous software packages that assist the collector with everything from forming an inventory to calculating the value of stamps or downloading pre-designed album pages. Magazines, journals and societies often publish reviews of the latest philatelic software, and their merits (or pitfalls) are regularly debated in online discussion forums – which are themselves one of the fastest-growing

France C22 (StampID: 403350831)

Air Mail, L H, Bird, VF-XF

Condition: Unused, H
Cover: Year: 1900-1940
Other Cat Name: Other Cat #:

Catalog Value: $42.50
Sale Price: $31.29

+ Add to Cart   **E-Mail To Friend**

Q Zoom   **◄ Back to Search**   **? Ask a Question**

resources available to the online philatelic fraternity. Another hotly debated topic is the advantages or disadvantages of purchasing stamps online, which is becoming an increasingly popular alternative to local, face-to-face dealing.

RESEARCH AT THE CLICK OF A MOUSE

One of the biggest problems facing the thematic or topical collector is finding out about the subjects of stamps. The basic details such as the reason for the issue are given in stamp catalogues, but for a topical collection you often need to get the whole story – the why and the wherefore as well as the hidden meaning. It is ferreting out such information that gains good marks in competitive displays.

This is where search engines such as Google and Yahoo come into their own. There is, seemingly, absolutely nothing under the sun that cannot be found in this way, providing you type in a clear and concise phrase rather than a single keyword, which might yield far more than you require, much of it irrelevant. The search engines are also invaluable for researching postal history, and can help you to locate masses of information on the places whose postmarks you are interested in, as well as simply drawing your attention to organizations that can help

Above: Some of the larger philatelic societies offer a rigorously organized form of online "club packet", which enables members to swap stamps and even submit queries about a purchase.

further. Long-established thematic societies, such as the American Topical Association, also have their own websites, with useful tips and links for the keen researcher.

DATABASES, INVENTORIES AND WANTS LISTS

Stamp catalogues remain key to the process of identifying and valuing individual issues or long-running series. Yet there exists an increasing demand among collectors to be able to tailor these set-format reference tools to meet their individual needs. Some of the biggest catalogue publishers, such as Scott, are now working in conjunction with philatelic software producers to combine the entire catalogue of a country with the benefits of a personal inventory, so that a collector can itemize their prized possessions and identify gaps in their collection.

The idea is that the collector will not only be able to sort and display stamps by numerous categories, such as catalogue number and issue date, but also use the software to generate a personal record of their own collection.

Viewing Stamps Online

Stamps for sale on the internet are often accompanied by digital images of such quality that it is possible to discern individual fibres in the paper and verify the distance between the perforations. This Bavarian stamp displays a number of missing, or "pulled", perfs, which can affect value.

Current software offers the opportunity to revise information on value, add further details on format, grade and condition, and even upload digital scans. The best packages offer considerable space for editing data on each stamp – sometimes up to one page per issue. The collector can also inventory reports, calculate the value of a bulk of stamps, and generate wants lists to mail to dealers and other collectors.

Some of this software can be downloaded direct from the supplier's website, although before purchasing it is worth checking that the dealer is reputable and that a full mailing address, with customer service contact, is given. There may be free trial downloads, so that you can check that you are happy with the format of the software before purchasing it.

BUYING AND SELLING ONLINE

The ability to trade online is probably the most significant part of the internet revolution in stamp collecting. Stamp dealers who scraped a bare living catering to customers living in their neighbourhood have now found that by creating their own website their stock is available to the world at large. Collectors have found thousands of dealers and auctioneers, large and small, general and specialized, whose wares are to be found simply by clicking on to their websites. Most philatelic bureaux have also embraced this technology and it has become a very simple matter to select what you want and pay for it by credit card.

Apart from the various auctioneers, who also have websites nowadays and enable you to bid online, there are larger, less esoteric organizations such as Ebay, where online sales are in continuous operation. Nor does buying online always require putting in a bid. In America, *Linn's Stamp News* runs a site at www.zillionsofstamps.com – open to all – that gives the collector the opportunity to input data on a wanted stamp and then search by dealer. The American Philatelic Society runs its own stamps store for members at www.stampstore.org, where the collector can browse stamps, selecting them by keyword, catalogue number, country or even type, such as "air mails". APS members can also submit information on stamps they wish to sell to other collectors.

For all forms of buying and selling, the computer scores heavily because it is now possible to download high-resolution images of stamps, which make even the most sumptuous of printed catalogues look crude by comparison. Fakes (stamps that have been tampered with to improve their appearance or altered by cleaning off the cancellation to convert a cheap used stamp into a valuable mint one) are no longer such a headache for potential buyers, because high-resolution images of stamps will immediately show up any imperfection, repair or other signs of alteration.

DISCUSSION FORUMS

One of the latest developments in this interactive hobby is for collectors to meet and chat with fellow enthusiasts from anywhere in the world via online messaging services. This can be done by posting notices to message boards, or by participating in a "live" discussion. Many philatelic forums have countless discussions running at any one time – on every subject from catalogue prices to the latest commemoratives, how to get started in collecting or experiences of online auction bidding. A code of conduct is usually encouraged during these discussions – namely that the participants stick to the subject at hand. Two of the busiest stamp collector forums, with spirited discussions, are the Virtual Stamp Club (www.virtualstampclub. com) and Frajola's Board for Philatelists (www.rfrajola.com). These sites also offer other standard facilities such as a bookstore and archive search facility.

Below: Global auction sites such as Ebay have embraced online philatelic trading. The number of bids is often displayed in a "counter" at the bottom of the screen. If you are not too familiar with the stamps you are bidding for, check that the seller has included their catalogue value with the lot, otherwise you may end up paying over the odds. Before getting involved in a bidding war, determine the maximum amount you wish to pay per stamp.

USEFUL SERVICES AND ADDRESSES

For the vast majority of collectors the standard stamp catalogues, published by long-established firms such as Gibbons (UK), Scott (USA), Michel (Germany) or Yvert et Tellier (France), are their bibles. The more advanced collectors are not content with one or other of the great general catalogues but require the specialized catalogues of their chosen countries – which may entail learning a foreign language as the best of the detailed catalogues, monographs and other reference works tend to be confined to the language of the country under study.

RESEARCHING THE MACHINS

The following example may help to illustrate the difference between the different levels of catalogues. The Machin decimal definitives of the UK, launched in 1971 and still going strong, occupy a column in the Gibbons *Stamps of the World* (2004 edition), which lists 120 stamps by denomination and colour only. The same stamps, classified by printer, printing process, perforation and phosphor, occupy nine columns in the Gibbons *British Commonwealth* volume 1, while volume 4 of the *Specialised Stamp Catalogue*, devoted entirely to the decimal definitives, now runs to almost 950 pages. This catalogue explains the differences in the stamps produced by Harrison, Enschedé, Questa and De La Rue (photogravure), Questa, Waddington and Walsall (lithography) and Bradbury Wilkinson, Enschedé or De La Rue (intaglio). It details the variations in the queen's effigy (high or

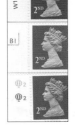

Left: Three British second class Machin definitives, printed by Walsall, Harrison and Questa, can be identified by the sheet markings.

low), whether chemically etched or computer engraved, and distinguishes the numerous types of paper, gum, perforation (normal or elliptical in different gauges), cylinder varieties, marginal markings, booklets and coils.

Many advanced collectors prefer the *Complete Deegam Machin Handbook* compiled by Douglas Myall, who is also the author of the *Deegam Catalogue of Machin Se-tenant Pairs* and even a catalogue of *Elizabethan Coil Leaders*. Beyond that, an absolute must is membership of the Great Britain Philatelic Society, which has a separate Machin chapter, or the Decimal Book Study Circle, which publishes *The Bookmark* detailing the latest research by members. In fact, it is the pooling of information by individual collectors, who devote a considerable amount of time and money to researching the latest printings, that helps to maintain the extraordinary momentum of interest in this series.

CHECKING PREVIOUS RESEARCH

There is a vast literature on all aspects of philately and postal history, from monumental treatises running to several volumes, to articles in general and specialist magazines. A great deal of research by countless students into the most subtle minutiae of stamps and more esoteric aspects of postal history is to be found. Much of it has probably never been distilled and published in even the advanced catalogues. One task for the collector researching his material in detail is to find out what has already been published on the subject; sourcing all this secondary material takes quite a lot of research in itself.

MUSEUMS AND ARCHIVES

Many countries have at least one museum devoted to philately. In the USA the Smithsonian Institution in Washington has one of the world's largest philatelic collections, or rather

a whole host of different collections pertaining to stamps, from a general whole-world reference collection to specialized studies and a wealth of postal history material. There are excellent facilities for studying these collections. The American Philatelic Society's extensive premises in State

---

Which Catalogue?

The following is an alphabetical list of the geographical areas covered by the key stamp catalogue producers. Although some of the larger publishers, such as Gibbons and Scott, also produce "world guides", they are listed here according to the country of which they have the most extensive coverage.

Australian Commonwealth Specialized Australia
AAMS US and Canadian Air Mail Covers
Bale Israel/Palestine
Barefoot European Revenues and British Revenues
Brookman United States
Campbell-Paterson New Zealand
Higgins & Gage Global Postal Stationery (10 yr)
Michel Germany
Minkus/Krause United States, Canada and United Nations
Nederlandsche (NVPH) Netherlands
Sanabria Airmail Catalogue Global Air Mail stamps (10 yr)
Sassone Italy
Scott United States
Springer Handbooks Non-Scott-listed US Revenues
Stanley Gibbons Great Britain
Steven's Mexican Revenues (10 yr)
Unitrade Canada and Provinces
World Perfin Catalogue Worldwide (printed in sections)
Yvert-Tellier France
Zumstein Switzerland

College, Pennsylvania also has some amazing reference collections, often donated or bequeathed by members, but its strong point is its library – one of the finest in the world.

At the other end of the spectrum is the National Postal Museum in London. This was located in the old General Post Office in the very heart of the City, but since the Post Office sold the building for redevelopment the museum has been in storage, under the management of the Post Office Heritage Collections. In the country that invented stamps and did so much to develop postal services this is a scandal of international proportions. The British Library is home to the Tapling Collection, containing many of the world's greatest rarities, as well as many other collections, available for research.

Elsewhere in the world, from Paris to Pretoria, there are postal museums and archives crammed with source material. The following associations may be able to offer advice on how to broaden the scope of your study.

Philatelic Societies
American Philatelic Society
100 Match Factory Place, Bellefonte, PA 16875, USA, www.stamps.org (*The American Philatelist, Philatelic Literature Review*)

American Poster Stamp Society
3654 Applegate Road, Jacksonville, OR 97530, USA

American Topical Association
PO Box 50820, Albuquerque, NM 87181-0820, USA (*Topical Time*)

Australian Philatelic Federation Ltd, PO Box 829, South Melbourne BC VIC 3205, Australia

British Philatelic Centre
107 Charterhouse Street, London EC1M 6PT, UK, www.ukphilately.org.uk
     Association of British Philatelic Societies
     British Philatelic Trust
     National Philatelic Society (*Stamp Lover*)

The Philatelic Traders' Society Limited, PO Box 371, Fleet, Hampshire GU52 6ZX

Right: The American Philatelic Research Library, based at the APS premises in Bellefonte, Pennsylvania, is the largest public philatelic library in the United States. It houses classic periodicals and catalogues, and is open to the general public.

The Cinderella Stamp Club
www.cinderellastampclub.org.uk
(*The Cinderella Philatelist*)

Collectors Club of New York
22 East 35 Street, New York, NY 100016-3806, USA, www.collectorsclub.org
(*The Collectors Club Philatelist*)

The Ephemera Society of America, Inc.
PO Box 95, Cazenovia, NY 13035-0095, www.ephemerasociety.org (*Ephemera Journal*)

Invalid and Lone Collectors Club
12 Appian Close, Kings Heath, Birmingham, B14 6DS, UK

Philatelic Foundation
21 East 40th Street, New York, NY 100016, USA

Royal Philatelic Society
41 Devonshire Place, London W1N 1PE, UK, www.rpsl.org.uk (*The London Philatelist*)

Philatelic Magazines
Canadian Stamp News
Trajan Publications, 103 Lakeshore Road, Suite 202, St Catharines, Ontario L2N 2T6, Canada, www.trajan.ca

Gibbons Stamp Monthly
5 Parkside, Christchurch Road, Ringwood, Hampshire BH24 3SH, UK
www.gibbonsstampmonthly.com

Right: The Bath Postal Museum, England, is situated in the building from which one of the first letters bearing a Penny Black was sent on 2 May 1840 – four days ahead of the official date.

Global Stamp News
PO Box 97, Sidney, OH 45365-0097, USA

Linn's Stamp News
PO Box 29, 911 Vandemark Road, Sidney, OH 45365-0065, USA, www.linns.com

The Philatelic Exporter
PO Box 137, Hatfield, Hertfordshire, AL10 9DB, UK, www.philatelicexporter.com

Scott Stamp Monthly
PO Box 828, Sidney, OH 45365, USA, www.scottonline.com

Stamp and Coin Mart
Trinity Publications Ltd, Edward House, 92-3 Edward Street, Birmingham, B1 2RA, UK, www.stampmart.co.uk

Stamp Collector
700 East State Street, Iola, WI 54990-0001, USA, www.krause.com

Stamp Magazine
IPC Media, Leon House, 233 High Street, Croydon CR9 1HZ, UK, www.stampmagazine.co.uk

Stamp News
PO Box 1410, Dubbo, NSW 3830, Australia

THE WORLD DIRECTORY OF STAMPS

Stamps function rather like miniature posters: they reflect what a country thinks of itself, or how it wishes to be seen by the world. In the following pages you will find a survey of the stamps of the whole world from 1840 to the present day. Each section covers the stamps of a particular continent, and, within these parameters, the stamps of individual countries, or a group of nations, that are related politically or geographically. The stamps often chart interesting developments. The United States, for example, has remained remarkably stable since the inception of its stamps, yet even in this instance the Civil War gave rise to the separate issues of the Confederate States. At the other extreme are countries that have frequently changed their political status (such as Albania, which has been a principality, a republic, an independent kingdom, an Italian colony, a people's republic and now a democracy), or have changed their name (such as Southern Rhodesia, which became Rhodesia and is now Zimbabwe). There are stamps that reflect the economic upheavals of the past century and a half and those that mark civil wars, or were issued by occupying forces in wartime or as part of plebiscites to decide a country's future. Each continental section includes a thematic feature illustrating stamps that reflect the culture, art or history of a particular region.

Above, from left: After Germany became a federation of 32 states in 1849, many towns and duchies issued their own stamps, including Brunswick (in 1852), Bergedorf (1861) and Mecklenburg-Schwerin (1856).

AMERICA

The American continent was quick to follow Britain in introducing adhesive stamps during the 1840s, and America took the lead in adopting pictorial stamps from the 1850s onwards. The continent's vast size and scattered population encouraged the early development of airmail.

CANADA

1   2

3

4

5

6

7   8

9

One of the world's largest countries, Canada was colonized by the French after 1534. Britain acquired Hudson's Bay, Newfoundland and Nova Scotia in 1713 and gained control of New France in 1763 after a decisive victory at Quebec in 1759. Thereafter, exploration and settlement extended British influence from coast to coast. Upper and Lower Canada (Ontario and Quebec) acquired self-government in 1837. They joined with New Brunswick and Nova Scotia in 1867 to form the Confederation of Canada; British Columbia (1871) and Prince Edward Island (1873) joined later, but

Newfoundland was not admitted until 1949. Until recently all Canadian stamps were printed by the intaglio process.

Left: This stamp of 1927, celebrating the 60th anniversary of the Confederation of Canada, shows how much its territory had grown over the period since the union was formed.

BRITISH NORTH AMERICA
Before confederation, the individual British colonies issued their own stamps. Canada led the way in 1851 by separating its postal services from the General Post Office in London. In the 1860s stamps were produced for use on both Vancouver's Island and British Columbia [1], but these were followed by separate issues due to differences in the value of their currency [2]. New Brunswick's diamond-shaped stamps (1851) were followed in 1860 by a pictorial series that was quasi-commemorative, the 1c stamp celebrating the opening of the railway [3].

Newfoundland's first stamps were issued in 1857 [4], with square, upright rectangular and triangular stamps featuring the heraldic flowers of the United Kingdom. Pictorial stamps, with a penchant for royal portraiture [5], followed in 1865, and from 1898 onwards there were long scenic sets. Newfoundland's last issues (1947) before joining Canada celebrated the

21st birthday of Princess Elizabeth and the 400th anniversary of Cabot's sighting of "the new found land" [6].

Nova Scotia issued the world's first diamond-shaped stamps in 1851, beating New Brunswick by four days. The advent of the dollar in 1860 resulted in a series issued by the American Bank Note Company of New York with a full-face portrait of Queen Victoria [7]. By contrast, most of Prince Edward Island's stamps were rather crudely typographed in London [8].

A LITTLE BIT OF FRANCE IN NORTH AMERICA
When France ceded all its territory on the mainland to the British it retained the two tiny islands of St Pierre and Miquelon, off the coast of Newfoundland, as a base for fishing on the Grand Banks. French colonial general issues were followed by distinctive stamps in 1885, most of them with motifs alluding to the fishing industry [9]. In more recent times a wider range

of subjects, such as scenery [10] and bird life, have been covered, reflecting the growing importance of tourism.

CONFEDERATION

The stamps of Canada introduced in 1851 were extended to the rest of the confederation from 1867 onwards. The dominion favoured portraits of Queen Victoria in a wide range that showed her at different stages throughout her long life. Her diamond jubilee in 1897 was the occasion for a set of 16, from 1/2c to $5, showing the Chalon portrait of 1837 and Von Angeli's bust of the 1890s [11]. The advent of imperial penny postage in 1898 gave rise to the world's first Christmas stamp [12] showing a world map with the territories of the British Empire coloured red. The history of Canada was charted by commemoratives, including a single stamp of 1917 for the golden jubilee of confederation [13]: this motif was reprised ten years later, along with others, for the 60th anniversary.

As with the issues of Newfoundland, a strong thread running through Canadian stamps is royal portraiture, notably for coronations, jubilees and royal visits [14]; to Canada belongs the only stamp ever to refer to Elizabeth II as Duchess of Edinburgh [15].

Stamps of 1951 and 1991 reproduced Canada's first stamp, the Threepenny Beaver. A long-running series consisted of pairs portraying former prime ministers [16]. Canada and the USA issued identical stamps for the opening of the St Lawrence Seaway in 1959, one of the earliest joint issues,

Below: Canada's first stamp inscribed solely in French marked the occasion of the Montreal Jazz Festival in 2004.

Works of Art
Since 1988 Canada has issued a large stamp each year reproducing an outstanding painting by a Canadian artist. These stamps are greatly enhanced by the use of gold or silver foil frames. The stamps have been produced in small sheets with descriptive text in the sheet margins, encouraging philatelists to collect them entire.

while the US bicentennial yielded a stamp portraying Benjamin Franklin, a reminder that he had been Deputy Postmaster General for the whole of North America [18].

Like the USA, Canada includes at least one stamp in the definitive range showing the national flag in various settings [17] but also has an alternative stamp at the basic domestic rate portraying Elizabeth II. Modern stamps are imperforate and produced in self-adhesive booklets. Canadian stamps were originally inscribed only in English, but from 1927 onwards they were regularly inscribed in French as well. Now stamps are captioned solely in French where relevant.

While it was once a conservative country with regard to stamp production, Canada broke new ground in 1994 with the world's first customized stamps, which offered the customer a choice of different circular labels to add to the basic stamp.

10

11

12

13

14

15

16

17

18

1
2
3
4
5
6
7
8
9
10
11
12

UNITED STATES DEFINITIVES

Although a New York private post had a stamp by 1842, and postmasters were authorized to issue their own stamps in 1845, it was not until 1847 that the US Post Office adopted stamps nationwide. At this time 5c and 10c stamps sufficed, and the USA chose portraits of Benjamin Franklin,

the first Postmaster General of the United States, and George Washington, the "Father of His Country". Every definitive series from then until the 1970s portrayed George Washington, and he has seldom been far from the scene since. Benjamin Franklin was included in every series up to the set of 1970–4.

Left: George Washington on America's "Penny Black", the 10c stamp of 1847, based on a portrait by Gilbert Stuart.

DEAD PRESIDENTS
Thomas Jefferson, the third president, was also the third man to appear on US stamps, on the 5c stamp of 1856, but in the series of 1860–1 he had to vie with Franklin on two values and Washington on the other five. The necessity for a 2c stamp in 1863, for local letters, led to the admission of Andrew Jackson on one of the oddest American stamps of all time, with a full-face portrait that seems to overflow the confines of the design [2]. A 15c in grey-black was added in 1866 and portrayed Abraham Lincoln within months of his assassination [1].

BROADENING THE SCOPE
Franklin [3], Washington and Lincoln graced the 1869 series, which introduced the concept of pictorial motifs [4], including creditable attempts to reproduce historical paintings of the landing of Columbus (15c) and the Declaration of Independence (24c). This novelty was short-lived, and the following year reverted to the portrait gallery approach, with images of politicians Edwin Stanton and Henry Clay, Daniel Webster, General Winfield Scott, the lexicographer Alexander Hamilton and Commodore Perry.

ADVENT OF PHOTOGRAPHY
All the 1870 stamps bore profiles sculpted like classical busts, but in 1875 a 5c stamp was added to the series that

bore a facing portrait of General Zachary Taylor taken from a daguerreotype. James Garfield, assassinated the previous year, was the subject of a 5c stamp in 1882, also derived from a photograph. Thereafter the classical profile gradually died out. In the series of 1890 only the three lowest values (1–3c) showing Franklin, Washington [5] and Jackson [6] and the two top values featuring Jefferson (30c) and Perry (90c) retained that style, while the six middle values (4–15c) were based on photographs. The only newcomers to this line-up were Ulysses Grant [7] and General Sherman on the 5c and 8c stamps. In 1894–5 the designs were modified and the opportunity was taken to add the fourth president, James Madison ($2) and the jurist John Marshall ($5), whose portraits were based on oil paintings.

For the new century definitive design took a backward step, setting the portraits [8] in very fussy frames, though the designs repay a second glance as Franklin on the 1c was flanked by allegorical figures holding electric light bulbs aloft. Newcomers included Admiral Farragut, hero of the recent Spanish–American War, and Martha Washington, the original First Lady, and first woman to appear [9].

There seems to have been a reaction against this surfeit of the great and good, for the definitives of 1912–22 were confined to profiles of Franklin

Non-portrait Definitives

Apart from portraiture, the series of 1975–81 (combining landmarks and symbols of the American Revolution with an assortment of musical instruments) and the coil series of 1985–93 (transportation from the Conestoga wagon to the school bus) have a strong thematic appeal.

13

14

15

16

and Washington. But by 1922 the public were ready for some variety and the series, which eventually ran to 23 stamps, ranged from the ½c [10] showing Nathan Hale (executed by the British as a spy in the War of Independence) to middle values portraying Teddy Roosevelt, William McKinley, James Monroe, Rutherford B. Hayes and Grover Cleveland [11], all of whom had died by that time.

The concept of portraying dead presidents reached its climax with the series of 1938–54, which portrayed every deceased holder of the highest office [12]. Furthermore, up to the 22c value, each president was portrayed on a stamp whose denomination accorded with his number. Above that, the presidents were shown in chronological order with their dates in office, ending with Calvin Coolidge on the $5 stamp. No doubt these stamps helped people to remember which president was which. Fractional values portrayed Franklin, Martha Washington and the White House.

PROMINENT AMERICANS
Dead presidents continued to dominate the 1954–65 series [13–14] but newcomers included General Pershing [15], Paul Revere [16] and Robert E. Lee, and from then on the presidential preference waned. To be sure, later series included Kennedy (1967) and Eisenhower (1970), but from that time

the themes would be Prominent Americans (1965–81) [17–19], Great Americans (1980–94) [20–22] and the current series of celebrities that began in 2000 [23–24].

Since May 1978 the US Post Office has issued undenominated stamps at times when the domestic first-class rate is being increased, to cover an anticipated shortage of stamps showing the new rate. The earliest featured a stylized eagle and were lettered A–D (up to 1985) but later stamps had distinctive motifs whose initial letter followed the same code. Thus the increase to 25c in 1988 was covered by a stamp showing the Earth. When the rate rose to 29c in 1991 a Flower stamp was accompanied by a "make-up" stamp inscribed: "This US stamp along with 25c of additional US postage is equivalent to the F stamp rate."

17

18

19

20

21

22

Above: Old images of Washington and Jackson were re-used in a diamond format on the $5 stamp in the 1990s.

23

24

1

2

3

4

5

7

6

8

9

10

11

UNITED STATES COMMEMORATIVE AND SPECIAL ISSUES

The first set of adhesive stamps intended for temporary sale, as opposed to the permanent series, was issued in January 1893, partly to commemorate

Columbus's arrival in the New World and partly to publicize the Columbian Exposition in Chicago. The set of 16 included values from 1c to $5, and was priced at $16 in total.

Left: The Columbian series traced the volatile career of Christopher Columbus.

EXPOSITION PUBLICITY

The Trans-Mississippi Exposition at Omaha in 1898 had a more modest nine stamps up to the $2 value [1], while the Pan-American Exposition at Buffalo in 1901 [2] had a mere six stamps, the highest value being 10c. The St Louis International Exposition, doubling up with the centenary of the Louisiana Purchase in 1904, rated five stamps (1c–10c); by the time of the Panama–Pacific Exposition in 1913 four low-value stamps sufficed [3].

The Jamestown Exposition (1907) rated only three stamps while the Alaska–Yukon–Pacific Exposition of 1909 had to be content with a single 2c stamp. Thereafter, most commemorative and special issues were singles [4], and the occasion had to be very special to merit more. In the 1930s there was a rash of small-format stamps celebrating the major anniversaries of the oldest colonies [5]. A return to expensive issues, last seen in the 1890s, came with the release in 1930 of three high-value stamps commemorating the Europe–Pan-American flight of the *Graf Zeppelin*, while the most prolific issue since the Columbian Exposition was a set of 12 for the bicentenary of the birth of Washington in 1932.

FARLEY'S FOLLIES

Most special issues before World War II took note of historic anniversaries or major current events, but in 1934 a set

of ten featured scenery in some of the national parks [6]. The issue was quasi-commemorative as it coincided with National Parks Year, although this was not actually mentioned on the stamps.

This was also the era of the Farley Follies, when Postmaster General James Farley, currying favour with Franklin D. Roosevelt (an ardent philatelist), presented him with imperforate blocks of commemoratives. When word got out, collectors clamoured that what was good enough for the president was good enough for them also, and Farley was forced to release special printings. The 1935 American Philatelic Society Convention in Atlantic City was favoured with sheets of six of the stamp showing Mirror Lake and Mount Rainier. In 1936 the third International Philatelic Exhibition in New York saw a miniature sheet of four recent commemoratives in an imperforate block.

COMMEMORATIVE THEMES

A more frankly thematic approach was evident in the four stamps of 1937 showing scenery and landmarks in US territories [8] and reached its climax in the sets of five honouring heroes of the Army and Navy [9]. Sets of five in 1940 honoured famous Americans: authors, poets, educationalists, scientists, composers and artists – a series of 35 in all [7]. This concept was put to good use in the 1943–4 set of 13 showing flags of the oppressed nations [12].

Above: Imperforate stamps of 1934–7, released on the authority of Postmaster General James Farley, were nicknamed Farley's Follies by collectors, whose protests forced the US Post Office to make them generally available.

SOCIAL FOCUS

In the immediate postwar era single stamps were the norm [11], but their frequency accelerated and reached a peak in 1948 [13]. Stamps were issued not only to mark historic anniversaries and contemporary events [10] but, increasingly, to focus attention on social issues and groups – from gold-star mothers [15] to newspaper boys. Different aspects of the American way of life were the pretext for numerous stamps through the 1950s and beyond [14], and this notion of using stamps to raise awareness of important social issues continues to this day, from the "Register and Vote" campaign to concern for victims of AIDS and breast cancer in recent years.

As everywhere else in the world, a topical slant has entered the new issue policy [16–17]. The 1956 trio showing wild animals may have had the laudable objective of making the public conservation conscious but its thematic appeal was overwhelming. Similarly the set of six in 1960–1 showing quotations and autographs attracted topical

collectors, although at the height of the Cold War its political message was its main objective. Sometimes the approach was more subtle: the stamp marking the Red Cross centenary in 1963 showed the Red Cross flag over the SS *Morning Light* – the ship that repatriated participants in the Bay of Pigs invasion of Cuba [18]. Most special issues are now self-adhesive [19].

Black Heritage

Protests that Black Americans had been neglected in US stamps led to the introduction of an annual stamp devoted to Black Heritage. Beginning in 1978 with Harriet Tubman, organizer of the "underground railway" for runaway slaves, the series has ranged from the civil rights activist Ida B. Wells to Jan Ernst Matzeliger, the inventor of the shoe-lasting machine, and W.E.B. Du Bois, founder of the Niagara Movement, precursor of the National Association for the Advancement of Colored People.

12

13

14

15

16

17

18

19

UNITED STATES POSSESSIONS AND TERRITORIES

A number of administrations, from mainland states and institutions to off-shore territories, formerly had their own stamps but are now part of the United States of America and employ the latter's issues. This includes even the extra-territorial post office of the United Nations, located in the head-quarters building at the eastern side of mid-town Manhattan, New York City. It should be noted that many similar stamps, inscribed in French or German, are used at the other UN post offices in Geneva and Vienna.

Left: To celebrate the 55th anniversary of the founding of the United Nations, stamps were issued in 2000 showing the headquarters building, both while under construction and at the present day. This stamp presents an unusual view looking southwards, with the East River on the left and Brooklyn in the distance.

CONFEDERATE STATES OF AMERICA

Eleven states seceded from the Union in 1861 over the vexed question of states' rights, with particular regard to slavery, and formed a federal republic under the title of the Confederate States of America. At first it was left to individual postmasters to furnish stamps to their own design. Many, such as the 2c stamp produced in Memphis, Tennessee, bore the name of the post-master rather than the town [1]. Other stamps, many unique or extremely rare, were crudely handstamped.

The first issues for general use were 5c and 10c stamps, printed by Hoyer & Ludwig of Richmond, Virginia; they portrayed Jefferson Davis [2] and Thomas Jefferson respectively. A supply of stamps was procured from De La Rue of London [3] – the only stamps of continental USA produced outside the country. Later stamps portrayed Jefferson Davis [4] and George Washington [5], a reminder that the Father of His Country had been a slave-owning Southern gentleman.

HAWAII

The Polynesian kingdom of Hawaii in the north central Pacific introduced stamps in 1851. Crudely typeset, they

are popularly known as Missionaries as most of them were used by Christian missionaries to send mail back to New England: some stamps bore the inscription "H.I. & U.S. Postage". Stamps portraying Kamehameha III appeared in 1853, followed by a veritable portrait gallery of Hawaiian royalty, including Kamehameha IV [6], Kamehameha V [7] and Princess Victoria Kamamalu [8].

In 1887 King David Kalakaua [9] was forced to accept a Western-style constitution that curbed native power. When his successor, Queen Liliuokalani, attempted a coup to restore the old laws, American business interests overthrew the monarchy and proclaimed a provisional government. On 4 July 1894, the Republic of Hawaii was proclaimed [11]. The islands were annexed by the USA on 12 August 1898. During this interim period (1899–1900) Hawaii's very last stamp portrayed the statue of Kamehameha I [10]. Ordinary US stamps have been used in Hawaii since 14 June 1900.

SPANISH–AMERICAN WAR

During the war between Spain and the United States in 1898 the US occupied the Spanish territories of Cuba and the Philippines. American stamps were

overprinted for use during the period of military administration, after which the islands were handed over to the indigenous authorities.

The USA also captured the islands of Guam in the Pacific and Puerto Rico in the Caribbean, both of which were ceded to it by Spain. Apart from occupation by the Japanese in 1941–4, Guam was under the control of the US Navy until 1950. American stamps were overprinted from 1899 to 1901 [12] and ordinary US stamps have been in use since then.

Puerto Rico used Spanish colonial keytypes in the latter part of the 19th century [13–14]. Having been ceded to the US on 10 December 1898, it was under military administration until 1900. Contemporary US stamps were at first overprinted "Porto Rico" [15], followed by the correct spelling in 1900 [16]. Ordinary US stamps have been used since April 1900.

UNITED NATIONS

Distinctive stamps for the use of the United Nations Secretariat in New York City were introduced on October 24 – United Nations Day – 1951. Since then the UN has produced a prodigious number of stamps, mainly publicizing the work of its specialized agencies and promoting causes of international concern. The UN building itself appeared in the first series [17] and has been the subject of many stamps since then, either in splendid isolation [18] or in relation to the neighbouring skyscrapers of Manhattan [19]. Several stamps feature the interior [20] or the gardens, statuary and stained glass windows. Stamps of 1952 [21] and 1995 [22] commemorated the signing of the UN Charter in San Francisco, and featured the Veterans' War Memorial Building in that city.

In the early years a valiant attempt was made to inscribe every stamp in the five major languages of the world – English, French, Spanish, Russian and Chinese – but by the mid-1960s this had been quietly dropped and English predominated in the stamps issued by the office in New York.

By 1967 a more thematic approach was evident, and a long-running series was devoted to works of art donated by member countries. In 1980 the UN embarked on a series depicting the flags of the member countries. These were released in sheetlets of 16, each containing four different flags. This marathon series came to an end in 1989, the final flag being that of the UN itself, but the accession of new countries in the 1990s as a result of the fall of communism led to the issue of a further 24 flag stamps between 1997 and 1999. The latest series is devoted to endangered species of the world.

Below: In recent years the UN has featured sites on its stamps, and the set of 2004 focused on Greece to coincide with the Athens Olympics.

14

15

16

17

18

19

20

21

22

1 2

3 4

UNITED STATES TRUST TERRITORIES IN THE PACIFIC

Germany acquired a number of Pacific island groups towards the end of the 19th century. The first were the Marshall Islands, which it colonized in 1855, and in 1899, at the end of the Spanish–American War, Spain sold the Caroline Islands to Germany. At the same time, the Mariana Islands, which had been administered by the Philippines, were transferred by the United States to Germany in November 1899. All three groups remained under German control until 1914, when the Caroline and Mariana Islands were occupied by the Japanese. The Marshall Islands were captured by New Zealand forces but transferred to Japan at the end of World War I. The Marianas were captured by US forces in 1944 and the other two island groups fell into American hands at the end of World War II. All three were declared the United States Trust Territory of the Pacific Islands by the United Nations on 18 July 1947.

Self-government was introduced in 1979 in the Marshall and Caroline Islands. The former group retained its original name but the latter was renamed the Federated States of Micronesia. The following year the Palau group in the western Carolines separated from Micronesia and became a republic in January 1981. In 1986 all three territories entered into the Compact of Free Association with the United States, which remained responsible for defence and external relations.

Left: A joint issue of stamps by the Marshall Islands and Micronesia in October 1996 celebrated the tenth anniversary of the Compact of Free Association; both designs featured a sailing boat alongside their respective flags.

5

6

7

8 9

10

In the Caroline and Mariana islands, which were under German rule from 1899 until 1914, stamps were issued in the contemporary colonial keytypes [1–2]. The Marshall Islands used ordinary German stamps until 1897, when overprinted stamps were adopted. These were followed by the Yacht stamps in 1901 [3]. Ordinary Japanese stamps were later used, followed by American stamps from 1945 onwards, and examples of these with identifiable postmarks of the islands are now much sought-after.

MARSHALL ISLANDS

Postal independence was inaugurated in May 1984 with a celebratory block of four stamps, followed shortly afterwards by a definitive series featuring maps of the various atolls. Subsequent issues have been strongly thematic, with fish, birds and ships [5] featured. In the early years of the Marshall Islands' independence commemorative stamps were issued relatively infrequently and, in fact, stamps relating purely to the islands are few in number [4; 6]. This was more than balanced by the stamps that increasingly looked to the outside world.

In 1989 an ambitious programme was launched chronicling all the major campaigns and battles of World War II. The series eventually ran to 157 stamps, including portraits of the leading figures on both sides of the war [7]. More recent issues include a sheet of 50 showing American warships, from the USS *Alabama* to the USS *Wyoming* – one for each state – and stamps showing solidarity with the United States in the aftermath of 9/11 [8]. Historic ships are a recurring theme [9] for stamps, while figures such as Winston Churchill and Tsar Nicholas II have also been portrayed.

MICRONESIA

The inaugural issue consisted of a block of four showing maps of Yap, Truk, Pohnpei and Kosrae, the groups making up the Federated States of Micronesia, all formerly part of the Caroline Islands. At the same time a definitive series portrayed explorers and island scenes, notably the famous stone money of Yap [11]. A moderate policy of new issues was pursued at first, with most of the stamps devoted to subjects of island interest [10] or commemorating salient events in the islands' recent history [13].

In the early period the stamps were designed and marketed by the Crown Agents in England, and this was reflected in the use of British designers and European printers. In 1991, however, the contract passed to the Unicover Corporation of Cheyenne, Wyoming, which was already printing the stamps of the Marshall Islands. Unicover had its own printing facilities and employed mainly American designers, notably the father-and-son team of Paul and Chris Calle. This inaugurated an era in which popular themes such as fish, butterflies and flowers were the subjects of long sets, often released in sheets of up to 25 different stamps side by side. In 1993 Micronesia introduced a series devoted to pioneers of aviation portrayed alongside their aircraft [14], from the Wright Brothers to heroes of World War II. These stamps were issued in *se-tenant* blocks of eight and continued to appear at regular intervals until 1996.

In the following year the contract passed to the Inter-Governmental Philatelic Corporation of New York, and since then a much more prolific policy has been pursued. There is now a greater focus on events and personalities of worldwide significance, from Elvis Presley to Princess Diana.

Caught in the Act

To mark the Ameripex stamp show in Chicago (1986) Micronesia issued five stamps illustrating the life and crimes of Bully Hayes. In addition to murder and mayhem, he forged rare stamps of Hawaii, as shown on the 33c stamp. Incidentally, the forgery, like the genuine stamp, did not have perforations (as shown below right).

PALAU

This republic had a head start on the others, adopting its own stamps in March 1983. It has maintained a more prolific policy ever since. Successive definitive sets have featured marine life [12], flowers [15], birds [16] and insects. As a popular destination for Japanese tourists visiting the war graves, Palau has made a number of issues relating to its links with Japan [17], and its connection with the USA has yielded stamps featuring Ronald Reagan [18] and Operation Desert Storm [19]. Many sheets vividly illustrated every phase of World War II in the Pacific, notably the fighting over Peleliu in 1944. A self-adhesive die-cut stamp in the form of a Bai gable marked the republic's tenth anniversary.

Palau has been a client of the Inter-Governmental Philatelic Corporation since its inception, and although the flow of new issues was relatively modest in the early years it has greatly increased recently. Sheets of 25–40 different stamps have been prevalent from 1986 onwards, with increasing emphasis on stamps with immense appeal to collectors worldwide, from Disney characters to footballers.

11
12

13

14

15
16

17

18

19

NORTH AMERICAN INDIANS IN STAMPS

When Europeans penetrated North America at the beginning of the 16th century there were probably about a million Native Americans spread across what is now Canada, the USA and Mexico. By the end of the 19th century that figure had been halved, but after 1910 the Native American population began to recover. Driven off their ancestral lands by the encroachment of Europeans, many tribes ended up living on large reservations in areas of little interest or apparent use to the incomers, such as the Dakotas and the arid regions of the South-west.

The first Native American to appear on a US stamp was Minnehaha, the heroine of Longfellow's epic poem *Hiawatha* – and as that was the $60 newspaper stamp of 1875 it is unlikely to figure in most pictorial collections devoted to this theme.

The earliest stamp to show indigenous people in their own right was the 4c value of the set of 1898 publicizing the Trans-Mississippi Exposition. The first Indians to be identified by name on stamps were Powhatan and his

Below: Blocks of four showing Pueblo decorated pots, 1977 (left) and shamanistic masks, 1979 (right).

daughter Pocahontas, whose microscopic effigies were worked into the framework of the 1c stamp of 1907 portraying Captain John Smith, marking the tercentenary of Jamestown. Pocahontas herself was portrayed on the 5c stamp, all dressed up in the height of Jacobean fashion as Smith paraded her in London.

While the low values of the 1922–32 US definitive series focused on famous Americans, and especially presidents, the 14c showed an unnamed American Indian in feather war bonnet. It later transpired that the image was derived from a photograph of Hollow Horn Bear, chief of the Brule Sioux. After

Above: Chief Hollow Horn Bear of the Brule Sioux (left) and an Indian Head cent on the definitive 13c stamp of 1978 (right).

Right: Pocahontas appears in Jacobean dress on a stamp of 1907.

Hopi: Heard Museum Phoenix
Pueblo Art USA 13c

Acoma: School of American Research
Pueblo Art USA 13c

Heiltsuk, Bella Bella
Indian Art USA 15c

Chilkat Tlingit
Indian Art USA 15c

Zia: Museum of New Mexico
Pueblo Art USA 13c

San Ildefonso: Denver Art Museum
Pueblo Art USA 13c

Tlingit
Indian Art USA 15c

Bella Coola
Indian Art USA 15c

Presidential Gallery

To mark the bicentenary of the US constitution in 1987 the Turks and Caicos Islands produced a series of sheetlets portraying every American president with a scene representing his time in office. Whereas presidents such as George Washington, Abraham Lincoln and John F. Kennedy have tended to hog the philatelic limelight, these little islands at last gave prominence to Millard Fillmore, Rutherford B. Hayes and others who had been largely forgotten.

himself emperor. Following his murder in 1806 the country split into a kingdom under Henri Christophe and a republic under Alexander Petion.

Stamps were introduced in 1881; the first, showing the head of Liberty, was followed by the national arms [10]. The centenary of independence was celebrated by two sets of 1904 portraying Toussaint l'Ouverture [11] and other patriots, and many later stamps depicted the impressive citadel of Christophe [12]. In recent years restrained intaglio has given way to gaudy lithography [13].

JAMAICA

The largest colony in the British West Indies, Jamaica had a postal service from 1671, using British stamps until 1860, when distinctive issues appeared. They followed the British colonial pattern, although a pictorial 1d stamp appeared as early as 1900. The definitives of 1919–21 took the colourful history of the island as their subject. Self-government was granted in 1945

and independence in 1962 [14], with Elizabeth II remaining head of state. Since then stamps have become much more colourful – not only the small-format definitives but also the special issues marking events of specifically Jamaican importance [16–17]. Even Christmas stamps are used to get across vital public messages [18]. The Jamaican dollar, adopted in 1969, remained fairly stable until the 1990s when it depreciated heavily. As a result, stamps since 1996 have been denominated in as many dollars as they were formerly in cents.

The Cayman Islands used Jamaican stamps until 1900, when distinctive issues were produced. Though best known today as a financial centre, the islands also rely heavily on tourism, reflected in the stamps. Stamps were issued by the Turks Islands from 1867 until 1900 [15] when they joined with the Caicos group (formerly under the Bahamas). Although stamps in joint names are still current, the Caicos Islands have occasionally had distinctive stamps since 1981.

Below: A high proportion of stamps from the Cayman Islands highlight the fauna and flora of the Caribbean, but the leisurely way of life also features.

BRITISH WEST INDIES

The islands generally grouped under this heading are scattered around the Caribbean and fall geographically into two main archipelagos known as the Leeward and Windward Islands. The Leeward Islands at one time formed a political union, consisting of Antigua and Barbuda, the British Virgin Islands, Dominica, Montserrat and St Christopher Nevis Anguilla. It was formed in 1871, putting into constitutional effect an informal federation dating from the 1670s. The Windward Islands, however, were always separate colonies. The West Indies, a major source of sugar for Britain, also assumed an important strategic role after the loss of its American colonies.

Left: Admiral Lord Nelson was commander of the West Indies station in the late 18th century and is commemorated to this day by the naval dockyard. It was from here that he set sail for his final decisive battle at Trafalgar in 1805.

LEEWARD ISLANDS

While each colony of the Leewards originally had distinctive stamps, a general issue was released in 1890 in the prevailing keyplate design. Stamps of this type, differing solely in the profile of the reigning monarch [1], continued until the federal union was dissolved on 1 July 1956. In 1903 the various islands, objecting to the loss of philatelic revenue, had resumed the issue of their own stamps, which were used in conjunction with the general series.

Antigua had its own stamps from 1862. Until 1982 they were thus inscribed [3], but since then they have also borne the name of its dependency Barbuda [4]. Stamps of the Leeward Islands overprinted "Barbuda" were briefly introduced in 1922 but Barbuda did not resume stamps of its own until 1968. A long series (1968–71) portrayed every British monarch since William the Conqueror [2], while stamps inscribed "Antigua & Barbuda" are now overprinted "Barbuda Mail" for specific use there. From 1979 to 1991 the uninhabited island of Redonda, forming part of this group, had prolific issues in its name that pandered to the most popular themes [5].

Dominica introduced stamps in 1874 and these continued in the usual colonial style until 1968, when the island was granted associated statehood and became more prolific and innovative in its issues, notably with the D-framed definitives of 1969 [6]. It became independent in November 1978, assuming the name of the Commonwealth of Dominica [7].

Montserrat's stamps date from 1876. At one time its sole claim to fame was the lime juice supplied to the Royal Navy to prevent scurvy (hence the American term "limey", originally applied to British seamen), but since 1971 it has acquired a reputation for prolific stamp issues, although these have been considerably moderated in recent years. Most issues are generally thematic [8] with a strong element of royal pomp and circumstance [9].

St Christopher [10] and Nevis [11] issued their own stamps from 1870 and 1868 respectively until 1890, then used the stamps of the Leeward Islands. When distinctive stamps were resumed in 1903 they chose the title "St Kitts-Nevis" for a joint series. After the island of Anguilla celebrated its tercentenary in 1950 its name was added to the title, which is now "St Christopher Nevis Anguilla" [12].

Following the grant of associated statehood in 1967, Anguilla agitated for independence and seceded that September, overprinting its stamps accordingly. Its secession was contested at first, but the dispute was resolved by placing Anguilla under a British Commissioner, hence the curious inscription [13]. Since June 1980 the other islands have had separate postal administrations, with stamps inscribed "Nevis" [14] and "St Kitts" [15].

WINDWARD ISLANDS
The Virgin Islands adopted distinctive stamps in 1866 and these continued to be thus inscribed until 1968 [16], when the epithet "British" was added to avoid confusion with the American Virgin Islands. Ironically, the US dollar (discreetly indicated on stamps by the abbreviation "U.S.Cy") has been the currency of the British Virgin Islands since 1962. Unusually for the West Indies, the islands' stamps continue to focus on local customs, marine life and flora, with a strong emphasis on the British royal family. A set of 1969 commemorated Robert Louis Stevenson, whose adventure story *Treasure Island* was set in the islands.

Grenada had a conventional philatelic history from 1861 to 1967, when it was granted associate statehood, but since then it has become one of the world's most prolific issuing countries, producing about 5,000 stamps by 2004. Many sets are produced in sheetlets of from 6 to 20 *se-tenant*, devoted to many subjects that have little relevance to the country, ranging from dinosaurs to American entertainers. The Grenadines of Grenada are almost as prolific, with separate issues

Below: The Virgin Islands paid tribute to the Princess of Wales (left), while Grenada honoured President Reagan's visit with an overprint (right).

Stamps for All Occasions
The smaller the Caribbean island, the more prolific the stamp issues. The Grenadines of Grenada and St Vincent rival each other in their bid to produce stamps for every conceivable occasion and celebrity. The islands that first put Michael Jackson and Madonna on stamps have even produced images of every team that reached the finals of the World Cup football championships in recent years.

---

for Carriacou and Petite Martinique that often cover the same topics as Grenada itself.

St Lucia began issuing stamps in 1860 and followed the prevailing colonial policy until it was granted associate statehood in 1967, followed by complete independence in 1979. Since 1983 it has liberalized its stamp policy, although there has been some attempt to maintain the integrity of stamps by a relative adherence to subjects of indigenous interest [17].

It pales into insignificance alongside St Vincent. Here, stamps in the colonial style were issued from 1861 to 1963, when the island was granted ministerial government and the stamp contract passed out of the hands of the Crown Agents to an American company. Complete independence was gained in 1979. Since then new issues have risen to several hundred each year. Equally prolific were the issues of the Grenadines of St Vincent (1973–94) [18], followed by the numerous stamps from individual islands Bequia, Canouan, Mustique, Union Island, Palm Island and the Cayes of Tobago.

10   11

12

13

14

15

16

17

18

MEXICO

The United States of Mexico lie south of the USA, geographically part of North America but culturally and linguistically part of Latin America. The area was the home of a highly developed civilization long before Hernando Cortés and his conquistadors toppled the empire of Montezuma early in the 16th century. Under Spanish rule, New Spain extended from Guatemala to Wyoming, but the secession of Texas in 1836 and war with the USA (1846–7) resulted in the loss of territory now forming the states of California, Arizona, New Mexico and parts of Utah, Idaho, Washington and Oregon, leaving Mexico's boundaries more or less where they are today, along the Rio Grande del Norte. Until the 1920s Mexico suffered frequent revolutions, breakaway regimes and changes of government, followed by a period of anti-clericalism and extreme socialism before the country emerged from anarchy.

Left: A map of Mexico appeared in the series of 1915 signifying the re-unification of the country after a period of civil war.

DICTATORS AND FOREIGN INTERVENTION

All the stamps issued from 1856 [1] until 1879, with one notable exception, portrayed Miguel Hidalgo, who had proclaimed Mexico's independence from Spain in 1810. The inherent instability of the country for much of the 19th century encouraged the intervention of the United States in the 1840s and European nations during the 1860s. When Mexico suspended its payment of foreign debts in 1861 it was occupied by British, Spanish and French troops. The French stayed on and, taking advantage of the American Civil War, installed the Austrian Archduke Maximilian as emperor [2]. In 1867 the USA invoked the Monroe Doctrine, forcing Napoleon III to withdraw his troops. Maximilian surrendered to the republicans, led by Benito Juarez [4], and was executed at Queretaro on 19 June.

Stamps in the 1870s were printed by the American Bank Note Company and share the characteristically florid frames found on US stamps of the same period [3]. A curious feature of many Mexican stamps from 1868 to 1883 was the overprinting of district names and numbers.

REVOLUTIONS AND CIVIL WARS

The dictator Porfirio Díaz held power in Mexico from 1876 to 1911, but was ousted by a popular revolt that began in 1910. He was succeeded by the liberal Francisco Madero [5], who was overthrown and murdered by his general Victoriano Huerta in February 1913. This outrage provoked a civil war that lasted until 1915 and involved various factions, led by Pancho Villa, Emiliano Zapata, Venustiano Carranza and Alvaro Obregon, who eventually joined forces as the Constitutionalists.

Numerous overprints and local issues appeared all over Mexico during this period, followed by a general series [6] in 1914. In October that year, however, Villa and Zapata broke with Carranza and proclaimed a provisional government by the Convention of Aguascalientes. Mexican stamps were overprinted by the Conventionists [7].

The Constitutionalists retook Mexico City in August 1915. Zapata and Villa were murdered in 1919 and 1923 respectively, and Carranza introduced a new constitution in 1917 that laid the foundation of the modern state. However, it fell to Obregon to realize the aims of the revolution.

MODERN MEXICO

Although the Revolution Monument graced the definitive series of 1934–6 [8], the vast majority of stamps from that time forward avoided contentious political issues. Old enmities with Mexico's powerful northern neighbour were forgotten by the time of the New York World's Fair in 1939 [9]. A traditional view of the country was deliberately fostered, even in the series of 1956 celebrating the stamp centenary [10], but by that time Mexico was tending to look back to its ancient roots for inspiration [11].

Mexico was the first country to portray President Kennedy, in connection with his state visit in June 1962 [12]. As a result of this visit, the Chamizal Treaty was signed in 1963, whereby the USA returned some land along the Rio Grande. A stamp of 1964 showed Kennedy and President Lopez-Mateos shaking hands on the deal [13]. A long-running series, introduced in 1973, highlighted Mexican exports [14]. More recent stamps resemble mini-posters, not only for Christmas [15] but for many anniversaries, though the quality of offset lithography has improved in recent years [16]. A series of 1993 portrayed Mexican film stars, although Dolores del Rio [17] was the only one to make it big in Hollywood.

A more subtle, delicate style of design emerged in the 1990s. Mexican patriotism was stronger than ever but colours were generally much lighter and more restrained than previously [18]. An interesting stamp of 1997 commemorated the St Patrick's

Below: A stamp issued in 1994 to publicize National Week of Patriotic Symbols features the Mexican flag.

One Small Step for Man
Many countries celebrated the achievement of the Apollo 11 mission to the Moon in 1969, and most depicted the astronauts Armstrong and Aldrin on the lunar surface. Mexico was alone in adopting a more symbolic approach, using Neil Armstrong's footprint in moon dust to create a very powerful image.

Battalion – Irishmen who volunteered to fight for Mexico in the war against the United States [19].

Like the USA, Mexico favours single stamps for commemorative purposes, and these are mostly denominated at the domestic letter rate, with the intention of informing and motivating the Mexican people rather than promoting a national image to the world at large. Stamps are released at frequent intervals and cover all manner of subjects and events. A relatively high proportion pay tribute to Mexican personalities, very few of whom are known outside their own country (or, in fact, all that well known within it either).

A spate of 50th-anniversary stamps since the 1990s testifies to the enormous social and economic progress of Mexico in the years following World War II. By contrast, a recurring series in recent years has featured the glories of Mexico's architecture from the Spanish colonial era, although this is exceptional: the vogue for thematic sets, so prevalent elsewhere, has never really caught on in Mexico.

12

13

14

15

16

17

18

19

1

2

3

4

5

6

7

8

9

10

CENTRAL AMERICA

With a long and unenviable reputation for revolution, the countries of Central America were the original banana republics, with one-product economies largely in the hands of foreign (mainly US) investors. They share a common profile, characterized by a mainly impoverished population ruled by a handful of landowners with US business interests paramount, most

notably over the development and operation of the Panama Canal. Not surprisingly, the character and subjects of their stamps often reflect their status as client states of the USA.

Left: President Jimmy Carter and President Torrijos of Panama signing the treaty that ceded the Canal Zone back to Panama in 1977.

COSTA RICA

The "rich coast" facing the Pacific began issuing stamps in 1863, and early issues tended to portray dead politicians [1]. Stamps overprinted for the remote province of Guanacaste were in use in the 1880s due to local currency differences [2]. Pictorial themes appeared in the 1930s, sport being a very early topic. Institutions such as Rotary [3] reflected the Americanization of the country. From 1947, when Roosevelt was honoured, the great and good of the USA were often portrayed, ranging from Father Flanagan, founder of Boys Town, on a children's charity set of 1959, to John Kennedy and John Kennedy Junior [4].

EL SALVADOR

The volcano of San Miguel appeared in 1867 on the first stamps of the country named in tribute to the Saviour [5]. The early stamps were often overprinted or surcharged for re-issue but more pictorial designs appeared in the 1930s. Some very attractive sets engraved by American and British firms appeared in the 1940s, notably the Roosevelt memorial issue of 1948, which comprised 12 stamps and two miniature sheets [6]. Stamps of more recent times have been lithographed in full colour and cover a wide range of topics, from sport to wildlife and scenery [7].

GUATEMALA

Another smoking volcano graced the arms stamps of Guatemala [8], adopted in 1871, but its most enduring image is the long-tailed quetzal. First appearing on stamps of 1881 [9], as a national icon it has been reprised on many issues down to the present time, usually in repose but sometimes in flight [10]. Philatelically one of the more conservative countries, Guatemala tends to stick closely to subjects of domestic interest. Such issues include several propaganda stamps laying claim to British Honduras (later Belize).

HONDURAS

The triangular seal of Honduras, with its sun rising over a volcano, formed the motif of the first stamps, issued in 1866 [11], but by 1878 the country had become infected with the craze for dead presidents [12], which continued until the 1930s. From 1946 onwards Honduras discovered a lucrative market in long sets honouring American heroes, starting with Roosevelt. The series of 1959 for the 150th birthday of Abraham Lincoln ran to 24 stamps and included his log cabin birthplace [13] and the Gettysburg address.

NICARAGUA

In the stamps of Nicaragua, from their inception in 1862, the smoking volcanoes really came into their own [14].

Presidential Visit
One of the few stamps to portray
Bill Clinton during his term in
office was this issue by El Salvador
in 1999, marking his presidential
visit to the republic. Both presidents, with their seals and flags, are
depicted on this *se-tenant* pair.

Unfortunately, the series of 1901 showing Momotombo issuing smoke [15]
deterred the US Congress from its original plan to drive the canal across
Nicaragua, and thereafter the Panama
lobby triumphed. Among the non-
political US celebrities honoured was
the humorist Will Rogers, with a piece
of subliminal advertising for Pan-
American Airways for good measure
[16]. Because of currency fluctuations,
stamps were overprinted "B"
(Bluefields) in the province of Zelayo
[17] and in Cabo Gracias a Dios.

PANAMA
The most southerly of the republics
was originally a province of Colombia
and from 1887 it issued stamps thus
inscribed but showing the isthmus of
Panama. In 1903, when Colombia
refused to lease territory to the USA for
the construction of the canal, Panama
declared its independence. The US
Navy prevented Colombia from taking
action and stamps were overprinted to
blot out the Colombian inscriptions.
Panamanian stamps grew lavish in their
coverage of US subjects. This has been
less noticeable since the fall of the
Noriega regime and emphasis is now
on modernization and social reform.
   The canal was not opened until
1915 but from 1904 onwards stamps
were overprinted or inscribed with the

words "Canal Zone" [18]. Many of
them portrayed the engineers who built
the canal [19] or depicted its landmarks
[20]. The US lease expired in 1999 and
ordinary Panamanian stamps have been
used since then.

BELIZE
The only British colony in Central
America, British Honduras had its own
stamps from 1865. Bicoloured pictorials showing local products and Mayan
ruins appeared from 1938 until 1962,
when a series featuring local birds was
printed by multicolour photogravure.
In 1964 the colony was granted self-
government and was renamed Belize in
1973, the series then current being
overprinted accordingly. Continual friction with neighbouring Guatemala
(which laid claim to the colony)
delayed the grant of full independence
until September 1981.
   Belize continues to pursue a conservative policy regarding new issues and
the vast majority of them concentrate
on subjects of indigenous interest. Its
stamps are firmly rooted in the colonial
past, with numerous issues featuring
the British royal family. Among other
themes, primary products such as log-
wood rank highly, but Belize is also
proud of its status as the originator
of chewing gum [21]. The Cayes of
Belize, a chain of islands off the coast,
had a typewritten local stamp in the
1890s and this seems to have inspired
the "regional" stamps that appeared
briefly in 1984–5.

*Below: Oliver Stanley was one of the
few British politicians to achieve
philatelic recognition. The airport of
British Honduras was named after him
when he was Colonial Secretary.*

11   12

13

14   15

16

17   18

19   20

21

1 2

3 4

5

6

7 8

9 10

11 12

COLOMBIA, ECUADOR AND VENEZUELA

Occupying the north-west corner of South America, these countries cover the area from the Atlantic coast to the equatorial region of the Pacific. Once part of the Spanish Empire under the name of New Granada, the region declared independence in 1813 and was united by Simon Bolivar to form the Republic of Greater Colombia, named in honour of the man who discovered it. However, it disintegrated in 1829–30 and the component states have been separate ever since.

Left: This Colombian stamp marked the 150th anniversary of the Spanish rout at Caribobo, which freed New Granada and led to the Republic of Greater Colombia.

COLOMBIA

Following the break-up of the short-lived republic, Colombia reverted to its old Spanish colonial name and by 1859, when its first stamps appeared [1], the country was a loose union of states known as the Granadine Confederation. Two years later it changed its name to the United States of New Granada and in 1862 adopted the name of the United States of Colombia [2]. It changed its name for the fourth and last time in 1886 to become the Republic of Colombia [3].

Relatively crude stamps were litho-graphed locally but from time to time Colombia went to the great American or British printers. The earliest attempt at a multicolour treatment was in 1947, when Waterlow of London printed a series featuring local orchids, combining intaglio with lithography [4]. Colombia was noted for stamps produced for specific services, such as the "Extra Rapido" service [5]. The vast majority of stamps pertain strictly to Colombia, with only the occasional nod at an international figure [6].

States Issues

The constitution of 1832 divided the country into 18 autonomous provinces, reduced in 1858 to nine. The federal government encouraged the provinces to establish their own postal services and all produced their own stamps at various times from 1865, but after 1886 this was gradually curbed and the last stamps were abolished in 1906.

Antioquia began issuing stamps in 1868 and although not the first to do so it was by far the most prolific, producing almost as many stamps as the other eight states combined. In the first decade the stamps concentrated on the state arms, followed by the head of Liberty in the 1870s and 1880s and finally a portrait of local hero, General Cordoba [7]. Bolivar was the first to adopt distinctive stamps, beginning in 1863 with a stamp showing the national seal that is arguably the smallest stamp ever issued. Later stamps bore a profile of Simon Bolivar, after whom the province was named [8].

Boyaca issued stamps only between 1899 and 1904 but in that short time produced the most varied of all the states issues: a medley of portraiture [9], heraldry and the monument to the Battle of Boyaca during the War of Independence. Cauca issued only two typeset stamps in 1902 [10] while Cundinamarca's stamps, issued from 1870 to 1904, concentrated on the national arms [11]. Heraldry was the principal feature of the stamps produced by Santander between 1884 and

1903 [12] and by Tolima from 1870 to 1904. Stamps were also issued by Panama from 1878 until it seceded from Colombia in 1903.

ECUADOR

At one time the Inca kingdom of Quito and later part of New Granada, Ecuador was liberated in 1822 but left Greater Colombia in May 1830 and was established as a republic, taking its name from the Equator, which runs through it. Stamps were introduced in 1865 [13], national arms being followed by presidential portraits [14].

The 1920s and 1930s were a period dominated by frequent overprints and surcharges. Design improved in the late 1930s and culminated in a set of 14 celebrating the 150th anniversary of the American constitution, recess-printed in New York in four colours – a tour de force for the time [15]. The American connection was reinforced a year later with a long set for the New York World's Fair and since then stamps have included the only one to show Vice President Nixon and one of the few to show little John Kennedy Junior saluting his father's coffin [16]. Nowadays, tourism is the most important industry, reflected in numerous stamps publicizing the Galapagos Islands and other attractions [17–18].

VENEZUELA

Columbus reached the north coast of South America in 1498 during his third voyage and named the region

Below: A stamp of Venezuela was issued in 1969 to mark the 150th anniversary of the Battle of Boyaca.

Cartographic Conflict
At various times since 1894 Venezuela has issued stamps laying claim to extensive tracts of neighbouring Guyana. A series of 1965–6 backed this claim by reproducing various maps published from 1775 onwards showing the disputed territory.

Venezuela (Little Venice) because of the numerous lagoons in the delta of the Orinoco. The first stamps were introduced in 1859 and showed the arms of the Venezuelan Federation.

The country changed its name to the United States of Venezuela in 1866 and stamps thus inscribed were released [19]. From 1871 to 1903 all but a handful of stamps portrayed Simon Bolivar [20]. Apart from a series of stamps issued in 1951–3, which featured the arms of the 24 provinces and ran to several hundreds, Venezuela has pursued a fairly modest policy, with a penchant for patriotic themes. It is interesting to contrast the restrained monochrome engraving of the stamps celebrating the centenary of independence in 1921 [21] with the multicolour lithography of recent years.

In November 1863 a Scottish entrepreneur, Captain Robert Todd, was awarded the contract to convey mail from Venezuela to St Thomas in the Danish West Indies (now the American Virgin Islands). Stamps depicting the SS *Robert Todd* and inscribed with all the names of the ports served were issued between 1864 and 1873. During the Civil War of 1899–1903 many local provisional stamps appeared.

13

14

15

16

17

18

19

20

21

BRAZIL AND GUYANA

Brazil occupies approximately half the continent of South America and is the only country in the Western Hemisphere to derive its language and culture from Portugal. It was discovered in 1500 by Pedro Cabral and settled in 1532. During the Napoleonic Wars, when João VI was driven from Portugal, he established his court in Brazil in 1808. In 1822, after his return to Portugal, his son Pedro I declared Brazil to be an independent empire, which continued until 1889 when Pedro II abdicated and a republic was proclaimed.

Left: One of several stamps issued in 1932 to celebrate the quatercentenary of the colonization of Brazil shows a map of South America with the Brazilian territory shaded.

BRAZIL: EMPIRE
Dom Pedro II succeeded his father as emperor in 1831, at the tender age of six, and reigned until 1889. When he was barely 17, Brazil became the first country in the world to follow Britain's example by introducing adhesive postage stamps, popularly known to collectors as Bull's Eyes on account of their circular shape. In 1943 stamps identical but for the inscription marked their centenary [1]. Dom Pedro appeared on stamps printed in New York [2], his beard becoming whiter as he advanced in years. Ousted by a military coup, he was exiled to Europe and died in Paris in 1891.

REVOLUTION AND REVOLT
Although its subsequent history was not as turbulent as that of many of its neighbours, Brazil had its share of rebellions in remote provinces, as well as occasional revolutions. A series of 14 stamps issued in April 1931 celebrated the revolution of 3 October 1930, with portraits of politicians and quotations from their speeches. Obscure at the time, they are well-nigh baffling today. Few now recall why Vargas said: "Rio Grande stands by Brazil", to which Pessoa responded, "I say No!" [3].

A revolt broke out in São Paulo in July 1932 and a provisional government was established. It was suppressed by federal troops on 2 October, but not before revolutionary stamps [4] had been issued. The United States of Brazil became a Federative Republic in 1946, but following a military coup in 1964 the country was a dictatorship until March 1985, when democratic government was restored. None of the later upheavals had any impact on stamps.

REPUBLIC
The vast majority of Brazilian special issues have been single stamps covering a wide range of topics and personalities. A strong feature is the issue of stamps marking visits by other heads of state, a tradition dating from 1920 when Albert, King of the Belgians, paid a visit. In addition to small-format definitives, Brazil has issued very tiny stamps for compulsory use to raise money for child welfare [5].

Most stamps are produced at the Brazilian Mint and the quality of production has improved considerably since the 1950s [6]. Symbolic motifs are frequently used and often demand a second glance [7–8], although the ban on drinking and driving could not be clearer [9]. At the same time there is considerable nostalgia for the past, as exemplified by the bilingual stamp recalling the age of steam [10] and the many stamps harking back to imperial glory [11].

GUYANA

The vast tract of territory on the north-west coast of Brazil, bordering with Venezuela, was colonized by the British, French and Dutch. The first stamps of British Guiana were the extremely rare Cottonreels of 1850. In 1898 the colony belatedly celebrated Queen Victoria's diamond jubilee with a set featuring local scenery [12]. A pictorial definitive series of 1934 included a portrait of Sir Walter Raleigh and his son [13]. British Guiana gained independence in May 1966 and adopted the ancient indigenous name, Guyana. Between 1981 and 1994 Guyana overprinted earlier stamps, yielding almost 3,000 different varieties. Since 1994 sanity has returned, although it still ranks among the most prolific stamp-issuing countries, with a predilection for popular themes [14–15].

The only French colony in South America, French Guiana lies between Brazil and Surinam. It formerly included the notorious penal settlement of Devil's Island, but nowadays the territory is better known as a base for European experiments with the Ariane space rockets. French Guiana began issuing distinctive stamps in 1886, when several of the French colonial general series were surcharged with new values and overprinted "Guy. Franc". By 1892 the general colonial stamps were being diagonally overprinted "Guyane", and these were shortly followed by the colonial keytypes inscribed with the name at the foot.

Below: Surinam was the first country to celebrate Commander Alan Shepard's sub-orbital flight of 5 May 1961.

Most Valuable Perhaps, but Not the Rarest

British Guiana is remembered philatelically for the unique 1c black and magenta stamp of 1856, which was reproduced on stamps of 1967. Though no rarer than any other stamp of which only one example is known, it was at one time the most valuable, having achieved a world auction record price of $935,000 in 1980.

A pictorial series, introduced in 1904, featured a giant anteater, a gold-miner and palm trees in the capital Cayenne; the series was followed by rather garish bicoloured stamps in 1929 and more attractive intaglio pictorials in the 1940s. A definitive series featuring the tricolour was printed in London for the Free French [16], followed by a series showing scenes of native life [17]. French Guiana became an overseas department of France in 1946 and ordinary French stamps have been in use there since 1948. The inland territory of Inini was separately administered and had its own stamps from 1930 to 1946 [18], when it was re-incorporated with French Guiana.

The Dutch colonized Surinam, which issued colonial keytypes from 1873 and later distinctive designs, especially after 1954 when it became an autonomous state. Since then stamps have honoured America's first astronaut, Alan Shepard, and the 30th anniversary of Amelia Earhart's flight to South America [19]. Surinam became an independent country in 1975 but the stamps have continued in the same style.

11

12

13

14

15

16

17

18

19

BOLIVIA, CHILE AND PERU

Much of the area occupied by these three republics once formed the mighty Inca empire, overthrown by the conquistadors led by Francisco Pizarro in 1531–3. Because of its immense mineral wealth the region became the most prosperous of all Spain's possessions in South America, and it was here that the struggle for independence was fiercest and most prolonged. War at sea eventually gained the countries' independence but it was another naval campaign, the Pacific War of 1879–85, that lost Peru her southern nitrate districts and Bolivia her access to the ocean.

Left: Victories on land by Simon Bolivar and José de San Martín were clinched by the defeat of the Spanish navy by the British naval commander Thomas Cochrane, 10th Earl of Dundonald. Unjustly convicted of fraud, imprisoned, disgraced and dismissed from the Royal Navy, he went to South America and used his considerable talents to secure the liberation of Chile, Peru, Brazil and later Greece. His exploits won him a pardon and reinstatement. Dying an admiral, he was buried in Westminster Abbey.

BOLIVIA

Released in 1867, Bolivia's first stamps featured a condor, symbolic of the Andes [1]. They were soon followed by allegorical and armorial designs recess-printed in New York [2]. In 1901 Bolivia switched to portraits of historical figures [3] but adopted pictorialism in 1916, with scenes of Mount Ilimani and Lake Titicaca [5]. Having lost its Pacific seaboard to Chile, it waged a stamp war with neighbouring Paraguay over the Gran Chaco [4]. Its claims to the Chaco Boliviano eventually led to the war of 1932–5, which left both countries on the verge of bankruptcy.

Many later stamps featured designs depicting the scenery, wildlife and culture of the Quechua Indians of the Altiplano [6]. Commemorative issues harked back to the battles of the War of Independence [7] but the Pacific War was best forgotten in Bolivia.

Like the other countries of UPAEP (the postal union of the Americas) Bolivia now issues stamps each year in the prevailing topic [8]. In 1986 the boliviano collapsed, resulting in hyperinflation. Since the currency reform of 1987 and the introduction of the new boliviano, the country's economy has been relatively stable.

CHILE

The longest of the Latin American countries, extending from the tropics to the sub-Antarctic, Chile is hemmed in between the Andes and the Pacific. Virtually all of its stamps portrayed Columbus from 1853 [9] until 1910. In that year the centenary of independence was celebrated by a long set [11] of which the highest denomination portrayed Admiral Cochrane. The admiral also appeared in ensuing definitive sets [10].

The Pacific War had been fought by Chile to gain access to the nitrate deposits jointly owned by Peru and Bolivia, and this valuable asset was the subject of many stamps in the 1930s and 1940s [12]. Commemoratives tended to concentrate on the struggle for independence, often tastefully recess-printed at the Chilean Mint [14]. More strident offset lithography tends to be favoured increasingly [15]. In the postwar period, Chile became embroiled with Argentina over rival claims to a slice of Antarctica, and this was a frequent subject for stamps.

Chile produced a set of four stamps in 1910 for use in the offshore islands of Juan Fernandez [13] and in more recent years has issued "regional"

Antarctic Rivalry and Co-operation

Both Chile and Peru followed Argentina's example and developed an interest in Antarctica in the years after World War II. While the stamps of Chile and Argentina became increasingly strident, with maps claiming the same territory, Peru's involvement was much more low key. Eventually the Antarctic Treaty of 1988, to which they all subscribed, took the heat out of the situation. They have since tended to co-operate in scientific research.

stamps for Easter Island, which is now a major tourist attraction.

The overthrow of the democratically elected Marxist President Salvador Allende in 1973 ushered in an era of military dictatorship under General Augusto Pinochet, but stamps of this period studiously avoided political controversy. After Pinochet was ousted in 1989, a more liberal policy ensued and a number of stamps portrayed the writer Pablo Neruda (who had been exiled) as well as Allende himself.

Although Chile pursues a relatively moderate policy with regard to new issues, in 1996 it released a set of 60 stamps each warning against a specific accident – in the home, on the roads, at school and in the workplace, as well as warnings on alcohol and drug abuse and hints on safety in leisure activities.

PERU

Pending the introduction of its own stamps [18] in 1858, Peru made use of freight labels supplied by the Pacific Steam Navigation Company. From 1866 most Peruvian stamps were recess-printed by rival New York firms. After the Chilean occupation in 1881 stamps were overprinted with the Chilean arms [16]. When President Morales Bermudez died suddenly in 1894, shortly before his term of office expired, stamps were overprinted with his portrait as a mark of respect [17]. These are arguably the first mourning stamps to be produced by a government postal administration (as opposed to the German private posts in 1888).

Peru was one of the first countries to adopt photogravure, in 1924, and throughout the 1930s many fine examples from England were released, notably the long series celebrating the quatercentenary of Lima in 1935 [20]. Since World War II, however, most stamps have been lithographed locally. Co-operation with other Latin American countries is a recurring theme [21], along with frequent references to the region's pre-Columbian civilizations. Boundary disputes with Chile and Bolivia [19] still fester and have several times brought Peru to the brink of war with her neighbours.

Below: This se-tenant pair of stamps was issued in 1992 mainly for tourists' postcards from Easter Island, but is also valid on mail from mainland Chile.

1   2

3   4

5

6

7

8

9   10

ARGENTINA, PARAGUAY AND URUGUAY

These three countries, lying south of Brazil, were first visited by Spaniards in 1512–20 but were not colonized until the late 16th century and were still relatively undeveloped when they threw off the Spanish yoke in 1810–11. Argentina and Uruguay lie on opposite sides of the River Plate, while Paraguay is one of South America's two landlocked countries, lying north-west of its neighbours.

Left: The Battle of Maipu in 1818 marked the turning point in the struggle for independence from Spain. Having liberated Argentina, José de San Martín crossed the Andes to free Chile and Peru.

ARGENTINA

Three of the Argentine states had their own stamps in the 1850s, those of Buenos Aires featuring a steamship. Cordoba [1] had an armorial design but Corrientes blatantly plagiarized the Ceres stamps of France. General issues for the Argentine Confederation [2] were issued in 1858–60, followed by stamps of the Republic [3]. Argentina stuck to dead heroes and presidents until the 1930s, San Martín predominating, but had the distinction of producing the first commemorative stamps in the Western Hemisphere in October 1892 to celebrate the quatercentenary of the first voyage made by Columbus [5]. Between 1913 and 1938, stamps were overprinted for the use of eight separate government departments [4].

A set of 25 marked the revolution of 1930 [6], the first of many issues that reflected the turbulent politics of Argentina in later years. Other stamps looked back to the heroic struggle for independence [7] or pursued the government's long-running battle with Britain over the Falkland Islands and territory in Antarctica [8].

PARAGUAY

This landlocked country had the misfortune to be ruled by a series of tyrannical dictators, the last of whom declared war on Argentina, Uruguay and Brazil (1864), almost destroying Paraguay as a result. The first stamps appeared in 1870, the year this disastrous war ended [9]. History repeated itself when Paraguay became involved in a dispute with Bolivia over the Gran Chaco. A war fought in the stamp album with rival map stamps [10] escalated into bloodshed in 1932–5; this time Paraguay won a Pyrrhic victory.

In the 1930s and 1940s many stamps were printed in England [11] but after World War II American printers predominated [12]. Relations with Argentina improved in the 1950s and stamps portraying the two dictators, Stroessner of Paraguay and Peron of Argentina, set the seal on this [13].

Since 1962 Paraguay has issued a prodigal number of stamps, from space research [14] to nude paintings [15], of little relevance to the country itself.

Below: Stamps issued by Buenos Aires in the 1850s bore a steamship, hence their nickname of Barquitos ("little ships").

URUGUAY

In the 17th century this region on the east bank of the River Plate was fought over by Spain and Portugal, and when Spanish supremacy was smashed in 1810 local hero José Artigas tried to create a separate state, known as the Banda Oriental. To maintain independence Artigas had to fight Spain, Buenos Aires and the Portuguese. In 1825 Brazil and Argentina went to war over the disputed territory, and the matter was resolved only when Britain intervened to force the belligerents to recognize Uruguay's independence in 1830. Uruguay, which won Olympic soccer gold medals in 1924 and 1928, hosted the first World Cup in 1930 and celebrated the centenary of independence by winning the trophy.

Uruguay's first stamps, introduced in 1856, are popularly known as the Montevideo Suns. They were followed in 1866 by a series in which the numerals were the dominant feature [16]. The full title República Oriental del Uruguay means "republic on the east bank of the River Uruguay", and it appeared on many later stamps. Unlike most Latin American countries,

Below: One of a series showing historic engravings of Montevideo (top) contrasts with the poster style of the 1990 stamp honouring the Engineer Corps (bottom).

Land of Fire and Gold Dust
The island of Tierra del Fuego at the southern tip of Latin America was discovered by Magellan in 1520 as he rounded Cape Horn, and named "Land of Fire" by him from the bonfires of the natives. Argentina and Chile partitioned the island in 1881 and six years later Julius Popper established gold-mines in both parts. Mail taken to Punta Arenas in Chile bore a 10c stamp – representing neither Chilean nor Argentinian currency but centigrams of gold dust.

which followed the US fashion for presidential portraiture, Uruguay preferred allegorical subjects [17] and historical vignettes, either lithographed locally or recess-printed in England. In recent years a more symbolic approach has been adopted, with designs rendered in a semi-abstract poster style. Visits from heads of state of many countries, from France and Italy to Israel [18], have been a fertile source of stamp designs, bolstering Uruguay's sense of its global importance.

Occasionally Uruguay has issued stamps and miniature sheets whose validity has been cast into doubt because they were not on general release in post offices. These include the sets marking the Montreal Olympics, the 30th anniversary of the United Nations and the Apollo-Soyuz joint space mission (1975), and the Nobel laureates, World Cup football championship, Lindbergh, Rubens and Zeppelin sets (1977). Apart from these lapses a fairly modest policy has been pursued, confined mostly to single stamps.

11

12

13

14

15

16

17

18

SOUTH ATLANTIC ISLANDS

Dotted around the South Atlantic are several remote island groups, the last remnants of the British Empire, consisting of the Falkland Islands and St Helena, with the dependencies of South Georgia and the South Sandwich Islands (to which is appended British Antarctic Territory) on the one hand, and Ascension and Tristan da Cunha on the other. The Falklands, which have been in British hands since 1833, have relied on sheep-farming, and St Helena has been a coaling-station. Only Ascension, with its communications and NASA installations of recent years, has real importance today. The Falklands and South Georgia were invaded and occupied by Argentina in 1981, precipitating war with Britain.

Left: Following the liberation of the Falklands and South Georgia, £1 stamps featuring maps of the islands were sold at a premium of 100 per cent in aid of the reconstruction of the islands. Such a high premium was contrary to UPU guidelines.

FALKLAND ISLANDS

The stamps of the Falkland Islands departed from the usual British colonial pattern in having distinctive designs, even though they stuck rigidly to the tradition of royal portraits. In 1929 a definitive series was introduced with a profile of George V over a tiny vignette of a fin whale and gentoo penguins, but it was not until 1933, with a long series celebrating the centenary of the British colony, that bicoloured intaglio pictorials were adopted. This remained the norm until 1968, when multicolour photogravure became fashionable. The stamps of recent years have sometimes referred to the war with Argentina [1], but birds and seals continue to be the dominant subjects [2], with occasional scenes of island life [3] and visiting ships.

FALKLAND DEPENDENCIES

Although a small undated stamp inscribed "South Georgia" (intended to be marked on letters below the postage stamp) was occasionally used to cancel mail to these territories, it was not an overprint in the true sense. The first stamps of South Georgia, with similar sets for the South Orkneys [4], South Shetland and Graham Land, were issued in 1944, followed by a general

series in 1946. In 1954 a pictorial definitive series featured scientific ships that had been associated with the area.

Stamps of the Falkland Islands Dependencies were replaced in 1963 by separate issues for British Antarctic Territory and South Georgia [5]. Stamps inscribed for the former remain in use, but from 1980 to 1985 South Georgia reverted to stamps of the Falkland Islands Dependencies. In 1985 it and the South Sandwich Islands ceased to be dependencies of the Falkland Islands and began issuing stamps bearing their joint names [6].

British Antarctic Territory has issued stamps continuously since 1963. The Silver Jubilee stamps of 1977 alluded to the time spent in the region by the Duke of Edinburgh, unusually portraying him bearded [7]. Other stamps allude to the area's wildlife [8] and the work of the scientific research stations.

ST HELENA

Blue stamps denominated 6d were introduced in St Helena in 1856, but between 1864 and 1880 they were printed in different colours and surcharged accordingly for use as various values from 1d to 5s. In later years the colonial keytypes were used, although some pictorial designs appeared from

1903 onwards. As in the Falklands, the centenary of the crown colony in 1934 was celebrated by a long set of bicoloured intaglio pictorial stamps, establishing a precedent for later issues. Multicolour photogravure was adopted in 1961 [9]. Apart from some stamps alluding to Napoleon's exile, most recent issues have been preoccupied with island scenery and flowers [10]. Stamps in support of the Hong Kong stamp show of 1994 featured islanders' pets, and a wide range of other topics includes sea slugs and medical scientists. The stamps celebrating Elizabeth II's silver jubilee in 1977 showed the royal family visiting the island [11].

ASCENSION

This remote island was an outpost of the Royal Navy and used ordinary British stamps until 1922, when overprinted St Helena stamps were adopted, followed by a pictorial series in 1934. It has since followed the same

Above: The garden on Green Mountain featured on a 1975 stamp marking the 160th anniversary of British settlement.

Below: Base B and the postmark of Deception Island appear on a British Antarctic stamp.

Ducal Connections
The "capital" of Tristan da Cunha is called Edinburgh, named in honour of Prince Alfred, the first Duke, who visited the island aboard HMS *Galatea* in 1867.

---

pattern, issuing more colourful stamps since the 1960s. Many issues refer to its importance as a communications centre, the 1986 Christmas stamps appropriately including an image of George V making the first royal Christmas broadcast for the BBC [12]. Scenery, bird life and landmarks [13] provide the staple fare for its stamps.

TRISTAN DA CUNHA

Named after the Portuguese navigator who discovered it in 1502, Tristan da Cunha remained a desert isle until Napoleon was exiled to St Helena. Its garrison was evacuated in 1816 leaving behind Corporal Glass, who became the patriarch of the little community.

Stamps of St Helena with an overprint were introduced in 1952, followed by pictorial issues that reflect the scenery and wildlife [14] or mark the few historic events, such as the evacuation in 1961 following the eruption of the volcano, or the visits of scientific expeditions [15]. While its first stamps were overprints on those of St Helena, the position was briefly reversed on 12 October 1961, when a quantity of Tristan stamps held in St Helena was overprinted "St. Helena Tristan Relief" and surcharged in sterling (although the stamps were denominated in South African cents). Only 434 complete sets were sold (mostly to passengers of a visiting liner) before the issue was suppressed.

8

9

10

11

12

13

14

15

EUROPE

The European contribution to philately is immense: it includes the first adhesive (1840), bicoloured (1843) and pictorial stamps (1845), as well as many technological advances, from intaglio in the 1840s and photogravure in 1914 to holographic stamps (1988) and heat-sensitive inks (2001).

WESTERN SCANDINAVIA

As a collective name for the countries of north-western Europe, Scandinavia is often used to include not only Denmark, Norway and Sweden but also Finland and the North Atlantic islands colonized by the Vikings in the Middle Ages: the Faroes, Iceland and Greenland. The Vikings were hardy seafarers who penetrated even North America around AD 1000; in the early 11th century Cnut (Canute), king of Denmark and Norway, also ruled England. In 1397 Queen Margrethe I united Norway, Sweden, Iceland, Greenland and Finland under the Danish crown, a union that lasted until 1523, when Gustavus Vasa drove the Danes out of Sweden. In the 17th century Sweden was the greatest power in the Baltic, but its expansion into

Russia was checked in 1709 and a century later it was forced to cede Finland to the tsar. Norway remained part of Denmark until 1814, when it was transferred to Sweden, but in 1905 the Norwegian parliament voted for independence, electing a Danish prince as Haakon VII. Iceland became a republic in 1944.

Left: The eruption of Hekla in Iceland in 1948 was marked by a set of seven stamps showing different views of the volcano.

DENMARK

The first of the Scandinavian countries to adopt stamps, Denmark's first issue consisted of the 2rbs and 4rbs (rigsbank skilling) stamps – small, square with a security underprint [1]. A feature common to the main Scandinavian countries is the use of a numeral motif for the low-value stamps that is retained in use for many years. The Danish waves design [2] has been in use, with modifications, since 1905. The first commemoratives appeared in 1920 to celebrate the recovery of Northern Slesvig from Germany [3]. The Nordic countries preferred a small format for special issues, such as the set marking the 400th anniversary of the Reformation in 1936 [4].

From 1953 to 1956 Denmark celebrated its millennium as a kingdom with ten stamps, one for each century.

The top value [5] showed the memorial to the war of 1864, in which Denmark was defeated and lost Slesvig to Prussia. Stamps honouring the Red Cross in 1966 bore the titles of international Red Cross organizations in 32 languages, plus a Latin motto – the largest number of different languages on a single stamp up to that time [7]. The postal printing works has continued to use intaglio to this day, but in recent years multicolour lithography has also been employed effectively, as in the stamps celebrating the silver jubilee of Margrethe II [6] and the Youth series, which included a close-up of a tongue with a stud in it [8].

NORWAY

Both Norway and Sweden introduced stamps in 1855 but while Norway portrayed King Oscar of Sweden [9]

Sweden preferred armorial designs. Both countries would later follow the same pattern as Denmark, using a numeral motif for the lowest values and heraldic design for the middle denominations and a portrait of the monarch on the high values. This meant that the only stamps that needed to be changed at the outset of each new reign were the relatively little-used high values.

For the most part Norway preferred the cheap letterpress process, reserving intaglio for the occasional high-value commemorative, but in 1928 the contract passed to Emil Mostue, who used lithography for a short period before introducing photogravure. This was used most effectively in the tourist propaganda series of 1938 [11] and the Queen Maud charity set of 1939 [12].

Both Denmark and Norway were overrun by Nazi Germany in 1940. While Christian X remained in Copenhagen to raise the morale of his people, Haakon VII went to Scotland to regroup his forces there. In Norway the Germans installed Vidkun Quisling [13], whose name has become a byword for treachery; the date on the stamp was that on which he was asked to form a government. The definitives were overprinted with a large letter V for Victory [14], but this boomeranged when the Resistance painted the slogan "Vi Vil Vinne" (We will win) on roads, a scene depicted on one of the stamps issued by the Norwegian government in exile [15].

Increasing use of multicolour lithography has brightened the appearance of Norwegian stamps in recent years [16]. The inauguration of the National Junior Stamp Club in 1997 was marked by two stamps crammed with different thematic subjects [10].

DANISH POSSESSIONS

Iceland had been a Danish colony since Viking times and its earliest stamps [17] were closely modelled on those of the mother country. In December 1918 it was declared an independent kingdom under Christian X but it became a republic in 1944. Since 1938 many of its stamps have featured geysers and glaciers [19], the volcanic destruction of Heimaey and the birth of the island of Surtsey.

Greenland had free postage until 1938, though parcels had to bear special stamps [18]. During World War II, when stamps were unavailable from Denmark, a series was recess-printed by the American Bank Note Company. Since 1950 Greenland's stamps have followed the Danish style but reflect the culture and traditions of the Inuit population. Bilingual inscriptions have been in use since 1963.

The Faroes had the unusual distinction of their own provisional stamps during World War II but did not get a permanent series until 1975 [20]. Since then the stamps have continued to depict the extraordinary scenery of these islands.

11

12

13

14

15

16

17

18

19

20

Record Longevity

The posthorn design of Norway's low values was introduced in 1871 – and is still in use. Over the years it has changed currency (1877), lettering (1893) and printer several times, and switched from letterpress to photogravure (1934), then intaglio (1962) and multicolour lithography (1997). Norway even celebrated its centenary with a pair showing the 3sk of 1871.

1   2

3   4

5   6

7

8

9   10

EASTERN SCANDINAVIA

Sweden was the dominant Baltic power from the Middle Ages to the end of the 17th century. Sverker I (*c.* 1134–56) united the Swedes and the Goths, and his crusade to Christianize the pagan Finns marked the beginning of the Swedish conquest of Finland. The Union of Kalmar (1397) united Denmark, Norway and Sweden under one ruler, but in 1520 the Swedish noble Gustavus Vasa raised a revolt against the Danish king that restored Swedish independence. Under his successors Sweden extended its rule over the whole of Finland and south of the Baltic. Sweden's power was checked when Poland, Denmark and Russia combined against Charles XII in a long war (1700–20), as a result of which it lost Estonia, Livonia and Ingermanland. Finland and the Aland Islands were ceded to Russia in 1809.

Left: Since 1956 the Nordic countries have issued stamps in uniform designs to symbolize their close postal co-operation. In 1967 the subject of these stamps was the Nordic House in Reykjavik, Iceland.

FINLAND

Until 1917 Finland was a Russian grand duchy and its early stamps were inscribed in both Cyrillic and Roman alphabets [1]; later issues were trilingual, with the name of the country in Russian, Finnish and Swedish [2]. When russification was at its height at the turn of the 20th century the stamps were identical to the Russian series [3], apart from the currency (the markka, divided into 100 penniä). Finland's first independent stamps were designed by its leading architect, Eliel Saarinen [4].

Most stamps were recess-printed in single colours [5] until 1966, when multicolour lithography was adopted [6]. Annual issues for the Red Cross and anti-TB campaign followed the same trend, with themes reflecting Finnish scenery and wildlife [7].

Most definitive issues since 1917 are in a small upright format and depict the lion rampant, a device seen on the tombs of the Vasa kings of Sweden. These have varied from time to time and designs featuring scenery and landmarks have been favoured for the high values [8]. Stamps portraying Marshal Gustav Mannerheim were overprinted for Eastern Karelia, occupied by the Finns from 1941 to 1944 [9].

ALAND ISLANDS

The Aland Islands in the Baltic were ceded to Russia in 1809. Of immense strategic importance, their great fortress at Bomarsund was destroyed by an Anglo-French fleet in 1854 and the islands were demilitarized and declared neutral. The mainly Swedish inhabitants were granted autonomy in 1922.

Regional stamps were introduced in 1984 [10] but since January 1993 the Aland postal service has been completely independent. Its stamps concentrate on the islands' scenery and distinctive culture, with a popular annual issue featuring island churches [11]. Their endearingly homespun character is reflected in genre scenes of island life. A beauty contest for cats in 2003 to elect "Missy Aland" resulted in the winners, Tovis [12] and Randi, being portrayed on a couple of stamps.

SWEDEN

Adhesive stamps were introduced in July 1855 and showed arms or numerals [13], a tradition continued in the low-value definitives to this day. No portrait of the king appeared until 1885, when Oscar II was shown on the higher denominations [14]. In 1920 stamp production passed from private firms to the Stamp Printing Office and Swedish stamps were subsequently recess-printed [15] in booklets or coils, distinguished by the lack of perforation on one or more adjoining sides, or two opposite sides [16] respectively.

Sweden was the home of Alfred Nobel, the armaments millionaire who created the prizes named in his memory. Nobel's image appeared on stamps of 1946 to mark the 50th anniversary of his death, and in 1961 Sweden began issuing a set each year portraying the Nobel laureates since 1901 [17].

A joint issue with Finland in 1967 publicized Finnish settlers in Sweden and Swedish settlers in Finland. Each country issued two stamps symbolizing solidarity, designed by Pentti Rahikainen and lithographed at the State Bank Note Printing Works in Helsinki [18]. Since this major turning point Swedish stamps have been much more colourful, increasingly employing offset lithography. At the same time their scope has widened considerably, from rock 'n' roll [19] to the endearing charm of Carl Larsson's paintings [20].

11

12

The Greatest Master of Line Engraving

In 1960 a young Polish engraver named Czeslaw Slania began work at the Swedish Stamp Printing Office. Over the ensuing 45 years he engraved more than 1,000 stamps for his adopted land and many other countries (including the UK and USA). Universally recognized as the maestro of portrait engraving, in 1991 he was accorded the singular

honour of a souvenir sheet as a 70th birthday tribute – which he engraved himself. Although at the time that was his greatest masterpiece, he surpassed it in March 2000 with this magnificent work, his 1,000th stamp engraving. Appropriately, he reproduced the painting *Great Deeds of Swedish Kings* by the 17th-century artist David Klöcker Ehrenstrahl.

13   14

15   16

17

18

19

20

VIKINGS IN STAMPS

The word "Viking" came to be synonymous with "warrior", but it originally meant "bay people" and alluded to those who came from the inlets and fiords of western Norway and terrorized all of Europe between 780 and 1050. The image purveyed by the monastic chronicles – of bloodthirsty murderers and ruthless pillagers of Christendom – dies hard, but Viking history has now been substantially revised. Their influence in Britain is evident in place names from Ipswich and Harwich in the south to Lerwick and Haroldswick in Shetland.

Today, the Vikings are depicted in a more positive light, with a highly developed civilization and a strict code of honour. They were not all looters and rapists but accomplished craftsmen in wood, stone and metal, and skilled builders of ocean-going vessels far ahead of their time.

The Vikings had a distinctive religion based on a rich mythology with its own pantheon of gods and lesser deities. Above all, it was their daring seamanship that has proved their lasting legacy. Not so long ago Christopher Columbus got all the credit for finding the New World; now the prior claim of the Vikings has been proven by archaeological discoveries.

Below: The Scandinavian countries issued miniature sheets in 2004 showing characters from Norse mythology, such as Thor and Ran on this sheet from the Faroes.

While Scandinavian philately has been much enriched by Viking subjects, their impact elsewhere has provided material for stamps from many countries. Significantly the longship is the most important symbol of that era, for it was this craft that made possible the extraordinary expansion of the Vikings between 900 and 1100.

Norsemen raided Brittany and Gaul, laid siege to Paris and were bought off by grants of land in what came to be known as Normandy. Although they acquired a veneer of civilization from the Franks, it was the same tough fighting men who invaded and conquered England in 1066. Half a century earlier King Cnut had also conquered England and briefly created a vast Norse empire that stretched from Arctic Norway and Sweden to western Scotland and much of Ireland as well as the Faroes, Iceland, Greenland and the north-eastern seaboard of America.

Above: Viking ship on an early stamp of Estonia (top) and an Arctic Viking stamp from Greenland, showing an Indian arrowhead from a Viking grave and a Viking coin found in Maine.

Below: Floki and his raven on an Iceland miniature sheet, 2003.

Right: Miniature sheet from the Faroes showing the Vikings' Atlantic voyages.

Below: Tynwald, named from the Norse for "assembly field", celebrated its 1,000th anniversary in 1979.

Above: The name Viking remains a byword for exploration: the space mission to Mars, honoured by this American stamp, recalls the intrepid Atlantic voyages of 1,000 years ago.

Right: In 2000 Iceland issued two stamps featuring Viking architecture, including this reconstruction.

Above: Dragon figurehead of a Viking ship on a Danish stamp (left); Leif Erikson's statue in Reykjavik, Iceland, featured on an American stamp in 1968 celebrating his arrival in and exploration of Vinland, believed to be Maine (centre); Viking warriors and longships arriving on the Isle of Man on a stamp of 1973 (right).

While Hrolf the Ganger (later Duke Rollo of Normandy) was carving a large fief in the lower Seine basin, others penetrated the Mediterranean, colonized Sicily and Malta and got as far as Constantinople, which they knew as Miklagard (big garden). The followers of Rurik sailed north into the Black Sea and penetrated the valleys of the rivers Don, Dnieper and Volga, laying the foundations of Russia and the Ukraine. The indigenous peoples invited the strangers, whom they called Rus (red-haired) to bring law and order. Rurik answered the call and founded Novgorod (new town), the first of many cities that included Kiev and Smolensk. Viking ships can be found on the first stamps of Estonia as

well as on more recent issues from Poland, Ukraine and Lithuania.

Of all the lands the Vikings settled, Iceland has remained most faithful to Norse culture. They first arrived in 874, driving out or enslaving the Irish hermits they found there. Icelandic stamps recall their arrival at Reykjavik and the establishment in 930 of the Althing, the world's oldest democratic assembly.

Banished from Iceland in 980, Erik the Red and his followers sailed to the far west, where he discovered southern Greenland. Three sets and matching miniature sheets from Greenland in 1999–2000 tell the story of the rise and fall of the Arctic Vikings. Though Greenland was treeless, the abundant driftwood in its bays encouraged Erik's

son Leif the Lucky to look for land farther west. Around 1000 he discovered three territories, Helluland (Baffin Land), Markland (Newfoundland) and Vinland (wine country, believed to be Maine). Stamps from many countries, including Canada and the USA, acknowledge Leif Erikson's discoveries.

Many stamps of the Isle of Man, under Norse rule until 1266, allude to its Viking heritage. Stamps of Ireland also reflect Viking history, from the founding of Dublin to the Battle of Clontarf in 1014. Numerous stamps with a Viking theme have been issued by Denmark, Norway and Sweden, illustrating Viking craftsmanship from the carved stones of Gotland to the Jellinge style of curvilinear ornament.

BRITISH ISLES

Eighty years ago there was a single stamp-issuing authority for the whole of the British Isles. Today, there are five, and of these Royal Mail (which is responsible for the stamps of the United Kingdom) also produces country or regional stamps for England, Scotland, Wales and Northern Ireland. The first division came in 1922, when the 26 counties of southern Ireland became the Irish Free State. Wartime provisional issues in the Channel Islands were followed by the regional issues of 1958, and postal autonomy in 1969 for Guernsey and Jersey was followed by that for the Isle of Man in 1973. At first, regional stamps, apart from those of the offshore islands, were confined to Scotland, Wales and Northern Ireland, but England has also had its own stamps since 2001. In 1840, when Rowland Hill introduced adhesive postage stamps, no country name was necessary, and in deference to Britain's premier position, the Universal Postal Union decreed in 1874 that Britain alone would be exempt from the rule requiring the country name to appear on stamps. Ever since then, the head of the reigning monarch has been sufficient identification.

Left: In 1995 Royal Mail issued two stamps to celebrate the bicentenary of the birth of Sir Rowland Hill, portraying him as a young man and in old age. The latter also incorporated the Penny Black.

CONSERVATIVE POLICY

The design of the Penny Black (1840) was regarded as so perfect that it remained in use for 40 years, changing colour in 1841, adopting perforations in 1848 and acquiring check letters in all four corners in 1858 [1]. When the rate for postcards and printed matter was halved in 1870 the solution was to issue a stamp half the size of the Penny [2]. Separate stamps for revenue purposes were introduced in 1853, but postage and revenue duties were combined from 1881 onwards. As a result, the Penny Lilac [3] is arguably the world's greatest stamp, at least in terms of its being produced in quite astronomical quantities up to 1902.

Attempts to improve the appearance of the Victorian stamps led to the mainly bicoloured Jubilee series of 1887. Most of the designs were retained in the reign of Edward VII, with his profile substituted [4]. The stamps from 1880 onwards were mainly printed by letterpress; the George V series [5] was adapted to photogravure in 1934 [6]. George V, a keen philatelist, requested that the intaglio process, which had been used from 1840 to 1879, should be revived for the high values, popularly known as the Seahorses [7].

FIRST COMMEMORATIVES

Although commemorative postal stationery had been produced in 1890 for the jubilee of penny postage, no adhesive commemorative stamps were issued until 1924, when new stamps were produced for the British Empire Exhibition [8], though sales were confined to the showgrounds. Britain produced very few commemoratives until the 1950s; those that were issued were confined to events of national, international or royal significance [9].

PHOTOGRAVURE

The definitives for the brief reign of Edward VIII broke new ground, using a design that was ideally suited to the photogravure process [10]. The clock turned back again a year later, when the

1

2

3

4

5

6

7

8

9

10

11

definitives of Edward's brother George VI added the heraldic flowers of the United Kingdom [11]. For the Coronation stamp of 1937 the king and queen were portrayed side by side [12] whereas the Silver Wedding stamps of 1948 featured conjoined busts [13]. Special issues in the immediate postwar years were heavily symbolic in character [14].

EARLY ELIZABETHAN STAMPS

The first definitives of the reign of Elizabeth II, introduced in 1952, were based on a facing portrait of the queen by the photographer Dorothy Wilding [15]. One of the four designs for the Coronation stamps, issued in 1953, showed a full-face portrait with the coronation regalia [17]. The first definitives were superseded in 1967 by a series that returned to the style set in 1936 by the Edward VIII series, using an effigy of the queen sculpted in plaster by Arnold Machin [16].

The tempo of special issues increased in the 1960s; at the same time the first bicoloured stamps since 1910 appeared [18]. Symbolism gave way to pictorialism [19] and the first stamps to commemorate a historic personality

Below: Four stamps issued in 1964 depicted characters from Shakespeare's plays to mark his quatercentenary, and in 1966 Robert Burns was belatedly commemorated (bottom).

The World's Most Prolific Series

No one could have foreseen that the British definitives first issued in 1967, known as the Machins after the sculptor who modelled the queen's head, would become not only one of the world's longest-running series but also the most prolific of all time. Even on a simplified reckoning there have been well over 200 different denominations and colours since 1967.

The design was retained when Britain introduced decimal currency in 1971. It has been produced by several printers, using photogravure, lithography, intaglio and even letterpress and embossing, in gummed sheets and self-adhesive booklets. But taking into account all the variations in paper, perforation and phosphor bands, the number of collectable varieties runs into thousands.

appeared in 1964, although the Post Office argued that these marked the Shakespeare Quatercentenary Festival (a major national event) rather than honouring William Shakespeare himself. Nevertheless, protests in Scotland that the bicentenary of the birth of Robert Burns in 1959 had been ignored led to the issue of two commemorative stamps in 1966. That year, in which Post Office policy on special issues broke free, also witnessed stamps in honour of the football World Cup, including a last-minute "special" to celebrate England's victory [20], and the first British Christmas stamps, featuring two designs by young children – another novelty [21].

BRITISH REGIONAL ISSUES

Historically the British Isles consisted of three kingdoms (England, Scotland and Ireland), a principality (Wales) and three crown dependencies (Guernsey, Jersey and the Isle of Man). For more than 80 years after the first issue in 1940 the stamps produced by the British Post Office were used in all of these areas. Today, however, separate issues appear for use through-

out the United Kingdom, in England, Scotland, Wales and Northern Ireland, and Guernsey, Alderney, Jersey, the Isle of Man and the Irish Republic, reflecting the different history, culture and outlook of each territory, yet often revealing subjects common to all. Many events and personalities that might not be considered to merit the issue of British stamps are celebrated by the offshore islands.

Left: The first of an Irish series issued in 1969 devoted to Irish Art reproduced The Last Supper and Crucifixion, *a stained glass window in the chapel of Eton College in England, designed by the Dublin-born artist Evie Hone.*

RECENT DEVELOPMENTS IN BRITISH STAMPS

In recent years the use of intaglio combined with photogravure has resulted in stamps with much sharper outlines. Many modern British stamps have designs that bleed off into the perforations, although the motifs are often obscure, such as the series of 2002 for the centenary of J.M. Barrie's *Peter Pan* [1]. Just how far British design moved in the latter part of the 20th century can be gauged by comparing the stamps of 1981 and 1986 celebrating the marriages of Prince Charles [2] and Prince Andrew [3]: the latter showed a much more informal approach to its subject. A series issued in 2003 entitled Extreme Endeavours broke new ground by portraying a living person other than royalty on a stamp – it showed Sir Edmund Hillary approaching the summit of Everest in 1953 [4].

REGIONALISM

Although the Channel Islands and the Isle of Man had been agitating for their own stamps since the 1930s, nothing was done to implement this until 1958, when distinctive stamps appeared not only in each of the offshore islands but also in Scotland, Wales and Northern

Ireland. Like the "unified" series they bore no name, and all had to bear the Wilding portrait of the queen as their dominant feature. But the stamps, designed by local artists, gained their individuality from the inclusion of heraldic devices and local symbolism: the ducal crown and lily of Guernsey [5], the arms and mace of Jersey [6], the triskeles (three-legged symbol) and ring-chain of Man [7], the crown, this-tle and saltire cross of Scotland [8], the dragon and leek of Wales [9] and the red hand of Ulster and flax blossom of Northern Ireland [10].

Following the advent of decimal currency in 1971 the remaining regions received standardized designs based on the Machin portrait with their national emblems in the upper left-hand corner [11–14]. The Manx series was discontinued in 1973 following the island's postal autonomy, but the others continued until 1999–2000, when different motifs were produced for each of four stamps covering the basic postal rates [15]. England joined in 2001.

IRISH FREE STATE

Following the Easter Rising (1916) and War of Independence (1919–21), the 26 counties in the south and west of

Ireland attained dominion status as the Irish Free State, which introduced its own stamps in 1922. At first British stamps were overprinted in Gaelic, using monastic uncials to signify the Provisional Government of Ireland. This was followed by an overprinted series inscribed "Saorstat Eireann" (Irish Free State) [16].

The first of the distinctive stamps appeared on December 6, 1922, the very day the Free State came into being. The designs, rich in Celtic symbolism, included one showing a map of an undivided Ireland [17]. They continued in use until 1968, when they were replaced by a series illustrating ancient Irish art treasures.

REPUBLIC OF IRELAND

The first step to complete independence came in 1936 when Eamon de Valera used the abdication of Edward VIII to draft a new constitution formally abandoning the Free State title in favour of Eire. In 1939 two stamps celebrated the 150th anniversary of the US constitution and the installation of the first US president – they were the first of many stamps that emphasized the close ties between Ireland and the USA [19]. The Republic of Ireland was formally inaugurated in April 1949 with the only stamp ever to use this title for the country [18]. Since then the name Eire has been retained, although the penchant for inscriptions in the Irish language (spoken by only 20 per cent of the population) has

Below: Irish stamps issued in 2004 celebrated the jubilee of Pope John Paul II (left) and combined the theme of Valentine's Day with the Chinese Year of the Monkey (right).

greatly diminished. Interestingly, it has been used on recent stamps that reflect Ireland's enthusiasm for the European Union [20–21].

Special issues take pride in Irish inventions such as the air pump, the tractor, the steam turbine and the submarine [22]. Major naval figures include Commodore Barry, co-founder of the US Navy, and William Brown who founded the Argentinian Navy, while the exploits of the polar explorer Sir Ernest Shackleton were the subject of an issue in 2004. The pantheon of heroes and martyrs in the long struggle for independence range from the leaders of the ill-fated Easter Rising to Wolfe Tone, Michael Collins and Eamon de Valera. Literary figures are legion on stamps and range from medieval chroniclers to modern poets and playwrights. Sporting attractions range from Gaelic football and hurling to sailing [23], while scenery and wildlife are well covered. Ireland's devotion to Catholicism is featured prominently but other faiths have also been honoured. Since 1985 Ireland has issued stamps for Valentine's Day, more recent issues linking this to the Chinese Lunar New Year.

BRITISH OFFSHORE ISLANDS

The Isle of Man and the Channel Islands are not, strictly speaking, part of the United Kingdom but are dependencies of the Crown with their own parliamentary systems. The Isle of Man, situated between Ireland, Scotland and England, was under Norse rule until 1266, then briefly ruled by Scotland. The Earls of Derby and later the Dukes of Atholl were the Lords of Mann (sic) until 1765 when the island passed to the Crown. The Channel Islands comprise the bailiwicks of Guernsey (with its dependencies Alderney and Sark) and Jersey – the last remnants of the Duchy of Normandy. The Channel Islands were under German occupation during World War II.

Left: In 2004 Jersey issued a set of stamps in se-tenant pairs to celebrate royal connections dating from the Norman Conquest. Each pair featured an island landmark alongside a portrait of the monarch in whose reign it was constructed.

GUERNSEY

Both Guernsey and Jersey were occupied by German forces in May 1940 and were not freed until May 1945, during which time they ran out of British stamps. In Guernsey 2d stamps were bisected – as shown on a stamp of 1990 marking the 150th anniversary of adhesive stamps [1] – pending locally printed stamps [2], which ceased to be valid after the liberation. British stamps were used from then until 1969, when both bailiwicks took over their own postal services and introduced distinctive stamps. Guernsey's first definitives showed portraits of medieval rulers based on silver pennies [4].

The stamps of the offshore islands often focused on subjects overlooked by the British Post Office. Guernsey's stamps marked the St John Ambulance centenary [5] and John Wesley's ministry to the island [6] among many other events. Connections with nearby France have resulted in many stamps, such as the series of 1992 showing the cartoon character Asterix the Gaul [7]. In 2004 a set marking the 60th anniversary of D-Day (which bypassed the islands) paid tribute to the Red Cross ship *Vega*, which brought provisions after the island was cut off by the Allied advance in Normandy [8].

Guernsey's dependency Alderney has had "regional" stamps since 1983. Though distinctive to that island, they are also postally valid in Guernsey [9]. Circular stamps marking the centenary of FIFA in 2004 showed "playground school footie" [10].

JERSEY

As well as the armorial stamps issued in 1941–3 Jersey had a set of six pictorial definitives in 1943–4, designed by the well-known local artist Edmund Blampied but printed in Paris. The artist even managed to incorporate the royal monogram GR (flanking the value) under the noses of the Nazis [3].

Scenery and royal portraiture were featured in the definitives of 1969, which were re-issued in 1970–1 with decimal currency, followed by those of the parishes (1976–80) and the arms of the island's prominent families in 1981–8. Flowers, scenery and bird life have been covered in more recent sets.

One of Jersey's first special issues marked the 25th anniversary of the liberation, a subject that has been alluded to in several subsequent sets. Loyalty to the Crown is manifest in the many stamps portraying members of the British royal family: Elizabeth II's golden jubilee was celebrated in 2002 by stamps depicting the Crown Jewels [11]. Short sets are also produced frequently, covering numerous topics from tourist attractions to the island's remarkably diverse wildlife [12]. Since 1996 a £1 miniature sheet has been released annually to mark the Chinese New Year. Designed by Victor Ambrus, these stamps feature the relevant animal of the Chinese zodiac wearing a multicoloured scarf.

ISLE OF MAN

Although it had the option of postal autonomy in 1969, at the same time as Guernsey and Jersey, the Isle of Man did not follow suit until 1973. Following the style of the regional stamps of 1958–71, the first definitives that were issued incorporated the triskeles, the three-legged emblem of the island, and a Hiberno-Norse ring-chain motif. A second series, introduced in 1978, retained the triskeles but dispensed with the curvilinear ornament in order to place greater emphasis on landmarks of the island [13]. Later sets featured island birds (1983–5), Manx railways and trams (1988–92) and ships (1993–7), including the *Waverley*, the world's last

Below: Isle of Man stamps have featured Princess Margaret in Guide uniform (1985) and Queen Alexandra as Princess of Wales in 1885.

Puzzle Pieces

Two stamps that often puzzle collectors bear the portrait of George VI. Without a country name, they must be British, but they are not to be found under Great Britain in the catalogues. They were issued by Britain, in 1948, but celebrated the third anniversary of the liberation of the Channel Islands and are thus regarded as the forerunners of the modern stamps. Both depict islanders gathering seaweed for manure, based on paintings by the Jersey artist Edmund Blampied.

sea-going paddle-steamer, which plies the route between Glasgow and the Isle of Man [14].

Special issues have explored the island's Norse heritage but also proudly show the Manx contribution to the world at large. The Lifeboat Institution was founded by Sir William Hillary, a native of the island [15] while Manx connections with the USA have yielded several sets [16]. The Isle of Man granted votes to women in 1881, before anyone else [17]. Members of the British royal family, in their official roles, have been a popular subject, and include the late Princess Margaret and Queen Alexandra, depicted as Princess of Wales for the centenary of the servicemen's charity SSAFA (Soldiers, Sailors and Air Force Association).

The island is world-famous for its Tourist Trophy (TT) motorcycle races and these have appeared on a number of sets since 1973. The most recent combines them with the comedian George Formby, who made his screen debut in *No Limit* (1936), filmed during the 1935 TT races.

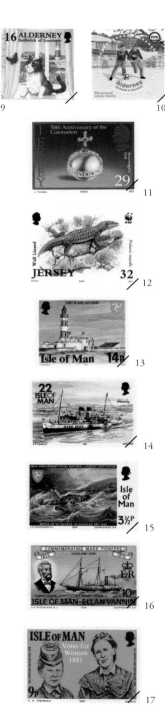

BRITISH EUROPEAN TERRITORIES

British stamps have been issued in a number of territories in continental Europe that it acquired as a result of various military campaigns. The first of these was Gibraltar, which had belonged to Spain since the expulsion of the Moors in 1492. Lying on the northern side of the straits at the western end of the Mediterranean, called the Pillars of Hercules by the ancients, it derived its name from Gibel Tarik (Tarik's rock) after the Moorish chieftain who seized it in the 8th century. It was captured by an Anglo-Dutch expedition in 1704 and remains British despite frequent attempts by Spain to regain it.

Left: The 1960 definitive series of Gibraltar featured a map of the straits, graphically illustrating the strategic importance of the Rock. The badge of the colony is, in fact, a bunch of keys, and it would be true to say that Gibraltar itself was the key to British mastery of the Mediterranean in both world wars, particularly during anti-submarine campaigns.

GIBRALTAR

The postal service was controlled from London until 1886 and used ordinary British stamps, identified only by an obliterator with the letter G in the centre. When control was transferred to Gibraltar itself the earliest distinctive stamps were merely those of Bermuda, overprinted [8]. Pictorial definitives were introduced gradually from 1931, using two-colour recess printing from 1928 to 1953 [1]. A more stylized approach was adopted in 1960 for a series showing the fauna and flora of the Rock, including the famous Barbary ape, the only higher primate found in Europe [2]. Ships [3], insects [4] and views of Gibraltar old and new were depicted on later issues.

Of the special issues, many alluded to the Great Siege of 1779–83 and the importance of the Rock as a British garrison and coaling station, but by the 1960s issues such as the Sea Angling Championships [5] were publicizing Gibraltar as a tourist destination. The first Christmas stamp reproduced a stained glass window from a Glasgow church [6].

Although only an associate member of the EU (through the UK), Gibraltar has produced a number of stamps that relate to it [7], including a sheetlet featuring the euro coinage, despite the fact that Gibraltar uses sterling currency.

MALTA

From the 16th century until 1798 Malta was the base of the Knights of St John, who had been ousted from Rhodes by the Turks. The French under Napoleon seized the island in 1798 but were driven out by a local rebellion assisted by the British, who then took over. Like Gibraltar, the postal service was run from London, and British stamps with the obliterator M were used until 1885, but from 1860 the island had a distinctive 1/2d stamp for local mail.

Pictorial stamps appeared from 1899 and included a view of the Grand Harbour at Valletta on the 1/4d stamps [9]. The strategic importance of the island fortress was shown during World War II, when Malta was besieged by Axis forces. George VI conferred the George Cross on the island in 1942, and thereafter it appeared on many of the stamps alongside the name [12]. Malta also received a commendation scroll from President Roosevelt [10].

Malta became an independent state in 1964, and its first definitive series featured landmarks illustrating its history since the Stone Age [11]. Many later stamps highlighted the glorious architecture and art from the time of the Knights [13]. On December 13, 1974, Malta became a republic within the Commonwealth [14]. In 1989 it hosted a summit conference between Presidents Bush and Gorbachev [16]. Its importance as a holiday destination goes back to the early 19th century, when Sir Walter Scott spent some time there [15]. More recent stamps have noted major international sporting events [17].

CYPRUS

During the Napoleonic Wars Britain gained control of the Ionian Islands in the Adriatic off the Greek coast. Ordinary British stamps were used in

Below: John F. Kennedy on a Cypriot stamp of 1965 (top). Stamps of Northern Cyprus cover international anniversaries (middle) as well as the annual Europa issues (bottom).

Refugee Tax
Compulsory stamps showing a child surrounded by barbed wire have been issued with various dates since 1977, in aid of refugees from Northern Cyprus.

Cephalonia, Corfu and Zante until 1859, when a set was produced of three undenominated stamps portraying Queen Victoria, with their values determined by their colour [18]. These stamps were withdrawn in 1864 when Britain handed the three islands over to Greece.

The Treaty of Berlin (1878) assigned the administration of Cyprus to Britain, and overprinted British stamps [19] were used until 1881. The island was nominally Turkish until 1925, when it was made a British crown colony. Pictorial definitives, dwelling heavily on the Greek classical period, appeared from 1934.

Cyprus became a republic within the Commonwealth in 1960. Although stamps since then have mostly alluded to the glories of its Greek heritage, issues mourning the death of John F. Kennedy quoted his speech on self-determination for Cyprus. Sadly, Cyprus was torn apart by ethnic violence, leading to the Turkish invasion and partition of the island in 1974. A breakaway regime known as the Turkish Republic of Northern Cyprus has had its own stamps since the island was partitioned. Mail to and from Northern Cyprus is routed through Mersin in mainland Turkey.

10

11

12

13

14

15

16

17

18

19

1

2

3

4

5

6

7

8

9

10

11

THE BENELUX COUNTRIES

Belgium, the Netherlands and Luxembourg, historically known collectively as the Low Countries, were at one time ruled by the same monarch, reigning as King of the Netherlands and Grand Duke of Luxembourg, but in 1831 the Belgians seceded and elected Prince Leopold of Saxe-Coburg-Gotha as their king. When William III of the Netherlands died in 1890 the union with Luxembourg was dissolved because Salic Law forbade the succession of a female. The grand duchy passed to Duke Adolf of Nassau, the nearest male heir. When Grand Duke William IV died in 1912 the law was changed to allow his daughter Adelaide to succeed to the throne. All three countries were overrun by the Germans in 1940; when they were liberated in 1944 they decided to form a commercial union known as Benelux.

Left: Since 1964 the Benelux countries have issued stamps in a common design to celebrate important anniversaries of the union, which served as a model for the EEC and EU.

BELGIUM

Adhesive postage stamps were adopted in Belgium in 1849, followed by Luxembourg and the Netherlands in 1852. All three countries have many similarities and parallels in their stamps, reflecting their common historical, political and cultural heritage. Each country has been responsible for innovations. While Luxembourg was the first country to issue stamp booklets (1895) and miniature sheets (1921), Belgium pioneered railway parcel stamps (1879) and continues to produce them to this day [1]. Between 1893 and 1914 stamps were issued with labels attached to signify that mail was not to be delivered on Sundays [2].

In August 1914 the Germans invaded Belgium in violation of the Treaty of London (1839), which had guaranteed its neutrality. The definitive series of 1919–20 shows Albert I wearing a steel helmet, alluding to his command of the Belgian Army during World War I [3].

All three Benelux countries have frequently issued stamps with a charity premium, a recurring theme being the younger members of the royal family. Baudouin of Belgium made his philatelic debut on the Anti-tuberculosis

Fund stamps of 1936 [5]. His mother, Queen Astrid, was killed in a car crash in 1935; a black mourning stamp [6] was followed by a set in different colours but with the same portrait edged in black. A stamp of 1957 for the 50th anniversary of the Edith Cavell Nursing School recalls the British nurse, shot by the Germans as a spy in World War I [7].

The Low Countries were overrun by the Germans in 1940. Belgium celebrated its liberation in 1944 with definitives showing the lion rampant and "V" for victory [4]. Since 1893 Belgian stamps have been inscribed in both French and Flemish, but two different versions of the liberation stamps were produced, with the titles rendered as "Belgie-Belgique" and "Belgique-Belgie" to satisfy Flemish and Walloon national pride. Despite deep-seated differences between the two communities, Belgium has been a model for European unity.

Brussels is the seat of the European Parliament, and the first elections were celebrated on stamps of 1979 [10]. Belgium's main artistic contribution to contemporary philately has been the extensive use of images from strip cartoons and comics [8].

The imperial free city of Bremen issued stamps from 1855 to 1867, showing the civic arms [7]. The duchy of Brunswick had stamps showing the white horse emblem from 1852 [9], switching to embossed stamps in 1861. Hamburg, a free city from 1510, adopted stamps in 1859, all showing its triple-towered badge [8]. Lübeck, a free city since 1226, joined Hamburg in 1241 to form the Hanseatic League. Armorial stamps were used from 1859 [11] and embossed from 1863 to 1867.

The kingdom of Hanover had armorial stamps from 1851 to 1855, then switched to a numeral design for pfennig values [12] and a profile of George V for the higher denominations. Hanover was on the losing side in the Austro-Prussian War of 1866 and its stamps were suppressed following annexation by Prussia. From 1856 the grand duchy of Mecklenburg-Schwerin issued stamps that could be divided into quarters [10]. The adjoining state of Mecklenburg-Strelitz introduced stamps only in 1864, using the embossed style then in fashion [13] and a similar pattern was followed by the grand duchy of Oldenburg [14].

Prussia adopted stamps in 1850, originally portraying Friedrich Wilhelm IV [15], but his successor Wilhelm I preferred embossed armorial stamps from 1861, setting the trend for other states whose stamps were printed at the Prussian State Printing Works in Berlin. Saxony began with numerals, progressed to royal portraiture and from 1863 used embossed stamps in the Prussian manner [16]. Schleswig and Holstein were German duchies ruled by the Danish monarch but they rebelled in 1848 and issued a stamp in 1850 [17]. In 1864 Austria and Prussia invaded and stamps were issued in each duchy [18]. Disagreement between the allies led to the war of 1866.

The kingdom of Württemberg began issuing stamps in 1851, using numerals followed by embossed arms [19] and numerals again from 1869. Although it joined the German Empire in 1871 it had its own postal service,

British Outpost

The strategic island of Heligoland was seized by Britain during the Napoleonic wars, but its postal service was operated by Hamburg. and stamps portraying Queen Victoria were printed in Berlin, with dual sterling and German values. The island was ceded to Germany on 9 August 1890.

with distinctive stamps, until 1902. When its posts were absorbed into the Reich service Württemberg continued to issue special stamps for government correspondence until 1920 and municipal service stamps until 1924 – the only states' issue to feel the effects of hyperinflation in 1923 [20]. There were even commemorative issues in each category for the jubilee of William II in 1916, featuring the royal arms and the king's portrait respectively [22]. The only states' pictorials were the official mail series of March 1920, showing views of Stuttgart, Ulm, Eilwangen or Tubingen [21].

THE MOVE TOWARDS UNIFICATION

The North German Confederation, led by Prussia, was established on 1 January 1868, and the stamps of the member states were replaced by numeral designs [23] in groschen or kreuzer currencies. A special stamp was provided for Hamburg which used its own schillings [24]. Stamps issued in French currency were produced for use in Alsace and Lorraine in 1870, absorbed into the Reich in 1871 [25]. Collectors also regard the semi-official air stamps as states' issues [26].

1

2

3

4

5

6

7

8

9

10

11

12

13

GERMAN REICH

The period from the unification of Germany in 1871 to the fall of Hitler in 1945 was one of immense material progress accompanied by political instability. Pulling together a ramshackle conglomeration of states with their own distinct history and culture was a superhuman feat, although it led to autocracy under Kaiser Wilhelm II. Germany's demand for "a place in the sun" and its commercial rivalry with Britain and France led inevitably to World War I. Resentment at the harsh terms of the 1919 Treaty of Versailles and mass unemployment in turn led to the rise of fascism. The collapse of the monarchies in 1918 had no impact on stamps, which were still inscribed "Deutsches Reich".

Left: Adolf Hitler, an Austrian who served in the Bavarian Army, founded the National Socialist German Workers' Party. Briefly imprisoned for an attempted coup in 1923, he gained power constitutionally in 1933, but rapidly destroyed German democratic institutions. Stamps were issued for his birthday each April, usually with exorbitant premiums for the Hitler Culture Fund. Nazi Germany often used philately for propaganda.

THE EMPIRE

The earliest stamps of the empire featured the German eagle [1], but in 1899 a series portrayed the actress Anna Führing in the role of Germania [2], epitomizing the aggressive style of the kaiser. Remarkably these stamps survived the empire by three years. Under the Weimar Republic the imperial inscription remained but definitives emphasized the working classes [3].

Germany began to suffer the effects of inflation during World War I and it escalated in the early 1920s, reaching its peak in November 1923. The 1 milliard (thousand million) mark stamp [4], released only in Bavaria, is known as the Hitler Provisional because it was issued a few hours before he staged his *putsch* in Munich on 9 November. There were few special issues in the Weimar period but significantly many had premiums in aid of the welfare fund to alleviate poverty [5].

THE THIRD REICH

By the beginning of 1933 the Nazis were the largest party in the Reichstag and President Hindenburg had no alternative but to appoint Hitler as chancellor. Once in power, the Nazis dissolved parliament, banned all political parties except themselves and imprisoned communists, socialists, trades unionists and anyone who dissented from their political philosophy. Hitler was hell-bent on reversing the terms of the Treaty of Versailles. Stamps of the 1930s became increasingly propagandistic, publicizing the annual party rallies [6] and showing the führer in belligerent mood. The stamps for the party rally of 1937 [7] formed a miniature sheet whose slogan translated as "He who will save a nation must think heroically." Other stamps charted the expansion of the Reich, from the restoration of the Saar in 1935 [8] to the union with Austria in 1938 [9].

Later in 1938 Hitler demanded the Sudetenland, the German part of Czechoslovakia; Czech stamps were overprinted "Wir sind frei!" (We are free!) with the swastika [10]. Danzig was subsequently absorbed into the Reich on 1 September 1939, its stamps being suitably overprinted [11], and the invasion of Poland the same day was the first act of World War II.

The definitives continued to portray Hindenburg until 1941, when Hitler put his own portrait on the regular

A Breakaway State

In 1923, when Germany was wracked by inflation, the French seized the opportunity to detach the Rhineland (then occupied by its troops) and create an independent buffer state known as the Rhineland Republic. German stamps were overprinted "R.R." for this purpose, but protests from Britain, the USA and Germany itself led to the plan being aborted.

series [12]. Wartime stamps continued the strident Nazi messages [13–14]. As the tide of war turned, Hitler renamed his empire Grossdeutsches Reich (Great German State) and this was expressed on the last issues of the Nazi regime [16]. Ironically the very last stamps, issued as the Russians were advancing through the ruins of Berlin, honoured stormtroopers of the SA and SS [15].

PLEBISCITES

After World War I many districts of the empire from Schleswig to Silesia held plebiscites to decide their future. Under Allied supervision plebiscites took place in Allenstein (East Prussia) and Marienwerder (West Prussia), both of which voted to remain German. Memel was placed under French administration but was seized by Lithuania in 1923. Schleswig was divided into two zones, the north voting to return to Denmark and the south voting to remain in Germany. Upper Silesia was partitioned between Germany and Poland. Distinctive stamps were issued in each district. The Saar, a special case, fell to the French, who wished to secure the rich iron and coal industries. German and Bavarian stamps were overprinted [18] pending pictorials printed in Paris [17]. When a plebiscite was finally held in 1935 the district reverted to Germany.

FREE CITY OF DANZIG

The Baltic port of Danzig had been part of Poland for centuries though it enjoyed considerable autonomy and its population was predominantly German, the descendants of traders who had arrived in search of amber. In 1795 it came under Prussian rule, following the third partition of Poland.

By the early 20th century Danzig was the capital of West Prussia and its inhabitants 95 per cent German, but the newly reconstituted Poland demanded the return of Danzig, a vital outlet for Polish trade and commerce. Under the Treaty of Versailles, the problem of satisfying Polish demands was met by creating the Free City of Danzig, in which Poland enjoyed considerable rights. This source of friction between Germany and Poland was violently resolved when Hitler invaded Poland and Danzig once more became the capital of West Prussia. The politics of the Free City mirrored those of Germany itself, with the local Nazis in power from 1934 onwards.

German stamps were overprinted [19] pending the supply of distinctive stamps showing the crowned double cross or a Hanseatic cogge [20]. The special issues reflected the essentially German character of Danzig, including a set for the 150th birth anniversary of the philosopher Schopenhauer [21].

OCCUPATION

By 1942 Hitler had overrun most of Europe, from the Pyrenees to the Arctic, from the Atlantic to the Black Sea. German definitives were overprinted for use in many areas, from Alsace [23] and Lorraine [22], which were soon reabsorbed into the Reich, to large parts of Russia, redesignated Ostland [24]. After the capitulation of Italy, the Germans occupied territories formerly under Italian control [25].

1

2

3

4

5

6

7

8

9

10

11

12

13

POSTWAR GERMANY

In May 1945 a defeated Germany was partitioned by the Americans, British, French and Russians, and the capital Berlin was divided into four sectors. What began as a scheme to prevent a united Germany from ever again threatening the free world soon turned into the battleground on which the Cold War was mainly fought. Germany split into East and West in 1948 and the breach widened with the Soviet blockade of Berlin and later the erection of the Berlin Wall, which never deterred the truly determined from escaping to the West.

Left: In 1965 the Federal Republic commemorated 20 years of refugees fleeing westward with this 20pf stamp. Mail addressed to the Democratic Republic bearing this stamp was either returned to sender or had the offending stamp painted over.

FOUR-POWER CONTROL

For the Anglo-American zones stamps inscribed "AM" (Allied Military) with a large "M" (Military) in the centre and "Deutschland" at the foot [1] were brought over from the USA, later reprinted in Britain and ultimately in Germany itself. The French had a general series [2] followed by separate stamps for Baden, Württemberg and the Rhineland-Palatinate [3]. The six regions of the Soviet zone each released their own stamps in 1945–6 [4], and many towns also produced their own issues. From February 1946 until 1948 the Soviet zone used the stamps of the Anglo-American zones [5].

Growing disparity in the value of the mark in the East and West led to currency reform in 1948, but it also precipitated the split between East and West. Stamps were overprinted to distinguish their respective use [6–7]. The three western zones became the Federal German Republic in September 1949 and a month later the Soviets created the German Democratic Republic. The western sectors of Berlin became a Land (province) of the Federal Republic on 1 September 1950, and this issued its own stamps until 1990.

FEDERAL REPUBLIC

Stamps with the inscription "Deutsche Bundespost" (German Federal Post) were used in the West from 1950 [8].

From time to time trouble flared between the two republics when the Bundespost issued stamps showing places in the East, such as the Treptow Gate in Neubrandenburg as part of the definitive series of 1964–9, whose theme was 12 centuries of German architecture [9]. One of the first multi-coloured stamps marked the centenary of the arrival of the political refugee Carl Schurz in America [10].

After the highly propagandistic stamps of the Third Reich, West German stamps concentrated on historical events and personages. Definitives bore famous buildings or presidential portraits, accident prevention (1971–4) and industry and technology (1975–82). From 1986–7 onwards two series ran side by side, featuring famous women (sheet stamps) and tourist attractions (coil stamps).

WEST BERLIN

Stamps used in West Berlin were often identical to those in West Germany, but with the inscription "Deutsche Bundespost Berlin". However, Berlin often produced distinctive stamps, especially with a theme that was particular to the city. One of the earliest issues featured the Freedom Bell, based on the Liberty Bell and the gift of the American people [12]. Other stamps charted the rebuilding of the city and such landmarks as the Kaiser Wilhelm

Memorial Church, preserved in ruins as a reminder of the war [14]. The Brandenburg Gate, shown on many stamps of the GDR as well as West Berlin [13], served as a symbol of the divided city.

Both the Federal Republic and Berlin issued stamps mourning John F. Kennedy [15], whose impassioned speech at the Berlin Wall struck a chord with his audience. The later stamps of Berlin highlighted the cultural heritage of the former German capital [16] but also paid frequent tribute to the Allies, whose airlift of supplies broke the Soviet blockade of 1949 [17].

DEMOCRATIC REPUBLIC

The stamps of East Germany reflected the doctrinaire politics of the regime almost to the end, with stamps commemorating Communist figureheads [18] and symbolism strongly redolent of the USSR in the Stalinist era [19]. In many ways, the GDR was the conscience of Germany, tackling issues – such as Kristallnacht, when the Nazis destroyed Jewish shops and synagogues [20] – that were ignored or glossed over in the West, such as the atrocities committed in the concentration camps. At the same time, however, many reflected the totalitarian and militaristic nature of the GDR itself [21–22].

In 1973–5 a definitive series featured famous buildings. The last definitive series, introduced in 1980, consisted of the same designs but in a reduced size [23]. A long-running series consisted of stamps issued each spring and autumn to mark the world-famous Leipzig Fair. Normally a pair of stamps was released in each case but an exception was the set of four with matching miniature sheet issued in 1965 to mark the 800th anniversary of Leipzig and an international stamp exhibition held at the same time.

The Ostmark was replaced by the Deutschmark on 1 July 1990, necessitating new stamps simply inscribed "Deutsche Post" [24]. Stamps bearing the letters "DDR" remained valid for postage until 31 December 1991 [25].

History Repeats Itself

After World War II, the Saar was administered by France from May 1945 and had distinctive stamps from January 1947, French currency being introduced in November 1947. The Saar reverted to Germany in 1957 and stamps were then issued with the German inscription "Saarland", often in the same designs as those of West Germany, until July 1959, when German currency was introduced.

UNITED GERMANY

On 3 October 1990, the Democratic Republic was absorbed into the Federal Republic and thereafter only one type of stamp was used throughout Germany. One of the first sets to appear was a pair issued on 6 November that year celebrating the opening of the Berlin Wall [11]. Since 1995 stamps have been simply inscribed "Deutschland".

A casualty of reunification was the separate postal service of West Berlin, whose stamps were discontinued in September 1990. The following January, a stamp of united Germany celebrated the bicentenary of the Brandenburg Gate. Thereafter Berlin, as the restored capital of the whole country, featured prominently. Many stamps since 1991 have portrayed historic figures. In 2003 a stamp portrayed Georg Elser, the man who tried to kill Hitler at a Munich rally in 1939, and previously a stamp showing the date "20 Juli 1944" behind bars alluded to the bomb plot of that year – both rare examples of Germany coming to terms with its past. Stamps of recent years have been more overtly thematic.

14

15

16

17

18

19

20

21

22

23

24

25

AUSTRIA AND HUNGARY

At the height of its power, the Habsburg Empire occupied most of the basin of the Danube, from Bohemia to Transylvania, from Galicia to the Adriatic. It was a conglomeration of many races, tongues and creeds, held together on the principle of "divide and rule". Hungary had been an independent kingdom since the 10th century but in the 17th century accepted Habsburg protection against the Turks. In 1848, the year of revolutions, the Hungarians rose in a revolt that was suppressed by Austria aided by Russia. Thereafter Hungary was absorbed by Austria, a situation that was inherently unstable. So completely assimilated were these countries that they used the same stamps when they were adopted in 1850 [1]. After the *Ausgleich* (compromise) of 1867 both countries had their own stamps.

Left: The embodiment of the empire was Franz Joseph I, who succeeded in the aftermath of the 1848 revolution, at the age of 18, and ruled his ramshackle dominions for almost 70 years. His private life was marred by tragedy: the execution of his brother Maximilian, the assassination of his wife and the suicide of his son Rudolf.

AUSTRIAN REPUBLIC

The empire survived the aged kaiser by only two years, collapsing at the end of World War I. Not only did Hungary break away, but Transylvania passed to Romania and the Alpine and Adriatic provinces went to Italy, while entirely new countries such as Czechoslovakia and Yugoslavia were created and Poland was reconstituted. Austria, once the heart of a mighty empire, was reduced to the size of Scotland, with a similar population. There was a strong movement in favour of union with Germany, and in 1918–21 stamps were actually inscribed "Deutschösterreich" (German Austria). In 1920 they were overprinted "Hochwasser" to raise money for flood relief [3]. The definitive issues of 1934–8 featured provincial costumes.

In the 1930s Hitler, the Austrian-born dictator of Germany, had ambitions to add his native land to the Third Reich, and in 1934 the Nazis murdered the Austrian chancellor, Engelbert Dollfuss [4]. The last stamps of the republic were the first Christmas stamps, issued in 1937. People imagined they could see the baleful image of Hitler in the rose [5], an ill omen.

In April 1938, on the eve of a plebiscite, the Nazis marched into Austria without a shot being fired.

Austria was liberated by the Allies in May 1945. The Russians issued stamps showing the hammer and sickle [6] while the French, British and Americans had an innocuous posthorn design, produced in Washington [7]. The second republic was proclaimed soon afterwards. Costumes were the subject of a long-running series [8], rendered this time in photogravure. Various subjects, from scenery and architecture to myths and legends, have been used since then, the current issue being aimed at the tourist industry [9].

Austria is a land of music, and numerous stamps from 1922 onwards have honoured the great composers such as Haydn, Mozart, Beethoven and Strauss, while very recent stamps have portrayed Oscar Peterson [10], Riccardo Muti and Seiji Ozawa as well as the Rolling Stones. Nostalgia for the Habsburgs has seen the release of several stamps portraying Franz Joseph and his wife Elisabeth, assassinated in 1898. Appropriately, "Sissi", as she was affectionately known, is the subject of a new musical [11].

HUNGARY

For a few years after the creation of the dual monarchy in 1867, Hungary and Austria had identical stamps that merely portrayed the man known in one country as Kaiser Franz Joseph and in the other as Kiraly Ferenc Joszef. The only inscription was the abbreviation "kr", denoting *kreuzer* in Austria and *krajczar* in Hungary. The first specifically Hungarian stamps were intended for the imperial tax on newspapers that enabled transmission free of postage. A series portraying the monarch with the Hungarian arms below but no inscriptions appeared in 1871 and it was not until 1874 that stamps bore the country name. A new currency, based on the *korona* (crown) of 100 *filler* was adopted in 1900; stamps thus denominated showed the aged king wearing the Hungarian crown or the Turul, the mythical bird of the Magyar people.

A series depicting harvesters was introduced in 1915 and bore the inscription "Magyar Kir. Posta" (Hungarian Royal Post). The design endured until 1926 but underwent changes of inscription and various overprints reflecting the turmoil of 1919–24. At the end of World War I, Hungary went rapidly from a people's republic [12] to a soviet republic under Bela Kun [13]. A right-wing coup led by Admiral Horthy established a separate government at Szeged [14] and when the communists were driven out their overprints were blotted out by a wheatsheaf [15]. Hungary remained "a kingdom without a king, ruled by an admiral without a navy", as the continued abbreviation for *kiralyi* (royal) in the later stamps indicated [16].

History repeated itself after World War II (in which Hungary had been allied to Nazi Germany) when a provisional government [18] was followed by a republic (1946) and a people's republic (1949). In the communist era Hungary gained notoriety for its large number of stamps, including strictly limited editions of imperforate varieties. From 1949 until 1990, when communism collapsed, stamps were

merely inscribed "Magyar Posta" [19–20] but since then "Magyarorszag" (Hungarian State) has been used. The output has been much more restrained but includes themes previously banned. Recent issues include stamps honouring Raoul Wallenberg, the Swedish diplomat who saved the lives of many Jews but died in a Soviet camp [17] and the countdown to Hungarian entry into the European Union in 2004 [21].

MISCELLANEOUS ISSUES

Stamps inscribed "K.u.K. Militärpost" were used in Bosnia and Herzegovina (*see* Yugoslavia) but stamps inscribed "K.u.K. Feldpost" were employed in World War I [22]. As well as a general issue there were separate sets for the occupation of Italy, Montenegro, Romania and Serbia, while stamps issued by the French, Romanians and Serbs marked their occupation of Hungarian territory. The Danube Steam Navigation Company had its own stamps for mail carried on its steamers along the river and in the Black Sea ports, originally denominated in kreuzer but later in the international currency of gold centimes [23].

CZECHOSLOVAKIA

Czechoslovakia, in the heart of Europe, was a creation of the Treaty of Versailles, uniting the Czechs of Bohemia and Moravia (formerly under

Austria) with the Slovaks and Ruthenes (formerly under Hungary). The inclusion of three million Germans and 700,000 Hungarians created problems in the late 1930s. The Czechs and Slovaks spoke very similar languages, but culturally, historically and economically they were very different. They won their independence in 1918 as a reward for helping the Allies against the Central Powers.

Left: The architect of the new country was a Moravian, Thomas Masaryk, who campaigned before and during the war to secure self-determination for Czechoslovakia.

PREWAR REPUBLIC

Before the creation of the republic, the Czech legions were present at the Western Front, in Italy and in eastern Europe, fighting on the Allied side. During the Russian Civil War the Czechoslovak army in Russia controlled the Trans-Siberian Railway and issued its own stamps [1]. After independence in October 1918 the first postal service was operated by the Boy Scouts [2]. Later, stamps of Austria and Hungary were overprinted [3]. Almost from the outset the republic was beset with problems, at first concerning the Slovaks, who felt they were the junior partner, and later with the large German community in the Sudetenland. In the 1930s both factions were manipulated by Hitler for his own ends.

DISMEMBERMENT

In 1938 Czechoslovakia was forced to surrender the Sudetenland to Germany. At the same time the demands of the Slovaks led to a compromise: to give the Slovaks equal billing, stamps were briefly issued with the country name rendered as "Cesko-Slovensko". That vital hyphen, however, failed to stem the tide. In January 1939 the Slovak parliament was inaugurated [5]. In March stamps of Czechoslovakia were overprinted "Slovensky Stat", soon followed by definitive stamps portraying the Slovak leader, Father Hlinka [4].

On 15 March 1939, the Carpatho-Ukrainian parliament was inaugurated with a stamp inscribed in Cyrillic [6]. By noon the same day the Hungarians had invaded and annexed Ruthenia. It was liberated by the Red Army in 1944 and briefly functioned as an independent republic with its own stamps [7], before it was absorbed by the USSR.

In March 1939 Germany invaded the rump of Czechoslovakia, establishing a protectorate under the name of Bohemia and Moravia. Czechoslovak stamps were overprinted, pending the supply of distinctive stamps inscribed in German and Czech [8]. Following the assassination of Reinhard Heydrich by members of the Czech resistance, a stamp showing his death mask was released [9]. Special stamps were provided for Theresienstadt concentration camp [11]. Many people fled to France and Britain, where an exile government issued its own stamps, including one portraying Josef Gabcik, who assassinated Heydrich [10]. The War Heroes set was subsequently released in Czechoslovakia itself in August 1945.

POSTWAR REPUBLIC

Czechoslovakia was reconstituted in 1945 following liberation by the Red Army [12], but by 1948 the country had been totally absorbed into the communist bloc. Stamps of 1945 marked the first anniversary of the

independence of Latvia was recognized by the USSR on 9 September 1991. Soviet stamps were overprinted and surcharged [13], augmenting an arms series issued shortly before [14]. Since then Latvian stamps have covered a wide range of modern themes [15].

LITHUANIA

Having proclaimed its independence in February 1918, Lithuania cast around for a German prince suitable to become king, but monarchy was on the wane and in November 1918 a republic was declared. Following some typeset stamps, Lithuania obtained stamps from Berlin [16] followed in 1921 by a series designed and printed in Kaunas [17].

A major setback was the invasion of Central Lithuania by a Polish volunteer corps under General Zeligowski. Stamps inscribed in Polish were issued in 1920–2 [18] before the area around Vilnius was annexed by Poland. When Poland was invaded and dismembered in 1939, Lithuania's share was the return to it of Vilnius, celebrated by an overprint on the stamps marking the 20th anniversary of independence [19]. In exchange, however, Lithuania had to accept a Soviet garrison and in August 1940 it was absorbed by the Soviet Union.

Independence was declared on 11 March 1990, but was not recognized by the Russians until 6 September 1991. The majority of stamps issued since then have been lithographed in Leipzig or Berlin, often emphasizing

Below: One of a series of stamps issued by North Ingermanland in 1920 shows a church burned down by Bolsheviks.

Still in Business

Many of Lithuania's prewar stamps were printed in Kaunas (the temporary capital) by the firm of Spindulys. Despite expropriation and nationalization under communist rule the company managed to survive and had the honour of printing the first stamps of the restored republic, but as it lacked a perforator the stamps had to be cut apart. In a subsequent printing, grey dots were added to simulate the perforations.

the country's long history. Annual issues have portrayed the men who signed the original declaration of independence in 1918 [20].

The overall character of the stamps since the restoration of sovereignty has been to catch up on the historic events and major figures denied philatelic recognition during the Soviet period [21]. The distinctive character of the country is also reflected in the long-running series devoted to provincial costumes, while illustrations from the Red Book of Lithuania cover the country's endangered fauna and flora.

NORTH INGERMANLAND

This territory north of Estonia briefly won its freedom from Russia in 1919–20 and issued its own stamps. The first series was closely modelled on contemporary Finnish stamps but was soon followed by a bicoloured pictorial set that alluded to outrages committed by the Bolsheviks. By the Treaty of Dorpat (Estonia), North Ingermanland reverted to Russia in October 1920.

1

2

3

4

5

6

7

8

9

10

11

12

RUSSIA

The world's largest country, Russia attained its greatest size, estimated at 22.5 million sq km/8.6 million sq miles, before the revolution of 1917. The loss of Finland, the Baltic States and eastern Poland in 1918–19 reduced it by 780,000 sq km/300,000 sq miles, but Stalin all but made that good by 1945. Even today, the Russian Federation, shorn of 14 of the republics that formerly made up the Soviet Union, still stretches from the Baltic to the Pacific, occupying the northern part of Europe and Asia. This vast, sprawling country of many different nationalities, languages and cultures, developed over two centuries. Its disastrous involvement in World War I

brought down the monarchy, and a moderate socialist republic was soon overthrown by the Bolsheviks led by Lenin, founder of the communist regime that endured for 70 years.

Left: Vladimir Ilyich Ulyanov, known as Lenin, was the Marxist revolutionary who led the Bolsheviks to power in 1917. Numerous stamps were issued from his death in 1924 onwards. This stamp of 1953, marking the 29th anniversary of his death, shows him during the October Revolution.

FALL OF THE TSARIST EMPIRE
Russia adopted adhesive stamps in 1858, having relied on pre-stamped envelopes since 1845. The format of the Russian stamps [1] was much smaller than that adopted by Britain and other countries and, indeed, has survived to this day. Variations on the theme of imperial arms continued up to the October Revolution of 1917, but in 1913 the Romanov dynasty celebrated its tercentenary with a portrait gallery of tsars from Michael I to the ill-starred Nicholas II [2], who abdicated in March 1917.

The Bolsheviks seized power in November 1917 and created the Russian Socialist Federal Soviet Republic (RSFSR). Tsarist stamps were overprinted with a hammer and sickle within a star and surcharged to cope with inflation [3]. Distinctive stamps symbolized revolution and liberty [4] and commemorated the fifth anniversary of the revolution [5]. Images of soldiers, workers and peasants [7] replaced tsarist symbols.

Civil war broke out in 1918 and dragged on until 1922. It was remembered philatelically by the ephemeral issues of breakaway governments from the Crimea to the Far East and the armies of Denikin, Wrangel, Avalov-Bermondt and others [8].

UNION OF SOVIET SOCIALIST REPUBLICS
Before his death in 1924 Lenin had clawed back a considerable part of the former empire, which had broken away at the revolution. In July 1923 he formed the Union of Socialist Soviet Republics, joining the RSFSR to the Ukraine, Belorussia and Transcaucasia. The Uzbek and Turkmen republics were added in 1924, the Tajik in 1929 and the Kazakh and Kirghiz republic in 1936. In 1940 Stalin added the Baltic States.

Following Lenin's death in January 1924 a set of four mourning stamps [9] appeared, and was reissued annually on the anniversary of his death until 1929. Lenin also appeared in many of the subsequent definitive sets, as well as countless special issues thereafter that formed part of the massive personality cult that grew up around him. By contrast, Stalin, his successor, appeared only twice – alongside Lenin on stamps marking the 10th and 20th anniversaries of the latter's death. For much of the Soviet period stamps were extremely propagandistic and introspective, either continually exhorting the workers to do better or trumpeting Soviet achievements, such as the mass flight over the North Pole in 1937–8 [10].

After the outbreak of the Great Patriotic War (set in motion by the German invasion of the USSR in 1941), the majority of stamps extolled the feats of Soviet heroes. However, a rare example of Soviet recognition of the Anglo-American contribution to the war effort came with two stamps of 1943 marking the 26th anniversary of the revolution and the Tehran Conference [6].

The issue of small-format definitives continued unabated from 1929 [11] to the 1960s [12] and beyond. In the post-Stalinist era stamps broadened in scope, noting cultural celebrities of other lands. The USSR was the first country to honour Scotland's national poet, Robert Burns, with a stamp in 1956 on the 160th anniversary of his death [13]. By the 1960s multicolour offset lithography went hand in hand with a more thematic approach and the Soviet Union's participation in international sporting events of the era [15], combined with occasional reminders of the Cold War [16].

RUSSIAN FEDERATION

One of the last issues of the USSR appeared in October 1991 and honoured heroes who helped defeat the attempted coup by communist hardliners [14]. By that time the Baltic States had declared independence and the USSR itself was formally dissolved on 29 December. Since January 1992 stamps have been inscribed "Rossija" and its Cyrillic equivalent. A small-format horizontal definitive series featured landmarks from the tsarist era [17] while special issues ranged from the splendours of old Russian decorative art [18] to wildlife [19] and children's cartoons [20]. Space achievements continued to rank high [21] and included a stamp celebrating a joint Russian–German space flight [22]. The

Stamps As Money
During World War I there was an acute shortage of small silver coins so the government reprinted the Romanov commemoratives of 1913 on cardboard with inscriptions on the reverse signifying their validity as coins.

500th anniversary of the discovery of America by Columbus was marked by a stamp showing the Stars and Stripes and the new Russian flag – actually the old tsarist flag revived.

Under the Soviet regime more than 6,000 stamps were issued, but in the years since the collapse of communism a more moderate policy has been pursued, omitting the political propaganda of the former era. Instead, like other former communist states, Russia has been engaging on a catching-up exercise, honouring personalities and anniversaries that would have been forbidden previously. Numerous sets in the past decade have extolled the glories and achievements of the tsarist period, culminating in the 3r stamp of 1998 commemorating the 80th anniversary of the death of Tsar Nicholas II. This stamp was issued with a *se-tenant* label portraying the entire royal family, murdered by the Bolsheviks at Ekaterinburg in 1918. Other issues have portrayed Peter the Great, notably the series of 2003 for the tercentenary of St Petersburg.

COMMONWEALTH OF INDEPENDENT STATES

The Commonwealth of Independent States was the name applied by Mikhail Gorbachev to the countries that emerged from the break-up of the USSR in 1991. In fact, the notion that the republics of the former Soviet Union would present any kind of image of solidarity was soon dispelled as the Ukraine came to the brink of war with Russia over the Crimea and numerous ethnic groups, from Abkhazia to Chechnya and Nagorno-Karabakh, attempted to secede and form independent states. Apart from the Baltic States only the Ukraine and the Caucasian republics had a previous existence as independent countries issuing their own stamps.

Left: The Ukrainian Soviet Republic was proclaimed in March 1919 and allied itself with the RSFSR in 1920. In July 1923 it became one of the constituents of the Soviet Union. Its only stamps were a set of June 1923 with premiums in aid of famine relief.

CAUCASIAN REPUBLICS

A national republic was proclaimed in May 1918 and used tsarist stamps overprinted with a national emblem. In March 1922 Armenia joined the Transcaucasian Federation and in this period issued stamps showing Mount Ararat [1] and other scenery. Since September 1991, when it declared independence, most of its stamps have been printed in England [2].

Briefly a national republic (May 1918 to April 1920) Azerbaijan became a Soviet republic when Red Army troops invaded. In this period it released a set for famine relief [3] before joining the Transcaucasian Federation in March 1922. Independence was declared on August 18, 1991, unissued stamps showing the Caspian Sea being overprinted [4]. Since then Azerbaijan has embarked on many "bandwagon" issues for John Lennon, Princess Diana and other international celebrities.

Nakhichevan, an Azerbaijani enclave entirely surrounded by Armenia, had its own government from 1924. It briefly had its own stamps in 1993 showing a map and portrait of President Aliev, who later became president of Azerbaijan itself [5].

Georgia was a national republic from May 1918 until February 1921 and in that time issued stamps showing St George [6]. It then became a Soviet republic and joined the Transcaucasian Federation, issuing stamps overprinted for famine relief in 1922 [7]. It regained its independence on April 9, 1991, and issued stamps originally inscribed "Gruzija" [8] but titled "Georgia" since 1993 [9].

When the Transcaucasian Federation was formed in 1922 each state continued to issue its own stamps until September 1923, when a general issue appeared [10]. These stamps were superseded by those of the USSR in 1924 and 70 years elapsed before separate issues were resumed.

WESTERN REPUBLICS

The political history of the Ukraine was broadly parallel to that of the Caucasus, with a national republic from January 1918 to March 1919. Most of the stamps issued in this period were tsarist stamps overprinted with the Ukrainian trident, and many variations of this appeared in different towns [11]. History repeated itself when the Ukraine declared its independence in

August 1991, with various trident over-prints on the Soviet definitives [12]. Many of the stamps issued since then have been printed in Canada [13].

Neither Belarus nor Moldova had a previous philatelic existence, although they were constituent republics of the USSR, previously known as Belorussia (White Russia) and Moldavia (whose name was changed to avoid confusion with the Romanian province of that name). They became fully independent in August and December 1991 respectively, although Moldova had previously asserted its sovereignty within the Soviet Union in 1990 and its first stamps celebrated the first anniversary [14]. Subsequently Soviet stamps were overprinted [15] pending the issue of stamps printed in Bulgaria, Hungary or Spain. The stamps of Belarus were printed in Moscow [16] but are now produced locally in Minsk.

ASIAN REPUBLICS
The remaining republics, which entered the stamp album only in the 1990s, were all within the territory formerly known as Soviet Central Asia.

Below: These stamps issued in 1992 were among the first independent issues by the former Soviet Central Asian states Turkmenistan and Uzbekistan.

A Feeling of Déjà Vu
The only distinctive stamps of the national republic of the Ukraine were those in a set of July 1918 showing the head of Ceres and various national emblems. After the Ukraine regained independence in 1991, the Ceres design was revived in a reduced size for the definitive series of 1992.

Kazakhstan declared independence in December 1991 and has had its stamps produced in Vienna [17], Paris, Berlin, Budapest, Oslo and Leipzig. Kyrgyzstan became independent in September 1991. Most of its stamps have been printed in Moscow [18].

Tajikistan asserted its sovereignty on 25 August 1990, and its independence on 9 September 1991, producing its own stamps from May 1992 [19]. Turkmenistan became independent on 27 October 1991, and issued a stamp portraying President Niyazov and the national flag to mark its first anniversary. Uzbekistan declared its sovereignty on 20 June 1990, and became independent in August 1991. In matters of stamp production it has remained faithful to Moscow.

PROVISIONAL ISSUES
In 1992–4 there was a tremendous flood of local provisional issues in the territories of the former Soviet Union, allegedly produced by the regional postal authorities during a period of political and economic turmoil, when postal rates rose sharply and there was an acute shortage of stamps. Apart from the definitives overprinted at St Petersburg, most of these have been ignored by the standard catalogues.

ALBANIA

The Balkans were the most unstable part of Europe in the late 19th and 20th centuries. The political upheavals of the dying years of the Turkish Empire, and the struggles between the various ethnic groups that continue today, are reflected in the bewildering array of stamps marking liberation from Turkish rule and the intervention of various European powers, as well as the rivalries of the different nationalities. Nowhere was this truer than in Albania, one of the most remote and backward outposts of the Ottoman Empire, where most of the inhabitants were Muslim and divided into two main tribes, the Ghegs and Tosks, but with large minorities of Greeks in the south and Slavs in the north and east.

Left: A pair of stamps marked the first anniversary of the death of Mikel Koliqi, the first Albanian cardinal, in 1998.

INDEPENDENCE, INVASION AND ISOLATION

During the First Balkan War, Albania declared its independence of Turkey. Its first stamps, issued in June 1913, were contemporary Turkish stamps overprinted "Shqipenia" (Albania) with the double-headed eagle. When these ran out, the Albanians resorted to makeshifts produced by typewriting and various rubber handstamps [1].

In February 1914 the provisional government invited a German prince, William of Wied, to be king. Stamps bearing his portrait were printed in Austria but never issued as such [2], and William returned to Germany when war broke out in August. Albania was a battleground between opposing forces in World War I, but for a time (1914–16) Essad Pasha ruled Central Albania until he was driven out by the Austrians [3]. In December 1916 French troops invaded from Salonika and established the autonomous province of Koritsa, which lasted until the French withdrew in 1920 [4].

A provisional government under Turhan Bey was established at Shkoder (Scutari) in December 1918, backed by an inter-allied commission to protect Albania from the Serbs. Austrian revenue stamps were overprinted and used until 1920 [5]. A regency was created at Shkoder in February 1920, continuing until January 1925. Ironically its first stamps were those of Prince William with the portrait obscured [6].

In December 1924 the national assembly voted for a republic and Ahmed Zogu Bey was elected president. The overprint signifies the return of the government to Tirana [7]. In 1928 the assembly voted for a return to a hereditary monarchy and elected the president, who took the title of King Zog I, the last republican series being appropriately overprinted [8].

On 7 April 1939, Italian troops invaded Albania and ousted Zog. Soon afterwards Victor Emmanuel III of Italy was proclaimed king of Albania [9]. The surrender of Italy in 1943 created a vacuum in the Balkans that was soon filled by the Germans. Stamps overprinted "14 Shtator 1943" (14 September) marked the German occupation [10]. Albanian partisans led by Enver Hoxha drove out the Germans and declared the Democratic State of Albania on 22 October 1944 [11]. The constituent assembly declared Albania a people's republic on 11 January 1946, effecting the country's 12th change of status in 35 years [12].

The doctrinaire communism of the Hoxha era was reflected in stamps portraying Marx, Lenin and Stalin [13] or showing wartime partisans and the triumph of socialism. Stereotyped motifs were not enhanced by the poor quality of the printing. From 1961, however, a more thematic approach was adopted in a bid to earn hard currency, and numerous sets featured birds, flowers, wild animals, cattle, dogs and other popular subjects. At the same time, Albania's gradual emergence from self-imposed isolation as the last bastion of Stalinism in Europe was reflected in stamps marking participation in the Olympic Games and other sporting contests. As the quality of printing improved, numerous sets reproduced paintings, mosaics and sculpture.

On 29 April 1991, Albania cast off communism and became a democratic republic. This change has been reflected in stamps honouring personalities and events banned in the communist era. Another sign of the times is the production of stamps in recent years by Alex Matsoukis, the leading Greek stamp printer.

ITALIAN POST OFFICES
In the closing years of Turkish rule Italy operated post offices in Albania, using Italian stamps overprinted "Albania" [14] or the names of the principal towns of Durazzo [15], Janina [16], Scutari [17] and Valona [18], but surcharged in Turkish currency. The last of them, in Scutari and Valona, were closed in 1918 but the Italians maintained a toehold in Albania, having occupied the island of Sazan (Saseno)

Below: A number of stamps were printed locally during the Greek occupation of southern Albania during World War II. This issue from the town of Erseka was based on the Greek flag.

Handstruck Stamps
The oddest of the Epirus provisionals was the set of four produced by Greek insurgents at Chimara in February 1914, with the skull and crossbones and the countermark of the area commander.

in the Gulf of Valona in October 1914 and remained there until 1943. Stamps were issued in 1923 [19].

GREEK OCCUPATIONS
In 1913 the European powers decided that Epirus should form part of Albania, but the mainly Greek population thought otherwise and rose in revolt. A provisional government was established in 1914 and stamps showing a rifleman were printed in Corfu [20] followed by stamps showing the double-headed eagle and Greek cross flag, overprinted at Koritsa [21]. Other issues were produced at Moschopolis [22] and other towns, including a set showing the Greek flag. In December 1914 the powers agreed that Greece should occupy the territory that had declared its independence, which was now renamed Northern Epirus. Greek stamps thus overprinted were in use from then until June 1916, when the region was occupied by Italian troops and returned to Albania in 1919.

In 1939 Italy seized Albania and from here the invasion of Greece was mounted in October 1940. However, the Greeks counterattacked and not only drove the invaders out but pursued them into southern Albania. Greek stamps overprinted to signify "Greek Occupation" were in use in Epirus until April 1941 [23].

12

13

14

15

16

17

18

19

20

21

22

23

BULGARIA AND ROMANIA

The countries bordering the Black Sea's west coast were important powers in the Middle Ages, but succumbed to Turkish rule until the 19th century. Moldavia and Wallachia united to form the kingdom of Romania in 1881. The principality of Bulgaria, created by the Congress of Berlin in 1878, remained under Turkish suzerainty until independence in 1908.

Left: After 1878 Bulgaria south of the Balkan Mountains remained under the Turks, who produced stamps for use in Eastern Roumelia, as this area was called. In 1885 the people rebelled and declared the state of South Bulgaria, overprinting stamps before uniting with the north.

KINGDOM AND PRINCIPALITY

The Danubian principalities of Moldavia and Wallachia [1] gained autonomy in 1858, later uniting to form Romania under local hero Prince Alexander Cuza. In 1866 he was forced to abdicate in favour of a German aristocrat, Prince Karl of Hohenzollern-Sigmaringen [2], who proclaimed himself King Carol I in 1881. In 1906 Romania celebrated Carol's 40 years on the throne by issuing no fewer than 43 stamps, including one of the earliest charity (semi-postal) sets showing Queen Elisabeth – better known as the poet Carmen Sylva – spinning, weaving and tending a wounded soldier [3].

The principality of Bulgaria, though nominally under Turkish suzerainty, was politically and economically dependent on Russia and France, as reflected in the centime currency of the first stamps [4]. Prince Ferdinand of Saxe-Coburg was chosen by the European powers to rule the principality, shown on the stamps of 1901. He assumed the title of tsar in 1909, reviving Bulgaria's ambitions to dominate the Balkans [5].

BALKAN WARS AND WORLD WAR I

Bulgaria achieved its greatest extent as a result of the First Balkan War of 1912–13, adding Western Thrace, which gave it access to the Aegean.

Stamps overprinted at the time [7] referred to it as a war of liberation, but it triggered off a second war in which Bulgaria faced its erstwhile allies Greece and Serbia and was shorn of Thrace, which went to Greece. Resentment at this led to Bulgaria's alignment with Germany and its old enemy Turkey in World War I. A set of stamps was projected in 1915, when Bulgaria again briefly occupied Macedonia and the Dobrudja, but was not actually issued until 1921 [6].

Romania entered World War I on the Allied side in 1916 but suffered heavy losses in 1917–18. Its reward, however, was the cession by Hungary of Transylvania, for which Romania overprinted Hungarian stamps at Cluj and Oradea in 1919 [8]. During the war Romania was largely overrun by troops of the Central Powers, and stamps were issued or overprinted by Austria, Bulgaria and Germany for those areas under their control [9–11].

THE SHADOW OF FASCISM

Both Bulgaria and Romania embraced fascism in the 1930s and were allied to Germany in World War II. In 1930 Boris III married Princess Giovanna of Italy, a political marriage that drew Bulgaria into Mussolini's orbit [12].

In Romania six-year-old King Michael succeeded his grandfather Ferdinand in July 1927. He was shown on the definitive series of 1928 [13], but abdicated in favour of his father Carol II, who had been passed over on account of his turbulent private life. He gained the throne in 1930 as a result of a coup but was forced to abdicate in 1940 [14]. Michael became king a second time and played a major role in the overthrow of the fascist dictatorship of Antonescu in 1944. Although Romania was occupied by the Red Army Michael held on to his throne until the end of 1947, when Romania became a people's republic [15].

Bulgaria changed sides when it was occupied by the Red Army in 1944 but remained a kingdom under the boy king Simeon [19] until September 15, 1946.

RISE OF COMMUNISM

For a brief period Bulgarian stamps were simply inscribed "Republic" [16] but soon it was officially styled a people's republic, denoted by the inscription "Narodna Republika", later shortened to "N.R." The communist propaganda of the early issues soon gave way to a revival of national pride in Bulgaria's long history [17]. Communism never supplanted the Orthodox faith, which was reflected in numerous stamps featuring monasteries and religious art [18].

As everywhere else in the communist bloc, early issues in both countries were dominated by propaganda, but by

Below: For The Europa Tales and Legends theme (1997), Romania depicted Dracula and Vlad the Impaler.

The Times Correspondent
In 1921 the first Englishman to appear on a foreign stamp was James D. Bourchier, the Balkans correspondent of *The Times*, whose despatches in 1877 helped to influence public opinion in favour of the Bulgars.

the 1960s a more liberal policy was in force. Romania played a prominent part in publicizing international cultural figures such as Shakespeare [20]. This policy has continued to the present day, especially since the overthrow of the Ceausescus in 1989 and the restoration of democracy. Stamps of 1999 portrayed Charlie Chaplin as well as Laurel and Hardy [21].

In the wake of the collapse of communism in eastern Europe, Bulgaria became a democratic republic on 15 November 1990. There was no change in the stamps, which had long since shed the "N.R." inscription and adopted bilingual captions.

12

13

14

15

16

17

18

19

20

21

1

2

3

4

5

6

7

8

9

10

FORMER YUGOSLAVIA

The kingdom of Yugoslavia was an artificial creation of the Allied Powers at the end of World War I. At its core was the kingdom of Serbia, a Turkish province from 1458 until 1804, then an autonomous principality under Turkish suzerainty until its independence was proclaimed by the Treaty of Berlin in 1878. It was closely allied to the tiny principality of Montenegro, which, alone of the Christian areas in the Balkans, retained its independence after the collapse of the Byzantine Empire in 1453.

Left: The first special issue of the new kingdom in 1921 was a set of three charity stamps for the disabled soldiers' fund. This stamp reproduced Uros Predic's painting of the Kosovo Maiden tending a wounded man on the battlefield in 1389.

SERBIA

While Montenegro had been ruled by a prince-bishop, Serbia was headed by one or other of two rival clans. In 1866, when stamps were introduced, the nation was ruled by Prince Michael Obrenovich [1], whose father Milosh had ousted Kara Georg (Black George). Michael was murdered in 1868 and succeeded by his nephew Milan, who proclaimed himself king in 1882 and abdicated in 1889. His son, Alexander I, succeeded him and reigned until 1903, when he and his consort were brutally murdered by a group of officers. This atrocity brought to the throne Peter, grandson of Kara Georg, whose first stamps were those portraying his luckless predecessor with the portrait blotted out by the royal arms [2]. Peter commanded the Serbian army in the Balkan Wars and the opening campaign of World War I [3].

Although Serbia was overrun by the Central Powers, the Serbian army managed to escape to Corfu, where it used French stamps overprinted [4] – the first instance of a postal service in exile. The Serbs shared this misfortune with their Montenegrin allies.

MONTENEGRO

In contrast with the bloody history of Serbia, Montenegro was ruled for 60 years by Prince Nikita and fought in the Russo-Turkish War (1877–8) and the Balkan Wars. Stamps were introduced in 1874 but to Montenegro goes the credit for issuing the first commemorative stamps by a European government, celebrating the 400th anniversary of printing, in January 1893 [5]. These overprints on the definitive series were followed in 1896 by a long set marking the bicentenary of the Petrovich dynasty [7]. Nikita proclaimed himself king in 1910 [8] but in 1919 he fled to the French Riviera where he died in 1921.

KINGDOM OF THE SERBS, CROATS AND SLOVENES

Nikita's kingdom merged with the new state that was known originally as the Kingdom of the Serbs, Croats and Slovenes. These peoples had been ruled by Hungary and Austria respectively. The kingdom also included part of Macedonia, a melting-pot that had been fought over by Serbia, Greece and Bulgaria in the second Balkan War (and which remains a bone of contention with Greece to this day).

They were joined by Bosnia and Herzegovina, Turkish provinces that had been occupied by Austria-Hungary in 1878. Their early stamps did not even bear a name, the Habsburg arms being sufficient identification [6]. The names (in German) briefly appeared in a pictorial series of 1906 [10] but during World War I an inscription

The Death Mask Stamps

A few months after the murder of Alexander I in 1903, Peter I celebrated his coronation and the centenary of the Karageorgevich dynasty with a set of stamps engraved and printed in France. They showed the conjoined profiles of Kara Georg and Peter but when they were turned upside down people imagined they could see the death mask of the murdered king. The stamps were hastily withdrawn from use as a result.

signifying the Royal and Imperial Military Post was substituted. To this period belongs the set of three stamps issued in 1917 in memory of Archduke Franz Ferdinand and his wife Sophie Chotek, whose assassination by Serb terrorists in June 1914 triggered off World War I [11].

At the end of that war the stamps of Bosnia and Herzegovina were overprinted "Država S.H.S." in Roman or Cyrillic lettering [12] to denote the union of Serbs, Croats and Slovenes. Hungarian stamps overprinted "Hrvatska S.H.S." were used in Croatia [9], pending the introduction of an Art Nouveau series [13]. Slovenia had a series of stamps popularly known as the Chainbreakers [14], as well as long vertical stamps with allegorical themes [15] or a portrait of King Peter [16]. A general issue for the whole kingdom, recess-printed by the American Banknote Company, appeared in 1921, portraying Peter or his son Alexander, who succeeded him that August [17]. A definitive series of 1926–7 portraying King Alexander [18] was printed in Belgrade from plates made in Austria.

YUGOSLAVIA

The name of the kingdom was changed to Yugoslavia ("land of the southern Slavs") in October 1929, in a desperate bid to hold together this ramshackle conglomeration of different religious, linguistic and ethnic groups. King Alexander realized that attempts at democratic institutions had failed and that the only solution was to impose a dictatorship based on fascist models. At the same time, strenuous attempts were made to give the different nationalities parity at all levels and this is reflected in the stamps.

The first issue of the new regime, in fact, celebrated the millennium of the ancient kingdom of Croatia; on two of the stamps King Tomislav, the first ruler of the kingdom in the 10th century, was portrayed alongside Alexander (who named his younger son after the medieval Croat hero). The stamps were released on 1 November 1929, and had obviously been designed and engraved before the political change; it was not until April 1931 that stamps inscribed "Kraljevina Yugoslavija" appeared. Commemoratives of the early 1930s highlighted events or anniversaries in Serbia and Croatia in equal measure. A new definitive series appeared in 1931 showing a facing portrait of Alexander in military uniform.

Alexander's policies, however, failed to appease growing demands from Croat separatists. Just after the fifth anniversary of the united kingdom Alexander was assassinated during a state visit to Marseilles. The entire definitive series was re-issued a few days later with a heavy black border [19] in mourning for the murdered king.

Alexander was succeeded by his 11-year-old elder son Peter. Peter had made his philatelic debut the previous year in the uniform of Sokol, a physical training and sports organization, to mark its meeting in Ljubljana [21]. A definitive series portraying the boy king appeared in 1935 [20], while a grown-up portrait of him appeared on the last definitives of prewar Yugoslavia, in 1939–40 [22].

1

2

3

4

5

6

7

8

9

10

YUGOSLAVIA: DIVISION, RECONSTRUCTION AND CIVIL WAR

As a country of peoples of widely differing linguistic, cultural, historic, religious and ethnic backgrounds, Yugoslavia was ruthlessly held together by strong men – King Alexander before World War II and Marshal Tito after it. Without such figures, it was bound to fall apart, first due to external threat and latterly due to implosion. As ancient rivalries between Serbia and Croatia surfaced, religious or racial tensions involving the Slovenes, Macedonians and Kosovar Albanians erupted into violent warfare, bringing a new expression – "ethnic cleansing", a euphemism for genocide – into common parlance.

Left: After being occupied by the Germans, the Yugoslavs freed themselves thanks to the partisans led by Josip Broz Tito, who formed the communist government that ruled the country until the 1990s.

WARTIME OCCUPATION

On 6 April 1941, Yugoslavia was invaded by German, Italian, Hungarian and Bulgarian forces. The Yugoslavs surrendered 11 days later and their country was dismembered by the invading powers. Germany annexed Lower Styria and Italy grabbed the rest of Slovenia, while also adding to the territory it had previously gained from the invasion of Albania. Hungary acquired territory north of the Sava and Bulgaria acquired those parts of Macedonia that Serbia had seized in 1914. Yugoslav stamps were overprinted by the Italians for use in Lubiana [1], but when Italy changed sides the Germans seized this area and overprinted Italian stamps with the German name of Laibach [2].

The rest of Yugoslavia was partitioned into three states. Croatia was nominally a kingdom but was ruled by the *poglavnik* (dictator) Ante Pavelich. Yugoslav stamps were overprinted with the Croat arms [3] followed by definitives portraying Pavelich [4]. The Croat Legion fought on the Eastern Front [5]. Montenegro used Yugoslav stamps overprinted by the Italians and later the Germans, while Serbia became a puppet state [6].

As in World War I, a government in exile was formed abroad, and distinctive stamps keeping alive the name of Yugoslavia were produced in England for the use of the Yugoslav Merchant Navy working with the Allies [7].

YUGOSLAVIA RECONSTITUTED

Resistance to the enemy was split between two movements: the royalist Chetniks under Draza Mihailovic and the communist Partisans led by Josip Broz, known as Tito. The latter triumphed in 1943; the Chetniks (often accused of collaborating with the Nazis) were discredited, and the communists seized power. Stamps of wartime Serbia and Montenegro were overprinted in December 1944 to signify the Democratic Federation of Yugoslavia [8], composed of the six republics of Serbia, Croatia, Slovenia, Montenegro, Bosnia–Herzegovina and Macedonia, with the federal territory of Kosovo, whose inhabitants were predominantly Albanian.

As everywhere else in the communist bloc, the early stamps were heavily politicized, a notable exception being those of 1948 marking the 80th anniversary of the death of Laurenz

Kosir, the "ideological creator" of the postage stamp. He had proposed the use of adhesive stamps some years before Rowland Hill but his recommendation was merely filed away. By the 1960s, however, a more thematic approach, with stamps featuring wildlife, flowers and Adriatic resorts, reflected an appreciation of the global stamp market and tourism as major sources of hard currency [9].

Obligatory tax stamps (with corresponding postage due labels for mail not bearing these stamps) were a recurring feature of the post-war years. Popular annual issues included stamps for Children's Week, while Yugoslavia was the first communist country to introduce Christmas stamps, in 1966.

A set of stamps marking Tito's 75th birthday in 1967 was retained and expanded as a definitive series, followed in 1971–3 by a long series featuring landmarks and scenery.

COLLAPSE OF COMMUNISM

The collapse of communism in 1991 led to the fragmentation of the Federation, and Croatia and Slovenia seceded in May and June respectively. Both were invaded by Serbia and for a time separate issues of stamps appeared in Kraina [10] and the Baranjska Oblast. Most of the early stamps of Croatia were obligatory tax stamps to raise money for national defence, but by 1993 stamps reflected global events and personalities [11]. This pattern was also followed by Slovenia, beginning with definitives featuring the national emblem [14] but soon paying tribute to UNICEF [13] and the United Nations for its support, or providing colourful images of international appeal.

Bosnia and Herzegovina declared independence in April 1992 and armorial stamps were issued by the Sarajevo government [12]. The country was soon embroiled in war, being fought over by Croats and Serbs, each issuing their own stamps. Recent issues from the Sarajevo government include a stamp for the AIDS appeal.

Diana Remembered

Following the tragic death of Diana, Princess of Wales, in 1997, Bosnia and Herzegovina issued a stamp in her memory. It was a reminder of her work for the eradication of landmines and of the visit she made to the war-torn country shortly before her death. The design featured an informal photograph of the princess in Sarajevo, with red roses and a map of Bosnia in the background.

Following a referendum, Macedonia declared its independence in September 1991. A high proportion of its stamps were for compulsory use, to raise funds for the Red Cross, or emphasizing the cultural identity of this ancient country [15] – a matter that has caused a major rift with neighbouring Greece.

SERBIA AND MONTENEGRO

Stamps inscribed "Yugoslavia" continued to be issued in Serbia and Montenegro, generally carrying on the colourful but bland policy of catering to the international market, but occasionally making a political point, such as the Destroyed Bridges series and Bombed Buildings pair of 1999, lashing out at NATO [16–17]. During this period, however, obligatory stamps were regularly produced for Serbia alone and thus inscribed [18].

The fiction of Yugoslavia ended in 2003 when stamps inscribed "Serbia and Montenegro" were introduced. Designs for these combine the image of a country striving to fit in with the international community [20] with a constant harking back to the glories of medieval times [19].

GREECE

The Greeks had been part of the Ottoman Empire since the fall of the Byzantine Empire in 1453, but in 1821 they rebelled and began a ten-year War of Independence in which Britain, France and Russia allied to defeat the Turks. In 1833 the European Powers selected Prince Otto of Bavaria to be King of the Hellenes, but he was deposed in 1862 and Prince William of Schleswig-Holstein-Sonderburg-Glucksburg replaced him, taking the title of George I.

Left: In 2004 the modern Olympic Games returned to Athens, where they had first been held in 1896. Numerous sets of Greek stamps publicized the Games ahead of the event and several others were issued during and after the Olympics.

CLASSICAL TRADITIONS
Stamps were introduced in Greece in 1861 [1]. Until 1911 all definitives portrayed Hermes, messenger of the gods, in various forms, and even thereafter a high proportion of stamps have drawn on the rich store of classical mythology and art. From 1927 onwards different motifs were used for the various definitive issues, and the vast majority were devoted to the glories of Ancient Greece. The 1935–9 airmails focused on mythological characters, while the airmails of 1942–3 drew on the spirits of the various winds. This tradition continues, as can be seen in the sets illustrating the labours of Hercules [3] or the 1988 definitives portraying the Olympian gods [4]. Even modern events and institutions are commemorated by designs that seek a parallel from the classical period.

BALKAN WARS
In the first hundred years of independence Greece doubled its territory. Britain ceded the Ionian Islands in 1864 and Crete (after a period of autonomy within the Turkish Empire but under Anglo-Russian administration) gradually passed into Greek hands after 1906 [2]. The largest accretion came in the Balkan Wars of 1912–13, which not only confirmed possession of Crete but also gave Greece western Thrace [5] and many Aegean islands,

such as Lemnos [6] and Samos [7]. In the second Balkan War Greece took Dedeagatz from Bulgaria [8].

Several compulsory tax stamps were issued in this period to raise money for war wounded and widows and orphans [9]. After World War I Greece seized eastern Thrace [10] but had to cede it to Turkey in 1922. This crushing defeat toppled the monarchy, marked by the overprint "Epanastasis" (Revolution), applied ironically to the remaining Victory stamps of 1913 [11]. Attempts to take over the Dodecanese Islands from Turkey in 1912 were foiled by the Italians, who held them until 1944.

MONARCHY RESTORED
The monarchy was restored in November 1935, signalled by the date and crown overprinted on all stamps then current [12]. During the period of the first republic Greece celebrated its centenary of independence with a long set portraying the heroes of that struggle [13]. Previously, two stamps of 1924 had marked the centenary of the death of Lord Byron at Missolonghi [14], and a 1927 set honoured the centenary of the naval battle at Navarino when the combined fleets of Britain, France and Russia defeated the Turks.

Preparing to invade Greece in October 1940, Mussolini issued an ultimatum, to which the Greeks replied with a resounding "Oxi!" (No!); this was

Eating His Words

In 1907 Winston Churchill, then Under-Secretary of State for the Colonies, visited Cyprus and said: "I think it is only natural that the Cypriot people who are of Greek descent should regard their incorporation with what may be called their mother country as an ideal to be earnestly, devoutly and fervently cherished…" When Britain refused the Greek Cypriot demands for *enosis* (unification with Greece) in 1954 his speech was quoted by Mrs Lena Jeger in a House of Commons debate on July 28. The relevant page from *Hansard* (the report of parliamentary proceedings) was reproduced on a set of Greek stamps, with a symbolic black blot across the middle.

the subject of two stamps on its fifth anniversary [15]. When the Italians invaded, the Greeks chased them all the way back to the Adriatic.

Coming to the aid of their allies, the Germans invaded Greece in April 1941. The royal family fled to Cairo, and Greece endured four years of occupation and privation that shattered the economy and reduced the population to starvation level. The currency collapsed and Greece suffered inflation, which was reflected in stamps that ran up to 5 million drachmae in 1944 [17]. A regency headed by Archbishop Damaskinos continued to September 1946, when a plebiscite voted to restore the monarchy.

POSTWAR PERIOD

Greece was one of the few countries to mourn the death of Franklin D. Roosevelt with an issue of stamps [16]. Although the royalist government was pro-western, a powerful communist movement arose out of the wartime partisans, which led to a long-running civil war that was reflected in several issues. A stamp of 1949 showing a column of women and children alluded to the abduction of Greek children to the neighbouring communist countries of Albania and Bulgaria [18].

From 1968 onwards Greek stamps were inscribed "Hellas", the Roman version of the country name, to conform to Universal Postal Union regulations insisting that countries should be identified in the universally recognized alphabet. In 1967 a military junta seized power, but apart from a set of 1972 marking the fifth anniversary of the revolution, the regime made little impact on stamps. In 1973 King Constantine II attempted a countercoup and when this failed he fled to Italy. The monarchy was abolished in his absence on June 1, 1973.

These political upheavals had remarkably little effect on the stamps, which continued to lean heavily on classical subjects. If anything, references to the glories of Ancient Greece have tended to increase in recent years, as suitable motifs derived from Hellenistic civilization are found for many subjects, from the Greek presidency of the EU (the allegorical figure of Hellas driving her chariot) to the second Pan-European Transport Conference (Hermes leading Selene's chariot). In addition to a wider use of the most popular themes [19] many very recent stamps have given prominence to the Macedon of Philip II and Alexander the Great [20] as a counter to the independent republic of Macedonia. Icons are a popular subject for Christmas stamps in general but especially for the Millennium series of 2000 [21], showing the birth of Christ. Greece issues Europa stamps each year in the prevailing theme [22].

1

2

3

4

5

6

7

8

9

10

TURKEY

Although most of Turkey is geographically in western Asia, it was formerly a great European power and in 1683 the Turks even laid siege to Vienna. At the height of their power, the Sultans ruled an empire that stretched along the north coast of Africa and included the whole of the Balkans. By the 1850s, however, Turkey was "the sick man of Europe", and it lost most of its European territory in a series of wars from the 1820s to 1914. Siding with Germany and Austria in World War I, it suffered humiliating defeats and lost its Asiatic dominions: Palestine, Syria, Iraq and the Lebanon. When the Greeks attempted to seize the coast of Asia Minor in 1922, the Young Turks rose in revolt. Led by Kemal Pasha, they abolished the sultanate and declared a republic. Kemal Pasha transferred the capital from Istanbul (Constantinople) to Ankara and embarked on a process of rapid westernization, abolishing Turkish dress and compelling everyone to adopt western-style surnames. He himself took the name of Ataturk, "Father of the Turks".

Left: One of Kemal's most important reforms was the replacement of Arabic by a modified form of the Roman alphabet. Stamps of 1938 show him teaching the new alphabet.

TURKISH ISSUES

Turkey introduced postage stamps in 1863 [1], the chief motif being the *toughra* (a combination of seal and signature) of Sultan Abdul-Aziz. Stamps showing the ruler's mark or the Moslem crescent continued for some years [2]. Stamps of 1908 were overprinted "*Behie*" (discount) to compete with the foreign post offices operating in Turkey. In 1914 a new series, recess-printed by Bradbury Wilkinson in England, featured scenery and landmarks [3]. Several World War I issues showed life at the battlefront [4].

Kemal raised the standard of revolt at Ankara in April 1920. Stamps showing the first parliament house of the republic [5] were issued in 1922. By November 1923 Kemal had driven out the Greeks and extended his nationalist regime to the whole country. Since then, Kemal has appeared on more Turkish stamps than Washington has on American issues. The two men appeared on the same stamp following the 150th anniversary of the American constitution in 1939, celebrated with a large Turkish commemorative [6].

Until 1951 stamps were inscribed "Türkiye Postalari" (Turkish Posts) and then "Türkiye Cumhuriyeti Postalari" (Turkish Republic Posts). From 1956 "Türkiye" alone was used but since 1966 "Türkiye Cumhuriyeti" has been preferred [7]. Modern stamps are lithographed in Ankara or Istanbul. While many special issues highlight the technological progress of the modern state [8], others cover historical events [9] and even foster the colourful regional costumes [10] that Kemal tried to stamp out. Tradition mixes easily with modernization [11]. Above all, Kemal himself is a constant thread running through Turkish philately; he is portrayed here on one of the stamps of 2003 celebrating the 80th anniversary of the republic [12].

ASSOCIATED TERRITORIES

Although numerous stamps reflect the invasion and occupation of Turkish territory that now forms part of Greece, Albania, Romania, Bulgaria and Russia, the process was reversed in 1898 when the Turks invaded Thessaly, a Greek province. Five octagonal stamps showing the railway bridge at Vardar were used by Turkish troops before they evacuated most of the area, which reverted to Greece [14].

In 1919 the French occupied Cilicia, formerly the *vilayet* (province) of Adana, and overprinted Turkish stamps [13] with the name and initials "T.E.O." for *Territoires Ennemis Occupés* (Occupied Enemy Territories). The territory reverted to Turkey in October 1921. In 1923 the French granted autonomy to the *sanjak* of Alexandretta and overprinted Syrian stamps for the purpose. When they planned to hand this Turkish enclave to Syria in 1938, the inhabitants rose in revolt. Following a plebiscite it became the autonomous republic of Hatay. Turkish stamps were overprinted in 1939 [15] before its re-incorporation into Turkey in June 1939.

FOREIGN POST OFFICES

For many years up to the outbreak of World War I the external posts of the Ottoman Empire were run by various foreign powers. Stamps surcharged in Turkish currency or inscribed "Levant" or the name of a town were used at the various foreign post offices.

Austria-Hungary maintained a number of offices in Constantinople, Smyrna and those parts of the Balkans that were under Turkish rule. Stamps of Lombardy and Venetia were introduced in 1867, but from 1880 Austrian stamps surcharged in paras or piastres were used [16]. The British offices used ordinary British stamps, identifiable by their cancellations, but

Below: This Syrian stamp was overprinted by the French for use in the sanjak *(region) of Alexandretta.*

Typewritten Stamps

Probably the oddest stamps to emerge during World War I were those produced by Lieut. Commander Harry Pirie-Gordon DSC, RNVR, who commanded a detachment of the Royal Navy that occupied the island of Cheustan, or Makronisi, in the Gulf of Smyrna for a few weeks in 1916. During that period the commander produced his own stamps on the office typewriter, inscribed "Long Island" (a translation of the Turkish and Greek names), with the royal monogram "G.R.I." at the top and denominated in sterling.

from 1885 to 1914 stamps were surcharged in Turkish currency [17]. France not only had a general issue, similar to contemporary French stamps but engraved with the name "Levant" [18], but also overprints for use at individual offices. German stamps surcharged in Turkish currency were adopted in 1870 [19].

The Italian post offices began with a general issue inscribed "Estero" (foreign) but from 1902 Italian stamps were overprinted with the name of the individual office and surcharged in Turkish currency [20]. Russia also favoured individual stamps for each of its 13 offices as well as a general series for the Russian Company for Steam Shipping and Trade, known by the abbreviation ROPiT. The British post offices were reopened in 1919–21, while Poland and Romania also operated post offices in this period.

11

12

13

14

15

16

17

18

19

20

ITALY

Like Germany, 19th-century Italy was divided into a number of separate kingdoms and duchies, while Lombardy and Venetia, the South Tirol and Italian-speaking districts north of the Adriatic were in Austrian hands. From the 1830s Giuseppe Mazzini's Young Italy movement encouraged the idea of unification. After defeat against Austria in 1848–9, Mazzini's followers

started the second War of Independence in 1859, aided by Giuseppe Garibaldi. By the end of 1860 southern Italy was unified under Victor Emmanuel II of Sardinia, though Lombardy and Venetia remained in Austrian hands until 1866 and Rome was garrisoned by the French until 1870.

Left: The battles of Magenta (appropriately depicted on a magenta-coloured stamp of 1959) and Solferino (whose carnage inspired Henri Dunant to found the Red Cross) were two of the great conflicts in the war that unified Italy.

ITALIAN STATES

Before 1860 the various states issued their own stamps. Modena and Parma [1] were duchies under Austrian rule, while Naples [2] and Sicily [3] formed the Kingdom of the Two Sicilies, ruled by Ferdinand II, nicknamed "King Bomba" from his habit of bombarding his unruly subjects from time to time. Since 754 the Pope had ruled Rome and the surrounding territory, known variously as the States of the Church or the Papal States [4]; it included the Romagna extending to the Adriatic coast [5]. The grand duchy of Tuscany [6] fell to the liberators in August 1859 and latterly had stamps featuring the arms of Savoy as a prelude to unification with Sardinia [7], whose ruler eventually became king of Italy. Stamps with his embossed profile were issued in the Neapolitan Provinces [8] following the unification of Italy, pending the introduction of lire currency there.

THE RISE OF FASCISM

Italy made further territorial gains, siding with Prussia against Austria in 1866 and winning Lombardy and Venetia, taking advantage of the Franco-German War of 1870 to drive the French garrison out of Rome, and also acquiring the South Tirol, Trieste and other Austro-Hungarian areas [9] at the

end of World War I. However, widespread discontent in the aftermath of the war led to the rise of fascism led by Benito Mussolini.

Mussolini's Blackshirts marched on Rome [10] in October 1922, and he became prime minister and subsequently dictator under the title of Il Duce ("the leader"). He was the role model for Hitler, although by World War II he was the junior partner in the Axis alliance [11]. In 1943 Victor Emmanuel III dismissed him and had him imprisoned when Italy changed sides. The Germans rapidly overran northern Italy, freed Mussolini and installed him as head of a puppet state known as the Italian Social Republic [13], which was overthrown by partisans in 1945.

POST-WAR REPUBLIC

Allied troops landed in Sicily in July 1943 and on the Italian mainland in September. In the occupied areas stamps produced in Washington [14] were issued by the Allied military government. Control was handed over to the king but in June 1946 Italy became a republic. The last of the royalist stamps [15] symbolized freedom, enlightenment, peace and justice and continued in use till 1948. A later series, known as *la Sircusa* because it

Commercial Advertising

Stamps of the 1901–22 series portraying Victor Emmanuel III were released in 1924 with commercial advertisements printed on labels. There were no perforations between the stamps and the labels, so that the public were encouraged to advertise various products every time they posted a letter.

was based on an ancient Greek coin of Syracuse, was adopted in 1953 and continued until 1980. On two occasions it was incorporated in stamps urging Italians to pay their taxes [12]. It was followed by a series featuring some of the many castles of Italy [16].

More recent special issues have been produced by intaglio or photogravure at the Mint in Rome [17]. Many Italian stamps are inspired by the sculpture of the Roman Empire, a legacy from the fascist period, rather than the influence of the Church, and religious themes are usually restricted to Old Master paintings, such as the stamps celebrating the 450th anniversary of the death of Raphael [18].

SAN MARINO AND THE VATICAN

The tiny landlocked republic in north-eastern Italy, independent since the fourth century, began issuing its own stamps in 1877. By the 1900s they were its principal source of revenue and became immensely popular worldwide because of their wide-ranging topics. They included a set of 20 in memory of Franklin D. Roosevelt in 1947 [19]. Numerous sets since the 1950s have catered to the thematic market.

San Marino was very much in the forefront of developments in philately, pioneering long sets devoted to popular themes such as sports, flowers, birds, veteran cars, vintage aircraft [20] and ancient ships, as well as more esoteric subjects ranging from medieval tournaments to dinosaurs. It was also one of the first countries to issue stamps in support of the Olympic Games (1955–6) and led the way in illustrating Disney characters. More recently it has produced sheetlets for Italian operas, comic strips and science fiction. Joint issues with other countries are now common, but San Marino and Italy scored another first in 1994 with a miniature sheet containing a pair of L750 stamps (one from each country) showing St Mark's Basilica in Venice. The stamps were arranged in the sheet upside down in relation to each other, giving the impression of a reflection in the water. An inscription on the back limited the validity of each stamp to the appropriate country.

The Vatican City State was created in 1929, giving the Pope temporal powers including the right to issue stamps [21]. Not surprisingly, the vast majority of these have had a religious theme, celebrating popes, saints and the achievements of the Catholic Church down through the ages. In recent times, however, they have also addressed social and political issues of global concern, such as aid for the refugees of the world's trouble spots.

Below: In 1999 the Vatican issued this stamp to raise money for refugees from Kosovo in war-torn former Yugoslavia.

13

14

15

16

17

18

19

20

21

1

2

3

4

5

6

7

8

9

10

11

FRANCE

A thousand-year kingdom, two empires and five republics, not to mention long periods in the 20th century when governments rapidly came and went, might suggest a lack of stability in France, but against this stands a record of affluence and material progress, of martial skills and technological superiority, centuries as the acknowledged centre of the fine and applied arts, and world leadership in literature, philosophy, music and the sciences. All have been explored thoroughly in stamps whose recurring theme is the glory of France, past and present. France rightly regards itself as the cradle of

modern democracy, with the fall of the Bastille in 1789 signalling the downfall of the *ancien régime*.

Left: The assault on the Bastille, the grim fortress that symbolized the autocratic rule of the Bourbons, marked the beginning of the French Revolution.

THE SECOND REPUBLIC

Revolutions in 1830 and 1848 toppled the last of the Bourbons and Louis Philippe respectively, ushering in the Second Republic, and France adopted adhesive stamps a few months later. Without a crowned head to adorn the French "Penny Black", a profile of Ceres, the Roman goddess of agriculture, was chosen instead [1]. Shortly afterwards Louis Bonaparte, president of the republic, staged a coup and proclaimed himself emperor, taking the title of Napoleon III. For twenty years his portrait graced the stamps [2] but, after the downfall of the empire in the Franco-German War of 1870–1, Ceres was restored. Thereafter France has opted for various allegorical females, brandishing *The Rights of Man* [3] or sowing seed [4], and Marianne, the epitome of France, has appeared in many guises to the present day.

Edmund Dulac, French-born but a naturalized Briton, engraved the set printed by De La Rue at the end of World War II – some of the few French stamps produced outside France [5]. This issue was briefly preceded by a series showing the Arc de Triomphe, brought over from America by the liberators in 1944 [6]. In the same period France embarked on a long series of stamps, originally showing the arms

of Nice, Corsica, Alsace and Lorraine (lost to the Italians and Germans in 1940) but eventually covering every part of France [14].

ARTISTIC EXPRESSION

Art is a recurring theme of French stamps, from Art Nouveau motifs at the beginning of the 20th century, to the geometric style for the stamps publicizing the Paris International Exposition of the Decorative Arts in 1925 (from which came the term "Art Deco") [7]. Several stamps from 1927 onwards show the Statue of Liberty, in one instance to raise money for refugees from the Spanish Civil War [8]. Who but the French would regularly issue charity stamps on behalf of Unemployed Intellectuals [9], providing an opportunity to portray eminent figures from the world of the arts?

France was (and still is) a leading exponent of intaglio printing. By the late 1950s two-colour recess-printing was possible [10], although monochrome was often preferred, as in the stamp portraying Auguste Bartholdi, sculptor of the Statue of Liberty [11], but by 1961 multicolour intaglio was spectacularly launched with the first of the extremely popular large-format paintings sets [12], which triggered a craze for fine art stamps all over the

To the Glory of France

Napoleon Bonaparte and Charles de Gaulle, the two towering figures who gave France back its pride in itself, have been the subject of numerous stamps. This strip, released in 1971, marked the first anniversary of de Gaulle's death. The images flanking the Cross of Lorraine chart his career from brigadier-general in June 1940 to president. In 2004 France issued a set for the bicentenary of Napoleon's coronation, reviving imperial glory.

12

13   14

15

16

world. In more recent years photogravure and offset lithography have made serious inroads, often accompanied by a surreal or whimsical approach [13].

The French Post Office also provides distinctive stamps for use at the Paris headquarters of UNESCO and the Council of Europe in Strasbourg [15]. France has joint suzerainty (with Spain) over Andorra and produces distinctive stamps for it, many of which reflect the impact of France on the tiny Pyrenean principality [16].

MONACO

A possession of the Grimaldi family since the 13th century, Monaco is a medieval relic that has managed to retain its independence and move with the times. Distinctive stamps [17] were introduced in 1885; before that stamps

Below: A Delahaye motor car of 1901 was one of 14 veteran automobiles depicted in a set issued in 1961.

of Sardinia or France were employed. Prince Rainier III [18], a keen philatelist, wed the actress Grace Kelly in a fairytale romance in 1956 [19].

The home of the Monte Carlo Rally, Monaco has issued many stamps depicting cars, as well as a sought-after series showing the starting points for the rally – though why Eilean Donan Castle in the Scottish Highlands should represent Glasgow is a mystery. Although Monaco prefers fine intaglio, some recent issues have been printed in multicolour photogravure or lithography, but always at the French Government Printing Works [20].

The astonishing diversity of landscape and buildings in the tiny principality is reflected in many of the stamps, including several sets reproducing engravings or paintings of bygone Monaco. Monte Carlo is an increasingly popular venue for international conferences and exhibitions, all of which are well publicized by stamps. The tragic death of Princess Grace in a motoring accident resulted in a steady stream of stamps in her memory, latterly giving prominence to the various charities and foundations of which she was the patron. The 700th anniversary of the Grimaldi dynasty was celebrated by a long set in 1997 portraying all the seigneurs since Rainier I in 1297.

17   18

19

20

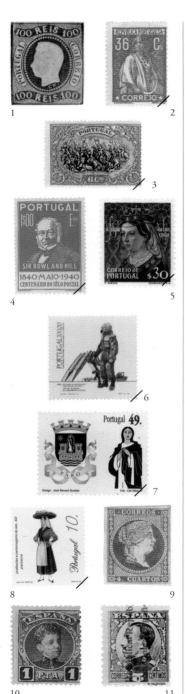

IBERIAN PENINSULA

The Iberian peninsula in south-western Europe is flanked by the Mediterranean and the Atlantic. In ancient times Europeans believed that the Pillars of Hercules (now the Straits of Gibraltar) marked the edge of the world and that there was nothing beyond. The Portuguese, under the guidance of Prince Henry the Navigator, were among the first to disprove this in the 14th and 15th centuries. Intrepid mariners explored the coasts of Africa, rounded the Cape of Good Hope and found the sea route to India and beyond, travelling to China and Japan. Others crossed the Atlantic and colonized Brazil. Spain, the larger partner in Iberia, would not be outdone.

Hiring a Genoese mariner, Christopher Columbus, Spain reached the New World and secured the untold wealth of the gold and silver deposits in Mexico, Peru and Bolivia. In both cases, imperial power and wealth proved to be short-lived.

Left: Many stamps of Portugal portray the navigators who gave it control of half the transoceanic world, the greatest (and most frequently depicted) being Vasco da Gama, who found the sea route to the Indies in 1497.

PORTUGAL

The stamps of Portugal from 1853 to 1880 bore albino embossed profiles of rulers [1]. After the collapse of the monarchy in 1910 the republic issued a definitive set depicting Ceres, goddess of agriculture [2]. Introduced in 1912, it continued until the 1930s: though not the longest-lived it was one of the most prolific series of all time, with numerous changes of colour and value.

In the 1920s Portugal favoured very long historical sets dwelling on past glories [3]. The centenary of adhesive stamps was celebrated in 1940 by a set portraying Rowland Hill [4]. A reminder that Portugal was England's oldest ally came in the set of 1949, which portrayed Henry the Navigator and his mother Philippa of Lancaster [5]. More recent stamps have been produced in multicolour lithography and range from the military sets of the 1980s [6] to the armorial issues of the 1990s [7]. Traditional crafts and vocations are also recurring themes [8].

SPAIN

The first stamps of Spain appeared in 1850 and bore the very homely features of Isabella II [9]. Corruption and misrule led to the abolition of the monarchy in 1873–4, but the House of Bourbon was restored by King Alfonso XII. He died without a male heir but his wife gave birth to a son several months later. The stamps of Alfonso XIII portrayed him from babyhood to adolescence [10] and into middle age.

In 1930 the centenary of the death of Francisco Goya was marked by a set of 32 stamps portraying the artist and reproducing some of his works. Three stamps featured *The Naked Maja*, which shocked the ultra-conservative Spaniards, and were effectively used as republican propaganda, insinuating that the image symbolized the decadent lifestyle of the monarchy. The furore eventually forced Alfonso XIII to leave the country, and a republic was proclaimed in April 1931.

Royalist stamps were overprinted [11], pending the introduction of republican issues [12]. Right-wing reaction led to a military coup led by General Franco [13]. This triggered the Civil War, which lasted for three years (1936–9), yielding a large number of local stamps issued by both sides. While fascist Italy and Germany gave

Forlorn Hope

Ever since the British captured the Rock of Gibraltar in 1704 the Spaniards have tried unsuccessfully to take it back. Having failed on several occasions, notably during the siege of 1779–83, in more recent times Spain has applied economic sanctions and even issued stamps in 1969, ostensibly in aid of Spanish workers unable to cross the line to their jobs in Gibraltar, although it was the Spanish government that prevented this traffic.

considerable support to the Nationalists, the Soviet Union and communists from many parts of the world flocked to the Republican colours in what amounted to a dress-rehearsal for World War II.

Under Franco Spain was theoretically a kingdom again but in effect it was a fascist dictatorship. Bypassing Alfonso's son and heir, Franco groomed his grandson for the throne and in 1975 Juan Carlos I succeeded on the death of Franco. These political upheavals were studiously ignored in the stamps, which have tended to draw heavily on the Spanish way of life and such sports as bullfighting [14]. Many have reproduced works of art, from cave paintings [15] to the avant-garde. Other very popular and long-running series were devoted to the castles [16] and provincial costumes [17] of Spain. A high proportion reflect its Catholic conservatism, though social problems such as domestic violence [18] have also been publicized in recent years.

Apart from the Civil War, Spain has had to contend with long-running unrest in the Basque provinces and Catalonia, which, in addition to separatist aspirations, formerly supported the claims to the throne of Don Carlos and his grandson. Carlist stamps were issued in 1873–4 [19].

ANDORRA

Spain had joint suzerainty (with France) over the Pyrenean principality of Andorra and opened post offices there in 1928. Ordinary Spanish stamps were used at first but since 1929 distinctive issues have been made. Originally inscribed in Spanish [20], they have been rendered in Catalan since 1979. Catalogues invariably describe the 1997 Christmas stamp as showing a Catalan crib figure [21]. The stamp itself is discreetly captioned "El Caganer" (the defecator), apparently a good-luck symbol in the Pyrenees.

Most Christmas stamps have concentrated on Old Master paintings of religious subjects or the decorative art of Andorran churches. Andorra is conspicuous for its new issue policy, one of the most conservative in the world, averaging only four or five stamps a year and invariably confined to subjects directly relevant to the principality. The only other regular annual issues are Europa stamps and one promoting the protection of nature. Andorra's main acknowledgment of the outside world is the occasional stamp for the Olympic Games or the football World Cup. Although it now has a single currency, the euro, separate issues of stamps are still made by France and Spain.

Below: Goya's The Naked Maja *was the first nude to appear on a stamp, and was hijacked by republicans eager to condemn the decadence of the monarchy.*

Principat d'Andorra

AFRICA

Africa was the last inhabited continent to adopt adhesive stamps, beginning with the celebrated Cape of Good Hope triangulars in 1853. Natal introduced stamps in 1857 but other states did not follow suit until the 1860s. By 1870 distinctive stamps were appearing in some Spanish colonies.

SPANISH AFRICA

As well as the Spanish-protected zone of Morocco, Spain acquired a considerable amount of territory in north-west Africa. However, most of this was in parts that were of little or no interest to the other European powers, mainly in the Sahara desert regions but also around the Gulf of Guinea.

Left: A general issue of stamps inscribed "Spanish West Africa", for use in Ifni and Spanish Sahara, was in use from 1949 to 1951. A portrait of General Franco was inset in designs featuring the scenery of the area.

GULF COLONIES

Spain's oldest colony was the offshore island of Fernando Poo in the Gulf, which it acquired from Portugal in 1778. From 1827 to 1834 Spain leased it to Britain as a naval base for the suppression of the slave trade. A British consulate was opened there in 1849 and a postal agency in 1858, using ordinary British stamps identifiable by the postmarks. This closed in 1877. Fernando Poo opened a Spanish post office in 1868 and issued a stamp portraying Isabella II (reproduced on a centenary stamp [1]) but it was soon withdrawn and from then until 1879 the stamps of Cuba were used instead.

From 1879 to 1960 the stamps of Fernando Poo consisted of contemporary Spanish stamps overprinted or inscribed thus. It was not until the creation of two Spanish overseas provinces in July 1959, one of which consisted of Fernando Poo and the island of Annobon, that distinctive stamps first appeared. The stamps were inscribed with the provincial name in letters smaller than those of the country name [2]. In October 1968 Fernando Poo joined Rio Muni to form the Republic of Equatorial Guinea.

Spain acquired the three islands of Elobey, Annobon and Corisco [3] from Portugal in 1778. Annobon is in the Atlantic south of the then Portuguese colony of St Thomas and Prince Islands; the other two are off the coast of Gabon. Spain established a protectorate over a part of the mainland of Guinea, also known as Rio Muni, in 1885, and from 1909 to 1960 the islands were joined with Fernando Poo and Spanish Guinea. Keytype stamps were used in "Spanish Continental Guinea" from 1902 to 1909 [4].

In that year both continental territory and offshore islands were combined as the Spanish Territories of the Gulf of Guinea, and stamps thus inscribed were then introduced [5]. Royal portraiture was superseded by pictorial designs from 1924 onwards [6]. The much shorter title of "Spanish Guinea" was adopted in 1949 [7] and continued until 30 July 1959, when the territory was divided into the overseas provinces of Fernando Poo and Rio Muni, covering the offshore islands and the continental portion respectively. Rio Muni issued stamps from 1960 to 1968, most issues being for Stamp Day [8] or Child Welfare [9].

Movie Stars

Typical of modern issues from the Republic of Equatorial Guinea are the stamps of 1996 honouring Marilyn Monroe, Elvis Presley and James Dean.

SAHARAN TERRITORIES

In 1885 Spain established a protectorate over the basin of the Rio de Oro (river of gold) in north-west Africa, just south of Morocco. The territory was administered from the Canary Islands and used ordinary Spanish stamps until 1905, when the keytypes were introduced [10]. The Rio de Oro region was renamed Spanish Sahara in 1924. In 1920 Spanish troops had occupied La Aguera on Cape Blanco with the intention of building an airfield for a projected route to Latin America, and for this stamps of Rio de Oro were overprinted accordingly [11]. The district was incorporated in Spanish Sahara in 1924.

In 1916 Spanish troops occupied Cape Juby at the southern end of Morocco. Stamps of Rio de Oro, Spain or Spanish Morocco were overprinted at various times [12]. Cape Juby was incorporated in Spanish Sahara in 1950 but ceded to Morocco in 1958.

Ifni was a Spanish enclave on the Moroccan coast from 1860 onwards. Before stamps were introduced in 1941, mail was franked by rubber stamp. Spanish stamps overprinted "Territorio de Ifni" [13] were used until 1950, when distinctive stamps were adopted. As in Rio Muni, most later stamps were issued for Child Welfare [14] or Stamp Day [15]. On 30 June 1969, Ifni was returned to Morocco.

Spanish Sahara started off with a distinctive series in 1924 [16] but thereafter relied on overprinted Spanish stamps until 1943, when attractive pictorials were resumed [18]. In 1975 Spain decided to relinquish the territory and it was divided between Morocco and Mauritania, but this was resisted by the Polisario movement, which proclaimed an independent Arab republic and has since issued stamps in areas under its control.

EQUATORIAL GUINEA

The Spanish colonies became the independent Republic of Equatorial Guinea in October 1968 and distinctive stamps were introduced the following year [17]. At first stamps with designs relevant to the country were issued [19] but since the early 1970s they have been frankly thematic and international in scope.

Below: In 1994 Equatorial Guinea issued this stamp portraying Neil Armstrong, Buzz Aldrin and Michael Collins to commemorate the first landing of men on the Moon.

10   11

12

13

14

15

16   17

18

19

NORTH AFRICA

The four countries of North Africa represented the furthest extent of Turkish rule from 1518 until the early 20th century, by which time they had become semi-independent and wholly lawless. They were the haunt of the Barbary pirates who preyed on Mediterranean shipping. European inroads began with the French invasion of Algiers in 1830 to extirpate piracy, leading to the direct annexation of Algeria in 1848 after a protracted and costly colonial war. The suppression of piracy led to the French protectorate over Tunis in 1881, although the Bey of Tunis remained as nominal ruler. As a result of the Italo-Turkish War of 1911 Libya fell to the Italians, and the following year France and Spain partitioned Morocco into protected zones, with Tangier as an international free port. Both powers had considerable difficulties with rebellious tribes. All but Morocco suffered the ravages of World War II and long, bitter conflict to attain independence in the 1950s.

Left: The North African campaign of 1942–3 was largely fought on Tunisian soil. Its liberation from German occupation was celebrated by a stamp of 1943 showing British, Free French and American soldiers.

ALGERIA

Ordinary French stamps were used until 1924 when Algeria was granted a measure of autonomy, and stamps were overprinted "Algerie" [1] pending a distinctive issue [2]. Administered by the Vichy French regime, the country was invaded by Allied forces in 1942; after the liberation stamps including the name of the French Republic were issued in 1944 [3]. Algeria continued to have its own stamps [4] until 1958, when it was again incorporated in France following the outbreak of rebellion in 1954. When the Algerians won their independence in 1962 French stamps were locally overprinted before distinctive stamps were resumed. Many stamps since then have referred to the struggles of that period [5], alternating with issues featuring landmarks [6] and the wide variety of scenery.

MOROCCO

By the late 19th century the Sherif of Morocco was virtually independent, but the strategic importance of his country led to it falling prey to rival European powers. The Agadir incident in 1911, involving the gunboat *Panzer*, almost triggered off a full-scale war between Germany and France. Britain [7], France, Spain and Germany all had their own postal services handing overseas mail, while internal services were operated by the Sherifian Posts [8].

After Morocco was partitioned between France and Spain in 1912 Tangier had its own postal services run by Britain [9], France and Spain [10]. The stamps used in the French and Spanish zones followed the styles of these countries but featured local scenes [11–12]. In 1956 both powers relinquished their protectorates and Morocco became a wholly independent kingdom [13]. Since then stamps have portrayed Muhammad V or his son Hassan II, interspersed with landmarks [14], scenery and wildlife [15].

LIBYA

Under Italian rule overprinted stamps were followed by distinctive designs that tended to highlight Libya's Roman history [16]. During World War II British stamps were overprinted "M.E.F." (Middle East Forces) for use in North Africa [17]. Later, similar overprints were produced for use in

Tripolitania. The French invaded Libya from the south and occupied Fezzan and Ghadames [19]. In 1949 Britain recognized the leader of the Senussi tribe as Amir of Cyrenaica and stamps thus inscribed appeared in 1950. In December 1951 Cyrenaica united with the states of Tripolitania, Fezzan and Ghadames to form the kingdom of Libya. It was the first country to achieve independence through the United Nations.

Stamps of Cyrenaica were overprinted, with the denominations in military administration lire [18]. Libya's stamps continued in the Italian tradition but increasingly espoused Islamic solidarity. In 1969 the monarchy was overthrown by a military coup that brought Colonel Gaddafi to power. Stamps of the Libyan Arab Republic (LAR) have boasted of its military preparedness to withstand western attempts to subvert the regime.

Below: Libya celebrated the centenary of the Universal Postal Union in 1974 with this stamp (top) showing a postrider and Concorde to contrast mail communications old and new. A stamp (bottom) from Tunisia marked the fifth annual week promoting the health of schoolchildren in the Maghreb (Arab region of North Africa).

Surreal Stamps

A characteristic of Tunisian stamps in the early years of the republic was their surreal quality, largely as a result of the work of one designer, Hatem Elmekki. Contrasting with the dour portraits of President Bourguiba, Elmekki's designs ranged from the whimsical to the bizarre and continued to flourish for almost 40 years.

TUNISIA

The French took over this Turkish province in 1881, recognizing the Bey of Tunis but establishing a regency because the region was on the verge of economic collapse as a result of the suppression of piracy, its main source of revenue. Stamps gave an outward semblance of independence [20] but it was not until 1955 that France bowed to nationalist agitation and granted it [21]. The following year the monarchy was abolished and Tunisia became a republic, one of the more moderate and westernized of the Arab states.

Tunisia pursues a moderate new issue policy, averaging about 30 stamps a year. Most are singles focusing on matters of national and international importance; their symbolic or allegorical motifs show the pervasive influence of Hatem Elmekki. Occasional stamps portray famous Tunisians, including women (such as the singer Saliha) which is relatively unusual in Muslim countries. Since 1997 short sets have reproduced paintings by indigenous artists, while a few sets of three or four stamps have adopted a thematic line, featuring horses, reptiles, shells, musical instruments and ancient ruins.

12

13

14

15

16

17

18

19

20

21

EGYPT AND SUDAN

The present-day Arab Republic of Egypt day is a world removed from the great pharaonic civilization of the Nile that was flourishing by 4000 BC when the upper and lower kingdoms of Egypt were united. After 525 BC Egypt was dominated by foreign powers from the Persians to the Turks, but was running its own affairs when the British became involved in the Suez Canal in 1869 and seized control in 1882. Although still nominally under the Ottoman Empire, Egypt became a British protectorate in 1914 following the outbreak of World War I. This arrangement continued until 1922, when it was declared an independent kingdom. The monarchy was abolished in 1952 and Egypt became a republic.

To the south, and three times the size of Egypt, lay Sudan, which Mohamed Ali, Pasha of Egypt, conquered in 1822. The Egyptians were driven out of Sudan by the Mahdist revolt of 1881, but the country was reconquered in 1899 and declared an Anglo-Egyptian condominium.

Left: A set of three stamps marked the signing of the Anglo-Egyptian Treaty of 1936. Ramsay Macdonald, British Prime Minister in 1924 and 1929–35, chaired the conference and is depicted at the top of the table; the future prime minister Anthony Eden sits beside him.

FROM KHEDIVE TO KING
When Egypt adopted stamps in 1866, they were totally oriental in appearance with Arabic inscriptions [1], but the Great Pyramid became the motif of all stamps from 1867 to 1914 [2]. Egypt was then ruled by a khedive (viceroy) for the sultan in Constantinople, but when it became a British protectorate in 1914, the khedive became a sultan in his own right. As well as the obligatory pyramids, stamps of this period showed other ancient monuments [3]. Sultan Ahmed Fuad became king on 15 March 1922, and stamps portraying him were produced by Harrison and Sons of London in 1923, using photogravure for the first time [4].

KINGDOM OF EGYPT
The kingdom lasted three decades, during which various special issues drew inspiration from the pharaonic period [5]. A stamp of January 1938 celebrated King Farouk's wedding to Princess Farida of Iran [6] while a similar stamp, with a wedding group substituted, celebrated the king's 18th birthday a month later. Farouk had ambitions to throw off British influence. He ejected their troops from the Nile delta in 1947 and confined them to the Canal Zone, then abrogated the treaty regarding Sudan in 1951, signalled by overprinting the stamps in Arabic to signify that he was king of both Egypt and Sudan [7]. From 1932 to 1941 special stamps were used by the British forces in Egypt [8–9].

ARAB REPUBLIC
Farouk was forced to abdicate in 1952 and a military junta proclaimed a regency for the infant Ahmed Fuad II, then declared a republic. The Farouk stamps were overprinted with bars to blot out his face [10]. After the Anglo-French Suez venture of 1956 the spelling of Egyptian stamps was changed from French [11] to English, although the Egyptians maintained that it was American [12]. Colonel Nasser merged Egypt with Syria in 1958 to form the United Arab Republic. It was shortlived but Egypt retained the title of UAR until 1971, when "Egypt Arab

Hollow Victory

Nasser nationalized the Suez Canal in September 1956, prompting the British and French to invade Egypt. Although the brief campaign was a military success, the Allies were forced to evacuate the country when the USA and USSR (in a rare Cold War truce) joined in condemning the action and threatening sanctions. Egypt celebrated its "victory" with a stamp showing soldiers and civilians, shoulder to shoulder, resisting the enemy invasion.

Republic" [14] was chosen. Modern Egyptian stamps continue to draw heavily on pharaonic images, contrasting them with modern buildings and logos reflecting the importance of Cairo as a global conference centre [15].

SUDAN

The reconquest of Sudan by an Anglo-Expedition army commanded by General Kitchener (Later Field Marshal Lord Kitchener of Khartoum) began in 1896 and was completed in 1899. The first stamps, issued in 1897, were Egyptian stamps overprinted [16], followed by a series depicting a camel postman [13]. This design was produced by E.A. Stanton, then a *bimbashi* (captain) in the khedive's army but later a colonel in the British Army and one of Britain's foremost philatelists. He persuaded the sheik of the Howawir tribe to pose with straw-filled sacks to represent mailbags. The bags were optimistically inscribed "Khartoum" and "Berbera", although these towns were still in enemy hands at the time. So popular did the image become that it remained on stamps until the 1950s and then became the

national emblem on Sudanese coins. An interlude in 1941 used a palm tree design [17] but the camel postman was restored in 1948 for the entire definitive series. Even when pictorial motifs were adopted in 1951 the camel postman was retained for the 50p top value.

The statue of General Gordon, murdered by the Mahdists in 1885, was the subject of the airmail series of 1931 [18], while a set of nine, released in 1935, marked the 50th anniversary of his death [19]. Self-government in 1954 was celebrated by three stamps showing the camel postman. Two years later Sudan became an independent republic, with stamps showing the wings of hope over a map [20].

In 1969 a pro-communist democratic republic was proclaimed [21]. Although this totalitarian regime was overthrown in April 1985 and an ordinary republic established [22], the country has been torn apart by ethnic and religious trouble in recent years.

SUEZ CANAL

During the late 19th century, France, Britain, Greece, Italy and Russia operated post offices in Egypt, but only the first of these issued stamps specifically inscribed or overprinted for use in Alexandria and Port Said. French involvement was largely concerned with the construction of the Suez Canal, begun in 1859 and completed ten years later. Stamps printed in Paris were used in connection with a mail service operated by the Suez Canal Company between July and the end of August 1868 [23].

Below: This French stamp of 1899 was overprinted for use at Port Said (left), and in 1902 French stamps were engraved for use at Alexandria (right).

ART AND ARCHITECTURE OF THE PHARAOHS IN STAMPS

The art and architecture of ancient Egypt is extraordinary and without parallel anywhere in the world. The tombs of the pharaohs are masterpieces of engineering that defy rational explanation and we still marvel at the methods used to raise such gigantic blocks of stone with such precision. The pyramids were one of the seven wonders of the ancient world, and it is small wonder that they have appeared on numerous Egyptian stamps since 1867.

Ranking in iconic stature with the pyramids is the colossal statue of the Sphinx nearby, which is often depicted in the foreground of stamps featuring the tombs. Although these famous structures are among the largest and oldest in the world, Egypt boasts many other architectural masterpieces, such as the great temple at Karnak, built by Seti I and Rameses II.

When the temples of Abu Simbel were threatened with inundation following the construction of the Aswan Dam in the 1960s, UNESCO mounted a worldwide appeal to raise the funds to have the temples dismantled and moved to higher ground. This provoked a flood of stamps from all over the world in its support. Egypt

returned the compliment with stamps showing aspects of the temples with the UNESCO emblem alongside.

The Sphinx and the gigantic seated figures of Abu Simbel are prime examples of architectonic sculpture that have never been surpassed, but dynastic Egypt also produced countless life-sized statues, heads and busts, from the exquisite head of Nefertiti, painted to re-create her fabled beauty, to the gold mask of Tutankhamun, the boy pharaoh. The discovery of his spectacular tomb in 1922 was one of the most important landmarks in archaeology

Below: A British stamp of 1972, marking the 50th anniversary of the discovery of Tutankhamun's tomb.

and it has been the subject of many definitive and special issues. The 50th anniversary of the find was celebrated by issues from Britain to Bhutan.

Not as spectacular, perhaps, but of immense importance to the emerging science of Egyptology, was the Rosetta Stone, whose parallel inscriptions in Greek and Aramaic enabled Jean-François Champollion to decipher hieroglyphics. This remarkable stone document was discovered during Napoleon's expedition to Egypt in 1798. When the French were defeated in 1801 the stone was handed over to Britain and is now in the British Museum, whose collection of Egyptian antiquities is second only to that of the Cairo Museum. The 150th anniversary

Left (clockwise from top): Egyptian stamps issued to mark the centenary of the opera Aida *in 1971, the International Conference on Population and Development, 1994, and the Cairo Statistical Congress, 1927, showing a statue of Amenhotep.*

Right (clockwise from top): Egyptian stamps featuring a gold chair back from Tutankhamun's tomb, 1972, Imhotep, god of medicine, 1928, and the World Under-17s football mascot, 1997.

AR EGYPT جمهورية مصر العربية

Above: Queen Nefertiti (1953) and Rameses II (1957) flanking a stamp of 1985 showing a slave kneeling with a tray of fruit, taken from a fresco.

Left: The souvenir sheet released by Egypt in 1972 to celebrate the 50th anniversary of the discovery of Tutankhamun's tomb shows his richly gilded second mummiform coffin.

Right: The elaborate court dress of a pharaonic messenger depicted on one of the annual issues for Post Day (1969).

50TH ANNIVERSARY OF DISCOVERY OF TOUT ANKH AMON'S TOMB

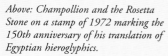

Above: Champollion and the Rosetta Stone on a stamp of 1972 marking the 150th anniversary of his translation of Egyptian hieroglyphics.

Above: Edfu Temple, depicted on an airmail stamp of 1985. Others in this series featured the pyramids of Giza and the colossal statue of Akhenaton.

Above: The Eye of Horus, flanked by the goddesses Nekhbet and Wadjet, on stamps for the 15th Ophthalmological Congress, held at Cairo in 1937.

of Champollion's breakthrough was celebrated by both Egypt and France in 1972. His discovery, and the booty brought back to Europe, triggered off a craze for all things Egyptian. It influenced everything from furniture to jewellery design in early 19th-century Europe. In the 1920s and 1930s, following the discovery of the boy pharaoh's tomb, there was an astonishing revival of Egytian style, which greatly influenced Art Deco.

The art of the pharaohs also exerted a tremendous influence on the development of Egyptian nationalism in the 19th century. Khedive Ismail commissioned Giuseppe Verdi to write the opera *Aida*, set in ancient Egypt, for

the opening of the Cairo Opera House in 1871; stamps marking its centenary depicted the opera's victory parade.

Egypt has been adept at harnessing pharaonic imagery to all manner of modern subjects. This fashion began when the statue of Amenhotep was used for the Statistical Congress stamps of 1927, while Imhotep graced stamps the following year for the Medical Congress in Cairo. The sacred Eye of Horus was an appropriate motif for the stamps of 1937 for the 15th World Ophthalmological Congress in Cairo.

These stamps set the trend for numerous more recent issues. In particular, wall paintings of the 18th dynasty from the tombs at Thebes have

provided a virtually inexhaustible source of pictures for the annual Post Day stamps. In one case, using a theme within a theme, pharaonic costumes were set within a frame derived from the great temple at Karnak.

Even events such as the Olympic Games have been given the pharaonic treatment. No matter what the topic or occasion, Egypt can invariably find a motif from pharaonic figurative or decorative art that is appropriate. The ceremonial headdress of the pharaohs has become almost a national symbol and has even lent itself to cartoon treatment, as in the mascot devised for the World Football Championships for Under-17s, held in Egypt in 1997.

1

2

3

4

5

6

7

8

9

FRENCH WEST AFRICA

The French colonies and protectorates in Africa were grouped into two large administrative units from 1944 until the various components became independent republics in the 1950s. They formed a vast area south of the Sahara that comprised Dahomey, French Guinea, French Sudan, the Ivory Coast, Mauritania, Niger, Senegal and Upper Volta. There was also a certain amount of adjustment territory. French Sudan was abolished in 1899 and its land was parcelled out among Senegal, Guinea, Ivory Coast, Dahomey, Senegambia and Niger, but it was reconstituted in 1921 and eventually merged with Senegal to form Mali.

Left: A stamp from the republic of Guinea shows a map of Africa with the four countries of the OERS (an organization of states bordering on the River Senegal) highlighted. This reflects the solidarity of the former colonies in French West Africa.

UNDER FRENCH RULE
Separate issues for the French colonies were replaced in 1944 by a single series inscribed "Afrique Occidentale Française" (French West Africa). They continued until 1958–9 [1] when they were superseded as the various colonies achieved independence. Before 1944 the various territories had their own stamps, mainly using one or other of the French colonial keyplate designs [2; 4–5] with the West African name as part of the permanent motif and the individual name added to the inscription. Later issues were distinctive to each territory. They were originally printed typographically in rather garish two-colour combinations [6], but intaglio was later used with the overall name reduced to the initials "AOF" [3; 7–8]. In general, these stamps provided a good insight into the scenery, landmarks, fauna and flora, tribal customs and culture of the region, yet had a distinctly French character.

INDEPENDENCE
The transition from colony to independent republic was achieved smoothly after the advent of the Fifth Republic under de Gaulle in 1958. At first the various colonies and protectorates became republics within the French Community and this was

reflected in the stamps of the period, which, for the most part, continued to be engraved and recess-printed at the Institut de Gravure in Paris.

The concept of a community of independent republics, modelled on the British Commonwealth, gradually disappeared, and the various countries went their separate ways. The political changes of the 1960s are charted by the switch to multicolour photogravure or lithography, as well as a number of name changes. Dahomey [9] became a popular republic in November 1975 and changed its name to Benin but a political change in 1990 led to the "popular" being dropped [10]. At the beginning of the 20th century Benin had been the name of a coastal strip that briefly had its own stamps before being absorbed by Dahomey.

The Ivory Coast [11] retained its colonial name after the attainment of independence in 1960, astonishingly as the name reflected the traditional trade in ivory, now highly illegal. The federation of Mali was formed in April 1959 by a merger of the former French Sudan and Senegal [12]. It had become independent within the French Community on 20 June 1950, but broke up when Senegal seceded two months later and resumed its own stamps [13]. Sudan, retaining the name

A Hard-won Struggle

Within ten years of their incorporation in Ethiopia, the Eritreans had risen in revolt and started a war that lasted 30 years. Two years before its independence was finally recognized by the world at large, Eritrea established a postal service, complete with stamps, in 1991. Stamps inscribed in English but printed in Italy reflect the support given to the new country by its former colonial rulers.

BRITISH TERRITORIES

British penetration of the area began in the 1880s as part of the Anglo-Egyptian Sudan, and Indian stamps were used until 1903 when the protectorate was transferred from India to the British government. Indian stamps overprinted "British Somaliland" [15] were used pending a supply of stamps more correctly inscribed "Somaliland Protectorate" [16]. Pictorial stamps were introduced in 1938 and continued until 1960, when the protectorate joined the newly formed Somali Republic [17].

ETHIOPIA

One of the oldest civilizations in Africa, Ethiopia was ruled by emperors who claimed descent from Solomon and the Queen of Sheba. The country retained its unique Coptic Christian culture and held aloof from the outside world until the late 19th century. It emerged from its isolation under Emperor Menelik II, portrayed on the stamps introduced in

1894. The country continued to make progress under his daughter, the Empress Zauditu (Judith) and her successor, Prince Ras Tafari, who was crowned emperor, with the title Haile Selassie, in 1930.

Many Ethiopian stamps of the early 20th century portrayed the members of the imperial family, along with exotic wildlife. Haile Selassie [18] reigned twice (1930–6 and 1941–74), steering his vast country into the modern world. Accusations of corruption levelled at the emperor, together with strikes and economic hardship arising from a severe drought, led to the abolition of the monarchy following a military coup, and Ethiopia became a republic [19]. In 1976 the ruling military junta proclaimed Ethiopia a socialist state, but in 1991, following a change of regime, Ethiopia emerged as a federal republic. Oddly, none of these political upheavals was reflected in any change of title on the stamps.

As a result of the new constitution of 1991 the province of Eritrea, which had fought a long and bitter civil war, was formally granted autonomy, and in 1993, following a plebiscite, it voted for outright independence from Ethiopia. Distinctive stamps appeared in 1991 to celebrate autonomy and the 30th anniversary of the armed struggle, followed by definitives showing the national flag and map. Most Eritrean stamps have been printed in Italy, the former colonial power.

Below: In 1995 Eritrea issued a set on the theme of the Council for Mutual Economic Assistance in Africa. The top value shows the emblems and flags of the member countries.

10

11

12

13

14

15

16

17

18

19

1
2
3
4
5
6
7
8
9
10
11

EAST AFRICA

This region, now comprising the republics of Kenya, Uganda and Tanzania, was colonized by the British in the 1890s and absorbed the former German East Africa (Tanganyika) during World War I. The postal services of this new British East African territory (later renamed the East African Posts and Telecommunications Corporation) were unified, although the component countries had political autonomy. This situation continued for some years after all three countries became independent republics within the Commonwealth. Nationalism developed rapidly after World War II in the "wind of change" that was blowing across the African continent. Kenya won its independence in 1963 after a long period of guerrilla warfare, and the other two republics soon followed.

Left: The architect of Kenyan independence was Jomo Kenyatta. Imprisoned by the British during the Mau Mau campaign in the 1950s, while in detention he was elected president of the national Kenya Africa Union party, becoming prime minister in 1963 and president of the republic a year later. His moderate policies and statesmanship conciliated the white community and made Kenya one of the most stable countries in Africa.

KENYA, UGANDA AND TANGANYIKA

East Africa was opened up by the Imperial British East Africa Company, which issued its own stamps [1] from 1890 to 1895, when it was taken over by the British government. In the same period a protectorate was proclaimed over Uganda, whose stamps featured a portrait of Queen Victoria by Baron Heinrich von Angeli [2]. The postal services of both territories were combined in 1903 and stamps portraying Edward VII [3] were introduced; the same frames were later used for stamps showing George V. The neater title of Kenya and Uganda was adopted in 1922 when British East Africa was transformed from a protectorate into a crown colony [4]. The former German colony of Tanganyika joined the postal union in 1935 and stamps bearing the names of all three countries were issued from then onwards.

It is important to note that, although collectors refer to this group as "Kenya, Uganda and Tanganyika" (KUT), the authorities were at pains to vary the order of the inscriptions so that no single territory assumed a dominant position. The inaugural series was in the prevailing colonial fashion for bicoloured pictorials, with a portrait of George V inset, and the series was re-issued in 1938 with the portrait of George VI substituted [5]. Stamps bearing the names of the three countries [6] continued until the 1960s, after they had become independent politically and even had their own stamps. From 1965 to 1975 stamps inscribed with the names of Kenya, Uganda and Tanzania were produced by the East African Posts and Telecommunications Corporation [7].

KENYA

Achieving independence in December 1963, Kenya became a republic a year later. The inaugural series inscribed "Uhuru" (Swahili for "independence") showed a mixture of subjects [8] but stamps since then have favoured natural history [9–10], handicrafts [12] and other subjects likely to attract tourists. They have also featured many universal organizations, such as Rotary, whose founder Paul P. Harris was portrayed on a stamp of 1994 for the 50th anniversary of the Mombasa club [11].

UGANDA

Distinctive Ugandan stamps were re-introduced in 1962, beginning with a set marking the centenary of the discovery of the source of the Nile [13]. Recess-printed, with a profile of Elizabeth II, these stamps were a far cry from the gaudy issues of later years, although the tyrant Idi Amin did not leave his mark on Ugandan stamps.

In later years stamps had a global outlook [14] but more recently Uganda has jumped on the thematic bandwagon with numerous sets – including the ever-popular Disney stamps [15] – aimed at collectors.

TANZANIA

Germany colonized Tanganyika in the 1890s and issued stamps inscribed "Deutsch-Ostafrika" [16] from 1893 to 1916, when the colony was occupied by British imperial forces. In this period stamps of the Indian Expeditionary Force were overprinted for use by troops on Mafia Island [17] blockading the Rufiji delta. From November 1917 German East Africa was under British administration and used stamps of East Africa and Uganda overprinted "G.E.A." [18]. Distinctive stamps featuring a giraffe [19] were introduced in Tanganyika in 1922 and continued until 1935, when the unified series was adopted. Though it was the last of the three countries to join the Commonwealth, Tanganyika was the first to gain independence, in 1961. Pictorial stamps inscribed "Uhuru" were issued in December that year.

Below: Lions of the Serengeti featured on one of Tanganyika's independence set of 1961 (left), and Sultan Kalif bin Harub on the Zanzibar definitive series of 1952 (right).

Missionary Mail

Uganda in the late 1880s was in a religious ferment as Muslim, Catholic and Protestant factions fought each other for converts. After the Anglo-German agreement of 1890, in which Britain exchanged Heligoland for a free hand in Uganda and Zanzibar, British influence increased and its missionaries were able to continue their work unhindered. One of these, the Reverend Ernest Millar at Mengo, organized the first postal service in March 1895, using sermon paper to produce stamps of a very basic design on his typewriter. Gum was supplied by the resin of a nearby tree.

The offshore island of Zanzibar, formerly centre of the Arab slave trade in Africa, had been a British protectorate since 1895 and originally used Indian stamps suitably overprinted. Later issues portrayed the sultans, dhows and distinctive Arabic architecture of the island. It gained full independence in December 1963 but only a few weeks later an African-inspired revolution toppled the sultan. Shortly afterwards Zanzibar joined Tanganyika to form the United Republic of Tanganyika and Zanzibar, soon shortened to Tanzania, but continued to issue its own stamps until 1967. During this period, despite the apparent unity represented by the stamps, Zanzibar was very much a law unto itself, with a Marxist regime that had its stamps printed in the German Democratic Republic and used strident images on them to promote its extreme left-wing politics [20].

12

13

14

15

16

17

18

19

20

1

2

3

4

5

6

7

8

9

10

11

CENTRAL AFRICA

A British expedition sponsored by the imperialist and financier Cecil Rhodes led the "scramble for Africa" in the late 1880s and resulted in the annexation of 1.25 million sq km/0.5 million sq miles of southern and central Africa in the name of the British South Africa Company. Out of Rhodes's ambition to create a British empire that stretched from the Cape to Cairo came the Bechuanaland protectorate (now Botswana in southern Africa)

and three countries, formerly Northern and Southern Rhodesia and Nyasaland, but now known as Zambia, Zimbabwe and Malawi respectively.

Left: Cecil Rhodes made a fortune from the Kimberley diamond mines before entering politics and becoming prime minister of Cape Colony. At the same time his imperial ambitions led him to found the British South Africa Company as well as endowing Rhodes scholarships for Americans, Germans and colonials at Oxford University.

COMPANY RULE

Stamps inscribed "British South Africa Company" were introduced in 1892 [1], followed by two later sets also featuring the company arms. A shortage of stamps during the Matabele rebellion of 1896 was met by overprinting stamps of the Cape of Good Hope [2]. Although stamps continued to bear the company name until 1909, the name "Rhodesia" was adopted in 1895. Cecil Rhodes thus joined the elite band of those, including Amerigo Vespucci, Christopher Columbus and Simon Bolivar, who had countries named after them, the only difference being that he chose the name himself.

Sadly Rhodes did not live long enough to see his name on the stamps for he died in 1902, worn out by his exertions in the defence of Kimberley during the Boer War. In April 1909 existing stamps of the British South Africa Company were overprinted "Rhodesia" [3], pending a supply of stamps with this name engraved at the foot, although the company name continued to appear at the top. The inaugural series of 1910 is popularly known as the Doubleheads, on account of its side-by-side portraits of George V and Queen Mary. This bicoloured series was not only very beautiful but also rich in its philatelic variety.

It was superseded by the Admirals, so-called because the series portrayed the king in naval uniform.

Further north, an expedition led by Sir Harry Johnstone occupied Nyasaland in 1893 to prevent the Portuguese from joining Angola to Mozambique. Sir Harry not only founded British Central Africa but even designed its stamps [4]. Stamps of this territory included a provisional issue in 1898 that utilized the upright oval designs normally embossed on cheques to create 1d stamps during a shortage of that denomination.

COLONIAL RULE

Following a proposal in 1923 by the British government to detach the main area of white settlement from company territory and join it to South Africa, the white settlers voted to become a separate crown colony with self-governing status. In 1924, therefore, the company's territories were divided into Northern and Southern Rhodesia and thereafter used stamps thus inscribed.

In both territories definitives portrayed the reigning monarch [5]. The Victoria Falls featured in several issues of Southern Rhodesia, including sets celebrating the silver jubilee of George V in 1935 [7] and the coronation of George VI in 1937. British Central

Illegal Stamps

The regime of Ian Smith in Rhodesia defied the British government by the illegal act of UDI (unilateral declaration of independence). When a stamp celebrating this event was issued, the British declared it invalid for postage, and any mail arriving in the UK with such stamps affixed was treated as unpaid and surcharged accordingly.

Africa was renamed the Nyasaland protectorate in 1907, and stamps portraying the reigning monarch were subsequently produced. A first tentative essay in pictorialism was the series of 1934, which showed a leopard on a rock, derived from the badge of the protectorate, with the profile of George V inset. The same motif, with a profile of George VI, was in use from 1938 to 1944 but then gave way to pictorial definitives [8]. In Northern Rhodesia small-format stamps managed to combine royal portraiture with a vignette of African wildlife [6].

FEDERATION

With the intention of creating an independent dominion, the three British territories in central Africa formed a federation in 1954 and introduced a joint issue of stamps inscribed "Rhodesia and Nyasaland" [9], followed by a small-format pictorial series [10]. Political disagreements emerged between the predominantly black countries and Southern Rhodesia, so this merger proved unworkable. When the federation broke up in 1964 each country resumed its own stamp issues. The only thing they had in common

was a penchant for small horizontal stamps, but whereas Southern Rhodesia [12] and Nyasaland [14] favoured a wide variety of subject, Northern Rhodesia produced a standard design showing the national emblem [13].

CHANGES OF NAME

Both Nyasaland and Northern Rhodesia attained independence in 1964 and reverted to names long used by their indigenous peoples. Thus Nyasaland became Malawi and Northern Rhodesia was renamed Zambia. Both celebrated their independence with stamps: Malawi portrayed Hastings Banda and the sunrise [11] while Zambia chose jubilant dancers [16]. Definitives under the new names continued existing patterns [15].

Most Zambian stamps since 1964 have been designed by Gabrielle Ellison [17]. This has given them an integrity that the stamps of many other African nations now lack, and until very recently they concentrated on subjects specific to the peoples of the country and their way of life, with attractive genre scenes [18–19]. Another unifying element in many stamps was the incorporation of a band of metallic ink alluding to the copper industry.

Southern Rhodesia merely dropped the "Southern" and retained the name of its founder, becoming a bastion of white supremacy. While affirming allegiance to the Crown, as exemplified in its Churchill stamp of 1965 [20], it was drifting apart from the mother country. In November that year it unilaterally declared independence. Stamps with an "Independence" overprint were followed by definitives omitting "Southern" [21]. Black majority rule eventually prevailed and in 1980 Rhodesia changed its name to Zimbabwe [22]. Stamps since then have either been thematic, with the usual themes of fauna and flora, or have highlighted the apparent technological progress of Zimbabwe [23]. In place of a portrait, these stamps feature the secretary bird, its national emblem, carved in soapstone.

1

2

3

4

5

6

7

8

9

10

11

WEST AFRICA

Four of the five countries on the west coast of Africa south of the Sahara were formerly British colonies, while the fifth, Liberia, shares with the others a common language (English) and a parallel history. Sierra Leone (1787) and Liberia (1822) were created by Britain and the USA respectively as homes for freed slaves, while the Gambia was, from 1808, a base for the Royal Navy in pursuit of slave-traders. The Gambia formed part of Sierra Leone until 1843, when it became a separate colony with a protectorate extending inland along the banks of the Gambia River.

The Gold Coast, which was first settled in 1821, was likewise administered by Sierra Leone until 1886. Nigeria first came under British influence in 1853, when a base was established at Lagos for the suppression of the slave trade. Later protectorates were proclaimed over the Oil Rivers and the Niger Coast. A chartered company penetrated the hinterland, which, in 1900, was formed into the separate colonies of Northern and Southern Nigeria; these were united in 1914.

Liberia had the distinction of being the first black African independent republic and it was from there that the concepts of nationalism and independence spread to the Gold Coast, the first of the British colonies to break away and become a dominion in 1957, assuming the name Ghana from an ancient African empire of that name.

Left: Dr Kwame Nkrumah (1909–72) was prime minister of Ghana from 1957 to 1960 and president from then until 1966, when he was ousted by a military coup while on a visit to China. Educated at Lincoln University in the USA, he is shown here posing in front of the Lincoln Memorial in Washington, DC.

THE GAMBIA

The first stamps are known as the Cameos, from the embossed profile of Queen Victoria [1]. From the 1920s pictorial stamps were recess-printed in the restrained two-colour settings fashionable until after World War II [3], giving way to multicolour photogravure with definitives following a single theme [4]. Since independence the Gambia has developed as a popular tourist destination [5]. It achieved autonomy in 1963, independence in 1965 and became a republic within the Commonwealth in 1970 [6].

GHANA

The first stamps of the Gold Coast were issued in 1875 and thereafter followed the prevailing colonial fashions for royal portraits. In 1928, however, it

became the first British colony to adopt photogravure, for a small-format series featuring Christiansborg Castle, a former Danish trading post in Accra, the capital [2]. Later definitives (1938–58) were recess-printed and reflected the British influence on the country [7]. Under Kwame Nkrumah [8], Ghana soon adopted an independent policy championing non-alignment and the cause of African freedom and unity [9], ideals maintained by his successors.

SIERRA LEONE

Sierra Leone introduced stamps in 1859, the first territory in West Africa to do so. They were confined to royal portraiture until 1932 when pictorial definitives were adopted [10–11]. Intaglio was employed from then until after independence was achieved in

1961. Since then a high proportion of the stamps have been colourful and exciting but seldom relevant to the country itself.

NIGERIA

Stamps were introduced at Lagos in 1874, portraying Queen Victoria [12]. Separate issues were discontinued in 1906 when Lagos joined Southern Nigeria. Ordinary British stamps were used in the Oil Rivers region pending the introduction of stamps overprinted after the territory was declared a protectorate in 1892 [13].

The protectorate was extended into the hinterland and renamed the Niger Coast Protectorate in May 1893, adopting stamps portraying the elderly Victoria the following January [14]. In 1900 Southern Nigeria was declared a crown colony and protectorate [15], while Northern Nigeria became a protectorate [16]. In January 1914 they were amalgamated to form Nigeria [17], which became an independent federation in 1960. Most stamps since then have been printed by the Nigerian Security Minting and Printing Company [18–19].

In 1967 the eastern region seceded from the federation under the name of Biafra and distinctive stamps were issued in 1968–9 before the area was overrun by federal forces. The stamps celebrating the first anniversary of independence depicted atrocities allegedly committed by the Nigerian army.

Below: Few charity stamps are as specific as this one from Liberia, which names a particular charity and shows Seán Devereux in action.

Free-form and Self-adhesive

Sierra Leone made philatelic history in 1964 when it produced the world's first self-adhesive stamps, die-cut in the shape of the country itself, with commercial advertisements on the backing paper.

LIBERIA

The first stamps appeared in 1860 and featured the seated figure of Liberty alongside a sailing ship, uncannily like the reverse of the British copper coinage of the period. By the 1880s pictorial designs were featuring scenery, wildlife and native types as well as presidential portraits in the American style. From 1894 onwards stamp designs [20] leaned heavily on the famous Cape Triangulars. Separate stamps for registered mail [21] were produced from 1893 to 1923, many bearing the names of individual towns. The earlier stamps even provided a space for the manuscript insertion of the registration serial number, but by 1919 a more pictorial approach had been adopted.

By the 1930s Liberia had virtually become the private fief of the Firestone Rubber Company and many stamps from then onwards had an American slant. The very prolific issues since the 1980s seldom allude to the chronic civil wars affecting the country, but more often express its indebtedness to the USA [22]. Although it is not a member of the Commonwealth, Liberia has even participated in colonial omnibus issues commemorating the British royal family.

PORTUGUESE AFRICA

The Portuguese had a head start on all other European nations in opening up the "Dark Continent". In the 15th century their seamen, encouraged by Prince Henry the Navigator, pushed far down the west coast of Africa, establishing the trading posts that would become the nuclei of colonies. In 1498 Vasco da Gama rounded the Cape of Good Hope and sailed up the east coast of Africa as far as Mombasa, Kenya, before striking east to India. The major Portuguese territories in West Africa ranged from Cape Verde in the north-west to Guinea and the Congo in the centre and Angola in the south. On the east coast the main colonies were in Mozambique and Nyassa. The rise of nationalism in the 1960s led to long-running warfare on both sides of the continent before Portugal granted independence in

1975. With the exception of Portuguese Guinea (now known as Guinea-Bissau), the former colonies have not changed their names since the grant of independence.

Left: Stamps for general use in the Portuguese colonies and protectorates in Africa were issued in 1898 for the quatercentenary of Vasco da Gama's discovery of the sea route to India.

ANGOLA

The earliest stamps of Angola, introduced in 1870, conformed to the prevailing keyplate types used throughout the colonial empire, only the name and currency being distinctive. Even as late as the 1930s special issues followed an omnibus pattern [1], but in the 1950s special issues [2] and individually styled definitives were coming into use. The first multicoloured set appeared in 1955 and featured a map of the colony [3]. Since independence, stamps of Angola have adopted a more frankly thematic approach, although few issues have been as minimalist as the birds series of the 1990s [5]. A set of 2000 featured post offices around the country [6]. The Portuguese Congo, now the province of Cabinda north of the River Congo, had its own keytype stamps [4] from 1894 to 1920, when it was absorbed by Angola.

CAPE VERDE

The Cape Verde archipelago consists of ten islands off the west coast of Africa. Discovered in 1456, they were colonized four years later by Diogo Gomes. They became a Portuguese overseas

province in 1951 and an independent republic in 1975. Standard colonial designs [7–8] were used until 1948 and new issues since then have been relatively moderate. The first full-colour stamps appeared in 1952, appropriately honouring the Portuguese navigators who used the islands as a staging post [9]. Tourism, wildlife and concern for the environment are recurring themes of more recent stamps [10].

GUINEA

The first stamps of Guinea consisted of those of Cape Verde overprinted in 1881. Thereafter, stamps of the keyplate types were inscribed for use until 1946, when a pictorial definitive series was adopted. In the 1960s stamps became more colourful and included an eye-catching diamond-shaped set devoted to indigenous snakes [11].

A revolt led by Amilcar Cabral against colonial rule erupted in 1963 and a decade later the republic of Guinea-Bissau was proclaimed. Its independence was recognized by the revolutionary government in Lisbon a year later, the first step towards the granting of independence to all the

other African colonies. Stamps since then have been predominantly thematic in nature, from fire engines [12] to cats and dogs [13].

MOZAMBIQUE

At one time the provinces of Inhambane [14], Quelimane, Tete [18] and Zambezia had their own stamps in the prevailing keytypes. Lourenço Marques, Mozambique's chief port, also issued colonial keyplate stamps, as well as a solitary stamp in 1952 [15]. During World War I Portuguese troops invaded German East Africa and occupied the district of Kionga; stamps of Lourenço Marques were overprinted for use there [20].

Separate issues were made by two chartered companies for territory under their control. The Mozambique Company was chartered in 1891 and issued stamps featuring the company arms, followed by pictorial definitives in 1918 [16] and a series designed and printed in England in 1937 [17]. The Nyassa Company was chartered in 1894. Pictorial stamps appeared in 1901, followed by a series of 1921 [19], both printed by Waterlow of London. Nyassa reverted to Mozambique in 1929. The stamps of Mozambique proper followed the colonial pattern, apart from some charity tax stamps during and after World War I, until 1944. Even thereafter, most issues

formed part of the Portuguese colonial omnibus series, but from 1951 attractive thematic sets appeared [21]. A restrained issue policy has been pursued since the country's independence. In 1995 Mozambique became a member of the Commonwealth.

ST THOMAS AND PRINCE

These two islands in the Gulf of Guinea were discovered by the Portuguese in 1471 and were used as a penal colony from 1493 onwards, accommodating common criminals as well as Jewish children forcibly taken from their parents and baptized. By the mid-16th century the islands were covered with sugar plantations. Continual raiding by the French and Dutch destroyed the islands' prosperity in the 17th and 18th centuries and the colony began to recover only after the introduction of cocoa cultivation in 1890.

The islands used the various Portuguese colonial types from 1870 to 1948, but in 1951 they attained the status of an overseas province with considerable autonomy, and a more liberal policy was inaugurated. Although many of the stamps in the ensuing period honoured Portuguese explorers and politicians there were also sets featuring wildlife, ships, military uniforms and other popular subjects.

The islands became a wholly independent republic on 12 July 1975. Since 1977, however, the country has produced prolific "bandwagon" issues of little indigenous relevance.

Below: Stamps portraying President Carmona of Portugal (left) were released to mark his visit to the African colonies in 1970. Even before joining the Commonwealth, Mozambique celebrated British events (right).

1

2

3

4

5

6

7

8

9

10

SOUTHERN AFRICA

Three countries adjoining, or even landlocked within, South Africa were formerly known as the High Commission Territories because they continued to be administered by the British High Commissioner in South Africa after that country became an independent dominion in 1910 and subsequently a republic outside the Commonwealth. Lesotho (formerly Basutoland) and Swaziland are enclaves within South Africa, while Botswana (formerly Bechuanaland) lies between South Africa and Zimbabwe.

Left: The position of these three countries in relation to South Africa and their other neighbours was vividly illustrated by this stamp of 1990, which celebrated the tenth anniversary of the Southern African Development Coordination Conference and showed the countries' boundaries and flags.

BRITISH INVOLVEMENT

The British developed an interest in the essentially tribal territories of southern Africa in the second half of the 19th century. British Bechuanaland was declared a crown colony in 1885 and at first used the stamps of the Cape of Good Hope with a distinctive overprint [1]. Two years later British stamps, similarly overprinted, were adopted and continued to be used in that region until 1895, when it was annexed by the Cape and subsequently became part of South Africa.

Tribal territory to the north of British Bechuanaland was made a protectorate in 1888. The British stamps that had previously been overprinted for use in British Bechuanaland were now additionally overprinted with the word "Protectorate" to denote their use in this area [2]. British stamps overprinted "Bechuanaland Protectorate" continued to be used there until 1932, when a series portraying George V showed cattle at a water-hole [3]. The "thirsty cattle" design was subsequently used for the definitives of George VI and Elizabeth II until 1961. Even the stamps celebrating the 75th anniversary of the protectorate showed thirsty cattle flanked by Queens Victoria and Elizabeth [5]. Sterling currency was replaced by South African rands and cents in 1961. At first, existing stamps

were overprinted pending a pictorial series featuring birds [4]. Most countries hail independence with a sunrise but here again the importance of water in a semi-arid region was reflected in the stamps of 1965 marking internal autonomy [6].

Up to 1933 Basutoland used the stamps of South Africa distinguishable only by the postmark, but in that year it followed Bechuanaland with a series portraying George V over a picture of a crocodile and the Drakensberg Mountains [7]. This motif was retained for the George VI series but in 1954 a pictorial series with different themes was adopted. All three territories adopted South African decimal currency in 1961. The inauguration of the Basuto National Council in 1959 was marked by three stamps and for the first time the indigenous name of "Lesotho" was inscribed alongside the European name [8].

BOTSWANA

Bechuanaland became an independent republic in 1966 and adopted the older form of the name. Early issues, such as the set of 1970 marking the centenary of the death of Charles Dickens [9], reflected continuing cultural ties with Britain. Later stamps, however, faithfully recorded every aspect of the life and culture of the country, from

Tradition Triumphant

The vast majority of Syrian stamps in recent years have maintained the tradition of blending military symbolism and portraits of President Hafez al-Assad with images drawn from the region's long and colourful history. A series of 1980 illustrated tales from the *Arabian Nights*, including Sinbad the Sailor (curiously captioned as Sindibad).

portrayed King Ghazi who, when he was killed in a car crash in 1939, was succeeded by his four-year-old son Faisal II [11]. Later definitives showed the boy king grown to manhood.

Faisal II's reign was brutally terminated when he was murdered on 14 July 1958. Stamps portraying him were overprinted to signify the republic [12] that installed General Karim Kassem, leader of the coup, as president [13]. Kassem eventually came to a sticky end when he was overthrown by Colonel Salem Aref in 1963. He in turn was ousted by the revolution of 1968, masterminded by Saddam Hussein, who had fled to Egypt after attempting to assassinate Kassem in 1959. Most stamps of Iraq in this turbulent period glorified the army [14–15], a trend that increased during the Saddam regime.

SYRIA

In 1919, following the Arab Revolt, the entire area of Syria and Lebanon was assigned to the French, who issued stamps overprinted to signify their military occupation [16]. A mandate by the League of Nations came into effect in September 1923, and stamps inscribed "Syrie" were then introduced,

of which the vast majority featured landmarks from Greek, Roman and Crusader times [17; 19]. In 1934 Syria became a republic under French control. Separate issues were made for the territory of the Alawites [18], which became the Republic of Latakia in 1930 but was absorbed by Syria in 1937 when the latter became a wholly independent republic.

The later history of Syria is one of revolutions and military coups. In 1958 Syria joined with Egypt to form the United Arab Republic and stamps were overprinted "UAR" pending the release of stamps thus inscribed. The union was dissolved in September 1961 and since then stamps have been inscribed for the Syrian Arab Republic, often denoted simply by the initials SAR.

Below: Syrian stamps were overprinted for use in Latakia in 1930 (top); the revolution of 30 March 1949, was celebrated by stamps portraying President Hushi el-Zaim (middle); and stamps were overprinted "UAR" in 1958 following Syria's union with Egypt (bottom).

10

11

12

13

14

15

16

17

18

19

1

2

3

4

5

6

7

8

9

10

MIDDLE EAST

The land at the eastern end of the Mediterranean was part of the Ottoman Empire until World War I. The Egyptian Expeditionary Force (EEF) under General Allenby advanced along the coast and took Palestine, while T.E. Lawrence organized the Arab Revolt, which liberated much of Arabia and the land east of the Jordan. Britain was granted a League of Nations mandate over Palestine and Transjordan. The British mandate over the latter ended in March 1946 when it became an independent kingdom. The mandate in Palestine ended on 14 May 1948, the day the State of Israel was proclaimed.

Left: Stamps of the EEF were overprinted in Arabic alone (far left), or in Arabic, Hebrew and English, for use in Transjordan and Palestine respectively.

JORDAN

Abdullah, son of the king of the Hejaz (later part of Saudi Arabia), was made Emir of Transjordan, becoming king when the mandate ended. Stamps of Saudi Arabia were overprinted in 1924 to signify "Government of the Arab East AH 1343" [1] while Abdullah's portrait appeared on stamps of 1927–44 [2]. When the British withdrew from Palestine the neighbouring Arab states declared war on the infant Jewish state. Jordan gained territory on the west bank of the river (including part of Jerusalem) and as a result the country was renamed the Hashemite Kingdom of Jordan. Abdullah's son Hussein succeeded in 1952 [3] and played a prominent part in the Arab League [4], where he was a useful counter to Egypt's Nasser (who tried several times to have him assassinated).

Many Jordanian stamps from the 1960s onwards were printed by Harrison's of England [5]. An interesting feature of the stamps after 1964 was their emphasis on Jordan's custody of the Christian holy places, notably the set of 14 in 1966 showing the Stations of the Cross [15]. Jordan played a major role in defusing tension in the Middle East. A set of ten devoted to Builders of World Peace (1967) included Pope John XXIII and Presidents Kennedy and Johnson as well as Hussein himself [6].

PALESTINE

During the British mandate, stamps featuring prominent landmarks such as King David's Citadel and the Dome of the Rock [9] were issued. The Hebrew version of the name Palestine terminated in the letters *aleph yud*, meaningless to anyone but the Jews, who realized that they were the initials of Eretz Yisrael (land of Israel). Yet when the first stamps of Israel appeared in May 1948 [8] they were merely inscribed "Do'ar Ivri" (Hebrew Post). By the time the Jewish New Year was celebrated that September, the inscription "Israel" was in use.

During the war of 1948 both Jordan and Egypt seized parts of Palestine, on the West Bank and the Gaza Strip respectively, and overprinted stamps for use in their occupied territories [10–11]. Egypt later released a number of stamps inscribed specifically for Palestine [7]. An Indian stamp overprinted "UNEF" (United Nations Emergency Force) was used by peacekeepers in Gaza. Victory in the Six Day War (1967) gave Israel possession of both territories.

ISRAEL

Although Israeli stamps are inscribed in Arabic as well as Hebrew, no stamps portrayed an Arab Israeli until 2004. The vast majority of Israeli stamps have either emphasized the country's military might [12] or drawn heavily on Jewish culture, often from Europe. A very few have portrayed Britons who played a part in the creation of the state, such as Lord Balfour or Orde Wingate [16]. Several issues have extolled the bravery of women, including Haviva Reik, a British agent killed by the Gestapo.

A unique feature of Israeli stamps is the tabs along the bottom row of the sheet, which often bear an apt Biblical quotation, as seen in the issue marking the 50th anniversary of the Balfour Declaration [14], or form an extension of the design of the stamp.

THE PALESTINE AUTHORITY

Control of Gaza and Jericho passed from Israel to the Palestinian Authority under Yasser Arafat in May 1994 and stamps printed in Berlin have been used there ever since. The first series was denominated in mils, the currency of Palestine up to 1948, but later issues have been valued in fils, the currency of Jordan. Most Palestinian stamps have, as in Jordan [15] previously, emphasized the Christian aspects of the Holy Land [17]. Stamps are regularly issued for Easter and Christmas [13].

Below: Israel issued a stamp in 1994 to mark the centenary of the "Dreyfus Affair". It shows the public disgrace of Captain Dreyfus, who was wrongfully convicted of treason. Emile Zola, whose newspaper article exposed French anti-semitism, appears on the tab below.

Wishful Thinking?

In 1964 Jordan issued a set of five stamps to publicize the Arab Summit Conference, which it hosted in Amman. The stamps portrayed King Hussein and a map of Palestine as it was in 1920, but unless you could read the minuscule Arabic inscription at the side you would be forgiven for thinking that the map represented an enlarged Jordan and that Israel simply did not exist.

Personalities featured on Palestinian stamps include Mother Teresa and the German politician Hans-Jurgen Wischnewski, who have appeared on annual issues made under the title of Friends of Palestine, invariably portrayed with Yasser Arafat.

Below: Every year Israel remembers its war dead with a stamp showing a different war memorial.

11

12

13

14

15

16

17

ARABIA

Four-fifths of the Arabian peninsula is occupied by Saudi Arabia, an absolute monarchy created in 1932 by Abdul Aziz Ibn Saud, Sultan of Nejd, who conquered most of eastern and central Arabia in 1923 and then occupied the kingdom of the Hejaz in 1924–5. The combined territories were renamed by him seven years later. To the south lay the kingdom and imamate of the Yemen. The whole of Arabia was nominally under Turkish rule but it broke up in the aftermath of the Arab Revolt during World War I. At the south-western tip of Arabia lay Aden, a British crown colony since 1839, together with the eastern and western Aden protectorate comprising a number of small sultanates. In 1963 they became the Federation of South Arabia, but four years later left the Commonwealth to form the Yemen People's Democratic Republic in November 1967.

Left: The designs for the first stamps of the Hejaz in 1916 were suggested by Lawrence of Arabia and were derived from carvings on doors or prayer niches in Cairo mosques, or stucco work over the entrance to Cairo railway station. The stamps were printed at the Survey of Egypt, Cairo.

SAUDI ARABIA

The ruler of the Hejaz was Hussein, Emir of Mecca, in whose reign stamps were introduced by T.E. Lawrence. True to Islam, they were non-figurative and relied heavily on quotations from the Koran [1]. In 1923 the Wahabis of Nejd, under Ibn Saud, began rapid expansion. In 1925 Hussein was forced to abdicate and go into exile in Cyprus, but his son Faisal was later made king of Transjordan. In 1924–5 the Wahabis of Nejd invaded and took over the Hejaz. Stamps for the joint territories showed the *toughra* of Ibn Saud [2]. Early Saudi Arabian stamps continued this tradition [3] but by the mid-1940s pictorialism was making a tentative appearance [4]. Pictorial definitives since 1960 have included the cartouche of the monarch in lieu of a portrait [5]. The first portrait stamp marked the installation of King Faisal in 1964 [7]; since then the palm tree and crossed swords emblem has usually been the only form of identification [8].

YEMEN

Imam Yahya became the spiritual ruler of the Yemen in 1904 and transformed it into a monarchy in 1918 when Turkish rule was overthrown. Stamps were introduced in 1926 and were non-figurative until 1946 [9], but a scenic definitive series appeared in 1951 [6] and thereafter stamps followed the western tradition. His successor, Imam Ahmed, died in September 1962 and his son Mohammed al-Badr proclaimed himself imam, but his palace was bombarded and rebels proclaimed a republic. The imam escaped to the mountains of the north-west and for several years there were two rival states: the Mutawakelite kingdom [10] and Yemen Arab Republic, often abbreviated to YAR on its stamps [11].

SOUTH ARABIA

The nucleus of South Arabia was the seaport of Aden at the south-western tip of the peninsula. It was originally occupied by the British in 1839 and used as a base to stamp out piracy, but following the opening of the Suez Canal in 1869 it became an important coaling station. It used Indian stamps, identifiable by their postmarks, until 1937, when a series featuring an Arab dhow flanked by curved daggers was introduced [12]. The series was re-issued in 1939 in an elongated format

PERSIA

The earliest stamps of Persia, introduced in 1868, were almost as primitive as those of Afghanistan. Although they were engraved by Albert Barre of Paris, they were printed in Tehran and the resulting impressions were very coarse [11]. Portraits of the Shah appeared from 1876 onwards, when stamps were printed in Vienna and later by Enschede of Haarlem [12]. Fine European printing contrasted with the numerous issues produced locally and their bewildering array of provisional overprints [13]. The coronation of Shah Ahmed in 1915 was celebrated by 51 stamps, the higher values with metallic gold frames [14].

IRAN

In October 1925 cavalry captain Riza Khan Pahlavi deposed Shah Ahmed Mirza and seized power; in December he was crowned Shahinshah of Persia and immediately began modernizing the tottering empire. Two-colour photogravure was adopted for the airmail series of 1930 [15] and stamps generally adopted a more westernized

Below: Many Iranian stamps celebrated the 2,500th anniversary of the Persian Empire (top) and a stamp of 1979 (bottom) designed by children, marked the International Year of the Child.

Mutilation Cancellation

Until the early 20th century the stamps of Afghanistan were cancelled by the postmaster or letter receiver by tearing a chunk out of them before mail went forward to its destination.

character. In 1935 Shah Riza changed the name of the country to Iran, an ancient term literally meaning "land of the Aryans". Despite westernization, Iranian stamps went through a phase when they were inscribed entirely in Farsi, including the set of 1939 celebrating the marriage of Crown Prince Mohammed Riza to Princess Fawzieh, sister of King Farouk of Egypt [16].

Shah Riza, intrigued with Nazi Germany, was ousted in favour of his son in 1941. From the late 1940s the stamps of Iran contrasted the glories of the ancient empire of the Medes and Persians with the achievements of the Pahlavi regime in modernizing such a vast and disparate country. On the whole, however, the stamps of the reign of Shah Mohammed looked back to ancient Persia, culminating in a veritable orgy of celebration for the 2,500th anniversary of the empire [17]. Stamps of 1968 marked the centenary of the first stamps with reproductions of the lion and sun design [18].

In January 1979 the Shah went to America for medical treatment and in his absence Ayatollah Khomeini returned from exile and began the revolution that transformed the westernized empire into a fundamentalist Islamic republic. Stamps in the era of the ayatollahs reflected their uncompromising religious fanaticism.

1

2

3

4

5

6

7

8

9

10

BURMA, PAKISTAN AND BANGLADESH

These three countries have had a common history, having been part of British India for very many years. The territories of Bangladesh and Pakistan came under the dominion of the Mughal emperors in the Middle Ages and thus passed into the hands of the East India Company in the 19th century. Burma was also part of British India, of which it was the largest province as well as the most easterly. It had been a powerful kingdom in its own right, but when its king invaded Bengal in 1825 the British retaliated and annexed Lower Burma in 1926. Two further Burmese wars, in 1852 and 1885, led to the entire country coming under British rule. It was granted autonomy in 1937, suffered Japanese occupation in 1942 and after liberation in 1945 adopted a nationalist government that attained full independence in 1947 and left the Commonwealth. Pakistan was created in the same year and consisted of the two predominantly Muslim parts of British India. However, as these were separated by India and ethnically different from each other, it was inevitable that they would split up. When West Pakistan resisted the secession of East Pakistan and tried to put down the revolt, the Indian Army intervened on the side of the rebels, whose independence as Bangladesh was confirmed in 1971.

Left: Stamps of 1955–6 showed maps of West and East Pakistan, the latter marking the first session of the Pakistani parliament in Dacca, the capital of Bengal. This was the region that seceded in 1970–1 to form Bangladesh. Stamps were usually inscribed in English and Arabic but this set was exceptionally inscribed in Bengali instead of English in an attempt to appease Bengali nationalism.

BURMA

Ordinary Indian stamps were used in Burma until April 1937, when it was separated from India and placed under direct British administration. Indian stamps were then overprinted for use there [1] pending a distinctive series released in 1938–40 [2]. Burma was the only country in the British Empire to celebrate the centenary of adhesive postage stamps, with an overprinted stamp issued in May 1940 [3].

The Japanese invaded Burma in 1942 and blotted out the portrait of George VI with a peacock emblem. In 1943 they set up a puppet government, which issued its own stamps. At the end of World War II the country was placed under military administration [4] prior to the creation of the Union

of Burma as a completely independent state [5]. While very few stamps were released in the ensuing years, they tended to emphasize the unique character of the people [6].

Following a referendum in December 1973 the military junta that had seized power in 1962 made way for a one-party socialist republic. Stamps with inscriptions reflecting this change were in use from 1974 [7] until the government changed the name of the country in 1990: "Myanmar", which had always been used in Burmese script, was adopted as the western form as well [8]. The country now holds the world record for the fewest new stamps, only about 20 having been issued since 1990, usually for the anniversary of independence.

Martyrs for the Cause

In 1991 Bangladesh celebrated the 20th anniversary of independence by embarking on a long series of stamps portraying Martyred Intellectuals – doctors, lawyers, politicians and teachers who lost their lives when Pakistan attempted by force to prevent the secession. These stamps were issued in sheets of ten different designs. A total of 240 different stamps were released, 30 at a time, up to 1999.

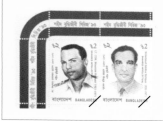

PAKISTAN

When the Islamic Dominion of Pakistan was created in August 1947 overprinted Indian stamps [9], many of them handstruck locally, were in use pending the supply of distinctive stamps in 1948 [10], recess-printed by the new Pakistan Security Printing Corporation, which has been responsible for the vast majority of stamps ever since. One of the earliest special issues marked the centenary of the Scinde Dawks, Asia's first stamps [11], as the formerly Indian province of Scinde now forms part of Pakistan.

In 1956 Pakistan became an Islamic republic [12] and thereafter stamps became more Muslim in character and content. By the early 1960s stamps were inscribed in English, Bengali and Urdu in a bid to placate the secessionist tendencies of East Pakistan [13]. A recurring theme was the quarrel with India over Kashmir, which had a mainly Muslim population but had remained in Indian hands [14]. From time to time the philatelic propaganda campaign has erupted into border incidents that have almost brought India

and Pakistan to open warfare. More recent stamps have reflected Pakistan's involvement in world affairs, including an issue publicizing its expedition to Antarctica [15]. One thing Pakistan has in common with India is a policy of issuing mainly single stamps, often portraying personalities little known by the rest of the world, although a 1990s series celebrated Pioneers of Freedom.

BANGLADESH

In time-honoured fashion the new country made use of overprinted Pakistani stamps before adopting distinctive stamps. The first series of these, issued in July 1971, showed a map of the new country [17] and portrayed the leader of the struggle for independence, Shaikh Mujibur Rahman [16]. Over the past 30 years the stamps of Bangladesh have been printed as far afield as Vienna and Melbourne. Many of them provide public service messages to the population [18] but the majority emphasize the distinctive cultural heritage of the country [19].

Below: The Bagha mosque of Rajshahi (top) was part of the 1997 Historic Mosque set, and a 2000 stamp (bottom) marked the tenth anniversary of the uprising for the restoration of democracy.

INDIA

The subcontinent of India has fostered civilizations for thousands of years and is home to almost a billion people of many languages, cultures and religions. The only factor common to all educated Indians is the English language, but in the scramble for India the British were late starters. The Portuguese got there first, in 1498, followed by the French and the Danes. The British founded the Honourable East India Company in 1600 to trade with India and the Far East, establishing its first settlement at Surat in 1612. Bombay was ceded by Portugal as part of Catherine of Braganza's dowry when she married Charles II in 1662. By 1700 Britain also had control of Madras and further expansion came at the expense of the French, who were defeated by Robert Clive in 1757. Over the ensuing century the East India Company gained control of the whole of India by bribery or force, ruling directly or through the feudatory princes. The Sepoy Mutiny (1857) led to the administration of India being handed over to the imperial government.

Indian nationalism grew after World War I, under the charismatic leadership of M.K. Gandhi. Britain agreed to independence in principle in 1931 but implementation was delayed by disagreement between the Hindu and Muslim factions. India eventually gained independence in August 1947, but was partitioned between India and Pakistan, with great bloodshed and ethnic cleansing, creating the greatest upheaval of population.

Left: Mohandas Karamchand Gandhi, architect of Indian independence, was assassinated by a Hindu fanatic on 30 January 1948, because he had failed to prevent the secession of Pakistan. The first of many stamps portraying him were released on 15 August 1948, the first anniversary of India's independence.

BRITISH INDIA

In 1852 India had the distinction of issuing the first stamps in Asia, the Scinde Dawks (derived from the name of the province and *dawk*, the Hindi word for posts). They were embossed and bore the emblem of the HEIC [1]. Stamps for the whole of India were introduced in 1854 [2] and from 1855 to 1926 were printed by De La Rue in England [3]. The inscription "East India" continued in use until 1877, when India was declared an empire with Victoria as Empress. Later definitives portrayed the reigning monarch [4] until 1947 and included the George VI series showing the many forms of mail transport in use [5]. India's first commemorative stamps appeared in 1931 to celebrate the inauguration of New Delhi as the nation's capital [6].

REPUBLIC OF INDIA

A set of three stamps was released on the day independence was proclaimed. The communal violence, which created an immense refugee problem, induced the Indian government to issue compulsory tax stamps in aid of refugee relief [7]. The same device was used in the 1970s to help refugees from the former East Pakistan.

Most definitives, such as those publicizing the Five Year Plan of 1955 [8], have retained the small size used under the British Raj. When the currency was decimalized in 1957 stamps showing the map were released [9]. Later sets were often didactic, educating the Indian public by focusing on social and economic matters from good husbandry to family planning. The latest series portrays prominent figures [10].

Most special issues are single stamps portraying historic personalities. Relatively few, such as Nehru [11], are known outside India. Subhas Chandra Bose was the leader of the Free India movement [12] who collaborated with the Japanese during World War II. The conquest of Everest in 1953 was marked by stamps showing the mountain, but it has also featured in several later issues [13]. Very few non-Indians have been portrayed, although they include Lord Mountbatten (the last Viceroy), Annie Besant (the founder of the theosophist movement), Abraham Lincoln [14] and Martin Luther King [15]. Philatelic tributes to the great and good of the past [16], as well as the religions and mythology of the subcontinent [17], are aimed at making Indians more aware of their diverse cultural heritage.

HIMALAYAN KINGDOMS
Nepal, the world's only Hindu kingdom, was welded into a single state in the late 18th century when the Gurkha ruler conquered a number of independent mountain principalities. Nepal had its own stamps from 1881 [18] but they were confined to internal mail until 1959, when Nepal joined the Universal Postal Union, and until then Indian stamps were used on mail going abroad. Everest, which lies partly in Nepal, features prominently on the modern stamps [19].

The kingdom of Bhutan also had stamps for internal use [20] until 1969, when it joined the UPU. Even before that date, however, it had embarked on prolific issues aimed at the international philatelic market.

EUROPEAN COLONIES
In the 17th and early 18th centuries France rivalled Britain for possession of India, but by the Treaty of Paris, which ended the Seven Years War, France relinquished all her territory except for Pondicherry and four other small outposts. These constituted the French Indian Settlements until 1954 when they were taken over by the Republic

of India. The French colonial keytypes, suitably inscribed, were introduced in 1892, followed by bicoloured pictorials in 1914 showing the god Brahma and a temple near Pondicherry. These stamps were overprinted "France Libre" in 1941 when the settlements joined the Free French, and subsequently a set of stamps produced in England was released [21]. A postwar series featured various Hindu deities.

The Portuguese territories of Goa, Damao and Diu on the west coast were all that remained of the territory acquired by Portugal from 1510 onwards, following Vasco da Gama's discovery of the sea route to India. Distinctive stamps, designed and printed in Goa, were introduced in 1871, and the local issues were superseded by colonial keytypes from 1877 to 1945, followed by a set portraying historic figures [22]. Portuguese stamps were withdrawn in 1961 when the territory was annexed by India.

13 14

15

16 17

18 19

20

21 22

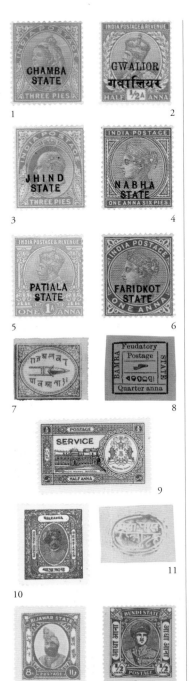

1   2

3   4

5   6

7   8

9

10   11

12   13

INDIAN STATES

In prewar India the British Raj ruled almost 400 million people, a fifth of the world total at that time. It was the most amazing mix of humanity, with 203 languages, many different ethnic groups and a dozen major religions. The British administration was divided into 17 provinces but the number of states ran to four figures. Some of the states were larger than many European countries, with their own armies; others were little more than tribal groups headed by chieftains.

More than 40 states had their own distinctive postage stamps at one time or another, a mere drop in the ocean compared with those that had rev-

enue stamps. Surprisingly, two of the largest states, Mysore and Baroda, did not have their own postage stamps, being content to use the facilities of the British Indian postal service.

Left: Charkari began with crudely printed stamps in 1894 but pictorials were in use from 1931 to 1948, when the state became part of Vindhya Pradesh.

CONVENTION STATES

Collectors divide the stamps of the states into two separate categories. The Convention States were those that signed postal conventions with the imperial administration, whereby the latter supplied them with Indian stamps overprinted for use in their states. These stamps were valid for postage within the state, to other convention states and anywhere within British India. The various conventions were negotiated between 1884 and 1887. The stamps of Chamba [1], Gwalior [2], Jind [3], Nabha [4] and Patiala [5] were still in use at the end of 1950, when they were replaced by the issues of the Republic of India. Faridkot [6] was the last state to adopt this system (1887), having previously issued its own stamps, and it was the first to abandon them, in 1901.

FEUDATORY STATES

The stamps issued by the princely states were valid only for postage within each state, except in a few instances. Stamps of Cochin [15], for example, were also valid on mail to neighbouring Travancore [39] and vice versa. Indeed these two states combined in 1949 and their joint stamps were then valid for mail throughout India and abroad [35].

Only one state in what later became Pakistan – Las Bela [29] – issued stamps in the imperial period, but one other began issuing stamps after the subcontinent broke up.

The stamps of the Feudatory States ranged from the extremely crude issues of Bhor [11], struck by hand, to the elegant stamps of Jaipur and Saurashtra [38]. They were printed by every method, including a high proportion of the very few printed by the halftone process [12; 20]. As many stamps have inscriptions only in their indigenous language they are identified here.

Alwar [7] issued stamps from 1877 to 1902, while the typeset stamps of Bamra [8] were in use from 1888 to 1895. Barwani did not commence until 1921 [10] but continued until the state was absorbed by Madhya Bharat in July 1948. Bhopal had ordinary stamps from 1872 to 1902 but continued to issue "Service" stamps for official mail until 1949 [9]. The hand-struck stamps of Bhor [11] appeared in 1879, while Bijawar's issues were confined to 1935–41 [12]. Bundi's stamps ran from 1894 to 1948 and ranged from extreme primitives to the last set, typeset by the *Times of India* [13]. Bussahir's stamps from 1895 to 1900 were overprinted with a security

Briefly Independent

Bahawalpur was independent between the partition of India on August 15, 1947, and joining Pakistan on October 3. No fewer than 46 stamps were issued in that period. Bahawalpur also had stamps for official mail from 1945, which remained valid until 1953.

monogram [14], as were those of Dhar in 1887–1900 [16]. Dungarpur had stamps from 1933 to 1947. Duttia (or Datia) had armorial stamps from about 1894 to 1920 [17]. Faridkot had very primitive stamps in 1879–86 [18] before adopting the Convention States' issues. Hyderabad's stamps ranged from 1869 to 1949 [19], but Idar's postal issues were confined to 1932–44 [20].

Indore or Holkar produced stamps from 1886 to 1948 [21], while Jaipur issued them from 1904 to 1949, both states ranging from the crude to the sophisticated. The stamps of Jammu and Kashmir from 1866 to 1894 [22] were non-figural. Jasdan's 1a stamps of 1942–7 featured the sun [23], while Jhalawar's stamps of 1886–1900 showed a dancing nymph [24].

Other states were Jind in 1874–85, Kishangarh in 1899–1949 [28], Morvi in 1931–48 [30], Nandgaon in 1891–4 [31], Nawanagar in 1877–93 [26], Orchha in 1913–48 [34], Poonch in 1876–88 [27], Rajpipla in 1880 [32], Shahpura in 1914–48 [36], Sirmoor in 1878–1901 [37], Soruth in 1864–1913 [33], when it became Saurashtra [38], and Wadhwan in 1888–94. Cochin from 1892 [15] and Travancore from 1898 [39] united to form Travancore-Cochin [35] in 1949.

INDIAN OCEAN

Dotted around the Indian Ocean are a number of archipelagos and individual islands, all of which are, or were, colonized by Britain or France. Some, like Sri Lanka, have a civilization dating back thousands of years, which saw the Portuguese and the Dutch come and go before falling into British hands. At the other end of the ocean, Mauritius was settled by Arabs and Malays before passing to the Dutch, then the French, before it fell to Britain during the Napoleonic Wars. Madagascar was contested by Britain and France before the latter triumphed. Other islands were gradually snapped up by the two major colonial powers in the 19th century. Relatively

undeveloped, their mainstay was fishing and coconut cultivation until the advent of tourism in more recent years.

Left: Sri Lanka, formerly Ceylon, is arguably the foremost preserver of Buddhism, as reflected in numerous stamps. This one of 1959 marks the inauguration of the Pirivena universities.

SRI LANKA

Formerly Ceylon, Sri Lanka was taken from the Dutch in 1802 and became a British crown colony, adopting stamps in 1857. They followed the prevailing British colonial patterns, using various portraits of Queen Victoria until 1900. Following the switch from sterling to a decimal system based on the rupee in 1872, Ceylon acquired an unenviable reputation for its enormous number of provisional surcharges throughout the 1880s and 1890s. After the Edwardian series the colonial keytypes were adopted for the stamps of George V, followed by scenic pictorials in 1935 with the king's portrait inset. The same designs were retained under George VI with his portrait substituted [1].

Although Ceylon became a dominion in 1948, ties to the British Crown remained strong, exemplified by stamps for the coronation and royal visit of 1954 [2]. It became the Republic of Sri Lanka in May 1972, and most stamps since that time have featured local personalities and institutions, with a strong Buddhist flavour [3–4].

MAURITIUS AND DEPENDENCIES

Although to this day French influence has remained strong in the language and customs of Mauritius, it was one of the few British colonies to celebrate the diamond jubilee of Queen Victoria with stamps [5]. After achieving self-government in 1967 the island became a republic within the Commonwealth in 1992 [6]. It continues a modest policy regarding new issues, which publicize tourism and an unchanging way of life [7–8].

The Seychelles were formerly a dependency of Mauritius and used its stamps, distinguishable only by their postmark, until they adopted distinctive stamps in 1890. Many stamps issued since gaining independence in 1975 have featured the wildlife of the islands, a major tourist attraction [9]. The Seychelles Outer Islands (Les Iles Eloignés Seychelles), comprising several outlying islands, had their own stamps from 1980 to 1992 and were served by a ship acting as a floating post office. During that period three different forms of the name in the local phonetic patois were tried.

The Chagos archipelago, formerly administered by Mauritius, became a separate crown colony in 1965 under the name of the British Indian Ocean Territory [10]. It included the Seychelles Outer Islands, but when the Seychelles became independent these outliers reverted to them.

MALDIVE ISLANDS

Lying to the south of Ceylon (Sri Lanka), this archipelago was a British protectorate and used stamps of Ceylon suitably overprinted before adopting distinctive stamps in 1933. In 1953 it briefly became a republic, but reverted to a sultanate later the same year. Since then it has become one of the most prolific stamp-issuing countries in the world. The vast majority of Maldives stamps have no bearing on the islands but are aimed at the world philatelic market [11–12].

MADAGASCAR AND DEPENDENCIES

An independent kingdom until the late 19th century, Madagascar's mail services were operated by the British consul (overseas post) and a syndicate of businessmen (inland mail), both using distinctive stamps [13]. These posts were suppressed by the French when they subjugated the island in 1895. French colonial stamps [15] were in use from then until 1958, when Madagascar attained independence as the Malagasy Republic, but it reverted

to its original name in 1992. Since then, like the Maldives, it has gone overboard on stamps that are more relevant to the USA than to the Indian Ocean, including a lengthy series cashing in on the *Titanic* craze.

North-west of Madagascar lies the Comoro archipelago. Each island in the group at first issued its own stamps, using the French colonial standard design with the name at the foot [14], but a general series was substituted in 1950 [16]. When the Comoros became an independent state, Mayotte was detached and became an overseas department of France. French stamps were used until 1997, when distinctive stamps were adopted.

Réunion, east of Madagascar, had its own stamps as long ago as 1852 but from 1891 used the French colonial keytypes. It used distinctive stamps from 1907 [17] as well as a Free French issue during World War II. Réunion became an overseas department of France after the war and the majority of its stamps were French, inscribed or overprinted in colonial francs. In 1975 it adopted the French metropolitan currency and separate stamp issues were then discontinued.

Below: The stamps of present-day Mayotte reflect the exuberance of the people (top). The Free French stamps of Réunion showed local produce (bottom).

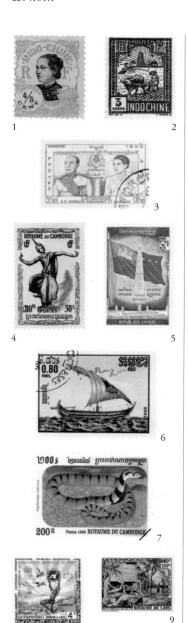

INDOCHINA

The French conquered Indochina in the late 19th century, the name being given from 1888 onwards to the colonies and protectorates of Cochin-China, Annam and Tongking (Vietnam) and Cambodia, to which were later added Laos (1893) and Kouang-Tcheou (1900). With an area greater than France itself, inhabited by peoples of diverse races with civilizations dating back many centuries, it is not surprising that colonial rule was resisted to a greater or lesser degree.

Resistance was greatest in north and central Vietnam, where Nguyen Ai Quoc (later known as Ho Chi Minh) campaigned for independence from the 1920s. Japan occupied Indochina in 1942–5 but allowed the Vichy administration to continue. During this period anti-Japanese resistance was organized by Ho. When French power was restored in 1945 France created the United States of Indochina, giving limited autonomy to each region. The Viet Minh waged war to unite the Vietnamese regions. In 1950 France tried to retain overall power in the area by giving greater autonomy to Vietnam and the kingdoms of Cambodia and Laos, but by that time its action was too little and too late.

Left: Ho Chi Minh (1892–1969), prime minister (1954–5) and president (1955–69) of North Vietnam, led the Viet Minh resistance movement from 1941 against the Japanese and later the French. "Uncle Ho" was also the driving force in the war between North and South Vietnam in the 1960s.

CAMBODIA

The French had produced stamps showing indigenous subjects for the whole of Indochina from 1889 to 1945 [1–2]. Stamps for the independent kingdom of Cambodia were introduced in 1951. King Norodom Sihanouk abdicated in 1955 in favour of his father Norodom Suramarit [3] but continued as president of the council of ministers. Stamps from this period concentrated on Cambodian culture [4]. When Suramarit died in 1960 Sihanouk refused the crown but ruled as chief of state. In 1970 he was deposed by the Khmer Rouge communist rebels, who established the Khmer republic [5] under Lon Nol.

In turn Lon Nol was overthrown by Pol Pot, who created Democratic Kampuchea. He abolished money, public transport and the postal service as well as murdering countless thousands of his own people. The country was liberated by Vietnamese forces, and the People's Republic of Kampuchea was proclaimed in 1969. The stamps of the ensuing period were apolitical and strongly thematic [6], a policy continued after the Vietnamese withdrawal in 1989 and reversion to the name of Cambodia [7]. The kingdom was restored, with Norodom Sihanouk once more on the throne.

LAOS

Compared with that of its neighbours, the history of Laos since independence in 1951 has been relatively stable. It remained a kingdom until 1975, when King Savang Vatthana abdicated and the Pathet Lao rebels proclaimed a people's democratic republic. Under the monarchy, most stamps were produced in France, mainly by intaglio [8] but latterly in multicolour lithography [9]. In the republican period they have been predominantly thematic [12].

VIETNAM

The Vietnam Democratic Republic was proclaimed by Ho Chi Minh [13] at Hanoi in September 1945 and was initially recognized by France, but relations deteriorated and erupted into guerrilla warfare. By 1947 the Viet Minh had withdrawn to northern Tongking [10]. In 1951 the French created Vietnam as an independent state within the French Union [11] but gradually the Viet Minh fought back. After they had decisively defeated the French at Dien Bien Phu in 1954 [14] a conference in Geneva partitioned the country at the 17th parallel.

The stamps of North Vietnam were extremely political, either attacking the USA directly for its support of the South, or praising those who protested against American policy, such as Norman Morrison, a Quaker who burned himself to death. Stamps supported Cuba and mourned the Marxist leader of Chile, Salvador Allende [15]. Separate issues were made in 1963–76 by the National Front for the Liberation of South Vietnam and these,

Below: A set of four stamps was issued by South Vietnam in 1968 to express thanks for international aid (top). Many recent issues of Vietnam feature wildlife (bottom).

Shooting Down the Enemy
During the Vietnam War the US Air Force carried out numerous air raids on North Vietnam and areas of the South controlled by the Viet Cong. A recurring theme of stamps in this period was the shooting down of American planes, often showing downed fliers as prisoners or anti-aircraft batteries in action, with the latest score.

if anything, were even more virulently anti-American [16]. By contrast, the stamps of South Vietnam highlighted the plight of refugees from the North [17] or promoted the solidarity of its allies in the long-drawn-out war.

Following the American withdrawal in 1975 the country was re-unified under the name of the Socialist Republic of Vietnam. Since then stamps have simply been inscribed "Viet nam" and have been devoted to the usual range of popular subjects.

KEEPING THE PEACE
In August 1954 the International Control Commission for Indonesia was created by the Geneva Declaration. It was chaired by India, regarded as the leading power among the neutral nations of the world, with Canada and Poland as the other members. Joint inspection teams of service personnel were provided with 1949 Indian definitives overprinted in Hindi, for separate use in Cambodia [18], Laos [19] and Vietnam. In 1960 the map series was overprinted for use in Laos and Vietnam [20]. They were replaced in 1965 by stamps overprinted "ICC" for use throughout Indochina [21].

12

13

14

15

16

17

18

19

20

21

1

2

3

4

5

6

7

8

9

10

11

12

CHINA

The world's largest country, China is inhabited by a quarter of the human race. The Manchu dynasty, which had ruled China since 1644, was overthrown by Sun Yat-sen in 1911 but the republic barely survived the trauma of World War I. Central government collapsed in the 1920s as China was polarized between communism and nationalism, led by Mao Zedong and

Chiang Kai-shek respectively. Breakaway provinces were ruled by warlords and the country was on the brink of anarchy. From 1931 onwards it was also prey to the aggression of the Japanese. At the end of World War II the Japanese returned Taiwan (which it had seized in 1895) just in time to provide the nationalists with a home after they were ousted from the mainland. The People's Republic of China was proclaimed in September 1949.

Left: Mao Zedong, the red flag and a military parade in Beijing were potent symbols used on many stamps from 1949 onwards.

EARLY POSTAL SERVICES

Although the Chinese emperors had a very sophisticated communications network for thousands of years, there was no countrywide postal service open to the public before 1897. The first stamps were issued in Shanghai in 1865, and were later overprinted to commemorate 50 years of international settlement [1]. The various towns with international communities under the terms of the Treaty of Nanking (1842) followed suit, and distinctive stamps were issued by Amoy, Chefoo [3], Chinkiang, Chungking, Foochow, Hankow, Ichang, Kewkiang, Nanking, Wei Hai Wei and Wuhu.

Several foreign powers operated postal agencies in China to facilitate the handling of overseas mail. Following the murder of German missionaries in Shantung, Germany occupied the port of Tsingtao and subsequently acquired a 99-year lease of Kiaochow, which had its own stamps [2], until the outbreak of World War I, when it was captured by the Japanese.

In 1863 Robert Hart was appointed Inspector General of the Imperial Customs and it was under this department that a new postal service was

introduced in 1878 [5]. Knighted in 1882, Sir Robert went on to organize the Chinese Imperial Post in 1897. The last issue of the empire appeared in 1909 and celebrated the first anniversary of the accession of the baby Emperor Hsuan T'ung. Appropriately it depicted the Temple of Heaven in the Forbidden City [4]. Deposed in 1912, Hsuan T'ung continued to live in the Summer Palace in seclusion but in 1932 he was plucked from obscurity by the Japanese to rule Manchukuo (formerly Manchuria) under the title of Kangde. Stamps of the puppet empire were issued from 1932 until 1945 [6].

NATIONALIST REPUBLIC

The first special stamps of the republic appeared in December and portrayed Sun Yat-sen, who had engineered the overthrow of the Manchu dynasty. Subsequently he appeared on most of the definitive sets down to 1949 [9]. An airmail series introduced in 1932 showed the Great Wall of China [7]. In addition to the mainstream issues of the republic, stamps were overprinted or surcharged for use in many of the provinces where the yuan fluctuated in value. From 1927, when war between

Gymnastics by Radio
A set of 40 stamps was issued in 1952 to illustrate a radio gymnastics programme, and everyone was expected to practise daily.

nationalists and communists broke out, there were many local posts in areas under communist control.

War with Japan erupted in 1931 and escalated in the ensuing decade. The value of the yuan plummeted [8], as shown by the inflated value of this stamp, and China suffered hyperinflation from 1946 until the nationalists withdrew from the mainland three years later [10].

COMMUNIST INSURGENCE
By 1937 the Japanese had occupied most of China but both communists and nationalists put up a strong resistance. The communist guerrilla armies operated in Japanese-held territory and organized a somewhat nomadic postal service, with many issues that fluctuated as the tide of war ebbed and flowed. These stamps are among the most complex in the world, issued by armies constantly on the move rather than associated with postal services in the accepted sense. Often crudely designed and printed under difficult conditions, they include many rarities.

As the communists gained control of many provinces after the defeat of Japan in 1945 postal services became more settled, and separate issues that read like the points of the compass appeared in different parts of China. Nevertheless, there were still many different issues, including seven in North-east China and ten in North-west China alone. Typical of these provincial stamps of 1945–9 were motifs of Mao Zedong and banner-waving troops [11–14]. Even after the proclamation of the People's Republic in 1949, separate stamps continued in North-east China because of the different value of money there.

PEOPLE'S REPUBLIC
The earliest definitives showed the Gate of Heavenly Peace in Beijing [15] or Chairman Mao [16], both themes that recurred frequently. Special issues reflected the rhetoric of the period, celebrating the 25th anniversary of the People's Liberation Army [17] and inauguration of the New Constitution [18]. The currency depreciated during the early 1950s but in 1955 it was reformed. In the ensuing period a more thematic approach crept in, gradually replacing endless Five Year Plan sets and portraits of communist heroes with sets reflecting the arts and crafts of old China [19]. During the Cultural Revolution (1965–71) quotations from Mao's little red book predominated [20]. Since the 1980s, recurring themes have been history and culture, among them stamps illustrating scenes from folk tales and Chinese classics. China's spectacular material progress since the 1990s has also been recorded [21].

Below: Supporting the Front *by Cui Kaixi featured on a 1998 stamp for the 50th anniversary of the Liberation War (top) and spectacular scenery is shown on a stamp of 2004 (bottom).*

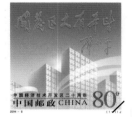

LUNAR NEW YEAR STAMPS

The Chinese calendar is based on the phases of the Moon and can be traced back 2,000 years to the time of the Eastern Han dynasty. The vast majority of China's predominantly rural people were illiterate, so astronomers worked out a dozen animal signs as readily identifiable symbols for the months, and these were also employed to describe the 12-year cycle of the years.

In Chinese culture the animal emblems are associated with the 12 earthly branches, representing nature or destiny. When combined with the five celestial stems or main elements – gold, wood, water, fire and earth – they produce a 60-year cycle known as a *chia-tzu*. Long after the construction of the calendar, the zodiac came to be applied to casting horoscopes, the reasoning being that every person born in a particular year would exhibit broadly similar character traits, governing their lives and affecting their future.

The 12-year cycle begins with the Rat (*Tzu*), which is followed by the Ox (*Chou*), Tiger (*Yin*), Rabbit (*Mao*), Dragon (*Chen*), Snake (*Szu*), Horse (*Wu*), Ram (*Wei*), Monkey (*Shen*), Rooster (*Yu*), Dog (*Hsu*) and Pig (*Hai*). These are the animals believed to have

been especially loyal to the Lord Buddha. According to Chinese folklore, their order of precedence in the zodiac follows the sequence in which they responded to the Buddha's summons to his power conference.

LUNAR NEW YEAR STAMPS

Although stamps marking the Lunar New Year were issued by Japan as long ago as 1936, this is a theme that developed only gradually from the 1950s onwards. By the 1980s they were regularly released by Japan, Korea, Taiwan, Hong Kong, Macao and Singapore, invariably featuring the relevant

animal in the Chinese zodiac. In recent years Japan's Lunar New Year stamps have been issued in two versions: a pair for ordinary postal use, and a matched pair in a longer format with serial numbers that are entered in a draw, the prizes being special miniature sheets.

In almost 70 years the Lunar New Year has spawned a formidable array of stamps, booklets, pre-stamped postcards and souvenir covers. Until fairly recently these were quite compact and manageable, being confined to the

Left: A rat and a snowman were shown on the New Year stamp from South Korea in 1995.

Below: Travelling pigs appeared on South Korea's stamp for the Year of the Pig, late 1994; the Hong Kong series (January 1995) showed pottery pigs.

Below: A stylized monkey is shown on a Macao stamp for the Year of the Monkey (2004); the 33c US stamp by Yuan Lee marked the Year of the Rabbit in 1999.

Below: Courting pigs from French Polynesia marked the Year of the Pig, 1995; Yuan Lee designed this 37c US stamp for the Year of the Goat, 2003.

Above: To mark the Year of the Dragon (2000) Micronesia released this $2 miniature sheet (left), reproducing a traditional Chinese image. Japan uses miniature sheets (right) as prizes in its annual New Year lottery.

countries of South-east Asia, but in the past few years the concept has spread like wildfire.

GOING WORLDWIDE

The United States, which has the largest Chinese population outside Asia (about six million), started the ball rolling with a 29c stamp in December 1992 to mark the Year of the Rooster (1993) and this has since become the theme for an annual issue. It spread to Canada in 1997 when the Year of the Ox was marked by a 45c stamp accompanied by a miniature sheet in the shape of a Chinese fan – this was a major innovation, as miniature sheets up to that time had invariably been rectangular in shape.

In recent years the concept has spread to every part of the globe, yielding Lunar New Year stamps as far afield as Ireland, the Marshall Islands and the Netherlands Antilles, and from Sweden to New Zealand and South Africa. Among the most attractive, and certainly most humorous, are those designed by Victor Ambrus for Jersey in the Channel Islands. They are in the form of £1 miniature sheets with the appropriate motif projected into the sheet margins. The Republic of China (Taiwan) has been issuing Lunar New Year stamps since 1969 (Year of the Dog). Latterly these issues have taken the form of two stamps showing different artistic interpretations of the appropriate animal.

Sweden seems about as unlikely a country as any to celebrate the Lunar New Year, but in recent years the event has been cleverly combined with tributes to children's literature. New Zealand likewise adopted an oblique approach to the Lunar New Year. In 1997 a set of six stamps featured different breeds of cattle, but the interpane gutters included the Chinese zodiacal symbol for the Year of the Ox. This established a precedent that is now followed every year.

For some years Ireland has produced stamps early in the year, primarily for Valentine's Day greetings. In January 1995 a booklet of four 32p stamps depicted various symbols of love, but the stamps were released simultaneously as a miniature sheet celebrating the Year of the Pig, with appropriate motifs and symbols for the Lunar New Year in the sheet margin. This established a pattern that has been maintained ever since.

A number of issues from the countries in the Inter-Governmental Philatelic Corporation group have also celebrated the Lunar New Year. These made their debut in May 1994, well into the Year of the Dog, and consisted of a number of sets depicting different canine breeds, but these stamps incorporated a tiny symbol in one corner inscribed "Year of the Dog", flanking the appropriate Chinese symbol.

More relevant were the issues of April 1995, designed by the leading Chinese-American artist Yuan Lee and featuring different aspects of pigs. Recent issues have tended to be more modest, confined to sheetlets of four and a matching souvenir sheet, with artwork by Yuan Lee predominating.

Below: One of the four stamps issued by Hong Kong for the Year of the Horse in 1990 (top) and the stamp from French Polynesia for the Year of the Dragon in 2000 (bottom).

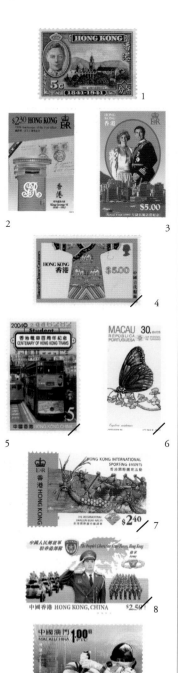

CHINESE TERRITORIES

In addition to China proper there are a number of territories that were at one time part of China (such as Mongolia) or, conversely, were European colonies but have now reverted to China (Hong Kong and Macao). Tibet, once autonomous, has been absorbed by the People's Republic, whereas Taiwan, which was occupied by Japan from 1895 to 1945, later became the

refuge of the Chinese Nationalists and survives to this day under the name of the Republic of China. The former British and Portuguese colonies of Hong Kong and Macao have enjoyed phenomenal economic growth in recent years; though now part of China again they are guaranteed autonomy for 50 years.

Left: The high-rise commercial buildings of Victoria, Hong Kong's capital, include several of the tallest structures in the world. Set against this background, the Peak Tram, opened in 1888, continues to transport tourists and commuters alike.

HONG KONG

In 1839 the Chinese tried to suppress the opium trade from India, but Britain retaliated and in 1841 forced China to cede Hong Kong island, which thereafter became the centre of drugs trafficking. The Kowloon peninsula was ceded in 1860 and a 99-year lease on the New Territories was granted to Britain in 1899. When it expired in 1997 Hong Kong's status was no longer viable and it was returned to China. Since then it has been a special administrative region and retains its own currency and stamps.

Hong Kong adopted stamps in 1862 and for almost a century most definitives were identical apart from the monarch's portrait. Although it actually produced the first commemorative stamp in Asia – the 2c definitive overprinted in 1891 to celebrate the 50th anniversary of British rule – a further half century would elapse before the first distinctive series appeared. This was a set of bicoloured pictorials marking the centenary of the colony in February 1941 [1], shortly before it was occupied by the Japanese.

Hong Kong participated in the various colonial omnibus issues from 1935 to 1966, an exception being the Victory pair of 1946: these utilized a design sketched by W.E. Jones in a

Japanese prison camp, showing a phoenix rising from the flames to symbolize the eventual re-emergence of Hong Kong after enemy occupation. Royal events, such as the wedding of Charles and Diana in 1981, and a visit of 1989 [3], were also covered.

Postwar commercial development and the influx of refugees from the People's Republic of China totally transformed the crown colony. Many stamps of this period presented a view of Hong Kong as a little bit of Britain in the Far East, with features such as Georgian pillar-boxes [2], but increasingly its Chinese heritage came to the fore. Numerous sets of recent years have featured costumes [4] and other aspects of the applied and decorative arts. Tourism is a major subject, reflected in scenery and local events such as the dragon boat races [7]. Since 1997 stamps have been inscribed "Hong Kong China", including a set celebrating the centenary of its waterfront trams [5]. The People's Liberation Army [8] took over the former British bases but generally keeps a low profile.

MACAO

The oldest European settlement in the Far East, Macao was settled by the Portuguese in 1557. As Portuguese colonial power declined in the 19th century Macao became a backwater, preserving its distinctive Iberian architecture. In 1999 it became a special administrative region of China and, like Hong Kong, retains its own stamps and currency. The early stamps from 1884 conformed to the Portuguese colonial designs, and distinctive motifs did not appear until the 1930s. After World War II they became much more colourful and thematic [6], but have latterly concentrated on indigenous art and culture, with numerous sets featuring the rapidly vanishing way of life [11]. Recent stamps, inscribed "Macau China", include a pair celebrating the first Chinese astronaut [9].

TAIWAN

The early issues of the Republic of China (ROC) were often inscribed entirely in Chinese, even when they related to international organizations [10], but later the name was rendered in English. When the nationalists fled from the mainland they took the vast bulk of the Chinese art treasures from Peking (Beijing) and these have been a fertile source of stamp illustrations ever since [12]. Many stamps from the 1960s to the 1980s highlighted Taiwan's siege mentality, but in the more relaxed atmosphere of recent years the emphasis has shifted to nostalgia, as in the old railway station series [13], and a revival of the penchant for illustrating the arts [14] and customs such as puppetry [15], folk tales [16] and children's pastimes [18].

Below: Damdinsuren's Camel Caravan *was one of several paintings on a 1969 Mongolian set for the tenth anniversary of the Co-operative Movement.*

Boxer Rebellion

When the Boxer rebellion laid siege to the foreign legations in Peking (1900), twelve countries, including the USA and Japan, formed a coalition to relieve them. Indian stamps overprinted "C.E.F." were used by the China Expeditionary Force which quashed the uprising.

MONGOLIA AND TIBET

Landlocked in central Asia, between Russia and China, is Mongolia, one of the oldest countries in the world. When at the height of its power in the 13th century Mongolia, under Genghis Khan, conquered the whole of China and expanded as far west as Poland and Hungary. After the Manchus conquered China in 1644 they absorbed Mongolia in 1681.

Following the Chinese revolution of 1911, Mongolia asserted its independence, which it attained in 1921 under the leadership of Sukhe Bator [17]. A people's republic from 1924, it overthrew its communist regime in 1990 and became the State of Mongolia. Since the 1930s, stamps have been an important source of hard currency.

Tibet was at various times tributary to China and its earliest stamps were those of China overprinted. Distinctive stamps appeared in 1912 and continued until 1950, when the Chinese invaded and annexed Tibet. The world's only theocracy has struggled ever since to regain independence, and stamps portraying the Dalai Lama and showing monasteries and the Potala Palace in Lhasa [19] have been produced by the government in exile.

1

2

3

4

5

6

7

8

9

10

11

KOREA

As a kingdom, Korea dates its origins to 2333 BC, and this is the starting point of its calendar. The country's history is well documented from 57 BC. The Yi dynasty had an unbroken record from 1392 until it was overthrown in 1910. In 1637, however, Korea was defeated by the Manchus and was a tributary of China from then until 1895. It was completely cut off from the outside world until 1876, when it was compelled to allow trade with Japan. In 1897 King Kojong proclaimed an empire. In 1905 Japan took over the postal service and five years later forced the emperor to abdicate. Korea was then annexed and remained part of the Japanese empire until 1945. Shortly before the war ended Russia declared war on Japan, and Soviet troops invaded North Korea. This proved to be the opening round of a conflict that has lasted ever since. The country was divided into Soviet and American zones of occupation by a line drawn across the peninsula at the 38th parallel.

Left: One of many tributes to its allies in the Korean War, a miniature sheet portraying General MacArthur and the Korean, UN and US flags was issued by South Korea in 1965.

UNITED KOREA

A postal service was introduced in November 1884 but a riot at the post office in Seoul a few weeks later led to the suspension of the service and the gradual infiltration of Japanese agents. The first stamps [1] are plentiful in mint condition but of the greatest rarity used, which is hardly surprising since they were in use for such a short time. A second attempt, in 1895, was more successful. The last series was designed and printed in Paris and bore the name of the Korean Empire in French. Under United States military government in 1945, distinctive stamps were revived [2].

SOUTH KOREA

The Republic of Korea, under Syngman Rhee, was proclaimed in August 1948, but in June 1950 it was invaded from the north. By September the enemy had overrun most of the country, but an American-led UN force landed at Inchon and the war raged back and forth for two years.

Eventually a truce was reached and a demilitarized zone established, initially patrolled by Indian troops, who had their own stamps [3]. Many of the stamps of South Korea since that time have referred to the war [4] and paid tribute to the USA for its support [5].

President Rhee was elected to a fourth term in 1960 but ousted by a military coup a month later [6]. By the 1970s South Korea was enjoying unprecedented prosperity and this is reflected in the stamps, which were not only well designed and printed but covered a wide range of topics, from fauna and flora [7] to cartoons [9] and comic book characters [10]. South Korea enthusiastically embraced the American way, from Boy Scouts to Lions Clubs [11], but its unique culture was not forgotten [12]. High-speed trains [13], motor manufacture and jet liners are recurring definitive themes. The country gained international prestige by hosting the Olympic Games (1988) and the football World Cup (2002), both marked by numerous stamps.

Cult of the Personality

The overriding theme of North Korean stamps has been the glorification of the Comrade Great Leader Kim Il Sung and now his son and successor Kim Jong Il. Not content with merely portraying these figures, the stamps incessantly depict them as role models and paragons of every virtue, in scenes that range from showing the peasants how to plant their crops to exhorting the factory workers to even greater efforts. Every other issue from the North seems to portray the two Kims.

12

13

14

15

16

17

18

19

20

NORTH KOREA

The polarization of the two Koreas is vividly demonstrated in their stamps. The Russian occupation ended in September 1948 with the institution of the Korean People's Democratic Republic. The stamps of this period were often crude imitations of contemporary Soviet designs, and they included numerous references to the

Below: This North Korean stamp was issued in 1998 to mark the 75th anniversary of Kim Il Sung's "250-mile journey for national liberation".

war, especially when it was going well for the communists [8]. Whereas the stamps of the South clung to the Korean chronology, the North adopted the Christian calendar. Many stamps alluded not only to victories and anniversaries of the Korean War but also commemorated earlier conflicts, from strikes and demonstrations [15] to outright guerrilla warfare against the Japanese [14].

More peaceful subjects began to appear in the late 1960s [16] but the onset of the Vietnam War gave North Korea more scope for its ongoing hatred of America. Anti-American propaganda included a stamp showing a monster in a GI helmet being skewered by bayonets [17]. In more recent years propaganda against the South has increased [18] although at the same time greater attention is given to popular themes [19]. Even UNICEF (if not the UN itself) gets some credit for relieving child poverty [20].

1

2

3

4

5

6

7

8

9

10

11

JAPAN

According to legend the empire of Japan was founded in about 600 BC by Jimmu Tenno, who was a descendent of the great sun goddess Amaterasu. All the emperors from that time until now have been in direct descent and their status as living deities explains why they are never portrayed on Japanese stamps, for to deface them with a postmark would be an act of sacrilege. Although the Portuguese first visited Japan in 1542 and Dutch traders subsequently got a toehold on Deshima, all foreign contacts were banned from 1630 until the visit of Commodore Perry of the US Navy in 1853. For 250 years the emperor was little more than a figurehead, while real power was vested in the shoguns, the xenophobic leaders of the mili-

tary caste, but under Emperor Meiji, who ascended to the throne in 1868, Japan rapidly industrialized, the shogunate was abolished and the country adopted western dress, technology and warfare, as well as a postal system, complete with stamps.

Left: The founder of the modern postal service was Baron Maeshima, who has been portrayed on many definitive stamps and special issues since 1946.

EARLIEST STAMPS

Four stamps covering the basic postal rates, denominated in mon, were introduced in April 1871 [1], but a few months later the currency was decimalized, based on the yen of 100 sen. Japan was not slow to introduce special issues: the first, in 1894, celebrated the emperor's silver wedding with a motif of cranes (symbolic of fidelity and long life). Victories over China in 1895 and Russia in 1905 were celebrated by stamps [2], while the battleships *Katori* and *Kashima* were featured on stamps issued in 1921 to celebrate the return of Crown Prince Hirohito from a tour of Europe [3].

WORLD WAR II AND ITS AFTERMATH

Japanese militarism gathered momentum in the 1920s and 1930s. Censured for its invasion of China in 1931, Japan left the League of Nations and formed an alliance with Nazi Germany. Rivalry with the USA in the Pacific led to the unprovoked attack on Pearl Harbor in December 1941, the start of Japan's own "lightning war" in the Pacific. The first anniversary of that "day of infamy"

was celebrated by stamps showing the air raid on Pearl Harbor and Japanese tanks in action at Bataan in the Philippines [4]. Although the tide turned at Midway in 1942 it took three long, hard years, and the use of two atomic bombs to destroy Hiroshima and Nagasaki, to bring Japan to its knees. Wartime definitives reflect the militaristic outlook of the period, but in the immediate aftermath stamps were poorly printed, often without perforations, because the usual printing works had been destroyed [5].

MODERN JAPAN

In contrast with the bellicose nature of the years up to 1945, postwar Japan concentrated on conquering the world markets, developing especially in the fields of electronics and the automotive industry. The vast majority of stamps are printed in photogravure, latterly in full colour. Definitives concentrate on antiquities, fauna and flora [6]. Since 1936 Japan has produced hundreds of stamps extolling the beauties of its many national parks [7]. Stamps have also been produced for New Year greetings, while annual issues of more recent

Letter Writing Day

To encourage Japanese children to write more letters, stamps in many different shapes have been designed by the Dutch artist Dick Bruna in recent years.

times have been aimed at popularizing letter writing, especially to pen-pals abroad [8]. Stamps are captioned only in Japanese [9], which creates difficulties for foreign collectors lacking a fully illustrated catalogue, but in compliance with Universal Postal Union regulations the country name "Nippon" has been inscribed in the Roman alphabet since 1966 [12]. The vast majority of Japanese stamps concentrate on the unique culture of the country, including its architecture, costume [10], theatre [11], art and music. However, western influences shine through in sport [13] and, of course, in technology [15]. For the Millennium Japan began a series of ten sheetlets (one for each decade of the 20th century) and has since produced similar sheetlets for the UNESCO World Heritage Sites in Japan, art treasures, and popular cartoon and comic-book characters.

Japan is divided into 47 administrative regions known as prefectures. In 1990 it released a sheet of 50 stamps to publicize the PhilaNippon international philatelic exhibition of 1991. Three non-postal labels advertised the exhibition but the rest of the sheet consisted of 47 stamps of the ¥62 denomination, each featuring a different flower associated with a particular prefecture, from the sweet briar of Hokkaido to the coral tree of Okinawa. This sheet was analogous to the sheets of 50 that have been issued by the United States since 1976, featuring the flags, birds and flowers of the 50 states. Japan, however, took the concept a stage further in April 1989 when the first batch of stamps pertaining to specific prefectures was released. Each prefectural stamp [14] is valid for postage all over the country but is sold only within its own prefecture and the other prefectures in one of the eleven postal regions into which the country is divided. In the main, these stamps are issued in conventional sheets, although some have also been released in booklets of miniature sheets. The number of different stamps fluctuates, from 19 in the inaugural year to 13 in some of the later years. Most of them feature landmarks, scenery and wildlife, but some have been issued to mark a special event.

WARTIME OCCUPATION ISSUES

Between 1942 and 1945, when Japan occupied China, South-east Asia and many of the Pacific islands, it overprinted the stamps of the occupied territories. These are noted elsewhere but a selection of the distinctive stamps of the period is shown here, including stamps for Burma [16–17], Malaya [18], Dutch East Indies [19], North Borneo [20] and the Philippines [21]. After the war Australian stamps were overprinted for the use of British Commonwealth Occupying Forces. In 1945 a US military administration was imposed on the Ryukyu Islands, including Okinawa, and distinctive stamps were used there until 1972 when the islands were handed back to Japan [22].

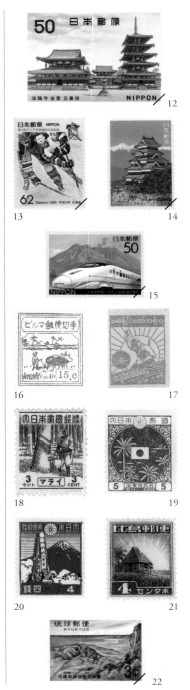

INDONESIA AND THE PHILIPPINES

These two large countries of the south-western Pacific have much in common and a parallel history. Both are archipelagos covering vast areas, which made communications difficult and encouraged the development of numerous petty states before they were conquered by European powers – Indonesia by the Dutch and the Philippines by the Spanish. Neither colonial ruler ever exerted full control and there were numerous rebellions. The modern republics have inherited many of these problems. In World War II both were overrun by the Japanese, who exploited latent nationalism. Both are nominally democracies, although in their recent past they have both been subjected to authoritarian rule.

Left: Achmed Sukarno founded the Indonesia National Party in 1927. Imprisoned and exiled by the Dutch, he was given power by the Japanese in 1942 and became president in 1945. In the 1960s luxury hotels contrasted with chaos and poverty and in 1965 an abortive communist coup led to his downfall.

DUTCH EAST INDIES

Portuguese traders discovered the spice islands in the 16th century but it was the Dutch who took over in 1602 and eventually ruled over an archipelago of 13,000 islands spread across 5,000 km/3,000 miles. Stamps were introduced in 1864, bearing a full-face portrait of William III, but from 1870 onwards the Indies, like other European colonies, conformed to the colonial keytypes. In 1902 stamps were overprinted specifically for use in Java [1] and six years later the same series was overprinted "Buiten Bezit" (outer possessions) for the outlying islands.

Airmail stamps were introduced in 1928 and charity stamps for child welfare became an annual feature from 1930 onwards, following the example of the mother country. Other early charity sets raised funds for a leper colony (1931), the Salvation Army (1932) and the YMCA (1933). A pictorial definitive series, with a standard design showing rice cultivation, appeared in 1933, while short sets depicting indigenous peoples and their customs appeared in the 1930s and early 1940s [2].

Although the Netherlands were overrun by the Germans in 1940, the colonial empire continued to function, being administered by the Dutch government in exile. In this period a charity set raised funds for the Dutch forces fighting with the Allies. The Netherlands Indies itself was under Japanese occupation (1942–5) and the nationalists then took over [3], but with the aid of British and Japanese troops Dutch rule was restored in Java. In 1950 the Dutch bowed to the inevitable and handed power over to the nationalists. Stamps portraying Queen Wilhelmina were overprinted "Indonesia" [4].

INDONESIA

A period of chaos followed in which different stamps were issued in Java, Sumatra and Madura and a series printed in Vienna was never put on sale [5], although it was at one time very common on the world stamp market. The various factions united in August 1950 to form the Indonesian Republic [6]. Until 1965 Sukarno, the founder of the country, remained firmly in control [7] but he gradually handed over to General Suharto. In turn Suharto was ousted in 1997, and Indonesia experienced true democracy for the first time in half a century.

The stamps of Indonesia have the usual themes [8] but also endeavour to bring together the country's many different ethnic groups [9]. Tourism is still a major industry, reflected in many sets featuring scenery and wildlife [10].

Separate stamps were issued in 1954–65 for the Riau-Lingga islands, whose currency was tied to the Singapore dollar [13]. After the Dutch handover to Indonesia they held on to West New Guinea and issued distinctive stamps [14], but from 1950 onwards Indonesia laid claim to this territory. To settle the dispute, it was placed under UN administration in 1962 and stamps were accordingly overprinted [11]. It was handed over to Indonesia in May 1963 and renamed Irian Barat, or West Irian [12].

The island of Timor in the Sunda group was partitioned between the Dutch and the Portuguese. Stamps of the Portuguese colonial type were used in east Timor from 1885 to 1975 [15]. Civil war erupted but when the Fretilin faction proclaimed independence Indonesian troops invaded and occupied the area. The oppressive regime was overthrown in 2003 and stamps inscribed "East Timor" are now used.

PHILIPPINES

Fernando Magellan was killed in the Philippine islands in 1521 during his voyage round the world. They were colonized in 1542 and named for the king of Spain. Stamps were introduced in 1854 [16], the last issue, during the Spanish-American War, portraying the young Alfonso XIII [17]. The indigenous population had fought a guerrilla war against the Spanish since 1873 and declared a republic in 1897, with distinctive stamps in 1898–9 [18].

The islands were ceded by Spain to the USA and placed under military administration. US stamps were overprinted [19], but were soon followed by stamps bearing the name of the

Good Relations

The close ties that exist between the USA and the Philippines have given rise to numerous stamps over the past century portraying American historical figures, but the Philippines alone produced a stamp showing not just John and Robert Kennedy but the entire Kennedy clan. The contract for the stamps, produced by an American agency with the agreement of the Filipino government, was cancelled at the last moment, and the stamps had no postal validity although they were on sale in the USA.

United States as well as the Philippines. Under the Commonwealth of the Philippines, established in 1935, the islands were granted autonomy. At first the previous pictorial definitive series was overprinted "Commonwealth" [20] and an entirely new series was just in the process of being released in 1941 when the islands were invaded.

After wartime occupation by the Japanese the Philippines became an independent republic in 1946, and the prewar overprinted series was reissued, overprinted "Victory". Many of the stamps from that time hark back to the heroic struggle of the war period [21], including several issues portraying General MacArthur, who was field marshal of the Filipino army from 1935 onwards and returned to liberate the islands in 1944. The modern stamps [22] reflect the unique cultural mixture of the Philippines, an amalgam of Spanish, American and Malay influences and of Catholicism and Islam, as well as the great diversity of landscape.

SOUTH-EAST ASIA

The Malay peninsula at the south-easterly tip of Asia is shared by three countries – Thailand, Malaysia and the tiny island republic of Singapore. Historically and culturally interlinked, their mutual interdependence was formalized when the menace of communism was at its height in the 1970s. Politically, Malaya consisted of three components: the Straits Settlements (a British crown colony consisting of Malacca, Penang and Singapore), the Federated Malay States (Negri Sembilan, Pahang, Perak and Selangor) and the independent states of Johore, Kedah, Kelantan, Perlis and Trengganu, all of which issued their own stamps at various times. A Malayan Postal Union, created in 1934, co-ordinated the postal services and issued postage due labels, but the issues of the various states continued. The Malay states were overrun by the Japanese in 1941–5, and at the end of World War II they came under British military administration until 1948. It was in this period that plans for closer integration and greater autonomy were formulated, leading to the creation of the Federation of Malaya in 1956.

Left: The Association of South-East Asian Nations (ASEAN) has expanded since its formation in 1977, as this 30th anniversary stamp from Brunei, showing the flags of the member states, demonstrates.

SINGAPORE

Founded by Sir Stamford Raffles in 1819, Singapore grew from a fishing village into one of the world's largest ports, a major centre for world trade. With Malacca and Penang, it formed the Straits Settlements, administered by the East India Company, which originally used Indian stamps surcharged in cents [1]. British influence over the Malay peninsula developed in the 19th century and after World War II Singapore was part of the Federation of Malaya [2], but in 1965 it seceded to form an independent republic within the Commonwealth. Its stamps reflect its astonishing urbanization [3], its multi-ethnic character [4] and its military preparedness [5].

MALAYSIA AND BRUNEI

Britain gradually brought the various Malay sultanates under its protection. Some of these were grouped together in the Federated Malay States [6] but each of the unfederated states had its own distinctive stamps [8–9] until the late 1940s. Thereafter uniform designs were used, differing only in the names of the states and the portraits of their rulers [7]. Labuan [10] and British North Borneo [11] combined to form the state of North Borneo [12], which subsequently joined the Malay Federation under the name of Sabah. In 1947, following Sarawak's transfer to the governance of the British colonial administration, its stamps were overprinted with the crowned cipher of George VI, pending a pictorial definitive series in 1950 with a portrait of the king inset. A new series, with Elizabeth II inset, was released in 1955 and continued until 1964, when Sarawak joined the Federation of Malaysia [13].

Stamps inscribed in Malay signified the Federation of Malaya [14], which was unique in having a king elected from the various sultans. The Federation changed its name to Malaysia in 1963. Apart from the states issues the national definitives have featured birds, fruits, fish and, most recently, butterflies [15], augmented by

The Land of the White Rajahs

For ridding his domain of pirates, the sultan of Brunei granted the Englishman James Brooke the title of rajah of Sarawak in 1842. Now a state of Malaysia, Sarawak has had its own stamps since 1869. After Japanese and British military occupation it was returned to the Brooke family in 1946, but the last rajah ceded it to Britain soon afterwards. All three white rajahs were portrayed on the stamps intended for the centenary in 1942 but delayed until 1946 as a result of the Japanese invasion.

short thematic sets ranging from birds of prey to marine life. Many of the recent stamps have shown the extraordinary development of the region, including one of the world's tallest landmarks, the Petronas Towers in Kuala Lumpur, depicted in a stamp marking the inauguration of the Putra light railway system in 1998 [16].

Closely associated with Malaysia is the sultanate of Brunei. Once an insignificant petty state in North Borneo, it is now one of the world's wealthiest countries due to the discovery of oil. Stamps showing a fishing village were current from 1907 until 1952, making them one of the world's longest running series [17]. Even today, Brunei operates one of the most conservative new issue policies in the world, with an average of 20 stamps a year, almost all of which are entirely pertinent to the country itself. Since his accession in 1967 Sultan Sir Hassanal Bolkiah has been portrayed on the vast majority of Brunei's stamps.

THAILAND

A postal service restricted to the royal court functioned in the mid-19th century, but an external service operated at the British consulate in Bangkok from 1858. Straits stamps overprinted "B" were introduced in 1882 [18] but were withdrawn in 1885 when Thailand joined the Universal Postal Union and introduced its own stamps [19]. Stamps bore the name of Siam until 1940, when the present name was adopted. Thailand has strong Buddhist and monarchical traditions, which have featured on numerous stamps [21]. Its military forces are highly trained and well equipped [22]. Most special issues are singles, with occasional longer sets.

JAPANESE OCCUPATION

During World War II the Malay peninsula was under enemy occupation from December 1941 until 1945. The conquerors began by overprinting stamps of the Malayan Postal Union, Malay states, Straits Settlements, North Borneo, Brunei and Sarawak with Japanese characters [20], but in April 1943 they produced a series of pictorials, printed by a Dutch company in Batavia.

Thailand was allied to Japan and was rewarded with the transfer of the northern Malay states (Kedah, Kelantan, Perlis and Trengganu), which had traditionally been under Thai influence. From October 1943 to September 1945 Thailand issued special stamps for use in these states, before they were returned to British administration.

Below: A tin dredger appears on one of the pictorials issued in Malaya during Japanese occupation in 1943 (left). The Thai war memorial featured on the stamps issued in 1944 during the Thai occupation of northern Malaya (right).

AUSTRALASIA AND OCEANIA

This term encompasses Australia, New Zealand and their dependencies in the Indian Ocean and Antarctica as well as the islands of the south, central and western Pacific. Adhesive stamps spread to Australia in 1850 and New Zealand in 1855, while the first stamp of New Caledonia appeared in 1860.

AUSTRALIA

The world's smallest continent is the only one that forms a single country. Australia was colonized by the British piecemeal following Captain James Cook's charting of the east coast in 1770. Eventually, six colonies were created under the British Crown, beginning with New South Wales in 1788. Originally allocated to the former territory, Van Diemen's Land (later renamed Tasmania) became a separate state in 1825, followed by South Australia in 1836, Victoria in 1851 and Queensland in 1859. The territory known as Western Australia was settled by 1829. The British parliament approved a federal constitution in 1900 and the following year the Commonwealth of Australia finally came into being.

Left: A set of three appeared in 1938 to mark 150 years since the first settlement of New South Wales. All the stamps were of a common design showing the landing at Sydney Cove on January 26, 1788.

AUSTRALIAN COLONIES

Each of the six colonies issued its own stamps, adopting a highly individual approach to the matter. In fact, New South Wales beat the mother country to it by introducing prepaid letter sheets, embossed with the colonial seal, in November 1838, 18 months before Britain adopted the Mulready wrappers. However, adhesive stamps were not introduced in New South Wales until January 1850. From 1851 stamps of New South Wales [1] generally portrayed Queen Victoria, with the exception of the centennial series of 1888. Other colonies followed suit [2–3]. Stamps inscribed "Van Diemen's Land" [4] were used in Tasmania from 1853 to 1857, and in 1899 Tasmania was the only colony to adopt a wholly pictorial definitive series [5]. Victoria likewise favoured portraits [7], whereas stamps of Western Australia [6] featured its emblem, the black swan.

The different postal rates in each colony meant that their distinctive stamps continued in use until 1913.

COMMONWEALTH ISSUES

From the outset the issue of stamps was a political tool. Labour were in power when stamps were introduced, hence the national motif of the kangaroo on a map of the country [8], but when the Conservatives returned to power soon afterwards the kangaroo gave way to the king [9]. When Labour returned to power, so did the roo, and so it continued through the 1920s and 1930s. Less controversial was the 6d stamp of 1914 showing a kookaburra [10].

Special issues, which appeared infrequently from 1927 onwards, marked the inauguration of the federal parliament in Canberra and the Sydney Harbour Bridge [11], while the trio celebrating the silver jubilee of George V in 1935 showed him in field marshal's

Australian Innovations

A self-adhesive booklet issued in 2004 took a rather whimsical look at some of Australia's ideas and inventions. These ranged chronologically from Racecam TV sports coverage, introduced in 1979, to the Baby Safety Capsule of 1984 and the world's first polymer banknotes, which were issued in 1988 for the bicentennial celebrations.

uniform mounted on Anzac [12], the horse named in honour of the Australian and New Zealand Army Corps, which had fought at Gallipoli in World War I. Fine intaglio printing continued until the early 1950s. The set honouring Australian Imperial Forces [13] was the only special issue of World War II until February 1945, when stamps marked the arrival of the Duke of Gloucester as governor-general [14]. From 1938 definitives were more pictorial, but continued the tradition of blending wildlife with royal portraits [15]; by the late 1950s less fussy designs were favoured [16].

Stamps for international occasions, such as the 75th anniversary of the UPU in 1949, were given an Australian slant [17]. Monochrome intaglio gave way to multicolour photogravure in the 1960s [19]. Annual stamps mark Australia Day [18] as well as the queen's birthday [20], indicating a strong monarchical feeling despite the rise of republicanism in recent years. Modern stamps reflect the laid-back, often irreverent, attitudes of Australians, whose off-beat humour is often expressed in both definitives and special issues. Not surprisingly, given the nation's many achievements in sport, this remains an immensely popular philatelic theme.

In recent years Australia has adopted a number of technical innovations, such as the use of holograms to convey the impression of Australian opals [21]. In 1994 Australia also led the way in developing self-adhesive stamps, in coils or special booklets. The Melbourne international philatelic exhibition of 2000 introduced personalized stamps, with adjoining labels bearing people's own snapshots, a technique that is now used worldwide. Stamps portraying the Australian gold medallists at the Sydney Olympics were on sale in their home states within 48 hours.

TWO HUNDRED YEARS IN STAMPS

While Australia's Aboriginal inhabitants have a history of many thousands of years, Britain's interest began only in the 18th century. About the time that it was losing its empire in what is now the United States of America, it was establishing another in the Southern Hemisphere. The first settlers of the new colony – 750 convicts – arrived in Botany Bay in 1788.

Until 1783 Britain had transported convicts to its American colonies, but robbed of this facility the government looked around for somewhere else to deport them. Then Joseph Banks, the naturalist on James Cook's first voyage to the South Seas in 1769–70, which charted the east coast of Australia, suggested Botany Bay as an ideal site. Late in 1787 HMS *Sirius*, with a flotilla of transport ships, set out from England bound for the land Cook had named New South Wales, from a fancied resemblance to the coastline of Glamorgan. On 26 January 1788, Captain Arthur Phillip and his officers disembarked at Sydney Cove and hoisted the British flag.

This incident would give rise to the world's first commemorative stamps issued by a government postal service: the set labelled "One Hundred Years"

by New South Wales in 1888. The 1d stamp showed a view of Sydney a century after that landing, while James Cook was portrayed on the 4d stamp. Interestingly, the 20s stamp portrayed not only Governor Phillip but also Lord Carrington, the governor in 1888. It would be well over a hundred years before Australia next portrayed a living person other than royalty.

None of the later colonies had the opportunity to celebrate their centenaries in this way, as by the time they came round colonial stamps had been superseded by the issues of the Commonwealth of Australia. In 1929 the centenary of Western Australia was marked by a single stamp featuring the state emblem, a black swan. Five years later, the original settlement of Victoria was marked with a set of three showing an Aborigine on the banks of the

Yarra gazing in wonder at the city of Melbourne. In 1936 South Australia's centenary was celebrated with a set of three showing the Old Gum Tree at Glenelg flanked by a view of Adelaide in 1836 and the modern thoroughfare of King William Street. Half a century later stamps were issued to mark the

Above: One of four stamps issued jointly by Australia and Britain in 1988 shows an early settler and a sailing clipper.

Left: Two stamps from the second Bicentenary series, with the theme of settlement, show navigator William Dampier and a globe and hand with an extract from Dampier's journal.

Below: A strip of five stamps issued on January 26, 1988, showed the arrival of the First Fleet.

Above: A stamp of 1927 celebrated the opening of the federal parliament in Canberra during that year.

Right: A miniature sheet of 1991 honoured the exploration of Western Australia by George Vancouver in 1791 and E.J. Eyre in 1841.

Above: Sir Edmund Barton and Sir Henry Parkes were portrayed on a se-tenant pair of 1951.

Above: The opening of the first federal parliament in Melbourne in 1901 was commemorated on its golden jubilee.

Above: A stamp of 1963 marked the 150th anniversary of the first crossing of the Blue Mountains.

150th anniversaries, and it is interesting to note how radically different artistic styles had become by the 1970s and 1980s.

In 1938 it was time to celebrate the 150th anniversary of the first settlement, with a set of three showing Arthur Phillip and his staff at Sydney Cove. Tasmania had failed to mark its centenary, but made amends with a sesquicentennial set in 1953, which consisted of two small-format stamps of Lieutenants-Governor Collins and Paterson, plus a large-sized 2s of the ships anchoring at Sullivan Cove near Hobart in 1804.

In May 1951 a set of four celebrated the Australian Commonwealth's golden jubilee. Sir Edmund Barton and Sir Henry Parkes, who led the campaign to unify the colonies, were portrayed on two small se-tenant stamps, while

the federal parliament building in Canberra appeared on the 1s 6d. The 5½d stamp reproduced a painting by T. Roberts showing the Duke of York (later George V) performing the inaugural ceremony in 1901. Since then many stamps have celebrated the centenaries of services that helped weld the continent into a single nation: the overland telegraph, the mail coaches, the railways and the first internal flights.

From 1968 several booklets portrayed famous Australians, beginning with the balladeer Banjo Paterson and the Aboriginal artist Albert Namatjira. The 75th anniversary in 1976 was marked by a stamp showing the arms of the commonwealth, but since 1978 a stamp has been produced each January 26 to celebrate Australia Day.

As the bicentenary approached in 1988 Australia pulled out all the stops.

No fewer than 13 sets of stamps were issued from November 1984, beginning with a set of eight paying tribute to the Aborigines, then charting European exploration, the voyage of the First Fleet in 1787–8, and the early years of the settlement. A joint issue with Britain showed the national flags and people who symbolized the common heritage of the two countries, from Shakespeare to John Lennon and the cricketer W.G. Grace. Joint issues were also made with New Zealand and the USA, using a cartoon treatment.

Australia celebrated the opening of its new parliament building as well as Expo '88 in Brisbane and also released a new definitive series jokily exploring the theme of living together. And, of course, many countries, from Ireland to Israel, also issued stamps in honour of Australia's 200 years.

AUSTRALIAN EXTERNAL TERRITORIES

Australia has four dependencies, which are classed politically as Australian external territories. Two are located in the Indian Ocean, one in the South Pacific and one in Antarctica. Christmas Island was originally part of the Straits Settlements and then of the crown colony of Singapore. Occupied by the Japanese in 1942–5, it reverted to Singapore following liberation but was transferred to Australia in October 1958. The Cocos (Keeling) Islands in the Indian Ocean were settled by the Clunies-Ross family in the 1820s, annexed by Britain in 1857 and transferred to Ceylon (now Sri Lanka) in 1878, then attached to the Straits Settlements in 1886. They were transferred to Australia in November 1955. Australian Antarctic Territory consists of a large sector of Antarctica with up to six bases in operation. The stamps of these three territories are provided by Australia Post and can also be used in Australia itself.

Norfolk Island was part of New South Wales from its inception in 1788 and was used as a penal colony for the most hardened convicts. In 1856 it was transferred to Tasmania and in 1914 became an Australian territory.

Stamps were introduced in 1947 and, unlike the others, are not valid in Australia itself.

Left: The ties between Tasmania and Norfolk Island were recalled by a pair of stamps in 1969 marking the 125th anniversary of the latter's annexation to what was then Van Diemen's Land.

CHRISTMAS ISLAND

This island got its first stamps cheaply, using the Australian definitive design modified to include different values typographed in black, with the name overprinted [1]. The set of ten definitives sufficed until 1963, when they were replaced by a pictorial issue distinctive to the island, showing a map, scenery and wildlife. The first special issue appeared in 1965 and was part of the Australian omnibus for the 50th anniversary of the Gallipoli landings.

From 1968 onwards stamps included "Indian Ocean" below the island name [2] to avoid confusion with the island of the same name in the Pacific. In more recent years stamps have tended to be confined to subjects of local interest. The few special issues relate mainly to Christmas, either showing totally secular motifs [3–4] or putting a highly individual slant on Santa Claus [5]. Christmas Island now also produces stamps for the Chinese New Year and these rank among the most spectacular of this genre.

COCOS (KEELING) ISLANDS

The only stamp-issuing country with alternative names (one enclosed in parenthesis), the islands used ordinary Australian stamps from 1955 until 1963, when a set of six pictorial definitives was introduced with the usual mixture of map, scenery and local life. Like Christmas Island, their first commemorative was the Gallipoli stamp. In 1979 a local council was established and at the same time the islands were given a greater measure of postal autonomy. Many of the stamps in the ensuing period pictured the birds, marine life [6; 8] and historic ships [7] associated with the group. The islands are of numismatic interest on account of the plastic tokens that passed for money at one time [9]. On 1 January

1994, responsibility for the postal service reverted to Australia. Since then stamps have included "Australia" in the inscription and are valid for postage in Australia, while Australian [10] stamps are also valid in the islands.

NORFOLK ISLAND

The stamps of Van Diemen's Land (Tasmania) were briefly in use in Norfolk Island (1854–5) and examples on cover with the island postmark are of the greatest rarity. Following its transfer to New South Wales, the stamps of that colony were used until 1913, followed by Australian stamps until 1947, when a set showing Ball Bay was introduced. Separate motifs were used for a short set of additional denominations issued in 1953, showing grim landmarks from the period when the island was a penal settlement.

Many subsequent issues have alluded to explorers who visited the island over the centuries [11–12], then a long cavalcade of all the ships that ever touched there [13] and finally the wrecks of ships that foundered there [14]. James

Below: A dog team pulling a sledge was one of the subjects of the Antarctic Scenes set in 1984 (top). A 1979 stamp (bottom) marked the 50th anniversary of Admiral Richard Byrd's flight across the South Pole.

Freeform Stamps
Between 1974 and 1978 Norfolk Island issued stamps in the shape of the map, and returned to the idea for the Christmas stamps of 1994, in the form of a scroll.

Cook is a popular subject, with eight issues in just ten years (1969–79) marking the bicentenaries of his voyages [15]. As in Christmas Island, a whimsical approach to Christmas has been used in recent years [16].

AUSTRALIAN ANTARCTIC TERRITORY

A solitary stamp showing a map was introduced by the territory in 1957 [17], followed by a few others from time to time covering basic postage rates. The switch to decimal currency in 1966 heralded an era of multicoloured photogravure or lithographed stamps, released annually and featuring scenery and scientific research [18].

The few commemorative stamps have marked important anniversaries. These have included the Australasian Antarctic Expedition of 1911–14, Captain Cook's circumnavigation of Antarctica in 1772, the first flight over the South Pole in 1929, the Magnetic Pole Expedition of 1909 and various anniversaries of the Antarctic Treaty of 1961. A particularly poignant set was released in 1994 to mark the departure of the last huskies from Antarctica.

11

12

13

14

15

16

17

18

NEW ZEALAND

Slightly larger than the British Isles but with a 20th of their population, New Zealand is often referred to by the British as the Antipodes (literally, the place lying at the opposite side of the world). Its climate and scenery are similar to those of Britain, if on a much grander scale. The North and South Islands were first populated by the Maori, Polynesians who sailed their canoes across the ocean from Hawaii between the 10th and 14th centuries. The islands were discovered by the Dutch in 1642 and charted by James Cook in 1769. The haunt of whalers in the early 19th century, New Zealand was annexed by the British in 1840, becoming briefly a dependency of New South Wales. It attained self-government in 1852 and, after refusing to join the Commonwealth of Australia in 1901, became a dominion in 1907.

Left: The centennial of annexation was marked by a long series of 1940 charting the country's history from the arrival of the Maori in 1350 onwards. This stamp shows the Treaty of Waitangi being signed by Captain Hobson and Maori chiefs.

EARLY STAMPS
Although a postal service was organized in 1840 it was not until 1855 that New Zealand adopted adhesive stamps. To mark the centenary the original design was revived, with a portrait of Elizabeth II replacing the Chalon portrait of Victoria [1]. Thereafter, most stamps were produced by the Government Printer in Wellington, although the dies were sometimes engraved in Australia. The first 1/2d stamp, introduced in 1873 when a low rate for printed matter was conceded, was a blatant copy of the contemporary British 1/2d stamp.

All stamps until 1898 bore portraits of Victoria, the last series portraying images of the queen from her teens to the Jubilee and Veiled Head portraits of 1887 and 1893 respectively. In 1893 the definitives were issued with advertisements printed on the back and these stamps, popularly known as "Adsons", are much sought-after. In 1898 New Zealand was one of the first colonies to issue pictorial stamps, featuring scenery, wildlife and a Maori war canoe [2]. The advent of the 1d rate to any part of the British Empire was marked by a stamp in 1901 that underwent numerous changes over the ensuing decade before the words "Dominion of" were

added, along with a series portraying Edward VII, who also appeared on the 6d [4]. Royal portraiture was the norm for the low values until 1935, when New Zealand returned to pictorials featuring scenery, wildlife and people [3; 7]. Pictorial and portrait definitives alternated until the 1960s.

BRITAIN OF THE SOUTH SEAS
The white settlers of New Zealand were predominantly from Britain and, until the 1960s, regarded that as "home", an attitude reflected in many stamps. A 1920 set marking victory in World War I used motifs from London statuary [5], setting a precedent for the Peace issue of 1946, which included a view of St Paul's Cathedral in the Blitz, with Churchill's assertion, "This was their finest hour" [8]. The Coronation set of 1953 showed not only the Crown Jewels and state coach, but also Westminster Abbey and Buckingham Palace [9]. Special issues also covered local landmarks and even incorporated Maori art in their borders [6], but the overwhelming impression is of stamps that were better at featuring the United Kingdom than British stamps were.

Sir Charles Kingsford-Smith pioneered air routes linking Australia and New Zealand and from 1931 onwards

Health Stamps

New Zealand's world-famous Health stamps began in 1929 with a stamp raising funds for the anti-tuberculosis campaign. It was reissued the following year with the caption altered to "Help Promote Health". Stamps have since been issued annually to raise funds for holiday camps, giving urban children in need the chance of a spell in the country. A recurring theme is the younger members of the British royal family, now extending to the third generation.

special stamps were produced for airmail. Few commemoratives were produced before World War II but the centennial of annexation in 1940 was the pretext for a long set reviewing the country's history and development. A long set of 1946 marked the return to peace, many of the stamps contrasting scenes in peace and war. From 1948 onwards many sets celebrated the centenaries of the settlement of various parts of New Zealand and later the charters of the various towns and cities.

New Zealand began issuing Christmas stamps in 1964, the first stamp appropriately marking the 150th anniversary of the first Christmas sermon, preached by the Reverend Samuel Marsden to a largely Maori congregation in 1814 [10].

MODERN NEW ZEALAND

Britain's entry into the EEC in 1973, and subsequent restrictions on trade between Britain and New Zealand, forced the latter to reassess its position as a country whose chief interests now lay in the Pacific region. This was increasingly reflected in stamps from this time onwards. The definitive series

of 1975 portrayed the queen on the 10c stamp but all other values had local subjects [11]. New Zealand sent troops to Vietnam [13] and developed closer ties with other countries of the Pacific Rim. Since 1988 New Zealand has issued a series of circular stamps showing its national bird, the kiwi. Designed in New Zealand, engraved in Canada and recess-printed in Australia, the Round Kiwis have continued intermittently to the present day [12].

RECENT DEVELOPMENTS

Most New Zealand stamps are now lithographed by Southern Colour Print of Dunedin. New Zealand is justifiably proud of the fact that it granted women the vote in 1893 and was the first country to do so [14]. Rugby football has been depicted on numerous stamps since the 1960s, even stamps for individual teams [15]. By contrast with the historical set of 1940 for the centenary, the 150th anniversary triggered off several sets devoted to the country's heritage, followed by the decades of the 20th century [16]. Scenery continues to predominate [18–19], interspersed with sets devoted to historic buildings [20] and antique farming equipment, but recent sets have also poked fun at typically Kiwi phenomena such as hokey-pokey (toffee crunch), jandals (flip-flops or thongs) and fish and chips, or some of the wacky letterboxes that dot the countryside. Special stamps were issued for the Government Life Insurance Department from 1891 to 1989, featuring lighthouses [17].

Below: A Burrell traction engine on a stamp of 2004 was part of a series showing vintage farm machinery.

11   12

13

14   15

16   17

18

19

20

PNG, NAURU AND VANUATU

New Guinea, the largest of the Pacific islands, was colonized by the Dutch. They annexed the western half of the island to the Netherlands Indies, but the eastern portion was divided between Germany and Britain. German New Guinea was occupied by Australian forces at the beginning of World War I and mandated to Australia in 1921 under the name of New Guinea. British New Guinea, better known as Papua, was under British civil administration until 1942 but came under military rule following the Japanese invasion of the northern coast. In 1945 both parts combined as the Australian trust territory of Papua and New Guinea, shortened to Papua New Guinea, or PNG, in 1972.

The island of Nauru was part of the Marshall Islands but following its occupation by Australian troops in November 1914 it became a British mandate. It was transferred to Australia in 1924 and became an independent republic in 1968. The New Hebrides were jointly ruled by Britain and France from 1906 until 1980, when the condominium became the Republic of Vanuatu and was admitted as a member of the Commonwealth.

Left: The bicentenary of the discovery of the New Hebrides by Captain Cook was celebrated in 1974 by stamps available in both English and French versions and denominated in gold francs.

NEW GUINEA

German keytype stamps were used in the colony of German New Guinea until 1914 [1]. Following the Australian occupation stamps and registration labels of German New Guinea, and stamps of the Marshall Islands, were overprinted "G.R.I." and surcharged in sterling. By March 1915 Australian stamps overprinted "N.W. Pacific Islands" [2] were substituted. Distinctive stamps showing a native village did not appear until 1935 [3]. A long set of air stamps, in denominations from 1/2d to £5, appeared in 1939, mainly for sending packets of gold dust from Bulolo to Rabaul [4].

PAPUA

Stamps of Queensland were used at Port Moresby from 1885 until 1901, when an issue inscribed "British New Guinea" [5] was adopted. Similar stamps, featuring a *lakatoi* (a sailing canoe) but inscribed "Papua", appeared in 1907. Four stamps were issued in 1934 to mark the 50th anniversary of the British protectorate [6] and the following year four definitives [7] were overprinted to celebrate the silver jubilee of George V [8].

PAPUA NEW GUINEA

From 1942 onwards Australian stamps were used in those districts of Papua and New Guinea that had not been overrun by the Japanese, and this situation continued until October 1952, when distinctive stamps bearing the names of both protectorates were introduced following the creation of the Australian trust territory. Up to 1972 stamps included the ampersand in the name [9] but thereafter it was omitted [10]. In September 1975 Papua New Guinea became an independent member of the Commonwealth, but this did not affect the style or content of its stamps, which have tended to focus on the country's flora and fauna [11–13].

COINS

The story of coins is as old as that of some of the greatest civilizations.
From ancient Turkey to India and the Far East, the earliest metal currencies
took on a wide variety of forms, often emulating the shapes of the bartered
goods they replaced. Round lumps of metal, struck with the emblems of
rulers, are known to have been in existence for almost three millennia – and
the basic design concept has endured to the present day. As with Stamps,
previously, this encyclopedic treatment of coins is divided into two
chapters. The first unravels the complex history of coinage around the
world, looking at the most influential currencies from iconic classical coins
through medieval innovations to modern-day series. This is followed by a
comprehensive world directory of coins, which represents all the
members of the coin-issuing world, from the most venerable contributors
to those whose very first coins are still less than a century old.

Left: coiners at work in Germany during the 16th century.
Above, left to right: guldengroschen of Austria, Algerian republican coins of 1964, Roman solidus of
Constans, Australian "holey dollar" commemorative, traditional tin coin of Burma.

INTRODUCING COINS AND NUMISMATICS

In his First Epistle to Timothy, St Paul declared that the love of money was the root of all evil. Clearly, he did not have numismatists (as coin collectors like to style themselves) in mind. Were there coin collectors back in the 1st century? Quite possibly, for the design and production of coins had risen to a very high level by that time and today we regard the Greek coins of the late pre-Christian era as some of the most exquisite works of art ever produced.

In St Paul's day the coins of the early Roman Empire were already showing their character, with accurate likenesses of emperors and their families on one side and generally a female figure representing some abstract concept such as Justice, Concord or Agriculture on the other. From the relatively large numbers of classical coins that have

survived in fine condition it must be assumed that wealthy Greeks and Romans were laying aside beautiful specimens to admire rather than spend. Certainly, by the Renaissance in the 15th century, princes and magnates had their coin cabinets, and it was the appreciation of classical coins that inspired the revolution in coin design and production from the 1450s.

Today the role of coins in everyday life is being supplanted by plastic in the form of credit cards and cash cards. There is a popular anecdote about a little boy who went into a grocery store, picked up a packet of ice cream and at the checkout proffered a used telephone card as payment. He had often seen his mother handing over something similar, which was accepted instead of cash. This story indicates

Above: New Zealand 3 pence of 1946 with a portrait of George VI and a reverse motif of Maori war clubs.

how a generation of children are growing up more accustomed to plastic than metal – they may never experience the tactile pleasure of jingling a handful of coins in their pockets.

Despite this gradual narrowing of the actual usage of metal money, coins as collectables have developed dramatically. Not only are the mints and treasuries of the world producing more and more deluxe items for collectors, but the coins in general circulation are more varied than at any time since the fall of the Roman Empire. For centuries coin collecting was the preserve of the upper classes, who had the wealth to indulge their passion, as well as the classical education to appreciate the designs and inscriptions. Today coin collecting is a hobby pursued by people of all ages and incomes.

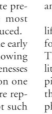

Above: An interesting coin of ancient Rome featuring a serrated edge and a sacrificial bull ritual on the reverse.

Above: An early Roman coin showing Apollo (left) on the obverse side. Later, portraits of emperors replaced deities.

STARTING A COLLECTION

A good place to begin is at home, with the small change in daily circulation. The collection can very quickly be extended to past issues of your own country, often readily available from local coin dealers, and then to the coins of related territories. These may be similar in denomination and appearance, but the coins of every country are distinctive, such as the 1946 silver 3 pence of New Zealand shown above, with the profile of George VI on one side, just like the British coins, but a pair of Maori war clubs on the other.

The names and nicknames of coins can give clues to their history. The American quarter dollar is still referred

Below: This 1st-century relief shows the kind of money bag a travelling moneyer would have taken to a Roman treasury.

Below: Coining is entwined with metal craft. The Gold Weigher, by Dutch artist Gerard Dou, appeared in 1664.

to as a two-bit coin, but few realize that the bit was originally the eighth part of a Spanish dollar, the *peso a ocho reales* (or "piece of eight" in pirate lore). The dollar sign ($) itself is a relic of this – it was originally a figure 8 with two vertical strokes through it.

Coins are usually identified by their inscription, and sometimes the denomination is helpful. Ancient coins are more of a problem; in the absence of any lettering, the effigy or emblem may be the only clue to identity. Where inscriptions exist and are legible, you can look for dates or the mint-marks identifying the place where the coins were struck. For example, American coins found without a mint-mark indicate that they were struck at the US Mint in Philadelphia, while those produced at the branch mints in Denver and San Francisco bear an initial letter D or S alongside the date.

The current range of American coins may seem limited – effectively the only coins in everyday use are the bronze cent (penny), 5 cents (nickel), 10 cents (dime) and 25 cents (quarter) – but in any handful of change you will find different dates and mint-marks. It is not

Below: A page from an American coin album designed to house Lincoln cents of each date and mint-mark.

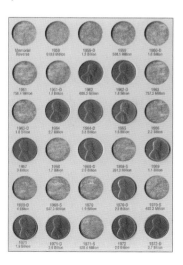

surprising, therefore, that coin collecting at its most basic, known by many as change-checking, should have developed into a national pastime in the United States.

This has led companies to produce a variety of housing options, such as albums of stout card pages with holes punched out to take the entire range of a particular denomination. The holes are annotated with the dates and mint-marks, and this encourages people to look for all the date and mark varieties.

Sooner or later you may want to start trading your coins, to finance new purchases and get rid of those in which you have less interest. Today there are many on-line businesses devoted to the sale of coins, while coin fairs – national and local – are great occasions to meet collectors and learn about your coins.

THE TRUE VALUE OF COINS

There are many opportunities nowadays to expand a coin collection at little cost, and the inclusion of related, noncoin items contributes colour, variety and context. My first trip abroad was to Greece in 1950, where there were no coins at all, just ragged paper printed with lots of noughts, reflecting the horrendous inflation of the immediate post-war years. In early 1950s, Holland I handled my first real foreign coins, but also saw massive silver 2½ gulden coins worn as buttons on the traditional jackets of Dutch men.

Above: Many mints now sell complete year sets, attractively packaged.

Rare vintage coins may sell for enormous sums, but most coins have a value of a different nature. When my father uncovered various copper coins of George III's reign in our garden, I took them to the local museum. The curator opined that someone, perhaps a farm labourer, had probably dropped his purse. Although I was disappointed to learn that the coins were very common and virtually worthless, I got a tremendous thrill imagining that they were the hard-won earnings of some poor ploughboy 150 years earlier. Today, when I handle a chunky Alexandrine tetradrachm of the 4th century BC I still get that tactile thrill, thinking that self-same piece of silver was earned, handled and spent by someone almost 2400 years ago.

Above: The reverse of a Netherlands 2½ gulden of William II, shown at actual size. These coins were often mounted and worn as buttons by Dutch people.

A GUIDE TO COLLECTING COINS

Coins have been in existence for almost 2800 years and, taking into consideration differences in dates, mint- and die-marks, the number of collectable varieties is countless. Even a general collection of world coins, confined to major differences in design, would run to many thousands. This chapter is divided broadly into three key sections. The first takes a look at how coins originated and evolved in different parts of the world, from the earliest currencies to the astonishing range of articles that have been used as substitutes for metal coins in times of crises. The second section helps the reader to understand the different factors that determine the identity and circulation of a coin: from weight and denomination to the metals used and methods of production, including the transition from hammering by hand to mechanical processes, the designs of coins and the security features employed to defeat counterfeiters. The final section traces the evolution of numismatics, especially from the late 19th century, gives advice on the care and conservation of coins. It also surveys some of the different approaches to collecting – by country, reign or period, or by theme or topic – and examines the byways of the hobby, including bogus coins, errors and oddities.

Left: Different methods of housing coins, plus magnification aids.
Above, left to right: Influential Greek design on an ancient Egyptian coin, a pictorial thaler of medieval Germany, and a gold mohur struck at Calcutta by the East India Company.

WHAT ARE COINS?

Pieces of metal stamped with a device guaranteeing their worth developed more or less simultaneously in China and Asia Minor (modern Turkey) in the 7th century BC. Generally round and flat, modern coins may have different designs and inscriptions but are akin to the coins used centuries ago, like this 12th-century copper 10 cash of the Chinese Song dynasty.

THE HISTORY OF BARTER

Long before coins were invented, goods were traded by other means. The earliest civilizations of the Middle East and the Mediterranean were pastoral and their wealth was represented by flocks of sheep and goats and herds of cattle. Naturally, the earliest forms of money used by these peoples consisted of animals, meat and hides. Many of the words used in connection with money originated in this way. From the Latin word *pecus*, meaning "herd", we get the adjectives "pecuniary" and "peculiar" (that portion of the herd assigned to the cowherd for his own use). The word "talent", which now means an asset or natural gift, denoted a sum of money in Biblical times, but long before that the Greek word *talanton* meant a cowhide. When metal began

Below: A 15th-century illustration of Russian and Scandinavian traders bartering, from the Historia Gentibus Septentrionalibus *by Olaus Magnus.*

to be used as money, these tended to mimic the traditional currencies. Large pieces of copper were shaped roughly like cowhides to form money talents.

The modern word "bourse" is used to describe a place where merchants and businessmen meet to buy, sell and exchange goods. This is also derived from cattle, the ancient word *byrsa* meaning "cowhide". Even some of the terms still used to indicate the denominations of coins are derived from animal skins. Thus, the Croatian unit of currency, the kuna, takes its name from the pine marten, whose pelt was the basis of trade, while the rouble is named from the Russian word for a strip of leather.

Salt was an indispensable commodity, highly prized for its use in the preserving of meat, and therefore very desirable in barter. From the Latin word for salt (*sal*) we get the modern term "salary", and we still use the expression "worth his/her salt". Bars of

Forms of Barter Currency
Native Americans, shown here at a trading post in Manitoba, bartered animal skins for guns. From beaver pelts and buckskins came the "made beaver" tokens of the Hudson's Bay Company and the continuing use of the expression "buck" to mean a dollar.

salt were still being used as currency in Ethiopia until the early 20th century.

When we discuss the fineness of gold coins, we use the term "carat" (US "karat"), which is derived from *keration,* the Greek word for a carob bean. These beans, being of a uniform size, were used for weighing things. The Greeks also coined the words *drachma* ("handful") and *obol* (from *belos*, meaning "dart" or "spit"). The Anglo-Saxons had coins called sceats and in the Baltic states a skatiku was a small coin, but both came originally from a Teutonic word *scaz*, simply meaning "treasure" (like the modern German *Schatz*). The German mark got its name from the scratch on a gold ingot, while "shilling" comes from Old Norse *skilja*, "cut".

Above: Tea-junks are loaded at Tseen-Tang, depicted in this 1843 engraving of a typical Chinese scene.

Below: Tobacco ships dock on the James River, Virginia in the 18th century, from Bryant's History of America.

PAYMENT IN GOODS

Barter is a system of trade whereby one commodity is exchanged for another, or for a service of some kind, without the use of money. It takes many forms, depending on whether it is carried out within a community or between different communities, and also according to the customs of the people and what goods they have to exchange. It probably arose informally but eventually led to indirect barter, where some objects were invested with a fixed value, whether traded or accumulated as status symbols or signs of wealth. Among the commodities that have acquired a monetary value at different times are almonds (India), rock salt (Rome and Ethiopia), dried fish (Scandinavia), tea bricks (China), cacao beans (Mexico), tobacco (North America, Central Africa, Indonesia and Melanesia) and potatoes (Tristan da Cunha). In Cambodia's recent history, Pol Pot's moneyless society banned all forms of currency except rice, which was traded or bartered in tins from 1975 to 1979.

Generally, barter eventually gives way to some form of money, but commodities have been pressed into service as money in times of emergency, in war or periods of economic upheaval. The best example of this is the cigarette, which was widely used as currency in Germany (1945–8) and the Soviet Union (1990) when money in the traditional sense had ceased to have any value. Candy and chewing gum circulated in Italy in the 1970s during shortages of small change. In 1811, Henri Christophe confiscated the Haitians' accumulated stock of gourds and made them the island's unit of currency, using them to buy coffee, with which he re-established foreign trade. To this day the unit is the *gourde*, alluding to this drastic measure.

Potato Stamp

During World War II the remote island of Tristan da Cunha was occupied by the Royal Navy. Previously the islanders had had no use for coined money, but for the convenience of the sailors the local barter commodity (potatoes) was integrated with sterling at the rate of four potatoes to the penny. This dual system was even expressed on the postage stamp, designed for local island mail.

Below: Soviet soldiers rolling cigarettes in World War II. Hard-to-find items such as tobacco and chocolate were often traded between soldiers and civilians.

EARLY CURRENCIES

From actual goods, such as potatoes, salt and tea, which were useful in themselves, it was a logical progression to use objects as currencies which, while lacking a practical use, came to represent an actual value against which the worth of goods and services could be measured. While an assortment of cigarettes or chewing gum may be of little interest to a collector of coins, the same is not true of various forms of early money, some of which are collected as "curious currencies".

SHELL MONEY

From a very early date, people have been fascinated by sea shells. They are often attractive in appearance and not easy to come by, so it is hardly surprising that they should have acquired a monetary value. Strings of *Dentalium* shells were used as money by the native American tribes of the north-western Pacific coast, while armlets composed of *Tridacna* shells were traded in New Guinea. Strings of polished shell discs were used as money all over the Pacific, variously known as *diwara* (New Britain), *pele* (Bismarck Archipelago), *biruan* (Solomon Islands), *mauwai* (Bougainville), *rongo* (Malaita) or *sapis-api* (New Guinea).

Above and right: "Money cowries" featured in J.G. Wood's Natural History, *1854. The cowrie continues to be used as a motif on coins, a rather crude design appearing on this 17th-century lead bazaruk of the Dutch East India Company.*

Above: An Egyptian tomb painting showing workers recording and banking payments in grain.

By far the most popular forms of shell money were the cowrie species *Cypraea moneta* and *C. annulus,* which were threaded to make necklaces. According to Chinese tradition it was the so-called Yellow Emperor, Huang-di (2698 BC) who established this ancient monetary system, though written records point to the ancient Shang and Zhou dynasties as the chief developers of the cowrie unit. The Chinese ideogram *pei* means both a cowrie shell and money in general. Cowrie shells were found only on the most southerly shores of China, which enabled the emperor to control the supply and thus maintain their value. As the population

Below: Two ancient currencies that circulated until quite recently: a Japanese silver chogin of 1865–9 (right) and a gold bar from Vila Rica in Brazil (below), used during the regency of Don João of Portugal, 1799.

expanded, the number of genuine cowries was insufficient to meet demand, so the Chinese resorted to various substitutes in stone, bone, ivory or jade, carved to resemble a cowrie, and later bronze cast in the shape of the shell. Cowries were used as money in China until about 200 BC, but their use spread to India and Arabia and thence to Central and East Africa, and the cowrie survived as currency until about 1950. The shells even circulated as small change alongside metallic coins, tariffed at 60–400 to the franc in French West Africa (1900), 200 to the Indian rupee in Uganda (1895) and up to 1200 to the West African shilling in the Gold Coast (now Ghana). They even inspired coins in India and Africa – the kori of Kutch and the cauri of Guinea. The cedi, used in Ghana, is named from a local word meaning "small shell".

It is strange that such a sophisticated society as that of ancient Egypt seldom used coins. However, the Egyptians had a highly complex currency system based on units of weighed metals, called *deben* and *qedet*, which enabled the values of goods to be compared with each other. Taxes could be paid in barley or other grains. The royal granaries acted as banks; people deposited and withdrew the goods, and interest-bearing loans of grain were also made.

ORIGINS OF METAL MONEY

A metallic standard was adopted in Mesopotamia (modern Iraq) as long ago as 2500 BC. By 1500 BC metal rings and copper utensils of standard quality, size and weight were being used as money and were interchangeable with articles of gold and silver. Deals were recorded in terms of copper bowls and pitchers, while gold and silver (originally valued equally) were worth 40 times their weight in copper. By the 10th century BC a ratio of 1:13:3000

Curious Currency

Bracelets in the shape of horse-shoes, known by the Spanish name *manilla* ("manacle"), circulated as money on the Slave Coast of West Africa. Far from trying to stamp out this currency, British traders imported vast quantities made in Birmingham in an alloy of copper, lead and pewter, and the indigenous tribes came to prefer these to their own productions. A manilla was originally worth 30 cents but fell to 20 cents by 1900.

---

was established in the Middle East for gold, silver and copper respectively.

Such systems were by no means confined to the ancient world. Small bars and ingots stamped with the weight, fineness and issuing authority circulated as money in the Portuguese territories of Brazil and Mozambique in the 16th to 19th centuries, rather than the standard coinage of Portugal. Curiously shaped silver bars known as Tiger Tongues and bent rings sometimes called Banana Bars were used in Thailand and Vietnam, while copper bars known as Bonks circulated in the Dutch East Indies. These areas had coinage, introduced from India in the 7th and 8th centuries, but by the 11th century it had disappeared and been replaced by silver ingots, of which these are just a few varieties.

It can be hard to understand why certain kinds of currency should sometimes have been preferred to coins. In some cases, as in colonial Brazil, the local currency was employed of necessity because of poor communications with the mother country. In another example, playing cards marked with values were used in 17th-century Canada instead of French coins. In South-east Asia, however, the curiously shaped pieces of silver were used, rather than flat discs, merely because that was the traditional style. For the same reasons, many of the petty kingdoms and states in India preferred copper and silver bars. It was traditional, and people had confidence in money of that kind, whereas coins in the Western sense were unfamiliar and not trusted.

During the Shogunate of the 17th to 19th centuries, Japan had the most elaborate metallic system of all, involving bars of copper (kwan-ei) and silver (chogin), rectangular gold ingots (ichibu and nibu kin) and large elliptical gold plates known as oban and koban. These had a ribbed surface on which symbols and inscriptions were countermarked. The oban were additionally inscribed with their weight and the mint-master's signature in black ink, using traditional brush techniques.

Above: A beautiful example of a gold koban of pre-Meiji Japan, with large piercing on the reverse.

NON-METALLIC SUBSTITUTES

Pieces of leather have served as money at various times in many parts of the world. As recently as 1923–4, during the German hyperinflation, pieces of shoe leather were stamped with values in millions of marks, and circular pieces of leather embossed with coin images were used in Austria. Pottery and porcelain tokens were used in China and Thailand in the mid-19th century, while in 1945 Japan resorted to terracotta coins of 1, 2 and 5 sen to combat wartime inflation. In the 19th and early 20th centuries the Chinese exchanged bamboo sticks stamped with brands to denote transactions from 100 cash upwards. Apart from a series of commemorative coins in 1977, the only currencies to circulate in the Cocos (Keeling) Islands are tokens of porcelain or plastic, which are used on the coconut plantations.

Below: Tokens exchanged on colonial plantations were often given actual currency values. This brass 1 dollar token is from the Dutch East Indies.

CHINESE COINAGE

The development of the earliest coinage was roughly simultaneous in China and Asia Minor. The first Chinese "coins" were small pieces of bronze, cast and fashioned into representations of the useful agricultural implements used in barter, such as spades and bill-hooks. The small knives, spades, keys and other domestic articles, symbols of the earlier barter system, were invested with a notional value and had no utilitarian purpose. But they represented a real value and could be exchanged for goods or services accordingly.

The knives were about 15cm/6in long and bore the value and the name of the issuing authority. The bu currency, a modified form of the bronze spades, circulated widely in the 5th and 4th centuries BC, and their image has even been reproduced on Chinese coins in modern times.

THE ARRIVAL OF CASH
By the 4th century BC, bronze circular discs with a hole in the centre were in circulation. Over several generations

Right: Bronze knife money used during the Warring States period.

Below: A cast imitation cowrie (with a central hole), and an example of the round-hooked "spade" money.

The Silver Yuan

Spanish, Mexican, British and American trade dollars circulated extensively in China and filled the need for coins of higher denominations, so it was not until the late 19th century that China began minting silver coins of its own. The yuan (dollar) was introduced in 1889 at par with the Mexican peso. It circulated alongside the foreign silver, but in order to provide pieces of the same weight and fineness as the other trade dollars already in circulation the Chinese had to produce coins of odd values, based on the traditional Chinese weight and value system of mace and candareens. A handsome piece, nicknamed the Sichuan rupee and issued in Tibet, appeared in the closing years of the century and was the only coin actually to portray the Manchu emperor.

Above: Pattern silver dollar produced by the central Tianjin mint in 1911.

Above: Silver dragon and phoenix dollar of the Chinese Republic, 1923.

---

these pieces evolved into the regular banliang (half-ounce) coins minted by the Emperor Shi Huang-di, founder of the Qin dynasty, in 221 BC and known as cash. In 118 BC the banliang were replaced by wuzhu (5 grain) coins by the Han emperor Wudi. These were used all over China, even after the empire was split into a number of smaller states in AD 220. In 621, after the empire was reunified, the Tang emperor Gaozu replaced the wuzhu with a new design with four, rather than two, characters. This style remained in use until 1911. Thus, the Chinese cash, with its distinctive square hole and inscriptions in ideograms, was in circulation for over two millennia. The four Chinese characters that appear on the traditional cash signify "current money of", followed by the

Right: An iron cash coin bearing Chinese and Manchu legends, produced by the Qing dynasty.

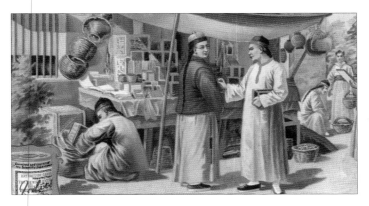

Above: A Chinese bazaar. Despite attempts by various governors to revive larger currencies, the portable copper cash coin remained part of everyday trade for more than 2000 years.

symbol of the appropriate reign. The currency name is not related to the English word for ready money (which comes from the French *caisse* and Italian *cassa,* meaning "money box"). Rather, it appears in slightly different forms in many Oriental languages, from the Sanskrit *karsa* and Persian *karsha* ("weight") via Tamil *kacu* and Portuguese *caixa,* denoting a small copper coin.

Below: Copper cash obverses from the reigns of Emperors Hongxian (1915) and Guangxu (1905).

Above: Reinstated bu (bronze knife and key) money of Wang Mang.

Bu money was briefly revived by the usurper Wang Mang (AD 7–23), but decimalized. Copper cash spread to Korea in the 3rd century BC and Japan (AD 708). Cash continued as the money of China itself and was not superseded until the overthrow of the Qing dynasty and the proclamation of the republic in 1911. Even then, Western-style bronze coins, introduced in 1912 and featuring the crossed flags of the new regime, continued to be denominated in cash, and it is believed that traditional copper cash continued to circulate in rural areas until 1925.

THE ARRIVAL OF CASH
Although various denominations of cash existed, the basic cash unit had a very small value, and the Chinese got into the habit of creating larger values by stringing them together into the shape of a sword. By the time of the Tang dynasty, between AD 650 and 800, merchants found the transportation of huge wagonloads of cash around the country not only cumbersome but insecure, at the mercy of bandits, so they invented *fei-ch'ien* (literally "flying money"), consisting of paper drafts negotiable in bronze currency. These drafts were not authorized paper money in the modern sense but undoubtedly paved the way for the bank notes introduced much later, that serve the world for higher amounts of money.

Above: A Chinese watercolour depicting a moneylender weighing out coins under the Qing dynasty.

Below: The Chinese were pioneers of the use of paper money. This 1000 cash note was issued in 1854, under the Qing dynasty. The rectangular red stamp is the seal of the Fukien Yung Feng Official Bureau.

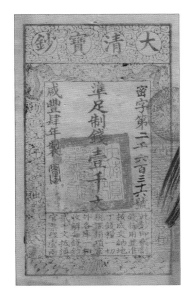

GREEK COINAGE

Copper was worked in Cyprus from at least 3000 BC (indeed, the name of the island is derived from the Greek word for the metal) and by the middle Bronze Age it was being cast into bullion bars, called talents. An ancient Greek talent of bronze (an alloy of copper and tin) weighed about 60lb/127kg. The talent used at the time of Homer, in the 9th century BC, was said to be made of gold, while the talent of Attica, the district surrounding Athens, was of silver, divided into 60 units known as *minae*, worth 100 drachmae each. These units of weight were widely used for high-value transactions in the ancient world.

LEAVING A MARK
Gold was regarded as being worth 13 pieces of silver of equivalent weight, or 3000 pieces of copper. An alloy of gold and silver called electrum, often referred to as pale gold or white gold,

Below: Leaden coin weights used in ancient Greece. The inscriptions on the bottom two suggest that they are equivalent to 8 and 2 drachmae.

Above: Electrum coinage of the Lydian kings with an open-mouthed lion on the obverse (top). The Turtles of Aegina (bottom) circulated widely through the Greek Empire and beyond. The reverse of this stater from 700–500 BC bears an interesting incuse (recessed) punch mark.

was popular in the earliest period. For centuries merchants were accustomed to weigh out lumps of metal at every transaction, but gradually a more convenient system was devised. A rich merchant, or a prince on whose land the metal was mined, would cast it into lumps of uniform size and weight and guarantee the weight of these lumps by applying his personal mark to them. At first this stamp consisted of an irregular mark, made by striking the metal with a broken nail. The jagged edge of the nail left an individual mark that served to identify the person who issued the metal. Sometimes these lumps had several marks struck on them in the form of a pattern. As a rule, the marks appeared on one side only, though the reverse might have a pattern of lines, where the anvil had dug into the metal during striking.

COINS IN A MODERN SENSE
According to the Greek historian Herodotus, the Lydians were the first people to use gold and silver coins. From the evidence of coin hoards and archaeological research it is now believed that the earliest coins of Lydia were produced in the late 7th century BC. By 630 BC the crude nail mark had developed into a proper design, the lion's head emblem of the Mermnad

dynasty of Lydia, of which King Croesus – whose wealth was proverbial in the ancient world – was the fifth and last ruler. This emblem was applied to the obverse, or "heads" side, by placing the lump of metal (called a blank or flan) on an anvil whose top had been engraved with the design. The flan had been heated until it was very soft, and striking it with a hammer impressed the image into the surface of the metal. At first the hammer had no mark on its surface, and the earliest coins were uniface (one-sided), but gradually it became customary to include a simple geometric design that bit into the reverse, or "tails" side, of the coin, giving an "incuse" reverse (a simple hammered design). The authority that these simple designs afforded came to be regarded as a guarantee of their value. The value was still linked to the

Below: Ancient Greek coins were highly innovative. This Corinthian stater (top) has a winged Pegasus with a concave reverse showing a helmeted Athena. The coin of Lucania (now Italy) bears a wheat ear with a simple incuse reverse (middle), while the coin of Miletus, a coastal colony in Asia Minor, bears interesting geometric designs (bottom).

The Ornate Shield of Macedon

Philip of Macedon welded the Greeks into a nation and his son Alexander the Great created an empire in the 4th century BC. After his death, the empire was divided and Macedon passed to his general, Antigonus. His descendant, Antigonus Gonatas (277–239 BC), struck this shield-shaped coin bearing the head of Pan. The reverse shows Athena Alkis holding a shield and thunderbolt. These ornate coins survived until Macedon was absorbed by the Roman Empire in the 2nd century BC.

This pattern survived until the early Christian era, though latterly the coins were confined to bronze and permitted by the Romans only for local circulation. The designs were faithfully reproduced in the coinage of modern Greece and survive to this day on the national reverses of the euro coinage.

By the 4th century BC coinage was in general use throughout the Greek world, including colonies as far afield as Syracuse (Sicily) and Marseilles. Silver predominated and coins ranged in size from the tiny hemi-obol to the massive decadrachm (10 drachmae). Portraiture was generally confined to gods and heroes, but after the death of Alexander his profile appeared on coins of the Hellenistic kingdoms created by his generals, and later they used their own portraits.

weight and precious metal content, but it was no longer necessary to weigh each piece at every transaction.

THE SPREAD OF COINS

The first electrum coins were found in the river bed of the Pactolus in Asia Minor and may have been struck under the authority of King Ardys of Lydia,

Below: Electrum and silver trihemibols of Phocaea (Ionia), in western Anatolia.

ancestor of Croesus. From there they spread to other parts of western Asia Minor, being adopted by the Greek coastal towns of Abydus, Chios, Miletus and Phocaea. These early coins needed no inscriptions, as they circulated only within their own territories, but their motifs were clues to their identity, such as the sphinx of Chios and the man-bull of Miletus. One of the earliest Greek coins showed the civic emblem of a stag and was inscribed "I am the sign of Phanes". It is still the subject of debate as to whether Phanes was a place or a person.

Coin production spread from Asia Minor to mainland Greece in the 6th century. Aegina led the way with its silver "Turtles", whose reverse had a geometric incuse pattern not unlike a Union Jack. Nearby Corinth followed with drachmae showing the winged horse Pegasus. Athens possessed silver mines that enabled it to strike a vast quantity of coins, which were soon accepted all over the Greek world. The earliest featured a range of motifs, but in 546 BC Pisistratus instituted the coins bearing a helmeted profile of Athena on the obverse and an owl, symbol of wisdom, on the reverse.

Above: One of many posthumous coins struck for Alexander the Great, after his death in 323 BC.

Below: The coinage of Alexander the Great, depicted in battle on this ceramic vase, greatly influenced ancient and medieval coins in Europe and Asia.

ROMAN COINAGE

Our connection with the Roman world can be detected in many of our units of currency and weight. The Latin word *pondus*, for example, has given us such words as "ponder" (to weigh up), "ponderous" (heavy) and "pound", used both as a weight (lb) and a unit of currency (£). The abbreviations for the pound in weight and money both came from another Latin word – *libra*, meaning a pound. This is preserved in many European currencies, as *lira* (Italy, Israel and Turkey) or *livre* (France).

Although an imperial mint to supply silver and gold coins was not established in Rome until 269 BC, the Romans had been striking bronze coins locally for several decades prior to this. These bronze currencies began with the aes rude, whose name refers to the crudeness of unmarked lumps of metal, which had to be weighed out at each transaction. Gradually, the lumps were replaced by bars or ingots of a uniform shape and weight. They were known as aes signatum ("signed bronze") because they bore the stamp of the issuing authority on both sides. Significantly,

Below: The Romans were highly skilled in financial dealings. This relief from a Gallo-Roman mausoleum shows a tax collector at work.

Above: Roman aes grave coins, denominated as triens and sextans.

one of these was a bull, alluding to the importance of cattle as a form of barter currency in earlier times.

After aes signatum came aes grave ("heavy bronze"). These pieces were roughly circular and fairly flat – like coins, but very much heavier. The basic unit was the as, weighing a pound (*libra*) and bearing the Roman numeral I. Half of this was the semis, indicated by the letter S. A third of an as was the triens, which, being worth four Roman ounces, bore four little pellets to indicate its weight and value. Smaller units were the quadrans ("fourth"), sextans ("sixth") and the uncia ("ounce", indicated by one pellet).

This heavy bronze coinage coincided with the inception of the Roman Mint, which issued a series of silver coins, influenced by the penchant for figures of deities and their familiars in Greek coin design. The series consisted of didrachms (2 drachmae) and their subdivisions of litra, half-litra and silver as. Ten asses of silver or bronze were worth a silver didrachm. The silver coins were inscribed "Roma" or "Romano".

At this point, bronze coins began to fall out of favour. Their weight and consequent value were progressively reduced, until the bronze as eventually weighed no more than the original uncia coin.

GOLD AND SILVER COINS

The Romans preferred silver coins because the metal was abundant, and could be made into a hard-wearing alloy by adding a little copper. Gold was regarded primarily as a medium for jewellery; it was very rarely used for coins. Gold staters were struck in 216 BC during a shortage of silver as a result of the wars against Carthage. (A small silver coin, equivalent to a drachma but known as a victoriate, was struck to celebrate the defeat of Carthage.)

Its victories in the Punic Wars made Rome the most powerful state in the western Mediterranean. Its prosperity led to the adoption of a new currency in 211 BC, based on the silver denarius – the forerunner of the deniers and dinars used by many European and Asiatic countries (and preserved in Britain until 1971 in the symbol "d" to denote the penny). The denarius of 10 asses was divided into the quinarius (5 asses) and the sestertius (2½ asses). A board of moneyers, consisting of three officials elected annually, was created, and their names, initials or family emblems began to appear on the coins.

PORTRAITURE AND ALLEGORY

From the 2nd century BC, Roman coins became more elaborate in their design. The most popular images were Roma and Bellona on the obverse and the heavenly twins, Castor and Pollux, on the reverse. From 146 BC, when the Romans finally destroyed the city of Carthage, Rome expanded rapidly, acquiring territory in North Africa, Gaul (France) and Iberia (Spain), suppressing the Greek colonies in southern Italy and advancing into the Balkans. Coins of this period featured Victory, Mars and Jupiter on the obverse, with elaborate designs illustrating characters and events in classical mythology.

In 141 BC the currency was revalued on the basis of the denarius of 16 asses. Scholars have many theories concerning the motive for this, the general view

Above: The coins of Antoninus Pius featured a seated Britannia (right).

Above: Some imperial gold coins circulated as far as India, like this holed gold aureus of Caracalla (top). A solidus of Valens appears below.

Coins in Memoriam
The Emperor Augustus struck coins in memory of his predecessor Julius Caesar, while the coin shown here was struck by Tiberius in memory of Augustus.

now being that silver had become much more plentiful, leading to a decrease in the value of the as. The increase from 10 to 16 asses in the denarius seems to have been a balancing adjustment.

Coins became more varied in design as the moneyers rivalled each other in depicting emblems and events alluding to their illustrious ancestors. By the first century BC, portraits of ancestors were appearing, while Rome was splitting into political factions under such men as Marius, Sulla, Pompey and Julius Caesar. Caesar struck coins in Gaul that included the numerals LII (52, his age) – one of the earliest attempts at putting a date on a coin. After 49 BC, when he became master of Rome, his coins took on a more personal character, with

Below: The expanding Roman empire struck denarii following acquisitions in France (Gallic shield on coin, top) and the Balkans (head of Victory, bottom).

lengthy inscriptions referring to his various public offices. The last coins under Julius Caesar's authority actually bore his portrait.

THE ROMAN EMPIRE
From Caesar's assassination in 44 BC until the battle of Actium in 31 BC, a period of civil wars was marked by coins struck on behalf of Brutus, Cassius, the sons of Pompey, the triumvirate of Mark Antony, Lepidus and Octavian, and finally for Octavian himself, having assumed the title of Augustus and set about transforming Rome into an empire. In 27 BC he accepted the title of emperor and instituted a new coinage based on the gold aureus, worth 25 silver denarii. Smaller coins included the brass sestertius and the dupondius (2 asses). Although the weights and sizes of these coins varied, the denominations remained in use for most of the Roman Imperial period.

Imperial coins were prolific and served as propaganda for the emperor, extolling his virtues and achievements and often portraying his wife and family as well as himself. They were generally well produced, with realistic portraits, and elaborate allegorical compositions on the reverse. The seated figure of Britannia shown on British coins since 1672 was actually modelled on the Britannia featured on coins of

Below: Seminal coins issued by the Roman Republic to mark the assassination of Julius Caesar (top) and the suicide of Mark Antony (bottom).

Antoninus Pius (138–61), in whose reign the Antonine Wall across the isthmus of the Forth and Clyde was built.

The double denarius, or antoninianus, was introduced in AD 214 under Caracalla. By that time inflation had caused the demise of the denarius and thereafter the antoninianus was the basic unit of currency. Although nominally silver, it was progressively debased and eventually was no more than a copper coin with a thin silver wash, which soon wore off. New coins were the follis (AD 294) and the gold solidus (309), ancestor of such European coins as the soldo, sol and sou, and the source of the "s" denoting the shilling in pre-decimal British currency.

The nummus, introduced by Diocletian between AD 295 and 310, played a major part in the development of Byzantine coinage. During the 4th century there were two new silver coins, the miliarense and the siliqua, and finally the tremissis, a gold piece worth a third of a solidus.

BYZANTINE COINAGE

In AD 364, Valentinian divided the Roman Empire into eastern and western provinces, assigning the Eastern Empire to his brother Valens. From that time there were two Roman Empires, based in the cities of Rome and Byzantium (Constantinople) respectively. The Western Empire came to an end in 476, when the last emperor, Romulus Augustulus, was defeated by the Ostrogoths. Their ruler, Theodoric, minted coins with his portrait on one side and a figure of Rome on the other, with the caption "Invicta Roma" ("Unconquered Rome"), but these coins were very crude by comparison with the classical issues, and they formed an ironic tailpiece to seven centuries of Roman coinage.

THE IMPERIAL TRADITION
In the east, the Roman Empire survived a further thousand years, until the capture of Constantinople by the Turks in 1453. At the height of its

Above: Crusaders at the walls of Constantinople in 1204, depicted in De la Conquête de Constantinople *by Geoffroi de Villehardouin.*

power, the Byzantine Empire extended over the eastern Mediterranean, including even parts of Italy. It retained the ancient Roman provinces in the Balkans and controlled Asia Minor, Syria and Palestine.

Byzantium became the repository of Roman technology, science and the accumulated wisdom of the classical world, and it was the flight of scholars and scientists from Turkish rule after the conquest that triggered off the Renaissance (the rebirth of learning) in the West. Just as the Byzantine Empire kept alight the lamp of learning and civilization in early medieval times, so did it continue the traditions of Greece and Rome in its coins. A new feature, however, was the portrayal of the emperor full-face instead of in profile.

Since the time of the Emperor Constantine (who believed that the victory that gave him the throne had been aided by the one God of the Christians), Christianity had been the official religion of the empire, and from its foundation in 324 his capital at Constantinople, on the site of the ancient Byzantium, had been a Christian city. This religious devotion found expression on the coins of the Byzantine Empire. The figure of Jesus Christ appears on the obverse of Byzantine coins from about 450, followed by the Virgin Mary. From the 9th century onward many saints of the Orthodox Church – Theodore, George, Michael and John among others – were portrayed on the reverses. Christian symbolism replaced the pagan allegory of the Roman Empire.

CHANGING STYLES
As time went by, Greek replaced Latin in the inscriptions on these coins, and it is interesting to note how the Greek letters gradually took over from their Roman counterparts. Inevitably the standards of design and production slipped over the centuries, although

Above: Constantine V (left) and a portrait of Christ (middle) on a coin that shows the joint rulers, Basil II and Constantine VIII on the reverse (right).

Below: Allegorical designs on coins of Anastasius and John II portray the emperors flanked by Victory.

> ### Saucer-shaped Coins
> Coins were produced on a flat disc flan until the reign of Constantine IX (1042–55), when a curious concave shape was adopted for all denominations except the smallest bronze pieces. These are known to collectors as *nummi scyphati* (literally "boat-shaped coins"). In succeeding reigns the flan became thinner and slightly cup-shaped, but the strange shape endured until the Latin conquest of 1204.
>
>

Byzantine coinage continued to be far superior to that produced anywhere else in the medieval world. Unlike their Roman predecessors, Byzantine coins were relatively neglected by collectors, who regarded their designs as stereotyped and rather monotonous, but recently collectors have developed a keen interest, discovering the subtle developments in design as well as the light they shed on a period of European history that is not well documented in written records. Not surprisingly, coins that not so long ago were comparatively cheap have soared in value.

Although it lasted a millennium, the Byzantine Empire was not a static entity but expanded and contracted, assailed by foreign invasion and torn by civil wars, and these highs and lows of its history are reflected in the coinage. Constantinople was besieged by the Arabs in 674 and the Bulgars in 923. In 1204, during the Fourth Crusade, it fell to these holy warriors and was under Latin (that is, Western European) rule from then until 1261.

The Byzantines minted coins in bronze, silver and gold, although their silver coins are comparatively scarce and usually debased by a high copper

Below: Emperor Justinian I and his wife Theodora, both of whom featured on Byzantine coins.

Above: Lengthy Graeco-Roman inscriptions on post-Justinian coins.

Below: Byzantine coin weights: a 2 solidi square weight (left), a nomisma square weight (right) and a ⅓ nomisma circular weight (bottom).

content. Justinian I was the first emperor to add a date to his coins, in the form of the year from the beginning of his reign, 526. As well as the increasingly bewildering mixture of Roman and Greek lettering, often reducing inscriptions to little more than an apparent jumble of initials, the collector has to contend with the use of letters to denote numerals in dates and denominations. New titles, such as "Autokrator" (Emperor) and "Basileus Romaion" (King of the Romans) in Greek capitals vie with the cryptic "MP QV" (*Meter Theou* or Mother of God) and "IC" or "XC" (Jesus Christ).

DENOMINATIONS
The currency was originally based on the gold solidus and its subdivisions, down to the tiny sixth, which was the equivalent of two silver hexagrams. Gradually, the Byzantines adopted a new name for the solidus, calling it

a nomisma. In the reign of Nicephorus II a lighter coin than the solidus was adopted, known as a tetarteron, on par with the Arab dinar. In the time of Michael IV (1034–41) the nomisma underwent progressive debasement. Its gold content had dropped to about 26 per cent by the time Alexius I reformed the coinage in 1092 and introduced the hyperper, nominally of pure gold but averaging 21 carat fineness.

The basic silver coin was originally the miliaresion. This word literally means a thousandth part – but of what remains a mystery, as it was tariffed at 12 to the solidus. It was replaced in the reign of Heraclius (610–41) by a crude coin of the same value known as a hexagram. By the 9th century the miliaresion was much thinner and lighter and seems to have been worth half a hexagram. Silver coinage did not recover until the end of the 13th century and was then modelled on contemporary Venetian types, reflecting Venice's control of Byzantine trade.

Copper coins were based on the follis of 40 nummia, the number being represented by a large M. The half (20 nummia) was indicated by the letter K and the quarter by the letter I. Billon (an alloy of copper with a small amount of silver) was used for the trachy, tariffed at 48 to the hyperper.

Above: The basic silver coin of the Byzantine Empire: the miliaresion.

Below: The follis of 40 nummia, a large and cumbersome coin, widely used as small change.

OTHER ANCIENT EUROPEAN COINAGE

Parallel with the main developments of coinage in the great civilizations of the Greek, Roman and Byzantine worlds were the attempts by the peoples beyond the fringes of the civilized world to emulate them. The groups discussed here are the ones of major interest to coin collectors. There were many others that are either obscure, or that produced relatively little coinage, or were content to copy the coins of their more powerful neighbours.

CELTIC COINAGE

The Celtic peoples settled the valley of the Danube and occupied the area now forming the countries of Switzerland, France, Spain, Germany, Belgium and the Netherlands. They migrated to the British Isles around 600 BC and their cultural legacy, especially in Ireland, the Scottish Highlands, Cumbria, Wales and Cornwall, remains strong to this day. Paradoxically, the Celtic fringes of the British Isles did not produce distinctive coinage, but elsewhere, including the southerly and eastern areas of what eventually formed Roman Britain, distinctive Celtic coins developed in the late pre-Christian era.

The Danubian Celts imitated the gold and silver coins with which they were most familiar, the silver

Below: Celtic coins of France and Spain include this Iberian coin of Osca with a horseman (top) and a Gallo-Belgic stater with a large flan depicting Apollo.

Above: Celtic designs: a vine leaf stater of Verica (top), the Phoenician goddess Tanit on a coin of the Danubian Celts (middle) and a stater of the Iceni with a horse and wheel (bottom).

tetradrachms and gold staters of the Alexandrine Empire and its Hellenistic successors, but because they were illiterate they blundered the inscriptions or abandoned them altogether. At the same time, the profiles of Philip of Macedon and Alexander the Great were reduced to caricature and then all but vanished, only curls and headbands surviving. Similarly, the horseman on the reverse was reduced to a stylized, abstract shape.

Not so long ago, Celtic coinage was dismissed as barbaric because of this abstraction of classical patterns, but now scholars and collectors are discovering the extraordinary vitality of Celtic art and the religious symbolism of the human heads and even the curvilinear motifs, which are startlingly avant-garde in appearance. British Celts latterly included brief inscriptions that identify the rulers of the Atrebates, Durotriges, Catuvellauni, Iceni, Trinovantes and others in the period immediately before the Roman conquest in AD 43.

THE FALL OF ROME

The minting of coins was one of the technologies lost in the collapse of the Roman Empire. Crude copies of Roman coins were produced by the Ostrogoths, Germanic people who

eventually ruled the Romans, from the end of the 5th century. Theodoric the Great not only paid homage to the memory of Imperial Rome but slavishly copied the gold coins of his Byzantine contemporary Anastasius, even going so far as to copy his titles and inscriptions. His successors, Athalaric and Theodahad, substituted

Below: A Celtic punch-marked coin of the Durotriges (top) and an Ostrogoth imitation of a Roman 40 nummia.

Above: Coins of early medieval France include this tremissis struck by the Visigoths in the name of Severus (top) and 12th-century billon deniers of Burgundy (bottom).

Above and right: The Vikings established extensive trade links. Viking pennies, such as these of Daegmund and Arus, have been found throughout Europe.

their own portraits. For a time the Byzantine rulers recovered the Balkans and Italy from the Goths and struck coins at Rome and Ravenna in the 8th and 9th centuries.

Elsewhere in the early medieval world, coins based on Roman models were struck by the Vandals in North Africa, denominated in both Roman siliquae and denarii, the Suevians in Spain, the Lombards in Italy, the Burgundians in northern France, the Visigoths in the south of that country, and the Anglo-Saxons in England.

In the majority of cases these coins followed Roman precedents, incorporating crude portraits of local rulers and a wide variety of local inscriptions. Whereas coin production was centralized at the Roman Mint, the rulers of the early medieval European kingdoms dispersed the process and granted the right to strike coins to many towns, and even to monasteries. In the Merovingian kingdom of the 6th and 7th centuries, for example, there existed more than 800 mints. The Merovingians, who ruled over parts of present-day France and Germany, introduced a new coin, the silver saiga, based on the Roman denarius. The legacy of this coin was far-reaching: it led to the denier or penny, introduced by Pepin the Short in 755.

VIKING AND ANGLO-SAXON COINAGE

The money that was used in Britain between the withdrawal of the Roman legions, early in the 5th century, and the advent of William the Conqueror, in 1066, is generally described as Anglo-Saxon, although distinctive types were adopted in the seven main kingdoms (Northumbria, Mercia, Kent, East Anglia, Essex, Sussex and Wessex), which emerged as a united England in 959 under Eadgar and adopted the silver penny as the standard unit of currency in 973.

The earliest coins were known as sceats or sceattas (derived from the Old English word meaning "wealth"), and were small pieces of base silver and latterly copper with a uniquely eclectic mixture of symbolism derived from Roman, Byzantine, Teutonic and Celtic coins. Offa of Mercia (757–96) introduced the silver penny, adapted from the Carolingian denier (denarius) with a crude effigy on the obverse and a cross on the reverse. The thrymsa was a small gold coin derived from the tremissis (or third solidus), which was struck between 575 and about 775.

The Vikings traded as widely as they raided and made use of the coinage of other countries, notably England, whose silver penny became the model for the earliest distinctive coins in Denmark, Norway and Sweden. Hedeby in Denmark and Birka in Sweden, the major trading centres of Scandinavia, produced vast quantities of silver pennies with distinctive motifs and runic inscriptions. English sterlings were also extensively copied, not only in the Danelaw (that part of England under Danish rule from the late 9th century), but also in the Norse kingdoms in Ireland and the Isle of Man.

Below: Anglo-Saxon silver pennies issued in Mercia (top) and by the authority of King Eadgar (bottom).

MEDIEVAL EUROPEAN COINAGE

With the collapse of the Roman Empire in Western Europe, social structures became more localized and the coinage system was fragmented. Under the Carolingian rulers, who rose to power as kings of the Franks in the 8th century, a new standardized system was imposed. The gold coins in the realm were demonetized, and in 752 Pepin the Short issued a new silver coin, the silver denier (based on the Roman denarius), which became the basic unit of currency.

BIRTH OF THE SILVER PENNY
The denier was a practical coin for the early Middle Ages, when barter was still prevalent and most people required coins only as a means of converting a small agricultural surplus into cash, and it remained the standard unit for nearly

Below: An enormous salut d'or of Henry VI, with the arms of England and France, to which Henry laid claim, and a depiction of the annunciation.

six centuries. In 793, Charlemagne increased the weight of the denier by a third, and as his empire grew, so his coinage was imitated in the denar of the Balkans (hence the dinar of Serbia to this day), the denaro of Italy and the dinero of Spain. It also provided the model for the penny, which travelled from 9th-century England to Scandinavia and northern Germany, giving rise to the pfennig or pfenning in the German states, the fenigow in Poland and the penni in Finland.

By the 11th century the use of the denier was more or less confined to France, where it was struck at many mints – royal, baronial and ecclesiastical. The inconvenience of having no larger coins led to the introduction by Louis IX (1226–70) of the gros (from the French for "large"), which spread across Europe in many different forms – grote, groat, groschen, groszy, grush and even the Turkish kurus.

Below: A 13th-century silver gros tournois of Philip III of France (top), and papal testones of Pius IV (middle), with St Peter enthroned, and Sixtus V (bottom), with St Peter standing.

Above: Workers of the 15th century being paid by the Commune of Siena, in a painting by Pietro di Sano.

Below: A cavallino d'oro of Sicily (top) and a 16th-century zecchino of Venice.

ITALIAN AND GERMAN COINS
After the collapse of the Roman Empire, Italy disintegrated into a multitude of petty principalities and city states. It was the crossroads of civilization and came under the influence of Romans, Byzantines, Goths, Franks and Arabs, reflected in complex coinage of many different types. Pope Adrian I (772–95) minted the first papal coins, which continue to this day.

By the 12th century the city states of Italy were in the forefront of the commercial revolution, and their prosperity was reflected in the size and quality of their coins, as well as the extent to which they were coveted and

Above: A Venetian silver ducato, showing the Doge kneeling before St Mark, and the winged lion.

Above (from top): Gold guldens of medieval Hungary and Germany; Crusader coins range from this copper type of Tancred of Antioch to this ornate silver gros of Bohemond VI.

because they were fragile and easily damaged, but it meant that a small amount of silver went a long way and enabled much larger coins to be struck.

ARABIC INFLUENCES

Gold coins were reintroduced in Western Europe from the 13th century, as the general level of prosperity recovered after the Early Medieval period. This was first evident in southern Italy, where the gold tari and copper follari, originally modelled on the Byzantine system, were inscribed in a mixture of Latin and Arabic. Byzantium was also the inspiration for the silver ducat, so-called because it was first struck in the Duchy (*ducatus*) of Apulia.

From the end of the first millennium the nation-states of Europe gradually emerged, but the process of centralizing coin production and introducing uniformity went on for several centuries. As well as the numerous coins issued by nobles in their own fiefdoms, Crusader coins emanating from the Latin kingdoms briefly flourished in various parts of the Balkans, Asia Minor, Syria and Palestine in the 12th and 13th centuries. Interestingly, it was in the Crusader kingdoms that the pattern of French feudal coinage was most closely followed, although while imitating the deniers of the West they were often influenced by the sizes, weights, specifications and designs of their Islamic contemporaries.

Below: A bilingual tram of Armenia with an inscription citing the Seljuqs of Rum (top) and imitation dirhams of the 13th century (bottom).

Bracteates

Coins so thin that they can be struck on only one side are known as bracteates, derived from *bractea*, the medieval Latin word for gold or silver leaf. Coins so described range from the "shadow" coins interred with the dead in ancient Greece to those used in Viking jewellery. The term is also used for the extremely thin silver coins popular in the German states in the 12th to 14th centuries, with emblems struck on one side showing through to the reverse. Popularly known as *Hohlpfennige* (hollow pennies), they circulated alongside more orthodox coins and may have served purely as local small change.

copied elsewhere. Venice, the greatest trading city of this period, introduced the zecchino or sequin, while its rival Florence produced a large silver coin in 1189 depicting a lily (the flower from which it derived its name). The coin, called a fiorino or florin, eventually passed into the currency of many countries, surviving until 2002 in the Netherlands (where the written symbol for a gulden was "fl"). From Genoa in the mid-13th century came the genovino, one of the first great trade gold coins. Worth 20 solidi or 240 denari, it helped to bolster the Roman £sd system, previously confined to money of account rather than actual currency.

In Germany the Franks were at first content to imitate the Romans and Byzantines. In the 14th century, Louis of Bavaria introduced the grossus, modelled on the French gros, and many of the German states adopted thin silver bracteates. It is hard to understand why these were so popular,

MIDDLE EASTERN COINAGE

The inhabitants of Arabia had no coins of their own and were content to use Sassanian drachmae of Persia and the copper folles of Byzantium. Even after they began their dramatic expansion throughout the Middle East, borrowed coinage remained the norm, but in the mid-7th century Caliph Abd al-Malik introduced coinage based on the gold dinar (denarius aureus), the silver dirham (drachma) and the bronze fils (follis). At first the caliph was content to use Byzantine gold solidi, but because they bore the image of Christ he decided to issue his own gold coins with non-figurative motifs, hence the dinar, whose appearance coincided with the rise of iconoclasm in Islam.

DYNASTIC COINS

By the mid-7th century the great empires of Persia and Byzantium had fought each other to a standstill. In the resulting power vacuum the religious zeal of the Arabs gave their aggressive expansion a powerful incentive and explains why they were able to overrun the Middle East so rapidly. Umar, the Commander of the Faithful, established Basra in Mesopotamia and Fustat in Egypt as major centres from which the Arabs spread across the Middle East and North Africa, and thence into Central Asia and the Iberian Peninsula.

Below: An Abd al-Malik dinar of AH 78 (top) and a dirham of AH 81.

Above: More than a thousand years of Arab influence on Spanish coin production can be seen in this 18th-century dirham of Marrakesh struck at Madrid (top) and in this Arab-Byzantine dirham circulated in 8th-century Spain (bottom).

First and foremost of the Arab dynasties were the Umayyads. At the height of their power they ruled over a vast territory from Seville to Bokhara, but they were overthrown in 750. From their chief mint at Wasit they produced the first of the silver dirhams with Koranic inscriptions on both sides, establishing a pattern that lasted for centuries, imitated by their successors, the Abbasids, and later rival dynasties such as the Fatimids of Egypt and the Ghaznavids of Afghanistan.

THE MONGOL INVASION

Early in the 13th century the Mongols under Genghis Khan swept out of the steppes of Central Asia and first over-ran China (1211–14), then in 1220 advanced westward against the Empire of Khwarizm (modern Iran, Turkestan and north-western India). Before he died in 1227, Genghis had conquered a vast territory from the Black Sea to Korea. In a series of lightning campaigns his immediate successors conquered most of Russia and, by 1241, had advanced into Poland and Hungary. By 1260 the Mongol Empire was divided among the descendants of Genghis and out of this developed separate dynasties in Siberia and the

Above: A Kay-Khusraw II type drachm (top) shows Byzantine influences, and the distinctive concentric design of an 11th-century Fatimid dinar (middle) is reflected in an anonymous silver dirham of the Golden Horde (bottom).

Above: An 18th-century Ottoman coin of Osman III.

Below: An Islamic street scene with a porter and a metalworker.

Crimea, and most notably in China under Kublai Khan. Their impact on coinage was considerable. They generally made use of the coins they seized as booty, or made crude copies of them, but later the khans of the Golden Horde produced small silver coins distinguished by their inscriptions, while the Ilkhans of Persia struck handsome coins in gold, silver and bronze reciting their titles and family tree. They did not contribute to European coinage and their impact on Islamic coins was slight, though coins of the Seljuks of Rum, struck at Qonya, include the adjective *mahrusat* ("well-defended" – against the menace from the east).

SELJUQS OF RUM

In 1055 Tughril Beg the Seljuq seized Baghdad and founded a dynasty that eventually controlled most of Anatolia, otherwise known as Asia Minor or Rum ("land of the Romans"). The Seljuqs of Rum were the most powerful of the Turkmen tribes and eventually prevailed over the others, establishing their capital at Qonya. In turn, they were defeated by the Mongols but remained significant until the early 14th century, producing a vast

Above: Modern coins of Islamic countries often show the ruler, as in this Iraqi coin of the 1950s portraying King Faisal II (top). Square silver dirhams of Morocco (bottom), a type introduced by Abd al-Mumin c. AH 550, were popular for 250 years.

series of coins mostly distinguished by square frames within a circle. Coins of a similar type were struck by the Mamluks of Egypt.

As Seljuq power declined, the Turkic tribes of western Anatolia became more independent, and distinctive coins were struck by the Qaramanids from about 1300, and the Jandarids soon after. Coins were also minted by the Sarukhan, Isfendiyarids and Eretnids, before the emergence of the Ottomans about 1350 under Bayazid bin Murad. His son Suleyman was the first Ottoman ruler to adopt the *toughra* or sign-manual of the sultan as a coin symbol; it survives in some Arab coinage to this day.

OTTOMAN EMPIRE

The Ottoman rulers of Turkey and western Asia began minting coins in the 15th century in gold, silver and bronze, featuring the toughra of the ruler and inscriptions in Arabic script. This type of coinage continued in Turkey until 1933, when the lira of 100 kurus was adopted. The portrait of Kemal Ataturk then began to grace the coins, emphasizing Turkey's transformation into a secular country, and henceforward inscriptions were in the modified Roman alphabet.

ISLAMIC COINS TODAY

Egypt, Morocco and the Yemen all have a long history of distinctive coins, clinging to Islamic tradition with lengthy inscriptions in place of portraiture, and numerous variations of the Bismillah ("There is no God but God and Muhammad is His Prophet"). Morocco's main concession to symbolism was the inclusion of the national emblem, a five-pointed star. All these countries have now adopted portraiture. By contrast, Saudi Arabia retains strong conservative traditions. It used Ottoman coinage until distinctive coins were minted in the early 1900s, apart from a few small copper pieces minted at Mecca from 1804. Foreign coins, notably the Maria Theresia thaler of Austria, were countermarked in Arabic.

Persian coins followed the Arab pattern, but under the reforming Shah Nasr-ed-Din (1829–96) a central mint was established at Tehran and coins on European lines were introduced.

Below: An early 20th-century dinar of Saudi Arabia.

Islamic Calendar

Most Islamic coins are dated from the Hegira, the flight of Muhammad from Mecca to Medina in AD 622. The Islamic calendar consists of 12 lunar months (as opposed to solar, or luni-solar), so it falls shorter than the Gregorian year. The date 1201, below, equates to 1786 in the Gregorian calendar.

INDIAN COINAGE

The Indian subcontinent developed a distinctive coinage, although at various periods it was influenced by political and artistic developments in other parts of the ancient world. Very little is known about hundreds of dynasties other than what can be gleaned from their coins. Ancient languages, such as Kharoshthi, have been deciphered from bilingual Indo-Greek coins.

EARLY INDIAN CURRENCIES

The earliest coins appeared *c.* 500 BC, when silver from Persia and Afghanistan began to flow into India. They were irregular in shape but of uniform weight. The use of such symbols as hills, trees, animals and human figures suggests issue by royal authority, rather than merchants' marks.

Coins recovered from a hoard at Mathura in central India, bearing up to seven punch marks, are regarded as the earliest known. Around the same time Taxila, which traded with Mesopotamia, produced curved ingots with punch marks at either end. Most punch-marked coins conform to the Karshapana standard weight of 32 rattis (1 ratti being 11mg/0.17 grains, the weight of a gunja seed). From the presence of coins of Alexander the Great in Indian hoards it appears that punch-marked coins continued long after the advent of Indo-Greek coins in the 4th century BC. Many were circular, showing the influence of Greek models. Later types included copper coins, relatively thick and often square, with various symbols punched on both sides.

Below: A conical copper currency item of ancient India bears designs also found on Mauryan coins.

Above: Indo-Greek tetradrachms and staters struck by the kings of Bactria.

HELLENISTIC COINS

Alexander the Great began his conquest of India in 327 BC and subjugated the territory as far as the Indus before his death in 323, when his vast empire was divided among his generals. Seleucus Nicator seized Persia, Bactria (Afghanistan) and Syria, and struck gold staters and silver tetradrachms, combining Greek and Indian inscriptions. He was checked by a powerful Maurya state ruled by Chandragupta, who married a daughter of Seleucus.

The Mauryan Empire covered most of India beyond the limits of Greek penetration and struck distinctive coins until its disintegration in 180 BC. Many other kingdoms and dynasties

Below: Allegorical subjects on Kushan coins range from Graeco-Roman figures such as Nike to the Hindu god Shiva.

(such as the Satavahanas, Kshatrapas and Maitrakas) then emerged, each producing its own coins. In southern India the best known coinage was that of the Ardhras, who used lead coins inscribed with native characters.

After the death of Seleucus in 281 BC, his empire broke up into several kingdoms, which continued with Indo-Greek coinage. Arsaces became king of Parthia, while Diodotus seized Bactria in 256 BC. The gold staters and copper tetradrachms of Bactria had inscriptions in both Greek and Prakrit. This Indo-Greek kingdom continued for more than a century before it was absorbed into the Kushan Empire.

The Kushans were a nomadic people of north-western China who moved into the Oxus valley in AD 78 and ruled most of what is now Afghanistan, Pakistan and north-west India. Kushan coins portrayed the ruler on the obverse, with a legend in cursive Greek, while the reverse featured Hindu deities with Sanskrit text. After AD 220 the Kushan Empire disintegrated into

Below: Gold dinars struck by kings of the Kushan.

Princely Coinage

Many Indian princes retained the privilege of striking their own coins until 1947, varying in content and denomination according to the ruler's whim. They range from crude, non-figural pieces to sophisticated coins on Western lines, often produced in London or Birmingham, such as this 1941 silver nazarana rupee of Faridkot, with the bust of Harindar Singh on the obverse and the state arms on the reverse.

numerous petty kingdoms, whose gold dinars and copper coins remained current until the 5th century, latterly with more emphasis on Hindu deities and inscribed in Brahmi script. Were it not for the extraordinary range and beauty of their coins, very little would be known about the Kushans.

THE GUPTAS

A Magadha (Bihar) kingdom, with its capital at Patna, emerged in the late 3rd century AD under Srigupta, founder of a dynasty that lasted for 300 years. His grandson, Chandragupta I (305–25), created the splendid Gupta Empire. The Guptas were noted patrons of the arts and their magnificent coins mirror

Below: Indian Islamic coins include silver horseman tankas of Delhi (bottom) and gold mohurs of the Mughals (right).

their taste, with beautifully executed inscriptions in Sanskrit, written in Brahmi characters. The empire, which extended over most of modern India, had collapsed by 650.

CENTRAL ASIAN INVASIONS

Internal dissension and rebellions made the Gupta Empire easy prey to the Hephthalites or White Huns, migrating westward in the 5th century. From time to time, various local dynasties briefly arose, such as the Vardhanas and Pratiharas, but the poor quality of their coins reflect the dark ages of Indian history under successive invasions.

From 717 to 920 several Turko-Hephthalitic kingdoms occupied what are now Afghanistan and Pakistan, and embraced Hinduism, reflected in the symbolism of their coins. Conversely, by the 9th century, many different coins in central India also reflected the influence of Islam, with motifs derived from Turkic and Sasanian coins, often combined with Hindu deities. In the 10th century various Hindu rulers founded petty kingdoms and minted their own coins, often depicting a seated goddess or a bull and horseman, the latter being a type popularized by the Rajput kingdoms.

ISLAMIC COINS

Arab penetration of India began in the 8th century, and by the end of the 9th century they had conquered Afghanistan, Baluchistan and the Punjab. Mahmud of Gazni (998–1030) raided India and struck silver dirhams at Lahore, with Arabic inscriptions on the obverse but Sanskrit text in Devanagri script on the reverse.

Muhammad Ghori (1173–1206) and his successor Qutub-ud-din Aibak created the Sultanate of Delhi. Qutub, originally a slave, founded the so-called Slave Dynasty, which welded together the petty kingdoms and laid the foundations of the mighty Mughal Empire. In the 13th and 14th centuries crude silver and gold tankas were struck, the forerunners of the beautiful gold and silver coins in which the Arabic script is particularly fine. They often bore verses of Persian poetry, and sometimes the signs of the zodiac. From the beginning of the 18th century, the quality of Mughal coins deteriorated. As the empire broke up, petty rulers began producing their own coins, a privilege that continued under British rule.

India holds the record for the world's largest coins, the stupendous gold 1000 mohurs of Shah Jahangir, struck at Agra in 1613, which weighed over 12kg/26lb. India also produced some of the smallest, the pinhead-sized gold coins of Colpata, weighing only 1 grain (65mg).

Below: A Parthian-style coin with a bearded king and a fire temple.

Above: A Gupta dinar with a king drawing his bow at a rearing tiger.

MINTS

The modern mint is a large complex of secure buildings, but early mints were little more than smithies equipped with a furnace for melting gold and silver, moulds for casting blanks, and hammers and anvils for striking the coins.

As soon as coinage came into being, representing the wealth and power of a country as well as providing a means of trade, coins assumed considerable importance. Reflecting the prestige of the ruler as well as creating commercial confidence, they had to be struck to exact specifications with clearly defined images and inscriptions. This could best be achieved in a central workshop, or provincial workshops using equipment supplied by a central authority. A typical mint, until the advent of mechanization in the 16th century, might consist of a small team of men engaged in melting and refining the raw metal, beating it into sheets and cutting it into roughly circular pieces, which were finally struck as coins by the hammermen. The anvils, with their coining irons (dies), were simple in design, and the equipment could be moved from place to place as occasion demanded.

As trade expanded and demand for coins grew, royal powers and privileges were often devolved to mint-masters or moneyers. In medieval Europe there was a proliferation of local mints, as the privilege of striking coins often passed to feudal lords and Church prelates.

Below: Solidi of Constans, struck at the Siscia Mint (left), and Valentinian III with the mark of the Ravenna Mint.

Above: A 2nd-century Roman coin shows Moneta holding scales and a cornucopia (top); a Phoenician tetrashekel of the Sidon Mint (middle); and half groats of Henry VII, produced by the ecclesiastical Canterbury Mint.

This trend was reversed in the 16th century as government became more centralized, and the coining privilege was restricted to the Crown.

AN ANCIENT TERM

The word "mint" is derived from the Latin word *moneta*, because the place where Roman coins were originally struck was the temple of the goddess Juno Moneta (literally Juno who monitors or warns) on the northern peak of the Capitoline Hill. The goddess had earned her nickname because she was said to have warned the Romans not to undertake any but just wars, promising in return that they would never run

Above: The 15th-century Austrian Emperor Maximilian I is given a tour of a German mint.

short of money. Moneta was personified in Roman myth and was usually depicted on Roman coins as a woman holding a balance and a cornucopia, or horn of plenty. Many Roman coins, from the reigns of Caracalla to Valens, have a reverse showing three figures of Moneta, holding scales and cornucopiae with lumps of gold, silver and bronze at their feet.

The name Moneta was later used to signify the workshop attached to the temple, and the bronze asses coined there were known as *monetae*. This use of the same term to describe pieces of money and the place where they were produced continues today in many European languages. In German, for example, the word *Münze* is used for "coin", "money" and "mint", and

Dutch *munt* and Swedish *mynt* have the same meanings. In the Romance languages the same word is used for coin and money but not the mint. Thus, French *monnaie*, Italian *moneta*, Spanish *moneda* and Portuguese *moeda* can all mean "coin" or "money", but "mint" is *hotel de monnaie*, *zecca*, *casa de moneda* and *casa da moeda* respectively. In English, "money", "monetary" and "mint" come from the same root. The word "coin" comes from the French word for a corner, which is derived from the Latin *cuneus*, a wedge.

ANCIENT MINTS AND MINT-MARKS

The names, abbreviated or in full, of the places where coins were issued began with Athens ("Athe") inscribed on coins of the 5th century BC, but it was not until the time of Alexander the Great that mint names were explicitly marked. By the end of the 4th century BC, standardization of coin types throughout the empire was the norm, and coins of the same design might be struck in many different mints. The coins of Alexander from Damascus and the Phoenician mints at Sidon and Akko, however, bore inscriptions that

Above: The circular symbol above the 'M' on this 18th-century Spanish reverse distinguishes the Mexico City mint from the Casa de Moneda, Madrid.

identified them. This system was revived by the Romans from the time of Probus (AD 276–82), the abbreviated names or initials of mints usually appearing in the exergue (the separate area below the design) on the reverse.

The Romans operated a highly complex system. Those cities that enjoyed the coining privilege had establishments that consisted of one or more monetary workshops (*officinae monetae*). On the coins of Valentinian II, Valens and Gratian in the 4th century the *officinae* were often designated by the letters P, S, T or Q (*prima*, *secunda*, *tertia* and *quarta*, denoting first, second, third or fourth). These letters may be found on their own in the field (the background of the design), in the exergue or before or after the initials of the mint town.

Mints in the Western Empire generally had a few *officinae*, though Rome had as many as 12. In the Eastern Empire, mints were much larger, and Constantinople had up to 11, while Antioch had 15 and Alexandria 19. Eastern workshops were sometimes denoted by 'OFF' on coins, followed by Roman numerals or Greek letters.

MEDIEVAL TO MODERN

After the fall of the Roman Empire in the west, European coin production was reduced to bare essentials, reflected in crude designs and irregular shapes. Early medieval production was split between numerous small workshops, and every town of any size had at least one. Over a thousand locations have been recorded in inscriptions found on the gold triens of Merovingian France.

In medieval England the names of mints were included on the reverse of coins from the 10th century onwards and at least 109 place names have been identified on Anglo-Saxon, Norman and early Plantagenet coins. Thereafter production became more centralized, and the number of mints decreased.

A similar pattern applied to other European countries in the same period. Medieval Germany consisted of many kingdoms, principalities and duchies, each with its own mint. Today, Germany is the only European country to divide production between several mints, in Berlin, Hamburg, Karlsruhe, Munich and Stuttgart. The United States has operated eight mints at various times since 1793, many of which have now ceased production.

Below (clockwise from top-left): Souvenir medals commemorating the assay office of New York and mints of San Francisco and Denver. (Bottom-left): The Royal Canadian mint has branches at Ottawa and Winnepeg (pictured), the former minting collector coins, the latter circulating coins.

COMMON CURRENCY AND TRADE COINS

There is a scene in Stevenson's *Treasure Island* in which Jim Hawkins and his mother sort through the possessions of the old buccaneer who has died at their inn. Mrs Hawkins wishes to collect what he owed her in board and lodging. "'I'll have my dues, and not a farthing over,'" she says as they count the coins: "It was a long, difficult business, for the coins were of all countries and sizes – doubloons, and louis-d'ors, guineas, and pieces of eight, and I know not what besides, all shaken together at random."

Above: A Mercia penny (top) and a 13th-century Scandinavian imitation of a radiate-type penny.

Below: Hernán Cortés and his Spanish troops discover Aztec treasure.

This sentence vividly conveys the manner in which coins of many countries were widely accepted because of the purity of their gold or silver content. This was not a new phenomenon, for certain gold and silver coins of ancient Greece circulated far beyond the boundaries of the cities that issued them. The Turtles of Aegina, the Foals of Corinth and above all the Owls of Athens were readily accepted all over the Mediterranean and probably even further afield, if the evidence of coin hoards is to be believed. Roman denarii and aurei, the staters and didrachms of Macedon and the darics and sigloi of Persia ranked among the leading trade coins of the ancient world.

From the time of King Offa of Mercia the English silver penny was prized for its high production values and metal content. The adjective "sterling", meaning of the highest character, is derived from the silver penny, which was 92.5 per cent pure. To this day sterling silver is an alloy of 925 parts silver to 75 parts copper, a composition that makes for great durability. The popularity of the penny caused some consternation for the local economy, however. As these good quality coins

Above: A speciedaler of Christiania (Oslo) of 1663 (top) and a jefimok rouble of Russia, counterstamped on a Salzburg thaler of 1625 (bottom).

began increasingly to drain abroad, periodic shortages resulted in England itself, and conversely the country was prone to invasions of poor quality imitations, known as pollards or crockards, from continental Europe. Successive monarchs were perplexed by the mixed blessing of producing a strong currency.

THE MIGHTY DOLLAR

The history of the world's most popular coin is an interesting one. Its origins are not in the New World but in an obscure valley in Bohemia (now part of the Czech Republic). Jachymov was known in German as Joachimsthal, and it was near this town, in 1519, that a large strike of silver was made. The Counts of Schlick coined the metal into large coins known as guldengroschen, which came to be nicknamed Joachimsthalers. Shortened to "thaler", the name was adopted for a wide range of large German silver coins, ranging from 60 to 72 kreuzer in value, some beautifully inscribed, which survived until 1872. The name was corrupted in other languages to talar (Saxony), tallero (Italy), tolar (Slovenia), talari (Ethiopia), tala (Samoa), dala (Hawaii),

Below: A Roman aes grave, marked with heads of barley and pellets.

Above: A sixpence of Charles II with interlocking Cs.

Above: Gold oban and koban coins being marked in 18th-century Japan.

evolved from the earliest monetary systems. The £sd system used in Britain until 1971 was derived from the Roman system, in which the libra was divided into 20 solidi or 240 denarii. Adopted by the Carolingian Empire, this survived in many European countries. Pre-Revolutionary France had the livre of 20 sols or 240 deniers, while Italy had the lira of 20 soldi or 240 denari.

In Germany, by contrast, the mark was divided into 4 vierding, 16 loth, 32 setin, 64 quentchen, 256 richtpfennig or 512 heller, but only the pfennig and heller existed as coins. However, all these units could be used as "money of account". The latter is, as its name suggests, any unit employed in the keeping of accounts: it is sometimes represented by actual coins but quite often not.

Above: George III shillings of 1787 and 1817 (back left and right), and silver Maundy pennies marked, unusually for the period, with Arabic numerals.

Just as metric and imperial systems are concurrent today, multiple value systems sometimes existed in the same country. In the later medieval period England had gold coins in different finenesses: 22 carat was used for the sovereign (20 shillings), half sovereign (10 shillings) and crown (5 shillings), but 23.5 carat for the noble (6s 8d) and its sub-divisions. The gold guinea (21 shillings) was replaced by the sovereign in 1816 but remained as money of account until the advent of decimal currency in 1971.

The denominations within each system were relative to each other, but different values could be attributed to the same units in different systems. In France the livre was worth 2 marks, but in England the mark was equivalent to two-thirds of a pound, both in weight (8 ounces) and value (13s 4d).

MARKS OF VALUE

The earliest coins bore no mark of value: this was implicit in their size and weight. Most Roman coins were undenominated apart from the aes grave, on which different values were indicated by varying numbers of pellets. Some Byzantine gold coins were inscribed OB, followed by Greek letters forming the number 72. This was an abbreviation for *obruson* ("pure"), and indicated that the coins had been struck at the rate of 72 to the pound of pure metal. Roman numerals XII, XXI or XLII

may be found on Vandal coinage to indicate denominations, while some English silver coins of Tudor and Jacobean times were inscribed with Roman numerals behind the monarch's head to denote their values in shillings or pence.

MULTIPLE DENOMINATIONS

Most countries get by with six or eight coins in everyday circulation. Before the general advent of paper money to represent higher values, coins played a much more prominent role, hence the need for high-denomination coins in gold and silver. Today the number of different coins in general use tends to be governed by the lowest paper denomination that is practical (which is dependent on the average life of a banknote). In Britain, for example, this is now £5: eventually the note may be replaced by a coin, as the life of a £5 note is only about three months.

The USA is virtually unique in persevering with a $1 bill (worth about 1 euro), whereas in Europe coins of 1 euro and 2 euros are in everyday use. Lower denominations merely serve the purpose of small change. Such factors as payment of taxes and the facilitation of trade, formerly served by large silver or gold coins, are now entirely supplied by paper or electronic bank transfer.

METALS AND ALLOYS

With very few exceptions, coins are made of metal. Pure, unadulterated metals are seldom used, although even the ancient Greeks managed to achieve a relatively pure gold for some coins. In the main, two or more metals are combined to form an alloy, giving greater durability. We think of copper, silver and gold as traditional coin metals, but a surprising range of other metals has been employed, ranging from platinum and palladium to pewter, tin, and even relatively dense compositions of lead.

METAL FINENESS

In the ancient world coins were simply pieces of precious metal, which could, of course, be weighed at each transaction. However, it was more convenient to accept the mark stamped on a coin as a guarantee not only of its weight but also its purity. For this reason, units of value were usually tied to specific

Right: A Russian platinum 3 rouble coin of 1830.

Below: Spanish settlers in Mexico smelting mined gold in imitation of the Aztecs.

Above: A Roman gold aureus with a lump of gold added to it to make up the correct weight.

Above: A platinum noble (1983) and a deluxe silver coin (1993) struck by the Pobjoy Mint in the Isle of Man.

weights and these, in turn, were derived from particular seeds or grains. Nowadays the fineness of precious coinage metals is measured in thousandths, using a much more precise system than the carat used in ancient times, though this unit has been retained in the assessment of jewellery.

ELECTRUM

The earliest coins of the Western world were made of electrum, a natural alloy of about 73 per cent gold and 27 per cent silver, found in riverbeds in the Tmolus Mountains of Lydia (present-day Anatolia in Turkey). Electrum was widely used for the coins of the 6th and 7th centuries BC. Latterly, the Greeks' love of white gold encouraged them to produce an artificial alloy consisting of one part gold and ten parts silver. The Celts copied electrum staters but severely debased them with copper and silver, and the Merovingians produced base electrum coins in which the gold content was minimal.

Theoretically any alloy of gold less than 75 per cent should be described as electrum, but in practice this is confined to classical and medieval coins. Some coins of the Isle of Man were struck in an alloy containing 9 carat gold (.375 fine), when the bullion price of gold was exceptionally high.

GOLD

The most popular of the precious metals was preferred by Croesus, King of Lydia (560–546 BC), who abandoned electrum for a bimetallic system with a gold–silver ratio of 40:3 (or 13.3:1). Coins were struck in relative weights, so that one gold piece was worth 20 of silver. This arrangement, fixed by the Lydians and Persians in the 6th century BC, continued in Rome and the Carolingian Empire and survived in Britain until World War I, the gold sovereign being worth 20 silver shillings.

The fineness of gold was based on the carat which, in addition to being a weight, came to represent a 24th part. Thus, pure gold is described as 24 carat fine. The purest gold for medieval coinage was 23 carat 3½ grains (.997 fine), which was as pure as the primitive metallurgy of the period could get. English gold was debased to 20 carat by 1545, but was eventually standardized at 22 carat (.9167 fine), originally

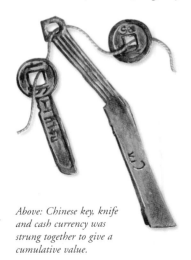

Above: Chinese key, knife and cash currency was strung together to give a cumulative value.

known as "crown gold" due to its first being used for the crown series. It was alloyed with .083 copper to produce a durable alloy with a reddish lustre and continues in the sovereign to this day.

The USA used the same fineness from 1795 to 1834 but later settled on .900. Mexico preferred .875, while France and Germany opted for .900 fine. The world's first major bullion coin of recent times, the Krugerrand, was minted to .9167 standard (the most practical and hard-wearing fineness), but later bullion coins strove for the utmost purity. Canada achieved .999 pure gold for the Maple Leaf (1979), but improved refining techniques led to the famous "four nines" gold first used in 1983. Bullion coins have both the weight and fineness of the metal inscribed on them.

SILVER
Used for coinage by the mid-6th century BC, mainly for the drachma and its sub-divisions, silver remained the preferred medium for the denarius, the denier and the penny, as well as most of the everyday coins of the world until the middle of the 20th century.

Medieval silver was .958 pure but was too soft to be practical, and .925 silver was the widely used sterling standard, usually alloyed with .075 copper. On many occasions, however, governments resorted to debasement of silver. Mexico, for example, struck coins in .903 silver until 1905 but, under pressure from inflation, then progressively debased it to .420 (1935), .300 (1950) and finally .100 (1957– 67). Low-grade silver alloys are often described as

Below: The "Rosa Americana" (1722), a British colonial brass 2 pence, was cheaply minted and consequently rejected by the American colonists.

Above: Wartime shortages led to the use of base metals for this Norwegian coin of the German occupation (top) and Belgian zinc 5 cents of 1915 (bottom).

billon. While base alloys are now used for circulating coinage, de luxe and collectors' coins are generally struck in silver of a high quality.

BASE METALS
As copper was tariffed at 3000 to 1 piece of gold, it was very cumbersome, and for that reason it was seldom used for coins at its intrinsic value. The strings of Chinese cash are an example; the enormous copper plates of 17th-century Sweden, known as plåtmynt, are another. More or less pure copper was used for subsidiary coins in Britain from the 17th century until 1860, but then the size was reduced and the copper alloyed with tin to form bronze. A small amount of zinc is often added.

Brass is an alloy of 80 per cent copper and 20 per cent zinc, used by the Romans and revived by Switzerland during World War I. Modern brass coins are alloys of bronze with aluminium or nickel. Aluminium, noted for its lightness, was first used in British West Africa (1⁄10 penny) and British East Africa (half cent and cent) in 1907–8. Adopted as an emergency measure in Europe during World War I and revived in World War II, it has since become much more widespread, usually for the lowest denominations.

Nickel has been used in coins since the 3rd century BC but was adopted by Belgium in 1860 as a substitute for billon in the smallest coins. Pure nickel

coins have been used as a substitute for silver in many European countries. Although Canada is the largest producer of nickel, it did not use it in coins until 1922, when nickel replaced silver in the 5 cent coin. The USA adopted an alloy of 75 per cent copper and 25 per cent nickel ("cupro-nickel") for the 3 cent coin of 1865. Cupronickel 5 cents appeared in 1866 and circulated alongside silver half dimes until 1873. The 5 cent coin is still popularly known as a nickel, but since 1964 this metal has also been used for the dime and higher denominations.

BIMETALLIC AND CLAD COINS
Clad coins have a core of one metal and an outer layer in another, such as stainless steel clad with copper (like most pennies and cents today).

Bimetallic coins have a centre in one metal and an outer ring in another. Tin farthings of Charles II (1684–5) had a copper plug in the middle. In the 19th century there were experiments with base metal coins with a silver plug to raise their intrinsic value. Since Italy pioneered bimetallic coins in 1982, alloys of gold and silver colour have been widely used for higher denominations. There are even trimetallic coins, but generally the central "plug" is of the same metal as the outer ring.

Coins on a Coin
This large gold-on-silver bimetallic coin from the Isle of Man reproduces an entire series of Cat crowns issued over the previous ten years.

SPECIFICATIONS

All coins are produced within particular parameters. As well as the purity of the metal or alloy, they must conform to particular weights, and certain specifications such as diameter and thickness. As well as the conventional round shape, many coins are polygonal or scalloped, with or without a central hole – all features that help users to distinguish the different denominations.

THICKNESS

In general, thick coins were common in ancient times because they started life as lumps of precious metal of a particular weight, which were cast in moulds and then struck. Only when the use of sheet metal became more practical were blanks cut with shears, enabling thinner coins to be produced.

Nowadays we are accustomed to coins that are neither too thick nor too thin, that handle easily and stack well. The surface of modern coins is relatively flat and great care is taken in their design to ensure an even balance between the obverse (heads) and reverse (tails). Modern coins have to be stackable in tall piles or, more importantly, operate smoothly in the acceptor–rejector mechanisms of pay-phones, slot machines and automats.

Below: Unusual shapes of modern coins (clockwise from top left) include scalloped (Israel), octagonal (Malta, and Macao) and heptagonal (Jordan).

Above: Silver Tiger Tongue money (top) and Leech money (bottom) from Thailand, and square and diamond-shaped coins of ancient India (middle).

SHAPE

The earliest coins were small electrum dumps of irregular shape. Some Celtic coins were globular, while the mameita gin of feudal Japan were bean-shaped. Thailand's so-called "bullet money" consisted of silver balls or gold cylinders, which were bent into rough balls.

Chinese sycee currency was given its name (*hsi ssu*, meaning "fine silk") in allusion to the purity of its silver. One form was a thick oblong oval, raised at the ends because it was rocked as the metal was cooled partially, before being stamped with maker's and assayer's marks. Sycee was current from the 8th century AD until 1933, when it was suppressed by the Kuomintang government.

UNUSUAL SHAPES

Oval coins have been produced in Japan and the ancient Persians had elliptical coins. The original kopeks of Russia were made from heavy silver wire, which was cut into short strips,

Above: A gold ingot issued by the Central Mint of China in 1945.

then hammered into ovals. They were extremely light and only about 15mm/⅝in long, providing small change from 1534 until about 1700. Many copper farthings of James I and Charles I (1613–42) had an upright oval shape.

Square or rectangular coins were common in Asia from pre-Christian times to the early 20th century. The style was popular in the Indo-Scythian and Indo-Greek coinage of the 2nd century BC, and continued under the Mughal Empire, down to the Indian feudal states. These coins were true squares with sharp corners, but in India and the Far East, modern square coins have rounded corners, which are much more user-friendly. The Netherlands is the only European country to have adopted this shape: 5 cent coins of 1913–40 had a diamond format, followed by a square format in 1941–3.

Rectangular coins were also popular in Asia and ranged from the long, narrow vertical gia long of Annam to the more elegantly proportioned silver cho gin and gold koban of Japan before the Meiji Revolution of the 1860s.

Klippe

Square or lozenge-shaped coins, known as *klippe*, were produced in many of the German states, and the form later spread as far afield as Poland, Hungary and Denmark. These coins were originally struck in times of emergency, when pieces were cut from silver plate, but later the shape became fashionable and coins were made as presentation pieces, with ornament in the corners. Pictured here is a klippe thaler of Friedrich Augustus I of Saxony, issued in 1697.

POLYGONAL COINS

The only true pentagons (with sharp corners) are the 1/16 and 1/8 ahmadi riyals of the Yemen (1947–60), but five-sided coins with rounded corners have been issued by Belize (1981) and the Solomon Islands (1983). Six-sided coins include the 50 cent coins in aluminium, zinc, brass or bronze from Djibouti (1920–2), the brass 2 francs of the Belgian Congo (1943) and Egypt's silver 2 piastres (1944). In all of these a format with flat sides at top and bottom was adopted. Hexagonal coins with points at top and bottom

Below: A Russian denga of the 11th century (top) and a Mongol silver dirham (bottom).

have been issued by the Yemen (1948), Sudan (1981) and the British Virgin Islands (1982–3).

In 1969, the Royal Mint created a 50 pence coin (worth 10 shillings) from the same weight and alloy as the obsolescent half crown, which had a quarter of the value of the new coin. The only variable in design was the shape; the new coin was given seven sides, a shape later extended to the 20 pence. Heptagonal coins later appeared in many Commonwealth countries. Octagonal (eight-sided) coins with flat top and bottom were favoured by some of the German states in the mid-18th century, and have been produced sporadically in more recent times, notably in Senegal (1920) and Egypt (1933). Octagons with points at the top and bottom have so far been confined to the $50 gold coin commemorating the Pan-Pacific Exposition (1915) and the gold $200 of the Netherlands Antilles (1976). Thailand (1972), Kenya (1973) and Tuvalu (1976–81) have had nine-sided coins, while Colombia (1967), Afghanistan (1979), the Dominican Republic (1983), Jamaica (1976) and Tanzania (since 1971) have had ten-sided coins.

Dodecagons or 12-sided coins are very popular and were pioneered by Britain for the nickel-brass 3 pence of Edward VIII (1936) and subsequent coins of this value until 1967. Just as Britain was abandoning the shape, it was taken up by many other countries, notably Argentina and Australia. When Canada changed the alloy of its 5 cent coin from nickel to tombac brass in 1942, a 12-sided format was adopted and retained until 1962. Its cent switched from circular to dodecagonal in 1982, saving 10.7 per cent in weight – before the change it was costing 2 cents to produce each cent!

Triangular coins with rounded corners have been produced by the Cook Islands and (appropriately) Bermuda, but the only three-sided coin with sharp corners was the 20 centime of Gabon (1883). The 10 centime had an over-all triangular shape but the points were truncated, so that the coin was actually six-sided.

SERRATED OR SCALLOPED EDGES

The Carthaginians and Seleucids had circular coins with serrated edges, but many modern coins have scalloped edges, a useful feature for distinguishing coins of different values but similar sizes. A "nicked" edge is a feature of the brass 20 euro cent, making it distinct from the 50 cent. Burma has even had polygonal scalloped coins.

Many Asian coins (notably Chinese cash) have a central hole, but this feature was not used elsewhere until 1883 (in Bolivia). It is a means of reducing weight and metal while retaining a relatively large diameter and is now widely practised all over the world.

Above: A square Indian rupee of the Indo-Scythian kings.

HAMMERED AND CAST COINAGE

Although a few coins were cast in moulds, most were struck by hand until the late 17th century, relying on the strength of the craftsman to hit the flan with a hammer. This technique sounds extremely crude, but, thanks to the skill of coiners, and the revival of intaglio techniques first developed in the classical world, intricate portraits, emblems and other designs were achieved long before the industrial age.

CAST COINS

In casting, metal is melted and then poured into a mould. The simplest moulds were merely hollows in a bed of fine sand, which produced the small, roughly circular lumps of metal that were then punch marked. Well into the 17th century, flans or blanks for struck coins were cast in this manner, although cutting blanks from thin sheets of metal gradually superseded this. A refinement was to carve a mould from a piece of stone, enabling detailed designs and lettering to be engraved. Double-sided moulds of this kind were used for double-sided coins.

This technique was used exclusively to produce Chinese cash until 1889, and some provinces continued to cast coins as late as 1908. Latterly multiple moulds were employed to cast several coins simultaneously. They resembled

Below: Early Italian cast coin (top); cast Korean bronze cash or mun (bottom).

Multiple Punch Marks

This coin of Asia Minor, dating from around 400–380 BC, shows similar designs on the obverse (crested Athena standing, left) and reverse (Apollo holding a bow). The reverse contains two rectangular countermarks made by the same punch. Early coins often bear various punch marks applied by different authorities to guarantee their value.

a tree with the coins as the fruit at the ends of "branches" created by the channels along which the molten metal flowed. A few of these "trees" have survived intact, but normally the coins were broken off and the rough edges carefully filed.

Cast coins were used in Japan until 1871, Morocco until 1882, Korea until 1888 and Vietnam until the 1930s. They were seldom produced in Europe, but noteworthy exceptions were the first coins of the Isle of Man (1709), where the halfpenny and penny were cast in a foundry at Castletown. These coins can be recognized by the flash marks on the rim and the slight excrescences where the connecting channels of molten metal were broken off. More recent examples are the copies of 8 real coins of Potosi cast by the garrison of Chiloe in South America (1822), coins cast from gunmetal at Terceira in the Azores for Maria II in exile (1829) and Andorran 1, 5 and 10 diners (1984).

The casting technique produced very crude coins compared to struck examples and was latterly used only in extreme cases when more sophisticated coining equipment was not available.

HAMMER AND ANVIL

The hammermen formed one of the most prestigious trade guilds of the Middle Ages, a measure of the importance and value of their skill. Generally, they worked in groups in which individuals were responsible for specific aspects of the process (smelting and refining, moulding the blanks or cutting them from sheet metal rolled out to a uniform thickness). The coining irons were generally supplied by the central government, but engravers sometimes used dies produced locally.

The earliest blanks or "flans" for hammered coins were cast in moulds, a natural progression from the original dumps and globules. The round blank was relatively thick. It was heated to make it malleable, then placed on an anvil of bronze whose face had been engraved with a device (the obverse). The upper die, a punch, was hit by a

Above: A Crusader "knight" follis from the 12th century with the design struck off-centre.

Below: In Venice, coins continued to be struck by hand until the 18th century.

face of the die. The discovery that steel could be chemically hardened, however, meant that it was possible to produce secondary dies, via an intermediate punch called a hub, from the master die. Alternatively, a positive image could be cut in relief on a metal punch and struck into a piece of softer metal, which was then hardened for use as a die. The technique of hubbing appears to have been known in classical times, although no hubs have survived from antiquity. This technique meant that working dies could be rapidly multiplied, greatly accelerating the mass production of coins.

Around 1715, Konstantin Nartov of the Moscow Mint invented a machine that could reduce a large sculpted model to the size required for a coin die. This revolutionized coin production by eliminating the hand engraving previously carried out on the master die, although it has been argued that the change of practice resulted in more stereotyped, less artistic designs.

Improved models were built in Paris between 1757 and 1824, and were applied with varying success to the production of steel dies from large plaster models. Perfected by M. Collas, these

Above: The large-scale plaster model is perfected before the design is reduced to create a hub of the correct size.

Above: The hub is coated with chemicals to harden it so that it can be used to produce a working die.

machines were in regular use at the Paris Mint from then onward, but it was not until 1839 that they were adopted by the Royal Mint; they spread to other European and American mints in the mid-19th century. The process is now carried out by the Contamin portrait lathe and the Janvier die-cutting machine.

FROM WAX MODEL TO FINISHED COIN

The progression from original concept to finished coin involves a number of different skills and processes, and since the 1830s, a series of mechanical processes have replaced the direct engraving of dies. A sculptor makes a wax model at least four times the size of the required coin. A plaster cast is created from the wax model, and from this a nickel-faced copper electrotype is produced. This is placed on the reducing machine, which operates on the pantographic principle. A tracer at one end of the proportional arm moves over the entire surface of the model. At the other end a cutting stylus, like the needle of a record player (but moving from the centre outward) cuts an exact but mathematically reduced reproduction to produce a positive punch, or hub. The hub is chemically hardened and driven into a cone of soft steel to produce the working die. In turn, this is also chemically hardened and is then ready for striking.

CIRCULATING AND PROOF COINS

Today, all coins intended for general circulation are produced on high-speed presses. The blanks are fed into the dial plates and pass through two checking points, which determine that they are of the correct thickness and diameter before they reach the coining station.

Each coin, as it is struck, passes a security counter, which keeps a record of the precise number of coins the machine has struck. The coins are then check-weighed and examined carefully for any flaws. After this examination they are counted again and hermetically sealed in the bags in which they will eventually be distributed to banks.

Proof coins were originally pieces struck to test the dies to ensure perfection before the start of production. They were struck individually by hand, often using specially polished blanks. From this arose the use of proof coins for presentation purposes, but since the mid-19th century they have increasingly been produced expressly for sale to collectors. Today, proof versions of coins are often struck in precious metals, while the circulating versions are in base metals. Although modern proofs are produced by machine like other coins, they are generally struck up to four times, using special dies with frosted relief and polished blanks to provide a sharper contrast between the image and the background.

Hubbing

Using a reducing machine, the enlarged image is transferred to a piece of steel known as the hub, in the precise dimensions of the coin. The next stage, known as hubbing, transfers the positive image from the hub to the working die, which is the negative image used to strike the coins.

SPECIAL PRODUCTION TECHNIQUES

Proof coins, intended not for general circulation but for collectors, are not only struck to a much higher standard than circulating coins, but are usually produced in precious metals and consequently sold at a much higher price than ordinary coins. In recent years many special techniques have evolved, which have revolutionized the production of coins intended for the numismatic market. These include the addition of coloured finishes, precious stones and even holographic designs.

PROOFS

It is probable that test impressions have been made from coinage dies since the striking of coins began. In the days of direct engraving they were struck for the purpose of checking details of the positive image, such as ensuring that the lettering was the right way round. Proofs were often pulled on blanks made of lead or some very soft alloy, which enabled the details to be more clearly seen. From this arose the custom of striking proofs in metals other than those that were to be used for the issued coins – variations now termed

Below: Working mints keep a large stock of coin blanks for striking proofs. These are handled with great care.

Jewel-Studded Coins
A very recent development has been the incorporation of precious stones in the surface of a coin to create a jewelled effect. One of the first coins of this type celebrated the centenary of the Diamond Jubilee of Queen Victoria, appropriately with a diamond inset.

"off-metal strikes". Nowadays, coins issued in base metals, such as cupro-nickel, are often struck as proofs in silver or even platinum, while gold is sometimes used for proofs of coins normally circulating in brass.

What was a widespread minting tradition has now become an important aspect of the numismatic business, as proofs are prepared specially for the collector. Proofs of this type were first marketed in the middle of the 19th century, the US Mint producing such sets for sale from 1858 onward. Royal Mint proof sets had first been produced in 1826 as presentation issues for a privileged few (such as members of the royal family and senior government officials), but in Britain proof sets sold to the public date from the golden jubilee of Queen Victoria in 1887.

The practice of issuing proofs has now reached the point at which many modern sets exist only in proof form and are not backed by any circulating coins. Modern proofs and deluxe versions of coins are struck on special

Above: A gilt copper proof 2 reas of the East India Company, produced in 1794.

slow-speed presses, in which each piece is struck up to four times to bring up the fine detail. The blanks are specially polished with mops made of linen, calico and swansdown to produce the "mirror table" effect, and the dies are often specially engraved so that the high points have a frosted relief that contrasts with the mirror-like surface.

Until not so long ago it was the norm for blanks to be prepared to produce an overall polished appearance. This is still employed but is often relegated to a version of the base-metal coins sold to the public under such descriptions as "specimen", "library finish" or "special select". These, with a better finish than the circulating coins, are usually marketed in special folders, whereas proofs may be contained in leatherette cases with a velvet lining.

The Franklin Mint (1975–77) frequently offered coin sets in three distinct versions, classified as "matte", "special uncirculated" and "proof". The Pobjoy Mint devised the terms "Proof 4" (proof coins struck four times), "BU2" (brilliant uncirculated struck twice) and "diamond finish" for base metal coins in a finish superior to the general circulating coins.

PATTERNS

In many cases, when a new coin is being considered, the authorities will commission several trial designs, developed all the way to actual production, so that the coinage committee can examine actual pieces before making their decision. Those pieces that are

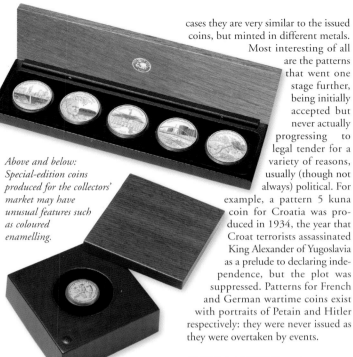

*Above and below:
Special-edition coins
produced for the collectors'
market may have
unusual features such
as coloured
enamelling.*

rejected and not put into production are known as patterns. Patterns may also arise if the design has been altered or modified in some way before going into production. Patterns of this type are often uniface or bear words such as "Specimen", "Trial", "Prova", "Prueba" or "Probe" (which actually signify "test" in other languages). Many mints, when tendering for a contract, would prepare sample coins to demonstrate design. If the contract were eventually awarded to a competing mint, these samples would be regarded as patterns.

The numismatic appeal of patterns is partly psychological; the rejected design often seems superior to the accepted one because the latter is debased by familiarity. On the other hand, though many patterns have been rejected because they were judged to be impractical as actual coins, they are beautiful works of art. Patterns have a special appeal to collectors as examples of what might have been. In many cases they are very similar to the issued coins, but minted in different metals. Most interesting of all are the patterns that went one stage further, being initially accepted but never actually progressing to legal tender for a variety of reasons, usually (though not always) political. For example, a pattern 5 kuna coin for Croatia was produced in 1934, the year that Croat terrorists assassinated King Alexander of Yugoslavia as a prelude to declaring independence, but the plot was suppressed. Patterns for French and German wartime coins exist with portraits of Petain and Hitler respectively: they were never issued as they were overtaken by events.

SPECIAL EFFECTS

Most modern coins have the design and inscription standing out in relief, but from time to time "intaglio" images occur, which appear as if cut into the surface, and an inscription may be "incuse" (cut into a raised surround). Incuse lettering on raised rims was a distinctive feature of the British Cartwheel copper coins of 1797, while the USA issued gold quarter and half eagles (1908–29) in which the Indian head (obverse) and eagle (reverse) were intaglio. Unfortunately such coins tended to accumulate grime in circulation and ended up looking rather dirty. The technique was revived by the Royal Mint for the 20 pence coin in 1982, but in this case only the inscriptions are incuse.

Raised edges with incuse inscriptions have been used to startling effect by the Pobjoy Mint since the 1980s. This private mint has been at the cutting edge of minting technology for many years and has pioneered the use of special surfaces. In 1990, for example, the crown coins celebrating the 150th anniversary of the Penny Black stamp had a black surface: the technique remains a closely guarded secret but the coin won the coveted Coin of the Year Award. Subsequent issues, appropriately coloured, have reproduced other famous stamps, such as the Blue Mauritius and the Black on Magenta 1 cent of British Guiana. The Pobjoy Mint has also, in recent years, led the way in the development of coins with holographic surfaces.

The Royal Canadian Mint pioneered coins in silver with a small motif inset in gold, used effectively in a series tracing the development of aviation, with portraits of aviators in gold. This technique has since been copied by other mints, notably Pobjoy, which took it a step further with insets of diamonds and other precious stones. Several mints, notably the Singapore Mint, have produced coins with latent images that change, like a hologram, as the surface is tilted.

While the enamelling of existing coins, to transform them into jewels for watch chains, earrings or brooches, has been practised for centuries, a number of special issues are now actually produced with multicoloured surfaces. The effect is usually achieved by adapting silk-screen and lithographic processes to this very exacting medium.

Below: The reverse of the silver crown celebrating the 150th anniversary of the Penny Black, the world's first adhesive postage stamp, in 1990. The surface was specially treated to produce an image of the stamp in black.

COMBATING THE COUNTERFEITER

For as long as coins have existed, there have been attempts to forge them, undermining public confidence as well as losing revenue for the issuing authority. The term "counterfeit" is derived from the French word for imitation and applies to copies of coins (and banknotes) that are intended to deceive and defraud people.

Throughout coin-producing history, strenuous efforts have always been made to deter counterfeiters, by threat of severe punishment as well as by making coins very difficult to imitate.

DEBASEMENT

Counterfeiting may not be the world's oldest profession but it has certainly existed as long as coinage itself: coin hoards dating from the 6th century BC have been found to include staters of Aegina with a copper core and a silver wash, passed off as genuine silver coins. There is even a case of official counterfeits, such as the lead pieces covered with gold, which Polykrates of Samos (532–21 BC) is said to have used to buy off the Spartans.

In the classical and medieval periods counterfeiting occurred frequently and was particularly prevalent in the Middle

Below: A clipped groat of Richard III (top) and clipped shilling of Charles I (bottom). The latter circulated until 1694, when they were finally demonetized and melted down.

Ages, when genuine coins were often poorly struck. The fact that many governments deliberately debased their coinage from time to time did not help.

The most blatant examples were the "crockards" and "pollards" manufactured by many petty lordships in Europe, which copied highly prized English sterling pennies. They flooded England in the 13th century, and when all attempts by Edward I to suppress them failed he made a virtue of necessity by legitimizing them and allowing them to pass current as halfpence. As the imitations contained more than a halfpennyworth of silver, this was a pretty shrewd decision. As a result, the crockards rapidly vanished, although they were not actually demonetized and declared illegal until 1310. This did not prevent a recurrence in the reign of Edward III (1327–77), when England was flooded with base coins known as "lushbournes" (a corruption of the name Luxembourg, whence they came).

CLIPPING COINS

Another age-old method of counterfeiting involved the slicing off of tiny slivers of gold or silver from the edges of coins. The edges were then filed down to give the appearance of normality. Sometimes forgers produced imitation gold and silver coins from base metals, but more often they bought clippings and melted them down to produce counterfeits with a reasonable proportion of precious metal, alloyed with copper.

COUNTER MEASURES

The major breakthrough against counterfeiting came with the widespread adoption of milled coins in Europe during the 17th century. This made it possible to employ sophisticated techniques to improve the appearance of coins generally, making it harder to produce accurate copies. The minting process also used specific methods to stamp out dishonest coining practices.

Above: The trials carried out by the Pyx office of the Royal Mint, London, were instrumental in distinguishing legitimate coins from copies.

SECRET MARKINGS

Various marks have been used to defeat the forger. Medieval English coins had tiny symbols, known as mint-marks, which appeared at the beginning of the inscription and denoted the period between Trials of the Pyx (the periodic assaying of coins at Goldsmiths Hall to test the gold and silver, named from the chest the coins were carried in). In more recent times mint-marks have identified the place where coins were struck and either appear as initials or tiny symbols in various parts of the design.

Privy or secret marks are intended for security purposes and include die numbers or letters engraved microscopically. In some cases privy marks have been used to transform definitives into commemorative coins, such as the baby's crib on Manx coins that greeted the birth of Prince William in 1982.

SECURITY EDGES

The milling process allowed the use of a specially engraved collar to impress an inscription on the edges of coins.

Counterfeit Coins Today

It has been estimated that more than 1 per cent of the pound coins circulating in Britain are counterfeits. They are easy to detect as even newly forged coins do not "ring true" when bounced on a table. Most lose their brightness very quickly and quite often the edge inscription does not match the reverse motif. Here, the tarnished English arms (left) are the reverse of a forgery, whereas the Welsh motif is the genuine article.

The milled coins that went into general circulation in Britain in 1662 bore a Latin motto around the edge – "Decus et Tutamen" ("An ornament and a safeguard") followed by "Anno Regni" ("in the year of the reign") and a date in Roman numerals. This effectively stamped out the practice of clipping. Many countries have resorted to edge inscriptions of this kind as a security feature. The lettering may be either raised or incuse, and often includes tiny ornamental flourishes.

Below: Today, subtle security inscriptions are incorporated into the designs of all coins to foil counterfeiters.

GRAINING

The most common form of safeguard against the clipping of coins is a pattern of fine grooves running across the edge, at right angles to the rim. In common parlance this is often referred to as "milling", but this is a misnomer.

The grain on British and American coins usually consists of fine vertical serrations, but some coins have been produced at various times with a coarser or finer grain, and having to count the number of notches threatens the advanced numismatist with a nasty headache and crossed eyes!

An interrupted grain may be found on some coins, with sections of vertical grooves alternating with plain sections. Its purpose is to assist partially sighted and blind people in distinguishing between coins of high and low value. In some countries graining takes the form of short lines set at an angle, and this is known as a cable edge. When Britain adopted pound coins in 1982 both graining and an incuse edge inscription were used.

PENALTIES

The treatment of counterfeiters has varied over the centuries and from country to country. Forgery was frequently a capital offence, and very special gruesome punishments were reserved for this crime. In England forgers were usually hanged, but the forgery of coins by women seems to have been regarded as particularly heinous, for several female counterfeiters were publicly burned at the stake as late as 1789. Boiling in oil was the preferred punishment in Germany, while in France it was breaking on a wheel; beheading was a common punishment elsewhere. In Russia counterfeiters had molten lead poured down their throats. First offenders were sometimes dealt with more leniently, merely losing a hand or an eye.

In Britain, the Coinage Offences Act of 1861 set out a series of penalties ranging from two years' imprisonment to penal servitude for life. The more severe penalties were meted out for

Above: The practice of graining or inscribing the edges of coins, to mark them as genuine, continues today.

counterfeiting gold or silver coins. Lesser offences included the gilding of farthings and sixpences to pass them off as half sovereigns, the possession of moulds, machines and tools clandestinely removed from the Royal Mint, and the impairment or diminution of gold and silver coins by filing or clipping (or even the possession of such filings and clippings). The Coinage Act of 1870 made provision for the counterfeiting of base metal coins of any kind. Today, US law dictates that counterfeiting is a felony, punishable by a large fine and a maximum of ten years' imprisonment.

Below: The arrest of a pair of coin counterfeiters in the early 19th century.

HISTORY OF PORTRAITURE

We talk about "heads" and "tails" to denote the obverse and reverse of coins. The former nickname derives from the fact that it is the side often reserved for the most important aspect of the coin, the effigy of the head of state.

By the time of the Hellenistic kingdoms, portraiture on coins was exceedingly lifelike. It attained its peak during the Roman Empire, but the Romans rarely attempted a facing portrait – something that modern mints attempt occasionally, but seldom with any real success. The full-face portraits on Byzantine coins tended to become stereotyped, and the full-face portraits on European medieval coins were very crude and undoubtedly symbolic rather than true likenesses.

During the Renaissance the large silver coins of Italy revived the art of portraiture. Modern portrait coins are still predominantly generated by the age-old method of sculpting a profile; photo-engraving has also been used in many instances, though the results are invariably much flatter.

EARLY PORTRAITS

There are examples of coins from the 6th century BC that show a human effigy, such as the head of a warrior (Ephesus), the head of a discus thrower (Cyzicus, *c*. 520 BC) and a helmeted profile (Kalymna), but it is not known whether these represented real people.

Below right: The Persian satrap Tissaphernes was the first ruler to appear on a coin, in 411 BC.

Below: Head of Apollo on a coin of the 4th century BC.

The earliest coins bearing identifiable portraits came from the Greek cities. Aphrodite and Athena were followed by Herakles, Zeus and a whole host of deities and heroes, but it was left to Persia to depict the first living person, Darius the Great (521–485 BC), on the gold daric and silver siglos. The figure appears as an archer and remained unchanged for 200 years, but is identifiable as Darius because he wears the spiked crown or *orthe* of the Persian ruler. Coins of Abdera (*c*. 425 BC) bear a profile identified by the inscription as Pythagoras, who flourished a century earlier, but the first coin to bear a close-up portrait of a living person was the silver tetradrachm of Miletus (411 BC) with the Persian satrap Tissaphernes.

After the death of Alexander the Great his generals carved up the empire into separate kingdoms and his profile began to appear on their coins. The horn of Ammon sprouting from Alexander's temple signified that he had now become a god. This established a precedent, and subsequent rulers of the Hellenistic kingdoms began portraying

Above: The Roman rulers Philip I (244–9, left) and Galerius (305–11, right) featured their wives on coins.

themselves. The notion spread to Rome in the late-Republican period, and Pompey the Great and Julius Caesar were thus honoured. Portraiture flourished in the Roman Empire, featuring not only the emperor but his wife and children, creating a veritable portrait gallery renowned for its realism.

Medieval coins were very crude by comparison, with stylized portraits of rulers on the verge of parody. Most were full-face portraits but they seldom bore any resemblance to the living ruler. There are rare instances of queens being mentioned, though not actually depicted, including Cynefryth, wife of Offa of Mercia (757–96) and Adelaide, wife of Emperor Otto (931).

REVIVAL IN THE WEST

The Byzantine Empire was indirectly responsible for the revival of realistic portraiture on the coins of Western Europe. Shortly before Constantinople fell to the Turks in 1453, Emperor John Palaeologus paid a state visit to Italy, an occasion commemorated by a handsome bronze medal. This triggered a fashion for large portrait medals in Renaissance Italy, which spread to other countries and also inspired the production of coins by the Italian city states. These relatively large coins came to be known as testone (from Italian *testa*, a head), and from this come the English words "testoon" and "tester", once synonymous with "shilling". In England the first testoon, of 1504, bore the first realistic profile of Henry VII, engraved by Alexander Brugsal, but it

Above: This full-face portrait on a Henry VIII testoon is a good likeness of the king. The testoon provided a good medium for larger portraits.

was not until 1544 that the stereotyped full-face portrait disappeared from the penny. Henry VIII adopted a full-face portrait and when he debased the silver content in his shillings the silver wore off the highest point – his nose – hence the nickname Coppernose given to these coins.

DIFFERENT STYLES
Since the revival of realistic portraiture in the 15th century most images have been profiles. In many monarchies, notably Britain, the custom developed of showing alternate rulers facing left or right. (Both George V and George VI faced left, because Edward VIII – whose coins were never issued – would have faced right.) Two or more facing portraits were fashionable in Byzantine coinage and this treatment is also found on many of the multiple thalers of the German states. The most spectacular examples were the Achtbruderthalers of Brunswick, which had side-by-side facing portraits of eight brothers, hence the name.

Vis-à-vis, or face-to-face, portraits have occasionally appeared. They include some Roman imperial coins, notably those of Septimius Severus.

Below: Successive British monarchs, Edward VII (left) and George V (right), facing alternately left and right.

Above: A multiple thaler of Friedrich I, Duke of Saxe-Gotha-Altenburg, of 1690, with seven busts in roundels.

The style was adopted by English coins showing Mary Tudor and Philip II of Spain, and Scottish coins showing Mary Queen of Scots and her first two husbands, either Francis II of France or Henry, Lord Darnley. A crown from the Turks and Caicos Islands (1976) has confrontational portraits of George III and George Washington, and the style was also used for coins marking the wedding of Prince Charles and Lady Diana Spencer in 1981.

Most coins that have two portraits show them as overlapping profiles, with the more important person (such as a king) at the front and the lesser profile behind. These are described as "jugate", "accolated" or "conjoined" profiles, and they have been in use since the gold staters of the Brutii (282 BC). In Britain the style was used for coins of William III and Mary II (1689–94), those of 1981, 1986, 2000 and 2005 celebrating British royal marriages and the Golden Wedding coins of 1997.

The strangest portrait coin of all time must be the Zurich thaler of 1512, with full-face standing portraits of the three martyred saints, Regulus, Exuperant and Felix, beheaded and holding their heads in their hands.

PORTRAITS OF PERSONALITES
The depiction of royalty other than the reigning monarch was popular during the Roman Empire, when relatives of

Right: Triple conjoined portraits of Carol I, Ferdinand and Carol II on a Romanian 20 lei of the latter (1944).

the emperor were often portrayed. The practice was revived in 16th-century Italy, when the large silver coins that were being produced afforded scope for it, but the portraits were still confined to royalty.

Bavaria appears to have produced the first coins commemorating historic personalities other than royalty, beginning with the thaler of 1826 mourning the deaths of the engineer Georg Friedrich von Reichenbach (1772–1826) and the physicist Joseph von Fraunhofer (1787–1826), whose face-to-face profiles appear on the reverse. Several Bavarian coins of 1840–9 depicted the statues of famous men from Albrecht Dürer to Orlando di Lasso. This notion was not copied elsewhere until 1893, when the USA struck a half dollar portraying Christopher Columbus (followed by many other similar coins) and Brazil similarly honoured Pedro Cabral in 1900.

Below: Personalities featured on recent coins include (clockwise from top left) sporting heroes (Roger Bannister, Britain), poets (Robert Burns, Isle of Man), explorers (Captain Cook, New Zealand) and royalty (Charles and Diana's engagement, New Zealand).

NON-FIGURAL MOTIFS

After their adoption of Islam as the prominent faith in the 7th century, Arab countries did not place any effigy of a living creature, either man or beast, on their coins. Although the portrayal of animate objects was considered to be closely linked to idolatry, and was thus declared taboo by the teachings of the Koran, there was no such ban on the depiction of inanimate objects. Nevertheless, until the middle of the 20th century, Islamic coins continued to be devoid of either portraits or pictures, and the space on both sides of the coins was entirely given over to inscriptions in Arabic. This restraint created a need to be innovative with the use of text, leading to some of the lengthiest – and most poetic – inscriptions ever to appear on coins anywhere in the world.

Above: The fusion of Persian and Arab styles has resulted in a few ancient examples of portraiture. This coin depicts Mus'ab bin al-Zubayr.

Below: Abbasid coins usually have the name of the current ruler's heir on the reverse. The bottom example is unusual for bearing the name of an unborn heir.

PIOUS INVOCATIONS

Not only did the countries that produced these coins develop increasingly ornate styles of script, but the inscriptions themselves became more flowery as time passed. The standard formula that appears on Islamic coins is known as the Bismillah, and is the first word of the affirmation, "There is no God but God, and Muhammad is His Prophet." By tradition Allah had 99 excellent names, but opinions differ as to what those 99 names were. In fact, no fewer than 132 epithets for Allah are recorded on Islamic coins. They range from the simple "The One" to "The Ever Self-existing One". Other versions found in inscriptions include "He Who Hath Not Been Begotten", "The Very Next Adjoining One" or the more prosaic "The Numberer" and "The Road Guide".

Muslims had no monopoly on the name of God by any means, but what made their coins so special was their purity of design: they were not sullied by portraits or images of animals or anything else that might distract the thoughts of the faithful.

WIDESPREAD USE OF ARABIC

Arabic was widely used, not only in Arabia and the lands conquered by the Arabs, from Spain to Mesopotamia, but also for the Farsi inscriptions on the coins of Persia and Afghanistan, and for the Malay texts on coins of Java, Sumatra and Malaya. Arabic was the script used by the Mughal emperors, the princely states and even the Honourable East India Company. On some coins of the Indian states Queen Victoria was named (though she was not portrayed) and styled in Arabic as Empress of India.

The earliest Islamic coins combined Arabic with Graeco-Roman or Sasanian (Pehlevi) inscriptions. Siculo-Norman coins were copied from Ayyubid coins but with a Christian formula in Arabic, "Victorious by the Grace of God" on

Above: Ornate punches replaced effigies on some post-Gupta Indian coins. The lotus motif is a good example of the use of recognized emblems.

Above: Zubayda, the wife of the Abbasid governor Al-Rashid, was perhaps the first woman to strike a coin in the history of Islam. The inscription reads: "By the command of the lady, mother of the heir apparent, may God preserve her, so be it."

gold taris of Tancred. Alfonso VIII of Castile struck coins inscribed in Arabic, "Amir of the Catholics and the Pope the Imam of the Church of the Messiah".

For the purposes of trade with Muslim merchants in Morocco, Portuguese copper ceitils were struck with a three-line Arabic inscription bearing the name and title of King Manuel I (1495–1521).

TITLES

Islamic coins bore the names and titles of rulers, and Abbasid coins often mentioned the heir to the throne as well – even if the heir was as yet unborn and unnamed. Titles, although extravagant and self-aggrandizing, were also carefully worded to underline religious commitment and the earthly confines of the territories over which a ruler presided. They included "Excellent King of the Surface of the Earth" (used by the Mongol rulers of Persia),

Sun Motif

While some coins of Hyderabad depicted the Char Minar gateway, its feudatory dependency of Indore struck coins with a smiling sun motif, the nearest thing to a portrait without actually being one.

"Emperor of the World" (for the Jahandar of Delhi) and "Lord of the World" (for the Atabeg of Mosul). By contrast, the most self-abasing title of all time was inscribed on Islamic coins, Shah Tahmasp I of Persia (1514–76) being content to refer to himself as "Slave of Ali". Not to be outdone, Shah Rukh was styled "Hound of the Threshold of the Pleasing One" and his successor, Shah Husain, went a step further with "Hound of the Threshold of Ali, of the Amir of the Faithful".

The most charming title found in an Islamic inscription was that favoured by some of the Indian princely states in the 19th century, after the proclamation of the Empire of India in 1877: "Queen Victoria, Adorning the Throne of Inglistan [England] and Hind". The saddest title was "Deceased", inscribed in Arabic on the coins of Aziz Sheikh of the Golden Horde and Tipu Sultan, ruler of Mysore, which were issued shortly after their deaths.

SIGN OF THE TOUGHRA

The *toughra* found on Turkish and Arab coins is the Islamic counterpart of the royal monogram on European coins. It consists of an elaborate Arabic inscription giving the names of a ruler and his father and incorporating three vertical lines. These date from the reign of Sultan Murad I (1359–89), who, when signing important documents, dipped three fingers into the inkwell and drew them down the page.

CHRONOGRAMS

A chronogram is an inscription in which some letters can be read as Roman numerals, which make a date when added together. (The term is derived from the Greek and means "time writing".)

This unusual practice was popular in Europe in the Renaissance and the 17th century, when it was often used to signify dates in inscriptions on tombstones and foundation stones, but it was derived from the Arab custom of giving the letters of the *abjad* (the Arabic alphabet) a numerical value. From this came the fashion for concealing the date in inscriptions on Islamic coins, which could be deduced

Below: The toughra is a feature of Ottoman coins (top) and Islamic coins of the Indian princely states (bottom); Egypt included an actual portrait of King Fu'ad I in 1921, and Morocco worked the national star emblem into an ornate reverse of 1900.

by adding up the value of the letters composing the word or words.

Thus, coins inscribed in the name of the ruler Fakhr al-Din Qara Arslan, Artuqid of Hisn Kayfa, contained a final word whose letters signified 500, 50 and 6, making the date 556 AH. On the reverse of coins of Nadir Shah appeared the inscription, "By the Tarikh, Whatever Happens is Best." The letters of this phrase as written in Arabic had the values 70 + 100 + 6 + 1 + 40 + 10 + 80 + 200 + 10 + 600 + 30 + 1, which together made 1148 AH.

A mohur of Jahangir bears the inscription: "The letters of Jahangir and Allahu Akbar's are Equal in Value from the Beginning of Time", and, indeed, when added up the letters of their names each total 289.

Below: Ancient Islamic coiners sought innovative ways of displaying their lengthy inscriptions, from hexagonal, circular and star-shaped arrangements to densely packed central legends.

HISTORY OF PICTORIALISM

The obverse of a coin was traditionally reserved for the portrait of a deity or ruler, while the reverse (the "tails") was used for an image of lesser importance. The distinction has been blurred in more recent times by the adoption of arms instead of a portrait (especially in republics) or, conversely, the use of portraiture on both sides.

Because of the symbolic importance of coins, pictorial elements often arise out of armorial emblems and they, in turn, may be traced back to mythology. The use of animals (particularly cattle and horses) may symbolize power and wealth. From the 1900s onward, as coins in general have become more pictorial, they have often illustrated national aspirations. By the 1930s a didactic or propaganda element was creeping in, particularly on coins of the USSR and fascist countries.

CLASSICAL IMAGES
The simple motifs on the obverse of the earliest electrum dumps probably represented the personal badges of the merchants and magistrates who authorized them. In the heyday of classical Greek coinage the civic emblem was the dominant feature of many issues. Among the earliest examples were the

Below: Motifs on ancient Greek and Persian coins include ordinary animals as well as mythical creatures such as a winged Pegasus or Gorgon.

winged boar (Klazomenai), boar (Methymna), calves' heads (Lesbos), lion's head (Lindos), amphora (Andros), frog (Seriphos), dolphins (Thera) and bull's head (Athens). Some of the emblems were a pun on the name of the city or district. Thus the *bous* or cowhide shield graced the coins of Boeotia, while a crab and a turtle were featured on the coins of Akragas and Aegina respectively. Others featured mythical figures associated with the area, such as the boy Taras riding a dolphin (Tarentum) and Athena with her owl (Athens).

Heraldic reverses related to portrait obverses developed in the 5th century BC, and from matching deities with their familiars, such as Zeus and the eagle, it was but a short step to the coins of imperial Rome, with the emperor on one side and an allegorical subject on the other. The Romans, however, eventually produced coins that had a wide range of subjects on the reverse, including the famous buildings and landmarks of the Roman Empire. It is on some of these that we find the earliest representation of the original Tower of London.

MEDIEVAL DEPICTIONS
Most medieval coins tended to show the stylized portrait of a ruler on the obverse and a cross on the reverse, partly out of Christian sentiment but also partly for the practical purpose of showing where the coin could be cut into halves or quarters. The revival of

Below: Favoured motifs for Roman coins included a standing bull (left) or landmarks such as the Temple of Jupiter (right).

Above and left: Dionysus, god of wine, is often depicted on ancient Greek coins of Thrace, the site of his sanctuary.

symbolism came in the early 10th century when Pope Benedict I sanctioned denarii whose reverse showed an open hand flanked by the letters R and O. The hand (*manus* in Latin) was a pictogram substituting for part of the word "Romanus". The hand of God raised in benediction was a popular theme on coins, especially as the dreaded millennium approached and people feared the end of the world. Extremely rare pennies of Aethelred the Unready had an obverse of the Lamb of God and reverse of a dove, and are believed to allude to the millennium.

Heraldic reverses were adopted by the Frankish rulers. Early coins had a stylized temple, but with the growth of chivalry in the 12th and 13th centuries it became fashionable to place the emblem from the ruler's escutcheon on the reverse. Thus began the convention, prevalent on many coins to this day, of having the ruler's portrait on the obverse and the national arms on the reverse. English gold coins may be found with the Archangel Michael slaying the serpent or the monarch armed and standing in a galleon, but it was not until the neo-classical Britannia (1797) and St George and the Dragon (1816) that pictorialism truly emerged.

MODERN PICTORIALS
In classical times, coins could be startlingly graphic in the subjects they featured. Drunkenness, rape and debauchery appeared on Greek

Above: A "death thaler" of the ruler August II of Saxony, showing a skull lying at the base of a tree.

staters from Thasos (Thrace) and Lete and tetradrachms of Mende and Naxos, reflecting a very earthy approach to subjects considered taboo in later times. Pictorialism as such, however, really began with the large thalers and guldengroschen from the 16th century. Their modern counterparts, dollars and crowns, offer considerable scope for elaborate pictorial motifs.

The large silver coins of the German states tended to be allegorical or propagandistic, particularly during the Thirty Years War (1618–48). Republican France's first pictorial coin, the 5 décime piece of 1793, was in the same genre. Popularly known as the Robespierre décime, its elaborate obverse depicts Nature as an Egyptian goddess expressing the water of life from her breasts. Robespierre (the President of the Convention) is offering a cup of the fluid to a delegate of the Assembly.

Austria and the German states took the lead in developing pictorial coins in the 19th century; the earliest issues

to depict ships and locomotives come from that area. But it was in the course of the 20th century that pictorial coins really came into their own. Pictorialism was no longer confined to large commemorative pieces but extended right down to the lowliest definitive circulating coins. The Irish Free State (later the Republic of Ireland) adopted distinctive coins in 1928 and these bore reverse motifs showing such subjects as a sow and piglets (halfpenny), a hen and chickens, a hare (3 pence), a hound (6 pence) and a bull (shilling). The Barnyard series, as it was nicknamed, continued for many years, surviving until 1968. Canada, Australia and New Zealand adopted pictorial motifs in the 1930s, while Britain introduced a series in 1937 depicting a wren (farthing), Sir Francis Drake's ship (halfpenny) and a clump of sea thrift (3 pence); other denominations retained the seated figure of Britannia (penny) or clung to heraldic themes.

Beginning with Lincoln in 1909 (the centenary of his birth), American coins have favoured portraits of dead presidents (obverse) and buildings associated with them, such as the Lincoln Memorial (1 cent) and Monticello, the home of Thomas Jefferson (5 cents), but otherwise heraldic and symbolic motifs predominate. The only truly pictorial United States coin was the

---

Sunrise and Hope

The world's newest country, the Democratic Republic of Timor-Leste, consists of the eastern part of the island of Timor. Formerly a Portuguese colony, it was occupied by Indonesia but fought a long campaign for liberation (1975–99) and, with the backing of a UN peacekeeping force, achieved full independence in 2002. It has the lowest GDP in the world, about $400 a year. The cockerel on the coin symbolizes the sunrise (Timor in Tetum means "sunrise") and hope for the new country.

---

nickel of 1913–38, which had the head of a Native American on the obverse and a buffalo on the reverse. In 2005 these much-loved motifs were revived after a gap of 67 years.

Pictorialism today is prominent in the coins of the emerging nations, but examples are also found in Scandinavia and Britain's crown dependencies. For Greece, Italy and Israel the wheel has come full circle, with heavy reliance on classical or biblical pictorial motifs.

Below: Coins of the Weimar Republic depicting Cologne Cathedral (top) and a scenic river reverse to mark the liberation of the Rhineland.

Below: A naval obverse of Virginia (top) and a mountain lion reverse of Vermont are just two of the pictorial subjects used on American commemorative issues.

HOW TO COLLECT

Numismatics boasts distinguished enthusiasts, many of whom used the hobby to develop a keen interest in history. Once you have decided on a focus for your collection, you can begin to make new acquisitions. Although it's tempting to seek out rarities, many issues of recent years – such as this enamelled coin of the Isle of Man – are truly resplendent.

ORIGINS OF NUMISMATICS

Numismatics is the name given to the study and collecting of coins and medals, and is derived from *nomisma*, the Greek word for coin. It is probable that coins were prized for their aesthetic qualities from the earliest times, while their importance in socio-economic development was appreciated by Herodotus and other early historians.

There were certainly coin collections during the earliest times – but not, perhaps, in the modern sense. In the era before banking existed, people stored their surplus wealth in leather bags or in earthenware jars, which could be buried in troubled times. Most hoards were presumably retrieved by their owners when the crisis passed, but many others were never recovered until turned up by the plough or (more likely nowadays) discovered by the

Above: Great royal coin collectors include (clockwise from top left) Carol I of Romania, Christina of Sweden, Habsburg Emperor Charles VI and Prince Rainier of Monaco.

metal detector. Coins from such hoards, large and small, have long held a fascination for the archaeologist and antiquary, and they are undoubtedly the source of much of the material now in the hands of museums and some collectors. Unfortunately, until relatively recently, such hoards were not carefully preserved and studied scientifically, although laws now exist in some countries to safeguard archaeological finds, including those of numismatic interest, until they can be properly catalogued by the appropriate authority.

EARLIEST COIN CATALOGUES
Although St Thomas Aquinas (1225–74) touched on coinage in his philosophical writings, the earliest works dealing with numismatics, or the antiquarian aspects of coins, as opposed

Right: Chocolate replica of the 1 euro coin, produced in 2000 to publicize the new currency.

Below: Chinese gold panda coin, distributed as a Lunar New Year gift in a red silk purse.

to the monetary and financial aspects of current coins, appeared early in the 16th century. The French antiquary Guillaume Budé (1467–1540) published *De Asse et Partibus Eius* ("Concerning the Roman As and its Parts") and *Libellus de Moneta Graeca* ("A Pamphlet of Greek coins").

Many other books appeared in the 17th and 18th centuries, in France, Germany and Italy, dealing with various aspects of ancient and medieval coins. By the early 19th century, the practice of coin-collecting was well enough established to support periodical literature. The earliest magazine devoted to numismatics was *Blätter für Münzkunde*, published in Hanover from 1834 until 1844 by Dr Hermann Grote. *The Numismatic Chronicle*, founded by John Young Ackerman, made its debut as a quarterly in 1836 and is still going strong as the journal of the Royal Numismatic Society.

The second half of the 19th century witnessed the publication of a profusion of catalogues and handbooks, consisting of either systematic listings of coins in the world's major public collections or studies of particular regions and periods, predominantly Greek and Roman but with a developing interest in medieval European and Islamic coins. From the tone and contents of these early works it is clear that the emphasis was on ancient coins, which collectors who had had the benefit of a classical education could appreciate.

Numismatics continued to be predominantly classical in character until the late 19th century. By that time, some wealthy collectors in North America were taking a keen interest in

the coins of the United States, yet the
earliest book on the subject was not
published until 1899.

Catalogues of the coins of the various European countries began to
appear in the 1880s, but a similar coverage of the coins of India, China,
Japan, Korea and other Asiatic countries did not develop until the turn of
the century. These catalogues varied
considerably in detail and illustration.
No attempt was made to produce
priced catalogues until the 1920s, when
such books covering specific countries
or periods began to appear regularly.
The only catalogues that cover world
coinage as a whole are the Krause catalogues, published in the USA (and
confined to the modern period).

GREAT COIN COLLECTIONS

From the Renaissance onward, it was
fashionable for gentlemen to possess a
coin cabinet (which in some cases was
an entire room, shelved from floor to
ceiling to house their treasures).
Outstanding among early collectors
were the Italian poet Petrarch, the
Medici rulers of Florence, Pope Paul II,
Queen Christina of Sweden and the
Habsburg Emperor Charles VI. In
Britain, King George III set a fine
example, and his interest in coins was
shared by his personal surgeon, Dr
William Hunter (1718–83), whose

wide-ranging collections, including
coins and medals, were the nucleus of
the Hunterian Museum in Glasgow,
opened in 1807. The collections
formed by his brother, Dr John Hunter
(1728–93), and their contemporary, Sir
Hans Soane, formed the basis of the
numismatic collections in the British
Museum. Britain is unusual in having
several great institutional collections,
including those in the Ashmolean
Museum (Oxford), and the Fitzwilliam
Museum (Cambridge), as well as the
Royal Scottish Museum (Edinburgh).
Elsewhere, large and all-embracing collections are housed in the Bibliothèque
Nationale (Paris) and the Smithsonian
Institution (Washington).

Among more recent monarchs who
had an abiding passion for coins were
King Carol of Romania and Prince
Rainier of Monaco, but King Victor
Emmanuel III of Italy was a lifelong
numismatist, whose studies and scholarly writings on the subject are still
widely respected. Conversely, King
Farouk of Egypt, another royal collector, was really the pack rat par
excellence, whose collections ranged
from stamps and coins to glass paperweights and ladies' underwear. Some of
the greatest collectors of more recent

*Above: Promotional sets and souvenir
folders are contemporary methods of
encouraging budding coin collectors.*

times were Americans, such as the
pharmaceuticals magnate Eli K. Lilly
and the Texan tycoon Nelson Bunker
Hunt, who famously tried to corner the
world silver market back in the 1970s.
The late Mary Norweb was arguably
the world's leading female numismatist,
and the sale of her incomparable collections in the 1980s was spread over
many auctions.

*Below: The coin collection of William Hunter (bottom-left),
anatomist and surgeon of fellow collector George III (pictured
on this 1796 guinea, right), formed the nucleus of Scotland's
oldest museum, the Hunterian in Glasgow. The museum, as it
was in 1807, is shown in the engraving (bottom right).*

GRADE AND CONDITION

Coins are the most durable of all the antiquities and have survived in remarkable condition considering their age. Gold coins have been dug out of the earth gleaming as brightly as the day they were minted. Conversely, modern coins may show rapid signs of wear due to frequent circulation and the rough treatment meted out in slot machines. It follows that the condition of a coin plays a major part in determining its value to a collector.

COIN GRADES

Newcomers to the hobby are often amazed at the enormous disparity in value or price between a coin in impeccable mint condition, with neither scratches on its surface nor irregularities in its edges, and its twin in worn condition. The effigy on the obverse of the latter may have lost its fine detail but surely it is still recognizable? And the coat of arms on the reverse may be reduced to a mere outline, but the date is still readable, so why should it be regarded as worthless?

Everything is relative. Collectors may be quite happy to acquire a medieval coin in generally poor condition because (a) it is a major rarity, or (b) that is the condition of all the known examples of the coin and it would be virtually impossible to find a specimen in a better state. It seems to be the case that, when it comes to medieval

Below: These 18th-century British spade guineas are judged by one auctioneer to be "fair to very fine", though it often takes an expert to discern variations in condition, and reach an overall grading.

Viewing and Assessing Coins

Above: A soft, lint-free cloth offers good protection against surface scratching when setting coins down to view.

Above: A range of magnification tools exist; generally x10 is the maximum strength required to view coins.

Above: If you must handle coins – not recommended for rarities or those in mint state – hold them at the very edges.

Above: Common, circulating coins will arrive in various states, and may be in need of cleaning before viewing closely.

coinage, you will often have to be content with a piece that would otherwise never be considered worthy of a place in your collection. Supply falls far short of demand in this particular area of numismatics. On the other hand, Greek and Roman imperial coins generally exist in such large quantities that their relative condition is a major factor in determining their value.

As for modern coins, anything less than the highest grades of condition should be unacceptable to a collector – a fact that is reflected in the coin catalogues, which usually confine their prices to the two top grades. At the apex of the pyramid, proof coins are collectable only in pristine condition, exactly as they left the mint; anything less makes them unacceptable to the discerning collector.

HOW TO ASSESS GRADE AND CONDITION

The ability to appraise a coin accurately comes only with years of experience. A good magnifier is an absolute necessity, but nowadays you can also scan coins at a high resolution and then view them on screen, focusing on the particular details you wish to examine more closely.

In the highest grade of condition a coin should still possess the original lustre characteristic of a freshly minted coin. Next comes a coin that may have lost some or most of its lustre but on which the finest detail of the design is absolutely sharp. Lower down the scale are coins that show slight evidence of wear on the higher points of the design, such as the hair on the portrait, the fine folds of clothing or the intricate detail

Classification of Condition

Because the conventional terms have tended to become subjective, the American Numismatic Association (ANS) has devised a more scientific and objective system, combining terms or abbreviations with numbers to give a more precise classification. This is now used worldwide by dealers when encapsulating or "slabbing" coins in sealed folders (pictured), to bolster confidence in buying and selling. These grades are as follows:

Proof-70   Perfect proof
Proof-67   Gem proof
Proof-65   Choice proof
Proof-63   Select proof
Proof-60   Proof

Uncirculated coins are graded by Mint State (MS):

MS-70   Perfect
MS-67   Gem
MS-65   Choice
MS-63   Select
MS-60   Uncirculated

The lower grades combine the traditional abbreviations with numbers:

AU-50   About uncirculated
EF-45   Choice extremely fine
EF-40   Extremely fine
VF-30   Choice very fine
VF-20   Very fine
F-12   Fine
VG-8   Very good
G-4   Good
AG-4   About good
BS-1   Basal state

will not necessarily lose value if the mark itself is sufficiently clear and complete. Both sides of the coin are assessed during grading: the final evaluation will be based on the slightly weaker of the two sides, if they are not particularly different, or the coin will be given a "split grade" in the catalogue entry. If the two sides are found to be more than one grade apart, this suggests that the design of either the obverse or reverse has been subject to greater wear and tear, and the coin will be graded on the weaker side alone. Coins bearing a small motif, such as a crown symbol, may be graded solely on the condition of this easily worn element of the design. A guide to nomenclature is given with the glossary to this book.

Below: This gold half-anna restrike of an 1892 copper denomination (top left), struck for use in British India, is judged to be in "brilliant" state as it has almost no surface markings. "Peripheral" weakness on the obverse (top right) of a 13th-century issue from Bukhara earns it a split grade of "good/very fine". The "unique" status of these Anglo-Saxon "bonnet-type" pennies (middle) increases value despite their time-worn condition, while this 2 shilling coin of George VI (bottom), sold with its original 1937 proof-set packaging, was graded "about as struck".

in a coat of arms. Below that, you will notice wear in the inscriptions, with the lettering looking thick or blurred.

Beyond that state, coins showing extensive signs of wear are not worth collecting unless they are very rare. The same is true for coins that bear signs of rough handling – scuff marks, scratches or edge knocks. Coins that have suffered actual damage, such as piercing

Below: Special peel-back holders are available to preserve the condition of individual coins.

for use as jewellery or clipping to remove slivers of gold or silver from the edges, should be avoided altogether, except as historical curiosities.

NOMENCLATURE

Over the years dealers and collectors have attempted to classify the condition of coins, adopting various terms to define the various states, from "brilliant uncirculated" to the lower grades of "fair", "medium" and "poor". The trouble is that the terms, like the coins themselves, have tended to become worn or debased with the passage of time and as a result new terms have been devised to upgrade the system. At one time, for example, the term "good" meant just that, but nowadays a coin given that epithet would, in fact, be pretty poor and not worth considering unless it was a very elusive item.

Auctioneers and cataloguers should include the quality of the strike with their description. Countermarked coins

LOOKING AFTER COINS

Coins are tough – they have to be in order to carry out their function. For this reason, they have been produced using hard-wearing materials designed to be handled frequently, and to withstand the grime and sweat of hands in every climate and working condition. They have to be robust enough to withstand harsh treatment, such as being shoved into slot machines or dropped on the ground or, worst of all, jostled constantly with other coins in purses and pockets.

PRESERVING CONDITION

Coins are often expected to circulate for decades and, unless there is a change in the currency or a denomination is withdrawn, only when they are too old and worn to be recognizable are they taken out of service. However, even coins bearing the marks of time should be preserved in the condition in which they are found.

Unless you are confining your acquisitions to coins neatly packaged in their pristine state by the mint or numismatic bureau, or slabbed by a dealer of high repute, you will acquire coins in their naked and unadorned state. At best they will have been passed from hand to hand to some extent, even if they are still bright and shiny and bear the current date. At worst they will have been in circulation for some time,

Right: Manage your expectations when caring for your coins. If, for example, they display signs of "copper sickness" such as the coins on the left of this picture, you will never be able to restore them to their original state, like those on the right.

perhaps for many years. They may latterly have reposed in a dealer's oddment tray, the convenient repository for so many unconsidered trifles, waifs and strays, which are too poor or of insufficient value to make it worth the dealer's time and trouble to sort and grade properly. Collectors love sifting through these bargain trays as the cheaper material generally ends up there, where quick turnover is the name of the game.

CLEANING WITH CARE

Once you have borne away your treasures and taken them home for closer examination and identification, before putting them into the appropriate place in your collection the first thing is to

attend to their appearance. The plain fact is that most coins that will come into your possession in the ordinary way will be dirty, dull and grimy, even if they still possess some of their original lustre. The oils secreted by human hands, atmospheric pollution and everyday dust and dirt all combine to give circulated coins a fairly unattractive appearance.

Generally speaking, a good degreasing solvent will work wonders in removing surface grime. A drop or two of a good quality lighter fuel on the surface of a coin, gently wiped off with a very soft cloth, will remove all or most of the dirt. For more persistent cases, especially when dirt accumulates in and around the lettering or the more intricate parts of the design, brushing with a soft brush with animal bristles – never use nylon or other artificial fibres – is efficacious.

The watchwords here are gentleness and persistence. It is preferable, when handling coins, to wear latex or fine plastic surgical gloves. If you are not wearing gloves, always hold coins at the very edge, as shown, left, so that any contact between your fingertips and the coin surface is minimal. You would be surprised how indelible fingerprints can be; once a fingerprint marks the surface of a coin, it can never be removed and is etched there for all time.

Cleaning Coins

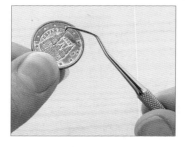

Above: A specially designed coin 'pick' will help to remove encrusted grime.

Above: This coin cleaning brush causes minimal damage to the metal.

SOLUTIONS FOR DIFFERENT METALS

If all coins were made of gold or silver the problems of caring for them would be simple. Gold does not rust, it is impervious to oxidation or atmospheric pollution and it resists most of the chemicals found in the soil. Of course gold coins do get grimy from constant handling, but surface dirt can be easily removed with a solution of lemon juice in an equal amount of warm water. Silver responds well to a bath in warm water to which you have added a few drops of ammonia.

Copper or bronze coins are more of a problem because these metals are prone to oxidation and form the green patina called verdigris. Where this is evenly distributed over the coin, it actually protects the surface from further deterioration, and it is not unattractive in, for example, Roman coins. But where verdigris appears as bright green patches, it is regarded as "copper sickness" and needs special attention. Fortunately, there are now various products on the market that are designed specifically for the cleaning of coins made of different metals. Read the instructions on the label and follow them carefully, and you should be able to cope with this problem.

Below: Basic household items such as an empty jam jar and caustic soda are useful for coin care.

The Perils of Polish

If cleaning should be approached with the utmost caution, polishing is definitely a bad thing! Beginners sometimes fall into the trap of assuming that a vigorous rub with metal cleaner will improve the appearance of a coin, but short of actually hitting it with a hammer and chisel, this is the worst thing you can do. Polishing a coin may briefly improve its superficial appearance, but such abrasive action will destroy the patina and reduce the fineness of the high points of the surface. Even if a coin is polished only once, it will never be the same, and an expert can recognize this immediately.

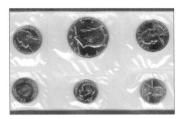

Above: You should never remove coins from any form of sealed packaging unless it is really necessary.

The lower down the electromotive series the metals are, the greater the problem, as these materials have a greater tendency to rust and corrode. This applies particularly to coins minted in times of shortage, such as wartime, which may be made of tin, zinc, iron or steel. In this case, immersion in a 5 per cent solution of caustic soda containing some aluminium foil or zinc filings works well, but care must be taken to rinse the coins thoroughly afterwards in clean water. Cotton buds can be extremely useful accessories for dealing with troublesome patches of dirt or grease. Dry coins carefully with a soft cloth – never use paper towels as these can scratch the metal surface – and always blot coins dry rather than rubbing them.

SALVAGED COINS

Coins recovered from being buried in the ground, or found on the sea bed, may present special problems due to chemical reactions between the metals and the salts present in earth or sea water. Buried silver coins, for example, will acquire a dark patina of silver sulphide. In such cases, the best advice is to take them to your local museum or friendly coin dealer and let the conservation experts decide what can or should be done to improve their condition and appearance.

Left and below: The packaging in which special edition mint sets are issued is designed to preserve the coins into perpetuity.

HOUSING COINS

Like any other collectables of value, coins need to be properly housed. Although they are far less bulky than even small antiques, they are much more cumbersome than stamps or postcards, and have their special requirements in order that they should be kept in a safe and orderly manner. Storage options range from special items of furniture to boxes, cases and albums. Each has its good and bad points, but, in the end, what you use is a matter of personal choice.

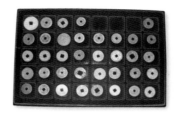

Above: Modern plastic coin trays have a felt lining and compartments, often with a transparent lid and slipcase.

BOXES AND CASES

For those seeking to establish a fairly extensive collection, with room to grow, boxes and cases not only give the "classic" feel of a small library, but are also a useful aid to cataloguing. Companies such as Abafil of Italy and Lindner of Germany produce a large range of cases suitable for coins. They are constructed of steel or stout plastic, and open to reveal several shallow trays, often stacked in such a way that each can be slid in or out of place without disturbing the other trays. The trays themselves have compartments of various dimensions tailored to fit coins of different sizes and are felt lined. Most of these boxes

Above and left: A set of Australian transport tokens in a presentation folder.

have a good locking system and a carrying handle, so they are particularly popular with dealers travelling to and from coin shows. When the case is locked the trays are held securely in place and there is no danger of the coins slithering around or falling out in transit. These cases often have separate

Left: There are a number of different ways to house coins, from felt-lined trays to ring-bound albums with clear plastic sleeves, with compartments into which individual coins can be slotted, enabling both sides to be viewed in the sleeve.

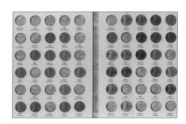

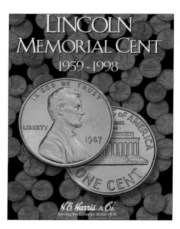

Above and top: A Harris & Co. Memorial Cent coin folder which, when opened, reveals holes to contain all the variants of a particular denomination, arranged by date and mint-mark.

compartments for such handy accessories as a good magnifier and callipers for accurately measuring diameters and thicknesses. Another useful feature consists of side pockets inside the box for hygroscopic crystals, which ensure that the coins are kept in a dry atmosphere.

The same companies also produce individual cases on the same principle, usually constructed in stout plastic lined with felt, with a sliding plastic lid and a handle. In turn, the case fits inside a slipcase on which you can write the details of the contents. Unlike the boxes, however, these cases seldom have a lock, so they are much less secure. While coin boxes are best simply stacked on the floor, the cases can be stored on bookshelves – always making sure that you do not overload them. There are also stacking systems that enable you to build up boxes and cases in a single all-purpose storing unit. The German company Mobel-Element, for example, produces a cabinet with a steel frame that can be adapted or added to as your collection grows.

COIN ALBUMS

Stout card coin folders produced by such firms as Harris and Whitman, with holes drilled for different denominations and the date, mint-mark and brief description printed below each hole, have long been immensely popular with American collectors. Similar albums have been produced for coins of other countries. While they are ideal for change-checkers intent on completing all the dates and mint-marks of a particular coin, they lack the flexibility required for a general collection.

In the 1960s, when coin collecting grew dramatically in popularity, a number of stationers began producing coin albums. These had a leatherette binder and a stout steel post with two or four

Below: A souvenir presentation case with a slipcase, housing a set of coins celebrating the Chinese Year of the Dog.

rings on to which transparent pages with pockets of various sizes could be threaded. These albums have the advantage of allowing you to see both sides of the coin merely by turning the page – a big improvement over traditional cabinet trays. If they are stored upright on bookshelves the weight of the coins tends to distort the pages and may even pull the steel post away from the spine, so for this reason they are best laid flat, like coin cases.

WALLETS

Plastic wallets are designed to hold individual coins, and are used in conjunction with larger containers such as albums. They often have a small sleeve into which a card giving details of the coin can be inserted. These wallets have largely superseded traditional manilla envelopes, but both can be stacked upright in narrow cases. You can buy cases for this purpose that build into storage systems, but many collectors are content to use any long, narrow box. Today many mints issue coin sets in special folders or wallets, and these can be stored in the compartments of coin cases, or slotted into albums.

CABINETS

Wealthy collectors of former times generally stored their treasures in a coin cabinet, a substantial piece of furniture in its own right. Splendid examples with marquetry doors and elegant cabriole legs come up at auction from time to time, and cost the earth, but plainer examples turn up occasionally in second-hand furniture stores, and as there is little general demand for them you might be lucky and get a bargain.

There are still specialist cabinet makers who produce modern coin cabinets in air-dried mahogany, walnut or rosewood (never oak, cedar or any highly resinous timber, which would react chemically with the contents). These cabinets have tiers of shallow drawers containing felt-based trays made of the same wood but with half-drilled holes of various diameters, suitable for every size of coin from the smallest copper to

Above: A souvenir wallet produced by the Royal Mint in 1968 to publicize the introduction of decimal coinage in 1971.

the largest crowns and dollars. As these cabinets are largely constructed by hand, they are more expensive than machine-made furniture, but prices vary widely, depending on size, number of drawers and such refinements as lockable double doors and brass fittings. Certainly, budget options exist.

The smaller cabinets will sit comfortably on a stout table (bear in mind the weight of the contents), but the more expensive versions are freestanding. When the doors are shut, these cabinets look no different from a drinks or television cabinet and can stand discreetly in your living room without attracting undue attention.

Hidden Dangers of PVC

PVC, once the preferred medium for sleeves, is not chemically inert. After a year or two, coins inserted in these sleeves begin to change their colour and appearance. Bronze coins turn green while "silver" turns to "gold", or, rather, acquires a sickly yellow slime. Thankfully, the rigid pages of albums are now plasticizer-free.

USING GUIDES AND CATALOGUES

Books dealing with aspects of coins and money have been in existence for many centuries, but in the past hundred years the spate of literature devoted to the subject has been enormous. There are thousands of books now available, ranging from beginners' guides to the subject to detailed studies of a single coin or series.

The old maxim "Knowledge pays off" is seldom truer than in the case of coin collecting and trading. A study of the literature appropriate to your chosen field will repay you handsomely. Coin dealers are very knowledgeable people, but numismatics is such a vast subject that no one could ever know everything. The money laid out on buying up-to-date catalogues alone will soon show an excellent return on the investment.

CATALOGUES

The essential tools that no collector should be without are the coin catalogues. Not so many years ago numismatics lagged behind philately in the provision of good catalogues covering the whole world, but this

Below: Comprehensive catalogues even include entries on contemporary imitations of coins, such as this poor copy of a George II halfpenny dated 1758 (top) and unofficial patterns, such as this issue portraying Edward VIII (bottom), released specifically for collectors years after his abdication.

Right: Popular contemporary coin literature ranges from the massive, and indispensable, compendia on coins of the world, published by the American company Krause (top of picture), to smaller guides detailing the coins of single countries, and specialist periodials and catalogues.

deficiency has been remedied by the splendid range now published by Krause Publications of Iola, Wisconsin.

It may seem strange that a small town in the American Midwest should be the centre of a publishing concern of global stature, but the *vade mecum* for most collectors is Krause's *Standard Catalog of World Coins*, published annually. It started out in 1972 as a single volume encompassing all the coins of the modern world, from about 1800 onward. Today it has expanded back in time to 1600 as well as right up to the present day and has been divided into four volumes, covering the 17th, 18th, 19th and 20th centuries respectively. Each of the current volumes is thicker than a London or New York telephone directory. Along the way the "phone book" (as it is affectionately known the world over) has spawned a range of more detailed catalogues, dealing with specific countries or periods

The Krause catalogues are in a class of their own, but at the next level there is an enormous range of rivals that concentrate on single countries or periods. In the USA, for example, the collector has the choice of several excellent works such as *The Handbook of United States Coins* (known as the "Blue Book"), and

The Guide Book of United States Coins, (known as the "Red Book"), both issued by Whitman Publishing of Atlanta.

In Britain the pre-eminent catalogues are those formerly published by B.A. Seaby but now kept up to date under the imprint of Spink & Son. These catalogues group coins by reign, but a different approach has been adopted by the Coincraft *Standard Catalogues*, in which coins are classified according to denomination. These two radically different approaches reflect the contrasting ways in which coins are collected and studied.

Below: Specialist catalogues may not tell the full story about mintage and availability of coins.

There are authoritative specialized coin catalogues for virtually every country now, most of them compiled and published in the countries concerned. Although many are not in English, they are generally well illustrated and include a glossary of terms in different languages, so using them is not difficult. Besides, the collector who wishes to concentrate on the coins of France or Germany, for example, will very soon acquire a working knowledge of the relevant language anyway.

A number of catalogue producers also publish yearbooks, which generally incorporate price guides as well as containing a wealth of other reference material. Auction catalogues for sales of important collections are invariably well illustrated, with scholarly descriptions of each lot, and these are much prized as permanent reference works.

CATALOGUE PRICES

A salient feature of catalogues is that they contain prices, which gives the collector a pretty good guide to current market values. Some catalogues are

published by dealers, and so the prices are essentially those at which coins in the different grades are offered for sale. Most catalogues, however, are produced by a team of dealers and experts and the prices quoted tend to reflect the prevailing state of the market more accurately and objectively.

Catalogues often include mintage figures, which can give a pointer to the relative scarcity of a coin, although these statistics have to be used with caution for they seldom take account of the vast quantities of coins melted down by the mints and therefore do not truly reflect the availability of material on the market.

WHERE TO FIND OUT MORE

Whereas catalogues tend to set out the bare details of coins with prices alongside, handbooks have a more discursive approach. Most of them do not provide prices (which would soon be rendered obsolete) but are designed as monographs that will stand the test of time. In this category come the sumptuous series published by the British Museum

Above: Try an on-line numismatic book store for helpful guides.

over more than a century, and now running to many volumes, dealing in considerable depth with the coins of Greece and Rome.

An impressive runner-up is the series compiled by members of the British and Royal Numismatic Societies and published under the generic title of *Sylloge of Coins of the British Isles,* which has been in progress since 1958. It started out as volumes that catalogued in detail the coins in the great national collections, beginning with the Fitzwilliam Museum in Cambridge and the Hunterian Museum in Glasgow. Ignoring the collections at the British Museum (which were already well-documented) apart from the Hiberno-Norse series, it covered the collections of other provincial museums in the British Isles, but also recorded British coins in the leading European and American museums and has latterly concentrated on the great private collections such as those formed by Emery Norweb, R.P. Mack and John Brooker. These handsome volumes were originally published by the British Academy but have recently been issued by Spink.

Browsing through these scholarly works makes you realize the complexities of British coins alone – and these are a drop in the ocean compared with the coinage output of the whole world. There is now a definitive handbook for just about anything, no matter how esoteric, from the *Pobjoy Encyclopedia of Isle of Man Coins and Tokens* (1977) to *Jewish Ghettos' and Concentration Camps' Money* by Zvi Stahl (1990).

International Coin Literature

The main English-language periodicals for coin collectors are published in the USA: *COINage* (Miller, Ventura, California), *Coin World* (Amos Press, Sidney, Ohio) and *World Coin News*, (Krause, Iola, Wisconsin). Krause also publish a range of more specialized titles such

as *Coin Prices* and *Coins and Numismatic News.* America also takes the lead with *Celator* (Lancaster, Pennsylvania), the only magazine aimed specifically at collectors of ancient coins. *Canadian Coin News* (Trajan, St Catharine's, Ontario) and *Coin News* (Token Publishing, Honiton, England) also have a worldwide readership. *Cronica Numismatica* (Domfil, Barcelona), *El Eco* (Vilanova) and *Cronaca Numismatica* (Bolaffi, Rome) are the leading magazines in Spanish and Italian, while *Revue Numismatique* and *Numismatique et Change* (Paris), *Münzen und Medaillen* (Berlin), *Münzen Revue* (Switzerland) and *Money Trend* (Vienna) serve French and German collectors respectively. *Munt Kourier* is published for collectors in the Netherlands.

COLLECTING BY COUNTRY

Traditionally, collectors have naturally tended to concentrate on the coins of their own country as the most readily available. They would begin with the coins they encountered in their small change in everyday life, gradually exchanging worn specimens for examples in better condition. Then they would work backwards in time, seeking examples of obsolete coins in second-hand or junk shops. Finally, they would begin buying from coin dealers and auctions to fill the gaps in the older issues; coins of a previous regime or those pre-dating economic upheavals and monetary reforms.

This is probably still the usual approach to coin collecting, but the rise of mail-order and on-line trading has made the choice infinitely wider. It is

now feasible for even the novice collector to acquire coins from any country that appeals on account of the diversity of its coinage, the type of coins or the subjects pictured on them.

CHOOSING A COUNTRY

Many collectors are attracted to a particular area for religious reasons. Thus the coins of Israel have an immense appeal to Jewish collectors all over the world. Similarly, Catholics are drawn to the beautiful and prolific issues of the Vatican City State. In both cases, there is infinite scope in the earlier coinage, on the one hand that of Judaea and the Nabatean kingdom as well as the coins of the Jewish revolts against Roman rule, and on the other the fascinating coins of the Papacy stretching back to early medieval times.

As the collection becomes more advanced, the collector may wish to narrow the scope to a single period or reign and concentrate on different coin types, die variants and mint-marks. Hand in hand with the amassing of

Above: The more research you do into the coinage of your chosen country, the better idea you will have of what is available to collect.

specimens goes the study of the history, geography, economic structure and monetary policies of the area, all factors that have an impact on the size, choice of metal or denomination of the coins at different times, not to mention the portraits of rulers and changes to inscriptions and armorial devices.

Other factors that may have some bearing on the choice of country may include the frequency of issue and the

Below: If the coins of a country run into thousands, you can opt to focus on the output of a specific region, such as these coins of Bengal: post-Gupta coins (top) struck under the authority of Sasanka, King of Gauda, 600–630; silver tankas of the Sultans of Bengal (middle); and gold mohurs of the East India Company, Bengal Presidency, struck at the Calcutta Mint (bottom).

Right: Ireland's history has been chronicled in coins: (clockwise from top left) the Hiberno-Norse penny, a Henry VIII "Harp" groot, a "Gun-money" half crown of James II, a halfpenny of William and Mary, a halfpenny struck during the Siege of Limerick, and the "St Patrick" farthing of Charles II.

balance between the definitive series and the number of commemorative or special issues. In general, the latter are phenomena belonging to the past half century, but even the most conservative coin-issuing countries seem to be producing more and more of these coins, which are essentially intended for the collectors' market rather than for general circulation.

THE IRISH EXAMPLE

When considering the variety of definitive issues you will find countries such as San Marino, which changes its designs each year, at one extreme and at the other countries such as the USA, whose basic series has remained unchanged for many years. In the middle are countries whose modern coinage does not go back very far, has not changed much since its inception, and which does not include too many special issues. These can be useful building blocks for putting together a comprehensive but not complex single-country collection.

A good example of this is provided by Ireland, whose modern coinage began in 1928 with a harp obverse and various animals on the reverses. Apart from the change of Gaelic title in 1939,

Above and left: The inscribed names on the 20th-century coins of Congo, Central Africa, chronicle its transition from French colony to People's Republic.

when "Saorstat Eireann" (Irish Free State) was replaced by "Eire" (Ireland), the Barnyard series continued until the advent of decimal currency in 1971. On the decimal coins, the harp obverse remained the same, and the animal motifs were retained on the cupro-nickel coins; only the bronze low values were given new reverse designs, based on ancient Celtic art, in a series that continued until Ireland adopted the euro in 2002.

Only a handful of Irish special issues have appeared since 1966. On the other hand, Ireland has a numismatic history that stretches back more than a thousand years to the Norse kingdom of Dublin. Interesting coins for collectors include the Anglo-Irish pennies, the "gun money" of the Williamite Wars and the tokens and coppers of the 18th and early 19th centuries.

THE INDIAN EXAMPLE

Apart from the usual country approach, many collectors in earlier generations gravitated towards the coins of ancient Greece and Rome. In the 1950s an interest in the Byzantine series began to develop, and recently an increasing number of collectors worldwide have been focusing on Islamic coinage, which had, naturally, always been popular with Muslim collectors. Now the

numerous issues of the dynasties of the Indian subcontinent are attracting a growing following outside India. It is interesting that, while Greek and Roman coins appealed to early collectors everywhere because they had all received a classical education, the attraction of Islamic or Indian coins is also transcending the barriers of race, religion or language, the lure of the relatively unfamiliar being a large part of their appeal.

CHANGING BORDERS

Sometimes it is difficult to define the scope of a country from the collector's standpoint. In Europe there have been sweeping changes in the latter part of the last century, as a result of the re-unification of Germany on the one hand and on the other the fragmentation of the USSR, Yugoslavia and even Czechoslovakia, resulting in many new names appearing in the coin catalogues.

The political changes in Africa have seen many former colonial territories adopting new names. The Congo is a particularly confusing example: the former Belgian Congo became the Democratic Republic of the Congo (1960), then Zaire (1977) and is now the Democratic Republic once more (since 1999). The neighbouring French Congo became the Popular Republic of the Congo and issued coins thus designated until 1993, when the name was changed to the Republic of the Congo.

It is important to note that most general catalogues list coins only from the 18th century onward. The collector delving into the coins of earlier periods therefore has to seek out more specialized handbooks and monographs to get the full story.

Above: Mints now produce country-themed sets of coins to tempt collectors and promote tourism.

Island Coinage

Another fairly manageable group that has considerable appeal is the Pacific islands. Apart from Hawaii (which had its own coins only in the 19th century) and former German New Guinea (pictured), none of these territories has a history of distinctive coinage going back before World War II, and in most cases their coins have only appeared within recent years.

COLLECTING BY GROUP

Rather than concentrating on the coins of a single country, many collectors prefer to study the coins of a group of territories that are related to each other, either geographically or politically. This might mean countries that have a shared colonial or Commonwealth history, or neighbouring countries with a shared language or culture. This approach provides more variety and interest in the collection generally, as well as allowing the collector to develop the theme of common interest, even exploring links in the design and production of the coins themselves.

SHARED IDENTITIES
A prime example of the geopolitical approach is to take a group of modern countries that, on account of their contiguity, have much in common, which is reflected in the development of their coinage. The Scandinavian countries – Denmark, Norway, Sweden and

Below: The "C5" monogram of Christian V of Denmark and Norway (1670–99) appears on the coins of both of these territories (top and middle). Christian V and his son Frederick IV appeared on the same coin of 1699 (bottom), Frederick on the obverse.

Above: Examples of religious imagery include a small cross on both sides of a coin of Canute (top), the hand of God on a penny of Aethelred (middle) and highly pictorial Christian imagery on a Habsburg thaler of Joseph II (bottom).

Finland – provide considerable scope for this kind of treatment. They have a shared cultural heritage, similar languages and a history that has frequently been intertwined.

Although they developed as separate kingdoms they were actually united under Margrethe I of Denmark (1387–1412) in a federation known as the Union of Kalmar. This lasted until 1523 when Gustav Vasa expelled the Danes from Sweden and founded a separate dynasty. Finland remained under Swedish rule until 1809, when it was ceded to Russia and became a separate grand duchy under the tsar.

When Finland gained its independence in 1917 it was the lion rampant emblem of the Vasa kings that became the motif on the coinage. Linguistically, Finland belongs to the Finno-Ugric group (which includes Estonia and Hungary) but there is still a large minority of inhabitants who are linguistically and ethnically Swedish, and ties across the Baltic remain strong.

American Colonial Coins
John Hull and Robert Saunderson operated a mint in Boston, which struck the first American coinage long before the United States gained independence from Britain. It was simply inscribed "NE" (New England) with denominations in Roman numerals, and was followed by coins featuring willow, pine (pictured) or oak trees. The Willow Tree shilling first appeared in 1652, but the other tree designs were not issued until the following decade. However, they all bore that original date to get around the fact that they had not been authorized by Charles II. Maryland, New York, New Jersey and Connecticut also produced coins during this period.

Norway was ceded by Denmark to Sweden in 1814, but resistance from Norwegian nationalists led to its rule as a separate kingdom under the Swedish crown until 1905, when it became a wholly independent sovereign state under Haakon VII, a Danish prince. Ties between the Scandinavian countries were strengthened by the adoption of a common currency based on the krona of 100 öre in 1875.

Below: Russian coinage of 1757 bore the arms of its conquered Baltic kingdoms, Livonia and Estonia.

THE LOW COUNTRIES

Belgium, the Netherlands and Luxembourg are another obvious choice for the subject of a group collection. Today they are separate countries, but they have a common history going back thousands of years to the time when they were settled by the Belgae, a Celtic people.

In the Middle Ages they formed the core of the duchy of Burgundy, which fell under Habsburg rule in the 1490s. The northern part broke away in the 1570s to form the United Provinces (now Holland) while the south became the Austrian Netherlands. By the Congress of Vienna (1815) the whole of the Netherlands was united under the king of Holland, but Belgium seceded in 1830 and Luxembourg was separated from Holland in 1890. Ties remained close and in 1945 they formed a commercial union (Benelux), a forerunner of, and model for, the European Union. Belgium and Luxembourg have had similar currencies (both struck at Brussels) and all three have issued coins in similar designs to commemorate events of common interest.

IMPERIAL COINS

The former territories of the French, Portuguese and British colonial empires are areas with strong political links. The French and Portuguese tended to use uniform motifs for their dependent territories, whereas apart from the profile of the reigning monarch, coins of the dominions and colonies of the British Empire, and later of the Commonwealth, were quite distinctive in their reverse types.

Then there are the colonies that federated. They would have enjoyed their own coins prior to uniting, and thus the colonial coinage can be collected as a separate entity, with or without the coins of the united country. There are quite a number of instances of this, the coins in each case varying considerably in scarcity and expense. At one end of the scale there are the coins of the

Above (clockwise from top left): United Provinces klippe, cut peso from Curaçao, gulden of the Dutch West Indies and thaler of the Austrian Netherlands.

American colonies produced in Massachusetts (1652), Maryland (1659) and New Jersey (1682), followed by the "Rosa Americana" series struck by William Wood at Bath in the early 18th century. Even after the Declaration of Independence in 1776, distinctive coins were circulating in Connecticut, Massachusetts, New Hampshire, New Jersey, New York and Vermont. Some of them were very similar to their British counterparts, with Britannia on the reverse but replacing the effigy of George III with George Washington or a Native American. From 1776 onward there were also various attempts at federal issues, such as the "Nova Constellatio" coppers and the "Fugio" cents, before the emergence of the Federal coinage in 1792. If the numerous tokens that also circulated in the late 18th century were also included, this would be a formidable group indeed.

A similar pattern obtained in British North America, where local issues, mainly bank tokens, were produced in Upper and Lower Canada (modern Ontario and Quebec), New Brunswick, Nova Scotia and Prince Edward Island, before the Confederation in 1867. Prince Edward Island continued to issue its own coins until it joined the Confederation in 1873; Newfoundland had its own coins, until 1947.

Above: A Dutch coin weight being used in the Caribbean. The Dutch economy was boosted by its involvement in the sugar and tobacco plantations there.

RELIGIOUS SYMBOLISM

Just as coins of the Islamic world conformed in design to the belief systems of that religion, across Christendom coins used a common Christian imagery, sometimes in a bid to convert pagans to Christianity and, later, Catholics to Protestantism.

Christian iconography was prevalent on Byzantine coinage, while in northwestern Europe subtle religious symbols appeared on coins in the territories subject to Anglo-Saxon influence. In Scandinavia, prior to the Viking Age, Harald Bluetooth employed Christian symbols on coins as a part of his efforts to convert the Danes. A handful of very rare coins produced around the first millennium depict brooding symbols of divine judgment, such as the hand of God on the English coins of Aelthelred. Nordic and Anglo-Saxon coins were again united in Christian symbolism by the imperial coins of King Canute, which featured the crucifix. This ubiquitous religious icon dominated the "Long-cross" and "Short-cross" pennies that circulated in Britain for centuries.

In later medieval times, Christian imagery was employed to highly picturesque effect on the coins of the great city states of the Habsburg Empire, and also on Italian coins such as those of Venice and the Papacy in Rome.

COLLECTING BY MINT

As an alternative to collecting coins of a particular country, a number of collectors are now examining some interesting and challenging alternatives. Such lateral thinking allows you to cut across national frontiers and find common factors to shape a collection. An obvious one is to study and collect the products of a particular mint. In most cases the larger mints (such as those operated under the US Treasury Department) produce coins only for their own country, or operate on such a global scale that the field would be far too wide, but others make interesting subjects for collections. Some mints have gained contracts to produce coins for territories too small to have their own national mint.

COLLECTING BY MINT-MARK
Collecting coins according to mint can stretch back to the time of the Roman Empire. Many collectors of classical coins, for example, concentrate on the imperial coins struck at the Roman mints in Alexandria, Carthage, Serdica, Constantinople or western Europe. All are clearly identifiable by their mint-marks and inscriptions.

At the other end of the spectrum you could concentrate on the coins that emanated from a particular mint in a

Above: Coins minted by royalist factions during the English Civil War had their own inscriptions, ranging from monograms such as "BR" on coins of the Bristol Mint (top), to motifs such as Oxford plumes on coins of that city (middle) and a lion of York (bottom).

Above: The Birmingham Mint was established in 1860 by Matthew Boulton. It still produces coinage, tokens and medals – like this commemorative issue for the mint itself – for the international numismatic market.

PRIVATE MINTS
This leaves the private mints, which, not being tied to national contracts, offer their services to any country or issuing authority that cares to use them. At one time the Birmingham Mint, the successor to Boulton & Watt's Soho Mint, later known as the Heaton Mint, struck coins for well over a hundred governments from Afghanistan (1886) to Zambia (1968). The company produced the first issues of many countries, from Chile in 1851 and

country where several mints were in simultaneous operation. This might, for example, mean confining your interest to coins bearing the S mark of San Francisco, the aqueduct mark of Segovia in Spain, or the letters A or D that identify coins from Berlin or Munich respectively.

During the English Civil War the Parliamentary forces controlled the mint at the Tower of London. This meant that the Royalists were obliged to rely on various temporary mints established at Aberystwyth, Shrewsbury or Oxford and later mints in a few pockets of resistance and Royalist strongholds such as Chester, Exeter, Truro and York. Identifiable coins from these places are much sought after by those occupied in collecting the antiquities of their own town or county, quite apart from their general numismatic interest.

Below: Imperial Roman coins bearing the mint-marks of Nikomedia (SMN), in what is now Turkey, and Treverorum (TROBS), now Trier in Germany.

Perth Mint

The Perth Mint remained under the jurisdiction of the Royal Mint until 1970, where it was transferred to the authority of the Government of Western Australia. Today the mint still operates from its original building, constructed from limestone extracted from the offshore Western Australian island of Rottnest, and it is one of the oldest mints in the world to do so.

Frequently Changing Designs

While most British coins in everyday use have had unchanged reverse motifs since decimalization in 1971, an exception is the pound coin, which has had a different reverse each year since its inception in 1983. The royal arms (1983) were followed by floral emblems of the four countries comprising the United Kingdom (1984–7), then heraldic motifs and, most recently, landmark bridges of Scotland (Forth railway bridge), Northern Ireland (Belfast–Dublin Railway), Wales (Menai Bridge) and England (Gateshead Millennium Bridge). Of these four architectural giants, the first three were built at various points during the 19th century, whereas the latter, which crosses the River Tyne in Newcastle, opened in 2000 and quickly became the pride of this northerly city.

Left: Pattern obverses of the recent series of pound coins, paired with their pictorial reverses. From left: the famous transport bridges of Scotland, Northern Ireland, Wales and England.

Above: A "basic currency unit" collection centred on the British farthing might include a tin farthing issue of William and Mary (top) and the many imitative tokens (bottom).

Above: The Greek drachma was an ancient currency unit, revived soon after Greece won its independence from Turkey.

value flanked by oak leaves, continued until the advent of the euro in 2001. With annual issues from up to six different mints, identifiable by a code letter, the major types of the mark would form a very large collection.

By contrast, coins with a very similar reverse, but struck in aluminium with the emblem of the German Democratic Republic on the obverse, were not adopted until 1956 and were very sporadically struck thereafter, reflecting the political division and economic disparity of the German states. The "Ostmark" disappeared when Germany was reunited in 1990. Both republics were prolific producers of 2, 5 and 10 mark coins for commemorative and special issues.

BASIC CURRENCY UNITS

Not everyone can afford to collect large, handsome silver dollars and crowns, and many numismatists focus on other, smaller denominations.

In England the "splendid shilling" of 12 pence sterling began with the testoon of Henry VII and survives today as the 5 pence in the decimal series, but it has undergone many changes of design, weight and composition over the centuries, as have its counterparts in the Commonwealth. Even the cent, usually the smallest coin in a currency range, offers immense scope, from humble US pennies to the

Below: Interesting and collectable ephemera often accompanies the introduction of a new denomination coin.

small bronze, steel or aluminium coins of many countries. Other minor issues include the öre coins of Scandinavia or the 1 and 5 centime coins of France. The humble pfennig of Germany was successively struck in copper, aluminium, bronze, zinc, bronze-clad steel and latterly copper-plated steel, reflecting the political and economic upheavals of the 20th century.

Such coins may have little or no spending power alone, but they are vital in making up odd amounts in everyday transactions. British numismatists have a special affection for the farthing (originally the fourth part of a penny). Redundant by 1956, many have survived in generally fine condition because people who got them in change tended to hoard them in jars. Similar hoarding of bronze cents in the USA caused a currency crisis in 1982 when the price of copper rose sharply, and the US Treasury was compelled to replace bronze by a zinc alloy.

Through the Ages

The first £1 coin was minted in 1489 by Henry VIIth. It remained until the £1 note was established in 1915, although the first note had appeared briefly during the Napoleonic wars.

Maxwell House are very pleased to be able to present to you, as one of our special customers, a new £1 coin.

One of the most striking features of the new coin is the inscription on its milled edge "Decus et tutamen", quite unique on British coins. Roughly translated, this means "An ornament and a safeguard".

We hope you will treasure this £1 coin as a memento of this historic occasion.

Your New One Pound Coin

COLLECTING PICTORIAL COINS

While coin obverses have, traditionally, been reserved for portraits – either allegorical or symbolic figures or lifelike effigies of rulers – pictorial reverses have predominated on coins since the very earliest currencies. The splendid silver coins of 16th century Europe – guldengroschen and thaler – stimulated the development of sophisticated pictorial designs by virtue of their large size, and numismatic pictorialism may be said to have attained perfection during the 20th century.

Landmarks of national or religious significance featured on ancient coins and on some of the beautiful city coinage of medieval trading centres, and continue to be commemorated on some of the world's most recent issues. Mythical creatures such as winged deities or dragons have also featured heavily, due to their links with national folklore and identity. Animals – once symbolic of trade and economic strength – remain a popular pictorial theme, though in a world economy that relies more on mechanization than livestock they are now likely to represent a topic such as conservation. Since the 1930s, the fashion for pictorials has become increasingly linked with commemoratives and coins produced for the collectors' market.

Below: A cock and a crab on an ancient Sicilian coin (top), and images of a heraldic bear and lion on medieval coins of Germany and Zealand (bottom).

Above: Many Roman coins feature allegorical figures or landmarks (clockwise from top left): an allegorical depiction of the Tigris and Euphrates with Armenia; the Ara Pacis; a personification of "City" carrying two temples; the market on Caelian Hill.

TWO POSSIBLE APPROACHES

Two recent books, R.G. Penn's *Aspects of Medicine on Ancient Greek and Roman Coins* (Spink & Son, London, 1994) and Marvin Tameanko's *Monumental Coins: Buildings & Structures on Ancient Coinage* (Krause, Iola, 1999), explore two distinct branches of thematic coin-collecting. Tameanko, an architect, has concentrated on coins, mostly from Imperial Rome, that show identifiable buildings, such as temples, shrines, forts and triumphal arches, or engineering structures such as roadways, aqueducts and harbours. His book classifies more than 600 classical coins, featuring such landmarks as the Temple in Jerusalem, the Colosseum and the Acropolis. Two of the Seven Wonders of the World appear: the Pharos of Alexandria (the world's first lighthouse) and the Mausoleum of Halicarnassus, but it is strange that the Hellenistic kingdom of Egypt never depicted the Pyramids or the Sphinx on its coins.

Penn, a doctor of medicine, has adopted a rather different approach and used pictorial coins to illustrate the origins and development of medicine in the ancient world. Certain Greek coins portray Hippocrates and Asklepios (Aesculapius), the real and mythological fathers of medicine, and coins with mythological subjects that have a bearing on the ancient perception of illness and cures. Many coins of both Greek and Roman periods depict medicinal plants. There are also coins advocating sanitation, depicting the goddess Hygeia, healing springs and aqueducts, as well as the Cloaca Maxima (the great Roman sewer) and even Cloacina, goddess of the sewers.

Both these writers have brought to bear their professional expertise to write about their chosen coins. In the same way, many collectors develop a thematic collection that reflects their professional or recreational interests, giving numismatics a new dimension.

OTHER CLASSICAL SUBJECTS

Because so many Greek coins do not bear an inscription identifying their origin, there are books that catalogue them according to their subject-matter, and this has stimulated interest in collecting them in this manner. *Greek Coin Types and Their Identification* by Richard J. Plant (Spink & Son, 1979) is a notable example of this genre. While it was primarily intended as an

Below: Animals are closely linked with perceptions of national identity, and continue to be a popular pictorial subject on modern coins.

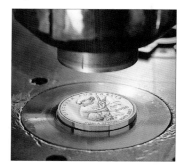

aid to identification, it serves as a very useful basis for a thematic collection. In it you can see at a glance the 116 coins showing Nike, the winged goddess of victory, or the numerous pieces that show helmeted warriors. The pantheon of Greek deities and associated heroes is set out clearly, from Aphrodite and Artemis to Zeus himself.

If animals are your choice, you can find coins showing animals fighting or feeding their young. In antiquity, bulls, either whole or in part, were a popular subject, perhaps an allusion to the value of cattle in the earliest barter economy, but dogs, wolves, sheep and goats are not far behind. Horses were a major subject, as were men on horseback or driving chariots and, of course, Pegasus the winged horse of mythology.

Lions, elephants, tigers and panthers form a veritable numismatic menagerie, while mythical beasts, such as the sphinx and the griffin, are also prominent. Eagles perching or in flight are a colossal subject, rivalling images of lions on coinage right down to the present day. Serpents, dolphins and fishes abound, as well as familiar flora.

Coins That Tell a Story

Several brass denarii of Vespasian and his son Titus have a reverse showing a date palm beneath which a woman sits weeping. To the left of the tree stands the emperor in armour, or a man with his hands tied behind his back – a captive taken in AD 70 when Titus suppressed a Jewish revolt, sacking Jerusalem and destroying the Temple. The sorrowful woman is an allegory for *Judaea capta* (captured) or *devicta* (defeated).

Above (clockwise from top-left): Coins have personified Africa, Helvetica, and Britannia both standing (middle) and seated (bottom), in female form.

MODERN PICTORIAL THEMES

The trend towards more pictorial reverses, which gathered momentum in the 1930s, yielded a good number of coins showing all kinds of shipping, from outrigger canoes to ocean-going liners. Although Germany struck some coins showing the Zeppelin airships, aviation as a theme only took off in 1983 with the celebration of the bicentenary of the first manned balloon flights; it received a tremendous boost in 2000–2, when many coins used the centenary of powered aircraft as an opportunity to show their development from the original Wright Flyer to Concorde. Both warships and military aircraft have been prominent in very recent years, on coins commemorating the military contingents fighting in World Wars and other conflicts.

Many contemporary coins are devoted to animals. Whereas earlier coins in this category merely showed them as typical examples of the fauna of a particular country, today the trend is didactic, highlighting species under threat of extinction. The People's Republic of China even launched its gold bullion series with motifs showing the giant panda, the elusive creature that has become the symbol of the World Wide Fund for Nature.

Above: A stunning medieval bishopric thaler of Münster (top), a landmark on a Turkish million lira coin and a temple on a Thai coin of Rama V.

Many pictorial coins are now issued in long thematic sets, which makes this kind of collecting all too easy. There is much more fun to be had in poring over coin catalogues, seeking out stray items on your favourite theme that will fit into your collection.

Above: This Iranian 1 rial coin is part of a series depicting mosques.

Below: A set of FAO coins issued by North Korea in 2002, depicting various modes of transport by land, sea and air.

COLLECTING PURPOSE OF ISSUE COINS

A major branch of thematic collecting is devoted to coins issued by several countries more or less simultaneously to celebrate a major anniversary of an event or personality of worldwide interest, or to publicize a contemporary event of global importance. These events are often the subject of colourful coins aimed at the collectors' market. The phenomenon of simultaneous or joint issues is relatively new, although there are some topics that, by their cyclical nature, have been the subject of coins from many countries at different times.

COMMEMORATIVES FOR COMMON PURPOSES

Philatelists describe issues by several countries celebrating the same event as omnibus issues. In numismatic terms the earliest instance of this occurred in 1617. The Thirty Years War, which split Europe on religious lines, was about to erupt when several states in Germany, Austria and Switzerland issued silver coins to celebrate the centenary of Martin Luther's Wittenberg Declaration, which launched the Reformation. Similar issues took place in 1717 and 1817. Even at the height of World War I, Saxony managed to

issue a silver 3 mark coin in 1917 under the auspices of the German Empire, but only 100 coins were struck, making this quatercentennial coin the key issue in any collection devoted to the Reformation. Sri Lanka marked 2500 years of Buddhism in 1957 with a set of coins.

BIRTHS, MARRIAGES AND DEATHS

Diana, Princess of Wales, was not the first international figure to be remembered by coins of more than one country. That honour went to John F. Kennedy, who not only replaced Benjamin Franklin on the American half dollar but was also portrayed on a silver 5 riyal coin issued by Sharjah, a remarkable feat since this Gulf sheikhdom had never issued any coins previously and by this gesture flew in the face of the Islamic ban on human representation in any form. The precedent was soon followed by other Gulf States, which produced coins portraying the late President Nasser of Egypt. The portrayal of famous persons, either soon after their death (as in the case of Pope John Paul II) or on a major anniversary, such as a centenary, has now become commonplace.

Above: Austria marked the bicentenary of Mozart's birth with this 1956 coin.

SPORTING EVENTS

Arguably the most important of all events in the numismatic calendar are those pertaining to sports. If shooting is counted as a sport, some of the earliest coins on this theme are those produced in the German states and Switzerland from 1590 onward, as prizes for annual shooting contests. They endured longest in Switzerland, where silver 5 francs and gold 100 francs were struck on behalf of various cantons as late as 1939, Lucerne being the last canton to issue them.

However, the Olympic Games tower over all other sporting events. As long ago as 510 BC distinctive coins for the Games were struck by Elis, the host state. By 480 BC coins showing the winged figure of Nike (Victory) alluded to the athletes who won the events. It is believed that the beautiful large decadrachms of Syracuse dating from about 465 BC were intended as prizes for athletes at the Demareteian Games.

The modern Olympic Games were inaugurated at Athens in 1896, but it was not until they were held in Helsinki that Finland produced special coins in 1951–2 showing the Olympic rings. Since then it has become axiomatic that coins marking the Games are released by the host country, often in lengthy series. Since the 1970s, special coins have also been released by many of the participating countries as well, with separate issues for the Winter Games and Paralympics.

Right: Popular sporting events celebrated on coins include the European and World Cup football championships.

Below: Classical subjects on coins marking the Olympic Games of Berlin (1936) and Athens (2004).

net a tidy sum for a night's work. The most desirable tokens bear the name of the town and dairy (an example from St Kilda, Victoria, recently sold online for $60), but usually they are inscribed or stamped with the initials of the dairy or even the individual milkman, with numerals indicating the number of pints. Now that milk comes in disposable cartons, these tokens are a thing of the past – and very collectable.

TOKENS FOR SLOT MACHINES

Coin-operated public pay-phones were another tempting target for the street bandit and the cost of repairing the damaged equipment induced the authorities in many countries (mainly in continental Europe and Asia) to adopt a system whereby the public purchased tokens from a post office or tobacconist's kiosk. As these could not be exchanged for coins, there was no point in breaking into the machines to steal them. Furthermore, the actual sale price could be varied or increased without the expense of altering the slot machines. Similar tokens were later devised for other machinery that would normally have been activated by a coin in the slot, from parking meters to car-washing and laundry facilities.

Below: Transport tokens from Dunedin, New Zealand (top), and Paris (1921, middle), and a range of American bus or subway tokens (bottom).

Tobacco and Beer Tokens
These brass tokens advertising Samson cigarette tobacco (1987) and Hofmeister Lager not only promoted the products but also represented a small discount off the next purchase.

GAMING TOKENS

Called jetons (from the French *jeter*, "to throw") or counters, gaming tokens have been in existence since the 15th century. They are used as money substitutes in games of chance, although they originated as the metal discs used in medieval accountancy on a chequerboard or counting table (the "exchequer"). Brass counters with an imitation of the heraldic device of so-called Spade guineas, and with the royal titles replaced by such slogans as "In memory of the good old days" were used in early 19th-century Britain.

Gambling chips afford security to casinos as they have no real value until converted into cash. Although most modern chips are made in coloured plastic they may also be found in aluminium, brass or cupro-nickel. Small tokens, also known as pub checks, have been used for games of chance in public houses and entertainment arcades.

TRANSPORT TOKENS

In 1549, metal tokens were adopted at Regensburg to control bridge crossings and to represent a fee levied on those who wished to enter a walled town after the gates were closed for the night. The system spread to the USA in the 1790s, and Pennsylvania was the first state to introduce tollgate tokens on the turnpike highways.

In the 19th century the use of tokens extended to public transport of all kinds, from ferries to trams, buses and

Above: American Civil War soldiers being punished for gambling.

Below: Gambling tokens from the West Point Casino, Tasmania (1974) and the Palm Beach Club, London (1968).

subway systems. They were often given to employees of post offices or other public utilities, enabling them to travel free on company or municipal business. Most bear a civic or corporate emblem, but many modern examples feature vehicles. Associated with them are the tokens used at public lavatories or restrooms in bus and railway stations, where they are given only to bona fide passengers on presentation of a travel ticket. There are also numerous checks, tokens and tallies formerly used by railway companies, coal mines and market traders. Usually utilitarian in design, they are actively collected for their historical interest.

Below: A bronze sugar estate token of Mauritius with the head of Victoria.

COLLECTING COIN LOOKALIKES

Sooner or later every collector acquires one or more puzzle pieces, which look like coins and may even have a name or value inscribed on them but cannot be located in any of the standard catalogues. It seems obvious that such pieces must have had a valid reason for their existence, otherwise why would anyone have gone to all that trouble and expense to manufacture them?

BOGUS COINS

Imitation Spade guineas made of brass instead of gold have already been mentioned. They bore the profile of George III on one side and the royal arms in a spade-shaped shield on the other. Anyone who could read the motto inscribed on the coins – "In memory of the good old days" – would have no problem recognizing these pieces for gaming counters, but trouble arose when unscrupulous people passed them off as real gold guineas (worth 21 shillings, or £1.05) on unsuspecting (and illiterate) members of the public.

In the same category comes a brass piece that very closely resembles the gold sovereign current in the 1830s, with the monarch's effigy on the obverse and a reverse motif which, at first glance, might be mistaken for St George and the Dragon but which actually shows a crowned horseman. In place of the usual inscription are the words "To Hanover", which provide the clue to the identify of this piece. Under Salic Law, which insisted that a male heir must always take precedence,

Below: Plastic play money from Hong Kong of the kind often used to teach children about different denominations.

Above: The obverse and reverse of mid-Victorian model coins struck by Joseph Moore of Birmingham, forerunners of today's bimetallic coins.

Queen Victoria could not succeed to the Hanoverian throne and her place was taken by her unpopular uncle, Prince George, Duke of Cumberland. It is believed that the "Cumberland Jack", as it is commonly known, was produced as a satirical piece, but it was often passed off as a genuine sovereign on the public.

MODEL COINS

At various times in 19th-century Britain the question of reducing the size and weight of the cumbersome copper or bronze coins was debated. The government was always reluctant to take such steps, clinging to the notion that even base metal coins should have an intrinsic metal value that was fairly close to the face value. It took well over a century for the authorities to abandon this notion and introduce the decimal coinage in small sizes, which weighed a fraction of their £sd predecessors.

As a possible solution to the problem, however, Joseph Moore, a Birmingham die-sinker and token manufacturer, produced a model coinage consisting of tiny bronze coins with a plug of silver in the centre. These model coins, portraying Queen Victoria, were intended to improve the

coinage in general, as well as providing pieces whose intrinsic worth was the same as their circulating value. Similar bimetallic model coins were produced by Harry Hyams. These had a brass centre in a bronze surround, and ranged from the crown of 5 shillings (about the size of the modern 2 pence coin) to the halfpenny.

A tiny bronze coin was produced in 1887, with Victoria's profile on one side and St George and the Dragon on the other. The inscription "Jubilee Model Half Farthing" indicates its commemorative nature. Another such item is the diminutive silver piece portraying the infant Prince of Wales (later Edward VII), which was struck as a toy coin shortly after his birth in 1841. Model and miniature coins of this sort were popular as novelties in Christmas crackers during the 19th century.

Very tiny replicas of American coins are sold as souvenirs in the USA. At the other end of the spectrum are gigantic replica coins, often in the form of money-boxes or paperweights.

Spoof Coin

From 1966 until his death in 1987 Leonard Joseph Matchan was lessee of the tiny island of Brecqhou in the Channel Islands. As well as issuing stamps for a local postal service to Sark he created this spoof bronze coin, denominated "one knacker". As it was clearly never intended to be taken seriously, it did not render him liable to prosecution, unlike the owner of Lundy Island, whose coins of 1929 got him into trouble with the law and had to be withdrawn.

Above: "Fantasy" Tibetan coins include this restrike of a quarter rupee by the Shanghai Mint (top) and a Sichuan fantasy dollar (bottom).

PLAY MONEY

Tiny replicas of current coins are produced in many countries for use as toy shop or dolls' money. Long ignored by numismatists, these pieces were sought out by collectors of dolls' house furniture and the like, but have now attracted the attention of coin collectors as well. Actual-size toy money, for teaching children arithmetic and the basics of shopping, is also collectable.

During the transitional period from sterling to decimal currency in Britain (1968–71) many types of instructional

Below: The publicity campaign that preceded British decimalization was aimed at businesses as well as the public, with measures taken, such as the release of 'play' coins, to ease the passing of the old currency system. In the event, the reforms were implemented within weeks.

money were produced, in plastic, metal or stout card, and these are now keenly collected as mementos of the greatest currency reform in Britain since Roman times. They were surpassed, however, by the instructional kits produced in the 12 European countries that adopted the euro in 2002. In many instances the kits, which included imitation coins, were supplied to every household.

FANTASY COINS

In 1925 a businessman, Martin Coles Harman, purchased Lundy, an island in the Bristol Channel, and proceeded to issue his own stamps. In 1929 he went so far as to issue his own coins, with his profile on one side and a puffin on the other. Because they were in the same metal, size and weight as the contemporary British penny and halfpenny, Harman was prosecuted under the Coinage Act of 1870, convicted and fined £5. The coins were withdrawn, but the dies were later used for an issue dated 1965, raising funds to preserve the island as a nature sanctuary.

In 1976, the self-styled Prince Leonard of the Hutt River Province (actually a sheep range in Western Australia) issued coins, from the aluminium 5 cents to the gold $100, which gained catalogue status, but not for long.

In Asia, the number of forged countermarks on Sichuan rupees and Tibetan coins during the early 20th century is such that a leading expert on Chinese coinage, Wolfgang Bertsch, self-published an entire volume dedicated to *Tibetan Fake Coins and Fantasy Countermarks* in 2003.

ELONGATES

Not really a coin lookalike but a novel way of converting a coin into a tourist souvenir or advertising piece, the elongate was invented by the American, Frank Brazzell, who also produced the machines to create them. The coin is

placed between two rollers, on one of which is engraved a motif. When the handle is turned the coin emerges in an elongated shape with the original obverse and reverse removed and a new image on one side. Thousands have been produced in the USA. Often termed elongate or 'flat' pennies, they feature a broad range of subjects, from publicity for local businesses to whole series on dinosaurs or baseball heroes. The idea eventually took root in Britain in 1981, when the law forbidding the defacement of coins was repealed. Elongates are now also popular souvenirs in France, Germany and other European countries, and often feature famous landmarks.

Above and left: A 2 euro plastic token and a German elongate from a 5 pfennig coin, as a souvenir of St Bartholomä's Church on the Königssee.

Below: A cased set of miniature replicas of American coins.

COLLECTING ERRORS AND VARIETIES

Serious collectors love to acquire items that are in some way off the beaten track or out of the ordinary. They look out for subtle differences in apparently similar coins, as well as various types of errors that arise in the course of manufacture but somehow get into general circulation, and sundry oddities such as coins hastily withdrawn from circulation because of a mistake in design.

DIE VARIATIONS

Right back in the days of the earliest hammered coinage, it soon became apparent that both the hammer and the anvil were liable to show signs of wear after the first few hundred coins had been struck. In many cases the designs engraved on the parts that actually struck the blanks could be sharpened up by re-engraving all or part of the surface. No matter how carefully this was done it gave rise to slight changes in the appearance of the coins.

As one side tended to wear out sooner than the other, scholars have often been able to trace the sequence of production by the combination of obverse and reverse impressions during the production of a particular coin. Hoards can often be a good source of large quantities of coins for such detailed studies.

This phenomenon is by no means confined to hammered coinage. Modern coins are produced in their millions, entailing the production of hundreds of dies. Theoretically, they should be identical but, inevitably, variations large and small tend to creep in. Sometimes these variations are quite deliberate, a prime example being the British gold sovereigns with shield

Left: This mis-struck Indian rupee of 1984 makes a curious sight, with its design around 75% off-centre.

Above: A cupro-nickel 1 baht coin of Thailand, with the design struck approximately 10 per cent off-centre.

reverse from 1863 to 1874, which bear tiny numbers engraved between the rose at the foot of the design and the knot tying the two laurel branches. All Shield-back sovereigns in this period should have a number ranging from 1 to 123 (though far fewer numbers were used in many years, while others may exist but have not yet been recorded). Some sovereigns of 1863 were issued without die numbers before the scheme started, and the same is true of 1874 coins after the practice was abandoned, but coins dated 1872 without die numbers are not uncommon. Conversely, a few sovereigns of 1863 have been discovered with the tiny numerals 827 impressed on the truncation of Queen Victoria's neck. Michael Marsh, the recognized authority on the gold sovereign, has recorded two examples with the die number 22 on the reverse and four without the die number, making the 827 coin one of the greatest rarities of British coinage.

Much more common are coins in the American series with the last digit of the date overstruck, a practice of the US Mint in the 19th century to change the date in line with federal law, which required coins to bear the actual year of striking. American coins also exhibit such die variations as large or small numerals. The coins of most countries feature die variants, ranging from slight changes in the actual design (such as the high and low horizons on British pennies) to the number of serrations in the edge, or the number of beads in the border of the rim.

Above: Victorian Shield-back sovereigns bearing die variation marks 36 and 52.

ERRORS

Accidents in manufacture give rise to some peculiar errors. A "brockage" is a coin with only one design, normal on one side and appearing incuse on the other. This occurs when a coin already struck adheres to the die and strikes the next blank to pass through the press. "Clash marks" are mirror-image traces on a coin struck by a pair of dies that have been damaged by having been struck together without a blank between them. Other mis-strikes occur

Below: Tibetan local government issues struck using different dies.

Above: A curved clip on a Sudanese 10 ghirsh coin of 1980.

Right: A British 10 pence struck by the Royal Mint in the scalloped collar of the Hong Kong $2, one of a batch shipped out to the colony, where the error was discovered.

when the dies are not properly aligned, and the design on one or both sides of the coin appears to be off-centre.

Such errors are ephemeral and are usually of little more than curiosity value. Much more interesting and desirable are hybrid coins, known to collectors as "mules", in which the obverse is not matched with its regular or official reverse. Mules have been recorded from Roman times, the obverse referring to one emperor and the reverse referring to a predecessor or another member of the imperial family. Accidental mules in recent times have resulted from the mixing of dies at mints where coins of several countries are being struck. This gives rise to such famous mules as the Coronation anniversary crowns with Ascension and Isle of Man dies, or 2 cent coins with Bahamas and New Zealand dies. Restrikes of rare American coins have been detected in which the dated die has been paired with the wrong reverse, such as the 1860 restrike of the rare large cent of 1804.

Sometimes the wrong collar is used, the most spectacular examples being British 10 pence coins with a scalloped edge, which actually got into circulation in Hong Kong as $2 coins before the error was detected.

COUNTERMARKS

There have been many occasions on which marks have been applied to coins after they were issued, analogous to overprints on stamps. This is a normal procedure in cases where the value of the original coin has to be changed, and it was a widespread practice in Britain in 1800–4, when Spanish and other foreign coins were stamped with the effigy of George III to pass current for 5 shillings. The Bank of England even overstruck Spanish coins with a new obverse and Britannia on the reverse, but traces of the original design usually showed through.

Unofficial countermarks make an unusual sideline. Although it was a serious offence to deface coin of the realm it was common practice to engrave or strike pennies with a lover's initials. In some cases more elaborate motifs, such as entwined hearts, were stamped. In Northern Ireland, many British and

Above: Mules, pairing Italian and Russian rulers from a 20 lira coin of 1863 and 20 kopeks of 1867 (top) and colonial issues for Sierra Leone (obverse, bottom left) and Macao (right), mistakenly paired in the 1790s.

Irish coins of recent years have been countermarked by the IRA, UDA, UVF and other paramilitary factions, a curious memento of the "Troubles".

A particularly large and fascinating group consists of Spanish coins, or more often pieces of them, countermarked with values and the initials of various islands in the Caribbean, officially authorized as currency there, mainly in the 18th and early 19th centuries, before the introduction of a more regular coinage.

Below: Pennies of George III and George V with engraved or punch-marked letters, perhaps intended as love tokens. One has the incuse stamp of a broad arrow, an official government mark but here applied quite illegally.

Countermarked Dollars

At the end of the 18th century there was a severe shortage of silver coins in Britain. A large quantity of Spanish-American dollars (8 reales) had been captured and these were pressed into service, circulating as 5 shilling pieces and officially authorized by means of a countermark consisting of the bust of George III in an oval, or later octagonal, frame.

COLLECTING PATTERNS, PROOFS AND EPHEMER

Serious numismatists are not content with the coins that actually circulate, but also seek out pieces that trace the development of a coin from the earliest concept to the finished article, as well as the various versions produced by mints to supply the collectors' market, and even the packaging and promotional material associated with each new issue.

PATTERNS

Pieces resembling coins, prepared by the mint to the specifications of a new design or on the authorization of the coin-issuing authority, but differing in some respect from the coin that actually reaches the general public, are known as patterns. This category also includes pieces produced by mints when tendering for a coinage contract – an actual piece of metal being a much more effective sales tool than a sketch or a photograph.

Patterns may differ from the final coins as issued in the type or quality of metal used, but more often than not they differ in details of the design. Sometimes these differences may be

Below: A presentation folder from Estonia with a proof set of coins encased, 1999.

quite minor, such as the addition of some small detail, but they may be quite radical, or show entirely different motifs to those used for the issued coins. Patterns, especially if they exist in a sequence, are of particular use in illustrating the evolution of the coin.

Allied to them are the test pieces that occur when a new die is being tried out prior to going into actual production. These have a superficial resemblance to coins, in that they are usually struck on blanks of the correct weight and size, but the impression may vary from a mere ghostly outline to a nearly perfect image as the minter adjusts the machinery. Many test pieces, however, are known in lead or some other soft metal, pulled as the engraving of the dies is in progress, in order to make sure that no mistakes have arisen.

PROOFS

The die test pieces were, in fact, the true origin of proofs, but by the 19th century it had become standard mint practice to make impressions of coins on specially polished blanks for presentation purposes, and in more recent years this has become just another medium for selling coins to collectors.

Above: A 17th-century Christiania pattern silver strike of a gold coin.

Left: A pattern produced by VDM (a German manufacturer of coin blanks), with a reverse depicting the fortress of Altena, where the company is located.

The practice has now reached the point at which many deluxe coins are released only in proof form. They are undeniably very handsome but some purists are interested only in coins that actually get into general use, and some catalogues classify proofs of this kind as "non-circulating legal tender" (NCLT). One suspects that many of these beautiful pieces have never been accorded legal tender status.

PIEDFORTS

Derived from the French for "heavy or strong foot", the term "piedfort" denotes a coin struck with normal dies but on a blank of a much greater thickness than usual. The practice originated in France in the 15th century, when gold coins of twice or three times the normal thickness were struck for presentation to royalty, courtiers and foreign dignitaries. It spread to England in the reign of Henry VII. Examples of the gold sovereign, introduced in 1489, are known in double or treble weights. So far, only one of each has been recorded, and it is assumed that the king intended them as presentation pieces rather than high-value coins for general circulation.

This practice, long dormant, has been revived by the Royal Mint in recent years. The 50 pence coin, normally struck in cupro-nickel, was

Eestis emiteerib münte Eesti Pank. Eesti Pank on asutatud 1919. aastal. Pank tegutses 1940. aastani, mil Eesti okupeeriti Noukogude Liidu poolt. Panga tegevus taastati 1990. aastal. Mündivoldikus on esitatud Eesti kaibemündid, mis lastakse ringlusesse 1999. aastal.

5 krooni   5 krooni
1 kroon   50 senti
20 senti   10 senti

this era rigid plastic cases were adopted, the coins within them being inserted into stout cards printed with the national arms and salient details. In other examples the coins were merely encapsulated in thin plastic envelopes, although in some cases these were then inserted in paper envelopes with stiffener cards bearing descriptions of the coins. The current trend is towards much brighter, more colourful coin folders, which can be housed intact in coin albums. Different forms of packaging are often used, distinguishing between simple sets of circulating coins, sets in a superior finish but still in base metal, and the deluxe proofs in precious metals.

Two other recent developments seek to draw the sister hobbies of philately and numismatics closer together. Both originated in Germany, where coins and stamps have long been collected by the same people. The first is the philanumismatic cover, examples of which are now produced all over the world, while the second is the *Numisblatt*, which has so far made little headway beyond the country of origin. It consists of a stiff colour-printed card bearing stamps with special cancellations, with a coin encapsulated for good measure. *Numisblätter* are very similar to PNCs but are generally much larger and more decorative.

Above: A piedfort silver jeton depicting the assassination of William of Orange in 1584 (top) and a gold coronation jeton of Moscow.

original artists' thumbnail sketches reflecting the initial design concept for a coin are very desirable but are understandably rare. Such items are keenly fought over when they occasionally appear in the auction rooms.

Below: Collectable ephemera might even include hand-held beam balances and brass coin weights; such pocket balances were a must in the days of coin-clipping to check that coins were of full weight.

released in 1973 as a silver piedfort but only about 20 pieces were produced and they now command four-figure prices. Even the small 20 pence coin, introduced in 1982, was issued as a piedfort silver proof and this is now standard practice for pound coins (whose designs are changed each year) and commemorative 50 pence coins.

PACKAGING
Traditionally, proofs and year sets were tastefully packaged in leather cases lined with blue satin or plush. While this is still the case for the more expensive items, most mints have resorted to other forms of packaging, which are not only cheaper but more eye-catching. The vogue developed in the 1960s when year sets became fashionable. In

Below: A Dutch bronze pattern coin of William III tendering two possible reverse designs.

EPHEMERA
Serious collectors also watch out for the various pieces of ephemera associated with coins. These range from press cuttings and leaflets about new or forthcoming issues to mini-posters used by banks. Coins incorporated in premium giveaways or advertising gimmicks are also worth considering. Even chocolate packaged in metal foil stamped to resemble coins is collectable – assuming you can withstand the temptation to eat the contents.

Acts of Congress or other parliamentary bodies authorizing coins, as well as government reports on proposed changes, are also eminently collectable. Photographs and the

BUYING AND SELLING COINS

Although it is possible to form a collection from coins picked up in change or in the course of foreign travel, sooner or later you are more likely to want to start planning acquisitions in order to add to your collection in a meaningful way. There are several ways of acquiring new specimens: by exchange with fellow collectors, from dealers and by bidding at auction.

COIN CLUBS
All collectors inevitably accumulate material that is surplus to their requirements: such coins can very often be exchanged with fellow enthusiasts and new items added to the collection in return. If you are at all serious about your hobby, you will want to subscribe to a periodical devoted to the subject, and through it you can make contact with others through the small ads. You can also place an advertisement yourself stating what you have to offer and what you are looking for in exchange.

Most towns of any size have a coin club or numismatic society. Joining such a club gives you the chance to

Fairs and Forums
National societies such as the American Numismatic Assocation are extremely active at local level, organizing events ranging from coin marts to seminars on the role of coins in education and research. These occasions offer collectors a great opportunity to interact.

meet other collectors and swap coins. Your public library or museum will have information on clubs in the area, as will coin collectors' magazines. Many countries have a national numismatic society, perhaps with a website, which may be able to advise on local societies. Failing this, try an internet search.

Some clubs set aside time before or after each meeting for swapping, and in many cases one or more dealers will be in attendance. Others confine this activity to auctions once or twice a year. Apart from the chance to add to your collection, a coin club is the ideal venue to broaden your interests and improve your knowledge of coins.

Many of the larger numismatic societies host regular exhibitions and talks, and will be able to advise on the programme of events for the coming months. Some have extensive libraries of coins and other research facilities open to the public, or to members.

BUYING FROM DEALERS
A measure of how the hobby has grown in recent years is the increasing number of coin dealers operating in many European countries and elsewhere in the world, while the USA (which always had many more coin dealers than other countries) has retained its position in this respect.

Many dealers regularly take classified advertisements in coin magazines and are also fully listed in the various coin yearbooks and trade directories. A number of websites provide details of dealers who specialize in the coins of a particular country, region, period, denomination, or theme. The fact that the majority of dealers – from international companies specializing in tax-free gold to smaller-scale collectors offering information on their speciality and the opportunity to buy – now operate over the web means that the location of an outlet is much less important than in the past. As a result, it's possible to view images of and information about, and

Above: National numismatic bodies often promote clubs at local level and offer searchable, on-line directories.

purchase, coins from anywhere in the world, greatly increasing the possibilities for making new acquisitions.

BOURSES AND FAIRS
These radical changes in trading practice, combined with high overheads, have meant that the number of actual coin shops has dwindled, but at the same time buying coins by mail order has escalated dramatically and many dealers now send out regular lists to their clients. In addition, there are now many bourses, fairs and dealer circuits, giving collectors and dealers frequent opportunities to meet face to face.

Below: You may be fortunate enough to live in a town with a local coin shop, where you can purchase coins and kit.

THE WORLD DIRECTORY OF COINS

This chapter provides a historical survey of coins across the whole world, from antiquity to the present day. Each section delves into the coins of a particular continent and, within these parameters, the coins of individual countries, or a group of nations that are related politically or geographically. Coins often chart interesting developments, among them the establishment and subsequent break-up of empires, the fight for supremacy among dynastic rulers, the arrival of religious or political doctrines from foreign lands, or the changing economic fortunes of once-prosperous, but later war-ravaged, nations. In the modern age, coins reflect the efforts of new republics to wrest themselves free of colonial power, or the rise and fall of Communism in the Soviet Union, Czechoslovakia and Yugoslavia. There are denominations that have become influential via foreign trade, or currencies born of economic unions among impoverished nations in Africa and South America. There are coins made of the precious metals favoured in centuries past, but gradually replaced by cheaper alloys. Each continental section includes a thematic feature with coins that reflect the culture, art or history of a particular region, and these offer rational options for building superior global collections.

Left: Piecing together the identity of your coins is one of the most enjoyable parts of the hobby.
Above, left to right: iconic silver coinage of newly-independent Mexico, gold trading ducat of Habsburg Hungary, the first 'struck' copper coinage of the central Chinese mint.

AMERICA

The earliest coinage consisted of crude pesos struck in the Spanish colonies from locally mined silver. The *peso a ocho reales* (8 real piece) later became the standard currency medium throughout the French and British colonies in North America and laid the foundation for the dollar system.

CANADA

One of the world's largest countries, Canada was colonized by the French after 1534. Although John Cabot discovered Newfoundland in 1497, it was not annexed by England until 1583, and no attempt was made to colonize it until 1610. Britain formally acquired Hudson's Bay, Newfoundland and Nova Scotia in 1713 and gained control of New France in 1763 after a decisive victory at Quebec in 1759. The early colonists used French, English, Spanish or Dutch coins, but suffered frequent shortages of money from France and resorted to using playing cards, stamped locally. In 1670 silver coins denominated in sols were struck at the Paris Mint, specifically for use in New France, but were unpopular as they could not be used to buy supplies from France. A second attempt to provide a purely local coinage was made in 1721, when the mint at La Rochelle struck copper deniers, but they were no more successful. The British colonies were supplied with gold and silver coins from England, but subsidiary coinage was in the form of tokens struck by the major banks. Federal coinage was adopted in 1870, following the Confederation of Canada in 1867. New Brunswick, Nova Scotia and Prince Edward Island issued copper or bronze coins before joining the Confederation in 1873, while Newfoundland had its own coins until 1949, when it joined Canada.

Left: The dollar of 1982, celebrating the 125th anniversary of Confederation, reproduces the painting entitled The Fathers of Confederation *by Robert Harris, showing delegates at the Quebec Conference of 1864, which led to the unification of the colonies in British North America.*

BANK TOKENS

From 1800 the chronic shortage of coins from Europe led tradesmen to issue copper tokens, but these were gradually suppressed from 1835 and replaced by copper or bronze tokens issued by the major banks. The first of these were the Bouquet Sous of the Bank of Montreal [1–2], followed by issues in Quebec showing the bank emblem with a farmer or bank building on the reverse [3], though the last issue had the farmer on the obverse and an allegorical scene on the reverse [4]. The Bank of Upper Canada (now Ontario) struck pennies and halfpence in 1850–7, with St George and the Dragon on one side and the bank's arms on the other [5–6]. The tokens were withdrawn in 1858, when bronze cents were introduced for the whole province of Canada.

PROVINCIAL COINAGE

Copper or bronze halfpence and pennies were issued by the Maritime Provinces before they joined the Confederation. New Brunswick had coins showing Queen Victoria on the obverse [7] and a shipping scene on the reverse, while Nova Scotia had coins featuring a Scottish thistle on one side and busts of George IV or Victoria on the other [8]. Both colonies also struck cents in the 1860s. Prince Edward Island produced only a single coin, a cent of 1871 [9–10], before joining the Confederation in 1873, but Newfoundland [11–12] had its own coins until 1949.

DEFINITIVES

The coins of the Confederation bear the effigy of the reigning monarch to this day. Prior to 1935 the reverses showed the value in words, set within a wreath and surmounted by a crown, but in 1920 a small cent was adopted with maple leaves flanking the value; two years later the nickel 5 cents replaced the tiny silver coin [13]. In 1937 a pictorial series was adopted: the reverses showing maple leaves (1 cent), beaver (5 cents), the schooner *Bluenose* (10 cents), caribou (25 cents) and national arms (50 cents) continue to this day [14–18]. The silver dollar first appeared in 1935, celebrating the silver jubilee of George V, and its motif of a Voyageur canoe was retained until 1987, when it was replaced by a circulating coin in aureate-bronze plated nickel depicting a loon [19]. A bimetallic $2 coin showing a polar bear was added in 1996 [20]. Gold coins began with a Canadian version of the British sovereign (1908–19) alongside $5 and $10 coins (1912–14). Gold bullion coins in the Maple Leaf series have appeared since 1983.

BULLION COINS

Canada is one of the world's leading producers of precious metals, and this inspired the development of the Maple Leaf in 1979, a coin containing a troy ounce of pure gold, originally struck to a fineness of .999. The reverse featured the national emblem, hence its name. The legal tender value of $50 appeared on the obverse. Since 1983 this coin has been struck in .9999 fine – "four nines gold" – which appears alongside the maple leaf. In addition to smaller gold coins, Canada has also produced platinum bullion coins since 1988.

From Barter to Beaver

Relics of the days when Canada's chief industry was fur trapping are the coins struck by the Hudson's Bay Company. These brass pieces, with the arms of the company on the obverse, had a cryptic reverse showing ligated H B over E M, then 1 or a fraction, with N B at the foot. The last initials were actually an error for M B ("made beaver") and denoted a value in terms of prime beaver pelts, which were highly prized for men's hats.

COMMEMORATIVE COINS

From 1935 the silver dollar was the preferred medium for commemorative coins, but since 1943 Canada has also produced many as base-metal circulating coins, beginning with the 5 cent coins in tombac brass or chromium-plated steel instead of nickel (which was required for the war effort). These substitutes featured the V-sign and had a victory slogan in Morse code around the rim [21–22]. The bicentennial of the nickel industry (1951) resulted in a special 5 cent coin, and this set the precedent for the entire series from 1 cent to $1, with motifs and double dates to celebrate the centennial of Confederation (1967).

More recently, 5 and 25 cent coins [23] have often been used as commemoratives, notably the 1992 series of provincial quarters [24] to mark the 125th anniversary. Special issues have proliferated since the 1970s, notably the series for the Montreal Olympics (1973–6) and the Calgary Winter Games (1985–7) [25–26], and the 150th anniversary of Toronto [27]. Gold and platinum have also been used in recent years for coins in thematic sets featuring Canadian wildlife.

UNITED STATES DEFINITIVES

Although the Continental Congress of 1777 resolved to establish a national mint, it was not until 1792 that the first mint was opened in Philadelphia. Up to that time the currency was chaotic, with base-metal subsidiary coins valued in pence or halfpence and silver based on the Spanish dollar. In common parlance the Spanish real was known as a "bit", and a quarter dollar was known as a "two-bit coin", a term still used to signify 25 cents. From the outset however, the infant United States adopted a decimal system (following the examples of Russia and France), although the original 10 cent piece soon changed its name from "disme" to "dime". An interesting feature of United States coins is the inclusion of initials denoting the various branch mints, which were set up to refine and coin gold and silver mined locally. This practice survives to this day, although most US coins are now confined to base alloys.

Left: Among the prototypes for a distinctive American coinage were the coins that have acquired the nickname of Fugio Cents, from the Latin word meaning "I fly" inscribed over a sundial. This reminder that time flies and the more trenchant legend "Mind Your Business" are believed to have been suggested by Benjamin Franklin. The reverse shows 13 rings, symbolizing the original states.

STATES OF THE CONFEDERATION

From the Declaration of Independence in 1776 until the introduction of a federal coinage in 1792, it was left to individual states to produce subsidiary coins. Massachusetts struck cents and half cents depicting a Native American and the eagle [1–2], but others, notably Connecticut, New Hampshire, New York and Vermont, imitated British and Irish coins, often with busts of George Washington laureated in the Roman manner and looking suspiciously like George III [3]. Even the seated Britannia was only slightly modified for many of the reverses.

EARLY COINS

The first coins consisted of cents and half cents, followed by silver dollars [5–6], half dollars [7–8] and half dimes (5 cents) in 1794, and the dime [11–12] and quarter dollar [13] in 1795. The half cent vanished in 1857 when the size of the cent was considerably reduced [4]. The remaining six denominations have continued ever since, although now for all practical purposes only the coins from 1–25 cents generally circulate. Some odd values have been struck from time to time, including the bronze 2 cents (1864–73) [14–15], the silver 3 cents with a shield in a star (1851–73) [16] and a larger piece in nickel with a head of Liberty and the value in Roman numerals (1865–89) [17–18]. Between 1875 and 1878, 20 cent coins appeared briefly, showing a seated figure of Liberty on the obverse and an eagle on the reverse.

The silver half dime, with the seated Liberty on one side [9] and the value in words on the other [10], continued until 1873 but was challenged in 1866 by a larger coin minted in nickel with a shield obverse and the value in numerals on the reverse. Both coins circulated side by side for several years and the latter acquired the nickname – nickel – by which it is still commonly known today, even though the circulating "silver" coins (dimes, quarters and half dollars) have been produced in a similar alloy since 1964.

The mid-19th century gold rush had a massive impact on US coinage, reflected by the dominance of gold in the eagle ($10), the double eagle ($20) [21–22] and its subdivisions of half ($5) and quarter ($2.50), deriving its name from the reverse motifs, which showed an American eagle in various guises, either heraldic or flying [19–20] or even walking. As if this were not sufficient, the 19th century saw tiny gold dollars as well as $2, $3, $4 and $50 denominations, though some of these were intended for commemorative purposes. Following the California gold rush of 1849, gold coins of 50 cents or $1 were struck locally in addition to the federal gold dollars. Many of these tiny coins were octagonal in shape and fairly basic in design [23].

MODERN COINS

Although the figure or profile of Liberty dominated American coins for many years, there were some attempts to replace her with other motifs. When the size of the cent was reduced in 1857 Liberty was replaced by a flying eagle, followed two years later by the head of a Native American wearing a war bonnet [30]. This motif continued until 1909, when it was replaced by a bust of Abraham Lincoln, marking the centenary of his birth [24]. Almost a century later it is still in use, second only to the world's longest-running coin design – Pistrucci's St George and the Dragon on the British gold coins. In 1943 cents were struck in zinc-coated steel [24–25]. In 1959, on Lincoln's 150th anniversary, the ears of wheat [25–26] were replaced by a Lincoln Memorial reverse [27–28].

The Indian Head Penny, as it is commonly known, inspired the changes made to the nickel in 1913,

Above: The profile of Dwight D. Eisenhower on the dollar of 1971.

When Precious Metal Replaced Base Alloy

Between 1942 and 1945 the nickel was actually struck in silver. It may not be a precious metal but nickel was vital to the war effort, hence its replacement by coins containing 35 per cent silver alloyed with copper and manganese. To distinguish the silver from the nickel coins a mint-mark was placed above the dome on the reverse; these marks included a P – the first (and for many years the only) time the coins from the main mint at Philadelphia had been thus distinguished.

when pictorial motifs were used for both sides. James Earle Fraser produced the head of a Native American chief based on profiles of John Tree, Iron Tail and Two Moon, but the "buffalo" on the reverse (which gives this coin its nickname) was actually Black Diamond, the American bison in the New York Zoo. In 1938 it was replaced by designs portraying Thomas Jefferson (obverse) and his home, Monticello (reverse). Nostalgia being what it is, the Buffalo reverse was revived in 2005.

George Washington [29] replaced Liberty on the quarter in 1932, the bicentenary of his birth, while Franklin D. Roosevelt was the first president to receive this honour barely months after his death [31]. Similarly, Kennedy (1964) and Eisenhower (1971) appeared on the half dollar and dollar, the former replacing Benjamin Franklin and the Liberty Bell, which had graced the half dollar since 1948.

AMERICAN COMMEMORATIVE AND SPECIAL ISSUES

Although the United States was one of the first countries to produce commemorative coins (1893), this practice was overdone in the 1920s and 1930s to such an extent that it was virtually abandoned in 1938. No fewer than 48 different half dollars were produced in this first period, but with variants in date and mint-mark the total rose to 142, which collectors eventually protested at as being excessive. In the same period there was one quarter and one silver dollar, plus a pair of quarter eagles and two massive $50 gold coins. Apart from three circulating, double-dated coins celebrating the bicentenary of the Declaration of Independence (1976), commemoratives were not generally revived until 1982. Output since then has far exceeded that of the first period.

Left: The United States struck a number of gold commemoratives for the Pan-Pacific Exposition in 1915, marking the opening of the Panama Canal. Many, like these half-dollar coins, had typically ornate designs.

Among the most collectable, however, are the gold $50 coins struck at San Francisco in 1915, which circulated in circular and octagonal versions [1–4].

EARLIEST COMMEMORATIVES

The first half dollars appeared in 1892 to celebrate the 400th anniversary of Columbus's voyage to America, as well as to publicize (and help finance) the Columbian Exposition in Chicago. This opened in 1893, hence coins of both dates were issued [7–8]. The half dollar bears the bust of Columbus on one side and on the other his flagship *Santa Maria* above the twin globes representing the hemispheres. The Ladies Committee of the Exposition pressed for a coin of their own, resulting in the silver quarter portraying Queen Isabella. Tiny gold dollars were struck between 1903 and 1922 to mark the centenaries of the Louisiana Purchase and the birth of Ulysses Grant [5–6]. William McKinley, assassinated in 1901, had the unusual distinction of appearing on one of the Louisiana coins of 1903 as well as coins of 1916–17 with his memorial on the reverse. The last of these tiny pieces marked the inauguration of Grant's memorial. Gold quarter eagles appeared in 1915 for the Pan-Pacific Exposition celebrating the completion

of the Panama Canal, and in 1926 for the 150th anniversary of Philadelphia as the cradle of the Revolution. A silver dollar bearing the conjoined profiles of Washington and Lafayette appeared in 1900.

SILVER HALF DOLLARS

A silver half dollar was included in the set of 1915 marking the Pan-Pacific Exposition, but no further commemoratives of this denomination appeared until 1918, when the centennial of the state of Illinois was marked by a coin portraying Lincoln and an eagle [12–13]. Two years later the tercentenary of the Pilgrim Fathers was marked by coins showing a Pilgrim (obverse) and the *Mayflower* (reverse). In the same year a coin celebrated the state of Maine, with its arms on the obverse and the value on the reverse, establishing the precedent for several others commemorating statehood anniversaries [14–17]. Native Americans featured on the reverse of the Missouri Centennial half dollar in 1921 (with frontiersman) [18–19], and on the obverse of the Oregon Trail memorial in 1926 (with covered wagon on reverse)

The Spirit of '76

Although the definitive obverses were retained in 1976, the quarter, half and dollar bore the double date 1776–1996, with entirely new motifs on the reverse. A drummer boy of the Continental Army and Independence Hall, Philadelphia, graced the quarter and half respectively, while the dollar featured the Liberty Bell with a full Moon in the background, alluding to the recent Apollo missions.

[20–21]. Ulysses Grant was again commemorated on a half dollar of 1922 [10–11]. In the early years the events honoured were relatively important and included the Huguenot-Walloon tercentenary (1924) and the 150th anniversary of Cook's landing in Hawaii (1928), but by 1930 the pace of issues was escalating as the importance of the events diminished: even individual towns petitioned Congress for coins to mark their anniversaries. This reached its nadir in 1936, when no fewer than 16 coins appeared, celebrating the centenary of Bridgeport, Connecticut, the opening of the Bay Bridge linking San Francisco and Oakland, and even the opening of the Cincinnati Music Center [22–23]. More portentously, a silver half dollar was struck in preparation for the 75th anniversary of the Battle of Gettysburg in 1938. It featured conjoined busts on the obverse, plus two

shields flanking a fasces (the ancient Roman symbol for authority and power over life and death) on the reverse.

Not only were these issues too frequent, but rumours of manipulation and speculation brought the programme into disrepute. Nevertheless, they are handsome examples of the numismatic art, and most are now quite expensive because the average mintage was very small. The post-World War II exceptions, honouring Booker T. Washington and George Washington Carver, were produced in plentiful quantities on a nationwide basis, and were even reissued in subsequent years to satisfy public demand.

MODERN COMMEMORATIVES

After a gap of almost three decades commemorative half dollars resumed in 1982, to mark the 250th anniversary of the birth of George Washington. Since then, they have been used sparingly, for the centenary of the Statue of Liberty, the bicentenary of Congress, Mount Rushmore's golden jubilee, the 450th anniversary of Columbus, the Bill of Rights and World War II.

The shape of things to come was manifest in the coins launched in 1983 for the forthcoming Olympic Games in Los Angeles, followed by coins for the 1994 World Cup soccer championship, hosted by the USA and, more recently, the Centennial Olympic Games in Atlanta. The last were celebrated by no fewer than six gold $5, ten silver dollars and six cupro-nickel half dollars [24–27]. Apart from these Olympic coins, half dollars have not been issued since 1996. The preferred denomination is the silver dollar, retaining its traditional size and weight.

Modern commemorative issues are much more prolific than the pre-war half dollars but tend to be restricted to events and personalities of national or international importance. Particularly poignant are the 1994 coins honouring US prisoners of war and Vietnam veterans. By contrast, the USA is now following Canada's example, with low-value circulating commemoratives [9].

THE STATE QUARTERS OF 1999–2008

Certain American coins, notably the commemorative half dollars of the early 20th century, alluded to particular states, but this was haphazard and piecemeal. Conversely, even individual towns and cities have been honoured solely because they petitioned Congress for a coin marking their jubilee or centenary. Every state of the Union is honoured equally for the first time in the ten-year celebration that began in 1999 and continues at the rate of five coins a year.

HOW IT ALL BEGAN

Although the 13 colonies declared their independence in 1776 and fought a long and bitter war to secure their freedom in 1783, a federal constitution was not finally drawn up until 1787 and then had to be ratified by each state. The first to do so was Delaware, on December 7, 1787. Pennsylvania followed five days later, and then New Jersey on December 18. Georgia ratified the Constitution on January 2, 1788, and Connecticut a week later. These five states were therefore selected for depiction on the quarter dollars released in 1999.

On December 1, 1997, President Clinton signed Public Law 105–124 (the 60 States Commemorative Coin Program Act), authorizing the United States Mint to celebrate each state with a special coin. The general circulating

Below (clockwise from top-left): state and keystone (PA), Charter Oak (CT), statutory George Washington obverse used for all quarters, Delaware River crossing (NJ), Caesar Rodney (DE).

versions of the five coins issued each year have a copper core and a cupro-nickel cladding. They are struck at Philadelphia and Denver, identified by the P or D mint-marks below the motto on the obverse. Proof versions of each coin are struck at the mint in San Francisco and bear the S mint-mark.

The quarter was chosen for this ambitious series because it is the most widely circulated coin, as well as the largest of the four coins in everyday use. The US Mint invited the governors of each state to submit suggestions for the designs on the reverse of each coin. These were considered by the Mint, the Citizens' Commemorative Coin Advisory Committee and the Commission of Fine Arts. They were then sent to the Secretary of the Treasury for final review and approval.

No other quarters are being struck during this ten-year period. Five quarters are being released each year, in the order in which the states ratified the Constitution or attained statehood.

DIVERSITY OF SUBJECTS

Obviously, when there is only a fairly limited amount of space for a motif, the choice of subject is very important. What is intriguing is the wide range of subject matter depicted on these coins, reflecting different outlooks and attitudes across the United States.

The designs for the first coins, issued on behalf of the states that were quick to ratify the new Constitution, have adopted a historical approach. Delaware chose a figure on horseback, Caesar Rodney, who, like the much more famous Paul Revere, made a midnight ride of 130km/80 miles in a thunderstorm on July 1, 1776, to break

Above (clockwise from top-left): Jamestown (VA), young Abraham Lincoln (IL), Helen Keller (AL), Kitty Hawk (NC), Gateway to Discovery (FL), pelican (LA), space odyssey (OH).

the deadlock in the Delaware vote for independence. A major-general in the Delaware militia, he held more public offices than anyone else in a career spanning 40 years. Connecticut chose its Charter Oak, but the most dramatic motif is to be found on the New Jersey quarter, with the caption "Crossroads of the Revolution" below the image of Washington crossing the Delaware to defeat the British at Trenton, the turning point in the war. A Minuteman – a member of the colonial militia, who fought the British from the outset, appears on the Massachusetts coin.

Above: Many states have chosen famous landmarks. Mount Rushmore appears on the South Dakota quarter.

HISTORIC EVENTS AND PERSONALITIES

Some of the states formerly ranked among the earliest colonies allude to events of another era. Virginia shows ships at Jamestown, which celebrates its 400th anniversary in 2007. By contrast, others have selected events and celebrities of much more recent vintage, ranging from a young Abraham Lincoln (Illinois) to Helen Keller (Alabama), who overcame both deafness and blindness to teach others. Appropriately the coin also bears her name in Braille. Ohio alludes to its role as the birthplace of aviation pioneers with an astronaut, John Glenn, in a spacesuit and the *Wright Flyer*. The latter is also featured on the coin from North Carolina, where the first flight actually took place near Kitty Hawk in December 1903.

Guitars and a trumpet celebrate the musical heritage of Tennessee, an oblique reference to jazz pioneer W.C. Handy and, of course, Elvis Presley. Florida has the slogan "Gateway to Discovery", contrasting a Spanish galleon with the Columbia Shuttle.

LANDMARKS

Some state quarters have picked an outstanding landmark. The strange geological feature aptly named the Old Man of the Mountain is shown on the coin from New Hampshire, while the Statue of Liberty was an obvious choice for New York. Other manmade features that appear include the most easterly lighthouse (Maine) and the dome of the state capitol (Maryland). Missouri has chosen the great arch at St Louis in the background to a scene showing the Corps of Discovery, led by Lewis and Clark, setting off on their expedition in 1804.

MAPS AND SPECIALITIES

Many of the designs incorporate a map of the state, often with the state bird such as the pelican (Louisiana), the great Carolina wren (South Carolina) or a loon on one of the 10,000 lakes of Minnesota. Arkansas features the mockingbird, an ear of corn and a diamond, alluding to the fact that it is the only state where diamonds are mined. Pennsylvania includes an allegorical statue with the caption "Virtue Liberty Independence", while Texas has the

Above (clockwise from top-left): Old Man of the Mountain (NH), Statue of Liberty (NY), Pemaquid Point (ME), Lewis and Clarke (MO), Statehouse Dome (MD).

lone star and Georgia has a peach. Other states omit the map and concentrate on what they are best known for: cattle and corn (Wisconsin), sailing (Rhode Island), magnolias (Mississippi), breeding horses (Kentucky) and car racing (Indiana).

By the time the series is completed in 2008, with coins representing New Mexico and Arizona, which gained statehood in 1912, and Alaska and Hawaii, which attained that status in 1959, collectors worldwide will have a better picture of the various maps, birds, landmarks and achievements that characterize each State of the Union.

Below (clockwise from top-left): Camel's Hump (VT), musical heritage (TN), Great Lakes (MI), Minuteman (MA).

Below (clockwise from top-left): Palmetto Tree and wren (SC), Lone Star (TX), cattle and cheese (WI), peach (GA).

Below (clockwise from top-left): Ocean State (RI), magnolia (MS), Indy Car Races (IN), thoroughbred (KY).

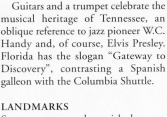

BAHAMAS, BERMUDA AND WEST INDIES

Contrary to popular belief, the Bahamas and Bermuda are not in the West Indies but lie in the North Atlantic rather than the Caribbean. Barbados was regarded as one of the Windward Islands but lies well to the east of the archipelago, while Trinidad and Tobago are at the southern end of the islands, off the coast of South America. In the 17th and 18th centuries, throughout the Caribbean, extensive use was made of Spanish, French and British coins, cut into pieces and countermarked for local circulation.

Left: The earliest coinage in this area consisted of the Hogge Money of Bermuda, produced in 1616 and so called on account of the image of a pig on the reverse, alluding to the wild hogs that succoured shipwrecked mariners. The image has been used on the reverse of 1 cent coins since their inception in 1970.

BAHAMAS

The Commonwealth of the Bahamas is an archipelago of about 3000 islands, cays, rocks and reefs east of Florida. The Bahamas have the distinction of being the first land sighted by Columbus in 1492, but they were colonized by the English in 1626 and, although they attained full independence in 1973, the British monarch remains the head of state.

A penny with the effigy of George III and the colony's badge was struck at Birmingham in 1806–7. British coins were legal tender until 1966, when distinctive coins from 1 cent to $5 were adopted with the bust of Elizabeth II on the obverse and images of island fauna and flora on the reverse [1–2]. The Bahamian sloop (25 cents) and blue marlin (50 cents) allude to the main tourist attractions. The same reverses were retained for a new series in 1974, with the arms of the Bahamas replacing the Queen's effigy [3–4]. The original series was struck at the Royal Mint; from 1974 to 1985 they were produced by the Franklin Mint and are now produced by the Royal Canadian Mint. Small gold coins marked the adoption of the new constitution (1967) while cupro-nickel or silver commemoratives have appeared since 1974, notably celebrating anniversaries of the arrival of Columbus.

BARBADOS

Although the island was discovered and named by the Portuguese in 1563, it was not settled until 1627. It remained in British hands from then until it achieved independence in 1966, Elizabeth II continuing as head of state.

Countermarked Spanish silver (1791–9) and copper tokens with a Negro head obverse and Neptune reverse (1788–92) [5–6] were followed by mainly British coins. Coins of the British Caribbean Territories (Eastern Group) were in use from 1955 to 1973, when a distinctive series from 1 cent to $5 was introduced [7–9], with the arms of the island (obverse) and landmarks, birds and fishes (reverse). Double-dated versions appeared in 1976 to mark the tenth anniversary of independence. Gold coins since 1975 and $10, $20 and $50 silver coins since 1981 have been struck as commemoratives, and they include the world's first cricket coin (1991).

BERMUDA

The "still-vex'd Bermoothes" of Shakespeare's *The Tempest*, the island was settled involuntarily when a shipload of British colonists bound for Virginia was wrecked there in 1609. The settlement became permanent in 1612. Apart from the crude Hogge Money (in denominations of 2, 3, 6 and 12 pence), Bermuda had a token coinage from 1793 [10–11] until 1842, when British coins became legal tender.

Bermuda abandoned sterling [12–13] in 1970 and adopted the dollar of 100 cents. Birds, fish and flowers form the subjects of the reverses, while various effigies of Elizabeth II have appeared on the obverse [14–18]. A brass $5 coin was added in 1983 for general circulation. A series of 25 cent coins appeared in 1984, with the arms of Bermuda or its ten parishes on the reverse, to celebrate the 375th anniversary of the colony. Large silver (and latterly cupro-nickel) dollars have served as a commemorative medium since 1970 while higher values ($2, $5 and $25) have been produced for the same purpose since 1975. Gold coins from $10 to $250 have also been issued for special events and anniversaries.

TRINIDAD AND TOBAGO

Discovered by Columbus in 1498, these islands were colonized by the French and Dutch but captured by the British in 1797 and formally annexed in 1814. Originally administered as separate colonies, they merged in 1888. They formed part of the British West Indies Federation until 1962, when they became an independent state, adopting a republican constitution in 1976.

Spanish, French or British countermarked or cut coins circulated in Tobago (1798) and Trinidad (1804 and 1811 respectively), followed in 1825 by British coins, which were replaced in 1955 by those of the East Caribbean. Distinctive coinage (1–50 cents) was adopted in 1966, with numerals of value on one side and the republic's arms on the other [19–20]. Higher denominations consist of $1 (1969), $5 (1971) and $10 (1976) in base metals, with silver and gold coins in higher values for commemoratives. Pictorial motifs were substituted from 1974 onwards, many featuring Caribbean landmarks, fauna and flora [21–24] but also giving prominence to cultural heritage, such as the steel bands for which Trinidad is world famous.

The Bermuda Triangle

Since 1996 Bermuda has produced coins to publicize the great mystery of navigation known as the Bermuda Triangle. The coins have, appropriately, three sides and are denominated as $3 or a multiple. The first coins ($3, $6 and $30) showed a map, a compass and a sinking ship; later issues have featured specific ships, such as the *Sea Venture*, wrecked in 1609, and the *Deliverance*, built by the survivors.

NETHERLANDS ANTILLES

These islands, forming part of the Kingdom of the Netherlands, comprised two groups: Aruba, Bonaire and Curaçao near the coast of Venezuela, and St Eustatius, Saba and part of St Martin south-east of Puerto Rico. Aruba became a separate state in 1986.

A general issue of coins for the Dutch West Indies appeared in 1794. Copper cents and silver stuivers were issued at Curaçao in the name of the Batavian Republic (1799–1803) and later, stuivers and reaals, often cut into segments under the Dutch kingdom. Cut or countermarked Spanish coins were used during the British occupation (1807–16) and after the restoration of Dutch rule, until 1821, when coins specifically minted for Curaçao were resumed.

Modern coins date from World War II, when the islands were cut off from Holland while it was under German occupation. These coins were similar to their Dutch counterparts, but with "Curaçao" inscribed on the reverse [25–27]. Distinctive coins inscribed "Nederlandse Antillen" have been in use since 1952, with a separate series for Aruba since 1986 [28–31].

CUBA, HISPANIOLA AND JAMAICA

The three largest islands of the Caribbean lie in its northernmost part, south of Florida and the Bahamas. Spanish-speaking Cuba is the largest and most westerly of the group. To the east lies the island of Hispaniola, the western third constituting the French-speaking Republic of Haiti and the remaining two-thirds the Spanish-speaking Dominican Republic. South of Cuba lies Jamaica, which is English-speaking and now a republic within the British Commonwealth. Associated with Jamaica are the Cayman Islands and the Turks and Caicos Islands, which were formerly its dependencies.

Left: Jamaica remained within the sterling area until 1969, and in this period produced its first commemorative coin, a crown-sized 5 shillings to celebrate its hosting of the 1966 Commonwealth Games.

CUBA

Reached by Columbus in 1492 and settled by the Spaniards in the early 1500s, Cuba remained a Spanish colony until 1898. The island was captured by the United States during the Spanish-American War and granted independence in 1902. The dictatorship of Fulgencio Batista was overthrown in 1959 by Fidel Castro, who instituted a communist regime. Although trade sanctions are still imposed by the USA, Cuba has become a popular tourist resort in recent years.

Distinctive coins based on the peso of 100 centavos were introduced in 1915, with an armorial obverse and a five-pointed star inscribed "Patria y Libertad" ("Fatherland and Liberty") on the reverse [1–2]. The Castro regime retained these motifs but changed the motto to "Patria o Muerte" ("Fatherland or Death") on some of the coins. In 1915 dollar-sized silver pesos were accompanied by a tiny gold coin portraying the martyr José Marti. Silver pesos ceased in 1939 but since 1977 smaller cupro-nickel coins have been extensively used as a vehicle for commemoration: by 2004 there

had been well over 400 different issues [3–8]. Since 1975, 5 and 10 pesos have been almost as prolific, with even larger denominations in silver or gold.

HAITI

Hispaniola ("Little Spain") was, like Cuba, claimed by Columbus on his first voyage and colonized by Spain, but in the early 17th century the western district was taken over by French pirates, who ceded it to France in 1697. The coffee and sugar plantations worked by slaves imported from Africa made Saint-Domingue one of France's richest colonies, but a slave rebellion led by Henri Christophe led to the creation of the Republic of Haiti in 1804, the oldest Negro republic in the world and (second only to the USA) the oldest republic in the western hemisphere.

Countermarked French, Spanish and Portuguese coins circulated in the 18th century, followed by a local coinage denominated in escalins. Coins in deniers and sols, introduced in 1807, were rapidly superseded by a decimal system based on the gourde of 100 centimes, a currency that continues to this day. Circulating coins have the arms on one side and Liberty (1881–94), followed by profiles of historic figures (since 1904) on the other. Apart from the circulating coins from 1 centime to 1 gourde in nickel- or brass-plated steel [9], Haiti has issued many gold and silver commemoratives since 1971.

DOMINICAN REPUBLIC

The larger part of Hispaniola, which the Spaniards called Santo Domingo, remained under their control until 1822, when the Haitians invaded it. They occupied the entire island until 1844. In that year Juan Pablo Duarte raised a revolt and drove out the invaders, establishing the independent Dominican Republic. It voluntarily submitted to Spain from 1861 to 1866 but has been independent ever since.

A Spanish mint was established at Santo Domingo in 1542 and struck silver and copper coins. Distinctive coins appeared in 1814–21 under the name of Fernando VII. Copper or brass quarter reales of 1844–8 were struck, but no other distinctive coinage emerged until 1877, when the peso of 100 centavos was adopted. The earliest coins were non-figural, with the date on one side and the value on the other, but an armorial design was introduced in 1937 [10–16], with a palm tree or native American head on the other side. Numerous commemoratives, in gold, silver or platinum, have appeared in more recent years.

JAMAICA

Columbus reached Jamaica in 1494 and it was colonized by Spain in 1509 but captured by Britain in 1655. It joined the West Indies Federation in 1958 but seceded in 1961, gaining full independence a year later. Cut or countermarked coins were in circulation in the 18th century, followed by the coins of the British West Indies in 1822. Sterling was introduced in 1834, represented by silver coins of small denominations. Cupro-nickel coins were introduced in 1869 with the effigy of the monarch (obverse) and colonial arms (reverse); these continued until 1969 [17–22]. The dollar was adopted in 1969; the arms moved to the obverse [23, 29] and pictorial motifs (fauna and flora) occupied the reverse of the cents [24], while Sir Alexander Bustamente, the first prime minister, was portrayed on the dollar [25]. Subsequently, other political figures were depicted [26–28, 30]. Since the 1990s inflation has led to a great reduction in the size of coins and the introduction of higher denominations for general circulation. Silver and gold commemoratives, up to $500, have also been produced.

FORMER JAMAICAN DEPENDENCIES

The Cayman Islands west of Jamaica and the Turks and Caicos group to the north-east were formerly Spanish but ceded to Britain in 1670 and 1799 respectively. The latter group was long a dependency of the Bahamas, then briefly a separate colony, before becoming a dependency of Jamaica in 1873. Jamaican coinage was used in both groups until 1959, when they joined the West Indies Federation. Distinctive coins have been issued by the Cayman Islands since 1972 [31–32, 34–35] and the Turks and Caicos Islands since 1969 [33], but both groups prefer US coinage in general circulation.

Colourful Coins

In 1994 Cuba became one of the first countries in the world to issue coins with a multicoloured surface. While the arms of the republic appeared in plain silver on the obverse, the reverse featured Caribbean fauna in full colour. The following year a similar series portrayed pirates of the Caribbean.

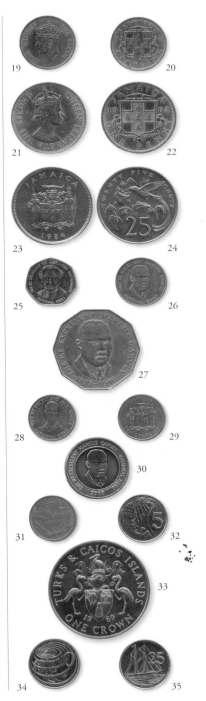

EAST CARIBBEAN

Columbus laid claim to the smaller islands of the east Caribbean during his second and subsequent voyages, and they were originally colonized by Spain but were frequently fought over by France and Britain in the 17th and 18th centuries, before finally coming under permanent British control. These crown colonies joined together in 1958 to form the West Indies Federation, but when that broke up they were granted associate statehood, with self-government, as a prelude to full independence within the British Commonwealth. They used British currency until 1955, when the coinage of the British East Caribbean Territories was introduced, followed by that of the East Caribbean Territories in 1980.

Left: The first coins inscribed for each territory of the British East Caribbean were the $4 coins of 1970, which formed part of the Food for All programme instituted by the United Nations Food and Agriculture Organization. These coins had standard obverse and reverse, depicting the East Caribbean arms [11] and bananas respectively, but individual names were inscribed below the arms.

The standard issues of the British East Caribbean Territories had a crowned bust of Elizabeth II on the obverse, and numerals (low values), Columbus's flagship the *Santa Maria* (5, 10 and 25 cents) or Neptune driving a sea chariot (50 cents) on the reverse [1–6]. The coins of the East Caribbean Territories bear the Machin bust of Queen Elizabeth and laureated numerals (1, 2 and 5 cents) and the *Santa Maria* (10 and 25 cents and $1) [7–10].

ANTIGUA AND BARBUDA
At the eastern end of the Leeward Islands, Antigua and its dependency of Barbuda achieved self-government in 1967 and became a wholly independent member of the Commonwealth in 1981, with the British monarch as head of state. Although copper token farthings, some struck in the Bahamas, were issued in the mid-19th century, the first distinctive coins appeared in 1982 to mark the 250th anniversary of George Washington's birth; they comprised three $30 silver proofs showing scenes of the American Revolutionary War. A $10 coin appeared in 1985 to celebrate Queen Elizabeth's visit, while more recent coins have focused on Caribbean wildlife.

DOMINICA
Lying in the Windward Islands, Dominica was confirmed as a British possession in 1805 and at that time had a curious currency consisting of rings, dumps or fragments of Spanish coins denominated in bits. Spanish dollars had a crenellated piece cut out of the centre to form the moco (1½ bits) [12] while the rest was tariffed at 11 or 16 bits according to size and weight.

Dominica was granted associated statehood in 1967 and became wholly independent in 1978. Coins were issued in 1970 to mark the signing of an agreement among 18 Caribbean states, to promote economic development in the region [11], and $10 coin, released that year to celebrate independence, featured carnival dancers. The relatively few commemoratives include those for royal and papal visits and the Middle East peace brokered by Bill Clinton (1979).

ST KITTS AND NEVIS
Though colonized by Sir Thomas Warner in 1623, St Christopher (usually known as St Kitts) became a permanent British possession in 1783. Billon French deniers were countermarked SK and issued in 1801. Known

coins (1879) had a pyramid emblem on the obverse and the value on the reverse [26]. Like the others, Honduras abandoned the peso (with its connotations of colonial rule) in 1931 and adopted a distinctive unit, the lempira, named after an Indian chief whose exploits against the Spanish were legendary. Lempira himself was portrayed on the obverse of the higher values [16, 19], with the arms on the reverse [15, 20]. On the smaller coins the arms occupied the obverse and the value appeared on the reverse [17–18].

NICARAGUA

This republic got by with Spanish pesos and the coins of its neighbours until 1878, when it acquired its own coinage, struck by the Heaton Mint of Birmingham, although the full range, from the half centavo to the cordoba [21–24], was not completed until 1912. The unit was named in honour of Francisco Fernandez de Cordoba who explored the area (1515–24). After the earthquake disaster of 1975 Nicaragua produced a silver 20 cordoba coin to raise funds for the victims, a very early example of a charity coin.

EL SALVADOR

Apart from an interesting issue of 1828–35, when the federation was collapsing, inscribed "For the freedom of Salvador", Central American federation

Below: Panama's silver 20 balboas was the largest coin in the world when it was issued in 1971, with a diameter of 61mm/2½in.

Country Named After a Town

British Honduras was settled by sailors shipwrecked in 1638 and later became the haunt of buccaneers who founded Belize, a town allegedly named after a pirate called Wallace. The country took the name of Belize in 1973 when it became independent. Coins portraying the reigning monarch were introduced in 1885, and since 1973 have had pictorial reverses.

reales and countermarked Spanish coins served El Salvador until 1889, when the peso of 100 centavos was adopted. While silver pesos and half pesos showing the flag or a bust of Columbus, and a gold series with the head of Liberty, were struck in San Salvador, some centavo denominations, in cupro-nickel, were produced by Heaton. In 1920 the colon replaced the peso as the unit of currency. Armorial obverses have alternated with a profile of Francisco Morazan, hero of the struggle for liberation and president of the Central American Republic from 1829 to 1840 [25]. Gold coins were revived in 1971, the prelude to many special issues of recent years [29–32].

PANAMA

After seceding from Colombia in 1903, Panama adopted the balboa of 100 centesimos [26–27], although an actual 1 balboa coin did not appear until 1947 [28]. Balboa himself has dominated the obverse of the coins since their inception; other historical figures have appeared since 1975. Panama has the distinction of producing both the region's smallest and (until recently) largest coins – the tiny silver 2 centesimos or "Panama pill" and the giant 20 balboas portraying Simon Bolivar.

COLOMBIA, ECUADOR AND VENEZUELA

Columbus reached the Atlantic coasts of Colombia and Venezuela in 1498 but no Spanish settlement took place there until the mid-16th century. These three countries in the north-east of South America originally formed the vice-royalty of New Granada, but revolted against Spanish rule in 1811. Although they achieved their independence in 1821, Spain did not recognize it until 1845. Initially the three countries united to form Greater Colombia or the Granadine Confederation, striking reales or using countermarked Spanish pieces, with numerous local issues during the war of independence. When the confederation disintegrated in 1830 each country went its own way. Panama seceded from Colombia in 1903, having used the coins of that country up to that time.

Below: Simon Bolivar (right), born at Caracas, Venezuela, in 1783, led the 1911 revolt against Spanish rule and is the great national hero of Colombia, Ecuador and Venezuela as well as Peru and Bolivia. The last of these was named in his honour, and from this derived the currency unit, the boliviano, while the Colombian state of Bolivar also perpetuates his memory. In his native land his name was given to the unit of currency, while that of his lieutenant, Antonio Sucre (left), was used for the currency unit in Ecuador.

VENEZUELA

Bolivar's homeland issued reales until the 1860s, although a reformed currency, based on the venezolano of 100 centavos, was in parallel use from 1873 to 1879, when it was replaced by the bolivar of 100 centimos. Early coins bore the head of Liberty, but since 1874 Simon Bolivar the Liberator has been portrayed instead [1], with a heraldic shield on the reverse [2–6]. Since 1975 a number of large gold or silver coins have commemorated historic events and personalities or appeared in sets highlighting nature conservation and other worthy causes.

ECUADOR

Francisco Pizarro penetrated the north-west Pacific coast of South America in 1526, and within a decade Ecuador had been pacified by Sebastian de Benalcazar, who founded Quito in 1534. Revolts against Spain were crushed in 1810 and 1812 and it was not until 1822 that Ecuador was liberated by Antonio Sucre.

Distinctive coins date from 1833 and were originally inscribed "Ecuador in Colombia", but "Republica del Ecuador" was substituted in 1837. The head of Liberty [7] and the sunrise over twin peaks were the main features of the early issues [8]. Decimal coinage based on the sucre of 10 decimos or 100 centavos was adopted in 1872, the obverses showing an elaborate coat of arms with the wreathed value in words on the reverse – a design that has endured for decades [9–11]. The effigy of Sucre appeared in 1884 and has dominated the higher values ever since [12], although pictorial designs still featured on the lower values [13–14]. Unusually, some coins of Ecuador include the word "Mexico" at the foot of the reverse to denote the place of minting [15]. Since 1988 nickel-clad

Leper Coins

Special coins were produced by Colombia from 1901 onward for the use of patients in the government-managed leper colonies at Agua de Dios, Cano de Loro and Contratacion. The standard obverse bore the name of the country with "Lazareto" across the middle. The coins, ranging from 1 centavo to 10 pesos, continued in use until the leper colonies were shut down in 1959. Venezuela also issued distinctive coins between 1913 and 1936 for each of its leper colonies at Maracaibo, Providencia and Cabo Blanco, and Panama produced coins for its leper colony at Palo Seco in 1907.

steel coins of Ecuador have matched a new armorial obverse [16] to images of the independence memorial [17] or indigenous sculpture and artefacts. Very few commemoratives have so far appeared, notably the series of 1991 for the Columbus quincentenary.

COLOMBIA

If the coinage of Ecuador and Venezuela has been relatively straightforward, that of Colombia has been exceedingly complex, reflecting turbulent times and periods of rampant inflation. A mint was opened at Bogota in the 1620s, striking silver pesos and also, from 1756, gold coins such as the beautiful 8 escudos portraying Charles III [18] with the crowned royal arms of Spain on the reverse [19], struck at the Bogota Mint in 1785. A subsidiary mint producing silver also functioned at Popayan from 1729. Spanish royalists and republican rebels struck coins in areas under their control during the prolonged wars of independence, the former at Popayan and Santa Marta

and the latter in Cartagena and Cundinamarca. A national coinage of escudos and reales appeared in 1820, richly symbolic with flowers, cornucopiae and doves of peace as well as the obligatory head of Liberty.

The first attempt to decimalize the currency (1847) yielded the peso of 10 reales or decimos. These coins continued the previous symbols but had the value on the reverse. The peso of 100 centavos was adopted in 1872, Liberty heads and arms or symbols providing the motifs, with profiles of Bolivar and other national figures more prominent from 1912 [20–22]. Bronze (and later copper-clad steel) subsidiary coins were introduced in 1962 with a wreathed Cap of Liberty on the obverse and a numeral of value flanked by flowers and a cornucopia on the reverse. Higher denominations with armorial motifs were struck in brass [24] while bimetallic high values were adopted in 1993 [23]. Recently, inflation has necessitated base-metal coins up to 5000 pesos. These have the value on one side and motifs derived from indigenous art on the other [25–26].

Special issues began in 1968, with cupro-nickel 5 pesos and gold 100 pesos to mark the Eucharistic Congress, while a 5 pesos of 1971 celebrated the Pan-American Games. The relatively few commemoratives issued since have mostly been of very high denominations (500, 1000, 1500 or 2000 pesos), struck in gold.

Colombia was rent by civil wars in the early 20th century, and the territory of Panama seceded with the connivance of the USA. In that period uniface coins of 10, 20 and 50 centavos were struck from thin sheets of brass at Santander under the command of General Ramon Gonzales Valencia. In the immediate postwar years the paper currency depreciated to the point at which a paper peso was worth no more than a centavo in silver coinage; 1, 2 and 5 peso cupro-nickel coins of 1907–16 are inscribed "P/M" below the value on the reverse, signifying "*papel moneda*" (paper money).

BRAZIL AND GUYANA

The largest of the Latin American nations, Brazil was claimed by the Portuguese explorer Cabral in 1500, and settled by the inhabitants of that country, who imported their currency based on the real. By the late 16th century sugar was serving as a medium of currency, with cowries (known as *zombo* or *gimbombo*) as small change. From 1580 to 1640 Portugal was under Spanish rule, and Spanish silver pesos circulated, followed in 1643 by countermarked coins. Mints were opened at Bahia (1694) and Rio (1698), where the 4000 reis coin of João V was minted in 1719 [1–2], and struck in gold and silver. Guyana is the generic name for the region north of Brazil and east of Venezuela, colonized by the French and Dutch, and later the British: these territories are now a French overseas department, Surinam and Guyana respectively.

Left: In 1900 Brazil celebrated the 400th anniversary of Pedro Alvares Cabral's arrival on its shore with a very large 4000 reis silver coin, the obverse showing the Portuguese explorer setting foot on dry land, cap in hand, while the reverse showed the sunrise flanked by the arms of Portugal and Brazil in upright oval cartouches.

THE EMPIRE
Some of the world's most poignant coins are those struck at the Rio Mint portraying the Portuguese royal family in the late 18th century. Queen Maria I suffered from severe melancholia, which descended into madness following the death of her husband, Pedro III. Their conjoined profiles appeared on the gold peca of 1782 [3–4], but the widowed queen appeared alone on later coins [5–6]. Coins were struck in the name of João VI, who served as regent from 1799 to 1816, including a gold peca of 1811 [7–8].

When Napoleon's armies invaded the Iberian Peninsula the Portuguese royals fled to Brazil and set up court in Rio de Janeiro. After Portugal was liberated by Wellington's troops in 1811, the Prince Regent, who would later accede to the throne as João VI, returned to Lisbon, leaving his son Pedro as his viceroy, but in September 1822 Pedro declared Brazil a wholly independent empire and proclaimed himself emperor. His son succeeded in 1831 and, as Dom Pedro II, ruled wisely until 1889. The abolition of slavery caused great discontent among the landowning classes and led to a military coup, which abolished the empire and deposed the monarchy.

Imperial coinage had a crowned shield on the obverse and the value on the reverse [9–10]. A singular feature of the early period was the plethora of countermarked copper coins [11] as the government strove to impose a standard system, although it was not until the 1860s that the coinage was reformed. Portraits of the emperor, from boyhood to old age, were confined to gold and a few silver coins.

THE REPUBLIC
As in Spain, Portuguese currency was based on the real, but it became so depreciated that it was counted in large multiples known as reis (the plural of *real* in Portuguese). Even in imperial times the lowest denomination was 5 reis, while silver coins ran up to 2000 reis and gold from 5000 to 20,000 reis. Under the republic the lowest coin was the bronze 20 reis, the highest the gold 20,000 reis minted between 1889 and 1922. Latterly money was counted in

Revaluation

Inflation and depreciation are nothing new to Brazil. Between 1667 and 1683, when the value of money fell in relation to the intrinsic worth of coins, Portuguese gold coins of 1000, 2000 and 4000 reis were countermarked in Brazil and stamped with new values of 1100, 2200 and 4400 reais respectively.

milreis (1000 reis) and the banknotes ran up to 1,000,000 reis, known as a conto. Liberty and the numerals of value dominated the coinage [12–14] but during the dictatorship of Getulio Vargas (1938–42) his profile appeared on the obverse [15]. A few special issues of the inter-war period commemorated the 400th anniversary of settlement and honoured celebrated Brazilians.

CURRENCY REFORMS

Despite the greatest natural resources of any South American country, Brazil has been hard hit by economic and political instability from time to time, coupled with periods of high inflation. This led to a reform of the currency in 1942 when the outmoded milreis gave way to the cruzeiro of 100 centavos. A feature of this series was that a different portrait of a famous Brazilian was used for each value from 10 to 50 centavos, while a map of the country or the federal arms graced the higher values. In every case the value, denoted by large numerals, occupied the reverse.

Inflation in the 1950s led to changes from cupro-nickel to brass and latterly aluminium, notably the series of 1965. Two years later the currency was reformed, the cruzeiro novo being worth 1000 old cruzeiros. In this period occurred the avant-garde coins marking the 150th anniversary of independence [16–17]. The currency was again reformed in 1986 when the new cruzeiro was superseded by the cruzado of 100 centavos [18–22]. Like its predecessors, this series was struck in stainless steel but by 1989 had also depreciated: 1000 cruzados were worth one cruzado novo, which was again replaced by the cruzeiro a year later. In 1993, 1000 cruzeiros equalled one cruzeiro real, but in July 1994, 2750 of these equalled 1 real of 100 centavos. So far, the real (plural *reis*) has managed to hold steady [23–24].

GUYANA

To a large extent coins of the mother country were used in the British, Dutch and French parts of Guyana, although during World War II Dutch coins were struck at the US Mint with a P (Philadelphia) mint-mark for use in Surinam. Appropriately countermarked Spanish coins, holey dollars and dumps were used in Essequibo and Demerara following the British occupation of 1796, made permanent in 1814. In the British colonial period stuivers and guilders portrayed the reigning sovereign [25–26]. British silver groats (4 pence) were superseded by distinctive coins of the same value, augmenting ordinary British coins [27–30]. When the territory gained independence in 1967 the dollar of 100 cents was introduced. The coins had armorial and numeral motifs [31–32], which changed to pictorial reverses in 1976.

The coinage of Dutch Guiana began at Recife in 1645, with gold florins inscribed "Brasil" (the first numismatic use of the name), followed by silver in 1654. These coins were rectangular, with the "GWC" monogram of the Dutch West Indies Company. Distinctive coins were introduced in Surinam in 1962, with an armorial obverse and value reverse. The former Dutch Guiana attained independence in 1975, and celebrated its first anniversary with silver and gold coins.

1

2

3

4

5

6

7

8

9

10

11

12

13

14

BOLIVIA, CHILE AND PERU

The former Inca strongholds were absorbed by Spain's colonial empire in the 1530s. In 1543 silver was discovered in Bolivia at Potosi in the Cerro Rico, which contained the largest silver deposit then known. Pesos were crudely struck at Lima, Peru, from 1565 and at Potosi from 1575, exemplified by the 1723 cob 8 reales of Potosi [1–2], intended mainly as a convenient medium for shipping bullion rather than for local circulation. Although independence was declared in 1809–10 and secured by 1824, Spain made many later attempts to regain the territory and did not finally recognize its independence until 1879. Ironically, by that time relations between the states had deteriorated, leading to the Pacific War of 1879–83, which resulted in victory for Chile, and territorial losses for Bolivia and Peru.

Left: The Andean condor, in flight or, as shown here, alighting on a lofty peak, has long been a popular motif for the coins of the countries dominated by this great mountain range.

BOLIVIA

Known as Upper Peru in Spanish colonial times, the country declared its independence in 1809, following a revolt in La Paz. It was the first of the Spanish territories to do so, but 16 years elapsed before it was secured by Bolivar's crushing defeat of the last Spanish army in South America, at Maipu in 1824. The republic, established in August 1825, took its name from its liberator.

Distinctive coinage began in 1827 with the escudo of 2 pesos or 16 soles, portraying Simon Bolivar with a palm tree on the reverse or the sun rising over the Andes (on gold escudos) [3–4]. A tiny quarter sol was added in 1852, featuring a llama (obverse) and an Andean peak (reverse). The coinage was decimalized in 1864, based on the boliviano of 100 centecimos, replaced by centavos in 1878. Arms, eagle or mountain motifs replaced Bolivar's effigies while the reverse bore the value. This series continued until 1919, although by that date only the 5 and 10 centavo coins were still being struck.

Attempts to re-introduce coins in 1935–7 and 1951 were hampered by rampant inflation. A drastic currency reform in 1963 led to the introduction of the peso boliviano and coinage was

resumed in 1965. The first commemoratives, in 1952, consisted of small gold coins celebrating the revolution of that year. By 1980 coins had disappeared from circulation, overtaken by inflation, but in 1987 a monetary reform, replacing 1,000,000 pesos with the new boliviano of 100 centavos, resulted in the first full range of coins in 80 years, with the arms (obverse) and value (reverse) [5–8]. A few special issues since then include the Ibero-American series of 10 boliviano coins and a 50 boliviano silver piece of 1998 for the 450th anniversary of La Paz.

CHILE

Coins were struck at Santiago from 1749 in the prevailing Spanish colonial styles; they included silver pesos and gold coins such as the handsome 8 escudo piece of Ferdinand VII minted in 1813 [9–10]. Following the revolution, distinctive coinage dated from 1817 and consisted of the peso inscribed "Chile Independent" with Santiago at the foot of a motif showing an erupting volcano. Other values from the tiny silver quart (quarter real) to the gold 6 escudos followed, but the peso of 100 centavos was adopted in 1835, with a star, condor or Liberty head (obverse) and value (reverse). Variations on these themes continued until 1942, when peso coins were introduced portraying Bernardo O'Higgins, dictator of Chile (1817–23). The peso was hard hit by inflation and by 1958 the condor or 10 pesos, originally a gold coin, was reduced to aluminium [11–12]. In 1960 the currency was reformed, introducing the escudo of 100 centesimos, with the centesimo worth 10 old pesos.

This series retained the flying condor obverse and value reverse, but since 1971 O'Higgins and other national heroes have been portrayed. In 1975 the coinage was again reformed, making the peso equal to 1000 old escudos. In this series the condor appeared in repose on the lower denominations [13–14], while O'Higgins graced the obverse [17] with a laureated value on the reverse [18]. Gold and silver coins showing a winged Victory appeared in 1976, originally celebrating the revolution of 1973, but the motif was subsequently extended to the base-metal coinage [15–16].

PERU

Low-denomination copper coins appeared in 1822–3 as a prelude to a regular series in silver. The tiny silver quarter real of 1826–56 featured a llama, but the higher values had the standing figure of Liberty (obverse) and arms (reverse). Coins inscribed "Nor-Peruana" or "Repub. Sud-Peruana Confederacion" appeared in 1836–9 and reflected a short-lived confederation with Bolivia.

A decimal system based on the libra (pound) of 100 soles, 100 dineros or 1000 centavos was adopted in 1863. The 1 and 2 centavos were struck in bronze, with a sunburst obverse [21] and a wreathed value reverse [22], but higher denominations were minted in silver with the seated figure of Liberty on the obverse [19] and the national arms on the reverse [20]. The dinero was phased out in 1916, but the gold libra and fifth libra survived until 1969. The brass coins of 1935–65, from the half sol upwards, bore the name of the Central Reserve Bank and a promise to

Tiny Gold

The peso was normally minted in silver, but from 1860 to 1873 Chile struck this denomination in 22 carat (.917 fine) gold, with the standing figure of Liberty on the obverse and a wreathed value on the reverse (see enlarged view, bottom). The tiny coin (14mm/⅝in diameter, top) proved unpopular and very few were struck after the production of silver pesos resumed in 1867.

pay the bearer in gold soles [23]. The promise gave way to an image of a llama on coins of 1966–75 [24–25].

Like other Latin American countries, Peru was hard hit by inflation, resulting in base-metal coins up to 500 soles by 1985. The currency was reformed in that year and adopted the inti (the Inca word for "sun") of 1000 soles de oro, with the value or arms on one side and a bust of the national hero Admiral Grau on the other [26]. Brass coins from 1 to 50 centimos and cupronickel 1 and 5 intis were struck until 1988. Yet another reform in 1991 produced the nuevo sol, worth 1,000,000 intis, and a range of brass coins from 1 centimo to 5 nuevos soles [27–28]. The arms and value were enlivened by the inclusion of tiny birds on the reverse of the highest denominations, while the lower coins incorporated the value in Braille. Among the relatively few commemorative coins should be noted the series of 1965 celebrating the quatercentenary of the Lima Mint, the reverse reproducing a coin of 1565 [29].

1
2
3
4
5
6
7
8
9
10
11
12
13
14
15
16
17

ARGENTINA, PARAGUAY AND URUGUAY

Spanish penetration of the countries bordering the River Plate and its tributaries began in 1515, but settlement was very slow and there was little European development, due largely to the preservation of the indigenous people by the Jesuit missions, which were brutally suppressed in 1767–81. In the decades that followed opposition to the tyrannical rule of Spain escalated and fuelled the movement for independence in 1810–11. Argentina won its independence in 1816. Paraguay followed soon afterwards, but Uruguay was conquered by the Portuguese from Brazil and did not gain its independence, with help from Argentina, until 1830.

Left: Veinticinco de Mayo (May 25) is to Argentines what the Fourth of July is to Americans, commemorating the date on which independence was declared in 1810. The 150th anniversary was celebrated by this peso showing the Old Town Hall in Buenos Aires and the national arms.

ARGENTINA

Republica Argentina (literally "silver republic") owes its name and origin to the mineral wealth in the basin of the Rio de la Plate ("river of silver") and the earliest coins (1813–15) were given Spanish inscriptions signifying "Provinces of the River Plate". They consisted of gold escudos and silver soles and reales with a radiate sun obverse and arms reverse. Continual civil war resulted in separate issues of coins in the provinces of Buenos Aires, Cordoba, Entre Rios and La Rioja at various times until 1867, and it was not until 1881 that a national currency emerged, based on the peso of 100 centavos. Arms and the head of Liberty [1–4] provided the dominant motifs until 1962, but as inflation took hold the need for higher denominations in base metal resulted in some coins portraying historic figures or the sailing ship *Presidente Sarmiento* (5 pesos) and a gaucho (10 pesos) [5–6].

The first of many currency reforms took place in 1970, when the old peso became the new centavo. Coins from 1–50 centavos showed Liberty [8] with the value on the reverse [7]. Inflation led to the re-introduction of peso coins in 1974, the radiate sun being revived [9]. José de San Martin, the father of independence, and the naval commander Almirante Brown appeared on the 50 and 100 pesos brass-clad steel coins of 1980–81 [10–11]. In 1983 the peso argentino, worth 10,000 pesos, was introduced, followed by the austral, worth 1000 pesos argentinos (1985), and the peso of 10,000 australes (1992); the currency has been reasonably stable since then [12–13]. The austral coins included fauna on the low values – a respite from the sun and Liberty head. In recent years Argentina has also produced a number of commemoratives, mainly in base metal, for general circulation.

PARAGUAY

Apart from a copper half real showing a lion and the Cap of Liberty (1845) Paraguay had no coinage until 1870, when the peso of 100 centesimos was introduced. A radiate star in a wreath alternated with the lion emblem on the obverse, with the value on the reverse, apart from the large silver peso of 1889, which used both symbols. A new system, based on the guarani of 100 centimos, was adopted in 1944 and struck in aluminium (centimos) or stainless steel (1–50 guaranies), with brass-plated steel 100 guaranies since 1992. The guarani series has a mixture of allegory and portraiture on the obverse, notably the figure of a soldier alluding to the disastrous Chaco War with Bolivia of 1932–5 [14]. Paraguay had lost half its territory to Argentina, Uruguay and Brazil in the War of the Triple Alliance (1864–70) and was not minded to give up any more. The Chaco War, fought in a harsh terrain, claimed more lives through malaria than combat. It was a pyrrhic victory for Paraguay, which decimated the population and almost bankrupted the economy. The soldier appeared on Paraguayan coins and banknotes from 1975 onwards. By contrast, the 5 guarani coin portrayed a typical Paraguayan woman [17].

The higher denominations, in stainless steel or cupro-nickel zinc, featured landmarks on the reverse, such as the Acaray River hydroelectric dam [15], ancient ruins [19] and modern buildings. The obverses bore national figures, such as Generals Estigarribia, Garay [16] and Caballero [18], beginning in 1968 with a 10,000 guarani coin portraying General Alfredo Stroessner.

Paraguay embarked on a prolific programme of special issues struck in gold or silver. These have portrayed not only local heroes but also a staggering range of international celebrities (Goethe,

Conquering the Desert
The pacification of the interior of Argentina was not completed until 1879, when a military expedition was sent to Central Patagonia to subjugate the native peoples at the point of a lance. The centenary of the "conquest of the desert", as it is euphemistically known, was celebrated by this coin showing a lancer on horseback.

Beethoven, Lincoln, Bismarck, Einstein, Garibaldi and Kennedy were among the earliest).

URUGUAY
Coinage in Uruguay was produced very sporadically in the 19th century, beginning with the copper 5 and 20 centesimos of 1840, followed in 1844 by the 40 centesimos and the silver peso. The copper 1, 2 and 4 centesimos appeared in 1869 and the silver 10 and 50 centesimos in 1870. The centesimos had a radiate sun obverse [20] and value reverse [21] but the peso had the republican arms. These types continued until 1953, when base-metal coins bore the national leader, José Artigas [22], previously portrayed in 1916–17. A brass 10 centesimo, issued in 1930 to celebrate the centenary of independence, had the head of Liberty (obverse) and a puma (reverse); it was re-issued in 1936 without the centenary inscription. A wide range of base alloys was used (bronze, cupro-nickel, aluminium-bronze or aluminium) for coins dated 1965, struck in very small quantities for the numismatic market.

Since the monetary reform of 1977, which exchanged 100 old pesos for one new one, aluminium or aluminium-bronze have been used for the circulating coins, with pictorial images and values on obverse and reverse respectively. The motifs were a curious mixture of the allegorical, such as the scales of justice on the 50 centesimo [23], and the agricultural, reflecting the importance of the cattle industry [24]. The nuevo peso denominations, however, featured José Artigas on the obverse [25–26]; Artigas was also the subject of a 5 nuevo peso coin issued in 1975 to celebrate the 150th anniversary of the revolutionary movement [27–28]. The currency was again reformed in 1993, when the peso uruguayano, worth 1000 nuevos pesos, was adopted. In recent years Uruguay has produced numerous medallic or bullion pieces in gold or silver [29–30]; they bear the revolutionary slogan "Libertad o Muerte" (Liberty or Death).

SOUTH ATLANTIC ISLANDS

The islands of the South Atlantic were some of the last outposts of the British Empire. Ordinary British coinage was largely used but in quite recent times distinctive sets in base alloys for general circulation have appeared. Since the 1970s they have also produced numerous commemorative or special issues. St Helena and its dependencies of Ascension and Tristan da Cunha were discovered by the Portuguese in 1501–2, while the Falkland Islands (named after Lord Falkland, Treasurer of the Navy) were discovered by John Davies in 1592. While St Helena (a staging post of the East India Company from 1659) was originally colonized by refugees from London after the Great Fire of 1666, Ascension and Tristan da Cunha were garrisoned in 1815 as a security precaution following the exile of Napoleon to St Helena.

Left: The Falklands, settled by Britain in 1833, have long been claimed by Argentina, resulting in the military invasion of April 1982 and the occupation of both the Falklands and its dependency, South Georgia. The South Atlantic War, which followed, led to the liberation of both island groups in mid-June. Crown-sized 50 pence in cupro-nickel, silver or gold celebrated the liberation and showed the arms of the colony superimposed on the Union Jack.

ST HELENA

Apart from a copper halfpenny of 1821 bearing the colonial arms [1–2], St Helena used coins of the East India Company and countermarked foreign coins until 1834, when British coinage was adopted exclusively for general circulation. In 1984, coins in the same weights and specifications as the British series were introduced with the names of both St Helena and Ascension inscribed on the obverse. The reverses feature South Atlantic fauna and flora.

In 1973, St Helena issued a crown-sized 25 pence in cupro-nickel or proof silver to celebrate the tercentenary of its return to British hands after a period of occupation by the Dutch [3–4]. A similar coin celebrated Elizabeth II's silver jubilee in 1977 [5] and in 1978 the 25th anniversary of her coronation was likewise celebrated. Since then relatively few silver or gold coins have marked royal anniversaries and occasions. Crowns valued at the traditional 25 pence continued to be issued, both for St Helena alone [6–7] and with Ascension [8], although other crown values have also appeared. In 1984, a crown-sized 50 pence celebrated the 150th anniversary of St Helena as a crown colony.

ASCENSION

This island, which derives its name from its discovery on Ascension Day 1501, was occupied in 1815 to prevent any attempt by Bonapartists to free Napoleon from exile on St Helena. It acquired a strategic value in World War II and more recently has been an important staging post for communications and a NASA tracking station.

Apart from the joint issues with St Helena, a number of which depict flora and fauna [9–11], Ascension has had several crown-sized coins, generally complementing the issues of St Helena. The first distinctive coin marked the 25th anniversary of the coronation and

The Queen's Beasts

In 1978 the 25th anniversary of the coronation was marked by an omnibus issue of stamps in the various crown colonies and dependent territories. Their theme was the set of 12 heraldic animals known as the Queen's Beasts. The stamps showed a facing portrait of the Queen flanked on one side by one of the original beasts and on the other by a creature relevant to the particular country. St Helena and its dependencies of Ascension and Tristan da Cunha went further by issuing coins to mark the event and made philatelic and numismatic history by reproducing the stamp designs on the reverse of the coins.

includes the error in which the Ascension reverse was muled with an Isle of Man obverse. The coin issued for the royal golden wedding in 1997 featured an equestrian event at the Montreal Olympics. Other Ascension issues marked International Year of the Scout (1983) with a portrait of Lord Baden-Powell, and the nature conservation programme of the World Wide Fund for Nature (1998), for which frigate-birds and long-tailed tropic-birds were shown on a pair of coins.

TRISTAN DA CUNHA

One of the world's remotest islands, situated roughly midway between South America and West Africa, Tristan da Cunha was named in honour of the navigator who discovered it, and like Ascension, it was garrisoned in 1815–16, though most of the present population are the descendants of shipwrecked seamen.

Barter currency of cigarettes or potatoes continued in use until the 1950s, when South African coins were adopted, but the island switched to British money after it was resettled in 1963, following the volcanic eruption of 1961. No circulating coins have been produced but a handful of crown-sized 25 pence and later 50 pence have marked royal events [12–13]. The sole exception is the gold £2 of 1983 for the Year of the Scout.

FALKLAND ISLANDS

British coins used on the islands were superseded by a distinctive series in the same weights and specifications in 1974, with the Queen's bust (obverse) and fauna (reverse) [14–15], including a gold sovereign and half sovereign featuring a Romney Marsh ram. Special issues began with the silver jubilee crown (1977) but began to proliferate after the South Atlantic War, including a lengthy series of 1996 entitled Royal Heritage, featuring monarchs from Egbert of Wessex (802–39) to Victoria (1837–1901). Very large silver coins (65mm/2⅝in diameter) tariffed at £25 have also appeared in recent years.

SOUTH GEORGIA AND SOUTH SANDWICH ISLANDS

Until 1985 these sub-Antarctic islands were dependencies of the Falklands, but they were then constituted a separate crown colony. Ordinary British coins are in everyday use, but since 2000 crown-sized £2 coins in cupro-nickel or silver, with occasional higher denominations in gold, have marked historic anniversaries, mainly pertaining to the islands, although also acknowledging royal events [16–19].

1 2

3 4

5 6

7 8

9 10

11 12

13 14

15 16

17

EUROPE

With a coinage that dates back to the 6th century BC, Europe is responsible for the largest number of different coins – far more than the rest of the world put together. This is due primarily to the multiplicity of petty kingdoms and principalities in the Middle Ages, each striking its own coinage. Even after the emergence of nation states with centralized coinage systems, political and economic upheavals, and the growth of commemorative and special issues, resulted in a vast output in the past century alone.

WESTERN SCANDINAVIA

This group includes the most south-westerly of the Scandinavian countries, Denmark, together with its colonies or dependencies in the North Atlantic. Iceland became autonomous in 1918 and a wholly independent republic in 1944. The unit of currency since 1874 has been the krone (crown) of 100 øre, replacing the daler (dollar) and skilling (shilling) of earlier times.

Left: Danish currency was reformed and rationalized with the foundation of the Rigsbank in 1813; the rigsspeciedaler of 96 skilling was replaced by the rigsbankdaler of 96 rigsbank skilling. The rigsbankdaler was worth half a rigspeciedaler, while five of them were worth a speciedaler d'or. Currency changed again in 1854, when the rigsdaler of 96 rigsmont skilling was introduced. Gold coins were known by the ruler's name followed by d'or *("of gold"), such as the Christian d'or.*

DENMARK

The kingdom of Denmark emerged under Gorm the Old in the 10th century, and his descendants have reigned ever since. King Cnut (Canute) united the Norse lands and even ruled over England (1016–35). Harthacnut, son of Cnut, ruled Denmark while his father reigned in England, and struck coins derived from Anglo-Saxon models [1–2]. About 800 the Danes began striking silver deniers and later imitated English pennies. The first distinctive coins appeared about 995 and followed the northern European pattern. Typical cross-type coins were the pennies issued by Eric of Pomerania at Lund in the 14th century [3–4]. In 1522 the first large coins appeared under the name daler. By the 16th century, Danish currency was in total chaos, with more than 150 different coins in circulation in the reign of Christian IV, many of which bore the crowned bust of the monarch on the obverse [5] and a

crown on the reverse [6]. A similar style was continued under his successor Christian V (1670–95), typified by fine portrait ducats [7–8] reflecting the growing importance of Denmark as a trading nation of world rank.

In the 19th century Denmark had a very complex monetary system based on the skilling, rigsbank skilling or rigsmont skilling as subdivisions of the rigspeciedaler, rigsbankdaler or rigsdaler. While the smaller coins featured a crowned monogram or shield, higher values portrayed the reigning monarch [9] with the value on the reverse [10].

DECIMAL COINAGE

On the formation of the Scandinavian Monetary Union the krone of 100 øre was introduced in 1874 and continued the style of the earliest coins, with a crowned monogram on the smallest denominations [11] and a royal effigy on the higher values [18], with the value on the reverse [12, 19]. Iron

the reverses. These large coins were accompanied by the annual issue of 5000 dinar gold coins.

South Korea did not wait until the end of the Los Angeles Games but began issuing its advance publicity coins in 1982 – thus lapping the previous Olympiad by two years. A total of eight gold, twelve silver, four nickel and four cupro-nickel coins was released over the ensuing six years, the pictorial motifs often having little or no relevance to the Olympic ideal. When Calgary hosted the Winter Games in 1988 Canada issued ten silver proof $20 coins from September 1985 onward, released in pairs at half-yearly intervals.

For the Albertville Winter Games (1992), France produced eight silver proof 100 franc coins showing various winter sports. In honour of the Barcelona Summer Games, Spain produced a superb collection of four individual issues, each consisting of three gold and four silver coins. Atlanta, Georgia was the venue for the Centennial Games, for which the US Mint produced two gold $5, four silver dollars and two clad cupro-nickel half dollars in 1995, all with attractive motifs showing aspects of Olympic sports as well as the Centennial logo of a torch, rings and the numerals 100. A similar programme appeared in 1996. Gibraltar, Bosnia and the Isle of Man were among the countries that released

Above: A set of crowns released by the Isle of Man for the Sydney Olympics, 2000, linking Australian maps and landmarks with various sports.

Below: A series of three crowns was issued by the Isle of Man on the occasion of the Los Angeles Summer Games in 1984.

Below: San Marino produced a silver 10,000 lire for the 2000 Olympics.

support coins in 1995–6. The most attractive of the support coins of recent years, however, have come from San Marino, often harking back to the timeless quality of the ancient Greek Olympic coins. In the same genre was the series of eight crowns from Gibraltar in 1992, with reverse motifs depicting events from the ancient Games, from boxing to chariot racing.

For the Millennium Games of 2000, Australia struck a prodigious series of coins in various metals. A total of 28 aluminium-bronze coins featured a wide range of Olympic sports: aquatics, archery, athletics, baseball, boxing, equestrian, gymnastics, hockey, pentathlon, rowing, sailing, volleyball, weight lifting, cycling, triathlon, football, canoeing, softball, wrestling, handball, taekwondo, basketball,

shooting, badminton, fencing and table tennis. A set of five coins from the Solomon Islands – two nickel $1, two silver $5 and a gold $50 – featured cartoon characters created by Brian Sage. Kenny the Kangaroo, Kylie the Koala and Eddie the Emu were shown taking part in various Olympic events.

To mark the Athens Games of 2004, Greece produced six sets of coins, each comprising a pair of silver 10 euros and a .9999 fine gold 100 euro piece. The obverses of the silver coins featured ancient and modern images of the same sports, to show the continuity of athletic contests over the millennia, while the gold coins concentrated on historically significant landmarks in Greece. The most recent issue is a set of coins from Italy, which hosted the Winter Games of 2006.

ENGLAND, SCOTLAND AND IRELAND

The three kingdoms of the British Isles maintained separate political identities for hundreds of years, and each struck their own coins before they were united. England and Scotland had distinctive coins until the Act of Union of 1707, while Ireland ceased to mint its own coinage when the United Kingdom was formed by the Act of Union of 1801.

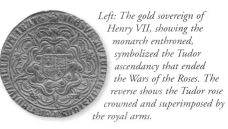

Left: The gold sovereign of Henry VII, showing the monarch enthroned, symbolized the Tudor ascendancy that ended the Wars of the Roses. The reverse shows the Tudor rose crowned and superimposed by the royal arms.

ENGLAND

Gallo-Belgic, Celtic tribal and Roman coins were used in Britain from the 2nd century BC until the withdrawal of the Roman legions in the early fifth century. These included gold Celtic ring money [1–2], Gallo-Belgic staters [3–4] and coins of the major tribes in southern Britain [5–6]. In succeeding generations, southern Britain was invaded by the Angles, Saxons and Jutes, who established petty kingdoms in Northumbria, Kent, Mercia (the Midlands) and East Anglia. The earliest coins were small gold thrymsas and silver sceattas [7] but Offa of Mercia (757–96) introduced the silver penny, which remained the standard coin until the reign of Henry VII (1485–1509), with a stylized full-face portrait (obverse) and a cross (reverse). While its obverse gave the name of the king, the reverse bore the name of the place where the coin was struck.

The Anglo-Saxon style of coinage was retained by the Normans and Plantagenets. Edward I (1277–1307) introduced the halfpenny and farthing [8–9] as well as the groat (4 pence). Edward III struck half groats and the florin, England's first regular gold coin. It was not a success, and was soon replaced by the noble [10], which

remained in use for almost a century. Edward IV introduced the gold angel [11] or third of a pound.

During the Hundred Years' War, coins in the English style were struck in those parts of France under English rule. Although the English king's claim to the French throne was effectively crushed by 1450, the French title and fleur de lis emblem survived on coins until the end of the 18th century.

English coinage entered a new era under Henry VII. He introduced the gold sovereign (1489) and the silver testoon or shilling (1500), the latter bearing the first realistic portrait on any English coin, influenced by developments in Renaissance Italy [12]. His grandson, Edward VI [13–14], introduced the large silver crown of 5 shillings, the first English coin to bear a date (1551). His sister Elizabeth (1558–1603) struck more denominations than any other British ruler – 20 different coins from the halfpenny to the sovereign [15–16]. Yet the number of types (about 60 in a 44-year reign) was comparatively small. During her reign the first tentative experiments in mechanization took place.

The Stuart dynasty, imported from Scotland in 1603, ruled England for little more than a century, but it was the most complex in British numismatic history. James I almost rivalled Elizabeth with coins of different names for the same value, such as the unite [17], laurel [18] and sovereign (pound), as well as new denominations like the thistle crown (4 shillings). During the reign of Charles I (1625–49) the Civil War broke out in 1642. While Parliament controlled London and thus the Tower Mint, which continued to strike coins in the king's name [19], the Royalists established mints at Aberystwyth, Shrewsbury, Oxford, York, Bristol [20], Exeter, Truro, Chester, Worcester and strongholds such as Hartlebury Castle. Makeshift coins were also produced in besieged towns, such as the diamond-shaped clipped coins of Pontefract [21–22].

Coins of the Commonwealth (1649–60) had the shield of St George on one side and the conjoined shields of England and Ireland on the other [23]. In 1662, shortly after the Restoration, milled coinage was adopted permanently, and, following the Act of Union of 1707, English coins extended to the whole country.

SCOTLAND
Scotland had no indigenous coinage until the reign of David I (1124–53), and only farthings, halfpennies and pennies were struck until the time of Robert II (1329–71), when gold nobles and silver groats [24] began to appear. Scottish coinage was remarkable for its diversity. Robert III added the lion (gold crown) and demy lion, while James I (1406–37) produced the demy and half demy. James III (1460–88) added the gold rider and its subdivisions, as well as the unicorn, the billon plack and the copper farthing [25–26]. Thereafter the use of base metal escalated, while gold and silver were often heavily debased. Inevitably the value of Scottish money fell in relation to sterling until ultimately the Scottish shilling (12 pence) was worth no more than an English penny [27–28]. After the Union of the Crowns (1603) the Edinburgh Mint continued to strike

Gun Money
Emergency coins were minted at Dublin in 1690 in the name of James II and were struck in metal from melted cannons in denominations of a crown, half crown, shilling and sixpence. Apart from the crown, these coins bore both their year and month of issue.

distinctive coins, but increasingly they conformed to English weights and fineness, which explains denominations such as 12, 30 and 60 shillings (equivalent to the English shilling, half crown and crown). The last Scottish coins were similar to those in England but bore the E mint-mark below Queen Anne's bust. The Edinburgh Mint closed in 1708.

IRELAND
Silver pennies were struck at Dublin by the Vikings in the 10th century. Following the Anglo-Norman conquest in the 12th century coins were struck showing Prince John as Lord of Ireland. Subsequent coins followed the English pattern but included oddities such as the tiny half farthing of Edward IV and a groat struck by Lambert Simnel, pretender to the throne under the name of Edward V. The harp first appeared on coins in the reign of Henry VIII and survived until 1822, when Irish coins were discontinued.

Below: An Irish groat of Henry VIII with the crowned harp on the reverse.

UNITED KINGDOM

The United Kingdom of Great Britain and Ireland was formed in 1801. In 1922, when the 26 counties of southern Ireland attained independence under the name of the Irish Free State, the United Kingdom of Great Britain and Northern Ireland came into being. Today it comprises the kingdoms of England and Scotland, the principality of Wales and the province of Northern Ireland, all but the first-named now having devolved powers exercised through a parliament in Scotland and assemblies in Wales and Northern Ireland. Scotland and Northern Ireland have their own banknotes, but the United Kingdom has a unified system of coinage.

Left: In 1989, £2 coins were issued to celebrate the tercentenaries of the Bill of Rights (England) and the Claim of Right (Scotland), which provided the basis for the constitutional monarchy under William III and Mary and laid the groundwork for the eventual union of the kingdoms.

HANOVERIAN RULERS

Her many children having pre-deceased her, Queen Anne (half farthing [1–2]) was succeeded by her cousin George Louis, Elector of Hanover, who ascended the throne in 1714 as George I. The quality of the engraving in British coins improved during the 18th century, with portraiture becoming more lifelike, if hardly flattering. Gold coins were struck in denominations of 5, 2, 1 [3–4] and half guinea (the name being derived from the Guinea Coast, whence much of the gold was imported). Although nominally rated at 20 shillings, the value of the guinea rose as high as 30 shillings before settling at 21 shillings, owing to fluctuations in the price of gold.

Silver became increasingly scarce in the Hanoverian period [10–11] and very few of the smaller coins (1–4 pence) were struck. Meanwhile, at the other end of the scale, small gold third and quarter guinea coins circulated, with respective values of 7 shillings, 5 shillings and 3 pence. A feature of British coins in this period was the inclusion of provenance marks, denoting the source of the bullion. In 1745, Admiral George Anson captured a Spanish treasure ship during his voyage round the world. Coins struck from the captured silver bore the word "Lima" below the king's bust [5–6].

Although base-metal halfpennies and farthings had been introduced in 1672, the Hanoverians were reluctant to issue base coinage, and the vacuum was filled by trade tokens. Not untypical were the heart-shaped tokens, bearing the London arms, issued by Sam Goodakers [7–8]. The first copper pennies and twopences (1797) were the Cartwheels struck by the private Soho Mint in Birmingham [9].

The parlous state of the coinage at the end of the Napoleonic Wars led to the reforms of 1816, re-introducing the sovereign of 20 shillings, much smaller and lighter than the guinea, with a corresponding reduction in the size of the silver coins.

VICTORIAN ERA

Most of the coins of Victoria's long reign portrayed her as a teenager [12] as she came to the throne in 1837, and it came as a shock to the public when the series released in 1887 to mark her golden jubilee showed her as an elderly lady [13]. There were some changes, notably the first attempt at decimalization, which resulted in the florin (1849), and the change from copper to bronze for the smallest denominations (1860), both utilizing more mature portraits [14–15]. The Jubilee bust was unpopular and was replaced by the Veiled Head in 1893 [16].

Timeless Classic

Benedetto Pistrucci's St George and the Dragon, featured on the gold coins of 1816–25, was revived in 1871 and has occupied the reverse of the gold coins ever since. It was also used for the silver crowns of 1818–23 and 1887–1902 and finally for the crown of 1951 marking the Festival of Britain. The model for St George was a waiter at Brunet's Hotel in Leicester Square, London.

EARLY TWENTIETH CENTURY

The coins of Edward VII followed the pattern of his predecessor, the standing Britannia motif of the florin being a notable concession to Art Nouveau (and inspiring the later Britannia bullion coins). A garlanded crown featured on the reverse of the George V crowns, but an Art Deco version of St George and the Dragon was used for the silver crown of 1935 for the silver jubilee [17]. Pictorial motifs were used on the low-value coins of George VI and Elizabeth II [20], while two different shillings (with English or Scottish heraldic lions) appeared in 1937 [18–19]. Few commemoratives appeared in this period, notably the crown honouring Sir Winston Churchill (1965).

DECIMAL COINAGE

Debated since the 1790s, British decimalization finally reached fruition in 1971. In the run-up to it several of the £sd series were not struck after 1967, while the first decimal coins appeared in 1968, the 5 and 10 new pence being struck in the same sizes as the shilling and florin. The half crown was withdrawn at the end of 1968 and in February 1971 the penny and threepence were superseded by the new ½, 1 and 2 pence coins [21]. In 1969 the 10 shilling note was replaced by the seven-sided 50 new pence. In 1982 the word "New" was dropped from the inscription and the small seven-sided 20 pence was introduced [24]. Two years later the halfpenny was discontinued.

The 50 pence was reduced in size in 1987, and the 5 and 10 pence were likewise reduced in 1990 and 1992 respectively. A nickel-brass circulating pound coin was introduced in 1983 and since its inception the reverse has changed annually [26]. Two pound coins were issued as commemoratives (1988–96) but a bimetallic coin of this value was added to the circulating series in 1997 [22]. The effigy of Queen Elizabeth has been changed four times. A bust by Mary Gillick was used for pre-decimal coinage [23], followed by effigies by Arnold Machin (1969), Raphael Maklouf (1988) [25] and Ian Rank-Broadley (1998). The crown was used for commemoratives and decimalized as 25 pence, but in 1990 it was revalued at £5. The 50 pence coin has often been used as a commemorative medium since 1973 [27].

Above: A crown released in 1981 to celebrate the wedding of the Prince of Wales and Lady Diana Spencer.

1

2

3

4

5

6

7

8

9

10

11

12

13

14

15

IRELAND AND OFFSHORE BRITISH ISLANDS

As well as the United Kingdom, there are four other countries in the British Isles that issue their own coins. The coins of Ireland issued before the Union of 1801 have already been discussed, but after 1928 the Irish Free State (now the Republic of Ireland) issued distinctive coins, while the Channel Islands (Guernsey and Jersey) and the Isle of Man each have a coinage history going back centuries.

Left: Guernsey released a square 10 shilling coin with rounded corners in 1966 to celebrate the 900th anniversary of the Norman Conquest of England, bearing the bust of William the Conqueror, Duke of Normandy. The Channel Islands are the last remnants of the Duchy governed by the British Crown.

JERSEY

Hoards of Armorican Celtic staters from 75–50 BC have been discovered in the Channel Islands, suggesting that they may even have been minted there.

Various bank tokens were issued between 1812 and 1831[1–2], but French currency circulated in Jersey until 1834, when the island switched to British money, and distinctive coins were adopted in 1841. Unfortunately, the money of account was the pre-Revolutionary French sol, tariffed at 520 to the pound. Jersey's largest coin was worth 2 sols – $\frac{1}{260}$ of a pound or $\frac{1}{13}$ of a shilling – hence the values on the early coins: $\frac{1}{52}$ (farthing) [3–4], $\frac{1}{26}$ (halfpenny) and $\frac{1}{13}$ (penny). In 1877 the currency was brought into line with Britain and the coins revalued at $\frac{1}{48}$, $\frac{1}{24}$ and $\frac{1}{12}$ of a shilling [5]. British coins served the higher values until 1957, when the quarter shilling (3 pence) was introduced. Since 1971 the decimal coinage has followed British standards.

GUERNSEY

French coins circulated in Guernsey for centuries, but halfpennies and farthings were imported from England from 1672 along with worn silver coins, which were not recalled until 1817. The vacuum was filled by a wide range of foreign coins and order was not restored until 1830, when the island introduced its own coinage based on

the ancient French *double tournois*, hence "Double" on the Guernsey coins [6–9]. Copper, and later bronze, issues of 8 (penny), 4 (halfpenny), 2 (farthing) and 1 double (half farthing) bore the arms of the bailiwick and the value.

A cupro-nickel threepence featuring a cow appeared in 1958–66 and the square 10 shillings in 1966. Since 1971 the full range of coins has conformed to British standards, the arms occupying the obverse until 1977, when Elizabeth II's profile was substituted. Gold and silver commemoratives have been struck for Alderney, Guernsey's dependency, since 1989.

ISLE OF MAN

Silver pennies modelled on the Hiberno-Norse coins of Ireland, but with blundered inscriptions and a crude portrait, were struck about 1025–35, but otherwise Scottish, English and Irish coins and tokens circulated freely and included Murray's Pence – local tokens declared legal tender in 1673. Distinctive pennies and halfpennies date from 1709, issued under the authority of the Earls of Derby [10–11] and later the Dukes of Atholl [12–13] as Lords of Man, with their emblems. The island was transferred to the British Crown in 1765 but regal coinage was not issued until 1786, with the bust of George III [14–15]. No coins were struck from

Above: The Isle of Man's close ties with Scotland are reflected in the set of four crowns issued in 1996 to mark the bicentenary of the death of Robert Burns, Scotland's national poet.

1813 to 1839, when coppers portraying Victoria were released [16]. Island money was tariffed at 14 pence to the shilling, but the Manx government brought it into line with Britain in 1840 and from then until 1971 British coins circulated. A gold series of 1965 marked the bicentenary of the Revestment Act, while a crown of 1970 featured the tailless Manx cat [19].

Since 1971 the island has issued the full range of coins for general circulation. The reverses often bear the national three-legged emblem and its motto, "Quocunque Jeceris Stabit", which translates as "Whithersoever you throw it, it will stand" [17]. While generally conforming to British standards, the Isle of Man pioneered £1 (1978), £2 and £5 coins (1981) in virenium, a special base-metal alloy [20]. Since 1972 it has been one of the world's most prolific issuers of commemoratives [18] and special issues, often in long thematic sets [21–22].

IRELAND

The first coins, designed by the noted sculptor Percy Metcalfe, appeared in 1928 with a harp (obverse) and various birds and animals (reverse), earning the nickname the Barnyard Series [23–25, 27–28]. The obverse was modified in 1939 when "Eire" (Ireland) replaced "Saorstat Eireann" (Irish Free State). In 1966 the 50th anniversary of the Easter Rising was marked by a 10 shilling coin portraying Padraig Pearse and the

statue of Cuchulainn. Ireland decimalized its currency at the same time as Britain, using the same specifications, but adopted distinctive nickel-bronze 20 pence (1986) and cupro-nickel pound coins (1990). The harp obverse was retained, as well as the horse, salmon and bull motifs on the 20, 10 and 5 pence [29–30], but Hiberno-Norse ornament graced the bronze coins [26], while the pound featured a stag and woodcock, formerly on the farthing, was promoted to the 50 pence. A 50 pence featuring the civic arms celebrated the Dublin millennium in 1998. The Millennium was marked by a pound coin depicting a galley surmounted by a cross, symbolizing the advent of Christianity in Ireland. Ireland adopted the euro in 2002, but medallic pattern ecus signalled the EEC Council Meeting in Dublin in 1990.

Portrait Gallery
One of the most spectacular coins of recent times was the crown released by the Isle of Man in 1987 to celebrate the bicentenary of the American Constitution. The reverse shows the Statue of Liberty surrounded by 11 portraits of US statesmen, from George Washington to Ronald Reagan.

16

17

18

19

20

21

22

23

24

25

26

27

28

29

30

1
2
3
4
5
6
7
8
9
10
11
12
13
14
15
16
17

BRITISH EUROPEAN TERRITORIES

Four Mediterranean countries with long and distinctive histories are grouped here because they came under British rule for many years and their modern coinage was therefore either closely linked to that of Britain or strongly influenced by it.

Left: The traditions of the Knights of St John of Jerusalem are continued to this day by the Sovereign Order of Malta, based in Rome. Since 1967 the Order has produced a large number of medallic pieces, denominated in scudi, illustrating the history of the Knights and raising funds for its charitable works.

CYPRUS

This island was of vital importance to Mediterranean cultures in the Bronze Age as the chief source of copper (from which the island derives its name); imitation cowhides cast in copper rank among the earliest forms of currency. In Greek classical times coins were struck at Amathus, Salamis, Paphos, Idalium and Citium. Typical of these coins was the silver of Evagoras II (361–351 BC) of Salamis [1–2] and Azbaal of Citium in the 5th century BC [5–6]. Coins of Alexander the Great were minted in Cyprus [3–4] from the 4th century BC.

Shown here is a Byzantine coin of Isaac the Usurper (1184–91), struck in Cyprus before he was overthrown [7–8]. Between 1192 and 1324, deniers, obols and gros were issued by the Crusader Guy de Lusignan and his descendants, such as Henry III, who struck large silver gros with facing portraits and cross motifs [9]. Distinctive coinage was revived in 1879 when Cyprus became a British protectorate. The Turkish piastre was tariffed at nine to the shilling, hence there were coins of 18, 9 and 4 piastres as well as smaller coins down to the bronze quarter piastre. These bore the effigy of the British monarch and the value or arms on the reverse. Latterly the reverse featured two lions passant gardant, the emblem of Richard the Lionheart, who seized Cyprus from the Byzantines in 1191.

Decimal currency based on the pound of 1000 mils was adopted in 1955, and pictorial reverses were then selected [10–11]. In 1960 Cyprus became an independent republic and introduced coins with the state emblem on the obverse [12]. The currency was reformed in 1983 and the pound of 100 cents adopted. A few commemoratives have appeared since 1976.

MALTA

Like Cyprus, Malta has a long numismatic history, its earliest coins being attributed to the Phoenicians in the 3rd century BC. Subsequently there was a limited (and very rare) coinage under Greek or Roman influence [13].

The Knights of St John of Jerusalem, having been driven out of Rhodes, occupied Malta from 1530 until they were expelled by Napoleon in 1798, and coins in various denominations from the tiny picciolo (72 to the penny) to the zechino (sequin, or third of a pound sterling) [14–15] were minted under successive Grand Masters from Villiers de l'Isle Adam (1533) to Count von Hompesch (1798) [16–17]. The French garrison produced siege coins in gold, silver and bronze during the British blockade of 1799–1800.

Ordinary British coins circulated from 1800 until 1972 but included third farthings (1827–1913), which corresponded to the copper grano. A decimal system based on the lira or obverse of the 1 and 2 franc coins. In 1878 a female profile replaced the cross on the 5 and 10 rappen, followed by the 20 rappen in 1881 [10–11]. In these coins the country name was rendered in Latin "Confoederatio Helvetica". The seated figure on the 5 franc coin was replaced by a garlanded profile in 1888, with the cross on a shield flanked by the value on the reverse. This type continued until 1922, when the bust of William Tell (obverse) and modified shield (reverse) was introduced. The bronze subsidiary

Shooting Festival Coins

From the late 16th century many German states and free cities issued special coins that were given as prizes at shooting festivals. This tradition spread to Switzerland in 1842, and while it died out everywhere else it continued there until 1939. The coins, variously denominated 4 francs, 40 batzen or 5 francs, usually had armorial or allegorical motifs, with figures of marksmen or crossed rifles as popular images. These handsome silver coins, which were struck for the annual festivals at a different venue each year, were last regularly minted in 1885 but were sporadically revived in the 1930s.

coins had a Swiss cross on the obverse and a wreathed value on the reverse [12–13]. Last, new designs were adopted for the 1 and 2 rappen coins in 1948, with a plain cross (obverse) and a numeral superimposed on an ear of corn (reverse) [14–15]. Apart from the replacement of silver by cupronickel in 1968, the Swiss coins have since remained unchanged [16–17].

COMMEMORATIVE ISSUES

Just as the permanent series has been very structured since its inception, so also the approach to commemorative and special issues has been very carefully orchestrated. Beginning in 1936, 5 franc coins were produced for special occasions [18–19], the first such coin publicizing the Confederation Armament Fund. The majority of coins have celebrated historic anniversaries or major current events and organizations, such as the Zurich Exhibition of 1939, the International Olympic Committee [20–21] and the Wine Festival of 1999 [22–23]. Since 1991, however, the chief medium for special issues has been the 20 franc denomination, usually confined to no more than two coins a year.

LIECHTENSTEIN

This tiny principality has had a lengthy association with Austria, whose currency it used until the end of World War I, augmented by the silver and gold vereinsthaler in the 19th century and similar coins in the kronen system from 1900, portraying the ruler (obverse) and princely arms (reverse).

In 1921 Leichtenstein entered a monetary union with Switzerland and adopted its coinage, followed by indigenous coinage of 100 rappen in 1924, portraying John II (1858–1929) or Franz I (1929–38). A series portraying Prince Francis Joseph II appeared in 1946. Since then there have been a few silver or gold commemoratives marking royal weddings, anniversaries [24–27] and the accession of Prince Hans Adam (1990) but Swiss coins are in everyday use.

1
2
3
4
5
6
7
8
9
10
11
12
13
14

GERMAN STATES

Within the boundaries of modern Germany there were hundreds of kingdoms, principalities, grand duchies, duchies, counties and free cities, which for almost 2000 years produced their own coins, ranging from Celtic and Roman provincial to the prolific Frankish and Saxon issues that preceded the medieval coinage. These coins range from the pilgrim denars of Cologne [1–2] to the regal issues of Otto III (982–1002) [3–4]. Although the number was greatly reduced as a result of mergers and territorial aggrandisement by the more powerful states such as Prussia [5–6] in the course of the 17th and 18th centuries, no fewer than 39 states were, nevertheless, still issuing coins by 1815. Even after the formation of the German Empire in 1871 many states reserved the right to strike coins with distinctive reverses, even if the obverse conformed to the imperial standard – a precedent followed by the European Union's common currency at the present day.

Below: Some of the most spectacular coins ever struck emanated from the Duchy of Brunswick and the Kingdom of Saxony, notably the great multiple thalers of the 17th and 18th centuries. Examples include the 1631 Purim thaler of Erfurt, with Hebrew inscription and radiate sign of Yahweh (left), and the 1661 thaler of the bishopric of Munster showing St Paul above a panoramic view of the city (right).

CURRENCY REFORM

Different systems of weights and measures as well as varying standards of gold and silver meant that each German state was a law unto itself, making interstate trade exceedingly complex. By the late 18th century this had been rationalized to some extent, with distinct patterns emerging in the northern and southern states, whose coinage was largely based on the thaler and kreuzer respectively. Thus, in the north, the thaler was worth 24 groschen, a groschen was worth 12 pfennige and 2 heller equalled a pfennig [7–8], but there was also the mariengroschen, worth 8 pfennige. Meanwhile, attempts to equate the gulden with the thaler resulted in a ratio of 2 gulden to one and a third thalers. In the southern states the kreuzer [9–10] was worth 4 pfennige or 8 heller, but 24 kreuzer Landmunze were equal in value to 20 kreuzer Conventionsmunze, while 120 Convention kreuzer equalled two

Convention gulden or 1 Convention thaler ("Convention" refers to an agreement of 1753, which first tried to bring the states into line). A new agreement (1837) reduced the complexity further. In the north the thaler was now worth 30 groschen or 360 pfennige (as recently as the 1960s Germans habitually referred to the 10 pfennig coin as a groschen). In the south the sole unit was the kreuzer.

VARIETY OF SUBJECTS

Several states produced a local coinage for provinces and other administrative subdivisions. Thus the kingdom of Prussia [11–12] also produced a subsidiary coinage for the province of Brandenburg and, within that, coins for Brandenburg-Ansbach-Bayreuth. The most notable of the subdivisions arose in Brunswick, where the practice of dividing a territory among all the sons of the ruler, instead of leaving everything to the eldest son, created a

Portrait Gallery

From 1957 onwards the 2 DM became more interesting as its reverse portrayed famous Germans. The physicist Max Planck was followed by a series of postwar politicians (clockwise from top left): President Theodor Heuss (dates of use 1970–87), Konrad Adenauer (1969–87), Chancellor Ludwig Erhard (1988–2000) and Dr Kurt Schumacher (1979–93). Also portrayed were Franz Joseph Strauss (1990–2000) and Willy Brandt, Mayor of West Berlin throughout the Cold War (1994–2000). As can be seen, these coins were often in simultaneous production and circulated widely.

DEMOCRATIC REPUBLIC

In the immediate postwar period the coins of the Bank of the German Provinces circulated in the Soviet zone, but economic disparity between the Soviet and Allied zones led to the currency reform of 1948, which recognized the difference between the money in East and West Germany. At this time distinctive coins began to appear in the Soviet zone. They comprised 1, 5 and 10 pfennige in aluminium and were simply inscribed "Deutschland" (Germany), with a numeral obverse and a reverse showing an ear of wheat superimposed on a cog wheel symbolizing industry and agriculture [14–17]. The German Democratic Republic was formally

instituted in October 1949 and by 1952 coins bore the emblem of the new state – a hammer and compass on wheat ears – with the country name "Deutsche Demokratische Republik" [18]. The 1 pfennig coin was modified in 1960, the central design now appearing within a border with the legend running around the outside [19–20]. Attempts to introduce higher denominations led to a short-lived 50 pfennig coin (1950 and 1958) [25], although this did not become a regular issue until 1968, followed by the 20 pfennige in 1969 [23–24]. Similarly, 1 and 2 mark [26–27] coins were sporadically produced from 1956 but did not become regular issues until 1973–4. The 1 pfennig was reissued in 1979 and remained in circulation until the switch to West German currency in 1990.

A 5 mark coin showing the Brandenburg Gate was minted in 1971 [21–22] and then annually from 1979 to 1990, but this denomination was mainly used for commemoratives [30–31], beginning with the 125th anniversary of Robert Koch (1968). From 1966, when the 125th anniversary of the architect Karl Schinkel was celebrated, 10 and 20 mark coins [28–29] were also released.

UNIFIED GERMANY

Ironically, the last issue of the GDR was a cupro-nickel 20 mark coin for the opening of the Brandenburg Gate in 1990 – the landmark that, with the breaching of the Berlin Wall, effectively brought the Democratic Republic to an end. The five eastern provinces were formally admitted into the Federal Republic on October 3, 1990.

No change was necessary in the coinage, which was merely extended to the East [32]. However, in 1991 a 10 DM coin marked the bicentenary of the Brandenburg Gate with an inscription signifying "Symbol of German Unity". For 40 years the gate had been the symbol of a divided nation. The commemorative coins issued since then tended to reinforce the concept of unity and a common heritage.

AUSTRIA AND HUNGARY

These two countries of Central Europe were at the heart of the Habsburg dominions, and for centuries they were administered as a single state. In the 19th century the rising tide of nationalism led to the Ausgleich (compromise) of 1867, whereby Kaiser Franz Josef of Austria also became Kiralyi Ferenc Joszef of Hungary. Henceforth, distinctive coins appeared under the Dual Monarchy, denominated in krone (korona) and heller (filler) respectively. The collapse of the monarchy in 1918 led to the establishment of two quite separate countries which, despite the political turmoil of the later 20th century, have retained close cultural and economic ties.

Left: Austria's pre-eminence in European history since the 15th century is reflected in many of the large silver commemorative coins of recent years; the standard obverse has the shields of the nine provinces with the national eagle at the top.

HABSBURG EMPIRE

Small silver coins known as *Wiener pfennige* (Vienna pennies), portraying the Dukes of Austria, were struck in the late Middle Ages, but the Habsburgs' outstanding contribution to numismatics was the development of large silver coins, the guldengroschen and the thaler [1–2] from the late 15th century, while gold ducats [3–4] ranked among the most popular trade coins until the early 20th century.

The circulating coinage of the Habsburg dominions was based on the thaler worth two gulden or 120 kreuzer [5–6], but the currency was decimalized in 1857 to the gulden or florin of 100 kreuzer, with the vereinsthaler worth 1 florin. These coins bore the bust of the emperor (obverse) and double-eagle emblem (reverse), but some of the smaller coins had the imperial arms (obverse) with a value (reverse). They were superseded by the krone of 100 heller in 1892, with arms and a value on the heller coins and the emperor's profile on the krone obverse and the imperial double eagle on the reverse [7–8].

Shooting festival 2 florin coins were struck in 1873 and 1879, while the opening of the Vienna–Trieste Railway in 1857 was marked by a double

vereinsthaler. Both silver and gold coins celebrated the emperor's diamond jubilee (1908). The humble heller and the silver coins vanished after 1916, while iron or zinc alloys were used for the 2 and 10 heller of 1916–18.

Hungary was a major source of both gold and silver in the Middle Ages [18–19], most of it exported to Venice, hence the lengthy series of ducats and florins of the Kremnitz Mint from 1324 onward [20]. After 1526, however, Hungary was claimed by the Habsburgs and thereafter its coinage followed a similar pattern to that of Austria, but inscribed "krajczar" (kreuzer) [21–22] or "forint" (florin). The filler denominations of 1892–1914 featured the crown of St Stephen on the obverse, while the korona coins showed it on the reverse surmounting the value.

AUSTRIA

The krone continued as the unit of currency after World War I but rampant inflation reduced the 100 krone to a tiny bronze coin in 1923–4 [9]. Like Germany in the same period, Austria resorted to *Notgeld* paper money, but, upon the reformation of the currency in 1925 [10], introduced the schilling of 100 groschen. Coins were struck in bronze, cupro-nickel or silver up to the schilling for general circulation, but from 1928 silver 2 and 5 schilling or gold 25, 50 and 100 schilling coins were struck as commemoratives.

Austrian coins were suppressed in 1938, when the country was absorbed into the Third Reich. When distinctive coins resumed after World War II, aluminium or aluminium-bronze were used for the lower values and cupro-nickel for the schilling denominations in general circulation [11–14]. Like their pre-war counterparts, these coins

International Coin
The silver thaler portraying the Empress Maria Theresia, with the date frozen at 1780 (the year of her death), was struck at Vienna until 1937 and also after 1956 to satisfy demand from the Arab countries. It was struck in Milan and Venice in the 19th century, at Rome (1935–9) for use in Ethiopia, and at Paris (1935–57), London (1936–61), Brussels (1937–57), Bombay (1940–1) and Birmingham (1949–55), as well as Prague and Leningrad until 1975. It has been estimated than more than 800 million coins have been struck.

had symbolic or pictorial motifs on the obverse and a numeral reverse. Commemoratives comprised base-metal 20 schilling coins (1982–2000) [15–17], silver 25, 50, 100, 200 and 500 schilling pieces (1955–2000) and gold 1000 schillings (1976–2000). In addition, gold 200 and 2000 schilling coins were struck annually from 1989 to 1999 in support of the Vienna Philharmonic Orchestra.

HUNGARY
Inflation hit Hungary in the aftermath of World War I, but it also suffered foreign invasion and the loss of much territory to its neighbours. A short-lived Soviet republic under Bela Kun was ruthlessly suppressed and Hungary became "a kingdom without a king, ruled by an admiral without a navy".

The currency was reformed in 1925 with the adoption of the pengo of 100 filler, and coins continued to feature the crown of St Stephen with a royal inscription. During World War II steel or zinc replaced bronze and cupro-nickel, while the pengo switched from silver to aluminium. A number of commemorative 2 and 5 pengo coins appeared from 1930, ranging from the silver coin of 1930 marking the tenth anniversary of Admiral Horthy as regent, to the aluminium coin of 1943 celebrating his 75th birthday.

After World War II Hungary suffered the worst inflation of any European country and the currency reform of 1946 restored the forint. The obverse inscriptions reflect postwar political changes: "Allami Valtopenz" (Provisional Government, 1945) "Koztarsasag" (Republic, 1946) [23–24], "Nepkoztarsasag" (People's Republic, 1950) [25–28] and "Koztarsasag" (Republic again since 1990) [30–31]. Most circulating coins under the communist regime were of aluminium, though the 2, 5 and 10 forint were in nickel alloys. The tenth anniversary of the forint was marked by a silver 10 forint in 1956, but 20, 25, 100 or 200 forint coins were the main commemorative medium [29].

CZECHOSLOVAKIA

Situated in the very heart of Europe, Czechoslovakia was formed at the end of World War I from the historic kingdom of Bohemia, with Moravia, Slovakia and Ruthenia, formerly part of the Habsburg dominions. Ethnically and linguistically Slavonic, these areas were administered under Austria or Hungary, which created an economic and political imbalance leading to dissolution in 1938–9 and again in 1993. The silver mines of Joachimsthal in Bohemia produced the raw material for the large coins that therefore came to be known as Joachimsthalers; the name was soon shortened to "thalers", from which the word "dollar" is derived.

Left: The Pragergroschen, which derived its name from the Latin inscription "Grossi Pragensis" on the original version, was the first of the large coins to circulate in Europe. The coins were originally struck at Kuttenberg (Kutná Hora). The kingdom of Bohemia played a major role in European coinage, its mines producing both gold for the Pragergroschen of the 14th century and silver for the great thalers that were minted from 1519 onward.

KINGDOM OF BOHEMIA
The early denars of Bohemia, struck at Prague in the 10th and 11th centuries, were a curious blend of Anglo-Saxon and German types, reflecting the commercial influences on this important duchy at the heart of Europe. In the 12th century, Bohemia produced bracteates in the German style. The discovery of silver at Kutna Hora in the late 13th century, and the establishment of a mint there in 1298, had a tremendous impact on European coinage thereafter [1].

In the 15th century the kingdom increasingly came under German domination, until in 1526 the throne was claimed by the Archduke of Austria. Thereafter, the Habsburgs ruled Bohemia until 1918, and the later coinage closely followed that of Austria and Hungary. The Prague Mint produced coins for the Habsburg Empire, including the famous Maria Theresia thaler of 1780.

FIRST REPUBLIC
The Czech lands of Bohemia, Moravia and part of Silesia were united with Slovakia and Ruthenia in October 1918 when the Habsburg monarchy collapsed. The coinage, introduced in 1921, was modelled on that of pre-war Austria and Hungary and comprised the koruna (plural *korun*) of 100 haleru. The obverse showed the lion of Bohemia, while numerals and quasi-symbolic motifs occupied the reverses [2–3]. Commemorative silver coins celebrated the tenth anniversary of the republic (1928) or mourned the death of Tomas Masaryk, the first president (1937) [8–9]. Gold ducats (known in Czech as *dukaty*) carried on a Habsburg tradition from 1923 to 1939 [4–5].

The dismemberment of the country began in 1938, when Czechoslovakia was forced to cede the Sudetenland to the Third Reich. Slovakia became a separate state and a fascist ally of Hitler. Carpatho-Ukraine was granted autonomy in March 1939 but was promptly seized by Hungary. At the end of the war, Ruthenia was briefly independent before it was absorbed by the USSR; it is now part of the Ukraine.

On March 15, 1939, Nazi Germany invaded what was left of the Czech lands and proclaimed the Reich Protectorate of Bohemia and Moravia.

Although the general appearance of the coins was similar to the Czech series, the wartime issues of Bohemia and Moravia bore the names of the protectorate in German and Czech.

POSTWAR CZECHOSLAVAKIA
The pre-war coinage was resumed in 1946 but with new reverse designs. It included several silver coins, commemorating the risings in Slovakia and Prague (1947–8), the 600th anniversary of the Charles University (1948) and the 30th anniversaries of independence (1948) and the Czech Communist Party (1951) [6–7].

In February 1948 the communists seized power and Czechoslovakia subsequently became a people's republic, then a socialist republic (1962) and finally the Czech and Slovak Federal Republic (1990) [16]. Within two years, however, the return to democracy led to a break-up, although ties between the Czech Republic and Slovakia have remained close. The coins of 1948–90 reflect the dichotomy between those in general circulation, which are mainly struck in aluminium or brass [10–11], and the prolific issues of silver commemorative coins, from 25 to 500 korun.

SLOVAKIA
Distinctive coins based on the koruna slovenska (Sk) of 100 halierov were struck at Kremnica from 1939 to 1945 [12–15]; zinc, bronze or aluminium was used for the lower values and cupro-nickel for the 50 halierov, and 1 and 2Sk. Despite wartime strictures, the Slovak state even produced a few silver coins marking anniversaries of independence and portraying Monsignor Joseph Tiso, the state president. Their obverse featured the double cross emblem, and this motif has also graced the coins of the republic since its restoration [22].

The present series was introduced in 1993 and has attractive scenic motifs in the background of the numerals on the reverse of the halierov coins [17–19], and images derived from

Stalin's Birthday
A sad reflection on the extent to which postwar Czechoslovakia was in the grip of communism was the release of silver coins in 1948 to celebrate the 70th birthday of Joseph Stalin. The reverse featured the bust of the Soviet dictator, who was never portrayed on any Russian coins.

ancient statuary on the koruna values [20–23]. Silver 100, 200, 500 and 2000Sk and gold 5000Sk coins have also been produced since 1993 to mark anniversaries of independence and pay tribute to famous Slovaks, as well as highlighting environmental problems and nature conservation.

CZECH REPUBLIC
Coins for the Czech Republic were introduced in 1993: the 10, 20 and 50 halierov in aluminium, the 1, 2 and 5 koruna czech (Kc) in nickel-plated steel and the 10, 20 and 50Kc in copper- or brass-plated steel [26]. The top value is a bimetallic coin with a plated brass centre and a copper-plated outer ring. The series has a standard obverse showing the lion of Bohemia [28], while the reverse motifs blend large numerals with symbols (up to 2Kc) [24]. The higher values show the Charles Bridge in Prague (5Kc) [25], Brno Cathedral (10Kc) [27], the equestrian statue of St Wenceslas (20Kc) [29–30] and a panoramic view of Prague. It constitutes one of the most aesthetically pleasing series of modern times. Silver (200Kc) or gold (1000–10,000Kc) coins have provided a rich variety of commemorative or special issues in the same period, including a 2000Kc in gold and silver with a holographic inlay to celebrate the Millennium.

POLAND

In the late Middle Ages, Poland expanded dramatically: at the height of its powers it extended from the Baltic to the Black Sea, encompassing Lithuania, the Ukraine and Belarus, but it declined in the 18th century and between 1772 and 1795 it was dismembered by Austria, Russia and Prussia. In 1807, Napoleon reconstituted much of the territory seized by Prussia as the Duchy of Warsaw, which briefly had its own coins portraying Friedrich August of Saxony, whom Napoleon installed as duke [6–7]. The duchy was overrun by Prussia and Russia in 1813 and partitioned between them in an arrangement ratified by the Congress of Versailles (1815), which also created the tiny republic of Cracow and granted the eastern lands to the Tsar as the so-called Congress Kingdom of Poland. The upheavals of World War I and the downfall of the three empires that had partitioned Poland enabled its reconstitution in 1917–18 as a republic.

Left: A 500 zloty coin of 1995 recalled the sufferings of Poland in World War II, when it was again partitioned, Nazi Germany taking the western provinces, including Warsaw, while the Soviet Union grabbed the rest – and retained most of it at the end of the war.

THE KINGDOM OF POLAND
The earliest coins emerged in the 12th century and consisted of bracteates [1–2] as well as small denars of a more orthodox appearance, such as the coin minted by Wladislaw II Wygnaniec [3]. The power and wealth of the medieval kingdom was reflected in the rich diversity of its coinage. This included the first coins with face-to-face portraits since Roman times (Charles I of Hungary and Elizabeth of Poland, 1308) and the coins of Sigismund I featuring the Golden Fleece (1601), after he was admitted as a member of that prestigious imperial order of chivalry. Under Sigismund III Vasa (1587–1632) the coins of Poland reflected Swedish influence, typified by the ort or 6 groschen [4–5].

The designs of the 17th and 18th centuries showed the influence of Germany, Spain and Italy. The coinage was exceedingly complex and included the szostak of 6 groszy and the tympf of 3 szostak, the polturak of 1 grosze or 3 poltura, and the gross of 2 poltura or 3 solidi or schillings. Under the Napoleonic Grand Duchy of Warsaw

the basic unit was the talara or zloty (from the Polish word for gold) worth 30 groszy, though 6 zlotych made a reichsthaler and 8 a speciesthaler. The reconstituted kingdom of Poland (1815) rationalized the coinage in 1832 [8–9] and linked it to the Russian system, so that 10 zlotych were worth 1 rouble and 30 groszy were worth 15 kopeks. Under the Grand Duchy and later kingdoms, coins in copper or silver had an armorial obverse and the value in words, but Tsar, as king of Poland, appeared in profile on the higher silver and gold denominations. After 1841, Polish coinage was suppressed and replaced by Russian currency. A crowned eagle obverse and numeral reverse appeared on coins issued in the districts occupied by Austro-German forces in World War I, based on the marka of 100 fenigow.

FIRST REPUBLIC
Because of postwar inflation and the problems of integrating the mixture of Austrian, German and Russian currencies in different parts of Poland, it was not until 1923 that a unified coinage

Siberian Copper

The city of Ekaterinburg, named in honour of Catherine the Great, was the centre of the Siberian copper mining district. The Ekaterinburg Mint was geared up to refine and coin Siberian copper in 1725–7, and during Catherine's reign it produced very heavy copper coins similar in size to the *plåtmynt* of Sweden. Although much favoured by the monarch, these coins were far too cumbersome for everyday use and were extremely unpopular with the merchant classes for that reason. As a result, they were withdrawn after two years and melted down.

silver coins marking the 1980 Moscow Olympics. Typically these coins had an obverse showing the Soviet arms with the value in the exergue [17], with an image and commemorative inscription on the reverse [18].

As the Soviet Union began to fall apart in 1991, an issue of coins was made by the State Bank in denominations from 10 kopeks to 10 roubles, with a standard obverse showing the Moscow Kremlin and a reverse bearing the value between an ear of wheat and oak leaves for the lower denominations [21–22]. They were struck in copper-clad steel (10 kopeks) or cupro-nickel (50 kopeks and 1 rouble), while the higher values were bimetallic. The issue even included a pair of 5 rouble coins for wildlife conservation, depicting an owl or a mountain goat on the reverse, with the value on the obverse. The State Bank also produced special issues such as the series featuring gems of Russian classical architecture [19–20].

unite", with "RSFSR" at the foot signifying the Russian Soviet Federative Socialist Republic [15–16], which gave way to the Union of Soviet Socialist Republics in 1923. Coins bearing the Cyrillic "CCCP" (USSR) appeared from 1924. A legacy of tsarist times was the wide range of denominations, with coins of 1, 2, 3, 5, 10, 15, 20 and 50 kopeks. Silver was replaced by cupronickel in 1931 and a brass alloy of cupro-nickel-zinc in 1961, with subtly changed designs.

From 1965, when a rouble celebrated the 20th anniversary of the end of World War II, the Soviet Union produced numerous commemorative pieces in denominations of 1, 2, 3, 5, 10, 25, 50, 100 and 150 roubles, culminating in the platinum, gold and

Above: Despite the negative experience of issuing very large and cumbersome copper pieces, Russia persevered with comparatively large copper coins, such as this 5 kopek of 1769, with the imperial double-headed eagle on one side and the crowned monogram of the Empress Catherine the Great on the other.

11 12
13
14
15 16
17 18
19
20
21 22

COMMONWEALTH OF INDEPENDENT STATES

The collapse of the communist regime in 1991 precipitated the dissolution of the Union of Soviet Socialist Republics. Mikhail Gorbachev attempted to hold the component republics together in a loose federation known as the Commonwealth of Independent States (CIS), but this concept was short-lived, as the various republics went their separate ways and even fought wars over disputed territory. Nevertheless it is convenient to survey the coins issued since 1992 under this heading. Outside Russia proper, indigenous coinage existed from the beginning of the Christian era in the Caucasus region, crude bronze pieces derived from Greek and Roman models being recorded from Georgia and quite sophisticated coinage in medieval Armenia, emulating the gold and silver of the Byzantine Empire. Although some of the states that briefly emerged in the early 1920s had their own paper money, none had distinctive coins until gaining independence in the 1990s.

Left: Levon, the Lion King of Armenia (1198–1226) allied himself to the Crusaders and married a Lusignan princess, founding a dynasty that expanded its territory in Asia Minor and was for some time a bastion of Christianity against Turkish aggression. Levon was a skilled diplomat, who forged alliances with the German emperors and Pope Celestine III. His westward orientation is reflected in his silver coins, such as this double tram showing him seated on the lion throne, holding the orb and sceptre, with the crowned lion in front of a patriarchal cross on the reverse.

RUSSIAN FEDERATION

By far the largest of the former Soviet republics is Russia, itself a federation of autonomous republics extending from the Baltic to the Pacific. It was hard hit by inflation when the USSR collapsed and a reform of 1992 led to the new rouble worth 10,000 old roubles. Brass-clad steel roubles were introduced that year, with the old double eagle emblem (minus imperial crowns) on the obverse [1–2] and the value on the reverse. Significantly, these and later coins were issued by authority of Bank Rossiya, the new state bank. Smaller coins, from 1 to 50 kopeks, featured St George and the dragon on the obverse [3–4]. The Soviet practice of issuing numerous commemorative coins has continued since 1992, including long thematic sets [5–7], such as the wildlife series of 1995–6. Some tiny 10 rouble gold coins have appeared since 1994.

CAUCASIAN REPUBLICS

As a once powerful kingdom geographically linked to Asia Minor and the Black Sea, Armenia's early coinage was subject to Greek, Roman and Byzantine influences. It struck its own coins from the 3rd century BC to the 16th century, but used Russian coins from 1801. Coins based on the dram (drachma) of 100 luma were introduced in 1994, with a double eagle obverse and value reverse [8–9]. A 5 dram silver coin of 1998, marking the fifth anniversary of the currency, reproduced banknotes on the reverse.

Azerbaijan's currency, based on the manta of 100 qapik, was launched in 1992 with symbols (obverse) and values (reverse) [10–11]. Gold and silver 50 manat appeared in 1996 to honour the national poet Mohammad Fuzuli.

In the 19th century, Georgian silver was mined for imperial Russian coins,

Return to Barter?

Tatarstan, an autonomous republic of the Russian Federation, declared its independence in February 1994. Since then, undated bronze coins with the state emblem on the obverse (top-right) have been introduced. These coins bear no inscibed value, but the smaller piece, which has ears of wheat on the reverse, is worth a kilogram of bread, while the larger coin, showing an oil well pump (bottom), is worth 10 litres of petrol (gasoline).

many bearing the Tiflis (Tbilisi) mint-mark [12–13]. Independent Georgia's coinage consists of the lari of 100 thetri; coins from 1 to 20 thetri in stainless steel, and 50 thetri in brass, have a wheel symbol (obverse) and various animals (reverse) [14–16]. A 500 lari gold coin appeared in 1995 to celebrate the 50th anniversary of liberation from Fascism.

WESTERN REPUBLICS

The Ukraine almost rivals Russia in its prolific coinage since 1995. It began with coins of astronomical denominations, but in practice, everyday money consisted of paper and the cupro-nickel 200,000 karbovanetz and silver coins denominated in millions were purely commemorative. The currency was reformed in September 1996, the hryven of 100 kopiyok being worth 100,000 old karbovanetz. Aluminium, steel or brass coins featured the trident emblem and value [17–20]. Numerous commemoratives from 2 to 500 hryvni in silver or gold have been released.

Belarus (formerly Byelorussia or White Russia) has stuck to the rouble of 100 kapeek and has had commemorative gold, silver and cupro-nickel coins since 1996, while relying on small paper notes for everyday use.

Moldova lies next to Romania and has adopted the currency of that country, the leu of 100 bani, but unlike Romania its lei have not assumed astronomical proportions as a result of inflation. Aluminium coins from 1 to 50 bani [21–22] and clad steel leu and 5 lei pieces were introduced in 1992–3. A few silver 100 lei commemoratives have appeared since 1996.

CENTRAL ASIAN REPUBLICS

If the Ukraine and the Caucasian republics enjoyed a brief existence after World War I, the republics of Central Asia had no political existence before their creation by the USSR. Kyrgyzstan became a Union republic in 1936 and, so far, its only coins (since 1995) have been silver 10 som or gold 100 som commemoratives. Kazakhstan introduced circulating coins based on the tenga of 100 tyn in 1993, with the state emblem and value on obverse and reverse respectively [23–24]. Coins of 20 and 50 tenge (cupro-nickel), 100 tenge (silver) and 1000 tenge (gold) have marked anniversaries of independence and honoured historic figures since 1993 [33–34]. Turkmenistan adopted the manat of 100 tennesi in 1993 and coins with the profile of President Saparmyrat Nyyazow have since been released in plated steel [25–29]. Silver 500 manat coins also circulate [35–36] and since 1996 have featured endangered wildlife.

Uzbekistan alone had distinctive coins before 1994, although these were only the tenga and falus struck in the khanates of Bukhara and Khiva during the last years of the tsarist empire. The contemporary steel-clad coins are based on the som of 100 tyin [30–32].

YUGOSLAVIA

The mountainous region of south-east Europe, inhabited by a mixture of ethnic, linguistic, political and religious groups, has been ruled by Greece, Rome, Byzantium, the Ottoman Empire and the Habsburgs. The Balkan mints at Ljubljana, Zagreb, Dubrovnik and Split were significant during the medieval period, producing coinage for local Venetian or Turkish rulers. Serbia was subjugated by the Turks after the decisive battle at Kosovo (1389) and did not regain independence until 1887. Montenegro was alone in precariously preserving its integrity from Turkish domination. As Turkish power waned Russia and Austria carved out spheres of influence, which led to War in 1914, triggered by the assassination of the Austrian Archduke Franz Ferdinand at Sarajevo. Out of the wreckage of World War I emerged the Kingdom of Serbs, Croats and Slovenes, which became Yugoslavia.

Left: Now known as Dubrovnik, in southern Croatia, Ragusa on the Adriatic coast was a major trading centre in the Middle Ages and the origin of the argosy, a large merchant sailing ship. Called the Pearl of the Adriatic, it was noted for the quality of its coinage, especially the silver blasius, named after the patron saint depicted on the obverse. In the 15th and 16th centuries it rivalled Venice in wealth and importance and was an independent republic until 1806, when it was suppressed by Napoleon.

SERBIA AND MONTENEGRO

In the 13th and 14th centuries the rulers of Serbia struck silver dinars as well as imitations of Venetian grossi at Belgrade [1–2]. Coins variously minted in Paris, Birmingham or Vienna were issued sporadically from 1868, based on the dinar of 100 para, with the ruler's profile or the eagle emblem on the obverse and the value on the reverse. After Prince Milan Obrenovich [3–4] assumed the title of king in 1882 coinage was more regularly struck, although under Peter I issues appeared only in 1904 and 1912 [9–10].

The coins of Montenegro, based on the perper of 100 para, began in 1906, with 1, 2, 10 and 20 para with a crowned eagle obverse. Higher values portraying Prince (later King) Nicholas appeared in 1909 with the arms on the reverse[5–6]. Gold and silver coins of 1910 [7–8] celebrated Nicholas's golden jubilee as titular prince-bishop.

YUGOSLAVIA

The Balkan kingdoms were overrun by the Central Powers in World War I, but regained their independence in 1918 and in December that year joined with the southern Slav dominions of the Habsburg Empire, Croatia and Slovenia, to form the Kingdom of Serbs, Croats and Slovenes under Peter I. His son Alexander acted as regent and ascended the throne in 1921. The problems of unifying such a disparate group of territories were immense and were solved only when Alexander assumed dictatorial powers and renamed the country Yugoslavia ("the land of the southern Slavs").

In the face of different languages and scripts (Roman and Cyrillic) the coins introduced in 1920 had an anepigraphic obverse with the royal arms alone, while the reverse had the numerals of value with "Para" in both scripts. Higher denominations, portraying Alexander I, appeared in 1925 [11–12]. When coins were next issued, in 1938, they merely featured a crown on the obverse but were now inscribed with the new country name.

Yugoslavia was overrun by Germany in 1941 and dismembered. Zinc coins with the double-headed eagle were issued in Serbia in 1942, while the puppet fascist state of Croatia issued zinc 1 and 2 kune as well as gold 500 kune in 1941. The half-Croat leader Josip Broz, known as Marshal Tito, eventually drove out the Germans and Italians and restored the country in 1945. Coins now bore the emblem of the Federal People's Republic. They were inscribed in Cyrillic alone [13–14] until the formation of the Socialist Federal Republic in 1963, when the equivalent in the Roman alphabet was added [15–16, 17–18]. From 1965 the denomination was rendered in all four different languages [19–22].

Beginning in 1970 with coins for the FAO "Food for All" programme, Yugoslavia produced commemorative and special issues in denominations from 5 dinara upwards, notably for the Winter Olympics at Sarajevo (1984).

Ancient Warriors

Macedonia, in the heart of the Balkans, has long been the subject of bitter disputes between Serbia, Bulgaria and Greece. It was from here that Philip of Macedon set out to conquer Greece, creating the empire later expanded by Alexander the Great. The Macedonian kingdom of Paeonia was one of the most important sites of ancient coin production and struck silver coins on the Greek model, such as this tetradrachm showing a head of Apollo (obverse) and a Paeonian cavalryman lancing a foot soldier, who is defending himself with shield and spear. Today it forms part of the Republic of Macedonia, which has the epithet "Former Yugoslavia" at the insistence of Greece, whose most northerly province is also called Macedonia.

DISINTEGRATION

After Tito's death in 1980 the six component republics began to drift apart, culminating in the break-up of 1990–1. The secessionist movement began in Croatia and swiftly spread to Slovenia, these republics having formerly been part of Hungary and Austria respectively. Macedonia [23] and Bosnia-Herzegovina also declared their independence, despite strenuous protests from Greece regarding the former and the rivalries of Croatia and Serbia over the latter. In the mid-1990s Serb Orthodox, Croat Catholic and Bosnian Muslim factions fought each other. The Serbs of southern Croatia even formed their own Serbian Republic of Krajina. Serbia and Montenegro alone maintained the fiction of Yugoslavia and coins thus inscribed appeared until 2002, latterly assailed by inflation, which witnessed coins up to 100,000 dinara. The currency was reformed three times in 1992–4 as ten, then a million and latterly a billion old dinara were revalued at one novi dinar [24–25].

Croatia had emerged as a fascist state in 1941 and introduced the kuna (from the word for a marten, reflecting the use of fur as currency in the Middle Ages). On regaining independence Croatia tariffed its kuna of 100 lipa at 1000 old dinara. Coins from 1 lipa to 25 kuna have the numerals of value superimposed on the national emblem on the obverse, with birds, animals and flora on the reverse [26–27]. Commemorative silver or gold coins of 25, 100, 200, 500 or 1000 kuna have appeared since 1994 [28]. Slovenia adopted the tolar (dollar) of 100 stotinov and has aluminium or brass coins with the value (obverse) and fauna (reverse) [29–30]. Many special issues from 5 to 500 tolarjev have appeared since 1991. Macedonia has had coins featuring wildlife since 1993, based on the denar of 100 deni [31–33]. Despite political divisions within the Croat-Muslim Federation of Bosnia and Herzegovina and the Serb Republic, a common currency is used [34–35].

ALBANIA, BULGARIA AND ROMANIA

These three countries lie in the southern Balkans, but apart from geography they have very little in common. Ethnically, culturally and linguistically, they are each unique. Distinctive coins appeared in the regions as far back as the 5th century BC, reflecting the successive influence of the Greek, Roman, Byzantine and Venetian worlds. Bulgaria was a major power until it fell under Turkish rule in 1395. In modern times, all three countries were kingdoms before World War II and people's republics from the 1940s until the collapse of communism in the 1990s. In the 1890s both Bulgaria and Romania issued gold coins that conformed to the French 20 franc piece, which was the standard in the Latin Monetary Union.

Left: In the 5th and 4th centuries BC the Greek colony of Olbia, a thriving port on the Black Sea, produced large coins cast from copper mined locally. Many of these curious pieces depict leaping dolphins and quasi-religious symbols. Quite unlike the usual Greek coins, they are believed to have originated as votive offerings to the god Apollo.

ALBANIA

The earliest coins in this area were struck at Apollonia (near modern Pojani), a colony founded in 588 BC by Greeks from Corfu. It struck its own coins until 229 BC, when it was annexed to the Roman Republic.

A Turkish province until 1912, Albania was fought over during the Balkan Wars and World War I. It was successively a principality (1914), a republic (1925) and a kingdom (1928). Coinage was not adopted until 1926, based on the lek of 100 qindar. The higher values portrayed President Ahmet Zogu, who later became King Zog I. The bronze or nickel coins were mostly struck in Rome and apart from the double-headed eagle on the 5 qindar and the half lek, motifs drew heavily on those of ancient Rome. The 20 franga of 1922 [1–2] had a reverse showing the Albanian double-headed eagle, but it was superseded in 1926 by a coin portraying medieval hero George Castriota Skanderbeg [3] with the winged lion of St Mark (a Venetian symbol) on the reverse [4]. In 1937–8

gold coins with King Zog facing right [5] had armorial reverses that celebrated the 25th anniversary of independence, the king's marriage and 10th anniversary of his reign [6], shortly before he fled the country. Victor Emmanuel III graced the coins issued in 1939–41.

Enver Hoxha led the partisans during World War II and emerged as head of the People's Socialist Republic, whose aluminium or zinc coins appeared from 1947 [7–9]. Steel or brass coins since 1995 have had various pictorial images on the obverse and a wreathed value on the reverse. Silver and gold coins proliferated from 1968, beginning with a series honouring Castriota Skanderbeg.

BULGARIA

The towns on the Black Sea coast of what is now Bulgaria struck Greek-style coins from the 4th century BC. Chief among them was Apollonia Pontica, which struck drachmae in 450–400 BC showing the Gorgon and maritime motifs such as a crayfish and an anchor [10–13]. Distinctive coins appeared in

Thrace from the 3rd century BC. Handsome drachmae were minted at Odessus (now Varna) in the period of the Mithridatic Wars with Rome (127–70 BC) with the head of Alexander and seated Zeus [14–15], and coins were minted at Serdica as a Roman and then a Byzantine province.

Straddling the northern Aegean and Black Seas, the area was settled by the Bulgars in the 7th century and flourished in the Middle Ages, striking its own coins from the early 13th century [16–17]. It became a principality in 1878, nominally under Turkish control, but joined forces with Eastern Roumelia in 1885 to form Bulgaria. Prince Ferdinand of Saxe-Coburg was appointed ruler in 1887 and proclaimed himself king in 1908.

Coins based on the lev of 100 stotinki were adopted in 1881 [18], with an armorial obverse. The silver (from 1891) and gold (from 1894) portrayed Ferdinand until 1916. Some 1 and 2 leva coins appeared between 1923 and 1941–3, but there were no other coins until 1951 when brass or cupro-nickel pieces from 1 to 25 stotinki were released by the people's republic, which abolished the monarchy in 1946 [19–22]. Further issues appeared in 1962 [23] and 1974 [24].

The return to democracy in 1992 was signalled by new coins from 20 stotinki to 50 leva, with obverses featuring ancient sculpture. In July 1999 the currency was reformed, 10,000 old leva being worth 1 new lev, and brass or cupro-nickel coins from 1 to 50 stotinki had a standard obverse. Numerous gold or silver commemoratives have been minted since the 1960s.

ROMANIA

The Roman province of Dacia bordering the Black Sea has retained the Latin influence in its language as well as its name, although the Christian principalities of Moldavia and Wallachia in the eastern Danube valley were under Turkish rule until 1877. A wide variety of coins was produced in this area from the 3rd century BC, long before the

Reflected Glory

Romania harked back to the time of Michael the Brave (1601) and Ferdinand I in World War I, portrayed alongside King Michael in the gold 20 lei coin of 1944 celebrating the restoration of territories formerly lost to Hungary and Russia. The reverse bore the arms of all 11 provinces, grouped around the crown.

arrival of the Romans. In the Middle Ages the princes of Moldavia and Wallachia struck coins, before and after the area came under Turkish control. Transylvania, now part of Romania, was successively under Hungarian or Habsburg rule, and an independent principality at various times. In each period, it produced distinctive coins.

The ruler of the Danubian principalities, Alexander Cuza, was ousted in 1866 and Prince Karl of Hohenzollern-Sigmaringen was appointed in his place. Karl (Carol) proclaimed himself king in 1881. Coins based on the leu of 100 bani, with the arms of the Danubian principalities and inscribed "Romania", were introduced in 1867 [25], followed by a series portraying Carol I (obverse) and the arms (reverse) [26–29]. Few coins below 50 bani were issued for general circulation between 1906 and 1952 [30–31]; in the interim Romania was ravaged by two World Wars, suffered inflation and ceased to be a monarchy in 1947. In the 1950s coins of the people's republic had the communist emblem and the value on the obverse and reverse. A new series in clad steel appeared in 1965–9, marking the change to a socialist republic, and since 1989 coins have reverted to the original title of Romania [32–35] with arms or symbols on the obverse.

1
2
3
4
5
6
7
8
9
10
11
12
13
14
15
16

GREECE

The cradle of Western civilization and a major contributor to the origin and development of democracy, the arts, architecture and, of course, coinage, Greece fell under the domination of the Roman Empire in the 2nd century BC and was part of the Byzantine Empire until 1453, when it came under Turkish rule. Thereafter coins were struck in various parts of what is now Greece, by the crusader Dukes of Athens [1–2], the Princes of Achaea, and under the auspices of the Knights of St John in Rhodes (until 1522), such as Grand Master Dieudonné de Gozon, who rebuilt the Kingdom of Rhodes in the 14th century [3–4]. Venetian and Genoese trading companies also struck coins in a number of Frankish principalities. Greece retained its distinct language and culture under Turkish rule and a revolt in 1821 triggered off the nationalist movement that led to the creation of a Greek state by 1827. In 1833 the European Powers recognized the sovereignty of Greece, choosing Prince Otto of Bavaria as its king.

Left: Many modern Greek coins use images from coins of ancient Greece: this brass 100 drachma piece of 1990–2000 portrayed Alexander the Great as king of the Macedonians – part of the ongoing propaganda campaign against the independent Republic of Macedonia.

FIRST KINGDOM

The newly independent state revived the ancient coinage system of the drachma of 100 lepta. Copper 1 and 5 lepta appeared in 1828 with a cross above a phoenix, symbolizing the rebirth of the country. Other denominations soon followed, with silver coins portraying King Otto in 1833 [5–6]. Otto was deposed in 1862 and in his place the Powers elected George, second son of King Christian of Denmark [7–10]. He reigned from 1863 to 1913, when he was assassinated during a state visit to Salonika, recently acquired as a result of the Second Balkan War. During his long reign his portrait was extended to the smaller coins. New types appeared in 1912, including holed 5, 10 and 20 lepta with the first essays in pictorialism, reviving the owl [11–12] and Athena motifs from ancient coins.

Relatively few Greek coins portrayed the reigning monarch, so the revolts and factiousness of the ensuing decade are not reflected in the obverses. Constantine I was forced to abdicate in

World War I for his pro-German sympathies. Restored to the throne, he was driven out again in 1922 following a disastrous campaign to seize the seaboard of Asia Minor from Turkey. He was briefly succeeded by his son, George II, but he too was ousted, and Greece then became a republic.

FIRST REPUBLIC

The monarchy was overthrown by Eleftherios Venizelos, who had worked closely with the British and French during World War I. The republic lasted until 1935, when George II was restored to the throne. During this period Greece abandoned royal symbolism on its coins; instead the country looked back to the glories of ancient Greece for inspiration, using the helmeted Athena from Corinthian coins for the series of 1926 from 20 lepta to 2 drachmae. In 1930 a nickel 5 drachma coin featured the phoenix derived from the coins of 1828 [13–14], while 10 and 20 drachmae revived ancient types respectively showing Demeter the corn goddess and an ear of wheat or Poseidon the sea god with the prow of a galley. The 5 drachma coin was struck in London and Brussels, distinguished by dots in the berries on the reverse.

MONARCHY RESTORED

Discontent with the republic led to a plebiscite on November 3, 1935, which voted in favour of restoring the monarchy. King George II returned to Athens and was formally restored to his throne on November 25. This was celebrated by gold and silver 20 and 100 drachma coins showing the king and the date of his restoration, although the coins themselves were not actually minted until 1940 [15–16]. The republican coins remained in general circulation and it is remarkable that, apart from these commemoratives, no further coins were issued until 1954 [17–18].

Greece was occupied by Nazi Germany in World War II and suffered inflation for many years, making coinage impractical. George II went into exile in 1941 but was restored for a third time in 1946 and succeeded the following year by his brother Paul, whose profile appears on the middle values of 1954–65 [19–20], though Selene the moon goddess was reserved for the 20 drachmae. Constantine II's reign began auspiciously in 1964 with

Blend of Ancient and Modern

The best example of the way in which modern Greece identifies with its ancient past is seen in the 10 drachma coins since 1976: the portrait of the philosopher Democritus (*c.* 460–370 BC), who devised the atomic system, is linked to a reverse showing a symbolic representation of an atom.

a 30 drachma silver coin showing the conjoined busts of the young king and his bride, Anne-Marie of Denmark. The permanent series bore his profile and the national arms [21–22].

SECOND REPUBLIC

When a military junta seized power in 1967 Constantine attempted a counter coup. It failed and he fled to Rome. The dictatorial regime of the Greek colonels deposed the king and abolished the monarchy in 1973. Ironically, new coins appeared in 1971 with Constantine's profile (obverse) and the phoenix emblem. Two years later a series appeared with the figure of a soldier superimposed on the phoenix, but the figure was soon removed [24]. The reverse of the series took motifs from ancient coins [23], including the owl and Pegasus, the winged horse [25]. The 1 and 2 drachma coins were inspired by the wars of independence, with portraits of Konstantinos Kanaris and Georgios Karaiskakis [26–7] on the obverse and various motifs symbolic of that period on the reverse [28], but the higher values reverted to classical motifs with Democritus, Pericles, Solon and Homer on the obverse and appropriate pictorial images on the reverse [29–30]. In the 1990s the circulating coinage became a medium for profiling Greek personalities of more recent times [31–32]. Classical motifs, however, have been used for the Greek versions of the euro coinage.

Commemorative coins from 50 to 1000 drachmae (silver) and 2500 to 20,000 drachmae (gold) proliferated from 1975 onward; many had sporting themes, from the Pan-European Games (1981) to the Chess Olympics (1988). For the Athens Olympic Games in 2004 Greece produced a prolific series showing Athenian landmarks and Olympic sports harking back to the Ancient Games. It included a 500 drachma piece portraying Pierre de Coubertin, father of the modern Games, alongside Demetrios Vikelas who organized the first modern Olympics at Athens in 1896 [33–34].

ITALY

The history of coinage in Italy goes back to the cumbersome cast copper coins of the 3rd century BC [1–2], but under the influence of the Greek colonies gold staters [3–4] and silver drachmae were struck in various parts of the Italian peninsula from the 4th century BC. As a political entity, Italy dates only from 1861. After the fall of the western Roman Empire in 476, the Italian peninsula was divided into petty kingdoms, city states and papal dominions, each with its own distinctive coins. In the Middle Ages Milan and Florence took a leading role in the revival of realism in coin design, while Venice created a great commercial empire in the Adriatic and eastern Mediterranean, and its coinage was a major influence in that area. Italy was finally unified under Victor Emanuel II of Piedmont, Savoy and Sardinia.

Below: In 1922 Benito Mussolini seized power in Italy and created the world's first Fascist country. While Mussolini wielded dictatorial powers as Il Duce ("the leader"), Victor Emanuel III continued as king. After the annexation of Abyssinia (Ethiopia) in 1936 Victor Emmanuel was styled as King and Emperor and the coins of this period bore dates in the Fascist era as well as the Christian calendar.

ITALIAN STATES

The Kingdom of Naples and Sicily emerged by 1130, but was under the rule of Spain or Austria from 1502 until 1733, when the Bourbon Prince Carlos became king [5–6]. It was sometimes called the Kingdom of the Two Sicilies, as on coins of Joachim Murat, styling himself Gioacchino Napoleon (1808–15) [12–13]. Sardinia was alternately ruled by Pisa and Genoa before falling to Aragon in 1297. It remained under Spanish rule until 1720, when it became part of the dominions of the House of Savoy and the nucleus of the future Kingdom of Italy.

Powerful families, such as the Sforzas of Milan, the Gonzagas of Mantua and the Medicis of Florence created city-states in the medieval period that came to wield enormous commercial influence and produced attractive gold and silver coins, such as this Florentine half tallero of Cosimo III (1670–1723) [7]. From the 16th century, however, the Italian city-states began to fall under the sway of France, Spain and Austria, and only the Republic of Venice maintained its independence until 1798. A silver ducat of 1676–84 shows the Doge of Venice kneeling before St Mark, the city's patron saint [8–9]. Napoleon Bonaparte briefly redrew the map of Italy in the 1790s, first creating a series of republics and then a kingdom under his personal rule (1804–14). Under Napoleon, coins bore his left-facing profile (obverse) and the crowned and mantled arms of his Italian kingdom (reverse) [10–11].

The Congress of Versailles of 1815 awarded Lombardy and Venetia to Austria; coins with the Lombard crown or the Austrian eagle, based on the scudo of 6 lire, 120 soldi or 600 centesimi, were issued from 1822 until 1866, when the kingdom fell to Italy. Naples and Sicily had a complex coinage based on the ducato or tallero (dollar) [14–15] of 100 grana, but 120 grana were also worth a piastra, 6 tari, 12 carlini or 240 tornese, while 6 cavalli made a tornese. In 1813 the currency was reformed and the franco or lira of 100 centesimi was adopted.

The Duchies of Parma, Modena and Tuscany, as well as the States of the Church, each had distinctive coinage. Piedmont and Sardinia each had their own currency systems, based on the doppia of 2880 denari or the doppietta of 1200 denari respectively, but from

1816 the lira of 100 centesimi was in use and it eventually extended to the whole of Italy.

KINGDOM OF ITALY

The campaign of 1859–60 known as the Risorgimento, led by Giuseppe Garibaldi, resulted in the unification of Italy under the House of Savoy, and coins portraying Victor Emanuel II were introduced in 1861 [16–17]. The Pope, under French protection, held out until 1870, but on the withdrawal of the French garrison Rome finally became the capital of a united Italy.

The reverse of the coins showed the value, but from 1908 onward, a more allegorical treatment was adopted, often using images that harked back to the Roman Empire [18–22]. Exceptionally, between 1894 and 1936, the 20 centesimi had either a crown, a Roman profile or the royal arms on the obverse. The use of imperial imagery increased from 1936 onward, with the rebirth of an empire that Mussolini hoped would encompass the Mediterranean [23]. Italy pioneered stainless steel as a coinage metal (1939) and bimetallic coins (1982).

REPUBLIC

During World War II, Italy was originally allied to Nazi Germany, but it changed sides in 1943 when Mussolini was overthrown, later to be captured and executed by partisans. Umberto II succeeded his father as king in 1946, but by referendum the monarchy was abolished and Italy declared a republic.

After the welter of wartime coins as the currency became depreciated, post-war Italy had a relatively stable coinage, with aluminium 1, 5 and 10 lira coins [24–25], aluminium-bronze 20 lire coins [26–27], stainless steel 50 and 100 lire and silver 500 lire. Allegorical portraits and imagery derived from classical motifs predominated. The size of the coins was reduced in 1951 and cupro-nickel was substituted for stainless steel in the 50 and 100 lira coins in 1993–6. A 200 lire in aluminium-bronze was introduced in 1977 and a

Vacant See

Distinctive coins are issued by the Vatican during the period between the death of a Pope and the election of his successor. These coins, inscribed "Sede Vacante" (Latin for "empty chair"), follow a tradition going back many centuries.

bimetallic 500 lire was adopted in 1982 [28–29]. Coins of this denomination continued to be minted in silver as collector's pieces. The 100, 200 and 500 lire were often struck as commemoratives from 1974 onward.

SAN MARINO AND THE VATICAN

The tiny mountain Republic of San Marino, which had been independent since AD 350, began issuing small bronze coins in 1864 and silver in 1898, but Italian coins predominated. Since 1972, San Marino has revived its coinage, producing a different series annually, mainly as tourist souvenirs but also including commemorative gold and silver scudi.

Papal coinage was suppressed in 1870 but revived in 1929, when the Vatican City State was created under the terms of the Lateran Treaty. These coins generally portray the Pope, with religious, allegorical or symbolic motifs on the reverse.

Above: A coin of Pope Pius XI from 1931, showing the papal arms and the Virgin Mary.

12
13
14
15
16
17
18
19
20
21
22
23
24
25
26
27
28
29

1

2

3

4

5

6

7

8

9

10

11

12

13

FRANCE

The Gaul of Roman times, France became the kingdom of the Franks and, under Charlemagne in the 9th century, the leading power in Europe. Central power weakened in the Middle Ages, with the rise of petty kingdoms such as Brittany and Navarre, and it was not until the early 17th century that France emerged as a highly centralized state. It attained its greatest power under Louis XIV, who came to the throne in 1643 at the age of five [1–2], but the autocratic monarchy was unstable and collapsed in the Revolution of 1789, which led to the First Republic in 1792. This was followed by the Napoleonic Empire (1804–14), the restoration of the monarchy (1814–48), the Second Republic (1848–52), the Second Empire (1852–71), the Third Republic (1871–1940), the fascist Vichy state (1940–4), the Fourth Republic (1944–58) and the Fifth Republic instituted by President Charles de Gaulle, which continues to this day.

Left: Louis Napoleon Bonaparte, nephew of Napoleon I, was elected president of the Second Republic but engineered a coup in 1852, restoring the Bonapartist Empire and taking the title of Napoleon III. On coinage his profile acquired victor's laurels in 1861, following a series of French victories in the campaign for the unification of Italy. France flourished under his rule but the monarchy collapsed as a result of the disastrous war with Germany in 1870–1.

MEDIEVAL COINAGE

Coin production was devolved to the towns and districts of medieval France. Many of the nobility struck their own coins, creating an immense field of study [7–9]. Anglo-Gallic coins were struck in the regions under English rule during the Hundred Years' War.

The regal coinage was reformed by Louis XI (1461–83) after he defeated the English and broke the power of the nobility. Separate coinage continued in Brittany and Navarre until Henry of Navarre took the throne as Henry IV in 1589. The third son of Antoine de Bourbon, Henry established a royal dynasty that was to rule France for the next two centuries.

REVOLUTION AND EMPIRE

In the period prior to the Revolution, French coinage became increasingly complex. The mouton d'or [3–4], a 14th-century gold coin, depicted the lamb of God, and was followed by the ecu d'or [5–6]. Others followed, including the angel, angelot, teston

[10–11], pavillon d'or, louis d'or and pistole. Latterly the currency was based on the gold livre of 20 sols or 240 deniers [12–13].

Following the abolition of the monarchy in 1792, some livres and sols were struck in 1793–4 with republican motifs. The transition of power is reflected in the coins portraying Louis XVI but with a reverse showing the

A Record of Longevity

The standing figure of Marianne as a sower of seed was adopted for the silver coinage in 1898 and continued until 1920, but following the currency reform of 1958 she was restored and continued until the advent of the euro.

Above: Marianne, the personification of the French Republic, has been a popular obverse motif. Some of her many guises are shown here on coins of 1872, 1849, 1904 and 1931.

Phrygian cap, fasces and Gallic cock flanking an angel writing a new constitution, with the date expressed as year 5 of Liberty [14–15] in the revolutionary calendar. In this period money rapidly collapsed and coins were replaced by paper currency known as assignats and mandats. In 1794 the currency was reformed and coins based on the franc of 10 decimes or 100 centimes were introduced. These had the head of Marianne, the allegory of Liberty, on the obverse while the reverse bore the value and the date expressed as *L'an* (the year) followed by a number from 4 to 9 (1793–1808).

Although Napoleon had proclaimed himself emperor in 1804, three years elapsed before the first coins bearing the initial N appeared [16–17]. Silver coins portrayed him as first consul and later as emperor.

LATER COINAGE
The Bourbon dynasty was restored in 1814 and silver and gold coins portraying Louis XVIII appeared in 1816 [18–19], followed by those portraying Charles X (1824–30) [20] and Louis Philippe (1830–48) [21–22]. No bronze coins for small change appeared until the overthrow of the monarchy in 1848. After this, Marianne was again portrayed. Silver 1 and 2 francs appeared in 1852, with Louis

Napoleon Bonaparte as president, but from 1853 Napoleon III (obverse) and the imperial eagle (reverse) were the norm [23–26]. After the downfall of the empire, the female allegory Liberty, in various guises, was restored.

France was the driving force behind the creation of the Latin Monetary Union in 1865, which created a coinage standard for Belgium, Italy and Switzerland that endured until 1927. The circulating coins of the French Republic rank among the most artistic in the world and from the 1870s reflected a gradual change from Neoclassicism [27–28] to Art Nouveau in the 1890s and Art Deco after World War I. There have also been a wide variety of base-metal alloys, from bronze and nickel before World War I, through the aluminium of the Vichy era and the postwar period before the advent of the "heavy franc" in 1958, to chrome steel, aluminium-bronze and nickel-brass. Many commemoratives have appeared in recent years, often in base metal for general circulation.

MONACO
The tiny principality on the French Riviera has had its own coinage since the late Middle Ages. Modern coinage, based on the French decimal system, dates from 1837, when 5 centime coins were cast in brass or struck in copper along with silver 5 franc pieces. Gold 20 and 100 francs appeared in the 1880s, but lower denominations were not released until the 1940s, conforming to the French specifications [29–30]. Coins were minted sporadically from then until 1974, but since then dates have been changed annually. Some high-denomination commemoratives have appeared in recent years.

Above: Prince Rainier III and the crowned arms of the Grimaldi family.

IBERIAN PENINSULA

The most south-westerly part of Europe was fought over and conquered by Phoenicians, Carthaginians, Greeks and Romans. Silver coins were struck at Gades (now Cadiz) on Greek lines [1–2] and copper denarii appeared before the beginning of the Christian era [3]. The Visigoths and Moors also left their mark on the coinage, but by the 12th century Christian kingdoms were beginning to emerge [4–5]. In the late 15th century the regions of Aragon and Castile were united by the marriage of their rulers, Ferdinand and Isabella [7–8], and the Moors were driven out in 1492 – the very year that Columbus set sail for the New World, whose mineral wealth would make Spain the richest and most powerful nation in Europe. Spain was also one of the major components of the Habsburg Empire in the 16th and 17th centuries and exerted a major influence on its coinage. Portugal was one of the kingdoms to emerge in the 12th century and managed to resist the encroachment of Spain, apart from the period 1581–1640. Both countries won and lost vast colonial empires, followed by political instability, the downfall of monarchy and the rise of fascist dictatorships before the establishment of democracy in the 1970s.

Left: The silver peso a ocho reales, or "piece of eight", featured the Spanish royal arms on one side and a depiction of the Pillars of Hercules (the Straits of Gibraltar) on the other, for which reason it is often known as the Pillar Dollar.

SPAIN

The silver and gold of the Americas flooded Europe from the 16th to the late-18th centuries and transformed the Spanish peso a ocho reales into the world's most popular coin and a role model for the dollar currencies ever since [6]. The gold escudo was worth 16 silver reales, while 34 copper maravedis equalled a silver real. This system was replaced by decimal coinage in 1848 based on the real of 10 decimos or 100 centimos, changed to the escudo of 100 centimos in 1864 and finally to the peseta of 100 centimos in 1868.

In the monarchical periods the obverse portrayed the reigning king or queen, with an armorial device on the reverse. Intermittent coinage during the 1870s [9–10] meant that the first republic (1873–4) came and went without note. Alfonso XIII, born after his father's death, was king from 1886 to 1931, and the early coins of his reign portrayed him successively as a baby and in various phases of childhood.

After the monarchy was overthrown in 1931 a few coins inscribed "Republica Espanola" appeared in 1934–7. In the early years of the nationalist regime, coinage was equally meagre, and it was not until 1947 that something like a regular series was adopted [11–12], with the portrait of General Franco as El Caudillo ("the leader") on the obverse [13] and national arms on the reverse. Although Spain was technically a kingdom from 1949, it was not until the death of Franco in 1975 that its monarchy was restored in the person of King Juan Carlos, grandson of Alfonso XIII.

Spanish coins often have a fixed date, the actual year of production being indicated by tiny numerals within an eight-pointed star, the mark of the Madrid Mint [14]. Conversely, letters after the date are those of mint officials. In recent years some handsome commemoratives have been released, notably for the World Cup football championship (1982) and the Barcelona Olympics (1992) [15].

Explorers Honoured

Many of Portugal's commemorative coins of recent times have focused on the exploits of the Portuguese explorers of the 15th and 16th centuries, not forgetting Prince Henry the Navigator who, though not himself an explorer, established the school of navigation that gave Portugal such a lead in opening up the world.

PORTUGAL

Like that of Spain, the currency of Portugal [16–17] was originally based on the silver real, but higher values were covered by *moeda ouro* (literally "gold money"), hence the term *moidore*. Portugal's commercial power was largely derived from the gold of the Guinea Coast, exemplified by this 4000 reis of João V, 1720 [18–19]. The monarch subsequently received the title "King of Portugal and Guinea".

As Portugal declined in uwealth and importance in the 18th century the value of the real fell to the point at which it vanished altogether. The smallest copper coin was the 3 reis (the Portuguese form of *reales*) but its multiples included the 10 reis [20], vintem (20 reis) [23], pataca (40), tostão (100), cruzado (480), escudo (1600) and the 8 escudo (6400) such as this coin of Carlos IV [21–22]. This cumbersome system continued until the overthrow of the monarchy in 1910, when the escudo of 100 centavos was adopted.

In the closing months of the monarchy, large silver coins celebrated the centenary of the defeat of Napoleon in the Peninsular War or honoured the Marquis de Pombal, the 18th-century statesman who rebuilt Lisbon after the earthquake of 1755. There was a great variety of types in the reis coinage, with the royal effigy or crowned shield (obverse) and value, arms or a cross (reverse). The same approach was adopted in the republican decimal coinage, on which various effigies of Liberty facing left or right [25] replaced the regal portraits. At first the reverses showed either the arms, minus the royal crown, or a wreathed value, but a more pictorial style gradually developed in the 1930s, notably in the silver coins that featured the flagship of the navigator Vasco da Gama [24].

While Portugal's circulating coinage has remained relatively conservative in style and treatment, the commemorative and special issues have escalated in recent years, recording anniversaries of numerous historic events, from the medieval explorations to the revolution of 1974 [26–7].

ANDORRA

The tiny principality of Andorra in the valleys of the Pyrenees is a feudal anachronism: the Counts of Foix (in France) and the Bishops of Urgel (Spain) have ruled it as co-princes since 1278. As a result, French and Spanish currency has circulated freely ever since. Since 1982, however, distinctive coins based on the diner (denier) of 100 centims have been struck, mainly as tourist souvenirs [28–30], along with silver and gold coins aimed at the numismatic market. Some of these coins bear the bust of the Bishop of Urgel (the role of the Comte de Foix has now passed to the President of France), but most feature the arms of the principality. Andorra even produced ecus, but now uses the euro.

Above: Recent motifs on coins of Andorra have ranged from wildlife (such as this Pyrenean goat) to historical figures such as Charlemagne, who granted the valleys their first charter.

AFRICA

Historically regarded as the Dark Continent, Africa is today home to many of the Third World's poorest countries. Exploited by the rest of the world for centuries and now hampered by colossal debt and unfair trade, it has experienced political turmoil, tyranny and corruption.

NORTH AFRICA

The portion of the continent on the southern shores of the Mediterranean came into contact with the civilizations of Greece and Rome, but long before that period the coastal regions were dominated by Egypt and colonized by the Phoenicians, who created the great power of Carthage, which challenged the might of Rome in the 3rd century BC. Coins struck to Greek standards date from the 6th century BC at Cyrene, such as the horned head of Karneios, counterpart of Apollo [1–2], and from about 410 BC at Carthage, bearing the profile of Tanit, the Carthaginian counterpart of Persephone (obverse) and a horse's head (reverse) [3–4]. Later coins featured entire horses or lions, and both gold and electrum pieces were also struck. The large silver coins, up to 12 drachmae, were heavily influenced by those of Sicily. By 146 BC, Carthage had been conquered and thereafter Roman coins were in use [5–6]. Some coins were also struck by the Berber kingdoms from the third century BC. In the Dark Ages Carthage was overrun by the Vandals but a Byzantine mint flourished briefly, and from the 8th century Islamic coinage was in use. After the death of Haroun al Rashid the power of the Caliphate was divided, and thereafter Ifriquiyah (Africa) became increasingly separate, with its own dynasties issuing Islamic coins in their own names, such as an 8th-century dirham in the name of Haroun's successor [7–8]. By the 14th century the Barbary states (Algeria, Morocco and Tunisia) were emerging; though continuing with the basic Islamic types, they gradually introduced their own distinctive features.

Left: Obverse and reverse of a silver coin of Juba I, king of Numidia in the first century BC. Juba, of Phoenician descent, ruled over Numidia, Mauritania and Libya. In pursuance of his ambitions to create an empire in North Africa he allied himself with the Roman Senate in their struggle against Julius Caesar and struck vast quantities of these coins to finance his campaign.

ALGERIA

The important city and seaport of Algiers was founded in 950 on earlier Phoenician and Roman settlements. Nominally subject to the sultans of Tlemcen, it achieved autonomy in the 15th century and became a commercial centre following the expulsion of the Jews and Moors from Spain in 1492. Although part of the Ottoman Empire from 1518 the Turks gave the Barbary corsairs a free hand, which is reflected in the distinctive coins struck at Timilsan (modern Tlemcen) by Murad III [9–10].

It was to suppress piracy that the French invaded in 1830, annexing Algeria in 1848. Coins modelled on Turkish weights and values were struck at Algiers and Constantine, and also at Mascara and Taqident during the revolt of Abd-el-Kader (1834–47). Latterly

Libya

Nominally part of the Ottoman Empire until 1911, the region of North Africa west of Egypt fell to the Italians in 1934, and they named it "Libia", the Latin name for the territory. Under Turkish rule the pashas, or governors, had struck copper and billon coins for small change, but it was not until 1952 that coins were adopted by this newly created kingdom, with the bust of Idris I on the obverse. The monarchy was overthrown in 1969, and Libya was declared a socialist people's republic, but coins with the republican emblem were not produced until 1975.

the coinage was based on the silver budju of 24 muzuna or 48 kharuba, along with the gold sultani and its subdivisions. French coins were normally circulated, but during World War I token coins were issued by the chambers of commerce. Coins with the head of Marianne, corresponding to the French style but inscribed "Algerie" on the reverse, were introduced in 1949–50. Independence was proclaimed in July 1962 and coins of the Algerian Republic appeared in 1964, based on the dinar of 100 centimes [11–12]. A new series, from the aluminium quarter dinar to the bimetallic 100 dinar coin, was adopted in 1992. A number of commemoratives have been issued since the tenth anniversary of Algerian independence.

MOROCCO

Of immense strategic importance at the western end of the Mediterranean, Morocco was successively ruled by Phoenicians, Romans, Vandals, Visigoths, Byzantines and Arabs.

Around 1062 Berber tribes, migrating northwards from Senegal, established themselves at Marrakesh. The Almoravids were so named from the Arabic for "those from the frontier posts". By 1086 they had extended their rule from Algiers to southern Spain. Various dynasties rose and fell, such as the Murabitid [13–14], but the Sharifs of Tafilat gained power in 1660 and have ruled ever since. From this period belongs the dirham struck at Madrid for issue in Marrakesh [15–16]. European rivalries resulted in the partition of Morocco into Spanish and French protectorates in 1912, but sovereignty was regained in 1957.

Coins, struck at Fez, Rabat, Tetuan and Marrakesh, conformed to Islamic styles, although from the early 19th century onward Solomon's seal (a five-pointed star) was a prominent feature [17]. The currency was reformed in the 1890s, based on the rial of 10 dirhams or 500 mazunas, with inscriptions entirely in Arabic except for a date of the Muslim calendar in western numerals. In 1921 the coinage was changed to the dirham of 100 francs, the only decorative feature being a five-pointed star. Following the resumption of independence portraits of Muhammad V appeared on the higher values [19–20]. The currency was changed in 1974 to the dirham of 100 santimat [18].

TUNISIA

The suppression of the Barbary pirates virtually bankrupted Tunis and enabled the French to establish a protectorate in 1881. Previously, successive beys (governors) had issued coins in the name of the Turkish sultan [21–22]. Similar coins, with the Paris mint-mark, were struck until 1891, when the franc was adopted. Thereafter, coins were inscribed in Arabic (obverse) or French (reverse). Tunisia became a republic in 1957 and introduced a coinage based on the dinar of 1000 millim [23–26], showing a tree or President Bourguiba on the obverse. A few commemoratives have been issued since 1976.

13   14

15   16

17   18

19   20

21

22

23   24

25   26

1

2

3

4

5

6

7

8

9

10

11

12

13

14

15

16

EGYPT AND SUDAN

Pharaonic Egypt had a sophisticated weighed-metal system, which did not require round pieces of metal but relied on standard weights of silver for certain transactions. Athenian tetradrachms were circulating in Egypt by the 5th century BC. Pharaoh Nectanebo II (359–343 BC) struck a gold stater inscribed "Neft Nub" ("good gold") in hieroglyphics and a few silver tetradrachms with indigenous inscriptions are known from around the same period. A distinctive coinage on Greek lines was adopted by Ptolemy I, one of Alexander the Great's generals, who in 304 BC established the Hellenistic kingdom that ended with the suicide of Cleopatra in 30 BC. Greek influence is clearly seen in the tetradrachms of Ptolemy I [1–2] and Ptolemy VI [3–4] of the 4th and 2nd centuries BC. Under Roman rule, Egypt was allowed a subsidiary coinage for local circulation, the output of these coins from the imperial mint at Alexandria being very prolific [5–8].

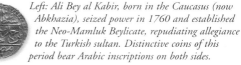

Left: Ali Bey al Kabir, born in the Caucasus (now Abkhazia), seized power in 1760 and established the Neo-Mamluk Beylicate, repudiating allegiance to the Turkish sultan. Distinctive coins of this period bear Arabic inscriptions on both sides.

BYZANTINE PERIOD
At the division of the Roman Empire Egypt passed under eastern control and Alexandria continued to strike copper nummia until 646 – some years after Egypt fell to the Arabs in 642. These coins were produced in unusual multiples of 3, 6, 12 and 33 nummia. Gold coins were minted sporadically, but later in some abundance towards the end of Byzantine rule, under Heraclius (610–41). The motifs conformed to Byzantine standards, with facing portraits of the emperor and his son Constans on the obverse and the stepped cross or a standing figure on the reverse. Coins portraying Heraclius flanked by the sun and moon were actually struck by Khusru II during the Sasanian occupation of 718–28.

ISLAMIC PERIOD
The Alexandria Mint was one of the casualties of the Arab conquest. When distinctive coins emerged under the Caliphate in the 9th century, coins of the Tulinids [9–10] and Ikshidids [11–12], independent governors in Egypt in the 9th and 10th centuries respectively, were struck at Cairo [13–14], Alexandria and other places.

In 969 Egypt fell to the Fatimids, who struck coins in entirely new designs at Cairo until the province was conquered by Saladin in 1171. Thereafter, coins followed the Ayyubid pattern until 1250, when Egypt became the realm of the Mamelukes [15–16]. They were in turn overthrown by the Turks in 1517. Thereafter the coinage followed the Turkish pattern. Ottoman control of Egypt declined in the late 18th century.

KINGDOM OF EGYPT
Though nominally khedive (viceroy) of the sultan, Mehemet (Mahmud) Ali created a dynasty that lasted from 1808 to 1953. The son of an Albanian tobacco merchant, he came to prominence in 1798 when he headed the Albanian–Turkish force despatched by the sultan to counter the French invasion. After the French were ousted by the British he became viceroy. He destroyed the Mamelukes (1811), conquered much of Arabia (1818) and annexed Nubia (1820). He extended his empire to Crete and Morea in Greece (1821–8) and Syria (1831) respectively, but his wish to become sultan of Constantinople was thwarted by the Quadruple Alliance (1840).

The coinage was reformed in 1835 and British coin presses were installed at the Cairo Mint. Nevertheless, the coinage continued to be very similar to the prevailing Turkish types, with the *toughra* on the obverse and elaborate Arabic inscriptions distinguished by the word "Misr" (Egypt) inscribed above the date on the reverse. The currency was based on the guerche or piastre of 40 para, but in 1885 it was extended to the pound of 100 piastres.

Egypt was under British military occupation from 1881 and formally became a British protectorate in 1914, following Turkey's entry into World War I on the side of the Central Powers. It became an independent sovereign state in 1922, when Fuad I was proclaimed king. Illustrated here is a silver 10 piastre coin with dates in both Muslim and Common Era calendars [23–4], struck by the Heaton Mint in Birmingham on behalf of Sultan Ahmed Fuad in 1920, two years before he was elevated to the kingship. Egyptian coins were dated according to the Muslim calendar until 1916, when the currency was reformed and based on the piastre of 10 milliemes; thereafter, dates were given in Arabic according to both calendars [17]. From 1924 onward the obverse bore the bust of the ruler [18–22].

Postman as National Emblem

The image on the Sudanese coins of 1956–71 is that of an Arab postman mounted on a camel, derived from the postage stamps issued from 1898 onward. So familiar was this motif (designed by Colonel E.A. Stanton during the re-conquest of the Sudan) that it became a national icon.

REPUBLIC

King Farouk reigned from 1937 until he was deposed by a military junta in 1952. He was briefly succeeded by his infant son Fuad II, but the monarchy was abolished in July 1953. The Sphinx replaced the bust of Farouk on the obverse of coins, which continued to be inscribed entirely in Arabic, the text reading "Jumhuriyya Misr Al Arabiyya" (Arab Republic of Egypt). Following union with Syria in the form of the United Arab Republic in 1958, the eagle emblem was adopted on the obverse. Syria left this union in 1961 but a decade elapsed before Egypt abandoned the grandiose title and styled itself once more as the Arab Republic of Egypt; the inscriptions on the coinage were suitably amended from 1971 onward [25–26]. The *toughra* was revived as an obverse type in 1984 [31] while higher denominations had a central hole [30], but a more pictorial approach was adopted for the circulating coins in 1992 [27–29]. Many commemorative coins have appeared since the 1960s, often harking back to the Pharaonic period.

SUDAN

This vast country south of Egypt was conquered by Mehemet Ali, seceded in 1881 during the Mahdist revolt, and was re-conquered in 1898. Gold and silver piastres were struck by the Mahdi at Khartoum (1885) and at Omdurman by his successor, the Khalifa (1885–98). From 1898 until 1954 it was an Anglo-Egyptian condominium. Autonomy was followed by the grant of full independence in 1956. Egyptian coins were used until then and the same currency, based on the pound of 100 ghirsh or 1000 millim, was retained. A democratic republic was proclaimed in 1969, signalled on the coins from 1971 by an eagle replacing the original camel motif [32–33]. Most of the special issues since 1972 marked anniversaries of independence or the 1969 revolution. The currency was reformed in 1992 and the dinar of 100 dirhems introduced [34–35].

17   18
19   20
21   22
23   24
25   26
27   28
29   30
31
32   33
34   35

SOUTH AFRICA

This large country at the southern tip of the continent was for centuries the most European part of Africa in its population and political character. Although the Portuguese first explored it in 1498 it was not colonized until the Dutch arrived there in 1652. The hinterland of the Cape of Good Hope fell to the British during the Napoleonic Wars and was formally annexed in 1814 as the Cape Colony. Discontent with British rule induced many of the Afrikaners (the Dutch settlers) to trek northward and establish independent republics. The subsequent discovery of gold and diamonds in these states led to friction between the Boers (Dutch farmers) and those they defined as Uitlanders (foreign incomers), culminating in the Anglo-Boer War of 1899–1902. Most South African gold was exported and had little effect on the indigenous coinage, and it was not until 1923 that a branch of the Royal Mint was established in Pretoria to produce sovereigns with the SA mint-mark [1–2].

Left: Jan van Riebeeck, portrayed on the obverse of the coins of the South African Republic (1961–9) led the expedition by the Dutch East India Company that founded Cape Town in 1652. His ship, the Dromedaaris, *was depicted on the reverse of the bronze halfpennies and pennies of 1923–60.*

EARLY COINAGE

Ordinary Dutch or British coins were used widely in southern Africa in the 17th and 18th centuries. The first distinctive pieces were issued by the Revd John Campbell, head of the mission station at Griquatown in the territory known as Griqualand, between the Kalahari Desert and the Boer republics. They consisted of copper farthings and halfpennies and silver 5 and 10 pence, depicting a phoenix on the obverse with the name of the mission and numerals of value on the reverse. They were undated but circulated in 1815–16 and are extremely rare. A pattern penny with the profile of Queen Victoria (obverse) and dove (reverse) was produced in Berlin in 1889 [3–4].

Distinctive coinage was first attempted in the South African Republic (Transvaal) in 1874, when gold pounds portraying President Thomas Burgers were struck. Only a few hundred of these Burgersponds were struck. Regular coinage, struck at Pretoria and bearing the bust of President Paul Kruger, was introduced in 1892 [11–12]; it consisted of the bronze penny, silver 3 and 5 pence, 1 shilling [13–14], 2 and 5 shillings [5–6] and gold pound [7–10]. Apart from the smaller silver coins (which showed the value in a wreath), this series bore the arms of the republic on the reverse.

UNION OF SOUTH AFRICA

British coins were in use from 1900 onward, extending from Cape Colony and Natal to cover the former Boer republics, now renamed Transvaal and Orange River Colony. Although the Union of South Africa was proclaimed in 1910 – the former colonies becoming provinces – a distinctive coinage was not introduced until 1923. This series, following British weights and specifications, ranged from the bronze ¼ penny (farthing) to the 2 shillings [15–18]. A curious feature of the 3 and 6 pence from 1925 onward was the depiction of three or six bundles of brushwood on the reverse to denote the value. The obverse portrayed the reigning monarch, with Latin titles, while the reverse was inscribed in English and Afrikaans. A silver 5 shillings was introduced in 1947 to celebrate a royal visit [19]. These coins, with a Springbok

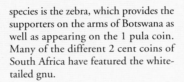

Above: In 2001 Sierra Leone released a set of five large silver coins with the national arms on the obverse and splendid specimens of Africa's Big Five – rhinoceros, lion, leopard, elephant and buffalo – on the reverses.

Equatorial and West Africa), the lyre antelope (French Territory of Afars and Issas, now Djibouti), Buffon's kob (Uganda), the sable antelope (Southern Rhodesia), the Bohor reed buck (Zambia) and, of course, the spring-bok, which is featured on many coins of South Africa. Africa's only equine

Below and below right: Silver $10 coins were produced in 1996 for "Preserve Planet Earth". Liberia's pair showed a grey parrot and two lovebirds.

species is the zebra, which provides the supporters on the arms of Botswana as well as appearing on the 1 pula coin. Many of the different 2 cent coins of South Africa have featured the white-tailed gnu.

OTHER ANIMALS

Africa is home to some of the great anthropoid apes, although few coins have so far been devoted to them. The best example is the gorilla depicted on a coin from the Congo. The aardvark may be found on coins from Zambia and the wildebeest on the 5 kwacha of the same country, while neighbouring Zimbabwe provides an example of a pangolin on the $2 of 1997.

Cattle, sheep and goats are shown on many coins, reflecting their importance to a pastoral economy, while a hare can be found on a Zimbabwean coin. Birds are relatively few, but include the horn-bill (Zambia), the crowned crane (Uganda), the heron (Malawi) and the sea eagle (several countries). The national emblem of Zimbabwe is a bird – not a real one but a stylized soapstone carving. Reptiles are represented by the turtle (Congo) and the Nile crocodile (the Gambia). The Congo has even depicted a butterfly on the 50 centimes of 2002 – a subject that has had very short shrift everywhere in the world.

PRESERVE PLANET EARTH

Concern over the endangered fauna of Africa has led to several recent issues of large silver coins giving prominence to species under threat. Many of these

Above: The obverse of Eritrean coins shows a dhow and a camel; the white-tailed sea eagle appears in the arms of Liberia. The reverses show wattled cranes and a Lanner falcon (Eritrea) and a leopard and storks (Liberia).

have emanated from such countries as Liberia, Eritrea and Sierra Leone and, as a group, they are renowned for their imaginative and realistic portraiture of the animals. From the same countries came a joint issue in 1997 devoted to dinosaurs that roamed Gondwanaland many millions of years ago.

Below: Coins on an ornithological theme from Eritrea in the "Preserve Planet Earth" programme included this Cape eagle owl.

CENTRAL AFRICA

The area of Central Africa, south of the Equator, consists of the two former Portuguese colonies of Angola and Mozambique, the former Belgian Congo and the territories mandated to Belgium by the League of Nations, and the former colonies and protectorates that made up British Central Africa. These countries were carved out by the various European powers during the "scramble for Africa" in the 19th century.

Left: A brief attempt to weld the colony of Southern Rhodesia and the protectorates of Northern Rhodesia and Nyasaland into a single dominion is recalled by the coins of Rhodesia and Nyasaland, which were issued between 1955 and 1963.

FORMER PORTUGUESE TERRITORIES

Coins for specific use in Portuguese Africa were minted from 1693 onward, while coins struck at Goa in Portuguese India, such as the 1000 reis of José I [1–2], were produced for circulation in Mozambique from 1725. Decimal coins inscribed "Republica Portuguesa" on the obverse, with the name of the territory on the reverse, were introduced in Angola in 1921 [3–4] and in Mozambique in 1936, gradually replacing the coins of the mother country, whose national emblems had given the colonial issues a degree of uniformity.

Both of Portugal's "overseas provinces" were in revolt from 1960 onward, but they gained their independence as people's republics only after the collapse of António de Oliveira Salazar's regime, and the advent of democracy, in Portugal in 1974. Following independence, Mozambique adopted the metical of 100 centimos, and Angola chose the kwanza of 100 lwei (1979). While Angola featured its national emblem on the obverse and numerals on the reverse of its coins [5], Mozambique chose the profile of President Samora Machel and various plants.

Both countries subsequently reformed their currencies. Mozambique switched from centimes to centavos in 1980, while Angola introduced the "re-adjusted" kwanza of 100 centimos, the equivalent of 1000 old kwanzas, in 1995.

FORMER BELGIAN TERRITORIES

Leopold II, King of the Belgians, was granted the Congo in 1885 and governed it as his personal property. This was reflected in the inscription on the coins introduced in 1887, which proclaimed him as Sovereign of the Congo Free State. Revelations of misrule led to it being annexed by Belgium in 1908 and renamed the Belgian Congo [7, 11]. The star emblem of the Free State was replaced by a profile of the king and crowned arms. A palm replaced the latter in 1920 [6], while an elephant replaced the portrait in 1944.

The Democratic Republic of the Congo gained independence in 1960 but was immediately plunged into civil war. Coins issued by the national bank appeared in 1965 [10]. The country's name was changed to Zaire in 1971 and the zaire of 100 makuta was adopted. In the ensuing period, coins portrayed President Mabotu [8–9], but following a civil war in 1997 the country reverted to the previous name and adopted coins featuring a lion (obverse) and various fauna (reverse). Rectangular or triangular coins (2000) publicized the campaign for animal protection.

During the civil war of 1961, bronze coins were struck in the breakaway southern province of Katanga, featuring bananas (obverse) [12] and the bronze crosses [13] used as money before the advent of coinage [14].

Belgium was granted a mandate over Rwanda-Urundi, formerly part of

German East Africa. Congolese coins were used there until 1952, when a series with these names was released. When the Congo gained independence in 1960, coins inscribed "Rwanda Burundi" were adopted. Separate issues in each country appeared in the Kingdom of Burundi (1965) [15–16] and the Republic of Rwanda (1964) [17–18]. Rwanda adopted a new series in 1974–7, with the national arms on the obverse and millet, coffee or bananas on the reverse [19–22]. In 1966, Burundi abolished its monarchy and replaced the portraits of Mwambutsa IV with the republican arms.

FORMER BRITISH TERRITORIES

British and South African coins circulated in the vast territories of the British South Africa Company headed by Cecil Rhodes. Rejecting incorporation in the Union of South Africa (1923) the territory was broken up into the

Above: Pictorial reverses of the 20 ngwee of Zambia, 1985 (left) and 1968-88.

colony of Southern Rhodesia and the protectorates of Northern Rhodesia and Nyasaland.

Distinctive silver coins were adopted in 1932 [23–24], followed by holed cupro-nickel halfpennies and pennies in 1934. Coins bore the head of the reigning monarch [25], with pictorial reverses [26–28]. Coins inscribed for use in the Federation of Rhodesia and Nyasaland (1955–64) followed a similar pattern. On the break-up of the federation, Nyasaland became Malawi and Northern Rhodesia became Zambia, both introducing distinctive coins in 1964. Both countries adopted a decimal system based on the kwacha [35–36], comprised either of 100 tambala (Malawi, 1971) [29–30] or 100 ngwee (Zambia, 1968) [31–32].

The former Southern Rhodesia dropped the adjective and then unilaterally declared independence in November 1965. Although the regime, headed by Ian Smith, was declared illegal, its coins continued to portray Elizabeth II until 1970, when a republic was declared and an armorial obverse was adopted. In 1978, Smith signed a pact with moderate African leaders and the country adopted the name Zimbabwe Rhodesia. No coins bearing the double name were ever issued, and in 1980 the country became the Republic of Zimbabwe. Coins thus inscribed, with the emblem of a bird carved from soapstone on the obverse, were issued that year [33–34].

While Malawi and Zimbabwe have produced very few special issues, Zambia has been prolific in releasing large silver coins, often multicoloured and in unusual polygonal or upright oval shapes.

Coins in Two Currencies

The coins issued by Rhodesia from 1964 to 1968 were denominated in both sterling and decimal currencies, on the basis of the pound of 20 shillings or 2 dollars. Thus the shilling of 12 pence was also worth 10 cents. Cupro-nickel coins, which ranged from the 3 pence (2 cents) to the 2 shillings (25 cents), were accompanied by gold coins solely denominated 10 shillings, £1 or £5.

1
2
3
4
5
6
7
8
9
10
11
12

EAST AFRICA

The countries of East Africa were formerly in the British or German spheres of influence and were created as a result of a series of pacts and treaties between these European powers and the various tribal rulers. The area included the offshore islands of Zanzibar and Pemba, governed by the Al-Busaid dynasty, originally from Muscat in Arabia and for centuries the centre of the Arab-dominated slave trade of Africa. The first regular coinage in this region consisted of the bronze pice and silver annas and rupees issued by the British East India Company at Mombasa in 1888–90 [1–6].

Left: Coins of the lower denominations of East Africa had a central hole, with the value and elephant tusks on the reverse and a crown on the obverse. They bore the names and titles of British monarchs, and thus had the distinction of being one of the few issues to be inscribed with the name of King Edward VIII, who ascended the throne in January 1936 and abdicated the following December.

ZANZIBAR
Coins were struck by various seaports along the Swahili Coast from the 11th century, and these remained in use until the arrival of the Portuguese in the 16th century. The sultans of Zanzibar had distinctive coinage in the 19th century. Barghash ibn Sa'id (1879–88) introduced silver ryals and copper pysa in 1882, with Arabic inscriptions on both sides [7–10]. The pysa, however, also featured scales on the reverse, copying the coins of the British East India Company. The rupee of 100 cents was adopted in 1908 and bronze or nickel coins of 1, 10 and 20 cents had a palm tree reverse. Otherwise the sultanate used the coins of the East African Monetary Union. A large silver medal marked the Zanzibar Exhibition in 1905 [11].

FORMER GERMAN EAST AFRICA
Germany obtained trading rights in Dar es Salaam and Witu in 1884 and declared a protectorate in 1891. Six years later the territory was proclaimed a German colony. At first the rupee of 64 pesa was used, and a copper pesa was released in 1890–2 with the name of the German East African Company with the imperial eagle on the obverse and an Arabic reverse. Coins inscribed

"Deutsche Ostafrika" were introduced in 1904, based on the rupee of 100 heller, and featured the imperial crown and a wreathed value (heller denominations) or the bust of Kaiser Wilhelm II (rupees). During World War I, German troops fought a skilful guerrilla campaign to the very end, and even produced emergency coins inscribed "D.O.A."

Under the name of Tanganyika, the territory was mandated to Britain in 1920 and became an independent republic in 1961. In 1964 it joined with Zanzibar (where the Arab sultanate had been overthrown) and adopted the name of Tanzania in October that year.

EAST AFRICAN MONETARY UNION
Instituted in 1906, the Union provided a common currency in five territories: British East Africa (the colony and protectorate of Kenya), Uganda, British Somaliland, Zanzibar and latterly Tanganyika. Coins inscribed "East Africa & Uganda Protectorates" were introduced: the low values had a central hole and a crown (obverse) [13], and elephant tusks (reverse) [12, 14], while the silver 25 and 50 cents bore the crowned bust of the monarch (obverse) and a lion and mountains

(reverse) [15–16]. Similar coins appeared from 1921 based on the shilling of 100 cents. This pattern continued until 1966, when it was replaced by the coinage of the component states as they gained independence.

INDEPENDENT REPUBLICS

Uganda was granted independence in 1962, followed by Kenya (1963) and Tanganyika (1964). Meanwhile the British Somaliland protectorate had joined with the former Italian colony to form the Republic of Somalia. Initially, the three republics within the Commonwealth continued with the coins of East Africa, but separate issues were adopted when the Union was dissolved in 1966.

The subsidiary coins of the Bank of Uganda retained the Union's ivory tusk motif but the higher values replaced the royal effigy with the arms of the republic [17], while a crested crane superseded the lion on the reverse [18] The composition of the coins was changed in 1976, with copper-plated steel replacing bronze in the lower denominations and cupro-nickel plated steel taking the place of cupro-nickel in the higher values. A new series in stainless or copper-plated steel (1987) had numerals in a floral reverse [19–20]. Inflation in the ensuing decade led to the 1998 series of 50 to 500 shillings, featuring wildlife on the reverse.

Kenya opted for a series with an armorial obverse and a bust of President Jomo Kenyatta on the reverse. In 1968 the reverse inscription was altered but Kenyatta's effigy stayed until 1978. After his death, the portrait of his successor, Daniel Arap Moi, was

Above: Imprisoned by the British during the Mau Mau campaign, Jomo Kenyatta became Kenya's first president.

Wartime Gold
In 1916 gold from the Kironda Mine at Sekengi in German East Africa was coined as 15 rupee pieces, popularly known as Tabora Sovereigns (from the railway workshop where they were struck). The dies were engraved by a Sinhalese prisoner of war, and German regulations decreed that they could be issued only to "residents of the better class."

substituted [21–22], and bimetallic coins from 5 to 20 shillings were added to the series between 1995 and 1998. The very few special issues have commemorated Kenyatta's 75th birthday (1966), the 25th anniversary of independence (1988), the tenth anniversary of Moi as president (1988) and the silver jubilee of the Central Bank (1991).

Julius Nyerere was portrayed on the coins of Tanzania from their inception [23, 25], with mammals, birds and fish on the reverse [24, 26]. As in other parts of East Africa, plated steel has replaced cupro-nickel in recent years [27–28]. The basic circulating series originally ran from the bronze 5 senti to 1 shilingi [29–30]. From 1974, a number of gold or silver high values, up to 2,500 shilingi, marked anniversaries of independence and the Central Bank of Tanzania or publicized wildlife conservation. A polygonal 5 shilingi, released in 1971 to mark the tenth anniversary of independence and contribute to the FAO coin programme, showed agricultural products grouped around the value. This motif was retained for the permanent coins of this denomination. Bimetallic circulating coins of 10 shilingi were introduced in 1987 and 20 shilingi in 1992; both portray Nyerere (obverse) and the national arms (reverse).

1
2
3
4
5
6
7
8
9
10
11
12
13
14
15
16
17
18
19
20

HORN OF AFRICA

The north-east corner of the continent, bounded by the Red Sea and the north-western part of the Indian Ocean, is described as the Horn of Africa. This region was predominantly in the Italian sphere of influence, since Eritrea and Somalia were Italian colonies or protectorates, while Ethiopia was under Italian occupation from 1936 to 1941. The French controlled the port of Djibouti and its hinterland, while the British established a protectorate over the area on the southern shore of the Gulf of Aden.

Left: Italian coinage was in use in Ethiopia from 1936 to 1941, but coins portraying the Emperor Haile Selassie, dated 1936 in the Ethiopian Era (1944), were issued following the country's liberation. They were struck in Philadelphia, Birmingham or London between 1945 and 1975.

ETHIOPIA

Formerly known as Abyssinia, this large country south of Sudan is the oldest independent nation in Africa, tracing its origins back to the 4th century BC, when it was founded by Menelik I, son of Solomon and the Queen of Sheba. The powerful kingdom of Axum was probably the first country south of the Sahara to issue coins, from the 2nd century AD, including exquisite little gold coins such as the tremissis of about AD 450 [1–2]. Brass or billon coins called mahallak were struck at Harar from 1807 to 1892.

Under Menelik II (1889–1913) Ethiopia emerged from centuries of isolation and rapidly modernized, adopting western-style coinage in 1892 based on the silver talari (derived from the Maria Theresia thaler) of 20 gersh (piastres) or 40 besa. In 1903 the talari was re-tariffed at 16 gersh or 32 besa. A decimal system based on the birr (dollar) of 100 santeems or matonas was adopted in 1931. Coins bore the effigy of the monarch (obverse) and the Lion of Judah (reverse) [3–4].

Haile Selassie was deposed in 1974 and the country became a people's democratic republic in 1976. Coins had a lion's head (obverse) and aspects of agriculture (reverse) [5–6]. A few gold or silver coins of more recent years have marked UN events, such as International Year of the Child (1980) or Decade for Women (1984).

ERITREA

The region on the south-west coast of the Red Sea was annexed by Italy in 1889, and merged with Ethiopia in 1936 to form Italian East Africa. Silver coins from 50 centesimi to 5 lire appeared in 1890, with the crowned profile of Umberto I on the obverse. A silver tallero (dollar) of 1918 showed an allegorical female bust (Italia), with the crowned arms of Savoy (reverse).

The area was under British military administration from 1941 to 1952, when the United Nations declared it an autonomous state federated with Ethiopia, whose coinage it used. This union, unpopular from the start, led to a long-running guerrilla war. By 1991 the Eritrean People's Liberation Front controlled most of the country and the independent republic was recognized in 1993. A series of coins based on the dollar of 100 cents was introduced in 1997, featuring wildlife (obverse) and soldiers with the flag (reverse) [7–16]. Cupro-nickel or silver coins with a camel and dhow on the obverse have proliferated since 1993, celebrating Eritrea's independence or promoting the "Preserve Planet Earth" campaign.

DJIBOUTI

French interest in the Red Sea resulted in trading concessions at the port of Djibouti in 1839. The same year, the British secured the port of Aden on the opposite side of the Bab el Mandeb strait. A protectorate was established in 1884 and the colony of the French Somali Coast proclaimed in 1896.

French coins were generally used, but a series of tokens was issued at Djibouti in 1920–1. Distinctive coins were introduced in 1948 and bore the effigy of Marianne (obverse), with a lyre antelope [17–18] or an Arab dhow and ocean liner (reverse), reflecting the growing importance of Djibouti as a port of call for cruise ships. The name was changed to the French Territory of the Afars and the Issas in 1967, and coins with this inscription but similar motifs (as well as high values depicting camels) were introduced in 1968–9. In June 1977, the country attained its independence as the Republic of Djibouti. Coins retain the reverse motifs of earlier issues but have the national shield and spears emblem on the obverse. [19–22]

SOMALIA
Indigenous coins date from the 14th century and were struck at Mogadishu by Arab traders, conforming to strict Islamic standards. Of particular interest are the undated brass tokens, which were extensively used as small change by Somali Muslims crossing the Red Sea on pilgrimage to Mecca, including types issued by the Italian colonial

authorities between 1895 and 1914 [23].Whereas British Somaliland used Indian rupees and coins of East Africa until 1961, when it was united with the former Italian Somaliland, the latter had distinctive coins from 1909. The rupia of 100 bese bore the effigy of Victor Emmanuel III, with the value in Italian and Arabic on the reverse.

Coins in the Italian currency system were planned, but only the silver 10 lire of 1925, with a crowned bust of the king, was issued. The resumption of Italian rule in 1950 was signalled by coins depicting an elephant or lioness from 1 centesimo to 1 somalo [24–25].

Following the unification with British Somaliland in 1960, to create the Somali Republic, the currency changed to the scellino (shilling) of 100 centesimi [26–27] with an armorial obverse and inscriptions in English and Arabic. Gold coins portraying President Abdulla Osman celebrated the fifth anniversary of independence (1965). After a military coup in 1969, however, Somalia became a democratic republic. Apart from some gold coins of 1970 marking the tenth anniversary of independence and the first anniversary of the revolution, the previous coinage continued until 1976, when the shilling of 100 senti was adopted, with an armorial obverse and various animals on the reverse [28–31]. Although in general circulation, this series was conceived as part of the FAO coin programme. Paradoxically, as true democracy was restored in the 1990s the word "Democratic" was dropped from the inscription. Since 1998 numerous bimetallic coins with multi-coloured centres have been produced in sets with such themes, as wildlife and world shipping.

Somalia has been wracked by civil war. The Somali National Movement controlling the former British Somaliland seceded in 1993, and began issuing coins inscribed "Republic of Somaliland" in 1994. The obverse shows a Somali stock dove, both a symbol of peace and the national emblem of the breakaway republic [32–33].

Unique Calendar
Ethiopia has its own Amharic characters to denote numerals, and a calendar that began seven years and eight months after the Common Era (AD). Dates are expressed by separate figures up to ten, then in tens to a hundred, using a combination of multiplication and addition to produce a five-digit date, as shown in the 1969 series.

21

22

23

24

25

26

27

28

29

30

31

32

33

1
2
3
4
5
6
7
8
9
10
11
12
13
14
15
16
17

WEST AFRICA

The countries surveyed here are located to the north of the Gulf of Guinea. Four of them were in the British sphere of influence and are now republics within the British Commonwealth, while the fifth, Liberia, was settled by freed slaves returned from the United States and is nominally English-speaking, with close ties to neighbouring Sierra Leone.

Left: Because the low-value coins of British West Africa did not portray the monarch, it was relatively simple to engrave new dies in 1936 bearing the name of Edward VIII as King and Emperor of India. This penny was one of the few coins issued in his name.

BRITISH WEST AFRICA

As in East Africa, a currency board, set up in 1912, provided the coinage in use throughout the British colonies and protectorates of West Africa. Previously, however, coins thus inscribed had been introduced in Nigeria in 1906 and had the distinction of including one of the world's first aluminium coins, the ¹⁄₁₀ penny with a Star of David about a central hole (obverse) and a crown over the value (reverse) [1–2]. From 1908 subsidiary coins were struck in cupro-nickel [3–4]. Coins from 3 pence to 2 shillings were initially minted in silver but switched to brass in 1920. On these denominations a crowned effigy of the reigning monarch (obverse) and an oil palm (reverse) were used for the shilling values [5] and a wreathed value for the 3 and 6 pence denominations [6]. Coins portraying Elizabeth II were in use from 1954 until the four countries achieved independence.

GHANA

The Gold Coast had a silver coinage based on the ackey of 8 tackoe, produced by the Royal African Company between 1796 and 1818. A copper proof tackoe of the first year of issue is shown here [7–8]. It was the first colony to attain independence, together with the mandated territory of Togoland, emerging in February 1957 as the sovereign nation of Ghana, which revived the name of an ancient West African empire. Pence and shillings, introduced in 1958, portrayed Kwame Nkrumah, first the prime minister and later (1960–6) president, of the republic. The currency was reformed in 1965, based on the cedi of 100 pesawas, retaining similar motifs [9–11]. After Nkrumah's overthrow, cocoa beans replaced his image [12], with the national arms dominating the reverses [13–15]. Some coins since 1979 have featured a cowrie, alluding to the currency of earlier generations.

THE GAMBIA

This tiny state along the banks of the River Gambia was purchased by London merchants in 1588 and thus became England's first colony in Africa. Originally a centre for the slave trade, it later became a base for its suppression. It gained independence in 1965, with Elizabeth II as head of state, hence her bust on the coinage [16], whose reverse featured fauna, flora and a sailboat [17]. It became a republic within the Commonwealth in 1970 and new currency, based on the dalasi of 100

Above: The cupro-nickel shilling of the Gambia has an effigy of Elizabeth II (obverse) and an oil palm (reverse).

bututs, appeared the following year, with the effigy of the former prime minister, now president, Sir Dawda Jawara on the obverse, and the republic's arms on the reverse [18].

NIGERIA

The first indigenous coinage of Nigeria (1959) was modelled on that of British West Africa, with the Star of David on the holed coins [19–20] and the crowned bust of the queen on the higher values, with agricultural themes on the reverse [21–22]. Nigeria became a republic in 1963 but the coinage remained unchanged until 1973, when the naira of 100 kobo was introduced. The series featured the republican arms, with pictorial reverses alluding to the country's mineral wealth and diverse agriculture [23–26]. Place of honour on the reverse of the naira was reserved for Herbert Macaulay (1864–1946), regarded as the father of independence.

In 1967, the eastern region broke away and proclaimed the Republic of Biafra. Aluminium coins from 3 pence to 2 shillings, with the palm tree emblem, appeared in 1969. A few silver and gold pieces were struck at the same time to celebrate the second anniversary of independence [27–28], although Biafra ceased to exist in January 1970 following a bloody war.

SIERRA LEONE

An important centre of the slave trade in the 17th and 18th centuries, Sierra Leone was chosen for the first experiment in returning freed slaves to Africa, the aptly named Freetown being established in 1787 [29–30].

Modern coinage, based on the leone of 100 cents, dates from 1964, three years after Sierra Leone achieved independence. Sir Milton Margai, prime minister and, later, the first president, appeared on the obverse with various fauna and flora on the reverse [31–32]. A leone produced for general circulation (1987) used an unusual octagonal format, which was originally applied to bicentennial coins issued to mark the anniversary of Freetown.

Earliest British African Coins

The Sierra Leone Company, set up to settle freed slaves, produced the earliest British colonial coinage issued anywhere in the African continent: the bronze cent (below) and penny; and silver coins from 10 cents to the dollar of 1791. All showed the lion and mountain (from which the country derives its name) on the obverse, and hands clasped in friendship (reverse).

LIBERIA

The country whose name means "the land of the free" was first settled in 1822 by the American Colonization Society, with the aim of repatriating freed slaves. Various settlements combined in 1839 to form the Commonwealth of Liberia, which became a republic in 1847.

A copper cent produced in 1833 showed a man planting a symbolic tree of Liberty, and this was the forerunner to the series of coins of 1896 with the head of Liberty on the obverse and a palm tree on the reverse. Coins were produced very sporadically prior to 1960 and many issues since then [33] exist only in proof sets.

Conversely, Liberia has produced numerous special coins since 1993, often in lengthy thematic series, such as the prolific Pioneers of the West, aimed principally at the American collector market. Other long-running sets since the 1990s have portrayed world statesmen, from Churchill and Roosevelt to Nelson Mandela, Formula One racing drivers, famous baseball players, from Babe Ruth to Reggie Jackson and even the leading characters in the *Star Trek* television series.

SAHARA AND EQUATORIAL AFRICA

Much of this vast region was formerly part of the French colonial empire, and was administered as French West Africa and French Equatorial Africa. To this day the common currency in these regions is issued by the West and Central African States, although some countries have their own distinctive coinage. Although most of the Equatorial region was in the French sphere of influence, both Spain and Portugal managed colonies here, and their successor states likewise now issue their own coins.

Left: Leopold Sedar Senghor, dubbed "the black de Gaulle" was a distinguished teacher, writer and poet who was prominent in the political development of French Africa after 1945, becoming the first president of Senegal (1960–80).

CENTRAL AFRICAN STATES
Ordinary French coins were used in French Equatorial Africa (Middle-Congo, Ubangi-Shari, Chad and Gabon) until 1942, when the region adhered to Charles de Gaulle and the Free French, and coins bearing a Gallic cock (obverse) and the Cross of Lorraine (reverse) were introduced. In 1948 a new type, with the head of Marianne (obverse) and a Loder's gazelle (reverse) was adopted [1–2].

Following the break-up of the French colonial empire in 1958–9, an attempt was made to form a political union comprising Chad, Congo, the Central African Republic and Gabon. Although this failed, an outcome was the monetary union known as the Equatorial Customs Unit, to which Cameroon acceded in 1961. Coins were struck by the authority of the Central Bank of the Equatorial African States, with a standard obverse of three giant eland and a wreathed value reverse [3–8]. The name was changed in 1974 to the Bank of the Central African States. Coins with the new title retained the original motif but from then until 1996 a letter was included to denote the country in which a coin was originally issued: A (Chad), B

(Central African Republic), C (Congo), D (Gabon) and E (Cameroon). Equatorial Guinea, a former Spanish colony, issued its own coins in 1969 [9] before joining the Central African States. Conversely the former French Guinea refused to join, and has issued its own coins [10–11] since 1962.

The bank also produces 100 franc coins with the great eland obverse and inscriptions signifying use in the Central African Republic [12–13], Chad, the Congo People's Republic and Gabon. All four have also produced distinctive commemoratives, notably Chad [14] which, in 1970 alone, honoured both Kennedy brothers as well as Martin Luther King, de Gaulle and President Nasser of Egypt.

WEST AFRICAN STATES
French West Africa comprised Dahomey, French Guinea, French Sudan, Ivory Coast, Niger, Senegal and Upper Volta, using French coins until 1944, when a series featuring Marianne and a horn of plenty was introduced. From 1948 to 1958 coins used the Marianne and Loder's gazelle motifs of Equatorial Africa, with the obverse inscription modified. The former mandated territory of Togoland (for which

Odd Man Out

Mauritania only became part of French West Africa in 1920, gaining autonomy in 1958, and becoming the Islamic Republic of Mauritania in 1960. It withdrew from the French Community in 1966 and left the West African monetary union in 1973. It has since issued coins based on the ouguiya of 5 khoums. These have an obverse showing the crescent and star of Islam with palms and the value, while the reverse bears inscriptions in Arabic.

separate coins were issued in 1924–6 and 1948–56) joined the French West African monetary union in 1957, and 5, 10 and 25 franc coins then included Togo in the inscription [15–16].

The coins of the West African States adopted a standard obverse showing an Ashanti gold weight [17], with wreathed values [18–19] or a Loder's gazelle [20] on the reverse.

Since 1980–1, the 10, 25 and 50 franc coins have had reverses showing food production, issued as part of the Food and Agriculture Organization coin programme [21–22]. These coins circulate in Dahomey (now Benin), Senegal, Upper Volta (now Burkina Faso), Ivory Coast, Mali, Togo and Niger [23–24]. Guinea had a currency based on the syli of 100 cauris from 1971 to 1985, when the Guinean franc was adopted [25–26].

In addition to the common currency, several member countries have issued their own coins. Sporadically, coins have been produced by Ivory Coast (1966), Niger (1960), Togo (1977) and Mali (1960–7). Mali's issue of aluminium 5 [28–29], 10 and 25 "francs maliens" underlined the nation's

new indepedence from France the previous year, and from the French-backed franc. Dahomey (Benin) and Senegal, meanwhile, have issued quite a number of gold and silver coins [27].

FORMER PORTUGUESE AND SPANISH TERRITORIES

In colonial times, the scattered possessions of Spain and Portugal in the Saharan and Equatorial regions used the coins of their mother countries, but since independence they have produced their own. In the north-west, the former Spanish Sahara was partitioned between Mauritania and Morocco in 1975, but after a long war of independence the Saharawi Arab Republic emerged in 1992. Coins from 1 to 100 pesetas have an armorial obverse and a camel reverse. There is also a prolific output of commemoratives aimed mainly at the Spanish market.

Distinctive coins are issued in the islands of Cape Verde [30–31] and São Tome and Principe, off the west coast of Africa, and in Guinea-Bissau (formerly Portuguese Guinea) on the mainland. São Tome issued coins in 1813, but both territories began issuing decimal coins in 1929–33 with the allegory of the republic and "Republica Portuguesa" (obverse) and arms with the name of the colony (reverse). The word "Colonia" was omitted during the 1960s when they became overseas provinces. In 1975 they became independent republics and have issued their own coins since 1977. All three began with modest series promoting the FAO coin programme but have since moved on to lengthy issues, often of little cultural relevance to their own countries, but aimed primarily at the overseas numismatic trade.

Above: The bronze 20 centavos (1962) of São Tome and Principe, with the Portuguese arms on the obverse.

ASIA

This vast continent, which stretches from the Mediterranean to the Pacific, was the birthplace of coinage. Scholars may argue as to whether it was the inhabitants of Asia Minor (modern Anatolia) or China who first adopted metallic currency, but there is no argument that this is where it all began.

TURKEY

Ancient Lydia, in the territory of modern Turkey, produced the first coins of the western world in the 7th century BC. By the time of King Croesus (561–545 BC) its coins had a lion and bull motif (obverse) and rectangular incuse marks (reverse) [1–2]. After Lydia's conquest by the Persian Cyrus the Great, tiny quarter-sigloi were struck under Darius I [3–4].

Although politically classed as a European country, Turkey lies mostly in western Asia, and from medieval to relatively modern times its coinage owed more to its Asiatic and Islamic background than to European influence. Under Ottoman rule the land of the Turks grew into a mighty empire, which stretched from the Danube to the Persian Gulf and from the Caspian Sea to the Barbary Coast of North Africa. The Ottomans controlled the trade routes between Europe and China and dominated the Mediterranean until their naval power was checked by the Battle of Lepanto in 1571. A century later they even besieged Vienna, but from 1700 their power gradually waned. The Ottoman Empire collapsed in the aftermath of World War I, and the republic that succeeded it was confined to Anatolia and a wedge of territory in eastern Thrace, the last remnant of Turkey in Europe.

Left: Out of an obverse type in which the Arabic letters of the ruler's title were interwoven developed the elaborate calligraphic toughra, or sign-manual of the sultan, a device that continued to be used on Turkish coins from the 11th to the 20th centuries.

HELLENISTIC AND ROMAN TURKEY

The Persian Empire declined in the 4th century BC under a succession of weak rulers. Asia Minor was invaded first by Philip of Macedon and then by his son Alexander the Great, who defeated the Persians and annexed the empire, ushering in a period of Greek settlement and rule. After his death, his generals divided his empire among them and struck coins bearing his effigy, such as the tetradrachm struck by Mithridates at Smyrna [5–6]. Under Roman rule (from 63 BC) local issues continued [7–8], latterly in the name of the emperor, such as this early 3rd century bronze coin portraying Severus Alexander [9–10].

MEDIEVAL TURKEY

Anatolia (Asia Minor) formed part of the Byzantine Empire and used its coins [11–12] but from the 10th century onward, it was frequently invaded and overrun by Mongols [13–14] and Turkmens, who established separate dynasties. The Seljuqs of Rum ("land of the Romans") [15], whose capital was the Byzantine city of Nicaea, the Qaramanids, Ilkhanids and others struck coins that were based on Byzantine models but inscribed in Arabic, and sometimes in Greek.

OTTOMAN EMPIRE

In 1453 the Ottoman Turks conquered the city of Constantinople and overthrew the Byzantine Empire. In the ensuing centuries the empire expanded dramatically, from the Caucasus to the whole of North Africa, but by 1914 Turkish dominions in Europe had shrunk to the hinterland of Istanbul (Constantinople), while alliance with Germany and Austria in World War I hastened the end of the empire.

The coins of the Ottoman Empire were struck in copper, silver and gold in a bewildering array of denominations based on multiples of the para, from 3 (*akce* or *asper*) to 240 (*altilik*). In the 17th century, Suleiman II introduced the kurus or piastre, originally a large silver coin worth 40 para. By the 18th century low-grade silver was being used for coins ranging from 1 para upwards, but between 1808 and 1840 the size and fineness of the coins were progressively reduced on eight different occasions as the economy collapsed [18–21]. The gold coinage was infinitely more complex, with numerous coins in different weights and fineness, each distinguished by its own name and issued simultaneously.

The coinage was reformed in 1844 by Abdulmejid, who introduced the gold lira (pound) of 100 silver piastres or kurus; the smaller coins, from 5 para upwards, were struck in bronze [22]. Large bronze piastres bore the Arabic numerals for 40, signifying their value in para. In this series the toughra of the sultan appeared on the obverse, with plain or elaborate surrounds, while the reverse bore the name of the sultan with a regnal year at the top and the date in the Muslim calendar at the foot. Gold coins [16–17] were produced in two types, for trade and mainly for jewellery respectively, the latter being generally thinner and pierced for adornment.

TURKISH REPUBLIC

The Greek invasion of Anatolia in 1921 provoked a resurgence of Turkish nationalism under Mustapha Kemal, who proclaimed a republic at Ankara in 1923 and overthrew the sultanate. The republic adopted the piastre of 100 para, omitting the toughra and

Currency Reform

The Turkish currency was reformed in January 2005, when the yeni (new) lira of 100 yeni kurus replaced a million old lira.

introducing the first pictorial elements: an ear of wheat (obverse) and a spray of oak leaves (reverse), with the crescent and star emblem at the top. These coins continued to be inscribed entirely in Arabic until 1934–5, when the lira of 100 kurus was inscribed in the modified Roman alphabet and the date appeared in the Western calendar [23–24]. In the early versions of the lower denominations the star appeared above the crescent, but from 1949 onward the emblem was rotated so that the star appeared on the left side. Silver coins bore the profile of Kemal Ataturk ("father of the Turks") and a wreathed value [25–26]. Gold coinage was resumed in 1943, with Kemal's effigy (obverse) and an elaborate Arabic inscription (reverse).

INFLATION

Turkey was overtaken by inflation in the 1980s; in the space of 20 years the 50 lira piece was reduced from a large silver coin to a tiny aluminium-bronze piece. In the 1990s base metal coins of 500, 1000, 1500, 2500 and 5000 lira briefly appeared, followed by coins denominated in *bin lira* (thousands of lira). By the end of the 20th century the 100,000 lira was a small aluminium coin [27–34].

In the same period commemorative coins appeared in gold or silver, culminating in the coin issued to celebrate the 700th anniversary of the Ottoman Empire (1999), which was denominated 60,000,000 lira.

PALESTINE, ISRAEL AND JORDAN

The region known as the Middle East forms the land bridge connecting Asia and Africa, and has therefore been an important crossroads of commerce since time immemorial. For the same reason, it has frequently been fought over and, indeed, remains an area of conflict to this day. Palestine (the land of the Philistines) was conquered by the Jews 3000 years ago. Since then it has been successively invaded and occupied by the Assyrians, Persians, Egyptians, Greeks, Romans, Byzantines and Arabs. For four centuries Palestine was part of the Ottoman Empire, before it came under British rule in 1917–18, following the demise of the empire. Britain was granted mandates by the League of Nations to administer the territories of Palestine and Transjordan. These mandates terminated in 1948 and resulted in the emergence of the State of Israel and the Hashemite Kingdom of Jordan.

Left: The Jewish Kingdom of Judaea was under Greek and later Roman rule, but rose in revolt on several occasions. The first Jewish revolt (AD 66–70) was suppressed by the Roman emperor Vespasian, who issued coins to celebrate this victory. He appears on the obverse. The reverse, inscribed "Judaea Capta", shows two Jews under a palm tree, symbolizing their defeat.

JEWISH KINGDOMS

For most of the period before the Common Era, the biblical lands of Judah and Israel used the coinage of foreign invaders and conquerors: the darics and sigloi of Persia, minted locally at Samaria [1–2]; the staters and tetradrachms of Alexander the Great and his successors, such as this coin depicting the goddess Athena but with a Samaritan–Aramaic countermark [3–4]; the Ptolemies of Egypt, exemplified by this tetradrachm of Ptolemy II, struck at Gaza [5–6]; and the Seleucids of Syria.

In 167 BC the Jews under Judas Maccabaeus rose in revolt against the Seleucid emperor Antiochus IV. At one time Jewish coins were attributed to this period, but it has now been proved that they belong to the first rebellion of the Jews against Rome in AD 66–70 [7–8]. In the interim, however, copper pruta circulated as small change and bore a Hebrew inscription on one side and twin cornucopiae on the other [9–10]. During the 1st century BC, Alexander Jannaeus assumed the kingship, and he and his successors struck bronze coins bearing various symbols, such as an anchor, wheel or stars. Although some coins were inscribed in Hebrew, most bore Greek titles. The coins of Herod the Great (37–4 BC) are particularly interesting, as they show increasing Roman stylistic influence. In AD 132–5 the Jews again rose in rebellion, led by Simon Barcochba ("son of the star"), hence the star symbols found on many of the coins of this period. After the revolt was crushed the Romans dispersed the Jews, beginning the Diaspora that continued until the early 20th century.

ISLAMIC RULE

Roman and Byzantine coins were used thereafter, but the encroachments of the Arabs were reflected in coins based on Byzantine models with Arabic inscriptions and motifs [11–12]. Islamic influence began in the 6th century AD, when the Sasanian Khusru II overthrew Byzantine rule. Byzantine gold and copper coins continued to be used in the region until supplies ran out. In the 10th century, Arab mints were established at Iliya Filistina (Jerusalem), Tiberias and Akka (Acre), striking Ikhshidid dinars [13–14]. By the end of that century the concentric designs of the Fatimids were prevalent, as seen in this gold bezant of Acre [15–16], and their coins were copied by much of the Islamic world.

KINGDOM OF JERUSALEM
By the end of the 11th century, the Fatimids had been overthrown by the Christian Crusaders. They established the Kingdom of Jerusalem, which initially extended over much of what is now Egypt and Lebanon. Typical of the Crusader coinage is a denier showing the Tower of David on the reverse [17–18]. The kingdom expired with the fall of Acre to the Mameluks in 1291. While Palestine remained under the rule of the Mameluks and later of the Ottomans, Syrian and Egyptian coins were in use.

BRITISH MANDATE
Under British rule coins inscribed in English, Hebrew and Arabic were issued in Palestine from 1927 to 1948. Those that did not have a central hole

bore an olive branch on the reverse [19–25]. Technically the mandate included Transjordan, so Palestinian currency circulated there as well, even though politically it was administered separately. In 1921 the British installed the Emir Abdullah, and in 1923 the lands to the east of the River Jordan became an autonomous state, although they remained under British mandate until 1948.

ISRAEL
The British mandate terminated in May 1948 and the State of Israel was proclaimed on May 14. Coins bearing dates according to the Jewish calendar were introduced, their motifs derived from the coins of the Jewish revolts [26–34]. The currency was originally based on the Palestinian pound of 1000 mils, but in 1949 the lirah israelit (Israeli pound) of 1000 prutah was adopted. Following the monetary reform of 1958 the lirah was divided into 100 agorot. Continuing inflation led to the reform of February 1980 that introduced the sheqel of 100 new agorot (worth 1000 old agorot), but since September 1985 the currency has been stabilized on the basis of the sheqel chadash (new sheqel) worth 1000 sheqalim. In all of these series the biblical themes have continued.

Israel has been a prolific producer of special coins, partly commemorative and partly didactic, upholding the image of the modern state with its roots in ancient Jewish traditions.

JORDAN
The coinage of the Hashemite Kingdom of Jordan, commencing in 1949, is based on the dinar of 10 dirhems or 1000 fils, with inscriptions in Arabic (obverse) and English (reverse) [35–36]. Non-figural motifs were used exclusively until 1968, when a profile of King Hussein appeared on the obverse. In 1996 the currency was reformed and the dinar divided into 100 piastres [37–38]. The few commemoratives since 1969 have mainly marked anniversaries of the kingdom.

Microprocessor Background
Since 1984 a number of definitive and commemorative Israeli coins portraying famous people, such as Theodor Herzl (below right), have had backgrounds formed by the continuous repetition of their names printed by microprocessor.

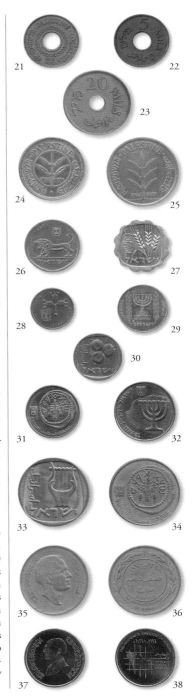

LEBANON, IRAQ AND SYRIA

This group of Middle Eastern countries did not exist until the 1920s, and yet the region has a numismatic history that goes back many centuries. It was successively conquered by the Persians, Alexander the Great, the Romans, Byzantines, Arabs and Crusaders, each of whom left their mark on the coinage of the area. For 400 years the territories remained under Turkish rule, until they were liberated by the Allies during World War I and mandated to the British or French by the League of Nations.

Left: The obverse of the 25 and 100 dinar coins of 2004, the only Iraqi issues since the fall of Saddam Hussein, features a map of Iraq – the historic Mesopotamia, or land between the two rivers, Tigris and Euphrates, which the Arabs styled Al Jazira ("the island") – with dates according to the Western and Muslim calendars.

ANTIOCH

Seleucus I Nicator, who founded the city of Antioch, naming it after his father Antiochus, was one of Alexander the Great's generals. After Alexander's death the generals divided his empire between them and Seleucus gained the territory of Syria and built the Seleucid Empire. Successive Seleucid kings struck coins on Greek models, typified by these tetradrachms of Antiochus II (261–246 BC) [1–4] and Antiochus IV (175–164 BC) [5–6].

No fewer than 12 towns or cities called Antioch struck coins in the classical period [7–8], but of these the most important was Antioch on the Orontes, the capital of the western Seleucid Empire and later of the Roman province of Syria (modern Antakiyah, transferred from Syria to Turkey in 1939). In the Roman and Byzantine periods it ranked third in importance after Alexandria and Constantinople [9–10]. The city was devastated by an earthquake in 526 and rebuilt under the name of Theopolis. It produced a large number of light-weight gold solidi [11–12] in the reigns of Justin II and Maurice Tiberius in the late 6th century.

In the early Islamic period Syria fell under the rule of the Umayyads and Abbasids and struck silver dirhams, notably under Caliph al-Malik, who struck coins at his capital, Damascus, as well as Basra [13–14]. Antioch was

liberated in 1098 during the first Crusade and became the capital of a principality that flourished in the 12th century. In this period copper folles [15–16] were struck by Roger of Salerno. Its fall to the Mameluk sultan Baybars in 1268 marked the end of an era that left a rich legacy of copper and billon coins [17–18].

MEDIEVAL DIVERSITY

Antioch was only one of several Crusader kingdoms and principalities that struck gold, silver and base-metal coins in the 12th and 13th centuries, modelled mainly on French deniers, and coins may also be encountered from Acre, Tripoli and Edessa, such as this follis of Baldwin II [19–20]. Meanwhile, Turkic tribes were migrating from Central Asia into the Near East. The Artuqids settled at Hisn Kayfa, while the Zengids occupied Mosul and Aleppo. Their coins are remarkable for their obverses, which bear astrological symbols [21–22] or are derived from classical Greek models [23], while the reverses conform to the Islamic style.

In the 11th century Tughril Beg, leader of the Seljuqs, advanced westward and made himself master of Baghdad. He and his successors extended their empire to the Caucasus and Anatolia. Islamic coinage was struck in many towns in and around Mesopotamia by Seljuqs, Urtuqids,

Royal Portraiture

Unusually for the period, the coins of Iraq portrayed the reigning monarch on the obverse and followed the British custom of profiles facing alternately to the right (Faisal I, 1931–3), then to the left (Ghazi, 1933–9).

Abbasids and Zengids. In the epoch of the Ottoman Empire, from 1516 onwards, coins were struck at Dimishq (Damascus) and Halab (Aleppo), in what is now Syria, and at Mardin, Al-Ruha and Amid in what is now Iraq. The rich variety of coins surviving from this period ranges from the 16th-century gold sultani of Mehmed III, struck at Dimishq [24–25] to the silver dirhams of Haroun al Rashid struck at Basra and the coins of the Zengid Atabegs of Mosul.

IRAQ

Mesopotamia was freed from Turkish rule in 1917 by the British, who were granted a mandate to govern the territory in 1920. It became an independent kingdom in 1921 under Faisal I, whose profile appeared on the coins introduced there in 1931 [26–29]. Similar coins portrayed Ghazi (1933–9) and Faisal II, who was murdered in 1958 when the monarchy was toppled in the first of several military coups. The reverse of the royal coinage, denominated in fils, dirhams, riyals and dinars, bore the value and inscriptions entirely in Arabic. Under the republic, royal effigies were replaced by a motif of palm trees. The relatively few commemoratives issued since 1970 have celebrated such events as peace with the Kurds (1971), oil nationalization (1973) and various anniversaries of the army or the ruling Ba'ath Party.

SYRIA

The League of Nations conferred a mandate on France to rule the Levantine states of Syria and Lebanon. A series of revolts in the 1920s led the French to concede an autonomous republic in Syria (1930), leading to complete independence in 1944. Faisal was briefly king before the French ejected him and the British placed him on the Iraqi throne, and in this period a gold dinar was minted.

Under the French protectorate piastres were inscribed in French and Arabic [30–32]. From 1948 onward, coins bore the eagle emblem of the republic, with Arabic values on the reverse. Subtle changes in inscriptions signified the United Arab Republic (1959–60) and the Syrian Arab Republic (since 1962).

LEBANON

Although the French had a mandate to govern Syria and Lebanon together, they were quick to distinguish between the predominantly Christian Sanjak of Lebanon and Muslim Syria, and as early as September 1920 established the former as the Etat du Grand Liban (State of Greater Lebanon). Coins thus inscribed were adopted in 1924; those without a central hole bore the cedar emblem on the obverse. Some coins from 1929 onward were inscribed "République Libanaise" (Lebanese Republic) although full sovereignty was not granted until 1946 [33, 36]. Few coins were struck during the prolonged civil wars of the 1970s and 80s; those issued since 1968 bear the name of the Banque du Liban (Bank of the Lebanon) [34–35]. A handful of gold and silver coins marked the Lake Placid Winter Olympics of 1980.

Above: Palm trees replaced royal portraits on the coins issued by the Iraqi Republic.

1
2
3
4
5
6
7
8
9
10
11
12
13
14
15
16

ARABIA

A geographical, rather than a political, entity, Arabia is a great peninsula of more than 2.5 million sq km/1 million sq miles between the Red Sea and the Persian Gulf, stretching from the Mediterranean in the north to the Indian Ocean in the south. At its core lies the kingdom of Saudi Arabia; to the south lies the Yemen, while along its eastern and northern borders are a series of smaller countries and petty states whose wealth and importance far exceed their size, as a result of the oil reserves that lie beneath them. Arabia was the cradle of Islam in the 7th century AD, and its language, alphabet, literature, arts and sciences have spread across the world, from Spain and north-west Africa to South-east Asia and the East Indies.

Left: The silver dirham (drachma) evolved in AH 79 (AD 698) and was to become the standard coin of the Islamic world for five centuries. The design of both obverse and reverse was composed entirely of Arabic inscriptions surrounded by circles and annulets. The obverse bears the Muslim declaration of faith while the reverse has a Qur'anic quotation surrounded by the prophetic mission.

CENTRE OF ISLAM

In September 622 Muhammad bin Abdallah fled from Mecca, his birthplace, where he was being persecuted by those who objected to his prophetic mission and teachings on monotheism, to join his followers at Yathrib, later renamed simply Medina ("the city"). This dramatic event was the Hegira or Hijra, from which Muslims date their calendar. Over the ensuing century the followers of Muhammad would create a movement that spread across the known world like wildfire and remains a potent force to this day.

Muhammad led his followers in war on Mecca, in which they were eventually victorious. He consolidated his rule over a unified Arabia, but when he died in 632 he left no son to succeed him. Instead, his powers were divided among two of his fathers-in-law and his two sons-in-law. To the senior father-in-law, Abu Bakr, fell the title of Caliph ("follower"), the spiritual head of Islam.

Arabia was an arid region inhabited by nomadic pastoralists, yet by the 8th century the Arabs had conquered the whole of North Africa and penetrated the Iberian Peninsula. They struck north, south and east, spreading the doctrines of Islam wherever they went. Inevitably as Islam spread, the centre of the religious and temporal power moved away from Mecca and Medina, and by the 9th century Arabia had reverted to the cluster of petty tribal states that had existed before the rise of Muhammad.

RIVAL CALIPHATES

Under the early caliphs, Arabia relied heavily on the gold and silver coins brought to Mecca and Medina by the faithful. By the 9th century, the Abbasids were striking coins at Sana'a and Aden in the Yemen as well as at Makka (Mecca), mostly silver dirhams [1–2]. They were followed by other dynasties such as the Rassids, who minted some beautiful gold dinars at Sana'a [3–4] and even larger coins at Sa'da about 910 [5–6].

Other dynasties that were prolific producers of gold and silver coins included the Ziyadids and Najahids of Zahid, the Sulayhids and the Fatimids. Constantly at war with each other, they fell easy prey to the invading Osmanli Turks who, by 1516, were in firm control. Thereafter Arabia was part of the Ottoman Empire. During this period, however, base-metal coins intended for small change were also struck by local *sharifs* (governors). They were pretty basic pieces, with simple motifs and mint-marks, such as this coin from Mecca [7–8].

SAUDI ARABIA

By the beginning of the 20th century Ottoman power was more nominal than real. From the late 18th century onward Arabia was in the British sphere of influence, the agents of the East India Company having concluded commercial treaties with local rulers from Aden to the Persian Gulf. In the 19th century a power struggle developed between rival factions, and the Turks supported the Rashidis against the Saudis. By 1887 the latter had lost most of their lands and went into exile in Kuwait. But in 1901 Abdul Aziz ibn Saud recaptured Riyadh, capital of the Sultanate of Nejd. He proclaimed himself sultan in 1905 and captured the Turkish province of Al Hasa in 1913.

Ibn Saud struck Hashimi gold dinars of good quality in AH 1334 (1915) [9–10]. Backing the British against the Turks in World War I, he embarked on the conquest of the Hejaz in 1925 and seized most of Asir the following year. To this period belongs the dinar minted in 1923 [11–12]. In 1932, Ibn Saud merged Hejaz and Nejd and founded the Kingdom of Saudi Arabia.

Countermarked coins were used at first, notably the Indian rupee and the Maria Theresia thaler, but a regular coinage based on the dinar of 5 riyals or 100 piastres was adopted in 1916, followed by similar coins, inscribed entirely in Arabic, for Hejaz and Nejd [13–16] and then the series of Saudi Arabia, distinguished by the palm tree and crossed swords emblem, from 1937 onwards [17–19].

A new currency, based on the riyal of 100 halala, was adopted in 1963. The innate conservatism of Saudi Arabia is demonstrated by the strict adherence to Qur'anic teaching and the total absence of any image, human or animal, on the coins [20–23].

United Yemen

In May 1990 the Yemen Arab Republic, also known as North Yemen, joined its southern neighbour to form a single nation state, the Republic of the Yemen. Coins depicting the eagle emblem, modern buildings and the ancient bridge at Shaharah were introduced in 1993.

YEMEN

Coins based on the imadi riyal of 40 buqsha or 80 halala were struck at Sana'a, the capital, from 1902 [24–27], the Mutawakelite Kingdom finally breaking free from the Ottomans in 1916. 1962 the imam was deposed and the socialist Yemen Arab Republic was proclaimed. There was little change in the coinage, other than the Arabic inscriptions, but in 1974 the currency was decimalized, introducing the rial of 100 fils, with an eagle emblem on the obverse [28–29]. A number of gold or silver coins since 1969 have commemorated such disparate subjects as the *Mona Lisa* and the Apollo landing.

The coins of the British East India Company and later of India circulated in British-ruled Aden prior to 1959, when it formed the core of the Federation of South Arabia and adopted the dinar of 100 fils. The reverses of these coins featured crossed *jambiyas* (curved daggers) or a dhow [30–31]. Following a revolution in 1970 the country became the People's Democratic Republic of Yemen, and its coins were subsequently inscribed in Arabic and English [32–33].

GULF STATES

This is the collective term for the small countries on the fringes of Arabia, along the western and southern shores of the Persian Gulf. They were inhabited by Arab tribes, the subjects of Persia or the Ottoman Empire at various times. They were first penetrated by the Portuguese in the 16th century but the British East India Company established trading posts in the early 19th century and in the wake of commerce came treaties of protection with Britain. These relations with the sheikhdoms and emirates of the Gulf terminated in the 1960s, leading to full independence a decade later.

Left: The 100 baisa bimetallic coin of Oman, issued in 1991, celebrated the centenary of coinage in the sultanate. The copper half-anna of 1891, showing a view of the port of Muscat, was reproduced on the reverse. The Arabic numerals signify AH 1411.

BAHRAIN

This country, ruled by the Al Khalifa family, consists of a cluster of islands that, prior to the discovery of oil in the 1930s, depended on pearl fishing. Revenue from oil has been wisely used to create an ultra-modern state and a major communications and commercial centre. Bahrain attained complete sovereignty in 1971 but introduced its own coins in 1965, with a palm tree obverse and value reverse based on the dinar of 1000 fils [1–2]. A new series, released in 1992, has the values in Western numerals on the reverse [3–10]. A few commemoratives have appeared since the UN Food and Agriculture Organization issue of 1969, including several silver coins portraying the ruler in Arab dress.

KUWAIT

Fearing Turkish encroachment, Sheikh Mubarak of the ruling Al Sabah family, who struck this Kuwaiti baisa in 1887 [11–12], sought British protection in 1899. The agreement was terminated in 1961 and Kuwait became a fully independent country.

Thanks to oil revenue, the Kuwaiti dinar is the world's strongest currency, fully backed by gold. The coins from 1 to 100 fils, introduced in 1961, feature a *sambuke*, or two-masted Arab dhow, with double dates (Christian and

Muslim) in Arabic numerals, while the obverse bears the value with the name of the country in Arabic and English [13–16]. A few commemoratives have appeared since 1976, when a silver double dinar celebrated the 15th anniversary of independence with portraits of Abdullah ibn Salim (1950–65) and his successor Sabah ibn Salim (1965–77) side by side. Gold and silver coins of 1981 marked the 1500th anniversary of the Hegira.

OMAN

Although the mint at 'Uman (Oman) operated only occasionally in the 10th century, both gold and silver coins were struck by the Wajihid governors of the province. The dirhams shown here were struck by Ahmad bin Hilal [17–18] and Muhammad bin Yusuf [19–20] between AH 299 and 310, but after about AH 350 coins were supplied from the Yemen.

In 1508 the Portuguese captured Muscat, the capital and chief seaport of the sultanate, in the first European penetration of the Gulf region. In 1650 they were ejected by the Persians, who ruled until 1741, when Ahmed ibn Sa'id seized power and established the dynasty that has reigned ever since. Muscat and Oman was the most powerful state in Arabia until the mid-19th century, when it was weakened by

Prolific Output

Immediately before the Federation of Arab Emirates was formed, many distinctive coins were produced in Ajman, Fujairah, Ras al Khaimah, Sharjah and Umm al Qiwain, a parallel to the unduly prolific stamp issues of the same period and likewise aimed at collectors. Subjects ranged from the World Cup to champions of sport. Sharjah's 5 rupee coin of 1964 was the first in the world to mourn the death of John F. Kennedy.

nomadic attacks. In 1798 it signed a treaty with Britain, which subsequently played a major role in its defence. Sultan Sa'id was overthrown in 1970 by his son Qabus, who dropped "Muscat" from the country's name.

The first coins were quarter and twelfth annas, struck in 1893. They had a pictorial reverse but the following year an all-Arabic non-figural type was adopted. The coinage was reformed in 1945, adopting the Saidi riyal of 200 baisa, with the national emblem, a dagger over crossed swords, on the obverse and Arabic inscriptions on the reverse. Qabus reformed the currency in 1972, adopting the Omani riyal of 1000 baisa. As well as a modified obverse inscription reflecting the change of

name, this series has the value in Arabic numerals on the reverse [21–24]. A conservative policy with regard to special issues was followed until 1995, when a lengthy series of 20 silver coins depicting Omani forts was released.

QATAR

This emirate was under Ottoman rule from 1872 until 1916, when the Turkish garrison was withdrawn. Sheikh Abdullah bin Qasim promptly sought British protection, which continued until 1971. The first coins were issued in 1966 and bore the names of Qatar and Dubai, with a gazelle on the reverse [25–26]. A plan to unite with Bahrain and the Trucial States was abandoned and since September 1971 Qatar has been fully independent. Separate coins were introduced in 1973 based on the riyal of 100 dirhem, with Arabic values (obverse) [27] and a dhow and palm tree (reverse).

UNITED ARAB EMIRATES

The sheikhdoms of Abu Dhabi, Ajman, Dubai, Fujairah, Sharjah and Umm al Qiwain [28–29] formed the Federation of Arab Emirates in December 1971, after the withdrawal of British protection over the area formerly known collectively as the Trucial States. In February 1972 Ras al Khaimah joined the federation, which became the United Arab Emirates and began issuing coins thus inscribed in 1973. Its coins are comparatively conservative, with Arabic values (obverse) married to reverses depicting date palms, dhow, gazelle, Mata Hari fish [30–32] and an offshore oil rig.

Above: The diamond-shaped 20 baisa of AH 1359 (1940) was struck by Oman specifically for Dhofar Province.

19 20 21 22 23 24 25 26 27 28 29 30 31 32

1
2
3
4
5
6
7
8
9
10
11
12
13
14
15
16

IRAN AND AFGHANISTAN

The Persian Empire embraced the lands now occupied by both modern Iran and Afghanistan, and at its height extended from Asia Minor to the north-west frontier of India, from the Caspian Sea to the Bay of Bengal. In its heyday, more than two millennia ago, it was one of the greatest civilizations and played a major role in the development of early coinage.

Left: Since 1994 Iranian coins of the higher denominations have been struck in bimetallic combinations. Their reverse motifs are derived from ancient art forms featuring stylized flowers.

ANCIENT PERSIA

The art of coinage spread eastward from Lydia, in modern Turkey, in the mid-6th century BC. The Greek historian Herodotus suggested that Darius Hydaspes (521–486) was the first ruler to strike coins, hence the name "daric" applied to the gold piece, equivalent to 20 sigloi (shekels) of silver. Both bore the kneeling figure of an archer – the king himself – on the obverse. These coins were roughly oval in shape and remained unchanged until the fall of the Persian Empire to Alexander the Great in the 4th century BC.

After Alexander, Persia was ruled by various satraps, or governors, who struck silver coins in abundance. In the mid-second century the Parthians overcame their Seleucid (Greek) masters and created a new empire in Persia. Silver coins on the Greek standard portrayed Arsakes, founder of the dynasty, exemplified by this coin of Osroes II dating from AD 190 [1–2]. Latterly, coins had inscriptions of corrupt Greek mingled with Pehlevi, the indigenous language.

The Kushans, a tribe originating in Xinjiang, China, created an empire that flourished from AD 105 to 250 and stretched from Tajikistan to northern India. At its height it produced gold and copper coins [3–4] but virtually no silver. The Kushan Empire declined early in the 3rd century AD, and much of its territory was absorbed by the Sasanians. Ardashir defeated the Bactrians and Parthians and established the Sasanian Empire, which ruled all of Western Asia and originally struck coins with a strong Kushan influence [5–6]. Gold and silver coins were modelled on Roman solidi and Greek drachmae respectively, the latter noted for their very wide, thin flans, later copied by the Arabs. Shown here are a gold solidus of Peroz I (459–84) [7–8] and drachmae of Khusru V (631–3) [9–12]. More orthodox in appearance were the billon tetradrachms of Elymais [13–14], a semi-independent kingdom in what is now south-western Iran, which was conquered by Ardashir.

MEDIEVAL PERSIA

In the 13th century the Mongols, under Genghis Khan, swept across Asia. The Ilkhans of Persia produced spectacular coins in gold [15–16], silver and copper at Tabriz, with the Shia creed of Islam (obverse) and the khan's title in Mongol (reverse). Shah Rukh introduced a new type of dirham, which remained popular from the 15th to the early 18th centuries [17–18] and provided the model for the thin silver coins, which later became smaller and thicker [19–20]. These coins were remarkable for their inscriptions and extensive use of rhyming couplets.

Regal coinage, confined to silver and gold, was struck at numerous provincial mints identified by Arabic abbreviations of their names. Many towns, however, produced their own copper falus, usually featuring animals or birds on the obverse, which serve to identify their origin.

MODERN COINAGE

The bewildering array of weights and values in the Persian coinage was rationalized in 1835 and the currency was based on the toman of 10 krans, 200 shahis or 10,000 dinars. The coins of Persia were consolidated by Shah Nasr al Din in 1876. All the branch mints were shut down and western machinery was installed at Tehran. Coins featured the radiate sun or lion and sunrise emblems [21–22] but from 1897 onward the portrait of the shah was often used.

In 1925 Reza Pahlavi overthrew the Qajar dynasty and proclaimed himself Reza Shah. He reformed the coinage in 1931, creating the toman of 10 rials, 1000 dinars or 5000 shahis. The name of the country was changed to Iran in 1935. In Reza Shah's reign coins reverted to the lion motif with the value in Arabic script [23–24]. His successor, Muhammed Reza Shah, had his profile on coins from 1966 until 1979, when he was overthrown [25–26]. Since then, the coins of the Islamic republic have eschewed portraiture, and mosques, tombs and other landmarks have appeared instead.

AFGHANISTAN

This remote country between Iran and India has been fought over for countless centuries. Distinctive coinage was produced in the area from the 4th century BC onward, notably the issues from the kingdoms of Bactria and Kabul. Lying between the Hindu Kush and the Oxus, Bactria occupied what is now northern Afghanistan and struck coins on the Greek standard, such as this gold stater of 250–230 BC [27–28]. Rectangular copper coins, such as the type by Menander of about 155 BC [29–30], were also produced.

The Kingdom of Kabul, ruled by the White Huns (5th century) and the Turko-Hephthalites (8th century) also minted coins. Afghanistan as a sovereign state developed only from 1747 under the Durrani dynasty, whose coinage aped that of the Mughal Empire, with the same fondness for

The Tyranny of the White Huns

The Hephthalites or White Huns were a nomadic people who invaded the Sasanian Empire in the 4th century. They captured Shah Peroz, ransomed him, then used the millions of Sasanian silver coins paid to them as the basis of their own coins, derived from Sasanian, Kushan and Greek types.

poetic couplets [31–32]. Copper coins were struck by hand in numerous provincial mints, while gold and silver pieces often appeared in the name of rival contenders for the throne.

A national mint was established at Kabul in 1891 and machine-struck coinage was adopted in a system based on the Kabuli rupee of 2 qiran, 3 abbasi, 6 sanar, 12 shahi, 60 paisa or 600 dinar. These coins bore the state emblem and an Arabic text. In the 1920s coins based on the afghani of 100 pul were struck bearing the *toughra* of Muhammed Nadir Shah. Following the overthrow of Zahir Shah in 1973, coins were issued with a wreathed eagle emblem.

Afghanistan became a democratic republic in 1979, and this regime, under Soviet protection, continued until 1989. In this period, coins with communist-style emblems were struck in Cuba. When Russian forces withdrew, Afghanistan descended into chaos as the Mujahideen fought the Taliban, who established a fundamentalist Islamic state in 1994. The most recent coins of the Islamic Republic of Afghanistan, denominated in afghanis, feature a mosque [33–34]. The date on the reverse is 1383, which approximates to the year 2004.

BURMA, PAKISTAN AND BANGLADESH

These countries were at one time part of British India, acquired by the Honourable East India Company by conquest in the course of the 18th and 19th centuries. Apart from this, the regions had little in common. Britain fought a long series of wars between 1824 and 1885 to subjugate Burma, which had its own long-established culture and political structure. The territory that is now Pakistan was a major component of the Mughal Empire. It had close ties with Afghanistan, and a coinage with a long and complex history dating back to the pre-Christian era.

Left: The independent Kingdom of Burma was renowned for its distinctive coinage, which had a peacock motif on the obverse and continued until 1885, when it was replaced by Indian coins. Highly prized were the silver kyats, which were subsequently decorated with coloured enamels to make a fashionable form of jewellery at the end of the 19th century.

BURMA

The Kingdom of Arakan struck coins based on Indian designs from the late 7th century, the conch being a popular motif [1–2]. In the Middle Ages, coins of the neighbouring Muslim sultans in Bengal were in use, but Arakanese coins were revived in the 16th century and continued until the 1790s; this 17th-century tanka bears the title "Lord of the White Elephants" used by the Arakan kings [3–6]. In southern Burma, influenced by Malaya, there was a tradition of tin coins from the 17th to 19th centuries [7–8].

Under the last kings, Mindon (1853–78) and Thibaw (1880–5), coins were struck in various denominations (kyat of 5 mat or 10 mu, 20 pe or 80 pyas), the silver kyat corresponding to the Indian rupee and the gold kyat to the mohur. Burma is one of the few countries in relatively modern times to have struck coins in lead for small change; the eighth and quarter pya of 1869 with a hare on the obverse. The quarter pe was struck in different metals: copper (1865), iron (1865), copper again (1878) and latterly brass. Higher denominations featured a lion or peacock on the obverse, with the wreathed value inscribed in words on the reverse [9].

In 1937 Burma was detached from India and granted autonomy, though it continued to use Indian currency. In 1948 it attained independence and left the Commonwealth. Cupro-nickel or pure nickel coins denominated in pyas or pe appeared in 1948–9, followed by the decimal kyat of 100 pyas from 1952. All these coins had the image of a *chinthe* (mythological lion guardian) on the obverse and the value in Burmese script on the reverse. Ironically, in 1966 a new series portrayed national hero Aung San, whose daughter Aung San Suu Kyi, winner of the Nobel Peace Prize, has been under house arrest by the ruling military junta, beginning in 1989. The country changed its name in that year to Myanmar (actually a more accurate phonetic rendering of the indigenous name) and coins with that name in European lettering have been issued since 1999 [10–11].

PAKISTAN

The territory of what is now Pakistan was ruled in turn by Parthians, Kushans and Hephthalites (White Huns), the last-named striking silver coins in the 5th century [12–13]. Later came the Sasanians and the Ghaznavids, who introduced Islam and struck coins at Lahore derived from Afghan types. From Afghanistan the Mughals conquered much of the Indian subcontinent. Multan, where this gold mohur was struck [14–15], was an important mint from the 16th to late 18th centuries. The Punjab was conquered in the mid-18th century by the Sikhs, who produced silver rupees at Lahore [16–17] and Peshawar [18–19] until the mid-19th century, when the region was brought under British rule.

When the British left India in 1947, the subcontinent was divided into the predominantly Hindu Dominion of India and the Muslim Dominion of Pakistan. Coins inscribed "Government of Pakistan" appeared in 1948, with a *toughra* or crescent and star motifs. The rupee of 16 annas gave way to the rupee of 100 paisa in 1961.

The Islamic Republic of Pakistan was proclaimed in 1956, and at first there was no change in the inscription, but English was dropped in 1964 [20–21]. A few 50 paisa or rupee coins have appeared since 1976, mainly to commemorate anniversaries of Jinnah, founder of the state [22–23], or the 1400th anniversary of the Hegira (1981). Gold, silver and cupro-nickel coins of 1977 publicized the Islamic Summit Conference. A set of three large coins in gold or silver appeared in 1976 to promote wildlife conservation.

Family Planning
The population of Bangladesh is increasing at an alarming rate, and even coins are harnessed to the government campaign for family planning. Several coins since 1975 have depicted the ideal nuclear family in an attempt to get this message across.

Pakistan has been under military rule for many years, punctuated by brief periods of parliamentary democracy, but political instability has not been reflected by any changes in the coinage.

BANGLADESH
Situated on the Bay of Bengal, between India and Burma, Bangladesh was formerly the province of East Pakistan. Although sharing the Muslim faith of West Pakistan, it was culturally and historically distinct. In the 2nd and 3rd centuries AD, local Bengal kings issued beautiful Kushan-style coins [24–25]. There were significant developments in the late Gupta period, notably under Sasanka, King of Gauda *c.* 600–30 [26–27], while the silver coins of the Akara dynasty of Bangla Desh in the 10th–11th centuries [28–29] are noteworthy.

In the medieval period, coins reflected Indian, Burmese and Islamic influence. The Ghorids (also dominant in Afghanistan) struck coins, as did the sultans of Bengal. Sultan al-din Iltumish revived the horseman motif in gold and silver tankas. Chittagong and Dacca (Jahangirnagar) were prolific mints in the Mughal period, while the East India Company struck traditional gold mohurs for circulation in the Bengal Presidency [30–31]

East Pakistan's sense of neglect by the more affluent West Pakistan led to an independence movement. Its people used the techniques of civil disobedience developed by Gandhi in India, provoking massive military retaliation. In support of East Pakistan India went to war with West Pakistan in 1971, and as a result the East declared independence as Bangladesh. Pakistani currency continued until 1973, when the taka of 100 poisha was introduced. Coins feature the *shapla* (lily) national emblem and various symbols of agriculture [32–33]. Significantly, many coins have been issued in connection with the FAO programme and since 1991 a few silver coins have celebrated anniversaries of independence or global concerns such as conservation.

EARLY INDIA

One of the world's largest and most populous countries, India is regarded as a subcontinent, bounded by the Arabian Sea and the Bay of Bengal, and it gives its name to the ocean that lies to the south. It is home to civilizations and religions that date back several millennia and it is probable that coinage originated there quite separately from that of Asia Minor or China, although it very quickly came under Greek influence.

Left: Typical of Indo-Greek coinage is this silver drachm of Radhasinha II (AD 305–13). It combines the sculptural and punch-mark techniques characteristic of the period.

EARLIEST COINAGE

Some of the earliest money in circulation in India consisted of gold discs with a central hole, which doubled as jewellery [1–2], but lead coins were struck by the chiefs of Karnataka in the second century AD [3]. Indian coinage developed along distinctive lines, consisting of pieces of silver or copper, often square or rectangular in shape, with flat surfaces into which various symbols or marks were punched on both sides [4–5].

During the period 600–300 BC, various petty kingdoms and states were producing distinctive coins that drew heavily on the Greek influences of the same period in their weight and style [6–7]. By the 4th century BC, if not earlier, both square and circular coins [8–9] were being cast in copper, with somewhat similar, though less diverse, symbolism. It is clear, from later discoveries of hoards, that these coins circulated all over India.

The empire created by Alexander the Great extended to the Indus and beyond, and the provinces of Parthia and Bactria (lying in what is now Iran) exerted a great influence on the development of Indian coinage, both the copper coins of numerous petty states and the tiny silver hemidrachms, which were rich in mythological symbolism. In the 2nd century BC the Greeks of Bactria encroached on north-west India and struck a wide range of portrait coins. The Greek inscriptions gradually gave way to Prakrit or became very corrupt, and the gods of classical Greece

were supplanted by Indian deities, reflecting the rise of the Indo-Scythian kingdoms and the great Kushan Empire, which flourished in the north-west from the 1st century AD and whose coins were apparently influenced by Roman models [10–11]. The Kushans' prolific gold and copper coinage was notable for inscriptions in Persian but written in a corrupt Greek form [12–13]. Portraits of rulers vied with images of the deities pertaining to all the religions of the period, in a style that endured for over 1000 years.

A great number of different types of coinage flourished in the various parts of India. In western India, satraps of Persian origin ruled from the 1st century BC and produced an abundant supply of silver coins featuring a bust of the ruler, down to the time of Swami Rudrasimha III, the last of the satraps of western India [14–15], who ruled in the late 4th century. The western satraps were overthrown by the Guptas, who began to imitate their silver. The Guptas originated in eastern India and spread northward. Their coins were elegant and often adapted Kushan designs [16–20], notably the Lakshmi and lion-slayer types of Chandragupta [21–22]. The White Huns swept aside the Gupta and other Indian civilizations in the 6th century but produced coins modelled on Kushan, Sasanian and Gupta types [23–24].

In central and southern India the Andras struck coins in lead around the beginning of the Common Era; later dynasties in the same area struck gold coins: these usually depicted the dynastic emblem [25–26], such as the elephant of Malabar or the boar favoured by the Chalukyas of the Deccan, who also produced punch-marked gold pagodas in the 11th and 12th centuries [27–28]. The Chola dynasty struck coins with a standing figure of the ruler on the obverse and the same figure seated on the reverse, a style that was widely copied.

Coinage declined in southern and eastern India in the 6th century, though kingdoms close to Bombay continued to mint coins for some time. A seated figure of Lakshmi was a popular motif for the Kalachuri gold coins of Tripuri [29–30].

MUGHAL EMPIRE

Islam spread to north-west India in the 8th century, but apart from some coins struck in what is now the Indo-Pakistan border area it was not until Mahmud of Ghazna conquered the Punjab in the 11th century that the new culture had much impact on Indian coinage. In 1193 Muhammad bin Sam conquered northern India and established a devoutly Islamic dynasty that lasted until 1399, when Tamerlane sacked Delhi. He created a great Mongol Empire, which stretched from the Mediterranean to the Ganges. As this disintegrated, the Mughals built up an empire that embraced much of modern Afghanistan but gradually spread over the whole of India. The coins of the first Mughal rulers, Baber and Humayun, accorded with the prevailing types of Central Asia [31–32]. However, new designs, sizes and weights were adopted by their successors, notably Jahangir, whose gold coins are among the most splendid in their artistic calligraphy as well as their poetic inscriptions. Square rupees continued under Akbar until the early 17th century [33–34].

Gold was struck only sporadically in the 15th and 16th centuries; there were brief experiments with brass coins but billon was preferred. Under Sher Shah (1539–45) there was a profuse issue of good silver coins, bearing the Kalima (the Islamic confession of faith) and the names of the Four Caliphs, and this set the style for the gold and silver coins that continued until the Mughal Empire was swallowed up by the French and British in the 18th century.

In 1613 Shah Jahangir commissioned the production at Agra of five gold coins with a value of 1000 mohur. These massive coins had a diameter of 203mm/8in and weighed over 12kg/26lb. Their value in modern currency would be £250,000–300,000/$440,000–525,000. Not intended for general circulation, they were presented to various foreign ambassadors. Gold 500 mohurs are mentioned in Jahangir's autobiography, while an electrotype of a 200 mohur is preserved in the British Museum in London. A 100 mohur coin, struck by Jahangir in 1639, had a diameter of 97mm/3.8in and weighed 1094g/2.4lb [35]. Aurungzeb (1658–1707) replaced the Islamic confession of faith with the name of the mint and the date, and this style prevailed until the end of Mughal rule.

Above: A gold coin issued in the reign of Muhammad bin Sam, Sultan of Delhi in the late 12th century.

INDIAN PRINCELY STATES

As the Mughal Empire declined from 1700 onward, many local dynasties sprang up, carving out independent principalities and often warring with each other or seeking alliances with one or other of the European powers gaining control in India. Although the Mughal Empire continued in name until 1857, by 1800 its powers had largely passed to the British East India Company, which exercised control to a greater or lesser extent over the princely states. After the suppression of the Sepoy Mutiny most of India came directly under British rule, but the rest was ruled indirectly through the medium of more than 1000 autonomous states. Even as late as 1947, when India gained independence, no fewer than 675 principalities remained. By 1950 the last of them had been abolished. At least 125 states produced their own coinage, mainly in the period from 1800 to 1900, though a number continued to issue coins until the 1940s.

Left: This gold mohur bearing the crowned bust of Victoria as Empress of India was struck at the Calcutta Mint in 1885. Copper and silver coins of this type were also issued from 1877 onward and were issued by the states of Alwar, Bikanir, Dhar and Dewas. Before she was proclaimed Empress of India in 1877, coins in the name of Queen Victoria had been struck in India from 1862.

MONETARY CONFUSION

Virtually every state had its own currency system, a situation complicated by the fact that there was very seldom a fixed ratio between copper, silver or gold. Values tended to vary according to the decrees of the local potentate, which could not have facilitated trade between the states. Certain denominations were widespread, such as the gold mohur, the silver rupee and the copper paisa, based on the coins of the Mughal Empire. Indeed, many coins included the name of the Mughal emperor in their inscriptions, presenting a nominal semblance of unity and adherence to the imperial principle. This silver rupee of Jaipur names the Mughal emperor Ahmed Shah Bahadur [1–2]. By the late 19th century, however, many coins bore inscriptions referring to Queen Victoria of "Inglistan" (England). As late as 1948 Jodhpur was still producing coins in the names of George VI and Hanwant Singh [3–4].

Some of the states in north-west India, such as Awadh and Hyderabad, produced copper falus [5–6] or gold ashrafi [7–8], reflecting their commercial and political ties to Persia or Afghanistan. States in the Kutch region, such as Bhavnagar, Porbandar and Junagadh [11–12], had silver kori and half kori and copper dhinglo, dokdo [13–14], dhabu [15–16] and trambiyo. Also shown is a gold coronation kori from Kutch [9–10]. The inhabitants of Cochin used chuckrams, puttuns and fanams, while neighbouring Travancore also had anantarayas. The silver tamasha circulated in Kashmir, while copper cash and the gold pagoda paralleled the silver rupee and its subdivisions (right down to the tiny 1/32 rupee) in Mysore. The pagoda was the chief gold coin of the southern Indian states, and the issues of Mysore were very prolific [17–20].

INSCRIPTIONS

Most of the state coinage had legends in Persian (Farsi) or Nagari script, but it was often crude and blundered and therefore difficult to read. Fortunately, various symbols, approximating to mint-marks, were also included, and it is on these that collectors generally rely in order to assign their coins to the correct state. In general, coins often present an appearance of Arabic, with one or more horizontal lines dividing the text. English inscriptions were confined to the coins issued in Bikanir, Travancore and Jaora.

IMAGES
The exceptional use of Queen Victoria's crowned bust has already been mentioned, but she also appeared bare-headed on the rupee and mohur of Bhartpur in 1858. In the Muslim states, the use of effigies was usually frowned upon, but the Hindu states made occasional attempts at portraiture. Sayaji Rao III, Gaekwar of Baroda, was profiled on gold and silver coins [21–22], while the last mohurs and rupees of Bikanir bore a full-face bust of Ganga Singh.

An exception to the exclusion of portraits is to be found on the coins of Bahawalpur (now part of Pakistan) whose ruler, Sadiq Muhammad Khan, appeared bare-headed or wearing a fez on copper coins and silver rupees minted in 1940, although most of his coins featured his *toughra*, or sign-manual [23–4]. Travancore stuck gold sovereigns and half-sovereigns with the bust of Maharajah Rama Varma V. His

---

Royal Portrait
Machine-struck cash and chuckrams of Travancore not only bore the denomination in English but also had the monogram RV on the obverse, denoting Maharajah Rama Varma VI (1885–1924). However, his successor, Bala Rama Varma II (1924–49), exceptionally placed his own portrait on the chuckram.

---

successor, Bala Rama Varma II, appeared in profile on the copper chuckrams of 1938–45.

The Hindu kingdom of Tripura in Bengal had a long tradition of pictorial coins. These were mostly silver tankas or ramatankas with a horse and trident reverse, but other motifs included an allegorical scene alluding to the conquest of Chittagong [25–26], and the ritual bath in the River Lakhmia [27–28]. The nazarana mohur of Dhar (1943) had an armorial obverse and a Farsi inscription on the reverse [29–30]. A coat of arms, along European lines, also appears on the mohurs (1912–14) and silver half rupee (1923) of Assam, the rupees of Tripura and the mohurs of Rewah.

Both a portrait obverse and armorial reverse occur on coins of Datia, Indore and Gwalior. Scenery and landmarks are conspicuously absent, with the solitary exception of Hyderabad, which featured its Char Minar monument on the obverse of most coins from 1903 to 1948 [31–32], although a toughra was used in the series of 1911–30. The silver coins of Mewar (1931–2), struck in the name of "a friend of London" (Bhupal Singh), are unique in having a panoramic scene on the obverse [33–34].

Most of the coins were non-figural, although occasionally a pictorial element crept in, as in the paisas of Baroda, which showed a dagger or sword, or the paisas of Derajat, Lunavada and Elichpur, with their crude figures of lions. The coins of Indore featured a sacred cow and also used the motif of a radiate sun, while Tonk showed a horse and Mysore favoured the elephant.

The Mughal emperor Jahangir (1605–28) produced a handsome series depicting the signs of the zodiac [35–36]. The only coin known to have been issued by Rajkot appeared in 1945 and had the state arms (obverse) and the rising sun (reverse). A sun face obverse, sometimes with a kneeling cow reverse, appears on many of the coins of Indore [37–38].

COLONIAL AND MODERN INDIA

In 1498 Vasco da Gama rounded the Cape of Good Hope and reached India by sea. Within a few years the Portuguese had established trading posts on the west coast, but they were soon overtaken by the Dutch, Danish, French and British, all of whom formed settlements on the east and west coasts. All the foreign settlements produced distinctive coinage.

Left: Coins with the crowned profile of George VI circulated until 1950, when the series inscribed "Government of India" was introduced. Among the patterns of 1947–9 were square 2 anna pieces, one with a peacock in side view and one face on, displaying its tail.

PORTUGUESE INDIA

Although Bombay passed from the Portuguese to the British as part of the dowry of Catherine of Braganza in 1660, Portugal continued to have a major interest in the subcontinent. Its settlements gradually declined but it retained Goa, Damao and Diu until 1962, when they were seized by the Republic of India.

Crude copper tanga [1–2] were produced at each settlement, each with its own currency system. Thus the rupia of 2 pardao or xerafim [3–4] in Goa was worth 480 reis, while in Diu the rupia was worth 10 tanga or 40 atias or 150 bazarucos or 600 reis. In 1871 the currency was reformed on the basis of the rupia [5–6] of 16 tanga or 960 reis, and coins inscribed "India Portugueza", with the profile of Luiz I (obverse) [7–8] and the royal arms (reverse) were introduced. After Portugal became a republic coins mainly featured the arms and cross emblems [9–12]; the escudo of 100 centavos was adopted in 1958.

DANISH INDIA

The Danes established trading posts at Pondicherry and Tranquebar, on the south-east coast of India, in 1620, but sold their remaining interests to the British East India Company in 1845. Crude copper or silver dumps denominated in cash and fano (fanams) respectively, with the crowned royal monogram (obverse) and the date and value (reverse), were produced until 1845, but they are now very rare.

DUTCH INDIA

The United East India Company of the Netherlands had a number of settlements that issued their own coins in the 18th and early 19th centuries. These included Negapatam, ceded to the British in 1784; Tuticorin, ceded in 1795; and Cochin, ceded in 1814. The last of the Dutch trading posts, at Pulicat, was transferred to British rule in 1824. Illustrated here is a tiny silver rupee of Jagannathpur [13–14] and a lead bazaruk of the Dutch East India Company [15–16].

FRENCH INDIA

The French did not take an interest in India until 1664, when the Compagnie des Indes Orientales was formed. Trading posts were established between 1666 and 1721, from Surat on the west coast to Balasore on the Bay of Bengal. There were inland settlements at Arcot in south India and at Chandernagore and Murshidabad in the north-east. Following the defeat of the French by Clive at Plassey (1759), France lost all its settlements apart from Pondicherry, which, in 1954, voted to join the Republic of India. Copper and silver coins based on the rupee of 64 biches (paisa) were augmented by fanons (fanams) and caches (cash). Apart from an issue of 1836–7 most coins were undated and very crude. The basic type of the silver fanon (2 royalins) showed a European crown on the obverse and the fleur de lys of France [17–18] but in deference to local custom a Hindu crown was later substituted, often reduced in the smaller coins to little more than a jumble of dots [19–22]. The copper cash showed a single fleur de lys, or a mere fragment in the smaller denominations. Coins of British India were used from 1848.

BRITISH INDIA

The territories of the British East India Company, developed from 1660, were divided into the Presidencies of Bengal, Madras, Malabar and Bombay (now Mumbai). Each produced coins that conformed to either the Hindu or Muslim coinage systems [23–24], based respectively on the pagoda of 42 fanams or 3360 cash, and the gold mohur (such as this coin of the Bengal Presidency in the name of the Mughal Shah 'Alam II [25–26]) of 16 rupees or 256 annas. The vast majority of coins were inscribed in Farsi, but Madras used Nagari script, as shown on this silver half pagoda of 1808 [27–28]. The Bombay coinage featured the bale-mark emblem (obverse) and scales (reverse) from 1791 onward, and an armorial obverse was gradually adopted from 1804.

Standard coins for the whole of British India were introduced in 1835. The copper denominations [29–30] featured the arms of the East India Company while the silver coins portrayed the reigning British monarch; all coins had a wreathed value reverse. Shown here is a gold restrike of the copper half anna of 1892, with Victoria as Empress [31–32]. A new reverse, featuring a tiger, was adopted in 1946 when nickel replaced silver in coins from 2 annas upwards. As a wartime economy measure the pice (quarter anna) was redesigned in 1943, retaining the original diameter but reducing the metal content by means

Architects of Modern India
Following the death of Jawaharlal Nehru in 1964 rupee coins with his dates of birth and death were struck for general circulation until 1967. This set the precedent for coins marking the birth centenaries of Mahatma Gandhi (1969–70) and Nehru himself (1969).

of a large central hole [33–34]. These coins continued until 1947 and are of immense interest as they were struck at Lahore, Bombay and Pretoria (South Africa) as well as Calcutta. As well as three different types of crown, there are variations in lettering and the presence or absence of mint-marks.

REPUBLIC OF INDIA

In August 1947 the British handed over power to the Muslims of Pakistan and the mainly Hindu government of India. The Dominion of India became a republic in 1950. In the first decade of independence the old coinage system, based on the rupee of 16 annas or 64 pice, was retained. The obverses of 1950–7 were inscribed "Government of India" around the Ashokan column, while the reverses bore the denomination in English and Hindi surrounding a pictorial motif.

In 1957 the rupee of 100 naye (new) paise was adopted. The column of Ashoka continued but now with the country name in Hindi and English, while the reverse motifs prominently featured the numerals of value [35–36]. The use of various shapes, begun under the British, was considerably extended, each value having a distinctive shape. The designs were subtly modified in the 1970s and 1980s, but in 1988 a new series of pictorial reverses was released [37–38].

INDIAN OCEAN

A number of islands in the Indian Ocean, which were formerly part of the British or French colonial empires, issue their own coins. They range from Sri Lanka (formerly Ceylon), which has a coinage dating back to the 1st century BC, to the territories that have adopted distinctive coins only in quite recent times.

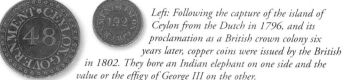

Left: Following the capture of the island of Ceylon from the Dutch in 1796, and its proclamation as a British crown colony six years later, copper coins were issued by the British in 1802. They bore an Indian elephant on one side and the value or the effigy of George III on the other.

SRI LANKA

The ancient coins of this island followed the pattern of the Chola dynasty of northern India, who subjugated the indigenous Veddahs and ruled until 1408. Ceylon then came under Chinese control until the arrival of the Portuguese in 1505. They, in turn, were supplanted by the Dutch in 1658. Local coinage was produced in each of these eras, mainly silver tangas such as this specimen from 1642 [1–2].

During the last year of the 18th century the British conquered the Dutch territories and made the island into a crown colony in 1802. The British retained the Indo-Dutch currency system, based on the rixdollar, on par with the rupee and divided into 48 stivers, each of 12 fanams. From 1839 to 1868 British third and quarter farthings [3–4] and silver threehalfpence also circulated in Ceylon, in addition to the local coinage. In 1872 the currency was decimalized, and the rupee of 100 cents was adopted. Bronze coins of this series bore the profile of the reigning monarch (obverse) and a palm tree (reverse) while the silver, or later nickel, coins had the value in numerals in an ornamental reverse [5–8].

Ceylon became a dominion in 1948 but continued to issue coins with the monarch's effigy until 1957. Thereafter the national emblem was substituted in a series introduced in 1963, with inscriptions in Sinhala and Tamil instead of English [9–11]. In 1972 the island became a republic under the name of Sri Lanka ("resplendent island"). A modified version of the coinage was adopted in 1975 [12]. A few commemoratives have been produced since 1957, when the 2500th anniversary of Buddhism was celebrated [13–16].

MALDIVE ISLANDS

This archipelago west of Sri Lanka was an independent sultanate from 1153 and had its own coins inscribed in Arabic from the 17th century. It became a British protectorate by agreement with the Governor of Ceylon in 1887. The rupee of 100 lariat (singular *larin*) became the rufiyaa of 100 laari in 1954, when the Maldives reverted to a sultanate after a brief period as a republic. Until 1968, when the second republic was proclaimed, coins bore the arms of the sultanate [17–20]. Since then coins have had pictorial motifs and numerals of value. Gold and silver coins in recent years have highlighted events or anniversaries of international importance.

MAURITIUS

Named after Prince Maurice of the Netherlands, this island was under Dutch control from 1598 to 1710, when it was acquired by the French,

Living Fossil

The coelacanth, a species of fish that existed 400 million years ago and pre-dated the dinosaurs, was believed to be long extinct when a live specimen was caught off the Comoros in 1938. Since then others have been found. This "living fossil" appears on a coin of the Comoros issued in 1984 to mark the World Fisheries Conference.

from whom it was captured by the British in 1810. At first the British retained the French currency of the livre of 20 sous; they then briefly issued coins in fractions of dollars [21–22] with a crowned anchor obverse, before adopting the rupee of 100 cents in 1877. Thereafter, coins portrayed the reigning monarch with the value on the reverse. From 1934, the silver coins had a pictorial reverse.

Mauritius became an independent state within the Commonwealth in 1968. Its coins continued to portray Elizabeth II until 1987, when the bust of Sir Seewoosagur Ramgoolam, the first prime minister, was substituted.

SEYCHELLES
Like Mauritius, this island group passed to Britain from France in 1810. It used the coinage of Mauritius until 1939, when distinctive coins, portraying the reigning sovereign, were introduced. These had the value on the reverse, but 5 and 10 rupee coins were added in 1974–9, with images of a beach scene and a turtle respectively. The Seychelles became an independent republic in 1976 and adopted a series of coins portraying the president, Sir James Mancham, with fauna and flora

on the reverse, but an armorial obverse was adopted the following year while retaining the same reverses [23–26]. Since 1983 there has been a prolific output of special issues marking all manner of events worldwide.

MADAGASCAR
A French protectorate from 1886 and a colony from 1896, Madagascar used French currency until 1943, when coins bearing the Free French emblem were introduced, followed in 1948–53 by a series showing the head of Marianne. The island became the Malagasy Republic in 1958 but did not issue coins thus inscribed until 1963, with poinsettia (obverse) and a zebu (reverse). It became a democratic republic in 1975 and reverted to the name of Madagascar in 1996, when the five-pointed star of the democratic republic reverted to the poinsettia emblem [27, 29]. Many coins are denominated in both French and local currencies, at 5 francs to the ariary [28, 30–32].

COMOROS
This archipelago came under French protection in 1886, and coins denominated in francs and centimes, but inscribed entirely in Arabic, were produced in 1890. Formerly a dependency of Madagascar, the Comoros attained self-government in 1961 and had coins with the effigy of Marianne and palm trees from 1964. It became a federal Islamic republic in 1975 and introduced coins inscribed in Arabic and French with the four stars and crescent emblem, with pictorial reverses [33–38]. Coins portraying Said Mohamed Cheikh celebrated independence.

Above: Gold crescent obverse, and silver pictorial reverse, issued as part of the Comoros 'independence series'.

INDOCHINA

The name Indochina was given collectively to the French colonies and protectorates in South-east Asia, on the eastern side of the peninsula shared with Thailand. The area was originally occupied by peoples from the Yellow River valley of northern China, who migrated as a result of ethnic cleansing during the Han dynasty. In the 2nd century BC, the Chinese conquered Indochina and controlled it until AD 938, leaving the indelible mark of Chinese culture. In more recent times the kingdoms and states of Annam, Tonkin, Cambodia, Cochin-China and Laos emerged. The French penetrated this area in the early 19th century and gradually gained control, creating the states of Cambodia, Laos and Vietnam.

Left: That the French regarded Indochina as the jewel in the crown of their colonial empire is reflected in the style of the coinage from 1879 to 1954, which is rich in the symbolism and allegory of the French Republic, with very little concession to local character.

FRENCH INDOCHINA

The extraordinarily diverse coinage of the region was gradually superseded from 1879, when the French introduced a uniform currency throughout the areas under their control. These coins had the inscription "République Française" on the obverse and "Indochine Française" on the reverse, the former usually accompanied by an allegorical subject and the latter with the value in European and Chinese characters. The coins were denominated in piastres of 100 sapeque, on par with the franc of 100 centimes.

Since it came under the control of the Vichy French government, Indochina was nominally an ally of the Japanese, who occupied it in World War II. French rule was restored in 1946 and new coins were then introduced. They were inscribed "Union Française" and "Federation Indochinoise", and bore the head of Marianne and ears of corn [1–4].

VIETNAM

This country occupying the eastern coast of the peninsula was formerly divided into Tonkin (north) and Annam (south). It gained complete independence from China in 1428 and developed into a mighty empire. Its prosperity was reflected in the wealth and diversity of its gold and silver coinage, which ranged from cast bent rings or "banana bars" and copper dongs to the beautiful tien and lang series of circular coins [5].

After the country came under French control, the emperors continued to rule. The last of them, Bao Dai (1926–55), was deposed in 1945 by the communist Viet Minh under the leadership of Ho Chi Minh. Ho established a provisional government in the north and struck dong, xu and hao coins with a five-pointed star [6–7] until 1954, when the Democratic Republic of Vietnam was established and aluminium coins with the communist emblem around a central hole were introduced [8–9].

Bao Dai fled from Hanoi to Saigon, where the French created the state of Vietnam in 1949. Aluminium coins of 1953 featured profiles or portraits of three women side by side [10–11]. In 1955, Bao Dai was deposed and (South) Vietnam became a republic. Coins inscribed "Viet-Nam Cong-Hoa" were issued, with rice plants or bamboo on the obverse and the value on the reverse [12–16].

CAMBODIA

The Khmer people have inhabited the region to the west of Vietnam for at least 2000 years. The Khmer Empire controlled much of South-east Asia at its zenith in the 12th century, but under attack from its neighbours it declined considerably. It sought French protection in 1863 and was incorporated in French Indochina in 1877.

Cambodia issued coinage based on the silver tical up to 1885, with tiny uniface pe depicting animals, birds or flowers. King Ang Doung imported British presses to mint coins such as the silver tical of 1847 with a view of Angkor Wat [17–18]. A series portraying Norodom I and dated 1860 (but not released until 1875) was produced in Belgium [19–20]. Independence was restored in 1949 under Norodom Sihanouk; coins inscribed "Royaume du Cambodge" appeared in 1953 [21–22]. The riel of 100 sen was adopted in 1959, but the previous motifs were retained.

In 1970, Sihanouk was deposed and the Khmer Republic was proclaimed by Lon Nol. No circulating coins appeared under this regime, although some gold and silver pieces were struck at the Royal Mint in 1974, shortly before the regime was toppled by Pol Pot. The People's Republic of Kampuchea abolished money. Apart from an aluminium 5 sen of 1979 [23–24], there were no coins until 1988 when some commemoratives began to appear. Pol Pot was ousted in 1989 and the State of Cambodia emerged the following year with coins thus inscribed. In 1993 Prince Sihanouk returned as head of state and the Kingdom of Cambodia was restored [25–26].

LAOS

Fa Ngum created the first kingdom known as Lan Xang ("land of a million elephants") in the 14th century and established his capital at Luang Prabang. The kingdom originally included parts of Thailand and Yunnan province in southern China, but it

gradually declined and by the early 19th century it had come under Thai control, whose coinage was widely used. The French established a protectorate in 1893. Autonomy was granted in 1949 but by 1953 the government was at war with the communist Pathet Lao. Laos gained independence in 1954, but civil war erupted in 1960 and continued until the creation of the Lao People's Republic in 1975.

Aluminium holed coins were introduced in 1952, based on the kip of 100 centimes [27–30]. Coins featuring the star and the hammer and sickle emblem were released in 1980 [31–32]. Large gold and silver coins were issued in 1971, and have reappeared since 1985.

Above: A silver bullion piece struck by the Chinese in 1943–4, denominated in kip, for trade in Laos.

CHINA

China is one of the world's largest countries, covering an area of almost 10 million sq km/3.7 million sq miles. It extends from Central Asia to the Pacific, and from the Gobi Desert to the Gulf of Tonkin. It is also the most populous nation on earth, with around 1.3 billion inhabitants. The Chinese were among the chief originators and developers of coinage. Their cash – distinctive copper coins with a square hole punched out of the centre – continued in use for nearly two millennia.

Left: The Dragon silver dollars, which were first struck at the Guangdong Mint in 1889, became the standard throughout the Chinese Empire. The weight of these coins was fixed at 7 mace and 2 candareens, the mace being a tenth of a tael.

ANCIENT CHINA

The bronze implements pioneered as currency by the Zhou dynasty were roughly contemporary with the very first coins of Asia Minor, but in China the former were actually predated by stone rings fashioned from limestone [1–2]. In addition to the well-documented "knife" and "spade" currencies, a variety of other implements circulated in the periods of the Zhou and Warring dynasties, including "bell money", "fish money" [3–4], imitation cowries and various other bronze artefacts used in barter [5–6].

The flattened, round copper discs known as cash [7], which more closely resemble today's circular coins, probably made their first appearance in the 4th century BC, although a handsome knife currency [8] reappeared at the beginning of the first millennium, thanks to the ruler Wang Mang. Cash often circulated alongside other items, such as the jewellery money of amulets and charms [9–10] exchanged under the Qing dynasty (1644–1911).

CHINESE EMPIRE

Although copper cash continued to circulate well into the 20th century, with many provincial variations, a standard unified coinage on western lines developed after the establishment of the central mint at Tianjin in 1905 [11–12]. Coins were struck rather than cast in the traditional manner. Subsidiary coins of values up to 20 cash were struck in brass, copper or bronze with a dragon motif, while silver coins were denominated from 10 cents to one dollar.

Tianjin manufactured the dies used at many of the provincial mints. In addition to the general issues for circulation throughout the empire, numerous provincial series were struck at regional mints in Anhui [13–14], Chihli [15–16], Fengtian, Fujian, Heilongjiang, Henan, Hubei, Hunan, Gansu, Guangxi, Guangdong, Guizhou, Jiangnan, Jiangxi, Jiangsu, Jilin, the Manchurian Provinces, Shaanxi, Shanxi, Shandong, Sichuan Xinjiang, Yunnan and Zhejiang. In some of these vast provinces there were several mints, each producing distinctive coins. In Xinjiang, for example, local coinage was produced at Aksu, Kashgar, Kucha, Urümqi and Wuxi in the latter period of the empire.

CHINESE REPUBLIC

The system of provincial and local mints continued after the republic was proclaimed in 1912. Indeed, it expanded in the 1920s and 1930s, as central government weakened and China disintegrated into regions controlled by warlords [17] followed by the long struggle between the Kuomintang ("national people's party") [18–22] and

Birds of Ill Omen

Silver dollars were issued in 1932, the reverse showing a junk with the rising sun in the background and three birds at the top. This seemed innocuous at the time, but the rising sun was the emblem of Japan and the birds were deemed to symbolize the Japanese air raids on Manchuria. The junk dollars were re-issued in 1933–4 with the sun and birds removed and in this form they were restruck during World War II in the USA, with an inscription added to celebrate victory over the Japanese.

the communists led by Mao Zedong. The situation was also exacerbated by wide variations in the value of currency in different parts of China, and latterly by inflation.

The bronze coins struck by the central government under the National Revenue Board had crossed flags on one side and the value in Chinese and English on the other, often incorporating a floral motif. Gold and silver coins portrayed Sun Yat-sen [23], Yuan Shi-gai [24] and other prominent figures. Interestingly, coins appeared in 1926 to commemorate the wedding of Pu Yi, the last emperor of China, who had abdicated in 1912. A new series portraying Sun Yat-sen was introduced in 1936 with a reverse reproducing an ancient bu coin.

Both the central government and the provinces produced numerous silver dollars portraying political and military leaders. Among the provincial issues, those coins issued under Japanese auspices in Manchukuo (Manchuria) in

the name of the Emperor Kang De (formerly Pu Yi) in 1932–45 are particularly noteworthy.

PEOPLE'S REPUBLIC

A soviet republic was proclaimed by Mao Zedong in 1931 and coins with a five-pointed star or the hammer and sickle superimposed on a map of China were issued in those areas under communist control. Extremely rare coins were also struck under communist auspices in various regions under local soviets [27–30], including some with very crude portraits of Lenin.

Although the People's Republic of China was proclaimed at Beijing in October 1949 it was not until 1955 that a regular coinage was introduced, based on the Renminbi yuan of 10 jiao or 100 fen, with a uniform obverse showing the state emblem and a wreathed value reverse. These motifs have been in use in the fen denominations for half a century without change. The jiao, first struck in copper-zinc in 1980, switched to aluminium in 1991 [25–26], when the 5 jiao, originally in the same alloy, switched to brass. In both values a new reverse incorporated a peony blossom. The yuan first appeared as a circulating coin in 1980, struck in cupro-nickel with mountains on the reverse, but changed to clad steel in 1991 with the peony reverse.

Silver and gold commemoratives have proliferated since 1980, mainly in yuan denominations, although they include the silver 5 jiao of 1983, which celebrated the seventh centenary of the sojourn of Marco Polo. Latterly, these commemorative and special issues have appeared in long series with specific themes, from the Olympic Games to the autonomous regions, founders of Chinese culture, poets and Chinese inventions. China has also produced tiny gold 3 and 5 yuan with a giant panda on one side and the Temple of Heaven in Beijing on the other. The Panda series has become immensely popular worldwide, even leading to issues in platinum since 1993 and large silver versions since 1997.

FLORAL COINS OF ASIA

More than in any other part of the world, the coins of Asia display a penchant for floral themes. The universal appreciation of flowers for their beautiful forms, colours and scents, combined with the fact that some species are associated with particular countries because they grow only in those regions, is reflected in the prevalence of flowers as national emblems. Thus, they provide a ready means of identification on coins.

FLORAL ORNAMENT

Because of the traditional Islamic objection to figural motifs based on living creatures (both animal and human), the preferred ornament on much of the coinage of Islamic states is floral. Plants and flowers, often stylized, may be found on the reverse of the contemporary coins of Pakistan. Whereas European and American coins might use laurel or oak leaves for wreaths, Asian countries often favour leaves of *padi* or rice plants, and these may be found on coins of many countries in South-east Asia. Rice plants at the flowering stage are featured on the coins of South Vietnam, Thailand and Burma

Below: Coins from Burma (top, and large central coin), East Timor (top-right and bottom-left), and Vietnam, showing rice blossom and panicles.

(Myanmar), while rice plants and a pineapple can be found on a coin from Thailand marking World Food Day.

The lower denominations of the coins issued by the People's Republic of China since 1991 feature sprays of peonies and other blossoms on the reverse. Flowers have also featured on the reverse of the large multiple tugrik coins of Mongolia since 1996, celebrating the Lunar New Year, as well as the series issued by South Korea to mark the Olympic Games of 1988. Since 1983, China has produced annual issues of bullion coins in silver or gold with the theme of the giant panda. As its diet consists solely of bamboo shoots, these plants invariably appear in the designs, showing the various stages of bamboo growth.

FLOWERS AS NATIONAL SYMBOLS

The chrysanthemum is the chief means of identifying the coins of Japan, and its similarity to the rising sun (a popular obverse motif) explains its appearance. For the Japanese the flower is a traditional symbol of the sun, and the symmetrical arrangement of its numerous petals represents perfection. It features in the Japanese imperial crest and the emperor's throne.

In the majority of coins issued in Japan since the arrival of Western-style coinage in 1873, a chrysanthemum blossom appears at the top of the reverse, but in the bronze sen of 1898–1915 it formed the central motif on the obverse. In many coins a wreath of chrysanthemum leaves surrounds the value. Other flowers have sometimes been featured, notably the *kiri-mon* (*Pawlonia imperialis*) on the sen of

Above (clockwise from top-left): A chrysanthemum on a Chinese 1 jiao, the Rose of Sharon from Korea, plum blossom on a 5 jiao, the Bauhinia motif on a Hong Kong dollar obverse.

Below: Kiri-mon blossom on the Japanese 100 yen (top). Phalaenopsis and cattleya orchids on coins of Taiwan (below).

1916–38 and the 500 yen since 1981, and the mass of cherry blossom on the 100 yen since 1967.

Many of the petty kingdoms of ancient India struck small copper coins with crude flowers. The reverse of the silver rupees under British rule had floral motifs, and in the George V and VI series the thistle, rose and shamrock of

Above (clockwise from top-left): Water lily (Iran), Hibiscus rosasinensis *(Malaysia), Jasmine (Indonesia) and Shapla (Bangladesh).*

the United Kingdom were surmounted by the lotus blossom of India. Among the coins of the modern republic, however, the lotus is the dominant motif in the Food and Agriculture Organization pair of 1970–1.

In Korea the five-petalled hibiscus known as the Rose of Sharon appeared at the top of the reverse in the issues of the empire (1898–1909) and has also featured as the chief motif in the high-value gold and silver coins of South Korea. The five-petalled plum blossom is the national flower of Taiwan and has appeared on the obverse of several coins, while the reverse of the yuan of 1960 also showed a dendrobium orchid. This theme was expanded in the 1 jiao coins of 1967–74, which featured a phalaenopsis orchid, while the 5 jiao depicted a cattleya.

The *shapla* or water lily is the emblem of Bangladesh and thus provides the principal motif for the obverse of the coinage, while a water lily may also be found on the reverse of the bimetallic 250 rials of Iran. The lotus is the emblem of Sri Lanka and thus appears above the value on the rupees since 1963. Gold-plated lotus flowers appear on the reverse of Nepal's silver 500 rupee coin of 1996.

The coins of Israel, derived from the ancient coins of the Jewish revolts, abound with plant life, from grapes to pomegranates, but the only true flower used on the coinage graces the obverse of the sheqel: this is the tri-lobed lily *yehud,* a pun on the word *yehudi* (Jew). Jasmine has appeared on several coins of Indonesia, usually in a subordinate position, but it takes centre stage on the reverse of the 500 rupiah coins issued since 1991.

Both Hong Kong and Macao, the former British and Portuguese colonies, adopted flowers as their national emblems, featured in the flags introduced when they became special administrative zones of China. The bauhinia orchid appears on the obverse of the entire series of Hong Kong, whereas the lotus of Macao has yet to be featured on its coins. The *Hibiscus rosasinensis* has appeared on the reverse of Malaysian coins as a wreath around the value, but in the 1989 series it is more prominent, appearing above the values on the obverse. The orchid *Vanda* 'Miss Joaquim' is the national flower of Singapore and two blossoms

Above (clockwise from top-left): full-colour Camellia (China), Pomegranate (Israel), Periwinkle (Singapore), a floral wreath (China) and the fruit salad flower on a Singapore 5 cents.

Above: Turkish coins of the 1990s had a wealth of floral designs, including (clockwise from top-left) the Carnation, Rose, Cedar and Tulip blossom.

have flanked the numeral on the reverse of the cent since 1986. Continuing this theme in the higher denominations are the fruit salad flower (5c), jasmine (10c), powder-puff plant (20c), yellow allamanda (50c) and periwinkle ($1). When a $2 coin was added to the series in 1992 the reverse featured *Vanda* 'Miss Joaquim' in all her glory.

Turkey has a long tradition of incorporating leaves into its coin designs, from the intricate leaf patterns drawing from Saracenic art in the Middle Ages to the olive, laurel and oak wreaths of many modern coins. In the 1990s, however, as inflation rose astronomically, a new series denominated in bin lira (thousands of lira) had a floral theme, with cedar blossom (2.5), tulip (5), carnation (10) and rose (25) motifs on the reverse.

PRETTY AS A PICTURE

Special or commemorative coins that have a flower as their principal motif are surprisingly few in number. When Thailand hosted the ninth World Orchid Conference in 1978 a silver 100 baht coin had a spray of orchids across the reverse. In 1999 China issued two large 10 yuan silver coins. One was gold-plated and depicted a Chinese rose on the reverse, while the other showed auspicious camellia blossoms in full colour.

1
2
3
4
5
6
7
8
9
10
11
12
13
14
15
16
17
18

CHINESE TERRITORIES

On the fringes of China are several countries that were once part of its territory and are now independent, or conversely are now part of China, having had an independent existence with distinctive coinage. They include the former British and Portuguese colonies of Hong Kong and Macao.

Left: The ruined façade of St Paul's Cathedral, depicted on several coins, is one of the most impressive sights in Macao. The edifice is a reminder of the heyday of this former Portuguese colony, and was a bastion of Christianity in the Far East in the 17th and 18th centuries.

HONG KONG

China ceded the island of Hong Kong ("fragrant harbour") to Britain in 1841 at the end of the First Opium War, and a 99-year lease on adjacent territory on the mainland was granted in 1898. On the expiry of the lease Britain ceded the colony to the People's Republic in 1997. It has since been a special administrative zone, retaining its currency based on the dollar of 100 cents.

Locally struck coins were introduced in 1863, all but the tiny mil (one-tenth of a cent) bearing the crowned bust of Queen Victoria [1–2]. This established a precedent for all the coins down to 1997, with a reverse showing the name and value in English round the circumference and the corresponding Chinese characters in the centre. The sole exception was the 50 cents with the bust of Edward VII [3–4] on the obverse: its value in English appeared in the centre, with the name and date around the top and the Chinese equivalent around the foot.

The traditional formula continued with the coinage of Elizabeth II, three different effigies being used between 1955 and 1992. A silver 20 cents with the bust of Edward VII appeared in 1902–5, and this denomination was revived in 1975 as a nickel-brass coin with a scalloped edge [5–6]. Cupronickel $1 (1960), $2 (1975) and $5 (1976) had a reverse type showing the crowned lion emblem of the colony surrounded by the name and value in English and Chinese [7–8].

In preparation for the retrocession, a new series, with a bauhinia flower (obverse) and numeral (reverse) was introduced in 1993 and this included a bimetallic $10 piece [9–12]. A coin of this type with a pictorial reverse was released in 1997 for the opening of the Harbour Bridge. Gold $1000 coins began in 1975 with the Queen's visit, and since 1976 similar coins have greeted the Lunar New Year [13–14].

MACAO

The Portuguese acquired the peninsula of Macao with the islands of Taipa and Coloane as a trading post in 1557, although it did not acquire full colonial status until 1887. Portuguese coins were used until 1952, when a distinctive series based on the pataca of 100 avos was adopted. The obverse showed the crowned globe and shield emblem of Portugal, while the reverse bore the value in European and Chinese scripts [15–16]. A new series, with a shield (obverse) and Chinese characters (reverse) came into use in 1982 [17–18], and a pictorial issue appeared from 1992–3 [19–24] in anticipation of Macao returning to China in 1999 as a special administrative zone.

Commemorative silver and gold coins since 1974 have marked the opening of the Macao-Taipa Bridge and the Macao Grand Prix as well as the Lunar New Year [25–26]. An unusual feature of many modern coins has been the depiction of the ruins of St Paul's instead of the customary arms.

TAIWAN

The island of Taiwan, formerly known as Formosa, was occupied by Japan in 1895 but returned to China in 1945. Thither came the remnants of the Chinese nationalist forces when the communists drove them from the mainland. Since 1949, Taiwan has been the seat of the Republic of China (ROC), led by Chiang Kai-shek and his successors. Most coins since 1949 have featured SunYat-sen (obverse) and a map of the island (reverse) [27–28], with inscriptions entirely in Chinese and dates in years since the foundation of the republic in 1911. The 5 and 10 yuan, introduced in 1965, depict Sun's mausoleum at Nanking on the reverse. Many of the yuan coins since 1966 have portrayed Chiang Kai-shek.

Relatively few commemorative coins (from 10 yuan upwards) have appeared, honouring leaders of Chinese nationalism [29–30] or marking anniversaries of the republic. A silver 1000 yuan of 1996 marked the first popular elections, with side-by-side portraits of President Lee Teng-hui and Vice President Lien Chan on the obverse.

MONGOLIA

Once a mighty empire that conquered China and extended as far as Hungary, Mongolia came under the rule of the Manchus in 1691. In 1921, with Russian support, it asserted its independence and became a people's republic. Coins based on the tugrik of

Above: Flowers and candles depicted on sample coins from the Central Mint of Taiwan in the 1960s and 1970s.

Commercial Advertising

Gold and silver coins were issued by Macao in 1978 to mark the 25th anniversary of the Grand Prix. They depicted racing cars blazoned with advertising for Seiko, Luso Banking and even Rothman Pall Mall cigarettes, which appeared in the photograph supplied to the coin designer. The colonial authorities took exception to this so the coins were hurriedly withdrawn and replaced by designs without advertisements. The "advert" versions are now extremely rare.

100 mongo were issued from 1925, with the national emblem, followed by communist symbols in 1945 when Mongolia severed its last links with China. The collapse of communism led to the creation of the democratic state of Mongolia in 1990. Since 1994 coins have reverted to the emblem of the 1920s [31–32]. Mongolia has also produced a vast number of special coins, ranging from the Chinese New Year to the Japanese Royal Wedding of 1993. While coins in general circulation are inscribed in Mongol, in both the indigenous script and a modified form of Cyrillic, special issues are invariably inscribed in English.

1 2
3 4
5 6
7 8
9 10
11 12
13 14
15 16
17 18

HIMALAYAN STATES

Two of the countries that lie in the Himalayas, between China and India, have managed to preserve their independence, despite having been under the protection of their more powerful neighbours at various times. On the other hand, although it is now classified as an autonomous region of the People's Republic of China, Tibet has been under Chinese control since 1950, when its distinctive coinage was suppressed.

Left: In 1966 Bhutan celebrated the 40th anniversary of the accession of Maharajah Jigme Wangchuk with the issue of a set of seven coins. The four lower values were denominated in Indian currency, but the top values were 1, 2 and 5 sertums and were struck in gold or platinum.

TIBET

Nominally a tributary of China for many centuries, Tibet embraced Buddhism in the 8th century and thereafter became increasingly isolated from the outside world. A British military mission from India, led by Sir Francis Younghusband, invaded it in 1903. Influenced by the British, Tibet formally declared its independence in 1913, but this was suppressed by China in 1950. Following a revolt in 1965 it was made an autonomous region.

The coins of neighbouring Nepal were used from 1570, but in the 1720s Nepal began striking coins with a lower silver content for use in Tibet, based on the tangka of 15 skar or the srang of 10 sho or 100 skar. This was unsatisfactory and around 1763 the Tibetans began producing coins for themselves. From this early period dates the Suchakra Vijana tangka [1–2], but such coins were produced by hand in small quantities. A mint opened at Lhasa in 1791 under local auspices and struck Kong-Par tangkas, but was quickly suppressed by the Chinese, who opened their own mint in Lhasa in 1792 and struck silver sho in the name of Emperor Qianlong [3–4]. Sino-Tibetan coins continued intermittently until 1909–10, when the copper skar [5–6] was struck in the name of the Chinese emperor Xuantong (Pu Yi).

In the independent period, the Tibetan authorities struck a wide range of coins, from the copper skar to the gold srang [7–8] with a lion obverse and various motifs, notably the prayer-wheel, on the reverse. Even after the Chinese invasion of 1950 a few coins with the lion on a background of mountains continued as late as 1953.

BHUTAN

This landlocked Himalayan kingdom was conquered by Tibet in the 9th century and had a similar theocratic form of government. The southern part was annexed by Britain to India, but the northern part became a hereditary kingdom in 1907 and attained full independence in 1971.

For countless centuries, Bhutan had a wholly agricultural economy: self-sufficient in foodstuffs it relied on barter in all transactions, and barter is still widely practised. It had no coinage of its own and, when the need began to arise in the 18th century, it made use of the silver debs or half rupees of the Indian state of Cooch-Behar. About 1790 it began striking its own coins, originally in the same weight and fineness as the Cooch-Behar coins, but from 1820 onward debased by an admixture of lead or other metals, so that latterly debs were mostly copper or brass, with a silver wash to give them the appearance of precious metal. The design was very simple, with three lines of characters separated by horizontal lines, but including a symbol that helps to place them in chronological sequence, rather like the mint-marks

Nepalese Symbolism

The coins of Nepal are rich in the aniconic symbolism of Buddhism and Hinduism. While the obverse of the 50 paise coin since 1994 has featured the plumed crown of the Shah Dev dynasty, the reverse incorporates some of the items that compose the *ashtamangala* (the eight auspicious symbols). The date, in Hindi and Devanagari script, is 2051 in the Vikrama Samvat Era, 57 years ahead of the Common Era (that is, 1994).

NEPAL

Distinctive coins, mainly square copper dams [15–16] were struck by several of the Himalayan mountain states from the late 15th century. Silver coins of good quality were produced at Patan [17–18] and Bhatgoan [19–20], while both circular and square mohars with their subdivisions were minted at Kathmandu [21–28].

In the late 18th century Prithvi Narayan Shah, ruler of Gurkha, welded these states into a single kingdom and struck silver mohars [29–30]. After his death Nepal suffered a long period of instability, reflected in the clay token inscribed in Newari, which was used as small change [31–32]. Order was restored in the 1840s when the Rana family established a hereditary premiership that took real power away from the king. This continued until 1950, when a popular uprising deposed the Rana prime minister and restored the power of the monarchy.

Prior to 1932 Nepal had a very complex currency system, based on the rupee of 2 mohar or 4 suka, 8 ani, 16 dak, 32 paisa or 128 dam [33–34]. Gold, silver and copper coins were struck on circular flans with geometric motifs contained in a square format (obverse) and a segmented device resembling flower petals (reverse). The currency was simplified in 1932 when the rupee of 100 paisa was adopted. Pictorial elements, such as crossed kukris, a hoe or a stylized lotus gradually crept in from that time. Symbols of the monarchy, such as the crown or sceptre, were depicted on the obverses [35–36]. Very few coins portrayed the ruler, King Tribhuvan, though he appeared on rupees of 1953–4.

A 2 rupee denomination was introduced in 1982 and thereafter became the preferred medium for commemoratives and special issues [37–38]. Previously, a few silver coins from 10 to 50 rupees had served this purpose. In more recent years both gold and silver coins of very high face values have appeared, including a gold bullion series denominated in asarfi.

on medieval English coins. They consisted mainly of the deb [9–10] and rupee [11–12] of debased silver.

This primitive coinage was replaced in 1928 by a series based on the Indian rupee of 64 pice. The obverse bore the bust of the ruler, Jigme Wangchuk, but the reverse was divided by horizontal and vertical lines to form nine compartments, with an inscription in the centre and ornate symbols in the others. They were undated but bore the symbol of the earth dragon in the Chinese zodiacal cycle. When re-issued they bore the iron tiger, dating them to 1950, though this symbol was retained when the half rupee was re-issued in a reduced weight to conform with the Indian coins current in 1967–8. In the interim a series based on the Indian rupee of 100 naye paise celebrated the ruler's 40th anniversary, followed in 1974 by a series portraying Jigme Singye Wangchuk, based on the sertum of 100 ngultrums or 10,000 chetrums [13–14]. Various Buddhist symbols appeared on the reverse.

Since 1974 Bhutan has produced numerous gold and silver coins for occasions ranging from royal anniversaries to international sporting events.

19 20
21 22
23 24
25 26
27 28
29 30
31 32
33 34
35 36
37 38

KOREA

The "land of the morning calm" occupies a peninsula in north-eastern Asia, bordering China. The country allegedly had its own distinctive civilization over 4000 years ago, but recorded details date only from the 1st century BC, while the name Korea (Koryo) appeared in 935, when three kingdoms were merged into one. It came under Japanese influence in the late 19th century, became a protectorate in 1905 and was annexed in 1910. Liberated in 1945, it split along the 38th parallel: the north, under communist influence, became the People's Democratic Republic of Korea, and the remainder the Republic of Korea. Despite the collapse of communism everywhere else, North Korea remains a totalitarian state and Korea is still divided.

Left: The bronze 1 chon, the basic currency unit, was introduced in 1902. Japan's growing confidence is reflected by the imperial eagle, crowned and armed with sceptre and orb, and the fact that the inscriptions were mostly in Japanese.

KOREAN EMPIRE

Korea had a copper cash currency, on Chinese lines, for many centuries from AD 996 [1–2]. In the 17th century a new series, known as *shang ping* (stabilization money), was introduced [3–4]. A second series followed around 1742. The coins were cast at numerous mints all over the country, while each of the government ministries in the capital, Seoul, also produced them. They are identifiable by marks in the form of Chinese ideograms derived from a book entitled *Thousand Character Classic* (because the text consisted of exactly 1000 characters, none of which was repeated). These coins continued until 1888 when small silver and bronze coins, from 1 to 3 chon, were introduced [5–8].

Coins struck from modern presses were adopted in 1888, based on the warn of 1000 mun. The currency was reformed in 1892, when the silver yang of 100 fun was struck [11–12]; in 1893, the hwan of 5 yang or 500 fun was introduced [9–10], but this system was superseded a decade later by the won of 100 chon. Apart from the denomination, which was in English, all inscriptions were rendered in Chinese characters, and a phoenix or dragon was depicted on the obverse. During the brief reign of the last emperor, Kuang Mu, a few gold 10 and 20 won coins were struck. Following annexation by Japan in 1910, only Japanese coins circulated until liberation in 1945.

NORTH KOREA

The Cairo Conference of 1943 had decreed that Korea should be "free and independent" and presumably a unified sovereign state, but towards the end of World War II the Soviet Union declared war on Japan and invaded Manchuria and Korea from the north in 1945. At the same time, American forces landed in the south, and later that year the Potsdam Conference decided that Korea should be partitioned at the 38th parallel.

When the Soviet authorities barred the entry of UN personnel to supervise free elections in 1948, leading to reunification, the elections went ahead in the south and as a result the Republic of Korea was formally proclaimed on August 15. Unsupervised elections took place in the north ten days later and the Democratic People's Republic, with its capital at Pyongyang, was inaugurated.

rupiah to one new rupiah) no coins appeared until 1970–1, by which time the rupiah was the smallest denomination. This series had different pictorial motifs (fauna [18–19], flora and landmarks [22–25]). In later years, 5 rupiah coins appeared sporadically, promoting family planning [20–21] and serving as small change, but it was not until 1991 that a general issue of coins was resumed. In this series, from 25 to 1000 rupiah, the garuda obverse was combined with pictorial reverses [26–27]. Relatively few gold and silver commemoratives, mostly celebrating anniversaries of independence, have appeared since 1970. Separate issues of coins with the bust of Achmed Sukarno on the obverse, were produced for the Riau archipelago (1963–4) and West Irian, formerly Netherlands New Guinea (1964–71). Both sets had fixed dates of 1962.

TIMOR

This island in the Lesser Sunda group was partitioned between the Netherlands (west) and Portugal (east) in 1859. West Timor was incorporated with Indonesia from 1950, but East Timor remained under Portuguese rule and had coins in the Portuguese colonial style. In 1976 it was occupied by Indonesia, triggering off a long-running war that culminated in the attainment of independence in December 1999. The Democratic Republic of East Timor was later proclaimed, and distinctive coins with pictorial motifs, based on the escudo of 100 centavos, were introduced in 2004 [28–32].

Cowboys

The reverse of the 100 rupiah of Indonesia since 1991 shows the national sport of cow-racing.

PHILIPPINES

An extensive copper and silver coinage was produced in the Philippines in the Spanish colonial period, based on the peso of 8 reales, with subdivisions of quarto and octavo real. The obverse showed a lion resting on twin hemispheres, while the crowned arms of Spain occupied the reverse. A wide range of foreign coins, with appropriate countermarks, circulated in the 19th century before the currency was reformed in 1861, and the peso of 100 centimos was adopted, with the head of the monarch (obverse) and crowned arms (reverse) [33–34].

Under American rule from 1898 the currency changed to the peso of 100 centavos, and this continued until 1967, when the names changed to piso and sentimo. The seated or standing figure of Liberty appeared on the obverse, while the reverse featured the American eagle and shield until 1935 [35–36], when the Commonwealth of the Philippines was proclaimed with a measure of autonomy. Although the shield on the reverse changed, the coins continued to bear the name of the United States of America.

Occupied by the Japanese in 1941 and liberated in 1944–5, the Philippines became an independent republic in July 1946, but coins reflecting this change did not appear until 1947 and most denominations did not appear with the republican arms until 1958. An entirely new series portraying national heroes was released in 1967 [37–38] and since then has undergone changes in metal, size and shape, with pictorial reverses replacing the original arms or seal devices in 1983. The current coins, introduced in 1995, have the value on the obverse and arms on the reverse.

In 1903 the Commission of Public Health established a leper colony on the remote island of Culion. Special coins, from half centavo to 1 peso, were struck by Frank & Company with the caduceus emblem on the reverse. In 1927 a new series portrayed José Rizal with the national arms on the reverse.

MALAYSIA AND SINGAPORE

The countries in this group were all formerly under British rule and have maintained close ties through membership of the Commonwealth since they attained independence in the 1960s. They formed part of the great Javanese empire of Majapahit and converted to Islam in the 14th century. From the 15th century onward the coins of the numerous petty states generally conformed to Islamic standards. Johor struck octagonal gold kupangs with Islamic inscriptions [1–2], but for small change Chinese-style cash, such as the tin jokoh of Perak [3], or the silver tanga, such as this example from Melaka of 1631 [4–5], were preferred. The Portuguese and Dutch penetrated the region in the 16th and 17th centuries, followed by the British East India Company, which acquired the strategically important island of Penang off the coast of Kedah in 1786.

Left: The tenth anniversary of the Republic of Singapore was celebrated by the silver $10 of 1975, with a pictorial reverse emphasizing its importance as one of the world's largest commercial ports.

STRAITS SETTLEMENTS

This British crown colony was formed in 1825 by combining the trading posts at Penang – shown here are copper pattern cents of 1788–1810 [6–9] and a quarter-dollar of 1788 [10–11] – and Melaka with Singapore, the settlement founded by Stamford Raffles in 1819. Coins bearing the name of the East India Company but denominated in the local currency, based on the dollar of 100 cents, appeared in 1845 with the profile of Victoria (obverse) and wreathed value (reverse) [12–13]. The name was changed in 1862 to "India Straits", then to "Straits Settlements" in coins from 1872 to 1935 [14–15].

BRITISH NORTH BORNEO

This territory was administered by a chartered company until it was over-run by the Japanese in 1942 and declared a crown colony in 1946. It changed its name to Sabah on joining the Federation of Malaysia in 1964. Coins bearing the company arms were struck by the Heaton mint from 1882 until 1941 [16–17].

SARAWAK

The land of the white rajahs came into being in 1840, when the Sultan of Brunei granted territory on the island of Borneo to James Brooke, a British adventurer who had quelled a rebellion on the sultan's behalf, and whose initials appear on this copper keping [18–19]. In 1888 the state of Sarawak was placed under British protection. It was occupied by the Japanese in 1942 and ceded to the British Crown in 1946 by Sir Charles Vyner Brooke, who is portrayed on the silver 20 cents of 1910 [20–21]. It joined Malaysia in 1963. Sarawak issued its own coins from 1841 to 1941, with the profile of the rajah (obverse) and a wreathed or encircled value (reverse).

MALAYA

The Currency Board of Malaya was established shortly before World War II and uniform coinage for use in the Straits Settlements and the Malay States was introduced in 1939, with the crowned profile of George VI (obverse) and the value (reverse) [22–23].

Although it was interrupted by the war, this coinage was resumed in 1945 and continued until 1956, though no coins were dated after 1950. A new series, with the crowned bust of Elizabeth II, circulated from 1954 to 1961 and was inscribed "Malaya and British Borneo" on the reverse [24–25].

MALAYSIA

The Malayan Federation was formed in February 1948 by Melaka and Penang with the nine Malay states. It became an independent member of the Commonwealth in 1957 and used coins of Malaya and British Borneo.

In September 1963 the Malayan Federation joined with North Borneo (Sabah), Sarawak and Singapore to form the Federation of Malaysia. Coins inscribed "Malaysia", in currency based on the ringgit of 100 sen, were introduced in 1967, when the Currency Board was dissolved. The standard obverse featured the parliament building in Kuala Lumpur and the crescent and star emblem, while the reverse bore the value [26–29]. A new series, with a floral obverse and indigenous artefacts on the reverse, was introduced in 1989 [30–31]. Commemorative coins have appeared since 1969.

SINGAPORE

This island at the tip of the Malay Peninsula became a separate crown colony in 1946. It joined Malaysia in 1963 but seceded in August 1965 to become an independent republic. Singapore continued to use the coins of Malaya until 1967, when a distinctive series based on the dollar of 100 cents was adopted. This followed the same pattern as the coinage of Malaysia, with the value on the reverse, but from the outset had different pictorial motifs on each obverse: birds and fishes on the middle values, with a fountain and high-rise apartment block (1 cent) [32] and Singapore's trademark mythical beast, the Merlion ($1). Armorial types with flora and fauna on the reverse have been used since 1985 [33–34]. Commemoratives have

South-east Asia's Own Olympics

Coins with seven interlocking rings have marked the four-yearly South-east Asia and Pacific Games, involving Malaysia, Singapore, Indonesia and the Philippines.

appeared since 1973, and there have been annual issues for the Chinese Lunar New Year since 1991.

BRUNEI

This sultanate arose in the 16th century and eventually ruled most of Borneo and even parts of the Philippines but declined in the early 19th century. It was eventually confined to a small area near the mouth of the Brunei River. Its fortunes recovered after World War II thanks to the discovery of oil in the region; it is now one of the world's wealthiest countries.

Cash or pitis of lead or tin appeared briefly about 1700, but it was not until 1868 that tin coins were re-introduced, with the state umbrella (obverse) and text in Jawi script (reverse). Western-style bronze coins, struck by Heaton of Birmingham, appeared in 1887, before Brunei adopted the currency of the Straits Settlements and later of Malaya. On the dissolution of the Currency Board distinctive coins were resumed, portraying Sultan Hassanal Bolkiah (obverse) [35] with ornamental motifs (reverse) [36–38]. New portraits were adopted in 1977 and 1993.

Gold and silver commemoratives have appeared since 1977, with various portraits of Sultan Hassanal on the obverse, mainly celebrating royal events or national anniversaries.

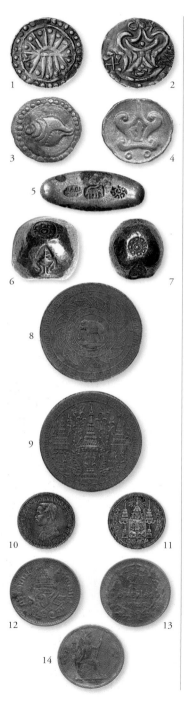

THAILAND

The ancient kingdom, known to its inhabitants as Muang Thai ("land of the free"), was the only country in South-east Asia never to fall under the control of a European power. Malay, Mon and Khmer kingdoms prospered in the region before the arrival of the Thai people, who began their migration from southern China and Laos during the 6th century. The emergence of a Thai-dominated nation began with the rise of the Sukhothai kingdom in the mid-13th century, under which distinctive bullet-shaped coins first emerged. In 1782 Rama I moved the capital to Bangkok and founded the dynasty that endures to this day. The Dutch, French and latterly the British played a part in the westernization of the country.

Left: The 10 baht coin of 1987, celebrating the anniversary of the Asian Institute of Technology, shows King Rama IX himself lecturing to students. It is one of many recent coins to show the hands-on approach of the royal family in everyday life.

SIAM

Silver and tin units were circulated in antiquity by the Indochinese kingdom of Funan [1–2], and later by the Mon people of Dvaravati [3–4]. In the north-east, the Kingdom of Langchang used bar-shaped coins of varying lengths, known as "leech money" [5] or "tiger tongue money", throughout the 16th and 17th centuries. More widely, gold and silver bullet-shaped coins developed from the original "bent rings" and endured as currency until the end of the 19th century [6–7]. The pieces had a standard weight based on the baht (15.4g/½oz), which was used as a unit of weight until the 1930s.

Bullet money was gradually superseded by western-style coinage from 1859 [8–9], the year in which Queen Victoria sent Rama IV a coining press as a gift. From then until 1937, coins were minted in a range of denominations, based on the baht on par with the tical and tamlung and worth 4 salung, 8 fuang, 16 sik, 32 pai, 64 att [12–13] or 1280 solot, while 20 baht equalled a chang.

From the outset these coins combined symbolism with images of Buddhist shrines and temples. In 1887 a series with the bust of Rama V (Chulalongkorn) was adopted [10–11], while the reverse of the lower values depicted a heavenly nymph, seated with a shield and spear, looking suspiciously like Britannia on British coins [14]. Buddhist symbolism continued on the higher values. The currency was reformed in 1908 and reduced to the baht of 4 salung or 100 satang, but similar types continued. Coins of this period were struck in many different metals, including tin, bronze, brass and cupro-nickel as well as silver and gold.

THAILAND

The new name was officially adopted in place of Siam by royal decree of June 1939. To this period belongs the bronze holed satang [15–16] followed by tiny tin or aluminium coins [17]. In September 1945 the country reverted to the older name but since May 1949 has been known as Thailand. Coinage continued to be inscribed solely in Thai characters until 1945, when western numerals were briefly used to denote value and date (in the Thai calendar). Most coins, however, have continued to be inscribed solely in the indigenous script. Definitive coins bear the effigy of the reigning sovereign. Rama IX (Bhumifhol Adulyadej) ascended the throne in 1946 as a teenager and many different portraits of him have been used. Sometimes the differences are very subtle, such as the effigies with one or three medals on the king's chest, or the portraits of the 1980s with or without a space between the collar and the lower hairline. The present series, from the tiny aluminium satang [17] to the bimetallic 10 baht, was introduced in 1987. It has the king's portrait on one side and symbolism, royal insignia or temples on the reverse [18–22].

COMMEMORATIVE AND SPECIAL ISSUES

An extraordinary feature of modern Thai coinage is the wide range of commemorative and special issues, the vast majority of which are produced in base metal for general circulation and add considerable interest to the everyday currency. They have been produced in denominations of 1, 2, 5, 10 and 20 baht in cupro-nickel. Although many have the portrait of Rama IX on the obverse this is by no means standard. In many cases, conjoined busts of the king and Queen Sirikit have been used, facing left or right [27–28]. Other coins have devoted the obverse to the Princess Mother [30] and the various princes and princesses of the blood royal. In effect, Thai coins are the nearest thing today to the portrait gallery of the Roman emperors. The coins that portray the junior members of the royal family are invariably intended to celebrate events in their lives, from the investiture of Prince Vajiralongkorn as crown prince (1972) [29] to royal birthdays and weddings. These are as assiduously chronicled in coins as the anniversaries of the king's reign. In some cases the formal portrait gives way to a more pictorial treatment. Thus the Food and Agriculture Organization coin of 1977 showed the king instructing a farmer, while coins of 1991, celebrating the award of a Magsaysay (Philippines) scholarship to Princess Sirindhorn showed her working with children (obverse) and the decorative scroll of the award (reverse).

When it comes to the centenaries of national institutions, an appropriate pictorial motif appears on the reverse, but conjoined busts or facing portraits side by side of Rama IX and one of his ancestors are commonly featured on the obverse. Triple portraits have been used in coins marking the centenary of the Thai Red Cross (1993) and the 72nd anniversary of Chulalongkorn University (1989). The reverses of these coins tend to be symbolic in character [23–26] – again the parallel with the allegories of the Roman Empire is close. A more pictorial approach has been used in coins publicizing wildlife conservation [31].

Graduation Coins

When Princess Sirindhorn and her sister Chulabhorn graduated from university, their success was celebrated by sets of three coins in 1977 and 1979, with their portraits on the obverse, and appropriate symbolism on the reverse.

Above: In the 19th century, multilingual trade coins, struck locally in cast tin, circulated in the port of Singgora (Songkhla). This example has Thai and Arabic characters on the obverse, and a Chinese legend on the reverse.

15 16 17 18 19 20 21 22 23 24 25 26 27 28 29 30 31

AUSTRALASIA AND OCEANIA

This vast area in the Pacific Ocean includes Australia, the world's smallest continent, together with New Zealand and a number of archipelagos scattered over the eastern and southern Pacific. The area was first traversed by Europeans in 1521 but was not properly surveyed until the 18th century, largely as a result of the three voyages of the British explorer and navigator Captain James Cook. All the territories have been subject to European colonization, primarily of British and French origin.

AUSTRALIA

Although Chinese, Spanish and Portuguese navigators sighted the great southern land it was not until 1770 that its east coast was properly surveyed by James Cook, who named it New South Wales because of an imagined similarity to that part of Britain. The first permanent settlement took place in 1788 when the penal colony at Port Jackson was founded. The six Australian states of New South Wales, Van Diemen's Land or Tasmania, Western Australia, South Australia, Victoria and Queensland were settled as colonies during the period 1823–59. They joined together in 1901 to form the Commonwealth of Australia. The country is a member of the Commonwealth, with Elizabeth II as head of state.

Left: A polygonal 50 cent coin was issued in 1970 to celebrate the bicentenary of Captain Cook's first voyage to the Pacific, during which he charted the east coast of Australia.

PRE-DECIMAL COINAGE
With a few exceptions, the Australian colonies used the coins of the mother country, and this continued for several years after the Commonwealth of Australia was formed. The silver threepence, sixpence, shilling and florin (2 shillings) were introduced in 1910 and bore the right-facing crowned bust of Edward VII, who died that year, with the Commonwealth arms on the reverse. The left-facing bust of George V was substituted the following year, when the bronze halfpenny and penny were added to the series [1–4]. These coins had a prosaic reverse with the value in words across the middle.

A new series appeared in 1938 with the bare-headed profile of George VI and pictorial images on the reverse. A kangaroo appeared on the bronze coins [5–6], while the silver featured ears of wheat (threepence) [7] or a merino ram (shilling), but the sixpence retained a modified version of the arms and the florin [8] had a more elaborate crowned version of the arms. These reverse motifs were retained for the series of 1953–64, with the profile of Elizabeth II on the obverse [9]. A crown (5 shillings) with a Tudor crown on the reverse was restricted to 1937–8. The florin was the medium for coins celebrating the jubilee of federation (1951) and the Queen's visit (1954) [10].

GOLD COINS
The only regular coinage produced in the 19th century consisted of gold sovereigns and half sovereigns [11–14]. Following the discovery of gold in South Australia, pound coins with a

crown (obverse) and value with the weight and fineness around the circumference (reverse) were minted at the Government Assay Office in Adelaide in 1852 [15–16]. Three years later a branch of the Royal Mint opened at Sydney and began coining sovereigns and half sovereigns with the profile of Queen Victoria (obverse) and a crown over "Australia" within a wreath (reverse) – the first coins to bear the name of the continent.

Australian coins continued until 1870 [17–18] but thereafter Sydney struck gold coins conforming to the prevailing British designs [19–20], distinguishable by the S mint-mark alongside the date. Branch mints were later opened at Melbourne (1872) [21–22] and Perth (1899). Production of gold sovereigns ceased in 1931.

DECIMAL COINAGE

Australia switched to the dollar of 100 cents in 1966. The bust of Elizabeth II by Arnold Machin appeared on the obverse [23], while reverses up to 20 cents featured examples of Australia's unique wildlife [24]. The circular silver 50 cents bore an elaborate version of the arms; when it next appeared, in 1969, the coin was struck in cupronickel with a polygonal shape. The series was re-issued in 1985 bearing the Maklouf profile [25] and in 1999 with the Rank-Broadley obverse [26]. The 1 and 2 cent coins were discontinued in 1991 and aluminium-bronze coins denominated $1 (1984) [27] and $2 (1988) [28] replaced banknotes.

Bimetallic $5 coins also appeared in 1988 but this denomination has since been largely employed as a commemorative. Australia has produced a vast range of commemoratives and special issues [29–31] in recent years, many in thematic series, in silver, gold and platinum and including, recently, coins with coloured surfaces.

KEELING COCOS ISLANDS

Ordinary Australian coins circulate in the overseas dependencies of Christmas Island and Norfolk Island. In the

Holey Dollar and Dump

The first distinctive coinage in Australia, authorized in 1813 by Governor Lachlan Macquarie, consisted of Spanish silver dollars with their centres cut out and tariffed at 15 pence, while the outer rings were circulated at 4s 9d. The work of cutting the coins and stamping them to denote their new value was entrusted to William Henshall, a convicted forger. In 1988, Australia issued a pair of legal tender silver coins, consisting of a 25g/1oz holey dollar and a 25 cent dump, as part of the celebrations marking the bicentenary of the first colony.

Keeling Cocos Islands, however, a distinctive series was issued in 1977, based on the rupee of 100 cents. It bears the bust of John Clunies-Ross (obverse), the self-proclaimed king of the islands in the 19th century, and a palm tree (reverse). Previously, various plastic and ivory tokens for use by workers in the coconut plantations were produced in 1910–13 and 1968 [32].

AUSTRALIA'S COMMERCE AND INDUSTRY

Australia is not much smaller than the United States of America, yet the ratio of population is 14.3 to 1. Most Australians live within a few miles of the coast and vast regions of the interior are either sparsely populated or uninhabitable. When the first British settlement was established at Botany Bay in 1788 the indigenous population of the continent has been estimated at about 60,000 Aborigines, nomadic tribes which had lived there for thousands of years. Although Australia had been discovered by the Chinese in the 15th century and sighted by the Portuguese a century later, colonization was hampered by its remoteness from the civilized world.

WOOL

Captain Cook explored and charted the east coast of Australia in the course of three voyages between 1770 and 1777, but it was only in 1788, after the loss of the American colonies, that Britain took serious notice of the great south-

Below: 200 escudo coin from Portugal, 1995 highlighting the Portuguese exploration of Australia in 1522–5.

Above: 50 cents portraying explorers George Bass and Matthew Flinders and the shilling showing a Merino ram.

ern land – and then only as a dumping ground for convicts. Its very isolation was originally regarded as its chief asset.

Attempts to penetrate the hinterland were baulked by the Blue Mountains and it was not till 1813 that Wentworth, Blaxland and Lawson (on a $5 of 1993) found a way through. They were rewarded by the sight of vast grasslands. As a result, pastoralism became Australia's first major industry, favoured by the flatness of the terrain. Vast areas of desert or semi-arid land, however, meant that the population density might be reduced to one or two sheep per square mile. Nevertheless, the number of sheep exceeded 100 million by the end of the 19th century. By 1940 there were 123 million – the largest sheep population anywhere in the world. By that time Australia possessed a quarter of the world's sheep resources (meat and wool). About 80 per cent of the wool exported is Merino, a fine wool highly favoured in the textile industry. A Merino ram appeared on the shillings of 1938-63 symbolizing an industry that generated a revenue of £55,000,000 a year in the 1930s, compared with about £20,000,000 for cattle and dairy products. Elizabeth MacArthur who introduced the breed, is portrayed on a $5 coin of 1995 with a flock of sheep in the background. Although these animals were bred primarily for their wool, the export of meat rose sharply after the introduction of refrigeration in the mid-19th century. Today, the lean meat of sheep bred in the Outback is particularly favoured in Islamic countries from Indonesia to Arabia. The great

Above: $10 of 2002 marking the 150th anniversary of the Adelaide pound.

Below: The original Adelaide pound of 1852, minted from locally mined gold.

importance of wool to the Australian economy is reflected in the 50c of 1991 issued to mark the 25th anniversary of decimal currency; the Merino ram was the motif on the reverse.

GOLD

The population of the Australian colonies remained small till the 1850s. In 1851 gold was discovered in Victoria more or less simultaneously at Bathurst and Anderson's Creek near Melbourne, shortly followed by the vast deposits at Ballarat. This triggered off a gold rush and by early 1852 prospectors from Europe, America and China were pouring through Melbourne at the rate of 2,000 a week. Though gold was the

Above (clockwise from top-left): George V sovereigns of 1921–6 with mintmarks above the dates: the Melbourne 'M', the Sydney 'S' and the Perth 'P' with obverse.

Below: Dollar celebrating the 130th anniversary of the Melbourne Mint, its gateway flanked by the two sovereigns.

Above: The reverses of coins marking the 150th anniversary of the Eureka stockade (left) and Cobb & Co mail-coach.

Below: Reverses of centennial coins marking the Darwin-Adelaide Railway.

in 1853 and struck gold sovereigns from 1855 onwards, with a profile of Queen Victoria on the obverse and a crown over AUSTRALIA on the reverse. These distinctive coins continued till 1870 when the Sydney Mint was redesignated as a branch of the Royal Mint in London. Thereafter, it struck British gold sovereigns, distinguishable solely by the initial letter S alongside the date on the reverse.

Another branch mint was opened at Melbourne in 1872 and struck sovereigns with the letter M. Finally a mint at Perth in Western Australia began striking sovereigns in 1899. The Sydney mint closed in 1926 and is now a museum. Although the production of gold sovereigns ceased in 1931 the Melbourne and Perth mints continue to this day, the former striking circulating and commemorative coins, while the latter concentrates mainly on bullion pieces such as the Kookaburra (silver), Nugget (gold) and Koala (platinum) series. In recent years, the use of mint marks has been revived, the letters C (Canberra), M (Melbourne) and S (Sydney) being found on some coins from 1993 onwards. And gold even accelerated the path of democracy; the miners' rebellion in the Eureka Stockade in 1854 (on a coin of 2004) marked the advent of workers' rights.

COMMUNICATIONS

Up to the 1850s, communication between the six colonies of Australia was by coastal shipping, but the gold rush of 1851-2 stimulated attempts to provide overland communications. In 1853, Freeman Cobb and three fellow Americans established the American Telegraph Coach Line, soon changed to Cobb & Co, and secured a Royal Mail contract to carry mail and passengers between Bathurst and Bourke. The network of mail-coaches spread rapidly across the continent, and the company enjoyed a high reputation for reliability. To this day Australians use the word 'cobber' to mean a good friend. A silver $5 coin was belatedly issued in 1995 to celebrate the 150th

most important metal in terms of value, copper, silver, lead, tin and later tungsten were also discovered, creating the core of Australia's wealth and greatly stimulating its population growth. The gold rush era is featured on a $5 coin of 1995.

This had a direct bearing on the money in circulation. Australia relied on British coins but it seemed logical to refine and coin gold in Australia itself rather than ship the raw metal back to England. In 1852, a mint which struck gold pounds was established in Adelaide. The obverse featured a crown while the reverse bore the value surrounded by the weight and fineness of the metal. A mint opened at Sydney

anniversary of the company and features a mail-coach on the reverse. The first railway opened in 1854, but today the major routes include the Indian-Pacific, from Perth to Sydney, and the 'Ghan', from Adelaide to Darwin, so-called because Afghan camel-drivers ran the supply route while the line was under construction. Coins of 2004 celebrated the 150th anniversary of the railway system, while subsequent commemoratives have marked the opening of air routes, including the Queensland and Northern Territory Air Service – better known today by its acronym QANTAS – and internal air services, including the Royal Flying Doctors (on coins of 1998).

NEW ZEALAND

The Dominion of New Zealand is a member of the Commonwealth and has Elizabeth II as its head of state. It consists of two large islands and has an area rather larger than that of the United Kingdom but with only a twentieth of the population. Its economy is based on agriculture, with wool, meat and dairy products accounting for the bulk of its exports.

Left: In 1977, New Zealand celebrated the Queen's Silver Jubilee with a silver dollar showing the house at Waitangi where the treaty of cession was signed in 1840, echoing the Silver Jubilee crown of 1935, whose reverse had depicted the signing ceremony.

The Maori who migrated from Hawaii between the 10th and 14th centuries called the islands Aotearoa, "the land of the long white cloud". Abel Jan Tasman was the first European to sight the land and named it after the Dutch province of Zealand. Its coast was surveyed in detail in 1769 by James Cook, who annexed it to Britain. This rash act was ignored by the home government and for more than half a century New Zealand was visited only by whalers and sealers. By 1814, missionaries were establishing posts around the Bay of Islands and adventurers came in search of gold. In 1840, Captain William Hobson signed the Treaty of Waitangi with Maori chiefs and New Zealand was annexed as a dependency of New South Wales. A silver crown issued in 1935 for the silver jubilee of George V pictured the meeting of Hobson and the Maori chief, Waka Nene.

New Zealand was detached from New South Wales in 1852 and granted self-government. In the 1860s the population rose sharply following the discovery of gold, but continuing wrangles over land resulted in the Maori Wars of 1861–71. In the 1890s, New Zealand declined to join the Australian colonies in federation and became a separate dominion.

EARLY COINAGE

Remarkably, New Zealand used British coinage well into the 20th century. Periodic shortages of coins were met by the traditional expedient of tradesmen's tokens, which began in 1857 and amounted to about 150 different types by 1881 when they were discontinued, although they continued to circulate until 1897. Later, Australian coins circulated alongside British ones.

New Zealand introduced distinctive silver coins in 1933, with the crowned bust of George V [1] on the obverse and various pictorial motifs on the reverse: Maori clubs (threepence) [3], the extinct *huia* bird (sixpence) [4], a Maori warrior (shilling) [2], a kiwi (florin) [5] and arms (half crown). Bronze coins did not appear until 1940, when the halfpenny featured a *tiki* or Maori idol [7] and the penny a *tui* bird [8]. These reverse types continued in later issues, with the profiles of George VI (1937–51) [6] and Elizabeth II (1953–64). Beside the centennial florin of 1940, silver crowns were issued on three occasions, for the silver jubilee (1935), the royal visit (1949) and the coronation (1953) [9]. To mark the centennial (1940) a half crown was issued [12], and half crowns were also issued in 1962 [10–11].

DECIMAL COINAGE

New Zealand adopted the dollar of 100 cents in 1967, with coins in bronze (1 and 2 cents) or cupro-nickel (5 cents to $1). The Machin bust of the Queen appeared on the obverse, while the reverse motifs were a stylized fern leaf (1 cent) [13], kowhai blossom (2 cents)

Non-Event

In 1949 a crown featuring a silver fern leaf and the Southern Cross was struck at the Royal Mint and shipped to New Zealand to celebrate the visit of George VI. The trip was cancelled on account of the king's illness, but the coins were issued anyway. When Queen Elizabeth and the Duke of Edinburgh visited New Zealand five years later no coins were issued to mark the occasion.

[14], tuatara (5 cents) [16], Maori *koruru* or carved head (10 cents) [15], kiwi (20 cents) [17], Captain Cook's brig *Endeavour* with Mount Egmont (Taranaki) (50 cents) [18] and the national arms crowned and flanked by fern leaves [19]. The 50 cent coin was re-issued in 1969 with an edge inscription to celebrate Cook's bicentenary.

Apart from the 1 and 2 cents (discontinued in 1988), the basic series has continued to this day, with the more mature effigies of the Queen by Maklouf (1986) [20] and Rank-Broadley (since 1999). In 1990 the large cupro-nickel dollar was replaced by a smaller aluminium-bronze coin featuring a kiwi [24]; at the same time a circulating $2 in the same alloy depicted a great egret [21] while the 20 cents now showed a tiki flanked by Maori curvilinear panels [23].

COMMEMORATIVE COINS

To mark the 150th anniversary of annexation in 1990 the circulating coins were temporarily replaced by issues showing a stylized bird (5 cents), a Maori sailing canoe (10 cents),

Cook's ship (20 cents) and tree-planting (50 cents); the dollar showed the signing of the Treaty of Waitangi.

Large dollars in cupro-nickel or silver were produced extensively from 1969 to commemorate historic anniversaries and events, including royal visits in 1970, 1983 and 1986, while royal birthdays, jubilees and wedding anniversaries [22] have also been assiduously celebrated. New Zealand hosted the Commonwealth Games in 1974 and 1989, issuing a single coin the first time and a set of four the second time. In more recent years coins have marked the Rugby World Cup and the Olympic Games. A series of 1992, ostensibly honouring Columbus, included coins in tribute to Kupe, the mythological leader of the Maori migration to New Zealand, as well as Tasman and Cook. A $5 coin of 1990 paid tribute to the Anzac forces of World War I, while a $20 of 1995 saluted the bravery of Charles Upham, the New Zealand double winner of the Victoria Cross.

New Zealand does not possess its own mint and has therefore relied mainly on the British Royal Mint for its coins, but this has given rise to some curious errors. In 1967 a consignment of bronze 2 cents was struck with the obverse of the Bahamas 5 cents instead. In 1985 a supply of cupro-nickel 50 cent coins was found to have the Canadian dollar reverse showing a Voyageur canoe. While examples of the Bahamas error are quite common, only nine of the Canadian hybrid coins have so far been recorded.

Above: A dollar depicting Mount Cook, known to the Maori as Aorangi, was issued to celebrate the 1970 royal visit.

NEW ZEALAND DEPENDENCIES

Several countries in the South Pacific are dependencies of New Zealand. Coins of the latter originally circulated in these territories – and still do, in the case of Niue – but in more recent years, indigenous coinages have developed, and these are inscribed with the names of the islands and relevant pictorial reverses.

Left: The British oarsmen and gold medallists Sir Matthew Pinsent and Sir Steve Redgrave are portrayed on the reverse of the $50 coin issued by Niue to mark the 1992 Olympic Games. Steve Redgrave holds the record as Britain's greatest Olympian, winning gold medals at five consecutive Olympic Games from 1984 to 2000.

COOK ISLANDS

This archipelago of 15 islands some 3000km/2000 miles north-east of New Zealand is named in honour of James Cook, although the Spaniard Alvaro de Mendaña was probably the first European to sight it, in 1595, while the Portuguese Fernandes de Quieros landed there in 1606. Cook visited the islands in 1773, 1774 and 1777 and named them the Hervey Islands, after one of the lords of the Admiralty.

The Cook Islands had their own monarchical system, but in 1888 Queen Makea Takau sought British protection. They were annexed by New Zealand in 1901 but were granted internal autonomy in 1965, though New Zealand continues to be responsible for defence and external affairs. The islands used New Zealand coins exclusively until 1972, when a series

Above: Dollar issued by New Zealand in 1970 to mark the bicentenary of the discovery of the Cook Islands.

bearing the Machin bust of Elizabeth II [1, 3, 5] was introduced. These coins followed the weights, alloys and specifications of their New Zealand counterparts, with pictorial reverses featuring a taro leaf (1 cent), pineapple (2 cents), hibiscus (5 cents) [2], orange (10 cents) [4], fairy tern (20 cents) [7], bonito fish (50 cents) [6] and Tangaroa, the Polynesian god of creation ($1) [8]. The reverse of the 20 cents changed in 1972 to depict a Pacific triton shell. The series was re-issued in 1978 with an edge inscription marking the 250th anniversary of the birth of Captain Cook, and the same device was repeated in 1981 to celebrate the wedding of Prince Charles and Lady Diana Spencer. In 1987 the Maklouf profile was substituted, the size of the dollar reduced and a scalloped shape adopted on the dollar, while a $2 coin depicting an island table and a $5 showing a conch shell [9] were introduced.

Numerous commemorative or special issues have appeared since 1986 [10–11], notably the series of 16 (1996) featuring world wildlife and the multicoloured coins depicting the cartoon character Garfield (1999).

NIUE

Discovered by Cook in 1774 and originally named Savage Island, Niue was originally administered as part of the

Cook Islands but has been a separate dependency of New Zealand since 1922. New Zealand coins are still in general circulation and Niue must be unique among the nations of the world in not having introduced a base-metal circulating coinage of its own. This defect, however, has been more than remedied since 1987 by the release of a considerable number of commemorative or special coins in denominations from $1 to $250, in cupro-nickel, silver or gold. The overwhelming majority are from $5 upwards and in fact it was not until 1996 that Niue got around to issuing a $1 coin, with a reverse depicting HMS *Bounty*, scene of one of the most famous mutinies in the history of the Royal Navy.

While some coins have the Maklouf profile of Elizabeth II on the obverse, the majority bear the crowned arms of New Zealand instead [12]. The first coins were of $5 denomination and portrayed the tennis stars Boris Becker [13] and Steffi Graf. This set the tone for subsequent issues; tennis is a sport that has been rather neglected on the coins of other countries, but from Niue have come coins honouring Martina

Navratilova and Chris Evert as well as Steffi Graf (1988), the final between Germany and Sweden in the Davis Cup (1989) and a further issue devoted to Steffi Graf (including silver $50 and $100 as well as $250 gold coins) in the same year. After that, Niue looked elsewhere and, discovering that soccer was a lucrative theme, issued coins portraying such football stars as Franz Beckenbauer and even the entire Italian squad (1990). Themes of other series range from endangered wildlife to war heroes such as Douglas MacArthur and Admiral William Halsey, and Cook's voyages of discovery vie with the Soviet Union's Luna 9 moon landing.

TOKELAU ISLANDS
About 3000km/2000 miles north of New Zealand lie the Union or Tokelau Islands – Atafu, Nukunono and Fakaofo – whose inhabitants are Polynesian by race and Samoan in language and culture. These remote atolls were acquired by Britain in 1889 and bandied about for many years, at times administered as part of the Gilbert and Ellice Islands Protectorate and then, from 1926 to 1948, attached to Western Samoa. Since then they have been a New Zealand dependency.

In 1978 a cupro-nickel dollar was issued, merely inscribed "Tokelau" with the date round the top, over the Machin bust of Elizabeth II (with neither her name nor titles) [14]. What appeared to be Morse code running round the rim were patterns of three dots representing the three atolls. The reverse depicted a breadfruit with the value in Samoan ("Tahi Tala") [15]. An edge inscription proclaimed "Tokelau's First Coin". This established the pattern for subsequent coins, from $1 [16–17] to $100, and though the Maklouf profile was adopted in 1989 the Queen's name remains conspicuously absent. The reverses depict aspects of island life, although a series of 1991 featured salient events in the Pacific War, from the attack on Pearl Harbor to the raising of the Stars and Stripes on Iwo Jima.

First Rounded Triangle

To the Cook Islands goes the credit for producing the world's first triangular coin with rounded edges, the $2 of 1987–94: both circulating and proof versions were minted in each year.

10

11

12

13

14

15

16

17

PNG, NAURU AND VANUATU

Apart from Nauru (formerly Ocean Island), these countries lie to the north of Australia. They include Vanuatu, formerly the New Hebrides, which was administered by France and Britain as a condominium, and the eastern part of New Guinea (the world's largest island after Greenland), which was formerly partitioned between Germany and Britain. The western portion of New Guinea was once part of the Dutch East Indies and is now Irian Barat, part of Indonesia.

Left: The toea, *or Emperor of Germany bird of paradise, is not only featured on coins of Papua New Guinea but has lent its name to the unit of currency.*

GERMAN NEW GUINEA

The southern portion of east New Guinea was annexed by Queensland in 1883. A year later Germany annexed the northern part, which became Kaiser Wilhelmsland. British and German coinage circulated in the respective territories, but in 1894–5 a distinctive series for use in Kaiser Wilhelmsland was produced by the New Guinea Company, whose German name appeared on the obverse of the bronze 1 and 2 pfennig coins, with the value on the reverse. The higher values, comprising the bronze 10 pfennig, silver half, 1, 2 and 5 marks and the gold 10 and 20 marks, had an obverse showing the *toea* (the national bird), with a wreathed value on the reverse [1–5]. Shortly after the outbreak of war in August 1914 German New Guinea was invaded and occupied by Australian forces. In 1920 Australia was granted a mandate by the League of Nations and ordinary Australian coins were adopted.

BRITISH NEW GUINEA

The administration of the southern portion, known as British New Guinea or Papua, passed from Queensland to the British Crown in 1888, but was transferred to the Commonwealth of Australia in 1901. It became a self-governing territory in 1906. British or Australian coins were used until 1929, when cupro-nickel halfpennies and pennies were introduced as small change, followed by the cupro-nickel

threepence and sixpence, and the silver shilling, in 1935. A singular feature of the coinage was that all five denominations had a central hole [6–7]. The obverse bore a Tudor crown flanked by two maces on the two lowest values and the shilling, while the others featured the crown and royal monogram flanked by the date. The reverses had the name of the territory, value and date, with cruciform or geometric patterns in the middle.

A bronze penny was adopted in 1936 with the monogram of Edward VIII, and was one of the few distinctive colonial coins of his short reign [8–9]. New pennies with the "GRI" monogram appeared in 1938 and 1944, with sporadic issues of higher values up to 1945 [10–11].

PAPUA NEW GUINEA

The Japanese invaded New Guinea in 1942 and a ferocious campaign ensued before Commonwealth forces regained control. A mandate from the United Nations was granted in 1946 and in 1949 Papua and New Guinea were united. In 1973 the territory was granted self-government, and full independence as a member of the Commonwealth was achieved in 1975.

Coinage was introduced that year, based on the kina of 100 toeas, the eponymous bird of paradise appearing on the standard obverse, with other examples of fauna on the reverse [12–13]. Simultaneously a gold 100 kina portrayed the prime minister, Michael Somare. Coins from 1 to 20 toeas have been issued in the same designs ever since [14–19].

A few heptagonal 50 toeas appeared in the 1980s, solely as commemoratives, but the crown-sized 5 and 10 kina are the preferred medium, together with gold 100 kina. The relatively few special issues have included coins for the visit of Pope John Paul II (1984) and the Commonwealth Games (1991). An enormous 25 kina in enamelled silver appeared in 1994 to mark the centenary of the first coinage.

NAURU

One of the world's smallest and most isolated countries, the Republic of Nauru has an area of just 21sq km/8sq miles and a population of 13,000. It has the curious distinction of being the only country in the world without a capital. Composed largely of phosphate deposits, now exhausted, Nauru could eventually disappear as the island succumbs to rising ocean levels resulting from global warming. Some of the phosphate revenue was invested in Australian real estate, notably Nauru House, one of the highest buildings in Melbourne, but having enjoyed the highest per capita income of any Third World country, Nauru is now on the brink of bankruptcy. In the 1990s the islanders attempted to create a tax haven, but this ended in 2004. Recently the island's main revenue has come from Australia, which uses it as a detention centre for asylum seekers.

Discovered in 1798 by a whaler, John Fearn, who named it Pleasant Island, Nauru continued as a tribal kingdom with mixed Melanesian and Polynesian inhabitants until 1888, when it was annexed by Germany as a dependency of New Guinea. The exploitation of the phosphate deposits began in 1905. Nauru was occupied and administered by Australia from 1914 and invaded by Japan in 1942. In 1947 the United Nations placed it under joint British, Australian and New Zealand government until it became an

independent republic in 1968 under the presidency of Hammer de Roburt. Australian coins are in everyday use but silver $10 and gold $50 pieces have been issued by the Bank of Nauru since 1993 to commemorate the Olympic Games, the World Cup, the Queen Mother [20] and other subjects of global interest.

VANUATU

Named the New Hebrides by Captain Cook in 1774, these islands east of Papua New Guinea were declared a neutral zone in 1878, administered jointly by British and French naval officers. A condominium was proclaimed in 1906, but the only distinctive coins were those provided by the French after 1966 (see "French Pacific Islands").

In 1980 the country became an independent republic within the Commonwealth and adopted the name of Vanuatu. Coins thus inscribed, with the national emblem (obverse) [21, 23] and flora or seashells (reverse) [22, 24], were struck in denominations from 1 to 100 vatu. Several FAO coins have appeared [25–26], along with coins from 10 to 100 vatu celebrating the end of the Victorian era (1995), the Olympic Games, Captain Cook and the 25th anniversary of the Voyager 1 spacecraft – an eclectic mixture.

Heptagonal Coins
In 1980 Papua New Guinea introduced a 50 toea denomination and adopted the seven-sided format pioneered by Britain. It has so far been confined to coins commemorating the South Pacific Festival of Arts (1980) and the Ninth South Pacific Games (1991).

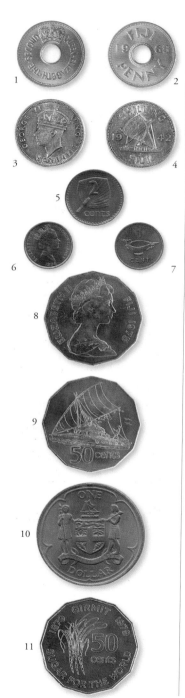

FIJI, SOLOMONS, KIRIBATI AND TUVALU

These countries are archipelagos scattered over the south-western Pacific. Though all three were sighted by European navigators in the 16th and 17th centuries they were surveyed by Captain Cook in the 18th century and thereafter fell within the British sphere of influence.

Left: Tuvalu, formerly the Ellice or Lagoon Islands, was claimed for the British Crown in 1892 by the captain of HMS Royalist, *depicted on the $20 of 1993.*

FIJI

In 1643, Abel Jan Tasman was the first European to sight Fiji, and the islands were visited by James Cook in 1774. William Bligh and the loyal members of the crew of HMS *Bounty*, set adrift in an open boat by the mutineers, sailed through the Fiji group on their epic voyage to Timor (1789), but it was not until 1840 that the islands were comprehensively surveyed.

Traders and adventurers arrived in 1801 in search of sandalwood, and by 1850 there was a sizable and cosmopolitan population in Suva, the capital. By that time the islands were united under King Cakobau, but in 1874 incessant tribal warfare induced him to seek British protection in order to restore law and order. In the colonial period the British developed the sugar industry, bringing in indentured coolies from India. When Fiji attained independence in 1970 the Indian majority were held back by the indigenous Fijians, a dangerous situation that resulted in two military coups in 1987, the declaration of a republic and Fiji's expulsion from the Commonwealth. It was re-admitted in 1997.

British (from 1881) and Australian currency (from 1910) was in circulation until 1934, when distinctive coins were introduced. The holed halfpenny and penny were originally struck in cupro-nickel, then brass (1942) and bronze (1949), with a crown and the name of the monarch on the obverse and the country name, value and date on the reverse [1–2]. Thus Fiji was one of the few colonies to issue coins in 1936 in the name of Edward VIII. The silver sixpence, shilling and florin appeared in 1934, with a crowned bust of George V on the obverse and reverse motifs of a turtle, outrigger canoe [3–4] and colonial arms respectively. A 12-sided nickel-brass threepence was added in 1947, featuring a thatched hut between palm trees on the reverse. These coins, with the crowned effigy of the monarch, continued until Fiji adopted the dollar in 1969. A new series bore the Machin bust of the Queen and artefacts representing indigenous culture: kava bowl (1 cent) [6–7], palm-leaf fan (2 cents) [5], ceremonial drum (5 cents), throwing club (10 cents), *tabua* (whale's tooth) on a braided cord (20 cents), sailing canoe (50c) [8–9] and arms ($1) [10], the specifications following the Australian standard. The Maklouf effigy of the Queen has been used since 1986.

Numerous commemorative coins have appeared since independence in 1970. In addition to conventional circular coins Fiji has experimented with pentagons, polygons [11–13] and even segments which, when fitted to similar coins from Western Samoa and the Cook Islands, form a complete circle.

Pacific Conflict

The Solomon Islands were the scene of some of the fiercest fighting between Japanese and US forces in 1942–3, especially on Guadalcanal. From 1991 onward, several coins were issued to mark the 50th anniversaries of the battles of the Coral Sea and Guadalcanal, beginning with a dollar commemorating the Japanese attack on Pearl Harbor.

SOLOMON ISLANDS

Discovered in 1567 by the Spanish, these islands were partitioned between Germany and Britain and were declared protectorates in 1885 and 1893 respectively. The German islands were occupied by Australia in 1914 and in 1976 the protectorate was abolished. Since becoming an independent member of the Commonwealth the islands have issued coins portraying Elizabeth II with indigenous artefacts on the reverse, as well as numerous commemoratives [14–19].

KIRIBATI

Pronounced "Kiribas", the islands' name is the Polynesian rendering of "Gilbert", as they were previously thus named after Captain Thomas Gilbert, who first visited them in 1778. With the Ellice Islands, the Gilberts were administered from Fiji as a British protectorate, becoming a crown colony in 1915. The Phoenix group was added in 1937 and the Central and Southern Line Islands in 1972. These sparsely populated islands are spread over more than 2.5 million sq km/1 million sq miles of ocean, but their total land area

is relatively small. The Gilbert Islands became a separate colony in 1976 and a republic within the Commonwealth in 1979, adopting the present name. Until then Australian currency was in use, but Kiribati has since issued its own coins, with arms (obverse) and indigenous fauna (reverse) on the low values and a sailing canoe and thatched hut on the dollar coins [20–21].

TUVALU

Formerly the Ellice Islands, this group has an area of 25sq km/10sq miles, and constitutes one of the world's smallest independent republics. In 1974 the inhabitants voted to separate from the Gilbert Islands and in 1976 became a "constitutional dependency" of the British Crown, under the name of Tuvalu. Complete independence for the population of 9000 was achieved in October 1978. Distinctive coins were adopted in 1976, bearing the Machin effigy of Elizabeth II with marine fauna on the reverse [22–23]. Since 1994 the Maklouf profile has been substituted. A few silver ($5, $10 or $20) and gold ($50 or $100) coins have appeared since 1976, marking anniversaries of independence or royal events, from the wedding of Prince Charles and Diana Spencer (1981) to the Duke of Edinburgh Award and birthdays of the Queen Mother.

Fitting the Pieces Together

Kiribati has produced relatively few special issues, although they include segmented Millennial coins resembling pieces of a jigsaw puzzle (1997), inscribed with the Latin for "times are changing".

FRENCH PACIFIC ISLANDS

Second only to Britain, France was the major colonial power in the South Pacific, and it still maintains a strong presence in that region. The Bank of Indochina established branches at Nouméa, New Caledonia, in 1888 and at Papeete, Tahiti, in 1905 and was responsible for paper money. French coins were in use until 1949, when separate issues for the French territories were introduced. The Bank of Indochina was succeeded in 1965 by the Institut d'Emission d'Outre-Mer (Overseas Issuing Institute), whose initials appear on the obverse of the nickel coins issued since 1975 [6, 14]. Separate issues are made for French Polynesia and New Caledonia, the CFP ("Change franc Pacifique" or "Pacific franc exchange") franc being tariffed at 1000 to 8.38 euros.

Left: An image of Moorea, one of the most spectacularly beautiful islands anywhere in the world, is featured on the 50 franc coins of French Polynesia.

FRENCH POLYNESIA

Porinetia Farani, as it is known in the local language, is a French overseas collectivity, comprising several island groups scattered over 2.5 million sq km/1 million sq miles of the South Pacific, with a total land area of 4,200 sq km/1,600sq miles and a population of 270,000. The largest island is Tahiti, which is also the location of the capital, Papeete. Captain Cook visited Tahiti in 1769, naming the archipelago the Society Islands, and Captain Bligh of the *Bounty* spent some time there in 1788–9 gathering breadfruit plants, which were to be established in the West Indies as food for the plantation slaves. Pomare II converted to Christianity in 1797 and British missionaries were in a favoured position until 1843, when France established a protectorate that became a colony in 1880 when Pomare V abdicated. The Society Islands joined the Marquesas and the Tuamotu archipelago in 1903 to form the colony known collectively as the French Settlements in Oceania.

French coins were used until 1949 when French Oceania attained self-government within the French Union. Aluminium coins from 50 centimes to 5 francs had the allegorical figure of Marianne on the obverse and a palm-girt scene on the reverse [1].

In 1957 the territory was renamed French Polynesia and chose to remain within the French Community. Coins in the same designs as those of 1949, but inscribed "Polynésie Française" on the reverse, were adopted in 1965 [2]. Higher denominations (10, 20 and 50 francs), struck in nickel, were added in 1967, with the head of Marianne (obverse) [5–7] and reverse motifs of a carved pole [3], frangipani blossom [4] and the jagged peaks of Moorea respectively. A 100 franc coin with the Moorea reverse, struck in nickel-bronze [8], was added to the series in 1976.

French coins also circulate widely, reflecting the continuing military presence associated with the testing of nuclear devices at Mururoa Atoll. Since January 1996, however, nuclear testing has been discontinued and the military garrison greatly reduced. Today the main sources of revenue come from tourism and the cultivation of *noni* fruit for the pharmaceutical industry.

NEW CALEDONIA

This archipelago 1800km/1100 miles east of Australia was discovered in 1774 by Captain Cook, who bestowed on it the name then used by poets to denote Scotland. As in Tahiti, British missionaries brought Christianity and a measure of Western civilization, but it was the French who established a protectorate there in 1853. They used it as a penal settlement, deporting many thousands of Communards in the aftermath of the abortive revolution of 1870–1. Normal colonial development began only in 1894.

New Caledonia used French coins exclusively until 1949 but, following its establishment as an overseas territory within the French Community in 1946, aluminium coins for small change were introduced. These had the same obverse as the coins of French Oceania [9] but the reverse featured the *kagu*, the national bird [10–11]. Nickel coins appeared in 1967 with the head of Marianne on the obverse [14] and on the reverse a Melanesian sailing pirogue, or flat-hulled canoe (10 francs) [12], zebu cattle (20 francs) [13] and a hut surrounded by Norfolk Island pines (50 francs) [15]. Nickel-bronze 100 francs with the pines reverse were added to the series in 1976.

Associated with New Caledonia are the three tiny volcanic islands of Uvea (Wallis), Alofi and Futuna, known as the Wallis and Futuna Islands, lying between Fiji and Samoa. The group was discovered by the Cornishman Samuel Wallis in the 18th century, but Christianized by French missionaries who arrived in 1837, and French protectorates were established over the islands in 1887–8. Each island has its own king to this day. In 1959 the inhabitants voted to become a separate overseas territory, thus severing political dependency on New Caledonia. A French overseas collectivity since 2003, the territory continues to use the coinage of New Caledonia.

NEW HEBRIDES
Named the New Hebrides by Captain Cook in 1774, because of a fancied resemblance to the islands off the west coast of Scotland, these islands east of Papua New Guinea had previously been visited by the Portuguese Pedro de Queiros (1606) and the Frenchman Louis de Bougainville (1768). Rival missionaries and sandalwood traders

Reference to Earlier Currency
The squiggles flanking the carved mask on the reverse of the 10 and 20 franc coins of the New Hebrides are pieces of *tridacna* or clam shell, used as money before the advent of coinage.

established themselves in the islands throughout the 19th century and urged their respective countries to annex them. Even British settlers favoured French protection when their own government seemed indifferent. An ad hoc dual system developed, but was unsatisfactory in regard to the settlement of civil disputes. The situation was aggravated by periodic uprisings by the indigenous inhabitants. In 1878 France and Britain negotiated a deal whereby the islands were declared a neutral zone, administered jointly by British and French naval officers, but this was impractical and led eventually to joint rule. A condominium was proclaimed in 1906, with two separate police forces and a judicial system headed by two judges (British and French) and a president, who could be neither British nor French, appointed by the king of Spain.

British, French and Australian currency was used but the only distinctive coins were those provided by the French authorities from 1966 onward, with the head of Marianne on the obverse and indigenous carvings on the reverse [16–20]. In 1980 the New Hebrides achieved complete independence, becoming the Republic of Vanuatu, a member of the British Commonwealth (see "PNG, Nauru and Vanuatu").

1

2

3

4

5

6

7

8

9

POLYNESIAN KINGDOMS

Polynesia (from the Greek for "many islands") is the generic name for the vast number of islands scattered across the central Pacific from Hawaii in the north, whence the hardy seafaring Polynesians set out to colonize the other island groups in the 10th and subsequent centuries. The tribal communities eventually developed into kingdoms with their own coinage.

*Left: The Hawaiian silver dollar (*akahi dala*) of King David Kalakaua, dubbed "the Merry Monarch" on account of his love of wine, women and song. Both he and Queen Liliuokalani, his successor, were gifted musicians.*

HAWAII

This archipelago was visited by Captain James Cook in 1778. At that time the eight main islands were under the rule of petty kings and tribal chiefs, but by 1795 Kamehameha I had welded them into a single nation. American missionaries and traders gradually transformed Hawaii, creating the sugar and pineapple industries and bringing in indentured labourers from Japan and the Azores. American businessmen engineered the downfall of the monarchy in 1893, and for a brief period in 1894 Hawaii was a republic before it was admitted to the USA in 1898, becoming a territory in 1900 and a state in 1959.

Copper cents with a facing bust of Kamehameha III on the obverse and the value in the Hawaiian language on the reverse appeared in 1847. A regular coinage was introduced in 1881–3, with the profile of David Kalakaua on the obverse [1–2]. The reverses featured a crowned value (5 cents), wreathed values (10 cents and ⅛ dollar) and the crowned arms (quarter, half and dollar). Coins with the bust of Queen Liliuokalani dated 1891 or 1895 (the latter bearing a striking resemblance to the Syracusan decadrachms of the 5th century BC, complete with dolphins surrounding the portrait) were commissioned by Reginald Huth, a wealthy British collector, and are regarded as

patterns. Restrikes or imitations of Hawaiian coins have been produced in recent years as tourist souvenirs.

TONGA

Named the Friendly Islands by Captain Cook in 1773, Tonga is an archipelago in the South Pacific, south of Samoa and east of Fiji. Intertribal warfare was brought to an end by Taufa'ahau, who adopted the name of King George Tupou I when he converted to Christianity in 1845. Aided and abetted by the British missionary Shirley Baker, who became prime minister, he united the islands into a single kingdom by 1862. Tonga became a self-governing British protectorate in 1900 and a fully independent kingdom within the Commonwealth in 1970.

The coinage of Britain, and latterly of New Zealand, circulated in Tonga, and the first indigenous coins were the gold pieces of 1962 called the koula (from the Tongan word for "gold") with its half and quarter. A standing figure of Queen Salote appeared on the koula and half koula and a profile on the quarter koula, with the royal arms on the reverse. Circulating coinage, based on the pa'anga of 100 seniti, was adopted in 1967, with Salote's effigy on the obverse [3] and various reverse motifs of a giant tortoise (1 and 2 seniti), wreathed value (5 and 10 seniti) and the coat of arms (20 and 50 seniti and 1 pa'anga) [4]. These coins were posthumous, as Salote had died in 1965. A series of seven coins, including the platinum hau (100 pa'anga) and its subdivisions, also appeared in 1967 to celebrate the coronation of her son and successor Taufa'ahau Tupou IV, with his portrait (obverse) and arms (reverse), followed by a permanent series with his profile replacing his mother's [5–7]. A series introduced in 1975 bore a facing bust of the king in military uniform, with motifs promoting the Food and Agriculture Organization programme [10–11]. Since then Tonga has produced numerous coins in all shapes and sizes [8–9] for a wide range of topics, often issued in thematic sets. These have ranged from veteran and vintage cars to celebrate the automobile centenary [12–13] to sporting events such as the Olympic and Commonwealth Games and the America's Cup yacht races, as well as tributes to members of the British royal family [14].

Christmas Coins

From 1982 to 1988 Tonga released heptagonal coins to celebrate Christmas, with appropriate reverse motifs ranging from Dürer's *Praying Hands* to the Three Wise Men. Struck in cupro-nickel for general circulation, they were also minted in silver, gold or platinum in very limited editions.

Despite its comparative remoteness, Tonga has made a big splash in the coin world with a number of startling innovations. As well as the first gold coins from Oceania, Tonga experimented with high-denomination coins (the hau worth 100 pa'anga) struck in palladium, a rare metal of the platinum group. In the 1980s, when the bullion value of silver rose sharply, a number of special issues were struck in silver-plated cupro-nickel. Some coins of 1967–8 were countermarked to commemorate the king's 50th birthday or the anniversary of Salote's death, in much the same way that stamps are overprinted for this purpose.

WESTERN SAMOA

The islands of Samoa were discovered by the Dutch Jacob Roggeveen in 1772 but were later the subject of a three-cornered tussle between Germany, Britain and the USA. Although the group had an indigenous monarchy, it was partitioned between Germany and the USA in March 1900, and the eastern portion remains under US rule. In 1914 German Samoa fell to forces from New Zealand, which was granted a mandate by the League of Nations. Western Samoa remained under this mandate until it attained independence in 1962.

Distinctive coins were introduced in 1967, based on the tala (dollar) of 100 sene (cents) [15–16]. The obverse bore the profile of Malietoa Tanumafili II, a direct descendent of the kings of Samoa, who holds his position for life, although it is intended that his successors should be elected for five-year terms. The reverses focus on various fruits [19–20], with the state arms on the tala. Since 1969 Western Samoa has issued a large number of special coins, commemorating the Queen's silver jubilee [17–18] and featuring sporting events such as the Commonwealth and Olympic Games [21–22] and the Americas Cup yacht races, while local heroes such as Robert Louis Stevenson (known as Tusitala – "the teller of tales") [23–24] and German governor Dr Wilhelm Solff are not forgotten.

GLOSSARY OF PHILATELIC TERMS

Adhesive Stamp issued with gum on the reverse for sticking on mail. *See also* Self-adhesive.

Bilingual pairs Stamps printed alternately in two different languages.

Bisect Stamp cut in half, horizontally, vertically or diagonally, for use at half the usual value.

Blind perforation Perforation in which the paper is merely dented, owing to blunt teeth in the perforating machine.

Block Four or more stamps joined together.

Bogus Label purporting to be a genuine stamp to defraud collectors. Bogus overprints may be found on genuine stamps.

Booklet One or more panes (small blocks) of stamps, usually held together with card covers.

Cancellation Postmark applied to stamps to prevent their re-use.

Cancelled to order (CTO) Stamps post-marked in bulk, usually for sale to philatelists below face value.

Centred A stamp whose design is equidistant from the edges of the perforations is said to be well centred.

Coils Stamps issued in reels or coils and often collected in strips. Usually imperforate on two opposite sides.

Colour trials Impressions, or proofs, of stamps created to determine the most suitable colours.

Comb perforation Perforation on three sides of a stamp made at one stroke of the perforator, resulting in perfectly even corner teeth, compared with line perforation.

Commemorative A stamp sold in limited quantities for a period of time, often honouring a person, place, or event.

Compulsory Stamp Charity stamps issued for compulsory use on mail.

Controls Letters and numerals found on British

sheet margins, 1881–1947, for accounting purposes.

Cork cancellation Obliterators cut from corks, usually with pictorial devices.

Corner block Stamps taken from the corner of a sheet, adjacent to marginal paper showing controls, cylinder numbers, plate numbers or printer's imprint.

Corner letters Double alphabet sequence of letters found in the corners of British stamps, 1840–87, indicating the position of the stamp in the sheet.

Cover Envelope or wrapper with stamps affixed or imprinted.

Cylinder number Tiny numeral printed in the sheet margin to denote the cylinder(s) used in production.

Definitives Stamps in general use over a period of years, as opposed to commemoratives, charity or semi-postal stamps and other special issues.

Demonetized Obsolete stamps declared invalid for postage.

Die The original piece of metal on which the stamp design is engraved.

Die proof Impression pulled from the die to check its accuracy.

Dumb cancellation Postmarks with the town name erased for security reason, often in wartime.

Embossed Stamps, or a portion of their design, die-struck in low relief, often colourless against a coloured background.

Error Stamps deviating from the normal in some respect: missing or inverted colours, surcharges and overprints in the design which may later be corrected.

Essay Preliminary design, not subsequently used.

Fake Genuine stamp that has been tampered with in some way to increase its value.

First Day Cover or FDC Envelope bearing stamps used on the first day of issue.

First Flight Cover Cover carried on first airmail via a new route or aircraft.

Fiscal Stamp intended for fiscal or revenue purposes.

Flaw Defect in the printing plate or cylinder, resulting in

a constant blemish on the same stamp in every sheet.

Frank Mark or label indicating that mail can be transferred free of postage.

Gum Mucilage on the back of unused stamps.

Gutter Area between panes of a sheet.

Half tone Black-and-white photographic image appearing on a stamp; often a feature of early 20th century essays.

Imperforate Stamps issued without any means of separating them, thus requiring them to be cut apart with scissors.

Imprint Inscription giving the name or trademark of the printer.

Intaglio Printing process where the design is engraved in "recess", or below the surface of the printing plate.

Issue New stamp or stamps issued by a postal authority.

Jubilee line Line of printer's rule reinforcing the edges of the plate. Appears as bars of colour in the margin at the foot of the sheet.

Key plate Printing plate used to generate the design of the stamp. Used in conjunction with a duty plate, which prints the value.

Keytype Collectors' term for stamps of the British, French, German, Portuguese and Spanish colonies which used identical designs, differing only in the name of the colony and denomination.

Line perforation Perforation where holes are punched out on one side of a stamp at a time, with the result that two sets of perforated lines do not register at the corners of the sheet.

Lithography Surface printing method where a design is photographically transferred to a zinc or aluminium plate. *See also* Offset lithography.

Locals Stamps whose validity is restricted to a single town or district.

Meter marks Marks applied by a postage meter used by some firms and other organizations, comprising imitation "stamp" with the value, the town die (with the date) and advertising slogan.

Miniature sheet Small sheet containing a single stamp or

small group of stamps, often with decorative margins.

Mint Unused stamp with full, original gum on the back.

Obsolete Stamp no longer on sale at the post office but still valid for postage.

Obliteration Post-marking of stamps to prevent re-use. *See also* cancellation.

Offset lithography Printing process whereby an image is transferred from an aluminium or zinc plate to a rubber blanket, and then from the rubber blanket to the paper.

Omnibus issue Commemoratives issued by several countries at once.

Overprint Printing applied to a stamp some time after the original printing, to convert it to some other purpose, such as charity, commemorative, or for use overseas.

Pane Originally a portion of a sheet (half or quarter) divided by gutters, but also applied to the blocks of stamps issued in booklets.

Perfins Stamps perforated with initials or other devices as a security measure to prevent pilfering or misuse.

Perforation Form of separation using machines which punch out tiny circles of paper. *See also* Comb perforation; Line perforation.

Phosphor band Almost invisible line on the face of a stamp, created by the application of a chemical, to facilitate the electronic sorting process.

Photogravure Printing process where the design is photographed onto the printing plate using a fine screen which breaks the copy up into very fine square dots. The tiny depressions that form around the squares retain the ink.

Plate Flat or curved piece of metal from which stamps are printed.

Plate proof Impression of a sheet, block or strip of new issues, pulled from the die, usually appearing in black ink, or sometimes in various trial colours.

Postage dues Labels denoting the amount of postage unpaid or underpaid (often including a fine).

Postage paid impressions (PPIs) Marks printed on mail, often used in bulk business mail.

Postal stationery Envelopes, cards and wrappers bearing imprinted or embossed stamps.

Proof Impression of a stamp design. *See also* Die proofs; Plate proofs

Provisionals Stamps overprinted or sur-charged to meet a shortage of regular issues.

Recess printing Term used in catalogues to signify intaglio printing.

Redrawn Stamps in which the basic design has been retained but various changes made in a subsequent edition.

Remainders Stocks of stamps on hand after an issue has been demonetized are sometimes sold off cheaply to the philatelic trade, with some form of cancellation to distinguish them from unused stamps sold at full value during the currency of the stamps.

Revenue Stamp intended for fiscal or revenue purposes.

Secret marks Tiny letters, numbers, dates and other devices introduced into the design of some stamps (notably the United States and Canada) for security reasons.

Self-adhesive A stamp in a coil or booklet with backing adhesive paper from which it is peeled and affixed to mail.

Selvedge Stamp edging or sheet marginal paper.

Se-tenant Two or more stamps of different designs, values or colours, printed side by side.

Sheet A complete set of stamps taken from a single printing plate. This may then be cut into individual panes for sale at a post office.

Sheetlet Small sheet of stamps, of varying quantities.

Specimen Stamp perforated or overprinted thus (in the appropriate language), for record or publicity purposes, and to denote its postal invalidity.

Straight edge Stamps with no perforations on one or more sides, mainly found in coils and booklets but also including sheets of stamps.

Strip Three or more stamps that have not been separated.
Surcharge An overprint that alters the face value of a stamp.
Tablet Adjoining section of a stamp bearing an inscription and, often, an advertisement.
Tabs Stamps with marginal inscriptions alluding to the subjects depicted, widely used by Israel, Switzerland and the United Nations.

Tied Postmarks that overlap the stamp and the envelope or card.
Toughra (also tughra) Calligraphic markings indicating the signature of the former Sultan of Turkey, prevalent on Turkish issues predating the Ottoman Empire's demise in 1920.
Typography Collector's term for letterpress printing, abbreviated in catalogues to

"typo".
Unused Stamp lacking a cancellation, but in less perfect condition than mint.
UPU Universal Postal Union.
Used Stamp bearing a cancellation.
Variety Any variation from the normal issue, relating to its shade, perforation, watermark, gum or phosphorescence. Usually

only listed in the more specialized stamp catalogues.
Vignette The main motif or central portion of a stamp design, as opposed to the frame, value tablet or inset portrait or effigy of a ruler.
Watermark Translucent impression used as a security device on paper on which the stamp is printed.
Zemstvos Russian local postal network which

prepaid postage from the many smaller towns to the nearest imperial post office.

PHILATELIC INSCRIPTIONS

Key-words and abbreviations found in inscriptions and overprints, with their country, state or region of origin.

A & T Annam and Tonquin
Acores Azores
Afghanes Afghanistan
Africa Portuguese Africa
Akahi Keneta Hawaii
Amtlicher Verkehr Wurttemberg
AO (Afrika Ost) Ruanda-Urundi
Allemagne/Duitschland Belgian occupation of Germany
A Payer Te Betalen Belgium (postage due)
A Percevoir postage due Belgium (francs and centimes); Egypt (paras, milliemes)
Archipel des Comores Comoro Islands
Avisporto Denmark
Azad Hind Free India (unissued stamps prepared for use in India after Japanese "liberation")
B (on Straits Settlements) Bangkok
Bani (on Austrian stamps) Austrian occupation of Romania
BATYM Batum (now Batumi)
Bayer, Bayern Bavaria
BCA British Central Africa (now Malawi)
Belgique/Belgie/Belgien, also **Belge** Belgium
Böhmen und Mahren Bohemia and Moravia
Bollo delta Posta Napoletana Naples
Bosnien Bosnia
Braunschweig Brunswick
C CH Cochin China
Cechy a Morava Bohemia and Moravia
CEF (on India) Chinese Expeditionary Force

CEF (on German colonies) Cameroons under British occupation
Centesimi (on Austria) Austrian occupation of Italy
Centimes (on Austria) Austrian POs in Crete
Centrafricaine Central African Republic
Ceskoslovensko Czechoslovakia
Chiffre taxe France
Chine French POs in China
Comunicaciones Spain
Confed. Granadina Granadine Confederation (Colombia)
Cong Hoa Mien Nam National Liberation Front for South Vietnam
Congo Belge Belgian Congo
Continente Portuguese mainland
Coree Korea
Correio Brazil, Portugal
Correos Spain, Cuba, Porto Rico, Philippines
Côte d'Ivoire Ivory Coast
Côte Française des Somalis French Somali Coast
Danmark Denmark
Dansk Vestindien Danish West Indies
DDR German Democratic Republic
Deficit Peru
Deutsch Neu-Guinea German New Guinea
Deutsch Ostafrika German East Africa
Deutschösterreich Austria
Deutsch Siidwestafrika German South West Africa
Deutsche Flugpost/ Reichspost Germany
Deutsches Reich Germany
Dienstmarke Germany
Dienstsache Germany
Diligencia Uruguay
DJ Djibouti

Drzava, Drzavna Yugoslavia
EEF Palestine
Eesti Estonia
EE UU de C Colombia
EFO French Oceania
Eire Republic of Ireland
Elua Keneta Hawaii
Emp. Franc. French Empire
Emp. Ottoman Turkey
Equateur Ecuador
Escuelas Venezuela
España, Espanola Spain
Estados Unidos de Nueva Granada Colombia
Estensi Modena
Estero Italian POs in the Levant
Etablissements de l'Inde French Indian Settlements
Etablissements de l'Oceanie French Oceanic Settlements
Etat Ind. du Congo Congo Free State
Filipinas Spanish Philippines
Franco Switzerland
Francobollo Italy
Franco Marke Bremen
Franco Poste Bollo Neapolitan provinces and early Italy
Franqueo Peru
Franquicia Postal Spain
Freimarke Wurttemberg, Prussia
Frimerke Norway
Frimaerke Denmark
G (on Cape of Good Hope) Griqualand West
G & D Guadeloupe
GEA Tanganyika
Gen. Gouv. Warschau German occupation of Poland, World War 1
General Gouvernement German occupation of Poland, World War II
Georgie Georgia
Giuba Jubaland
GPE Guadeloupe
GRI British occupation of New Guinea and Samoa
Grossdeutsches Reich Nazi

Germany
Guine Portuguese Guinea
Guinea Ecuatorial Equatorial Guinea
Guine French Guinea
Gultig 9 Armee German occupation of Romania
Guyane Française French Guiana
Haute Volta Upper Volta
Hellas Greece
Helvetia Switzerland
HH Nawab Shah Begam Bhopal
Hrvatska Croatia
HRZGL Russia
IEF Indian Expeditionary Force
IEF 'D' Mosul
Imper. Reg. Austrian POs in Turkey
Impuesto de Guerra Spain (war tax)
Inde French Indian Settlements
India Port. Portuguese India
Irian Barat West Iran
Island Iceland
Jubile de l'Union Postale Switzerland
Kamerun Cameroons
Kaladlit Nunat, Kalaallit Nunaat Greenland
Karnten Carinthia
Karolinen Caroline Islands
KGCA Carinthia
Kgl. Post. Frim. Denmark, Danish West Indies
Khmere Cambodia
Kongeligt Post Frimaerke Denmark
KK Post Stempel Austria, Austrian Italy
KPHTH Crete
Kraljevina, Kraljevstvo Yugoslavia
Kreuzer Austria
KSA Saudi Arabia
K.u.K. Feldpost Austrian military stamps
K.u.K. Militärpost Bosnia and Herzegovina
K. Württ. Post Wurttemberg

La Canea Italian POs in Crete
La Georgie Georgia
Land-Post Baden
Lattaquie Latakia
Latvija Latvia
Lietuvos Lithuania
Litwa Srodkowa Central Lithuania
Ljubljanska Pokrajina Slovenia
L. McL. Trinidad (Lady McLeod stamp)
Lösen Sweden
Magyar Hungary
MAPKA Russia
Marianen Mariana Islands
Maroc French Morocco
Marruecos Spanish Morroco
Marschall-lnseln Marshall Islands
Mejico Mexico
Militär Post Bosnia and Herzegovina
Mocambique Mozambique
Modonesi Modena
Montevideo Uruguay
Moyen-Congo Middle Congo
MViR German occupation of Romania
Nachmarke Austria
Napoletana Naples
NCE New Caledonia
Nederland Netherlands
Ned. Antillen Netherlands Antilles
Ned./ Nederl. Indie Dutch East Indies
NF Nyasaland Field Force
Nippon Japan
Nieuwe Republiek New Republic (South Africa)
Nlle Caledonie New Caledonia
Norddeutscher Postbezirk North German Confederation
Norge, Noreg Norway
Nouvelle Caledonie New Caledonia
Nouvelles Hebrides New Hebrides
NSB Nossi-Be (Madagascar)

NSW New South Wales
NW Pacific Islands Nauru and New Guinea
NZ New Zealand
Oesterr., **Oesterreich**, Österreich Austria
Offentligt Sak Norway (official stamps)
Oltre Giuba Jubaland
Orts Post Switzerland
OS Norway (official stamps)
Ottoman, Ottomanes Turkey
P, PGS Perak (Government Service)
Pacchi Postale Italy (parcel stamps)
Pakke-Porto Greenland
Para Egypt, Serbia, Turkey, Crete
Parm[ensi] Parma
Pesa (on German) German POs in Turkey
Piaster German POs in Turkey
Pilipinas Philippines
Pingin Ireland
Poblact na hEireann Republic of Ireland
Poczta Polska Poland
Pohjois Inkeri North Ingermanland
Port Cantonal Switzerland (Geneva)
Porte de Conduccion Peru
Porte Franco Peru

Porte de Mar Mexico
Porteado Portugal and colonies
Porto Austria, Yugoslavia
Porto-pflichtige Württemberg
Post & Receipt/Post Stamp Hyderabad
Postage and Revenue United Kingdom
Postas le n'ioc Republic of Ireland
Postat e Qeverries Albania
Poste Estensi Modena
Poste Locale Switzerland
Postes (alone) Alsace and Lorraine, Belgium, Luxembourg
Poste Shqiptare Albania
Postgebiet Ob. Ost German Eastern Army
Postzegel Netherlands
Preussen Prussia
Provincie Modonesi Modena
Provinz Laibach Slovenia
PSNC Pacific Steam Navigation Co., Peru
Qeverries Albania
R Jind
Rayon Switzerland
Recargo Spain
Regno d'Italia Venezia Giulia, Trieste
Reichspost German Empire

RF France and colonies
RH Haiti
Repoblika Malagasy Malagasy Republic
Republica Oriental Uruguay
Repub. Franc. France
Republique Libanaise Lebanon
Republique Rwandaise Rwanda
Rialtas Sealadac na hEireann Provisional Government of Ireland
RO Eastern Roumelia
RSA Republic of South Africa
Rumanien (on German) German occupation of Romania
Russisch-Polen German occupation of Poland
Sachsen Saxony
Scrisorei Moldavia and Wallachia
Segnatasse Italy
Serbien Austrian or German occupation of Serbia
SH Schleswig-Holstein
SHS Yugoslavia
Shqipenia, Shqipenie, Shqypnija, Shqiptare Albania
Sld., **Soldi** Austrian Italy, Slesvig Schleswig
Slovensky Stat Slovakia
SO Eastern Silesia

SPM St Pierre and Miquelon
S. Thome e Principe St Thomas and Prince Islands
Suidwes Afrika South West Africa
Sul Bolletina, Sulla Ricevuta Italy
Sultanat d'Anjouan Anjouan
Suomi Finland
Sverige Sweden
SWA South West Africa
TAKCA Bulgaria
Tassa Gazzette Modena
Te Betalen Port Netherlands and colonies
TEO Cilicia. Syria
Terres Australes et Antarctiques Françaises French Southern and Antarctic Territories
Territoire Français des Afars et les Issas French Territory of the Afars and Issas
Tjanste Frimarke Sweden
Tjeneste Frimerke Norway
Tjeneste Frimaerke Denmark
Toga Tonga
Toscano Tuscany
UAE United Arab Emirates
UAR United Arab Republic (Egypt)
UG Uganda
UKTT United Kingdom Trust Territory (Southern

Cameroons)
Uku Leta Hawaii
Ultramar Cuba. Porto Rico
UNEF Indian Forces in Gaza
UNTEA Western New Guinea
Vallees d'Andorre Andorra
Van Diemen's Land Tasmania
Venezia Giulia (on Italian stamps) Trieste
Venezia Tridentina Trentino
Viet Nam Dan Chu Cong Hoa North Vietnam
Vom Empfanger Einzuziehen Danzig (postage due)
YAR Yemen Arab Republic
YCCP Ukraine
YKP. H. P. Ukraine
Z Armenia
ZAR South African Republic (Transvaal)
Z. Afr. Republiek South African Republic (Transvaal)
Zeitungsmarke Austria, Germany (newspaper stamps)
Zil Eloine Sesel Seychelles Outer Islands
Zuid West Afrika South West Africa
Zulassungsmarke German military parcel stamp

GLOSSARY OF NUMISMATIC TERMS

Accolated *see* conjoined.
Ae Abbreviation of *aes* (Latin, "bronze"), used to denote copper, brass or bronze.
Aes grave (Latin, "heavy bronze") Heavy coinage of the Roman Republic from 269 BC.
Aes rude (Latin, "rough bronze") Irregular lumps of bronze used as money before the adoption of regular coinage, c. 400 BC.
Aes signatum (Latin, "signed bronze") Regular bars or ingots cast to a standard weight, stamped to guarantee their weight, 289–269 BC.
Alliance coinage Coins struck by two or more states in conjunction.
Alloy Mixture of metals, e.g. bronze (copper and tin).
Altered Deliberately changed, usually to increase the value of a coin (such as changing a common date to a rare one by filing one of the digits).
Aluminium Lightweight silver-coloured metal used for

coins of low denominations.
Aluminium-bronze Durable, gold-coloured alloy of aluminium and copper.
Amulet Coin whose design confers talismanic properties, often pierced and worn to ward off evil spirits. *See also* touchpiece.
Angel Gold coin named for its image of Archangel Michael, first used in France in 1340 and introduced to England in 1465, with a value of 6 shillings and 8 pence.
Annealing Process of heating and cooling metal to relieve stresses before it is processed.
Annulet Small circle used as an ornament or spacing device in inscriptions.
Antoniniani Roman imperial coins named after the emperor Caracalla (Marcus Aurelius Antoninus) in whose reign they were first minted.
Ar Abbreviation of *argentum* (Latin, "silver").
Assay Test to determine the fineness of precious metal.

Attribution Identification of a coin by such data as the issuer, date, reign, mint or denomination.
Au Abbreviation of *aurum* (Latin, "gold").
Barbarous Descriptive of coins struck by Celtic and Germanic tribes in imitation of Greek or Roman coins.
Base metal Non-precious metal or an alloy containing neither gold nor silver.
Bath metal Inferior bronze alloy used at Bath, England, for casting cannon, but also employed by William Wood of Bristol to produce tokens for Ireland and colonial America.
Beading Border of raised dots round the rim of a coin.
Billon Alloy of copper with less than 50 per cent silver.
Bimetallic Made of two different metals or alloys; such coins usually have a centre in one metal and outer ring in another.
Bimetallism Descriptive of coinage consisting of coins in

two different metals with a fixed ratio between them, such as gold and silver or silver and bronze.
Bit (1) Segment of a coin that has been cut up in order to circulate at half or one quarter the value of the entire coin. (2) Nickname of the 1 real piece that circulated in North America in the 17th and 18th centuries, worth one eighth of a dollar, or 12½ cents.
Blank Disc of metal cut or punched out of a strip or sheet, on which a coin is struck. Also known as a flan or planchet.
Blundered inscription (1) Jumbled lettering in inscriptions on barbarous coins, reflecting the illiteracy of the makers copying Greek or Roman coins. (2) Unreadable inscription as a result of a mis-strike.
Bon pour (French, "good for") Inscription on 1920s French tokens used during a shortage of legal tender coins.

Bourse Area in a coin exhibition where dealers sell their wares.
Bracteate (from Latin *bractea*, a thin piece of metal) Coin struck on such a thin blank that the image impressed on one side shows through on the other.
Brass Alloy of copper and zinc.
Brockage Mis-struck coin with only one design, normal on one side and incuse on the other, caused when a struck coin clings to the die and strikes the next blank to pass through the press.
Bronze Alloy of copper and tin.
Bullet money Globular pieces of silver with impressed marks, used as currency in Thailand from the 14th century until 1904.
Bullion Precious metal whose value is reckoned solely by its weight and fineness.
Bullion coin Coin struck in precious metal, now usually

with an inscription giving its weight and fineness, whose value fluctuates according to the market price of the metal.

Buyer's premium Percentage of the purchase price at auction paid by the winning bidder to the auction house.

Carat (US karat) Term used to denote the fineness of gold, being 1/24 of the whole. Thus 22 carat gold is .916 fine.

Cartwheel Nickname of the British penny and 2 pence copper coins with raised rims of 1797, weighing respectively 1oz/28.35g and 2oz/56.7g.

Cased set Set of coins in mint condition, packaged by the mint.

Cash (from Portuguese *caixa* and Tamil *kacu*, a small coin) Cast circular coins in copper or bronze with a square central hole, used as subsidiary coinage in China.

Cast coins Coins made by pouring molten metal into moulds, rather than by striking discs of metal with dies.

Clad Descriptive of a coin with a core of one metal covered with a layer or coating of another.

Clipping Removing slivers of silver or gold from the edge of coins, an illegal but widespread practice until the 1660s, when milled coins began to be struck with grained edges.

Cob Irregularly shaped silver piece sliced from a bar of silver and crudely stamped for use in Spanish America in the 16th to 18th centuries.

Coin Piece of metal marked with a device and issued by a government for use as money.

Coin weight Piece of metal of exactly the weight of a known coin, used to check weight and fineness of matching coins.

Collar Ring within which the obverse and reverse dies operate to restrict the spread of the blank between them; it is often engraved with an inscription or pattern that is impressed on the edge of the coin.

Commemorative Coin struck to celebrate a historic anniversary or personality or publicize an event.

Conjoined portrait Obverse portrait with two heads or

busts in profile, facing the same direction and overlapping. Also known as accolated or jugate.

Convention money Coins struck by neighbouring states and mutually acceptable; specifically the issues of Austria and Bavaria, which spread to other German states in the early 19th century.

Copper (1) Metal widely used for subsidiary coinage for more than 2500 years, usually alloyed with tin to make bronze, but also alloyed with nickel or silver. (2) Nickname for small denomination coins.

Coppernose Nickname derived from the debased English silver shillings of Henry VIII because the silver tended to wear off the king's nose, the highest point of the obverse.

Counter Piece resembling a coin but actually intended for use on a medieval accountancy board or in gambling.

Counterfeit Imitation of a coin for circulation, intended to deceive the public and defraud the state.

Countermark Punch mark applied to a coin to change its value or authorize its circulation in a different state.

Crockards Debased imitations of English silver pennies, produced in the Low Countries and imported into England in the late 13th century.

Crown gold Gold of 22 carat (.916) fineness, so called because it was first used in England in 1526 for the gold crown; it remains the British standard.

Cupro-nickel (US copper-nickel) Alloy of copper and nickel.

Currency Money of all kinds, including coins, paper notes, tokens and other articles, passing current in general circulation.

Current Descriptive of coins and paper money in circulation.

Cut money Coins cut into smaller pieces to provide proportionately smaller values for general circulation.

Debasement Reduction of a coin's precious metal content.

Decimal currency Any currency system in which the basic unit is divided into 10,

100 or 1000 units.

Demonetization Withdrawal of coins from circulation, declaring them to be worthless.

Denomination Value given to a coin or note of paper money.

Device Term derived from heraldry for the pattern or emblem on a coin.

Die Hardened piece of metal bearing the mirror or wrong-reading image of a device, used to strike one side of a blank.

Die break Raised line or bump in a relief image caused by a crack in the die.

Dodecagonal Twelve-sided.

Dump Coin struck on a very thick blank.

Eagle US gold coin with an American eagle obverse and a face value of $10, circulating until 1933.

Ecclesiastical coins Coins struck under the authority of an archbishop or other prelate, prevalent in the Middle Ages and surviving in coins of the Papacy.

Edge The side of a coin, perpendicular to the obverse and reverse surfaces, which may be plain, inscribed or grained.

Edge inscription Lettering on the edge of coins designed to prevent clipping.

Edge ornament Elaboration of the graining on milled coins designed as a security device.

Effigy Portrait or bust appearing on the obverse of a coin.

Electrum Naturally occurring alloy of gold and silver prevalent in the ancient coins of the Mediterranean region; it was also known as white gold.

Encased money Stamps enclosed in small metal discs and used in lieu of coins during the American Civil War and in Europe during and after World War I.

Engraving Technique of cutting designs and inscriptions in dies used for striking coins.

Epigraphy Study of inscriptions engraved in stone or metal, usually to determine the date and provenance of an artefact so inscribed.

Erasure Removal of the title or effigy of a ruler from coinage issued post-humously, notably in Roman coins of Caligula

and Nero.

Error Mistake in the design or production of a coin.

Exergue Bottom segment of the face of a coin, usually divided from the rest of the field by a horizontal line and often containing the date or value.

Face Obverse or reverse surface of a coin.

Face value Value of the denomination applied to a coin, distinct from its intrinsic value.

Facing Descriptive of a portrait facing to the front instead of in profile.

Fantasy Piece purporting to be a coin but either emanating from a non-existent country or never authorized by the country inscribed on it.

Field Flat part of a coin between the legend and effigy or other raised parts of the design.

Flan *see* **blank**.

Forgery Unauthorized copy or imitation, usually created to deceive collectors.

Frosting Matt finish used for the high relief areas of proof coins to contrast with the polished surface of the field.

Globular Descriptive of a coin struck on a very thick dump with convex sides.

Gold Precious metal used for coins since the 7th century BC.

Grade Description of the condition of a collectable coin for the purposes of valuation and trade.

Graining Pattern of close vertical ridges around the edge of milled coins, originally devised to eliminate the fraudulent practice of clipping. Also known as reeding or milling.

Gun money Emergency Irish coinage of 1689–91 struck from gunmetal by the deposed James II in order to pay and supply his troops during the Williamite or Jacobean War.

Hammered Descriptive of coins struck by a hammer to impress the dies.

Holed coin (1) Coin minted with a central hole. (2) Coin pierced after striking, to wear as jewellery or a talisman.

Hub Right-reading metal punch used to strike working dies.

Incuse Descriptive of an impression that cuts into

the surface of a coin.

Ingot Piece of precious metal, cast in a mould and stamped with its weight and fineness.

Intrinsic value Net value based on the metal content of a coin, as opposed to its nominal or face value.

Iron Metal used in primitive currency such as the spits of ancient Greece, and for emergency coinage in both World Wars.

Jeton (from French *jeter*, to throw) Alternative term for **counter**.

Jugate (from Latin *jugum*, yoke) Alternative term for **conjoined**.

Key date The rarest date in a long-running series.

Klippe Coin struck on a square or rectangular blank hand-cut from sheet metal, originally in a time of emergency.

Laureate Descriptive of a design incorporating a laurel wreath, either adorning the brows of a ruler or enclosing the value.

Legal tender Coin declared by law to be current money.

Legend Inscription on a coin.

Long cross coinage English pennies first issued by Henry III, on which the arms of the cross on the reverse reached to the rim.

Lustre Sheen or bloom on the surface of an uncirculated coin.

Maundy money Set of small silver pennies distributed by the British sovereign to the poor on Maundy Thursday (preceding Good Friday), a medieval custom still enacted. Ordinary coins were originally used but special 1, 2, 3 and 4 pence coins were first minted in 1822.

Milling Mechanical process for the production of coins, in use from the 16th century.

Mint Establishment in which coins are produced. Also used as a grading term.

Mint set Coins still enclosed in the package or case issued by the mint.

Mint-mark Mark on a coin identifying the mint at

which it was struck.

Mirror surface Highly polished, flawless surface of the field of a proof coin.

Mis-strike Coin on which the impression of the die has been struck off-centre.

Moneyer Mint official in pre-industrial era responsible for striking coinage of legal weight and quality.

Mule Coin whose obverse and reverse designs are wrongly matched. Can be comprised of different denominations or even separate foreign currencies.

Nickel Base metal used extensively in coinage as a substitute for silver, frequently alloyed with copper to make cupro-nickel.

Non-circulating legal tender Coins that, though technically valid for use, do not circulate in practice (such as silver and gold commemoratives). Abbreviated to NCLT.

Numismatics (from Latin *numisma*, coin) The study and collection of paper money, coins and medals.

Obverse "Heads" side of a coin.

Off-metal Descriptive of a coin struck in a metal other than that officially authorized.

Overdating Method of

changing a date without the expense of engraving an entirely new die. One or more digits are altered by superimposing other numerals using a punch.

Overstrike Coin produced when a previously struck coin is substituted for a blank, on which traces of the original design remain. Collected by some.

Patina Surface quality acquired as a result of environmental interaction over time, such as the oxidation of metal.

Pattern Design piece prepared by a mint for approval by the issuing authority, not actually put into production. Patterns may differ from issued coins in metal or minor details, but many bear designs quite different from those eventually adopted.

Pellet Raised circular ornament, sometimes used as a spacing device in the inscription.

Pieces of eight Nickname for Spanish silver 8 real coins.

Piedfort (US piefort) Coin struck on a blank of two or three times the normal weight and thickness.

Pile Lower die bearing the obverse motif, the opposite of the trussel.

Planchet *see* **blank**.

Platinum Precious metal first used for coins in Russia in 1819 and occasionally in recent years for proof coins.

Plate money Large, cumbersome copper plates used as money in Sweden, 1643–1768.

Privy mark Secret mark incorporated in a coin design as a security device or to identify a particular die used.

Profile Side portrait often used on the obverse of coins.

Proof Originally a trial strike but in recent years a coin struck to a very high standard, often in precious metals.

Punch Piece of hardened metal bearing a design or lettering used to impress a die or a coin.

Recoinage Process of recalling and demonetizing old coins, which are then melted down and made into new coins.

Reeding *see* **graining**.

Relief Raised parts of the design.

Restrike Coin produced from the original dies, but long after the period in which they were current.

Reverse "Tails" side of a coin, usually featuring arms, the value or a pictorial design.

Rim Raised border around the outside of a coin's face.

Scyphate (from Greek *scypha*, skiff or small boat) Cup-shaped, used to describe Byzantine concave coins.

Sede vacante (Latin, "vacant see") Inscription used on issues of ecclesiastical mints between the death of a prelate and the election of

his successor.

Series All the issues of a coin of one denomination, design and type, including modifications and variations.

Short-cross coinage English pennies on which the arms of the reverse cross fell far short of the rim.

Siege money Emergency currency issued under siege.

Silver Precious metal widely used for coinage from the 6th century BC onward.

Slabbing Method of encapsulating a coin permanently, particularly in a rectangular plastic case, to prevent deterioration.

Specie (Latin, "in kind") Money in the form of coins, especially of precious metals.

Steel Metal refined and tempered from iron and used in a stainless or chromed version for coinage since 1939. Copper-clad steel is now extensively used in place of bronze.

Tin Metal used for small coins in Malaysia, Thailand and the East Indies, and in British halfpence and farthings (1672–92). It is more usually alloyed with copper to form bronze.

Token Coin-like piece of metal, plastic or card issued by merchants, local authorities or other organizations, often during periods when government coinage is in short supply, but also produced extensively as a substitute for money.

Touchpiece Coin kept as a

lucky charm and often pierced to wear as jewellery, notably the English gold angel, which was believed to cure or ward off scrofula, a skin disease known as the King's Evil.

Trade coin Coin produced for use outside the country of origin as part of international trade, such as British and American trade dollars.

Truncation Stylized cut at the base of the neck of a portrait, sometimes the site of a mint-mark, the engraver's initials or a die number.

Trussel Upper die used in hammered coinage bearing the reverse design, the opposite of the pile.

Type A major variety of a series of coins.

Type set Set comprising one coin of each type in a series.

Uniface Coin with a device on one side only.

Vis-à-vis (French, "face-to-face") Descriptive of a double portrait in which the two heads face each other.

White gold Ancient term for electrum, which differs from the modern definition.

Year set Set of coins produced annually by a mint, usually containing a specimen of each coin issued by the mint during the year.

Zinc Metal alloyed with copper to produce brass; zinc-coated steel was widely used in Europe during both World Wars.

NUMISMATIC GRADES

You will find below the various terms given in catalogues and dealers' lists to denote the perceived state, or 'grade', of a coin, with the higher grades given first.

Fleur de Coin (FDC) or Brilliant Uncirculated (BU or B. Unc.) Denotes coins in the very finest possible condition with full original lustre, no surface marks or edge knocks. Usually reserved for descriptions of proof and de luxe coins.

Uncirculated (Unc.) The highest grade applicable to coins struck by high-speed presses for general circulation. These coins should have full original lustre, which may have darkened with age to produce an attractive patina. Otherwise the surface should be flawless.

Extremely Fine (EF) Indicates a coin in virtually pristine condition but showing slight signs of handling. It should have every detail of the engraving clearly delineated but will have lost some of its original lustre.

Very Fine (VF) Coins show slight evidence of wear on the highest points of the design, notably the hair on portraits and the ridge at the truncation of the bust. In modern coins this is the lowest grade for practicable purposes and to purchase a coin in any lesser condition would be a waste of money. Dealers do not normally offer modern coins in lower grades unless they are very scarce. Older material, however, may be acceptable.

Fine (F) To the uninitiated such a coin may seem perfectly acceptable, but look closely and you will see that

the higher points of the design are worn smooth and the lettering is noticeably thicker and less clearly defined, especially in the serifs (the little spurs on capitals) which may have all but disappeared.

Very Good (VG) A misuse of language as a coin with this description would be in pretty poor condition. In such coins little of the fine detail will be present and the overall impression would be blurred and worn.

Good (G) Similarly, this grade now means the complete opposite. A coin in this state would be worn smooth all over and the date would be just readable. For that reason alone collectors will keep such a coin if a particular year is so scarce that the chances of finding a better specimen might be remote.

Lower grades, such as **Fair**, **Mediocre** and **Poor** have almost vanished from the scene and would only be considered if the coin was seldom available in a better condition. These terms are usually reserved for medieval coins which have been clipped or have irregular shapes with chunks missing – which is, in fact, a not uncommon situation for many coins from the 10th to 16th centuries. Also included in these categories are coins which have been pierced for wear as pendants, the only exception in this case being the gold angels of medieval Europe, which were believed to guard the bearer against disease, and which are still highly valued by auctioneers and collectors.

PICTURE ACKNOWLEDGEMENTS

STAMPS (pages 10–255): All stamps illustrated in this part of the book and on the prelims, endmatter and on the jacket were kindly supplied by Dr James Mackay, from his private collection, unless indicated below. The main image appearing on page 10 shows a Swedish miniature sheet of 1991 reproducing "The Coronation of Gustav II" by Carl Gustav Pilo, designed by Czeslaw Slania, and is in the private collection of Dr James Mackay.

Key: l=left; r=right; t=top; m=middle; b=bottom

American Philatelic Society (http://www.stamps.org): 77tl (all pictures in box), 82 (all pictures), 83br, 84t, 84bl, 86 (all pictures), 88 (all pictures), 91t, 93br

Bath Postal Museum (http://www.bathpostalmuseum.org) : 13tr, 16bl, 18tr, 20bl, 20br, 22bl, 28bl, 29tl, 29bl, 31bl (in box), 46bl (both pictures in box), 54 (all pictures), 50tr (three pictures), 56br (in box), 58tr, 58bl (in box), 59ml and 59bl, 64tl, 64bl, 65tr (in box), 79 tl

Arthur H Groten, MD (from his private collection): 61 (all pictures), 68mr (in box)

Trevor Lee took the photographs appearing on pages 31tr and 91tr

National Philatelic Society, UK (http://www.ukphilately.org.uk): 81br, 83bl, 85bl (in box), 87bl (in box)

Philatelic Traders Society Ltd, UK (http://www.philatelic-traders-society.co.uk): 85tr

All recent British stamps illustrated in this book are Royal Mail British Stamps © Royal Mail Group plc.

Royal Mail Heritage (http://www.postalheritage.org.uk): 48bl, 51bl, 76br, 80bl

© Royal Philatelic Society London, UK (http://www.rpsl.org.uk): 87tr

The publishers would also like to thank:

The Bath Stamp & Coin Shop, 12–13 Pulteney Bridge, Bath BA2 4AY, United Kingdom, for supplying the equipment featuring on pages 32, 33, 34bl, 35ml, 35tr (in box) and 37tr (in box)

Linns Stamp News, Sidney, OH 45365, USA (http://www.linns.com): for allowing us to reproduce extracts from Philatelic Forgers: Their Lives and Works by Varro E. Tyler (1991) on page 64

Stanley Gibbons, 5 Parkside, Christchurch Road, Ringwood, Hampshire BH24 3SH, United Kingdom (www.stanleygibbons.com) for allowing us to reproduce images of their equipment on pages 32, 33 and 34

COINS (pages 256–501): All coins illustrated in this part of the book and on the prelims, endmatter and on the jacket were either supplied by Dr James Mackay or are © A H Baldwin and Sons Ltd (http://www.baldwin.sh), London, unless otherwise indicated below.

The following images are © Mary Evans Picture Library, London (www.maryevans.com): 256, 258bl, 262tr, 262bl, 263t, 263m, 263b, 264bl, 267tl, 273bl, 275tr, 282tr, 298tr, 298bl, 302t, 303br, 311bl, 311br, 315br, 323tr, 334bl, 335tr

The following images are © Art Archive in conjunction with the following:
Museo della Civilta Romana Rome/Dagli Orti: 258bl, 264t, Musée du Louvre Paris/Dagli Orti (A): 258br, Dagli Orti: 264t, Victoria and

Albert Museum London/Eileen Tweedy: 267tr, Archaeological Museum Naples/Dagli Orti (A): 269br, Rheinische Landesmuseum Trier/Dagli Orti: 270b, Bodleian Library Oxford: 272t, Sienese State Archives/Dagli Orti (A): 276t, Bodleian Library Oxford: 278br; American Museum Madrid: 284bl, Musée Carnavalet Paris/Dagli Ortii: 286br, Musée du Louvre Paris/Harper Collins Publishers: 288bl, Ministry of Education Tokyo/Laurie Platt Winfrey: 289tr, Templo Mayor Library Mexico/Dagli Orti: 290bl, Museo Correr Venice/Dagli Orti: 294br, Dagli Orti (A): 295t, Archaeological Museum Ferrara/Dagli Orti (A): 308tr, Dagli Orti (A): 310t (coin of Holy Roman Emperor Charles V), 327t: Culver Pictures

The following images are © the Perth Mint, Western Australia: 299, 300bl, 301tl, 303bl, 316m (Discover Australia collector's folder), 317bl, 321br (Discover Australia coins), 324br (in panel), 330br, 333tr

The following web pages are © the American Numismatic Association 2006, and have been reproduced with their permission: 319tr, 320tr, 343tr, 343bl (in panel), 344tr

The following images are © Heritage Galleries and Auctioneers, Dallas, TX, USA (http://www.ha.com), 352 (coins 1–6)

The following images are © New World Treasures, Iron Mountain, MI, USA: 367 (coins 18–19)

The following image is © Emmanuel Said & Said International Ltd, Valletta, Malta (http://www.emmsaid.com): 388 (coin inset, top)

The following images are © Guenter Roeck (http://www.mtt.roeck-us.net/en): 401 (coins in panel)

The following image is © Chard (1964) Ltd (http://www.24carat.co.uk): 495 (coin 20)

Paul Baker (http://www.wbcc.fsnet.co.uk) kindly supplied images on the following pages:
331mr (Iranian rial showing mosque), 336bl (Hong Kong 'play

money', 337tr (Euro plastic token), 337mr (elongate coin), 339tl (curved clip on Sudanese coin), 360 (coins 11, 14 and 15), 367 (coins top-left, in panel, coins 21–22), 372 (coins 12–13), 374 (coins 3–4, 6–11), 375 (coins 12–15), 385 (coins 24–26), 393 (coins 12–13, 16–17, 20–23), 396 (coins 3–6), 397 (coins 15–20), 398 (coins 6–7, 10–11), 399 (coins 21–32), 403 (coins 12–15), 404 (coins 12–13), 405 (coins 16–19, 24–25), 406 (coins 8–9, 12–17), 407 (coins 22–27 and 29–30), 411 (coins 34–37), 412 (coins 9–14, 17–18), 427 (coins 32–33), 430 (2–7, 9, 14–17), 431 (coins 25–26, 36–7), 438 (coins 7–18), 439 (coins 26–27, 30–33), 440 (coins inset, bottom-right, 16–17), 441 (coins 27–28), 442 (coins 1–2, 15–16), 443 (28–29), 450 (coins 15–16), 451 (coins 22–27, 32–33), 453 (coin bottom-right, inset), 454 (coin top, inset), 455 (coins 33–34), 460 (coins 13–16), 461 (coins bottom-left, in panel, coins 33–34), 465 (coins 27–38), 466 (coins 1–4, 8–9) 467 (coins 23–26, 31–32), 470 (top-right Korean coin depicting Rose of Sharon), bottom-right group of three Japanese and Taiwanese coins), 474 (coins 13–14), 476 (coins inset, top-left, 13–14), 477 (coins 15–16, 29–32), 479 (coins 20–23, 28–33), 480 (coins 10–13), 485 (coins 35–36), 490 (coins 1–2, 10–11), 492 (coins 1–6), 493 (coins 10–11, 14–17), 494 (coins 6–11), 495 (coins 21–22), 496 (coins 1–4, 8–9, 11), 497 (coins 12–19, 22–23), 498 (coin inset, top-right, 2, 6), 499 (coin in panel, coins 14–19), 500 (coins 1–4, 6–9), 501 (coins 17–20, 23–24).

INDEX: STAMPS

INDEX: COINS